ERNEST W. MCFARLAND

ERNEST W. MCFARLAND
ARIZONA WORKHORSE

ERNEST W. MCFARLAND

MAJORITY LEADER OF THE
UNITED STATES SENATE
GOVERNOR AND CHIEF JUSTICE
OF THE STATE OF ARIZONA

A BIOGRAPHY BY
JAMES ELTON MCMILLAN, JR.
WITH A FOREWORD BY
BRUCE BABBITT
AND AN INTRODUCTION BY
JANET NAPOLITANO

Sharlot Hall Museum Press
Prescott, Arizona

DEDICATION

to
Jewell McFarland Lewis 1929-2003
and
Delbert Lewis

TABLE OF CONTENTS

Part I
THE MAKING OF A SENATOR *1894-1940*

Part II
UNITED STATES SENATE FIRST TERM *1941-1946*

Part III
UNITED STATES SENATE SECOND TERM *1947-1952*

Part IV
THE GUBERNATORIAL YEARS *1953-1958*

Part V
LATER ARIZONA YEARS *1959-1984*

FOREWORD

I FIRST MET SENATOR ERNEST W. MCFARLAND at summer picnics when I was a child in Flagstaff. What brought our families together, even more than Democratic politics, was the perennial Arizona obsession with water. My uncle Jim, then a state senator from Coconino County, was leading an unpopular effort to ratify the Colorado River Compact as a necessary condition to persuading the Congress to authorize what would become the Central Arizona Project.

At the time, however, most Arizona political leaders were refusing to acknowledge that the federal government controlled the Colorado River. Standing on a shaky state's rights platform, they defiantly urged Arizonans to ignore the federal compact and instead go it alone on the river. Some day, they promised, Arizona would build the project all on its own. Governor Benjamin Moeur, in a theatrical gesture of defiance, had even sent the National Guard down to the river to block federal construction at Parker Dam. It made great press, but in the meantime California kept on taking and diverting more and more water.

Arizona was strangling in its own political rhetoric. It was past time to abandon the state's rights invective that elected generations of Arizona politicians. And it was Mac, as he was popularly known, who courageously took the lead, quietly circulating around the state, patiently explaining the reality—Arizona could not hold out any longer. It was time to get behind a federal project. Finally, in 1944 the Arizona legislature ratified the compact. The path was now open for McFarland to draft and introduce the Central Arizona Project legislation and to use his power as majority leader to push it through the Senate.

Forty years later when I presided over the ceremony celebrating the arrival of Colorado River water flowing down the aqueduct into Phoenix, Mac's singular role had been pretty much forgotten. But the history of our state will record the undeniable fact that his leadership finally turned the state around and set us on the pathway to eventual success.

xi

Mac's life story should inspire young Arizonans for generations to come. He was raised on an isolated homestead in the open spaces of the Pottawatomie Strip in Oklahoma. As a young man, he migrated to Arizona in search of wider opportunities. Those came rapidly, mainly the result of hard work, a thirst for education, and a fortuitous decision to settle in the small town of Florence where a newcomer could easily spread his political wings. By the time he retired from political life, Mac had served as majority leader of the United States Senate, governor of Arizona and chief justice of the Arizona Supreme Court, a trifecta of heading all three branches of government on the state or federal level. It is a record of service without parallel in American history.

Mac lived to be nearly ninety years old, the last sixty in the public eye. He left an immense body of personal and public records for historians to ponder. This engrossing, definitive biography was nearly twenty years in the making as Dr. James E. McMillan scoured manuscript collections from coast to coast, including the presidential libraries of Franklin Roosevelt, Harry Truman, and Lyndon Johnson, and searched through vast numbers of government documents, periodicals, books, and over fifty-five thousand personal items from McFarland's papers.

McMillan has fused these various sources into a seamless picture of how McFarland's private life shaped his public career. The habits and values he acquired as a young frontiersman struggling to gain an education guided him for the rest of his life: the worth of friendship, the stability of family, the efficacy of the work ethic, the magic of reading, the tragedy of human suffering, and most especially, the joy of liberty. As Mac told me long ago, he found that these precious ideals were all embedded in the Preface to the Constitution: ". . . to form a more perfect Union, establish Justice, insure domestic Tranquility, provide for the common defence, promote the general Welfare, and secure the Blessings of Liberty . . ." His vision of America came out of these ideals. He discovered early in his public career, however, that reform usually comes in small steps rather great leaps, so he mastered the art of political compromise where his skill was evident in the fact that he seldom gave away as much as he gained.

On at least one occasion, though, Mac did not give any significant ground. The initial GI Bill of Rights, passed in June 1944 after about a year of maneuvering, was a "great leap," and Mac was saluted by his Senate colleagues as its "father." The measure and its successors have been used by over forty million veterans. Mac saw it primarily as an investment in the future, and, indeed, its ultimate benefits far outstripped its initial promises. Historians now see the GI Bill as a congressional landmark—the progenitor of the vast, prosperous middle class that has distinguished America since WWII. McFarland, as author of the sections on education and on business and home loans, simply refused to compromise on those provisions. On this count alone, he deserves his stature as one of the most important figures in Arizona history.

I cherish the memory of one of the last visits that Mac made to the governor's office that he had occupied during two memorable terms a quarter of a century before. He was in a wheel cahir and looked all of his eighty some years, but you could never have guessed that from listening to him. I was preoccupied that morning with some now forgotten issue relating to State Parks, and he responded by reminiscing about his successful effort as governor to create the state parks sysem that I was now administering.

But he was not there to dwell on the past. He had come, he explained, to make the case for developing a seaport at Yuma to draw commerce up the Gulf of California and into Arizona. Yuma, he reminded me, had once been a river port where steamboats made their way up and down the river in the days before the railroads.

Throughout his long life Mac seldom looked back. He faced personal loss and political defeat with grace and humility and he never retreated off to the sidelines for a life of leisure. What he had learned in the vanished world of the Midwestern prairie and in the precincts of Pinal County was that there was always work to be done and additional ways to be of service to Arizona. Now that I have too closed out my days in public office, Mac remains a personal inspiration, reminding me there is still more to be done; in the words of Tennyson, "Come, my friends, 'tis not too late to seek a newer world.'"

Bruce Babbitt
Former Governor of Arizona and
US Secretary of Interior

INTRODUCTION

ERNEST W. MCFARLAND, DESPITE HIS HUMBLE ORIGINS in Oklahoma's Pottawatomie Strip, was not of the common crowd. Indeed, he stands alone in American history as the only person known to have led all three branches of government on the state or federal level: majority leader of the United States Senate (1951-53), governor of Arizona (1955-59), and chief justice of the Arizona Supreme Court (1968).

Historians rigorously research the past to determine how we have reached our present circumstances for the practical purpose of better preparing for the future. No one wants to repeat past mistakes and most want to emulate past successes. It is the same with politicians, and Ernest McFarland, throughout his extraordinary career was both farseeing and practical. From the Winnie Ruth Judd "Trunk Murderess" trial to the famous Miranda decision, Mac stood among the luminaries of Arizona and national public servants.

As a United States senator, he co-authored the GI Bill, facilitated progress on the Central Arizona Project, and ultimately rose to head that body. He conscientiously served the Native Americans of the Southwest and the elderly of the nation, and he modernized communications legislation to include television as well as radio. Another measure of effectiveness is how much federal activity and funding is brought into a senator's state. During Mac's twelve years in the Senate, Arizona had the highest per capita allotment of federal funds in the nation. He and Senator Carl Hayden, who advised Mac to be a workhorse and not a show horse, knew how to promote Arizona on Capitol Hill.

As governor, Mac made great strides in health, education, and welfare for Arizonans; he also opened the state for industrial expansion and revised the entire law code. Rose Mofford often has termed McFarland Arizona's best governor ever and one who could have been re-elected interminably if he had so chosen—high praise indeed coming from one who has occupied the office herself and served under many other governors. People looked to him for direction, and got it; Mac's initiatives have benefited the executive office to this day.

He then went on in his seventies to a six-year term on the Arizona Supreme Court, including a period as chief justice. He distinguished himself by writing more opinions than any other justice during that time, even while working for a year and a half on the presidential National Commission on the Causes and Prevention of Violence in America.

After his 1971 retirement, he continued as a lawyer, farmer, and chairman-founder of KTVK-TV (Channel 3); he wrote his autobiography, founded McFarland State Park, donated generous scholarships to all Arizona colleges and universities as well as Stanford and his Oklahoma alma maters, and continued as revered family patriarch until his death in 1984. His characteristic stewardship has been passed on to his family, particularly Del and the late Jewell Lewis who have carried on his philanthropic tradition with such projects as the restoration of Phoenix's Orpheum Theater, Jewell Lewis's Fresh Start Women's Resource Center, and continued contributions to the state's universities.

Mac has long been less recognized than others like Carl Hayden and Barry Goldwater, but that oversight is now being corrected. Two recent polls listed McFarland as the fourth most important person in the state's history behind Hayden, Goldwater, and Padre Kino. He also had one of the highest approval ratings of former Arizona politicians, while, at the same time, having low name recognition. However, as stated, this is all changing. A beautiful memorial has been erected to honor his life on Wesley Bolin Plaza at the Capitol and another in Mesa recognizing his work on the GI Bill; a bust of Mac rests under the Arizona Capitol Dome and the silver service of the *USS Arizona*, which he procured for the state's people, is on prominent display nearby. Upstairs are his offices while governor and chief justice. Indeed, the Old Capitol is plangent with Mac memories.

This well conceived and scrupulously researched biography by historian James McMillan, allows us, as readers, to walk these statehouse corridors with him and the halls, offices, and chambers of the U. S. Senate, and to accompany Mac on his worldwide journeys, traveling through history with FDR and Truman, Eisenhower and Churchill, MacArthur and Marshall, LBJ and JFK, and in Arizona with the Udalls, DeConcinis, Babbitts, and, of course, Hayden and Goldwater. Mac is now sure to be accorded appropriate historic scrutiny and respect. He more than deserves it; Ernest McFarland was simply a legend in Arizona history and a major player in the nation's twentieth-century development.

Janet Napolitano
Governor of Arizona

PREFACE

ERNEST WILLIAM MCFARLAND FASHIONED an exemplary
public service career during the crucial years of modernization in
the American Southwest.   As a political and judicial force, he
wielded enormous influence from the Arizona Statehouse in
Phoenix to Capitol Hill in Washington, D. C. His length of political tenure is matched by only a few, for the popular Mac served
state and nation from 1923 to 1971, nearly a half-century.
Moreover, his interests and areas of expertise were eclectic and
included irrigation and reclamation, agriculture, communications,
social services, veterans' affairs, and complex areas of jurisprudence that encompassed all of these. Throughout his years of
service, McFarland exhibited qualities of leadership that were
called upon to guide Democratic party organizations both in
Arizona and in Washington. He always rose to whatever challenge
he confronted, and though he did experience defeat and had political weaknesses, the entirety of his career was characterized by success and informed by the qualities of compassion and stewardship
and the concrete results drawn therefrom.

Born to a family of southern background in a newly
opened section of the American West, McFarland displayed qualities of both regions. As his forbears had, he supported the
Democratic party while determining policy for the West as it
moved out of the nineteenth-century past into a twentieth-century
future of enormous potential and extreme change.

As South and West merged in McFarland, so too did varying tendencies of Democratic party politics. As a legislator he
responded to the conservative interests endorsed by his southern
colleagues when he needed their support to reap advantages for
his own constituents in Arizona. In the rapidly developing West,
however, he supported liberalization of social, economic, and fiscal policy.

Open to both conservative and liberal ideology and
demands, McFarland could appropriately be termed a political
moderate. His personal life reflected the vision of a conscience lib-

eral, but Mac recognized the necessity of becoming adept at negotiation and compromise between political poles, an activity that kept government functioning constructively. McFarland loomed large among those who expedited this work, while others — better known, but less effective — pontificated more than produced.

Political recognition and effective legislation evolves slowly, and a stable longevity in politics can be crucial to both. McFarland was not so blessed. While his political career gave evidence of a deep underlying balance, this came more from the person than the fluctuating times. His calm demeanor and steadfast equipoise enabled him to bear up under political misfortune and rebound from defeat with agility. He did have to learn how to change political roles with frequency. Change undermined stability to a degree, yet McFarland always contributed in an active capacity whether it be local politics in the 1920s and 1930s, the United States Senate of the 1940s, the Arizona executive office of the 1950s, or the Arizona judiciary of the 1960s. Although such change can limit long-term effectiveness, McFarland accomplished tasks of enduring significance, notably his work on the GI Bill and the Central Arizona Project. His influence touched heavily on the careers of those endowed with greater political stability and recognition, namely Carl Hayden, Lyndon Johnson, and, in an adversarial sense, Barry Goldwater.

The hardships of an Oklahoma upbringing led young Ernest to an aggressive educational quest that resulted in a brief teaching career in prairie schools and then preparation for the legal profession. When World War I interrupted, he enlisted in the U. S. Navy where respiratory ailments kept him out of combat and led to an early discharge. The same ailments and a keen awareness of future possibilities led him to trade his Oklahoma home for new prospects in the desert Southwest. He brought with him a rounded experience of farm, academic, and military life.

During his early Arizona years, McFarland continued to develop his interests, grasping at opportunities, not occupations. From bank teller to young farmer to law student, he plunged ahead. Never lacking confidence in himself, he gained a Stanford law degree and entered the Arizona Bar. He proved a lawyer of talent and was appointed assistant state's attorney in 1923. His baptism into electoral politics occurred two years later as a county attorney and continued as superior court judge.

Politics and law coalesced into a positive formula for McFarland during the 1930s. He complemented these legal and political interests with his growing knowledge of farming and water issues in his adopted state. Most notably, though, for his political career, he developed an acute sense for divining constituents' needs and the means to fulfill them. The path led ever upward; he always aspired to the challenge of higher positions and new experiences. To those who knew him well, it came as no surprise when McFarland announced for the U. S. Senate in 1940 and pulled off a stunning upset over incumbent Henry Fountain Ashurst to get there.

The move to Capitol Hill proved a giant political step for McFarland. He reversed the usual procedure of being well known before attaining the Senate, for he garnered broad recognition only after arriving there. In this respect, he was fortunate, for he was given a rare opportunity as a freshman senator to win broad favorable public exposure by successfully defending the Hollywood film industry against censure. Unlike many senators, before and since, he deigned not to stay in the national spotlight, but chose the relative obscurity of the senate backrooms where his work brought him larger measures of collegial approbation than popular notoriety.

McFarland established himself as a reliable and consistent worker during the war years. Keeping state interests in mind, he and senior Senator Carl Hayden began an unsurpassed record in gaining federal attention for Arizona. Exploiting Arizona's climate, they assured the state major government appropriations earmarked for service camps and air bases. Arizona contributed in kind with agricultural and mining production as well, and the appropriations continued in the postwar years—more per capita than any other state during McFarland's tenure. Most importantly, during the war, he turned his attention to the needs of U.S. servicemen, particularly regarding postwar readjustment to civilian life. Many, including President Franklin Roosevelt, addressed this issue, but no one worked harder than McFarland, who earned himself the accolade "Father of the GI Bill."

McFarland easily brushed aside competition in the U. S. Senate race of 1946. He then returned to Washington where he continued to establish himself among the more dedicated and productive senators in his areas of influence and expertise, including communications, social security, and particularly irrigation and reclamation.

His all-consuming passion during the second term involved bringing Colorado River water to the arid lands of central Arizona and realizing the vision of a productive agricultural economy in the desert valleys of the Southwest. Plans for this prospect had been drawn up and debated for a quarter-century, but for Arizona, the water remained captive in the riverbed. Now, with Mac in the Senate, these plans began to move toward fruition. He superseded even senior-Senator Carl Hayden in developing and stating Arizona's water strategy, twice obtaining senate passage of the Central Arizona Project (CAP) in 1950 and 1951. But all of his work and Hayden's influence could not dislodge the impediment of the House of Representatives where, also desirous of Colorado River water, mighty California continually thwarted Arizona's claims. Yet these early efforts proved ultimately crucial by 1968 to eventual acceptance of CAP by both the Supreme Court and Congress.

In January 1951, his Democratic colleagues selected McFarland as U. S. Senate Majority Leader, a singular honor, but one that had limiting aspects. McFarland was a majority, not a unanimous choice, and he owed his selection to the conservative southern bloc. As such, he was out of step with the liberal Fair Deal program advocated by President Harry Truman. McFarland's leadership has been criticized for being ineffective for its failure to expedite this program, but in reality, it had already been rejected in the previous Congress which had a more liberal make up and a Democratic majority of twelve rather than the mere two that McFarland held. Furthermore, he had to face the full force of McCarthyism during his tenure. Most importantly, the overriding concern and responsibility faced by this Eighty-second Congress lay in meeting the demands of the Korean War. McFarland brought order to chaos and kept the Senate focused during these two years amidst almost constant controversy among liberals and conservatives, Republicans and Democrats, and president and the American public, particularly over the firing of General Douglas MacArthur, an action McFarland fully supported.

As majority leader, McFarland remained tied to the fading image of Truman, who plummeted to an unprecedented low rating in public esteem. McFarland's political opponents in Arizona took advantage of this and of the changing demographics of the sunbelt Southwest, which indicated a growing Republican constituency. In a 1952 upset of major implications to the future of American politics, Majority Leader McFarland suffered a narrow defeat at the hands of Republican Barry Goldwater, who subtly commenced the new rise of his party's conservative wing, which had been in abeyance and now would continue to exert its growing influence until dominating party politics thirty years later.

After this unexpected end to a quite extraordinary senate career, Ernest McFarland displayed characteristic agility in rebounding from defeat and leading a resurgence of Arizona Democrats in a 1954 triumph over popular Republican incumbent Governor Howard Pyle. Constitutionally, the Arizona executive branch remained weaker than the legislative, and, although the Democrats controlled the legislature, conservatives dominated, and the more liberal governor had difficulty in fully implementing his program. Nevertheless, Mac pushed through increases in health, education and welfare benefits and assured racial equality in public hiring practices. Moreover, in an unprecedented move for a state governor, McFarland personally argued and won an important case in the Arizona-California water rights controversy before the United States Supreme Court. Additionally, in two first term special sessions of the legislature, the governor directed the re-codification of the entire Arizona law code and assured the continued expansion of industry into the state by repealing restrictive sales taxes.

Elected to second term by a landslide in 1956, McFarland continued to demonstrate his personal commitment to hard work. Associates commonly held that Mac did not drive men, but only himself, and others followed. Very popular as a governor, he probably could have been re-elected interminably, but chose instead to attempt to regain the U. S. Senate seat from Goldwater in 1958. He failed in a hotly contested election notable for questionable tactics of misrepresentation directed against him by the Goldwater Republicans and Phoenix's Pulliam press.

A return to law practice, farming interests, family-time, and the television station he had founded in 1953 could not keep the old political warhorse down long, and in 1964, McFarland successfully ran for the Arizona Supreme Court. Now in his seventies, he kept up his furious pace writing hundreds of judicial opinions, including one in 1965 that was overturned by the U. S. Supreme Court in the famous *Miranda v. Arizona* case. Mac served as acting chief justice in 1967, chief justice in 1968, and in 1968-69, he added to this heavy work burden as a member of the thirteen-man National Commission on the Causes and Prevention of Violence in America, serving under Presidents Lyndon Johnson and Richard Nixon.

Ernest McFarland retired from public life in 1971 after having represented his state in its highest positions in the legislative, executive, and judicial branches of government, a unique public service record unsurpassed in American political history. Many rewarding golden years awaited Mac, who continued his diverse roles as a respected legal counselor, an honored television executive, a prosperous farmer, a writer, an advocate of historical preservation, a generous philanthropist, and a doting grandfather. Perhaps Stanford University Law School best summed up McFarland's life when six years before his June 8, 1984 death, it certified Mac as its "Most Distinguished Living Alumnus."

McFarland's significant contributions to his state and nation are well recognized by contemporary political leaders. Former Senate Majority Leader and still-current Senator Robert M. Byrd of West Virginia stated, "his life encapsulates the essence of modern U. S. history." Former thirty-year congressman, the late Morris Udall, remarked, "Perhaps more than any other individual, Ernest W. McFarland has written the story of modern Arizona." Former Governor and Secretary of the Interior in the Clinton Administration Bruce Babbitt wrote in tribute, "He served as a bridge between the old and the new Arizona as we grew from a pioneer to a modern state." In a final tribute, retired United States Senator Dennis DeConcini praised McFarland as "truly a man of the people. Perhaps the proof of which is that all who met him, from presidents to paupers, knew him simply as Mac."

Part I

The Making of a Senator
1894-1940

CHAPTER ONE

OKLAHOMA YOUTH
1894-1919

ERNEST W. MCFARLAND'S RISE TO PROMINENCE in the politics of the American Southwest evolved from both his and his forbears' quest for achievement and contentment in new lands. The family continually moved west from the Atlantic coast to the plains to the deserts and mountains. Born of southern heritage in a newly opened section of the western prairies, McFarland went on to display qualities of both regions in terms of personal values and Democratic party politics. From an Oklahoma log cabin to Capitol Hill to the Arizona Statehouse, he bridged the years of late nineteenth-century frontier experience to those of late twentieth-century modernization. Indeed, the lessons of one were integral to the actualization of the other.

Robert and Sarah McFarland, his paternal great-grandparents, emigrated from Scotland in the late 1700s, settling in North Carolina. They later moved on to Bedford County beyond the mountains in south-central Tennessee where grandfather William was born at the dawn of the new century on September 26, 1800. He married late in life in 1839 to a woman, Elizabeth Wilkins Kelton Good, twenty years his junior. Their first child, William Thomas McFarland, Ernest's father, was born another twenty years later on August 28, 1859, in Manchester.

McFarland's mother, Keziah, was born in 1863 at Athens, Tennessee, just over the Carolina border and Appalachian barrier, to Ewell and Julia Ann Owens Smith. During the Civil War, Ewell had obtained the rank of captain and had fought for

3

the Confederacy under Generals Braxton Bragg and James Longstreet in the western theater. At war's end, the "Captain" as he was called, and his family moved out to Pelham, about twenty miles south of Manchester. Here the Smiths and McFarlands came into contact, and William and Keziah were married on December 1, 1881.

Rural Tennessee had remained economically depressed in the postwar period, and after three years residence in Pelham, the young farming couple decided to move to the open country of Texas. They arrived in 1884, lured by the promise of a stable and secure life, possible now after the subjugation of the Indians, and a potentially profitable agricultural economy assisted by the advancing railroads. Three years later, a son, Forrest G., was born in McGregor, just to the west of Waco. Buffeted by the fickle Texas weather, the McFarlands searched for greener pastures to the north near the Red River border with Oklahoma and Indian Territories. Here, in Nocona, Texas, a daughter, Etta Pearl was born on June 28, 1891.[1]

Texas droughts and other agrarian hardships persisted, and so did William McFarland's restlessness, his undimmed hope that the next move would bring prosperity. The optimistic idea of progress ran deep and strong in the stream of McFarland Family tradition. William was one of the conduits who carried this tradition from eighteenth-century Scotland to twentieth-century Arizona. Almost predictably, his wandering eye caught notices of the pending opening of the Pottawatomie Strip. The strip lay a hundred miles to the northeast in what had been Indian Territory, but was now to be opened to white settlement and affixed to Oklahoma. Oklahoma Territory had been founded only recently in 1889 and continued to be enlarged and carved out of former Indian lands.

Through a combination of white political and economic pressure, the enforcement of the Dawes Severalty Act of 1887, and Indian reserve and, in rare cases, enterprise, Oklahoma went through the transition from Indian Territory to state between 1889 and 1907. The first opening or land run had occurred on April 22, 1889, into lands in central Oklahoma which had been previously unassigned to specific tribes. Now, lands of the Pottawatomie, Shawnee, Iowa, and Sac and Fox (Meskwakie), collectively known as the Pottawatomie Strip, were scheduled as the second land opening on September 22, 1891. The terms for settling the new area remained the same as the original run: at a uniform signal, prospective pioneers gathered on the border of the strip could enter the new lands and, for a small fee, file a claim to a quarter-section (160 acres) of land to be occupied for five years and paid for in the amount of $1.25 per acre, or $200 total. As opening day arrived, twenty thousand people (about three times more than the available quarter-sections) eagerly awaited the signal to stake a claim to part of the 1.12 million available acres.[2]

William Thomas McFarland waited among those anticipating the signal, his pioneering blood rising once again in expectation. People readied themselves on horse and oxen, aboard carriages and buggies, some even on bicycle or on foot. McFarland, like many, made the run in a covered wagon. Leaving his wife, four-year-old son, and infant daughter behind, he carried only the necessities for staking a claim: pick, hammer, saw, axe, shovel, wood boards for marking boundaries, food for animals and man, basic sleeping gear and tent shelter, and, of course, weapons. Indeed, McFarland had to run off one early arrival or "sooner" who had jumped the signal gun. Another "sooner" proved more troublesome and had to be bought off with one hundred dollars, a considerable sum in those days for this agrarian family.

McFarland entered the Pottawatomie Strip from the east and the lands of the Seminole Nation, one among the Five Civilized Tribes retaining title to most of eastern Oklahoma, still called Indian Territory. With an eye for the land, he established his claim in Sec. 8, T-9N, R-5E. The eastern boundary of his 160 acres lay just one-half mile to the west of the Seminole Nation border. Here, the Oklahoma prairie was not wholly typical, being more than rolling, even hilly, rather heavily covered by oak forests, and interlaced with numerous streams both large and small. These flowed down to the

Canadian River some twenty miles to the south, up several miles to the North Canadian, or into the Little River running through the middle of the strip. The abundance of wood and water in the area made pioneering somewhat easier to bear than in the more arid regions west of the 98th meridian — areas such as the Cherokee Strip which were settled later in the 1890s.

McFarland settled his claims and affairs in Tecumseh, the newly founded seat of "County B," later to be called Pottawatomie. He established friendships in the vicinity of his claim to watch over it, as he would theirs, upon returning to Texas later in the fall to gather his family and make the move to the virgin farming soil of Oklahoma. The family arrived on December 10, 1891 — William, Keziah, Forrest, and Etta — a representative homesteading group:

> The typical frontier family consisted of a big-boned, shaggy father with a determined wife and several small children. Their prairie schooner bulged with chickens, farm implements, furniture and mattresses, and the ubiquitous family dog. A leather trunk or box might hold mementos of other and perhaps happier days, a few worn books, some fragile china, or a bit of wedding lace.[3]

The family moved into a crude, one-room log cabin that William had constructed over the previous months -- an edifice that would be improved upon but suffice without expansion for the next few years. Here near Earlsboro, Oklahoma, in the small pioneer home, Keziah gave birth to her second son, Ernest William, on October 9, 1894, three years after the frontier disappeared from the Pottawatomie Strip. McFarland thus became one of the last American politicians who could claim the Lincolnesque distinction of a log cabin birth. Robert S. Kerr, born two years later and a few dozen miles to the south, could make the same claim, but it was Ernest McFarland who attained the honor of being the first native-born Oklahoman to serve in the United States Senate.

* * *

Family life in Pottawatomie County centered on the eco-
nomics of the farm. As a growing boy, Ernest learned the ways
of the woods, streams, and fields, both cultivated and unculti-
vated, the ways of wild and domestic birds and animals, and very
early on the physical demands placed upon a son of a prairie
farmer. The young field hand plowed furrows for cotton and
corn. He rode horseback through tall stirrup-high prairie grasses herding and tending scattered dairy and beef cattle to milk or
market, always helped by an ever-present dog. He grew inured
to fencepost digging and board construction, and he harvested
plants and trees as the modest, self-sufficient farm also produced vegetables, fruit, and poultry products. He adapted to
daily and seasonal routines of hard work. It was the only way to
get by and the McFarlands did. The rigorous demands of farm
work molded the habits of industry and steadfastness that so
characterized Ernest's later political career when he gained fame
as a "workhorse" senator, governor, and supreme court justice.

The family's material possessions grew as well. Father and sons
added a stable-barn and outbuildings and dug a storm cellar to
protect from hot summers, cold winters, and the ominous prairie
tornado and, most importantly, they expanded the home center.
By the turn-of-the-century, the single-room log cabin had been
finished into a frame home of five rooms with side porches, glass
windows, ornamental shrubbery, a sidewalk, and front gate.
Collections of old photographs depict a strong unified family
standing by the home. At a 1907 reunion attended by dozens
from Tennessee and Texas as well as Oklahoma, Father William,
at near fifty years, stands out as tall, thin to an extreme, with
healthy short-cropped brown hair, with a paintbrush mustache
and a long narrow head set off by the McFarland ears seemingly
readying for flight. Like the father, Mother Keziah appears stern
and judgmental with narrow set mouth and deep sharp eyes.
Older brother Forrest, too, appears serious at twenty years while
sixteen-year old Etta Pearl provides some much needed softness

and indeed beauty to the scenario. Ernest at thirteen, freckle-faced and like Forrest in homespun suit, looks every bit the callow farm youth uncomfortable with formal pose and camera, waiting to be released to explore the fields and streams with the shepard dog at his side. By this time the family had been increased by a third son, Sterling Carl, born in 1900. At seven and with the same designed suit-coat, he is in shorts, barefoot, croquet mallet in hand, ready for work, play, or posing. It is an impressive family group.[4]

Vestiges of frontier life abounded in Oklahoma. Spanish longhorns still roamed the tall grass prairie and covered wagons continually moved westward through the area. But just as these symbolized the frontier past to the wide-eyed McFarland boys, they marked progress as well. Likewise, the nearby growing village of Earlsboro provided some modernized amenities for the farm family.

Earlsboro was founded shortly after the opening of the strip in 1891 when the Choctaw Coal and Railroad Company extended its tracks westward from the Seminole Nation lands and deposited a boxcar there to serve as a depot. Settlement already existed in the area, and the McFarland cabin lay one-half mile east of what became the town center. Hopping on and off the slow moving trains, which ran in sight of the farmhouse provided youthful entertainment for Ernest and his brothers.[5]

As the train created tiny Earlsboro, so too did the proximity of Indian Territory, just a mile away, create its character. Seminoles and members of other tribes were always present along with a number of Black Seminole freedmen who counted among the original town inhabitants. The freedmen were former slaves who had escaped from Georgia and Alabama into the Florida swamps retained by the Seminoles. The escaped slaves were gradually incorporated into the tribe as equal members, including a share in later land rights. When a large segment of the tribe was forcibly removed west in the 1830s, many freedmen accompanied them to what became Oklahoma.[6]

Earlsboro's racial flair — black, white, and Native American — achieved increased visibility via the proliferation of saloons along its one main street. Alcohol was illegal in Indian Territory and as a bordering village, Earlsboro became one of many "whiskey towns." Although there were never more than five taverns operating at one time, that was enough to establish the town's reputation as wide open. Most everyone drank. Whiskey sold for ten cents a glass, and the drinking men carried six-guns. Bullpens with high fence enclosures were found behind every bar where the most satisfied customers could sleep off their libations watched by town youth who also wandered unrestricted in and out of the whiskey establishments.

Ernest McFarland did not appear among these wayward Earlsboro youth, for the town had another face, and his family formed an integral part of it, namely the church. William and Keziah were steeped in the Southern Baptist tradition, which had been particularly strong in their former roots in Texas. They and thousands of others brought their stern upright religion with them on the trek north to the newly opened lands. Equally in evidence was the religious influence of Kansas to the north, which contributed a large portion of "Jayhawker" settlers and their Methodist religion.

Earlsboro contained two churches, Baptist and Methodist, but neither could support a full-time preacher, so they held alternate Sunday services. The McFarlands attended both denominations, often inviting the preacher back for supper, and the family attended also a "protracted" confessional meeting on Thursday nights. Later, after he moved to Arizona, Ernest McFarland decided to join the somewhat less restrictive and fundamentalist Methodist Church.

By 1905 Earlsboro had peaked at a population of about five hundred. Along with the whiskey trade (ninety percent of the merchants dealt profitably in some facet of it), the town functioned as the commercial center for hinterland farmers, who themselves engaged primarily in cotton and cattle. Besides saloons, community businesses included three hotels, three cotton gins, a grist mill, a sawmill, blacksmith shops, livery stables, various smaller shops and groceries, and a bank, later robbed in the 1930s by the locally and ironically popular Pretty Boy

Floyd, who was known to share his stolen largesse with the needy. Besides the local farmers, townspeople, and Indians, railroad workers comprised the most prevalent group.

As statehood approached in 1907, the town underwent a rather radical change as liquor dealers began an exodus, aware of the prohibitionist sentiment in Oklahoma. Prohibition did, indeed, carry with the voters 130,361 to 112,258, and Earlsboro's first decline began, the population dropping to just above three hundred by 1920, a year after Ernest McFarland's departure from the area. For over two decades, the town and surrounding country had provided a pleasant and constructive environment for his growth to manhood, whether it was the exciting territorial days or the more staid era immediately after statehood.

Earlsboro later experienced another growth period that exceeded all predictions shortly after the McFarland family left. On March 1, 1926, the Earlsboro section of the Greater Seminole oil field was tapped into, precipitating an oil boom that brought the population in the immediate vicinity up to as many as ten thousand people. Ironically, the recently sold McFarland homestead had sat square in the middle of the wealthy area dotted with hundreds of oil rigs. The boom gave out early in the depression years, however, and Earlsboro settled back into the small village existence that remains today.[7]

Limited school facilities in Earlsboro and the demands of farming life informed McFarland's early education, but his parents, neither of whom had gone beyond the eighth grade, were determined to provide the best available. Ernest began schooling in the one-room schoolhouse on the east edge of town and continued there as classrooms were added until a new brick structure replaced the old wooden one in 1905. The new school offered studies only through grade ten, but it was exciting nevertheless with modern iron-legged desks rather than crude splintery benches, a gymnasium, and a pasture converted into a baseball field - a sport which Ernest avidly pursued as a young player and later as a longtime fan. Between innings, or classes, he and his classmates discussed current topics like local sports hero Jim Thorpe, who later in 1912 would dominate the Olympics. Thorpe, a Shawnee Indian, was born and raised a few miles to the north in Pottawatomie County. The young boys also dipped into the past to the days, only three decades removed, when the James and Younger gangs rode, camped, and hid in the area.[8]

School recreation and academics were oft interrupted by farming demands when the students gave priority to the planting and harvest. When McFarland turned eight, the family moved forty miles northeast to Okemah to attempt a new venture while still leasing the Earlsboro fields to other farmers. After a year, the family returned to the homestead, but the children missed a year of schooling, for Okemah had none.

After Earlsboro's grade ten, Ernest was forced to go seven miles away to Seminole for eleventh grade. Young McFarland and his cousin, also a student, "batched" it for the year, living independent of parents and working as janitors at the school. The lands of the Seminole Nation had been incorporated into Oklahoma at statehood in 1907, and now the town of Seminole had grown twice as large as Earlsboro, but the young independents avoided temptation enough to pass the grade, though as janitors, they proved far less worthy. In fact, it was the only job from which McFarland was ever fired.

The next year, McFarland returned to Earlsboro, where the high school had been completed. One of three members in this first graduating class of 1914, he ranked third. His report card for his senior year showed the following yearly grade averages: history — 88.3, literature — 80.7, physics — 82.7, mathematics — 89.3, Latin — 80.7, and German — 83.7. McFarland was over nineteen and one-half years old upon high school graduation, a year or two older than his classmates, because of farming demands and the lost year in Okemah.[9]

In the spring of 1914, farming chores took up much of Ernest's time as he finished high school. His father had put in an extra-large cotton crop and given his son an interest in it to finance his higher education. Unfortunately, drought depleted the crop, but money was found, nevertheless, and, in the fall of 1914, amidst the excitement of the new war in Europe, Ernest matriculated at East Central State Normal School in Ada, Oklahoma, fifty miles south beyond the South Canadian River from Earlsboro.

Up until this time, McFarland's life had been extremely insulated except, perhaps, for his junior high school year in Seminole. He had met very few people, particularly those of his own age, and traveled in only limited areas. Indeed, he was described by Ada classmates as simply "a quiet country boy bent on getting an education." But his lonely days were soon to end. He proved a hard worker and began to enter into activities and studies, which led in turn to meeting new people.[10]

Coincidentally, one of these new acquaintances, Robert S. Kerr, would later serve with him in the United States Senate. They began their close, lifetime friendship at this time when both joined the Phi Delta Debating Club. The Phi Delts contested issues with the older campus organization, the Forum Debating Society, which dated from the school's beginnings in 1909. Spirited competition ensued and the new club won its share, boasting "among the wearers of PD pins are some of the most prominent students of ECSN." McFarland took his public speaking very seriously and adhered to the discourse dictums of his day as presented in such books as *Lessons in Vocal Expression: Processes of Thinking in the Modulation of the Voice*, and *The Speaking Voice: Principles of Training Simplified and Condensed* (the only two Ada Normal textbooks that remain in the McFarland collection today). He referred to these later in life, for in formal situations, and there were many, his discourse was painfully correct, clear, and concise, and delivered in a rather monotone style. Informally and when relying on down-home colloquial vernacular, he was much more effective. The tall domineering Bob Kerr learned this lesson well, and after joining McFarland in Washington in 1948, went on to an imperious career as "King of the Senate" until his death in 1963. Kerr's college mates had him described well in the yearbook noting that "He likes to fight, and this spirit will likely lead him into politics. Once in, we venture that he will not stop before adding to his name M.C. or U.S.S."[11]

The reference to McFarland in the same 1915 yearbook is also of interest:

> Following the bent of his reckless disposition, Ernest becomes an   aviator, and his heedless sense of adventure inspires him with the desire to "circumnavigate" the globe in twenty-four hours.   This experiment leaves him hanging in the pines of the Rockies. Thereafter, McFarland is more conservative in his ideas, and he becomes the head of a small parish in Arkansas.

College years can be particularly impressionable, certainly to one so insular as Ernest. Though just over twenty, his country background narrowed his experience and, as the yearbook slogan suggests, he vacillated between recklessness and conservatism in his college life. When tricked into getting drunk with his classmates, he enjoyed it, a not surprising fact regarding a youth from two-faced Earlsboro. Young Ernest listened and experimented with all sides, as he would later with considerable skill as a politician.[12]

Ernest also became well acquainted with the school's first president Charles W. Briles, who was to doubly influence his early career. Briles took a personal interest in McFarland's progress. Learning that the young student lacked funds and was reluctant to ask his father for help after the failed cotton crop, Briles lent him twenty-five dollars to complete fall quarter studies. The president detected something of a pedagogue in Ernest and directed him towards the teacher preparation curriculum. By the end of the quarter, Ernest had accumulated enough courses for a one-year teaching certificate. Still needing funds, he took a teaching position at the minuscule crossroads town of Schoolton at the top of Seminole County. Moving north, and back into the country, McFarland kept Briles's adage in mind that there existed no finer profession for "keeping boys and girls on the right track."[13]

This could not be accomplished without some diplomacy, and the young teacher-on-horseback soon faced a problem with a prairie version of juvenile delinquency. Encouraged by local young rowdies and cowboys, the Schoolton students, some older and larger than Ernest, had succeeded in running the former two teachers out of town and were determined to set McFarland on the same course. Ernest proved able, through homespun humor, a cool, unfluttered manner, and physical presence, to frustrate the young rowdies. Later, he would bring these same qualities to politics, when he was recognized in the Senate for his unflappable bearing and subtle humor.

The position lasted only for the winter, however, and spring 1915 found McFarland back on an agitated Ada campus, troubled by Charles Briles's political alliances. The president had picked the wrong man in the Democratic gubernatorial primaries of 1914, and the victor, new Governor Robert L. Williams, targeted Briles for removal from the state position. Associates of Williams brought formal charges of malfeasance against Briles, including preferential treatment of Methodists over Baptists and his wife's domination of "the moral life of the community and the Girl's Basketball team."[14] Classes adjourned and students joined townspeople for the excitement of the June 1915 trial that acquitted Briles of the charges. However, his professional stature was permanently damaged, and he was dismissed a year later in the summer of 1916.

In the meantime, Ernest finished spring quarter studies while filling out the balance of a math teacher's year at Ada High School. McFarland preferred mathematics and engineering in his academics but drifted from the latter because of shortcomings in mechanical drawing. Indeed, any kind of script from blackboard to drawing board seemed difficult for him, and his adult hand became close to indecipherable. Overcoming these difficulties and piling on the work, he graduated from East Central at summer's end. The next year the normal school had a teaching position open, and Ernest applied to President Briles but did not get the job. Although the president said he would like to have hired McFarland, he declined because of his pending ouster and the expectation that Ernest, whose appreciative friendship for the president was well known, would not be allowed to retain the position. A victim of politics for the first time, McFarland abandoned his teaching aspirations, explaining "I then decided I wanted to be in a profession where I could fight back and not in one where I could be fired and have to keep still 'for the good of the cause.' "[15]

The year spent at East Central Normal had proven productive, bringing McFarland a lifetime teaching certificate, experience on two teaching jobs, and a broadened network of Oklahoma friends. He now determined to continue his studies, majoring initially in mathematics, at the top of the state educational system, the University of Oklahoma, which had been founded in 1892 at Norman. Once again his father stretched to come up with tuition and living expenses, deepening Ernest's commitment to escape the farm. Hard farm work, though, had left its mark upon him. The old Puritan economic virtues had been deeply etched on his psyche by both the Bible and the plow. He knew how to bear down and do what had to be done on the farm and at Ada. Now he continued the pattern in Norman, double-timing on several jobs as well as classes. As he put it, "It's better than being at home, looking a mule in the tail from sunrise 'til sundown."[16]

Working as a janitor, waiter, and grocer, Ernest completed his initial year at the university and hoped for the permanent position at Ada. Turned down in the wake of Briles's problems, he sold insurance that summer and made the career decision to forgo teaching and engage in pre-law studies at Norman. Work as librarian in the law school's new Monnet Hall and membership in the Wilson Law Review Club complemented his studies. He also maintained his interest in public speaking, joining the junior and senior debate societies, called the House and the Senate. After a second year's preparation, Ernest graduated from the University of Oklahoma on June 5, 1917, with a bachelor's degree and a major in law preparation.[17]

Two months previously, President Woodrow Wilson had

led the United States into the Great War, which had erupted in 1914. McFarland and dozens of his fellow graduates eagerly joined the American war effort, Ernest enlisting for a term of four years in the United States Navy as a second-class seaman at Oklahoma City on December 11, 1917. Two months beyond twenty-three years of age, he presented a lean figure at five foot, ten inches and 145 pounds. College and military era photos reveal a youthful, handsome face set off by the protruding family ears. Assigned to the Great Lakes Naval School on Lake Michigan, just north of Chicago, Illinois, McFarland left his native state for the first time. In fact, his geographical past had been limited to a small circle around Earlsboro, including Norman to the west, Ada to the south, and Muskogee the furthest point, one hundred miles to the northeast.

Navy life failed to suit the strapping farm youth. Although he did not experience the dangers of submarine or trench warfare, he had his own nemesis in the northern winter weather. The freezing winds blowing off the lake eclipsed in power the chilly gusts of the southern plains. Within months, he contracted pneumonia and was placed in the naval hospital listed as "seriously ill."[18]

Admitted on March 3, 1918, and placed on a liquid diet, Ernest's condition improved by March 12, and two days later the hospital notified the family in Earlsboro that no more telegrams on his health would be sent. Happily back on solids by March 16, Ernest felt "just dandy" and looked forward to a sick leave home in Oklahoma. His letters expressed concern over the farm's operation, Forrest having moved to nearby Shawnee leaving only younger brother Carl to help his father. Ernest hoped to send the family money from unused navy and saved teaching pay.

The illness lingered, however, and a relapsed second stage necessitated an operation on March 23. This rear-entry lung surgery removed part of a rib, drained built up fluids, and became a vicarious war wound McFarland carried the remainder of his life. Unfortunately, post-operation complications developed and his condition deteriorated. Periocarditis, pleurisy, and emphysema racked his body for weeks, and letters written by nurses to family members only increased their anxiety. On April 27, the hospital reported his condition as "not improved," and the next day a dreaded telegram arrived at the McFarland farm: "Condition serious. Recovery doubtful."

Keziah McFarland immediately entrained to her son's bedside and remained to nurse and comfort him for the remainder of May. The mother's touch proved effective and her intuition perceptive as she continued at her post while Ernest slowly backed away from death. Keziah monitored another relapse, but by June her son stabilized, and she returned to Earlsboro.

The ensuing months of recovery passed slowly and painfully for McFarland, and homesickness exacerbated the ordeal, but he had been far too ill to be released on a sick leave. As the war expired in November 1918, Ernest remained bound to the hospital. Finally, on January 31, 1919, the navy honorably discharged him. The Board of Medical Examiners had recommended disability in the line of duty. In total, McFarland had served 330 of 416 days on the sick list. The discharge papers also noted that he achieved top 4.0 ratings in obedience and sobriety and a 2.8 proficiency due to his illness, and that he had drawn out only $14.50 in salary during the year's service, saving the remainder to assist the farm or set aside for the future.

In later years, McFarland refused any elaboration of these dark months and his close brush with death, perhaps having had seen too much of the same since. He himself remained endowed with good health for the balance of his life. Indeed, according to one close associate, he had "the stamina of an ox."[19] He also retained a lifelong dedication to the United States Navy.

The months spent in the base hospital afforded McFarland much time to ruminate on future plans, and when he returned to Earlsboro, these crystallized into making the move away from the Oklahoma homestead to the newest state in the union, Arizona. Arizona had a reputation for a salubrious climate, particularly for those with lung problems. But, this was not all that the "Baby State" represented. In 1919, the underpopulated desert Southwest still held the old frontier promises of opportunity and hope, the same visions that had inspired his family elders to migrate from North Carolina to Tennessee, to Texas, to Oklahoma, indeed all the way from Scotland — goals to contribute and achieve — so young McFarland continued the family tradition of moving west.

The plains years had been enriching but filled with hardships for the McFarland family. While still in Ada, Ernest had chosen education over farming; at Norman he gave up education for an as yet undetermined "independent" profession such as law. Politics had not yet crystallized in his thinking. He did, however, reveal a desire and capacity to acquire more knowledge and experience with whatever means available and at whatever expense necessary. He did not stand pat. Learning tasks superseded farming chores, mathematics took preference over engineering studies, and finally pre-law preparation replaced teaching. He laid aside all of these ambitions for military responsibilities in World War I. Returning from service shaken, but not broken from his severe illness, he allowed the wanderlust that took him from his birthplace home of a quarter-century. McFarland took with him positive and basic attributes from Oklahoma: a sense of independent responsibility and self-reliance and a willingness to extend beyond the capabilities of others and dedicate himself to the most difficult tasks ahead. These characteristics had been inculcated by the family life on the prairie. McFarland now broke Sooner ties as he faced new challenges and development in the forty-eighth state.

CHAPTER TWO

EARLY ARIZONA YEARS
1919-1930

AFTER A FEW MONTHS OF REST AND FAMILY COMPAN-
IONSHIP at the Earlsboro homestead, Ernest McFarland put his
moving plans into operation and left for Phoenix, Arizona, in
early May 1919. Traveling by rail on the Rock Island Line
down to the Southern Pacific, the twenty-four year-old veteran
wore his uniform and carried ten dollars in his pocket and hopefully enough food to last the journey. Traversing the West Texas
expanses to El Paso, Ernest declined to wire ahead to an uncle
about his impending arrival when informed of the $1.10 price
tag. Leaving the unsent telegram on the counter, he re-board-
ed the train and departed into New Mexico adding new territory to his experience with each passing mile. His "navy blues"
must have had the appropriate effect on a compassionate telegraph girl, who sent the arrival message on without Ernest's
knowledge. Crossing the New Mexico-Arizona border, he ran
out of food but the ten dollars remained untouched.
Tightening his belt, he traveled up through Tucson musing on
potential employment opportunities — or lack thereof — in the
dry desert country. He had no set plan for obtaining a job, but
would use his intuition. In the back of his mind, there was
always the possibility of somehow entering law school.

McFarland arrived in Phoenix on May 10, 1919, the ten
dollars in hand, to be met by his Uncle Poliet Smith, brother to
Keziah. Uncle Poliet had been the first of the McFarland-
Smith relations to move beyond Oklahoma to the Far West, and
he now opened his Peoria home (just west of Phoenix) to his

young nephew. It was only for a short time, however, as within a few days Ernest managed to find employment at the Valley Bank in downtown Phoenix, moving there as well to begin a job as bookkeeper that would carry him through the sweltering summer months.[1]

McFarland's initial impressions of Arizona were negative as indicated in a poetic note aptly labeled "Exile" found among his papers:

> I am down in Arizona on its cactus-covered plains away down upon the desert. It is a God-forsaken place where you fight with the odds against you when you've taken your last stand. Where you live out in the open among the sagebrush and mesquite with a rattler as a neighbor, not the friendliest to meet — where you fling yourself on a bunk to rest your weary head and you shake the blooming scorpions from the covers of your bed. Oh, I look out upon the sagebrush as I stretch my yearning hands over the long unbroken reaches of the desert's burning sands to a land where brooks are honest. When your lips are parched and dry — not the canyons clear deceptive streams of tasteless alkali. Oklahoma has no mountains full of wealth, mines and drills, but I'd give this whole damned country for one sight of its rolling hills.

For the moment, homesickness and doubt lingered, but Mac, as he would come to be known to everyone in Arizona, soon changed his mind. In a later interview, he stated: ". . . one thing that appealed to me when I first came to Arizona. You could look out and see a country just like nature made it - in which beautiful sunset or sunrise were the rule and not the exception. All blended together for natural beauty of a country with large vistas."[2]

The seven-year-old "Baby State," though barely out of the nineteenth century economically and culturally, presented open opportunity. Ernest's new hometown, Phoenix, held a population of twenty-nine thousand and had just recently eclipsed in size, the "Old Pueblo" Tucson, which numbered twenty thousand. The entire state's population stood under 250,000. Mountains and desert dominated, and water remained scarce. Still, a viable agricultural trade had been developing based on alfalfa and the state's newest top farm crop, cotton.

Cotton joined cattle and copper as the foundational "three 'C's" of Arizona's economy. Indeed, as ranching continued an older style of western life, mining commenced an era as the state's leading economic component. Arizona already ranked first in the nation in copper production. McFarland found himself well placed in a state on the brink of vast potential and growth. He looked forward to developing his stake in this future and over the next sixty years would play a dominant role in all areas of Arizona's growth and maturation. Particularly concerning water use, McFarland's reasoned planning would prove influential in the state's future.[3]

Water scarcity was evident everywhere, except to a degree in Maricopa County where the Salt River had been harnessed and channeled by 1911 with the completion of the Roosevelt Dam. This Salt River Project, the first national reclamation effort under 1902's Newlands Act and one of Theodore Roosevelt's major conservation successes, provided Phoenix and its surrounding towns of Mesa, Tempe, and Scottsdale, with adequate water to leap ahead of other environs in agricultural production. To the north and west, the great Colorado River of the West ran free but contained in its banks for most of its length, controlled only by the Laguna Dam on its lower reaches near Yuma and the Mexican border. McFarland numbered among the many who speculated on the vast potential and reward of bringing these waters to a much-extended portion of Arizona.

Air conditioners were non-existent and evaporative "swamp" coolers only in developmental stages in this climate of daily temperatures in excess of one hundred degrees over five-month periods. As he tallied cattle, cotton, and copper accounts at the Valley Bank amidst the heat, Ernest considered the alternative of a law career to that of banking, commenting to a fellow clerk, "We belong on the other side of the bank. I don't think I'll ever make it there so I'm going to Stanford to finish my law." He successfully applied for admission to the Stanford University Law School and moved to Palo Alto, California, for the fall 1919 semester, but he never entertained any ideas of abandoning his newly adopted state. Using his veteran status, he filed a homestead claim on 160 acres of land near Casa Grande, humorously referred to later in life as his "jackrabbit farm."[4]

Using his savings from teaching and the service, McFarland plunged into his academic work in his usual vigorous fashion. Stanford held classes on the quarter system, and he attended four straight sessions through the summer of 1920, augmenting his legal preparation with courses in political science. Taking constitutional law, international administration, and analyzing topics such as the origin, nature, and purpose of the state, natural law, sovereignty, and theories of property and slavery, he read his way through Plato, Aristotle, Cicero, Thomas Aquinas, Machiavelli, Montesquieu, Locke, and Rousseau.[5]

Such a regimen would seem to leave little room for recreation, but Ernest found time to explore the streets of San Francisco and attend sporting events at nearby Berkeley as well as on his own campus where a huge new athletic stadium was then under construction. He waxed eloquent about the environs: "Today is a wonderful day, and as I look out upon the rising foothills, the red roofs of Stanford University, and the bay in the distance from my window, I am filled with the splendor of it, all the good and great things our Maker has given us."[6]

Ernest found time for parties as well, and at a Christmas 1919 soiree, met former Stanford student Clare Collins, a talented musician and aspiring teacher then attending Arizona Teacher's College in Flagstaff. Her name crops up in the few remaining Stanford letters from Ernest to his family and soon she met his parents who had moved to Arizona.

Indeed, Ernest had initiated a familial migration to his adopted state. Perhaps sensing something of vision and anticipation in the young man, all family members followed the middle son to the Phoenix area. While Ernest toiled over his books at Stanford, Keziah and William, with teenage son Carl in tow, made the move in April 1920. Before the year expired, sister Etta, her husband Melton Lawrence Hammen, and their children joined the Arizona McFarlands, leaving Seminole, Oklahoma, to set up a lumber business outside of Phoenix. By the next year, older brother Forrest, his wife, and children further expanded the contingent, leaving Shawnee, Oklahoma, bringing the number of parents, children, and grandchildren to a dozen, a closely bound group still pioneering in a sense.[7]

McFarland communicated often with his transplanted parents offering encouragement and advice on their new Arizona surroundings. Of course, his letters acknowledged homesickness and a desire to be by their side at their new home. He also, not surprisingly, expressed some insecurity in the wide world of the Pacific Coast, so far removed from the familiar plains and his short-lived desert home, noting, "As I looked out upon 2,000 students this A.M. I thought of the aims and desires of each of us. Each of us has a jewel we want to pick. . . . A small percent of us will reach that goal, so do not be disappointed if I am one of those who, in the eyes of the world, fail, but try and be content if each of us do our best. . . ." In this Mother's Day 1920 letter, he continued:

> So when you are thinking of the possibilities of your children and you happen to think of my possibilities, please do not expect much of me, because I am only one among many and all cannot succeed in this word the world calls success. But you should be content if each of us in our humble way succeeds in doing just a little toward making the world a better world. After all that is real success.[8]

At other times, Ernest lightened up his message while advising Carl on his vegetable garden or his father not to get "blue" over lung pains — "he had the same pains" — and noting proudly his weight gain to 160 pounds — admonishing "Carl, you had better get there" — or indicating surprise that late evenings no longer agreed with him — "guess I am getting old or something," at age twenty-five years. Ernest looked forward to returning to the new homestead, but not before he had the opportunity to attend his first of many Democratic National Conventions — as an usher — in San Francisco, the year the party nominated James Cox in a futile effort against Republican Warren G. Harding.[9]

Stanford recommended that its law students spend a quarter's time as a clerk to a law firm and offered to arrange such opportunities in the Bay area, but Ernest, both homesick and with a full year of academic achievement under his belt, determined to return to Arizona and serve his apprenticeship there in the fall of 1920. He was invited to clerk for the Phoenix office of Phillips, Cox, and Phillips, headed by Republican Judge John C. Phillips, who went on to serve as Arizona Governor from 1929 to 1931. Here McFarland came in contact with state politics for the first time. He also sat for and passed his Arizona Bar exam as he had planned. He fully intended to enter the legal field with all flags unfurled and requirements met when he completed his Stanford studies.

Returning to Palo Alto for the winter, spring, and summer quarters, 1920-21, he continued his law program adding to it studies on public utilities and water law. He also took enough political science courses to earn a master of arts degree in that discipline upon completing his thesis a few years later. Once again, during this second lengthy stay at Stanford, Mother's Day elicited thankful feelings from Ernest who wrote:

> We are sometimes not as appreciative of mothers as we should be and it is nice to have this one day to remind us of our shortcoming. Our futures are determined, to a great extent . . . 1st by heredity and 2nd by environment. We inherit certain traits, which are molded and trained by environment. The kind of parents one has determines, to a large extent, his environment for he is under their care while young – and impressions last afterward. The Roman Catholics say, give me the child until he is nine and then you may have him, but I think later years in a

boy's life are even more important. That while my
parents have not been blessed with the wealth of
some, if it be a blessing . . . [I] would not trade for
those of others. The great many ideals you have
taught me are worth more to me than wealth. . . .
Lincoln said `all I am and ever expect to be came
from my dear old mother'. . . . I shall substitute the
word parents for mother. It hardly seems possible
for me to be a grown man 26 yrs. Old.

Indeed, McFarland still wrote as a youthful student but
he had garnered great preparation for the abrupt shift to the
matured career that would come. Adding Stanford legal and
political science training to the discipline of the military, class-
room, and farm, he presented a diversified, well-rounded aspect.
He was anxious to return to Arizona, however, concluding this
letter: "Well I will soon be with you and glad to. Though college is a great place, I have had enough. I am convinced I have
had enough to start my life on."[10]

Ernest McFarland hung out his law shingle in the little
town of Casa Grande about forty miles to the southeast of
Phoenix in the fall of 1921. He made improvements on his
"jackrabbit" farm, but his in-town law office received little work
as Arizona faced hard times in the postwar recession. Returning
to Stanford in the summer of 1922, he completed and received
a juris doctor degree and began his master's thesis in political
science. Back in Arizona that fall, he, for the first time, took a
serious interest in politics, supporting the Democratic slate in
the upcoming elections.

Up to this time, McFarland had shown little inclination
for a political career, but he had demonstrated a notable ability
to shift interests and roles. Never one to restrict himself, he
grasped at opportunity more than occupation. Now he decided
to "play a little politics" with the ensuing election in hopes of
gaining a better job.[11]

Since entering the union in 1912, Arizona had been represented predominately by Democrats both in Washington and

the state capital Phoenix. By the 1920s, however, a viable two-party system had emerged, and since 1919, the Republicans had held the governor's chair with Thomas E. Campbell, and since 1921, one United States Senate seat with Ralph Cameron. Democrats Henry Fountain Ashurst and Carl Hayden held the other senate seat and the single house position respectively. While Cameron was not up for re-election until 1926 and Ashurst and Hayden were regarded as virtually unbeatable, the race for the governor's chair promised to be one of great competitive interest.

Already an Arizona political legend, former governor George W. P. Hunt, opposed the incumbent Campbell. Thirty years before, Hunt had been elected to the territorial legislature in 1892, and then had presided over the state constitutional convention in 1910, a well-placed stepping stone to his election as Arizona's first governor in 1911. When Arizona became a state in February 1912, Hunt served out that single-year term, being re-elected in November 1912 to serve the first of three consecutive two-year terms, the last after a disputed 1916 election opposing Campbell. After the 1918 elections in which Campbell defeated Hunt's chosen successor, Fred T. Colter, Hunt left state politics for the position of Minister to Siam during the Woodrow Wilson administration. He found this exotic and elite position "boring" and after the Harding victory of 1920 returned home determined to reclaim the governor's office at the next opportunity.

McFarland, unfamiliar with Hunt's earlier years, now closely observed and supported his party's nominee. As Hunt campaigned throughout the state's desert, mountain, and valley districts, the old politician once again revealed his grassroots instinct for a symbiotic understanding touch with the common people. Although his imperious appearance seemed to belie this ability, he was an expert at working the crowds in conventions and rallies, in the streets and cafés, and out on the farms and ranches. He seemed to possess an unlimited depth and memory of his constituents' names, occupations, interests, and concerns while in reality working hard to maintain this knowledge with a meticulously recorded index card system. McFarland watched closely and in time clearly absorbed much of Hunt's technique, which he exhibited to others' wonderment in his later career.[12]

McFarland picked the right man with Hunt's victory over Campbell and was suitably rewarded with an appointment as assistant attorney general under Attorney General John Murphy. The appointment also reflected on the young lawyer's abilities, which, with limited experience, had been capably demonstrated and noticed. Packing his bags, McFarland moved from Casa Grande to offices in the Arizona statehouse in Phoenix, dominated by the powerful Hunt who would hold onto the executive office for eight of the next ten years.

McFarland's work as assistant state's attorney was routine, but it did provide appellate experience, such as arguing cases in front of the Arizona Supreme Court, and the job familiarized him with a broad range of state issues and politicians. Again, he acquitted himself well, particularly concerning water cases, but his mind also searched elsewhere for increased political opportunity. He found it when the office of Pinal County Attorney opened. The incumbent Democrat had announced retirement, so Mac filed to be a candidate in the 1924 elections. Casa Grande lay within Pinal County and his eye was also drawn to the county seat of Florence where Clare Collins, with whom he continued to correspond, had a teaching position. If elected, he would be required by law to reside at the county seat.

Before the election, however, McFarland put the cap on his Stanford years by completing his thesis and receiving the Master's of Arts in Political Science. His thesis, entitled "The Operation of the Initiative and Referendum in California," recommended a restructuring of the California State Constitution. For decades, the effectiveness of these public political tools had been debated, with most Los Angeles and San Francisco newspapers coming out against their use, but the public's mood still seemed to favor both practices. The result of years of use of the initiative and referendum had nearly emasculated the power of the state legislature. Although McFarland was theoretically sympathetic to the idea of direct democracy, his study, in general for the years 1879 to 1911 and in detail from 1912 to 1922, indicated that as practiced in California it could lead to a tyranny of the majority with substantial damage to minority rights and the effectiveness of special interest groups. Therefore, he recommended that the state adopt a new constitution giving the legislature necessary freedom of action while still maintaining its responsibility to the people.[13]

Stanford endeavors complete, McFarland returned to Arizona and began a relatively easy campaign for Pinal County Attorney. Equipped with a farming background, quality legal training and experience, an affable manner, and good political contacts, he had become a very popular man in the rural county towns. He easily emerged the victor in the September Democratic primaries. Running without opposition in the general elections, he became, at age thirty, the youngest county attorney in the state of Arizona. Though triumphant, election-day, November 4, 1924, also proved a sad one for McFarland, as his father William passed away in Phoenix at age sixty-five.

Upon moving to the Pinal County seat, Florence, in late 1924, newly-elected County Attorney McFarland embarked on a productive sixty-year relationship with this small community on the banks of the Gila River. Florence possessed a unique ambience where the old West retained a living presence even as the town endeavored to embrace a significant modernized future in the state as a potential transportation and trade center. Like so many pioneer-era villages, Florence was to be largely disappointed in this hope. Juggled by the whims of transportation route choices and depletion of mining resources, the town, outstripped by other communities, never realized its dreams. It endured, however, encapsulated in its historical past and a viable present of agriculture and county politics. McFarland proved a stalwart townsman of Florence and kept its interests and comforts at heart for the remainder of his life as its most distinguished citizen.

In 1920, Florence and its hinterlands embraced a population approaching fifteen hundred, thus being considerably larger than the old homestead of Earlsboro when McFarland resided there. It also had a deeper past. Situated on the south bank of the Gila River, the lands that became the town were part of Old Mexico until the Gadsden Purchase of 1854 added this last chunk of the contiguous United States to the main body. Although this southern Arizona tract had been acquired to facilitate a transcontinental rail route, the main line of the Southern Pacific eventually bypassed Florence, as had the Butterfield Overland Stage route before it. Nearly half the population was Hispanic, many of whom farmed the area before the village was officially settled in 1866, just three years after Arizona achieved territorial status.

With the arrival of Anglo pioneers at that time, Florence became the sixth oldest settlement in Arizona, after Tubac, Tucson, Yuma, Prescott, and Fort Defiance. Civilization had long been established in the vicinity, however, as the Gila waters had been tapped by the ancient Hohokam and more recent Pima-Papago Indian cultures, and the environs had been trapped by mountain men and further explored by early Jesuit missionaries under Padre Kino around 1700 and later the U.S. Army under Col. Stephen Watts Kearny in 1846. After the 1866 founding, Anglos joined Hispanics and scattered Indians in developing an adequate agricultural economy fed by the irrigated waters of the river and providing for local inhabitants and the transient U.S. Army.

Mining, not agriculture, however, provided Florence with its initial boom period with the discovery of silver and the 1875 opening of the Silver King Mine about twenty miles away. For over a decade, the village prospered and became a prototype western town — open, wild, and violent — with a reputed twenty-eight saloons on the main street, not infrequent gunfights, stage robberies, lynchings, and Indian depredations committed by Apache tribes always hovering in the vicinity.

This colorful period came to an end, however, during the 1890s. The quality of the ore being mined at the Silver King declined steadily, and the Depression of 1893 hit the community very hard. After the turn-of-the-century, Florence returned to agriculture, producing cotton, grains, and cattle, all three ventures boosted by the demands of World War I.

As the nineteenth century receded, Florence returned to a sleepy agrarian atmosphere broken by occasional local excitement. One such time involved the construction of the Pinal County Courthouse in 1892, where McFarland would ply his trade. The courthouse, a tall structure dominated by a cupola that could be seen for miles in the Gila Valley, was touted as the finest in the state. Singularly appointed, built of red brick, and trimmed in white, it serves still in the twenty-first century as a source of community pride, the oldest operating courthouse in Arizona. Still standing on the northern edge of town and looming large in McFarland's future was the original territorial courthouse dating from 1878, which by this time had been converted to a hospital.

Recognition of a different kind came to Florence in 1909 when the Arizona Territorial Prison relocated there from remote Yuma. Benefits in the local economy failed to materialize quickly from the move as hoped, although convict labor contributed to town construction and maintenance improvements in ensuing years. Rather, the prison, a disengaged community, lent a somber and serious aspect to the environs. Prison and courthouse dominated and symbolized the town when McFarland moved there in 1924. He would see much of both as Florence, once again bypassed by the new Phoenix-Tucson highway, carried on as a backwater desert and farm town.[14]

McFarland took up residence in a frame house on the old Phoenix-Tucson Highway 89, which ran along the eastern edge of town. Across the road and removed a few hundred yards loomed the foreboding walls, towers, and cell blocks of the penitentiary, and beyond rose the extreme western abutments of the continent-spanning Rocky Mountain chain cut through by the upper reaches of the Gila River. There existed a frontier line of demarcation here, for to the east lay wilderness, while civilization took root at Florence and roads, towns, and farms loosely proliferated amidst desert lands one hundred miles to the west along the Salt and Gila River valleys. Beyond, the desert once again reclaimed the lands rolling to the Colorado.

The state's youngest county attorney established his private law office in a small adobe building on a side street just off the courthouse square. Here and in the courthouse, the popularly recognized Mac handled a myriad of cases ranging from cattle rustling to those unique to the era, moonshining and bootlegging violations of the prohibition laws. In his work, McFarland always made a point of never trying a person unless he felt he had a solid case and avoiding prosecution based solely on community or personal prejudice. Victories in subsequent county elections put the stamp of popular approval on his policies. In 1926 and 1928, he ran without opposition in the Democratic primaries and easily outdistanced his Republican rivals in the general elections by margins ranging up to seventy percent of the popular vote. These results reflected his popularity and skill, as the Democratic preponderance was not guaranteed in these years. In 1928, Pinal County supported Republican Herbert Hoover over Al Smith in the presidential elections, 1,536 to 1,324. Democratic incumbent Henry Ashurst defeated Ralph Cameron for the U.S. Senate only 1,451 to 1,218, and Governor Hunt, turned out of office statewide after three more terms, narrowly edged McFarland's old legal mentor and ultimate victor John C. Phillips, 1,499 to 1,354.[15]

Outside of the law office and courtroom, along the streets and wooden sidewalks, McFarland became one of Florence's most visible and active citizens in the affairs of the town and its people. "Mac was always there" in an important capacity at every public function whether it be supporting the local baseball team, riding in the notable town Parada, or initiating and encouraging community projects. He saw what needed attention and went ahead, often without request, and attended to the matter, always shaking hands and greeting people in his garrulous manner. Making contacts and lending support became his metier and valuable for future political considerations. According to the late Billie Early, a six-decade Florence resident, "Mac had more off the top of his head than any man

I've ever known."

A humanitarian instinct strongly emerged. Devoted to town concerns and the people, he made sure that no one went hungry during these often hard years of the 1920s and 1930s. Not totally a soft touch, he firmly advocated self-help in positioning the indigent and unemployed in jobs about town that only he knew of or that he conjured up for the occasion. During his years as a county attorney, Mac also kept his law office open for training purposes to aspiring lawyers from the University of Arizona Law School, and in 1928, he took on Tom Fulbright as his deputy. In 1931, Fulbright became a full partner in the private law office that operated in Florence into the 1970s. This "man about town" side of McFarland's life, his honest interest in the people, regardless of status, equally complemented his work as attorney and later judge in the eyes of the community.[16]

McFarland's service to the First Presbyterian Church of Florence was both typical of his community endeavors and noteworthy. He had already, in 1919, joined the Central Methodist Church in Phoenix, where he remained a lifelong member and continued his church upbringing from Oklahoma. No Methodist congregation existed in Florence, however, where central Arizona's first Catholic Church had been established in 1870 and the First Presbyterian Church in 1888. Whereas the Catholic Church ministered to the needs of the large Hispanic population in the area, the Presbyterian Church concentrated on the Anglo majority and extended its concerns to the Pima Indians. McFarland, who increasingly mastered water law complexities, here assisted work for guaranteed tribal water rights. As the congregation grew, larger facilities became necessary and McFarland, who never did officially become a church member, was appointed to chair the Church Building Committee, sell off the old properties, and construct a new edifice. Raising money, lining up inmate labor, consulting with architects, and overall coordination and guidance for the project fell to McFarland, who oversaw groundbreaking ceremonies on April 10, 1930. He and various family members continued to attend services there into the 1980s.[17]

* * *

For an all too brief period during these early Florence years, the professional Ernest McFarland enjoyed complete happiness as a family man, husband, and father. His eye had been drawn to Clare Collins as far back as 1919 at Stanford, and on January 1, 1926, they married. By all accounts, Clare was an exceptional person. Born in Illinois and valedictorian of her 1915 graduating class at Crookston (Minnesota) High School, she matriculated at Stanford University that fall for studies in music, concentrating on voice. Proficient enough to be considered a candidate for grand opera, Clare saw her musical aspirations dashed by a developing throat condition. For health reasons, like Ernest and before his arrival, she moved to the drier climate of Arizona and completed her studies in music and elementary education at Arizona Teacher's College in Flagstaff. Moving in the early 1920s to Florence with her mother Ann Collins Smith, Clare started her first teaching job at the new high school built in 1915 and purchased some property in the community. Earlier, impressed with the young student and attorney, she had kept up a correspondence from both Flagstaff and Florence, urging, amid political and religious comments, McFarland visitations, picnics, and a close relationship. Her wishes were granted when she terminated her teaching position and commenced her role as wife and manager of the McFarland house on the old highway.[18]

The family grew with the birth of a son in 1927, William Ernest, named after McFarland's recently deceased father. In 1928, Clare became pregnant again, but happiness was short-lived as the new baby, Jean Clare, died two days after her February 1929 birth. The tragedy was doubly compounded as the local newspaper commiserated: "It was the second loss by death to visit their home within a few days. Their oldest child, a son, was stricken with a serious infantile disease and passed away after only a short illness."[19]

With the loss of Mac's "lovely little boy" and the newborn, the childless couple endured unrequited grief while the husband worried over the wife's condition, both physical and mental. In McFarland's words this "broke her heart and she never fully recovered." In order to alleviate the depression with activity and a change of scene, Ernest hastily made preparations for a trip to Europe for the couple via the Panama Canal and New York City. He managed the expense, not from his county attorney's salary, but from investment profits made in his brother-in-law's lumber business. The round trip by ship cost the McFarlands $345 each, exclusive of land and ferry transportation.[20]

Ernest and Clare boarded the *S.S. Mongolia* in Los Angeles and on July 8, 1929, commenced their first ocean and European voyage. In letters indicating concern about Clare's weakened and nervous condition, Ernest also expressed near childlike glee over the new maritime environment of "large turtles, flying fish, porpoises, sharks, and whales." The *Mongolia*, itself, was a rather ill fitted ship with small, stuffy rooms, and the heat and humidity grew increasingly oppressive as the travelers neared the equator. They were, however, spared seasickness on the abnormally calm waters of the Pacific summer.

The voyage to New York City took sixteen days and included highlights of traversing the Panama Canal and stops in Balboa, Panama and Havana, Cuba, where Ernest smoked fine cigars to assuage his impatience over what he termed "jip artists" in local land transportation. Clare remained conspicuously silent on this leg of the trip suffering from "smothering and nerves."

Her condition improved, however, on the trans-Atlantic voyage from New York to Plymouth, England. The accommodations were far superior aboard the *S.S. George Washington*, the same ship used by Woodrow Wilson a decade earlier on his voyage to the Versailles Peace Conference. McFarland compared the quarters to local Phoenix hostelries, "nicer than the Adams Hotel . . . about like the San Carlos." Clare resumed writing lengthy letters and the couple attended shipboard concerts and church services on Sundays when Ernest wrote that his "thoughts just naturally turn homeward."

Extensive land tours by rail followed their arrival in

England and included London and the Celtic capitals of Belfast and Dublin, Ireland, and Edinburgh, Scotland, where Ernest stocked up on McFarland Clan ties. Impressed by the beauty of the British Isles, he also endured visiting "sufficient old churches and cathedrals to last me the rest of my life." Then the McFarlands embarked for the continent visiting Germany, Belgium, and Paris, and enjoying their first plane ride, a short flight between Brussels and Rheims. Later McFarland regretted only not visiting the Holy Land on the tour.

The return voyage across the North Atlantic left something to be desired, the *S.S. Leviathan* being so overcrowded with twenty-six hundred passengers and one-thousand crew that the couple were assigned to separate group rooms. Both experienced bad spells of seasickness, and Ernest wrote "Have not missed a meal and returned all of them. The Atlantic is rougher than the Pacific." Nevertheless, he more than endured the discomforts, so obviously enthralled with the world of travel.

Mac rigorously sought out the company of fellow travelers, particularly foreigners, rubbing shoulders with them in the warmth of the lounge or on a heaving deck by the windy ship's rail. He seemed at home and at ease with all types as he plied them for information on their governments, societies, law, farms and business, taxes and profits, and how they were faring during the worldwide depression. He mentally filed away reams of disparate information on European social, political, and economic practices, theories, and problems, much of which he would later call up for his own purposes. Without question, Mac was a "people-person," and meeting and experiencing other cultures became a constructive passion. This first lengthy trip established many of his lifelong travel patterns.

Closely monitoring his wife on the difficult return journey, he wrote "Clare has stood the trip pretty well although she has gotten pretty tired at times. I think as a whole, it has been good for her. I believe it has helped get her mind off things." However, while the voyage may have alleviated Clare's mental depression, it is debatable whether it had such a salubrious effect on her physical well being. McFarland's letters are filled with detail on the hardships of packing, unpacking, and making travel deadlines via boat, train, plane, car, subway, and cab, particularly in the big cities.

Arrival in New York in September marked only the beginning of the final leg of the lengthy ten-week journey. As was to become his custom, McFarland had purchased a new car direct off the factory line in New York to save the substantial shipping fees to Arizona. He and Clare drove back across the continent soaking in the atmosphere of the eastern United States, extensive regions that they had never seen, before returning home to Florence, a weary but satisfied couple.

Back to work in his county attorney's office as the new decade began, McFarland was quickly faced with one of the more distasteful aspects of his job, a capital crime. Thus far, during his five-year career, he had not prosecuted anyone whose life hung in the balance. Now, in February 1930, a unique circumstance arose that would involve him in one of Arizona's most bizarre court battles.

In 1927, Eva Dugan, a fifty-two-year-old domestic worker, had been tried and convicted of the first-degree murder of her employer, aged Tucson rancher A. J. Mathis. The Pima County Superior Court had sentenced her to die, and she awaited her fate at the state prison in Florence. Dugan had exhausted her appeals to the Arizona Supreme Court, and her only chance of escaping the noose would be if she were to be declared insane and unable mentally to understand the judgment. The prison warden certified this to be the case, and the situation required a sanity trial on the eve of execution. McFarland's responsibility as county attorney was to uphold her sanity so sentence could be enacted.

Reason did exist to suspect Dugan's sanity. A large, unattractive woman, hardened by years of servile work, she displayed bitterness, anger, and a potential for violence. The defense rested its case on these characteristics and other personal quirks. In a heated trial, McFarland damaged this position by inducing the defense's expert physician witness to anger during intense cross-examination on the stand and then insisting successfully that this type of temperamental display in no way demonstrated insanity. The jury concurred, and in three ballots voted that Dugan was indeed sane. Execution of the first woman in Arizona history took place the following day February 20, 1930, and changed the course of capital punishment in the state. McFarland later described the event in his autobiography: "I could imagine her hanging by the rope, but this she never did, because they gave her too much rope. As a result, she was decapitated. Her head went one way and her body went another. The sight was so gruesome to those who saw it that the law was changed to the use of gas rather than death by hanging."[21]

The trial and execution helped McFarland make a decision to change the direction of his career. As he put it, "I became tired of pushing people into the penitentiary." He decided to run for Pinal County Superior Court Judge in the upcoming 1930 elections. Looking forward to this challenge, the McFarlands also brightened at the prospect of a new baby, for Clare had again become pregnant. The election, however, did not run well for him, and he suffered his first of three electoral defeats. Running under the slogan "A Trial Lawyer for Judge of a Trial Court," McFarland in the primaries faced incumbent Judge E. L. Green who had served Pinal since 1924. Green prevailed by a close vote of 1,464 to 1,358, and McFarland, who had relinquished the county attorney's job upon the term's expiration, contemplated going into private practice.[22]

Disappointed by the results, Ernest and Clare looked forward to the birth of a child in December, but improbably tragedy struck again, and in staggering fashion. The baby, Juliette, was stillborn, and Clare was crushed mentally and physically by the ordeal. Already in a weakened state for the past year, she never recovered. Post-birth complications developed into pneumonia, and she died days after Juliette on December 12, 1930, at age thirty-three years. The old hospital (the original county courthouse, 1878-91) on the north edge of town had become a place of pain and death for McFarland who was totally devastated by the loss of his four family members in a space of twenty-two months.

Now, he and the community turned their attention to funeral ceremonies at the Presbyterian Church and burial at the Florence Cemetery. It was the largest such affair in the history of the town. The Florence newspaper eulogized Clare:

> . . . she has lived in our midst, keenly interested in church and community work, an inspiration to all with whom she came in contact. Few people are attuned to the beautiful as Clare McFarland was. Whether a daughter, sister, wife, or mother, she was unfailingly sweet, gentle and loving. So modest was she that only to her closest friends did she reveal the quality of her charm and the depth of her culture. Only the best in the arts, in her surroundings did she choose, and from others she attracted only the good qualities, either ignoring or covering up gross. She has lived this life before us and we are all better that she has lived.[23]

Clare and Juliette were laid to rest flanking the small graves from the previous year of William Ernest and Jean Clare, all overlooked by the large McFarland stone that Ernest had purchased for the family plot. The cemetery contrasted bleakness and beauty. It had been left so neglected over the years that a community drive and prison labor became necessary a few years later to partially restore it. In 1930, decayed fence-posts, rusty gates, and dilapidated grave markers over sunken graves predominated. Yet the whole tragic scene was surrounded by the sublimity and completeness of the deserts and mountains, the Superstitions lying formidably to the north, the Pichachos to the south, the Buttes to the east, and the Sans Tans and Sacatons to the west. The 360-degree panorama did nothing to alleviate the despair of McFarland. He threw a symbolic handful of dirt in the graves before leaving them to be filled by gravediggers. Then he stood dazed as the crowd left, alone with disconsolate thoughts of the past, present, and future.

The loss of family had a devastating effect on McFarland. His religious beliefs and decorum were nearly shattered by the enormity and suddenness of the tragedies. On one occasion, a townsman found him hopelessly inebriated and despondent underneath the bridge crossing the Gila, watching the high winter waters rush pass as he perhaps contemplated suicide.[24]

But the community cautiously rallied to his side, allowing him room for grief but demonstrating firm spiritual support. Gradually as the weeks turned into months of 1931, healing began to take place. Mac assisted himself with long walks in the solitude of Florence's nighttime streets or in the nearby desert and farmlands. He read purposefully about human travail and tried to find meaning in his own experiences. He sought understanding that could again give reason and definition to his plans for the future. A hardened but sympathetic character emerged. The family was gone, but he remained, as did his work. The time came to commit himself more ardently to it, not just for himself, but the community and county and more. Redoubled effort in law coupled with maturing vision put McFarland on the path of return, a decade-long path that would lead to the United States Senate.

CHAPTER THREE

THE ROAD TO THE SENATE
1931-1940

AFTER THE EMOTIONAL CRISIS OF THE DEATH of his family, Ernest McFarland, now thirty-six years of age, struggled to pick up the pieces of his life and leave the tragedy behind, not an immediately achievable task. He had more time on his hands without family or official responsibilities for the first time in eight years and found value in directing his full energies to developing his fledgling law practice with partner Tom Fulbright. He also became private counsel for the San Carlos Irrigation and Drainage District. Too, his past seemed to call as he returned to his roots by taking an increased interest in farming, purchasing a quarter section of land just east of town and planting it in alfalfa and cotton. As heir and co-owner, he also managed the estate of Clare as well as the property of her mother Ann Collins Smith, which included land homesteaded in the early 1920s to the south of Florence. McFarland continued to support and watch over Clare's mother until her death in 1941. Sometime in 1931, he moved from the home of sad memories on the old highway, taking up residence in a modest frame house he purchased adjacent to his town-center law office. He then bent to his work and began a decade of commitment that made his name familiar throughout the entire state as an expert in water law and a judicious personage on the bench. Out of the ashes of tragedy, these efforts in the 1930s would propel him not only toward a new career as a United States senator but also to a new family.

While the Great Depression years jolted Arizona's economy, Florence avoided the worst problems. Statewide, the mining industry plummeted, particularly copper which fell from 18 cents to 5.5 cents a pound by 1932. But Florence had already endured its mining catastrophe with the collapse of the Silver King Mine during the depression years of the 1890s. The agri-culturally-oriented community suffered less than those depend-ent on industry. To be sure, profits did decline, but the farmers could support themselves even though money was scarce.[1]

Even during hard times, civic pride asserted itself. The town acquired ornamental street lighting and a new sewage sys-tem, paved the main streets, and carried out improvements on the courthouse, high school, and local churches. McFarland busied himself with these community concerns and kept apace with litigation involving New Deal programs such as farm relief, rural resettlement, irrigation, and rural electrification made possible by the San Carlos Project.

Mac also joined his fellow townspeople in the simple pleasures of the Thirties: dances, barbecues, baseball games, and the town Parada, a parade that grew in reputation drawing spec-tators from beyond the county lines. Newer amenities includ-ed the opening of a cinema on Main Street and the proliferation of evaporative "swamp" coolers which became commonplace in the decade. Refrigerated air conditioning remained a novelty but did make its appearance in the Pinal County mines near Superior and the movie theaters of Phoenix.[2]

The state capital was still a long and dusty drive through desert and sparse farmlands, but one that McFarland frequent-ly took for business reasons and also to visit his mother Keziah and other relatives and friends. In fact, he became quite enam-ored of motoring and continued to handle the wheel in later days as senator and governor when most in his position pre-ferred chauffeured limousines. On his vacations from work, Mac often took long drives around the United States. After his European tour, he had gained the impression that Europeans knew more about the United States than most Americans. Determined not to be among these, by 1940 he had visited all but three of the forty-eight states as well as sections of Canada and Mexico.

Mac also numbered among the Florence citizenry who enjoyed the repeal of the nation's prohibition laws. A few new saloons sprouted on Main Street and although he kept a discrete distance from the daily regulars of farm workers and prison employees, he did join a group of young professionals who enjoyed occasional "slumming." After one such episode of late-night carousing, a prize turkey disappeared from the backlot of Mac's future son-in-law Del Lewis, then a Florence teenager. One must only imagine Mac's group of friends plucking and dressing the bird in the wee hours, for no evidence remained to link the revelers to the turkey devouring.[3]

Such injudicious frivolity, though, was out of sync with Mac's growing reputation as one of the community's stalwarts. As he moved slowly beyond his grief, he again enjoyed status as an eligible bachelor, and by mid-decade, he frequently sought the company of Edna Eveland Smith, a high school teacher who had come to Florence in 1930.

But before Mac and Edna became an item, the small town tranquility of Florence was briefly and dramatically altered in the spring of 1933 by a sensational trial that received national attention. Criminal activity fascinated the public mind at this time. Radio had drawn its first broad national audience with its hyper coverage of the Lindbergh kidnapping, and young J. Edgar Hoover was just beginning to capture the public imagination with his carefully scripted accounts of daring FBI encounters against all manner of criminals. "Ten Most Wanted" broadsides hung in post offices, and Hoover held the public's rapt attention as he constantly changed the list. The attention took on a recreational aspect as subscribers of the press and radio buffs avidly followed the exploits of "Pretty Boy" Floyd, "Machine Gun" Kelley, and John Dillinger, as their forebears had those of Billy the Kid and Jesse James a half-century earlier. The more ominous activities of Al Capone and Lucky Luciano drew the public's interest as well, and trials were sensationalized: Sacco and Vanzetti, Leopold and Leob, the Lindbergh kidnapping, even the Scopes "Monkey" trial, and, in

Arizona, the ordeal of Eva Dugan. Now the state again came into the spotlight with the trial of Winnie Ruth Judd, the "trunk murderess." This time McFarland appeared for the defense, though not in the initial trial, but in a later sanity hearing.

Judd, a twenty-six-year-old medical secretary, stood accused of the October 16, 1931 murder of two close acquaintances, Agnes Leroi and Heldvig Samuelson, in Phoenix. What brought the case its extra notoriety concerned the manner in which the bodies were found later in Los Angeles: dismembered and stuffed in two shipping trunks emitting a viscous leakage and an imponderable odor. Maricopa County Superior Court Judge Howard C. Speakman, an old Oklahoma acquaintance of McFarland, conducted the trial in Phoenix, drawing upon evidence concerning adulterous love affairs, insanity, lesbianism, and the roles of outside accomplices. Winnie Ruth, a very attractive woman supported by her clergyman father, physician husband, and six attorneys, drew attention for the nature of the crime, her alluringly beautiful appearance, and her courtroom conduct, which ranged from the stoical to the hysterical. Eventually the jury found her guilty of the first-degree murder of Leroi after a three-week trial ending on February 8, 1932. Judge Speakman handed down the death sentence and scheduled the execution for May 11. Arizona still mandated hanging as the public had not yet certified lethal gas as the official means of capital punishment. Professional out-of-state hangmen submitted offers of their services to the prison in order to avoid the embarrassment of the Eva Dugan execution.[4]

A reprieve was granted while Judd appealed first to the Arizona Supreme Court and then to the Board of Pardons and Paroles. Action on these used up the rest of 1932, but both appeals were ultimately denied as the experienced team of Maricopa County Attorney Renz Jennings and State Attorney Arthur T. LaPrade prevailed over a newly selected defense fronted by O. V. Willson of Phoenix. A January 1933 execution date was further postponed, first to February to avoid a Friday the 13th punishment and eventually from early April to April 21 to sidestep Good Friday. Judd's only remaining hope lay in being stipulated as insane by Arizona State Penitentiary Warden A. G. Walker and having this position upheld at a sanity trial. After a year-and-a-half of adjudication, McFarland entered the case at this juncture.

Warden Walker, upon the advice of several physicians and attendants, did certify Judd's insanity, and the new trial in Florence commenced on April 15, 1933, under the gavel of Pinal Superior Court Judge E. L. Green. McFarland's successor as County Attorney, W. C. Truman, conducted the prosecution to uphold sanity, while O. V. Willson continued to head the defense which now included Phoenix lawyer Edwin Karz and from Florence, H. G. Richardson, McFarland, and his partner Tom Fulbright. During this holding period, Winnie Ruth, under close observation, experienced nervous breakdowns and continued to threaten suicide. The hangman's rope, too, underwent its ordeal of being soaked in water and stretched by a weight of 300 pounds, a process lasting seven to ten days. Outside the prison walls, reporters from the United Press, Associated Press, Hearst's International News Service, the *Los Angeles Times*, and the *Los Angeles Examiner* joined those from Arizona in linking the Pinal County Courthouse to the rest of the nation by wire, phone, and print.[5]

The Reverend H. J. McKinnell, Winnie Ruth's father, personally requested McFarland's assistance with the defense case. The elderly, stooped man whose hair had turned grey during the lengthy trials, had no funds for payment, but McFarland accepted the job on the condition that he use only the evidence presented in lieu of a personal interview with the accused. This was agreed upon, and Mac never spoke to Judd until after the rendering of the verdict.

During this near mirror image of the Dugan sanity hearing, McFarland acted as the point man for the defense becoming quite vocal at times in the courtroom and assisting with strategy sessions. At one stage of the proceedings, just after Easter Sunday, he evoked the image of the thief on the cross asking the forgiveness of Jesus. Mac stated, "That is what we are asking for Ruth Judd. If she is to be executed, it would be at a time that she is sane and able to ask forgiveness." The *Los Angeles Times* maintained this speech to the jury won the case. The court found Winnie Ruth Judd insane and committed her to the Arizona State Hospital after the sanity hearing. Here she remained, except for seven successful escape attempts (one lasting six and one-half years), for nearly four decades until her pardon in 1971. In light of the Dugan trial and the shadows of his own family tragedy, McFarland received satisfaction at having been instrumental in sparing the life of this woman, whom he firmly believed to be mentally ill after having finally met and talked to her.[6]

While trials such as those of Dugan and Judd gave McFarland's name increased public exposure, his primary area of expertise concerned interpretation of and writing water law, both as a lawyer and judge. This complex and methodical work would later reap him great rewards as a senator.

As early as 1923, McFarland, as assistant state's attorney, closely studied the issue of how Colorado River waters were and ought to be apportioned in the American Southwest. The previous year, the Colorado River Compact had been negotiated at Santa Fe between the upper basin states, Wyoming, Utah, New Mexico, and Colorado, and lower basin states Arizona, Nevada, and California. (A small portion of northeastern Arizona actually lies in the upper basin). The Arizona legislature questioned the terms of the compact and members consulted with McFarland on these and the 1928 Boulder Canyon Act, which divided lower basin waters in the amounts of 4.4, 2.8, and .3 million annual acre-feet of water between California, Arizona, and Nevada respectively. At this time in the late 1920s, McFarland agreed with Arizona water experts who felt that the state should not sign the compact until the status of the Gila River could be determined.

The Gila already supplied irrigated water to Pinal County farms via the Ashurst-Hayden Dam opened in 1922, and its tributary the Salt River had been tapped into by the Salt River Valley Water Users' Association (Salt River Project) since the opening of the Roosevelt Dam in 1911, providing waters for Phoenix and Maricopa County. Large-scale plans for the future lay on the drawing board as well, involving the San Carlos Irrigation and Drainage District and a projected San Carlos (later Coolidge) Dam. At issue was whether these waters of the Gila, a tributary of the Colorado and amounting to 2.2 million acre-feet, should be included in Arizona's allocation of 2.8 million.

California desired as much Colorado water as possible for its greater population even though the river only bordered and did not flow in the state, and California contributed no major tributary streams. Limiting Arizona's water rights provided one method of guaranteeing the maximum for California. The Gila system, however, flowed almost entirely within the boundaries of Arizona, and emptied into the larger river only near its mouth, thus adding little appreciable flow to the Colorado until it had nearly reached the United States boundary with Mexico. McFarland and Arizona felt that Gila waters properly belonged to the state and should not be included in the 2.8 million acre-feet allocation unless the state were compensated at least one million acre-feet of additional Colorado River waters. Arizona, alone, refused to sign the compact, and the thorny issue of dividing the waters would receive McFarland's attention for most of the rest of his life until the Central Arizona Project bill finally became law in 1968, forty-six years after the original compact.[7]

While the Colorado question loomed large and long, McFarland also played an important role in local water development, initially as Pinal County Attorney and now as counselor for the San Carlos Irrigation and Drainage District. This district evolved out of the efforts of early Florence farmers who followed the lines of an elaborate irrigation system of the ancient Hohokam Indians, which dated to as early as 500-700 A.D. By 1888, plans for improving these ditches had been drawn up and a large main canal constructed soon after. This Florence Canal Company diverted the Gila waters to local farms and a reservoir from a rock dam near the Box Canyon and

Buttes area twelve miles east of town. Legal and financial problems led to a merger with another group in 1893 when it became known as the San Carlos Canal and Irrigation Company. Ultimately, this firm, too, experienced problems with maintenance and supply, and in 1916, water users filed a suit that resulted in the San Carlos company being declared a public service corporation required by law to render adequate service at reasonable price.

"Adequate service" necessitated immediate improvements, but the company lacked funds. Its directors, therefore, applied to the Indian Affairs Office of the Department of the Interior and obtained an appropriation of $250,000 to build a new dam. Debate over the division of the waters between Indians and White settlers ensued, with the Indians receiving water for thirty-five thousand acres of irrigated land to twenty-five thousand for the farmers. Then, at the behest of Senator Henry Ashurst, construction began as a measure to relieve unemployment among World War I veterans. The Ashurst-Hayden Dam commenced operation in 1922 after dedication ceremonies led by Secretary of the Interior Albert B. Fall of New Mexico, and the program featured a victrola rendition of a recorded address by President Warren G. Harding. The dam marked the first major step in the initiation of the San Carlos Project.

In 1924, Congress appropriated $5.5 million for the next step, construction of the much larger San Carlos Dam further up the Gila. Once again, the major question centered on division of the waters between the Indian and White population. The Florence Presbyterian Church monitored the Indians' water rights and McFarland, as *de facto* church member and Pinal County Attorney, played a major role in negotiating the "Gila Decree." This mandated sixty thousand irrigated acres for White farmers and forty thousand acres for the Indians in what was termed, by some, an "excellent and fair" decision, although many Indian spokesmen disagreed. However, without this settlement, the dam would not have been constructed. By 1930, the huge unusual edifice was complete and dedicated by ex-President Calvin Coolidge, for whom it was renamed.

Ultimately the San Carlos Project brought electricity and employment to a vast area of east-central Arizona, and like the Roosevelt Dam on the Salt, the Coolidge Dam on the Gila did much to guarantee adequate water for regional farming. After his leaving the county attorney's office, McFarland, in a logical hiring move, became private counsel for the San Carlos Irrigation and Drainage District.[8]

In 1934, McFarland again decided to run for Pinal County Superior Court Judge, goaded by his narrow defeat four years earlier and challenged to rise in the legal profession. Once again incumbent E. L. Green provided the opposition in the primaries. Green had served well since 1924, and the Florence newspaper endorsed neither, maintaining, "Both are good capable men worthy of your support." McFarland emphasized his fourteen-year county residency, experience, and education, and the electorate responded with a lopsided 2,543 to 1,542 vote victory for him. County returns for the same Democratic primaries showed a preference for Senator Henry Ashurst over Sidney Osborn, 1,535 to 933 and challenger B. B. Moeur over incumbent Governor George Hunt 1,935 to 1,215. Both prevailed statewide, Moeur bringing to a conclusion Hunt's fifty-year career and the most dominating gubernatorial administration in Arizona history. Franklin Roosevelt's New Deal efforts had impressed voters nationwide, and Arizona had once again reverted to a one-party state. All Democrats were easily re-elected in the general elections, McFarland running without opposition.[9]

As judge, McFarland distinguished himself by his availability and popularity, "the kind of judge lawyers liked to practice for, even if the ruling went against them." Work was light in Pinal County, so Mac accepted cases from all over the state, further familiarizing himself with the issues and a broad-based constituency. Ultimately, he occupied the bench in every county before his tenure concluded, and he was reversed on appeals to the state supreme court only three times. He later maintained that he enjoyed this work as much or more than any other endeavor during his long career.[10]

McFarland plunged into the complexities of water law rendering decisions of lasting significance that affected nearly all of the water rights in the state. Through a series of cases, he set forth the history and definition of the three water sources available in Arizona: normal flow, stored (lakes), and pumped. A major point of contention existed in defining underground water. Since all normal flow and stored water had been previously appropriated to Indian tribes and farmers with priority to those who had settled areas initially, underground water remained the only source for newer residents who, therefore, desired unfettered pumping privileges. Farmers with prior appropriation felt that all underground water lying in definite channels constituted in reality the underflow of the various streams and rivers. Such water should be off-limits to pumping. Latecomers and those without sufficient water maintained that much of the underground water was "percolating" in natural aquifers and not part of the underflow and thus available for pumping.

McFarland worked scrupulously on these problems, and, in effect, created new concepts of water law distinguishing between underflow and percolating sources. He did so in a fashion to not alter prior appropriations while allowing those in need and without appropriations to receive adequate supply via pumping. His interpretations affected all flowing waters in Arizona, and according to then Pinal County Attorney Brock Ellis, were "largely responsible for much of the evolvement of the economy of the entire state." As farmer and jurist, McFarland kept his eyes on the future and made his judgments accordingly.[11]

During his years as judge, McFarland entered a more settled and contented stage in his life, allowing past memories to continue to recede. A major reason for this was his relationship with Edna Eveland Smith, which evolved about the time he took the bench. Edna had come to Florence in 1930 from her native Iowa after graduating from Parsons College there. A recent widow, with a one-year-old daughter, Jewell, she found employment at Florence High School teaching history, civics, and mathematics. Eventually she chaired both social studies and math departments, and by 1935, she had completed a master of arts degree in history from Iowa State University. Like Clare before her, Edna became very community-oriented, and must have appeared a likely match for Florence's forty-year-old judge. The townspeople felt surprised by the length of the courtship, but not by the marriage, which occurred June 1, 1939, in Tucson. For his own reasons, Mac had wanted to keep the ceremony from becoming a spectacle, as assuredly it might have been if held in hometown Florence. Associates felt that Edna was "one of the things that actually made Mac," she being "straight-laced," and he "inclined to enjoy himself." Now he "settled down and really worked."[12] No stranger to work, McFarland perhaps manifested a new shade of commitment in his activities.

In 1938, McFarland had been re-elected to the superior court without opposition in either primary or general elections. He was now becoming something of a Florence institution, followed around town by his secretary's collie dog, Wimpy, to courthouse, church, movies, and other affairs. Judge Mac complained affectionately "Can't get rid of him — going to shoot him someday." The judge's appearance had changed over the decade. The leanness of his college and navy days had been maintained through the 1920s, but as he neared forty and after, he grew into a stocky, slow-moving man of about 5 feet 11 inches and two-hundred-plus pounds. He continued to display a down-home, country demeanor that many who first met him felt a bit unusual for a man of his position. But the slow movements, voice, and homespun manner only partially hid the quick and interested mind that took in all around him, from peoples' personalities and concerns to the issues involved. "Dumb like a fox" served as a fair and frequent description of Mac.

In chambers, McFarland kept an open door adjusting to his callers' hours, day and night, as they walked around or over the prostrate Wimpy guarding the entrance. After hours he engaged in his favorite relaxation of driving around and over-seeing the farming until returning home when he "went to bed late" (midnight) and "got up late," (7 or 8:00 A.M.). He explained, "I get more regular sleep that way."[13]

From his offices on the second floor of the courthouse, Mac could look out across the street to his house and by decade's end, he took pleasure in observing adopted daughter, eleven-year-old Jewell, working her horse in the backyard fol-lowed around by his new family dog, a cocker spaniel. Indoors, Edna tended to domestic chores, having given up her teaching position. She did so because major plans were afoot in the McFarland household as the new decade arrived. Mac had decided to challenge the venerable Henry Fountain Ashurst for the U.S. Senate in the upcoming 1940 Democratic primary elections.

Like ex-Governor Hunt, Senator Ashurst had built a formidable political reputation over several decades. A hard-riding former Coconino County Sheriff in the territorial nine-teenth century, he had emerged in the twentieth as one of the new state's first two U.S. senators. A twenty-eight year incum-bent, he now ranked second in senate seniority and chaired the powerful Juciciary Committee. Moreover, he was the acknowl-edged "silver-tongued orator of the Senate," a worthy reminder of the days of great senate debate, of Webster, Clay, and Calhoun.

On June 15, 1940, Ashurst rose in the Senate Chambers and announced his candidacy for re-election. Stating that he was opposed by able and worthy opponents, he expressed a desire to return to his home state. However, he concluded that he would be unworthy of his position if he did so during the stressful times the nation was facing. His reservations con-cerned military preparation and rearmament as the war in Europe escalated. After Adolph Hitler's September 1, 1939 invasion of Poland, the Nazi leader had subsequently dominat-ed the Low Countries and Norway and now in June 1940 posed a threat to France.[14]

Ashurst's decision did not surprise his colleagues in Washington, D.C. He possessed one of the most familiar names on Capitol Hill, while McFarland was termed by Ashurst supporters as "merely a county judge of one of Arizona's least important counties."[15] Underlying his obvious attributes, it was rumored that the senator, grieving over the loss of his wife the previous year, did not want to return to scenes of old memories. In fact, the Ashursts had been seeing less and less of their native state as the Washington years progressed. The bottom line of his campaign inactivity proved self-evident — he felt himself invulnerable to the challenge of a seemingly obscure opponent and devised no specific strategy for the contest.

Perhaps the senator should have been more perceptive, for on the same day of his speech, an editorial entitled "Political Perfidy" appeared in the Phoenix weekly newspaper, *The Messenger*. The piece examined the official returns of the 1934 Arizona U.S. Senate Democratic primary. The results showed an Ashurst plurality of 36,646 votes to 24,065 for his major challenger, future governor Sidney P. Osborn. However, when the votes for other Democratic contenders, Renz L. Jennings-16,743, William Coxen-8,653, and C. H. Rutherford-4,026, were added to those of Osborn, it became clear that a large majority of Democrat voters preferred an alternative to the incumbent, fifty-nine to forty-one percent. The editorial did not mince words in charging trickery and deception on the part of the 1934 Ashurst camp to break up the block of potential Osborn supporters by offering a slate of at least two additional candidates. The editorial compared that election to the current 1940 campaign regarding three additional Democrat nominees now on the ticket with Ashurst and McFarland. The paper dismissed the credentials of these periphery candidates and concluded "a vote for Judge McFarland was a vote for Arizona."[16]

Indeed, McFarland presented a viable threat to Ashurst, and appeared most cognizant and capable of continuing to step upward in his career, this time in politics. He was current on all the issues of the day and anxious to do political battle. As early as U.S. Representative Isabella Greenway's retirement in 1937,

Mac had checked out the possibilities of running for the House. But the urging of his friends could not alter the facts that he did not yet have the stature for such a race, nor the funds. Now both handicaps had ended with the new decade. Conditions had changed; McFarland had earned more money, made more acquaintances, and gained more recognition statewide after holding court in all of Arizona's counties. Most importantly, the 1934 primaries indicated the potential for a change in the state's Washington delegation, and Ashurst seemed vulnerable on other accounts as well.[17]

On April 26, 1940, McFarland officially announced his candidacy with "Arizona needs another senator who is interested primarily in Arizona." His campaign strategy rested on three basic foundations: his own confidence and capabilities, voting demographics, and the perceived deficiencies of his opponent. McFarland correctly noted and took advantage of the inherent rivalry between the "Old Pueblo" Tucson, and the ascendant city of Phoenix, contending that being from a neutral town like Florence would enable him to garner votes from both urban areas. Much in the fashion of George Hunt, Mac assiduously cultivated the interest of his conglomerate of acquaintances throughout the state, and opened his campaign on August 7 in Casa Grande, the site of his first law practice.[18]

McFarland's platform advocated strong national defense and preparedness, appropriate aid to Great Britain, aggressive action against fifth columnists, a protective tariff particularly for mining concerns, less government involvement in stock and range management, preservation of American markets for domestic labor and industry, federal aid to agriculture and cotton in particular, and full development of Colorado River water for Arizona use. He could not match Ashurst's flowery oratorical flourishes, but the stocky, homespun lawyer had his own style, undramatic yet effective — he simply personalized grass-roots issues with "common sense" explanation, and his audiences listened attentively. Although similar points existed in their platforms, Mac played upon differences of degree of commitment and, most importantly, used Ashurst's record of inconsistency, a trait that the senator, in fact, regarded as a positive attribute: "My faults are obvious. . . . I suffer from *cocoethes loquendi*, a mania or itch for talking. . . . But there never has been super-added to these vices of mine the withering embalming vice of consistency."[19]

McFarland quickly established these inconsistencies. Ashurst had shifted from a "dry" to a "wet" concerning prohibition and had changed from a low to a high tariff supporter. The issue was clearly one of inconsistency, McFarland being both a "wet" and a high-tariff man. Ashurst's oratorical excesses handed McFarland virtually an unbroken stream of opportunities to make political hay. On a cotton subsidy, Ashurst expressed confusion because the senators on whom he usually depended were in dispute. He stated, "I presume I must resort to the rather unpleasant idea of making up my own mind." On silver he commented, "Nothing has ever been able to make a breach in the wall that surrounds and protects the reservoir of ignorance I possess on the money question." Concerning his tariff shift, he echoed Aaron Burr, whom he revered, in saying, " I do not rise to exclaim or disclaim anything. My policy in life has been to never explain because if today one explains, tomorrow he will be explaining his explanation."[20]

Clearly these were instances when Senator Ashurst became victimized by his own *cocoethes loquendi* and half-serious jests. The audiences, however, responded to McFarland's campaign technique. More importantly, he stressed Ashurst's equivocation from opposition to support of the rejected Townsend social security plan for the elderly, and Mac particularly emphasized the 1937 Supreme Court fight. In this instance, Senator Ashurst initially stood against President Roosevelt's court-adjusting ideas. Then, as the head of the Judiciary Committee, he worked hard to push the "court-packing" plan through before ultimately voting with the majority against the proposal. McFarland pounced upon all of these issues.[21]

Closer to home, McFarland suggested that the incumbent acted too slow on the water issue, having taken twenty-eight years before only recently recommending a survey to determine the feasibility of bringing Colorado River water to central Arizona. He also questioned the depth of Ashurst's commitment to defense and preparedness, and the source of his campaign funding. He pointed out that in 1934, the senator had received several large contributions from eastern bankers and businessmen including one thousand dollars from Bernard Baruch. McFarland, himself, deplored eastern colonialism of the West and disclaimed any connections with eastern interests. He spent twelve thousand dollars for the campaign evenly divided between his own pocket and in-state contributions. It was a moot point. In 1940, Ashurst spent only $2,072.66 including $412 of his own, because of his decision not to campaign in Arizona.[22]

For his final campaign issue, McFarland frequently alluded to Ashurst's remaining in Washington. The senator exacerbated matters by stubbornly opposing Majority Leader Alben Barkley's (D-KY) proposal to recess Congress so that the congressmen "might go home and get back to the people." Ashurst responded "those who vote to go home should be kept there . . . for the remainder of their career," and he threatened to delay pending legislation if necessary to keep Congress in session. McFarland openly criticized all of these matters, effectively wearing down the credibility of the candidate and his campaign-in-absentia.[23]

The challenger was not always so overtly critical, however; he kept some delicate items about the incumbent out of sight. McFarland had meticulously researched Ashurst over the past several months in terms of finances and patronage. Beginning in early May, he kept in touch with Washington acquaintances to examine property taxes and value and salaries of Ashurst's office appointees. The research led to some interesting discoveries. Previous to the senator's chairmanship of the Judiciary Committee, he had been allotted the usual office positions of one secretary and three clerks. He employed only two people, using his wife's and another's name to draw the complete four salaries. As a chairman entitled to seven and then eight positions, he filled them in a manner that varied from five to nine workers including his wife, who did not perform any official work. Moreover, McFarland's contacts suspected that the salary of an Ashurst staff employee from Mesa was surreptitiously put towards an automobile, which had been used for at least one transcontinental trip for the Washington couple. Finally, a domestic worker in the Ashurst home drew government salary, and, except for a single assistant office doorkeeper, the senator had never employed anyone from Arizona. Not wanting to embarrass the popular Ashurst unless absolutely necessary, McFarland avoided disclosure of any of this information, relying instead on criticism of eastern influence, inconsistency, and lack of concern for Arizona affairs.[24]

As McFarland's campaign picked up steam, Ashurst's decision to remain in the capital appeared increasingly to jeopardize his position. He dispatched personal secretary Anthony O. Jones posthaste from Washington to bolster the apparently sinking Ashurst organization in the state. The senator, himself, toyed with the idea of returning, and warnings were issued to "Stop McFarland!"[25]

The challenger interjected a fresh issue into the campaign when the first peacetime conscription bill stood before the Senate after having passed the House. The Phoenix Junior Chamber of Commerce urged both candidates to support conscription. McFarland said the issue was above politics and would speed up national preparedness and increase the probability of avoiding war. Ashurst telegrammed the Chamber with a negative response: "With true respect and esteem for all, I should be lacking in candor and deficient in frankness if I failed to say that I could not vote for this bill." He based his verbose reservations on the illusion of American strength, the pervasive and negative influence of European militarism, and the threat of a peacetime draft becoming a permanent fixture on the domestic front. The candidates' replies were widely circulated to the public, which applauded both men for their stance, but when the Senate passed the bill, McFarland once again appeared more in line with the Roosevelt administration and public opinion.[26]

In replying to one of his supporters on the conscription

bill, Senator Ashurst showed a slightly less confident hand by referring to "this distressing primary campaign." He felt that since he had made his June 15 speech, he was obliged to "make good" his statement and remain in Washington regardless of the situation in Arizona. Indeed, he turned down an invitation to attend a Pima County Young Democratic Club rally scheduled for Labor Day. He also cancelled a speaking engagement at the convention of Arizona Small Mine Operators Association in Globe.[27]

Labor did not become discouraged by the senator's immobility, however, and continued its traditional support. The Washington, D.C-based *Labor* newspaper put out a special Arizona edition on September 3, commending Ashurst's stance against conscription, for the Townsend old age pensions, and for placing a greater burden of income tax on the wealthy. It applauded his work for the unemployed, the veteran, and the copper industry, and William Green, President of the American Federation of Labor (AFL), termed Ashurst's record perfect. Finally the paper elicited lengthy statements of support from some of the senator's more powerful Democratic colleagues, including Majority Leader Barkley, who lauded his historical knowledge, Interstate Commerce Committee Chairman Burton K. Wheeler (MT), who stated "he is a sane liberal," Foreign Relations Committee Chairman and President *Pro Tempore* of the Senate Key Pittman (NV), who took "special pleasure in supporting the re-election," Sheridan Downey (CA), who was "thrilled" by Ashurst's great oratory, Robert Wagner (NY), who called him "among the foremost statesmen of his day," and James Byrnes (SC), who commended his efficiency. Supportive in-state press echoed these sentiments, and as late as September 5, five days before the primary, the *Phoenix Gazette* editor predicted an Ashurst victory.[28]

More realistic political observers, including McFarland, thought otherwise even though the number of Democratic contestants appeared to cut into the challenger's potential constituency. The other nominees, all from Phoenix, were lawyers Henderson Stockton and Edwin Karz and pharmacist Robert Miller. McFarland campaign headquarters distributed and mailed fifty thousand copies of the editorial "Political Perfidy," which dismissed Miller as "utterly unequipped by training or experience." Karz dismissed himself, withdrawing from the race on August 30 and recommending his votes to McFarland. The editorial more harshly condemned Stockton, linking him to a probable repetition of 1934 ticket-splitting tactics and characterizing him as a "man of straw" involved in a "sham" effort to split the anti-Ashurst vote. Perhaps more telling in retrospect was Stockton's reporting no contributions and no personal expenditures on his campaign effort. He left this unexplained. McFarland did not exploit the issue.[29]

Stockton's "no-expense" campaign appears more peculiar in light of his August 30 speech in Tucson where he stated "the race for the U.S. Senate has simmered down to Senator Ashurst and me. . . . Judge McFarland is not eligible to try for the office." Stockton presented a serious threat by filing suit against McFarland's eligibility in Maricopa County Superior Court on September 1, basing his case on the state constitution which stated "Judges of the supreme court and judges of the superior courts shall not be eligible to any office or public employment other than a judicial office of employment during the term for which they have been elected." McFarland served in the middle of his second term as Pinal County Superior Court Judge, the term scheduled to expire January 1, 1943.[30]

The judge, on September 3, asked for dismissal of the suit as "groundless and wholly devoid of merit." The court set a hearing for that same afternoon when McFarland based his case on the United States Constitution, which stated, "Each house shall be the judge of the elections, returns, and qualifications of its own members." The court led by Judge Arthur T. LaPrade unanimously agreed, stating the state constitution provision "could be applied only to offices created by the Arizona Constitution and therefore could not be applicable to posts set up in the United States Constitution."[31]

Henderson Stockton's abortive court action had the unexpected result of crystallizing McFarland's campaign, and the results of the September 10 primary election proved to be a landslide. The challenger received 63,353 votes to Ashurst's 37,955. Stockton received only 5,220, while Miller and Karz picked up 4,306 and 1,022 respectively. On the Republican ticket, Irving A. Jennings edged out Burt H. Clingan 5,487 to 4,062. McFarland took ten of fourteen counties including his home area Pinal by a twelve-to-one margin and the urban enclaves Maricopa and Pima by 35,243 to 17,748. Ashurst barely succeeded in winning in the less populous northern counties surrounding his home base Flagstaff-Prescott. His defeat clearly resulted from initial overconfidence and lack of preparation throughout the campaign. His positive reception upon returning to Arizona in October showed an undiminished popularity that might have been exploited to victory under different circumstances and strategy. Conversely, McFarland successfully demonstrated determination and preparation, addressing the issues directly without vacillation and playing well the trump card of Ashurst's apparent disinterest in the campaign and the internal affairs of Arizona.[32]

Both candidates reflected positively on the election results, Ashurst magnanimous in defeat and McFarland generous in victory. They exchanged telegrams across the continent, Ashurst offering "heartiest congratulations" and stating he would "come home to campaign joyously for you and the entire state ticket." McFarland wired back, "Most sincere thanks for your very kind wire. It represents the highest type of sportsmanship." An embittered Henderson Stockton sent the victor a telegram of a different sort:

> Being a Democrat I shall support all the nominees of my party, notwithstanding the false charges that I was Senator Ashurst's stooge and that he financed my campaign made by you and your associates throughout the state, knowingly and maliciously with full knowledge of their falsity and notwithstanding your deliberate and premeditated assassination of my character.[33]

In Washington, D.C., Henry Fountain Ashurst was down

but certainly not out. On September 11, he attained one of his greatest personal triumphs weaving a spell with a resounding "Farewell to the Senate" speech, again in probable emulation of Aaron Burr's famous exit. The Senate, clearly moved, paid rapt attention as one of its most popular members spoke in a grandiloquent and sincere manner. Condolences, regrets, and requests for the farewell speech poured in to Ashurst from across the United States from such notables as William McAdoo, Cordell Hull, Carter Glass, Henry Morgenthau Jr., J. Edgar Hoover, and even cowboy film hero William S. Hart. A young Arizona merchandiser and photographer wrote:

> The one error of your life has been that you were not a Republican. This fact has prohibited those voters in Arizona who border on the intelligent from voting for you by virtue of the fact that they are Republicans. In the past it has always been necessary for us to wait for the general elections to give you our support. No one was more surprised or disappointed than I when I was denied that privilege this year by the recent catastrophe. [Signed] Barry Goldwater.[34]

While Ashurst deservedly gloried in the sun of his impending retirement in Washington, campaign activity kept up in Arizona where the new Democratic nominee prepared for an early trip to the nation's capital. McFarland expressed particular concern over a two-year drought then afflicting the Southwest and worried over the apparent strength in Arizona of Republican presidential nominee Wendell Willkie. Feeling it would be beneficial for all parties concerned, he sought Senator Carl Hayden's assistance in arranging a meeting with President Roosevelt. On October 2, the Hayden-McFarland tandem that would ultimately clear the Central Arizona Project through the Senate, first swung into action. Roosevelt expressed "sympathy" for Arizonans and promised funds, surveyors, and engineers for a preliminary study to be undertaken in the field within ten days. With this commitment in hand, McFarland returned to the state for the general election campaign.[35]

Arizona had been dominated by the Democratic party since 1912. Yet the Democratic contingent did not hold back in its campaign, dividing into two groups with Ashurst accompanying McFarland, and Hayden traveling with gubernatorial candidate Sidney P. Osborn. Ashurst's popularity worked effectively as he toured the state commenting, "I want to say that the young gentleman who defeated me is entitled to your vote and I am going to vote for him." The Arizona Senate sat in special session to honor its defeated five-term U.S. senator, while both parties kept to rigorous touring schedules between October 9 and November 3. Typical of old-style campaigning, McFarland stopped (in order) at Tucson, Bisbee, Douglas, Tombstone, Wilcox, Benson, Clifton, Safford, Globe, Miami, Ajo, Scottsdale, Tempe, Salt River Valley, Tolleson, Glendale, St. Johns, Springerville, Holbrook, Winslow, Williams, Flagstaff, Ash Fork, Seligman, Kingman, Somerton, Yuma, Buckeye, Cottonwood, Jerome, Prescott, Chandler, Mesa, Wickenburg, Superior, and Phoenix - thirty-six cities in twenty-six days - with only three days off. His platform remained essentially the same, while newly emphasizing wildlife preservation and assuring the interests of Ashurst's important supporters, labor and copper mining.[36]

By comparison, Republican efforts seemed perfunctory in criticizing the New Deal, organized labor, and an army commission for FDR's son. The Republican nominee for senator, Irving Jennings, did make overtures to gain the support of the defeated Democratic camp, but Ashurst's secretary Tony Jones turned down any arrangements. In fact, Jones soon commenced work for McFarland, whom he later referred to as "the most generous and forgiving politician I have ever met."[37]

The results of the general election of November 5, 1940, were never really in doubt. As President Roosevelt comfortably carried both the nation and the state, Judge McFarland carried all fourteen counties and major urban areas, easily prevailing with 101,495 to 39,657 votes for Irving Jennings. The

Democrats also elected Sidney Osborn as governor and four-year incumbent John Murdock to the U.S. House of Representatives.[38]

The 1940 U.S. Senate election in Arizona, coming on the eve of massive changes to be wrought by World War II, marked the commencement of a shift from an older to a more modern era in terms of the state's history and development. Capable men were needed to bring about this transition by interpreting events and initiating legislation. Ernest McFarland stood in the forefront of these. His background had prepared him well. He had known the hardships of an agrarian upbringing, but had persisted under trying circumstances to become a teacher. He had endured the physical discomforts of a serious illness while in his country's service, yet had emerged undaunted in his determination to create a new life in the Southwest. After relocating in Arizona, he had endured great personal tragedy with family deaths but had made providential decisions to continue his education and rise in both law and politics, embarking on successful careers in these pursuits. At the same time, he remained a farmer, never losing touch with the land, the people who cultivated it, or the crucial role of water in their future. These were the ingredients of the McFarland persona in 1940, a forty-six year old senator-elect with a vision of American potential, awaiting his opportunity to serve in the nation's capital.

PART II

UNITED STATES SENATE FIRST TERM *1941-1946*

CHAPTER FOUR

FRESHMAN SENATOR
1941

ERNEST W. MCFARLAND COMMENCED HIS SENATE CAREER on January 3, 1941, with the convening of the First Session of the Seventy-seventh Congress. Exiting Vice President John Nance "Cactus Jack" Garner of Texas called the session to order and administered the oath of office to McFarland, who was escorted by Arizona's now senior senator, Carl Hayden. McFarland resigned his position as Pinal County Superior Court Judge on that same day invoking the displeasure of Arizona's governor-elect, Sidney P. Osborn. By not waiting until January 6 to resign his position, the new senator allowed lame-duck Governor Robert Jones to fill the vacancy. Technically McFarland was correct, but this seemingly insignificant occurence forecast the potential for future division between the Osborn-controlled state party machine and the senator in the nation's capital.

The new senator spent much time during his early weeks in Washington finding lodgings and office space, appointing a staff, securing committee assignments, and attempting to establish suitable influence in terms of patronage. After finding a temporary apartment for his family, he appointed a staff that, unlike Ashurst's, which had had none, consisted entirely of Arizonans. The contingent moved into a small three-room cluster on the Senate Office Building's second floor across the hall from the Vice Presidential Suite soon to be occupied by Iowa's intrepid Henry Wallace.[1]

Although McFarland did not receive precisely what he

67

desired concerning committees, he expressed satisfaction with his assignments. In post-election letters to Senator Hayden, he had requested in order: Judiciary, Naval or Military Affairs, and Interstate Commerce or Agriculture and Forestry. With the final decision, Majority Leader Alben Barkley recognized Mac's background experience and concern for Arizona affairs by appointing him to the major committees Judiciary and Interstate Commerce, along with minor committees Indian Affairs, Irrigation and Reclamation, and Pensions, one more than the normal load for this second category.[2]

Initially Senator McFarland expressed great concern with establishing patronage and influence commensurate with a new U.S. senator. In a letter to Maricopa County Superior Court Judge Howard Speakman, he wrote of the foolishness of spending money, time, and effort to get to the capital and then not be able "to keep my fences built up and take care of my friends." Speakman reassured him that he was "laboring under a misapprehension" that he was not doing enough. More importantly, Speakman's letters alluded to divisions within the Arizona Democratic party. He urged McFarland to establish himself early concerning Colorado River water projects, or Senator Hayden and Governor Osborn would take "all credit for whatever is accomplished" and attempt to "steal your thunder." Speakman pointed out the three-way division of Ashurst, Hayden (and Osborn), and McFarland men with Hayden controlled by the Salt River Valley Water Users' Association and Central Arizona Power and Light Company and in turn controlling the Arizona State and Maricopa County Democratic Committees and the governor's staff. Speakman concluded, "They will try to rob you of any credit for any action on your part. Therefore, I would suggest you do not overlook these matters. . . ."

The extent of these party divisions did not become fully apparent for another dozen years, and during the ensuing decade of the 1940s, McFarland's equanimity proved largely responsible for providing Arizona with a solid congressional front. He remained determined to work smoothly and avoid an "out and out break" with the "popular" Hayden, allowing him first choice on mutual appointments, yet insisting on as close to fifty percent of choices as possible and rigorously maintaining the inside track on all judicial appointments.[3] Hayden's long service to his state required this deference. Along with Hunt and Ashurst, the Tempe native had fashioned an unrivaled career in Arizona politics, rising from Maricopa County Sheriff to the state's first U.S. representative (1912-27) and now a veteran three-term U.S. senator.

McFarland's major effort to establish patronage and influence reached to defeated Senator Henry Ashurst, but to no avail. Ashurst remained in President Franklin Roosevelt's "doghouse" for opposing administration policies like FDR's "court-packing." McFarland unsuccessfully joined eighty-four of ninety-five senators in petitioning the president to appoint Ashurst to a vacancy on the United States Court of Claims. Then, over Hayden's caution that Ashurst lacked adequate finances for the position, McFarland next advanced Ashurst's name for the ambassadorship to Great Britain, recently vacated by Joseph Kennedy. Failing this, McFarland joined in-state groups in forwarding his name for a vacancy on the U.S. Supreme Court, but all that was found available for the twenty-eight year senator and former head of the Judiciary Committee was membership on the Immigration Board of Appeals, a position from which he resigned in early 1943.[4]

While McFarland dealt with the red tape and bureaucracy of committee assignments, patronage and influence, and arranging Washington affairs in these early weeks, his mind, like all the others on the Hill, remained preoccupied with the great questions of the day concerning national defense and foreign policy. Roosevelt quickly directed Congress's attention to the deteriorating international situation at the beginning of the first session.

On January 6, 1941, FDR called a joint session of Congress to espouse his ideas on Lend-Lease to upgrade aid to a beleagured Great Britain, then standing alone against Hitler's menace, and to enunciate the "Four Freedoms" — of speech and religion and from want and fear. Senator McFarland later reflected on that momentous occasion, speaking of "the calm before the storm" and "the tense drama" as the members of the Senate marched in a body to the House Chamber, altogether an "unprecedented experience."[5]

Soon after this famous presidential speech, McFarland officially went on record in support of the president's policy. On January 23, 1941, he inserted in the *Congressional Record* a letter he had written to constituent E. J. Duhame of Phoenix on January 16. In this, the senator emphasized two major points for national protection: speedy completion of the national defense program and prompt and adequate aid to Great Britain. He did not favor sending men overseas to engage in combat but insisted that preparedness and assistance, indicating a position of strength, would not result in a war, but, in fact, would have an intimidating effect upon the Axis Powers, stating: "Germany has not forgotten that the entry of the United States into the last World War was determinative of its outcome. . . ."[6]

McFarland recalled the weeks of hearings on Lend-Lease as a time when "feelings ran high and impatience hung over Capitol Hill," and noted that opposition was "strong and untiring," although he never doubted these senators' sincerity and patriotism. The freshman senator displayed a consistent pro-administration front voting against amendments prescribed by the Republican and Democratic isolationist opposition that included geographic, financial, presidential, and fund-usage limitations. In each case he voted with the majority to strike down the amendments and for the final bill. Lend-Lease, allocating up to seven billion dollars aid for Great Britain, passed the Senate on March 8 during the season's heaviest snowfall, 60-31. It passed the House on March 11 by 317-71, the president signing it the same day.[7]

Senator McFarland concluded that the final bill comprised a composite judgment and opinion of the executive and the legislative branches embodying both supportive and opposing views. He pointed out that Congress could curtail presidential powers by concurrent resolution and that congressional approval was necessary for transferal of any goods amounting to over $1.3 billion in value. At a Jackson Day speech back in Phoenix later in March, he quoted from a speech by German Minister of Agriculture Walter Darre, who had expressed enmity to the U.S. and outlined plans to confiscate the European land and industrial property of all non-Germans for redistribution among citizens. McFarland also alluded to Hitler's own statement: "I guarantee that at the right moment a new America will exist as our strongest supporter when we are ready to take the stride into overseas space." Senator Josh Lee (D-OK) placed McFarland's speech in the *Appendix to the Congressional Record.*[8]

Two months later, Senator Claude Pepper (D-FL) continued the recognition by inserting McFarland's June Flag Day speech in the *Appendix*. Appearing before an audience of two thousand Floridians in Miami's Bayfront Park, Mac lashed out at opponents of preparedness. He also assailed communism, complimenting Florida for following Arizona's lead and striking the Communist party off the state ballot. He claimed that the United States should have no place for a party that stands for:

1) hatred of God and all forms of religion
2) destruction of private property and inheritance
3) promotion of class hatred
4) revolutionary propaganda
5) destruction of all forms of representative or democratic governments
6) the ultimate and final objective, by means of world revolution to establish the dictatorship of the proletariat into one world union of Soviet socialist republics with the capital at Moscow.

Ironically, the Flag Day speech occurred only days before Hitler's ill-fated invasion of Russia. McFarland had already voted against the prohibition of loans to the Soviets, and regardless of his attitude toward the Communist party, he stood behind those fighting a common foe with Great Britain, and he later voted to extend Lend-Lease to the Soviet Union.[9]

The session's high point for Senator McFarland's personal initiative in foreign policy occurred with his first major floor speech on July 24, 1941. He delineated the need for a better understanding among nations, particularly those who would prepare a peace treaty and postwar plans. He also expressed hope that if other nations knew the specific motives, goals, and plans of "Great Britain and her allies," they would be hesitant to engage in war against the United States. In emphasizing the importance of studying this postwar subject, Mac urged the Senate to exercise its duty to advise and consent by offering the following resolution:

> That a committee composed of 10 members be appointed by the President of the Senate to study, recommend, and report terms and conditions to be placed in any treaty of peace which results from a victory by Great Britain and her allies in the present conflict: also, if said committee shall find it advisable to study, recommend, and report whether an agreement to accept such terms and conditions should be made a condition of aid by the United States to any of the warring nations, and whether the United States should withhold aid against any nation which fails to accept and agree to such terms and conditions.[10]

The resolution seemed premature to the Senate, which rejected it. Nevertheless, it marked the first congressional proposal calling for a study of the postwar subject, and it drew the attention of President Roosevelt. A month later he and Prime Minister Winston Churchill met at sea off Newfoundland and agreed upon the Atlantic Charter, which perhaps coincidentally embodied the gist of McFarland's own recommendations.

In August, the Senate voted on the extension of the draft, and McFarland held to the administration's preparedness line by voting against amendments limiting the length of extension and for amendments increasing servicemen's pay. The Selective Service Extension Act as passed (by one vote in the House and 45-30 in the Senate) called for an extension of the draft by eighteen months beyond the original twelve. Returning home to Arizona at the end of the summer, the senator described this vote as "not a pleasant task and one of the hardest things I have had to do." Nevertheless, he took the unanimous advice of high ranking armed forces officials who maintained the extension was for the trainees' own good and that the training they did receive was insufficient and must be bolstered if they were to have appropriate means of self-protection. Using this reasoning, McFarland felt obligated to vote for the bill. Under the circumstances, he also felt compelled to vote for increased compensation during the time of extended service.[11]

During these months of heightened international activity, McFarland kept active with national and state domestic issues involving labor, mining, range management, agriculture, and particularly water. He established himself as a pro-labor senator slightly out of step with a Congress beginning to consider more restrictive legislation.

Union-management relations concerning production and wages during times of increased preparedness and potential warfare gained the apt attention of Congress in 1941. Worried about the possibility of disruptive strikes, the Senate began to consider legislation that would ultimately result in the restrictions of the Smith-Connally Act of 1943. During efforts to amend the 1940 Selective Service Act and place limitations on unions in key industries, McFarland voted against condemning strikes as contrary to the public interest and against authorization of presidential seizure of plants if production failure would be threatened by a labor dispute. In both cases, the amendments carried, but Mac kept his allegiance in line with labor, which had opposed him in the 1940 primaries.[12]

McFarland also held agricultural interests at heart. His farming experience fostered his regard for agriculture as the key to Arizona's future and water as the key to agriculture. Urging parity with the industrial East, he backed all legislation designed to aid the farmer and asked the government to "assist Arizona and other western states to conserve their water supplies by every feasible irrigation project," thus heeding the earlier advice of his friend Judge Speakman to establish himself immediately in water affairs.[13]

On April 29, McFarland got into an amusing exchange over water with the Senate's senior member, "Cotton Ed" Ellison D. Smith (D-SC), who had served since the century's first decade. Smith fought for flood control projects that would curtail natural threats to the cotton industry, and in doing so his speech disparaged McFarland's home territory:

> We spend money on the arid regions of the West, which God did not intend people to farm. They do not have any rain there in 4 or 5 years, and then they sit down and howl to be fed and clothed and housed when God did not intend anything but gophers and prairie rats to live there.

The southwestern senator took umbrage:

> I must take issue when he says that the deserts of our western states are not fit for anything but rats. That is a term that is usually applied to Members of Congress, and I do not think it ought to be applied to my people. I must say that Nature has so constituted the other places that they need protection. I for one am in favor of giving them that protection, and placing the water back in the river. In Arizona when the time comes, we shall want assistance in taking water out of the river and putting it in the soil.

This kind of laid back humor coupled with mild rebukes and a likeable demeanor ingratiated Mac with his colleagues and furthered his rise in the Senate.[14]

Just two weeks earlier, McFarland had attended Public Lands Committee hearings held in Phoenix and Kingman, which provided a forum for the complaints of public land users in the state. Over seven hundred people attended, mostly livestock and sheep ranchers who registered a general protest against increased grazing fees and a reduction system that cut stock numbers and land availability by ten percent on any transfer or sale. Influenced by the hearings and after his return to Washington, Mac sponsored his first bill to become law. Approved later in the 1942 second session, the legislation changed the old Taylor Grazing Act, which had stated that the government held no obligation to pay for the cancellation of grazing leases. These cancellations were on the rise in Arizona as more air and military training areas were established in what had been public grazing lands. McFarland's legislation adjusted this situation by providing compensation for losses, including improvements, to holders of the confiscated leases and permits.[15]

McFarland, already considered an expert on local and state water litigation, now engaged in determining a water issue of regional proportions and national implications, the allotment of the waters of the Southwest's greatest river, the Colorado. Beginning in April and continuing on into July 1941, he frequently appeared before senate committees considering allotments and appropriations of water and finances for irrigation and reclamation projects among western states. This activity marked the beginning of his congressional efforts, which eventually led to senate passage of the Central Arizona Project a decade later. No major decisions were made and no significant legislation passed in 1941, but senate water leaders began to group, draw battle lines, and plot strategies. McFarland emerged in the forefront of these, well qualified by his legal expertise in Arizona water affairs over the previous decades. Carl Hayden comprised the other half of the tandem, handling the intricacies of getting favored bills through committees to the floor (and sidetracking, if possible, those not in Arizona's interest) while McFarland handled the grueling chores of floor and committee debate and all legal formalities. Both senators were ably assisted in the House by Arizona's Congressman John Murdock. An aggressive California contingent led by Democratic Senator Sheridan Downey often opposed the Arizonans, occasionally joined by

Nevadans led by Democratic Senator Pat McCarran.[16]

Senator McFarland made his second trip back to Arizona in late August 1941, giving his major attention to the river, but he was more sought after for comments on the European war and preparedness. In Prescott, the senator addressed the twenty-third annual convention of the Arizona American Legion; in Flagstaff, he presented the commencement address at the State Teachers College; and in Phoenix, he spoke before a crowd of two thousand assembled by the Committee to Defend America. This organization had been founded to oppose the isolationist America First group, and McFarland under the Encanto Park bandshell was joined by Senator James E. Murray, who castigated his fellow Democrat and Montanan Senator Burton K. Wheeler, leader of the isolationists in Congress. Throughout all of these speeches McFarland eagerly flayed the isolationist stance and supported the administration's program of national preparedness.[17]

As his Arizona visit came to a close, McFarland returned to the nation's capital to achieve his greatest recognition as a freshman senator. Ironically, perhaps, this recognition was due to his appointment by Burton K. Wheeler to a subcommittee chaired and dominated by isolationists.

On the hot summer afternoon of August 1, 1941, in St. Louis's air-conditioned Municipal Auditorium, Senator Gerald P. Nye spoke on the hazards of President Franklin Roosevelt's growing tendency to intervene in the affairs of Europe and World War II. Nye, a Republican from North Dakota, had a national reputation as an isolationist and ranked among the America First Committee's most effective speakers. On this day he formed part of a two-fronted attack on Roosevelt's interventionist policies that he maintained were not only leading the nation to war, but also building a presidential dictatorship at home on the pretense of opposing dictatorships abroad. The senator specifically targeted the Hollywood moguls and their film industry, calling it "the most gigantic engine of propaganda in existence." Nye made three specific charges during his national radio address: the movies expounded pro-war propaganda; the industry constituted a monopoly controlled by a handful of men, mostly of foreign [Jewish] background; and there existed excellent reason to believe that the U.S. government had influenced the propagandistic direction. His speech generated supportive cheers along with lusty boos for the president.[18]

In Washington, D.C., on the same day, Senator Bennett Champ Clark (D-MO) introduced Senate Resolution 152, reiterating Nye's charges and asking that the situation be referred to the Interstate Commerce Committee, chaired by Senator Wheeler. Sanctioned by the Senate, Wheeler appointed an isolationist-dominated subcommittee to determine the feasibility of a full senate investigation. His selections included D. Worth Clark (D-ID) as chair, Homer T. Bone (D-WA), Charles W. Tobey (R-NH), and C. Wayland Brooks (R-IL). The only Wheeler-appointee who had supported the administration on such issues as Lend-Lease was Ernest McFarland. Because freshman senators were normally seen and not heard, most viewed the Arizonan's appointment as window dressing.[19]

There seemed adequate reason for concern over the film industry's ability to propagandize because of the current activity of Hollywood's Anti-Nazi League, the 1940 investigations by the House Committee on Un-American Activities, the previous support of the Motion Picture Artists Committee for the communist-backed Loyalists in the Spanish Civil War, and Hollywood's successful manipulation of the campaign against Socialist candidate Upton Sinclair in the 1934 California gubernatorial election. Chairman D. Worth Clark, therefore, summoned the resolution's author, John T. Flynn of New York City's America First branch, the resolution cosponsors, Nye and Champ Clark, and Hollywood gossip columnist Jimmie Fidler to testify against the film community. He also subpoenaed the press books and advertising material for seventeen films and placed the newsreel *March of Time* under suspicion. The anti-film witnesses would appear first, followed by Harry M. Warner (Warner Bros.), Darryl F. Zanuck (Twentieth-Century Fox), Nicholas Schenck (Loew's, Inc.) and Barney Balaban

(Paramount), who were to testify in Hollywood's behalf.[20]

The film community responded vigorously to the summons. On August 30, Will Hays, the industry's leading spokesman since the 1920s and president of the Motion Pictures Producers and Distributors Association, addressed a letter to Chairman Clark, welcoming the opportunity to prove "the baselessness of the false and shameful accusations."[21]

Two days later, Hays' colleagues unloaded a bombshell. Fearing that the industry spokesman might be too moderate and appeasing, the producers went over his head to retain Wendell Willkie as special counsel. The film community expressed shock at the engagement of such a prominent person and at the courage of the company heads for the move. Wendell Willkie had only recently been defeated by FDR in the 1940 presidential election while running on a noninterventionist ticket. Since that time, ten months earlier, he had turned coat, outraging the isolationists, and most particularly Gerald P. Nye, who had carried his home state for Willkie in the elections. Now the charismatic commoner would find little-known Ernest McFarland a welcome ally in the impending showdown with his irate former supporters in the stage-like setting of the Senate Caucus Room.[22]

To allow time to prepare a proper defense, Willkie had the hearing opening moved back to September 9. He then drafted a letter to Chairman Clark in which he agreed with Senator Nye that the motion picture industry opposed Naziism and cooperated with the government in preparing national-defense films. He also conceded that Jews (as well as Gentiles) composed an important segment of the film community. He denied, however, that the Roosevelt administration had in any way coerced the studios into producing interventionist propaganda.[23]

Willkie's assertive and unequivocal stance keynoted Hollywood's new aggressive policy toward those who sought to smear the motion-picture community. The industry questioned the legality of the subcommittee, its impartiality, and the intended manner of its proceeding. Terming the investigation "harassment of free expression in the United States," Willkie demanded that his letter be placed side by side in the record with Senator Nye's speech and Champ Clark's resolution. With that opening salvo, the scenario was set for the hearings in Washington. The script, however, did not take into account the unexpected role Senator McFarland would play as defender of the motion-picture industry.

The subcommittee convened on Tuesday, Septemper 9, 1941, in front of a packed gallery. Homer Bone of Washington was absent for the duration of the hearings due to illness. The remaining principals were present, including the four investigating senators, Wendell Willkie, and the day's witness, Senator Nye. Determined opponents immediately established positions when chairman Clark denied Willkie the right to cross-examine or call witnesses, a decision reached with McFarland as the only dissenting vote. Thus gagged, Willkie sat back amidst disappointed murmuring from the audience.[24]

With procedural matters out of the way, Senator Nye approached the bench. The North Dakotan looked the part of the senatorial pugilist who had successfully confronted millionaire financier J.P. Morgan, Jr., in this very room a half-decade earlier, during investigation into the World War I munitions industry. Tall, suave, pinstriped, and grasping a cigarette, the senator sported a a large bandage on his chin, masking a shaving accident. Nye commenced by denying that movies were entitled to the protection of the First Amendment. They provided entertainment, not information. His central thesis held that a small group of monopolistic producers controlled the production, distribution, and exhibition of material viewed weekly in seventeen thousand theaters by over eighty million Americans who desired only entertainment, not propaganda. The producers comprised the "most potent and dangerous Fifth Column in our country," he admonished before criticizing specific films *Sergeant York* and Charlie Chaplin's *The Great Dictator*, a parody of both Hitler and Mussolini. He then went on to deny charges of Jew-baiting, while at the same time adding fuel to the fire by stating, "If anti-Semitism exists in America, the Jews have themselves to blame."[25]

Senator McFarland functioned as the major cross-examiner, continually trying to pin the witness down on what legislation might be expected from the investigation and what exactly constituted propaganda. Nye equivocated on possible censorship legislation, and McFarland drew laughs by asking if it was "merely publicity" that the committee desired. Concerning the distinction between propaganda and accurate information, Nye decried films that produced "a spirit of hate" against a race. Pressed by McFarland, Nye revealed that he had seen only two of the films then under scrutiny and that he couldn't remember the name of one. *Variety*, the Hollywood trade magazine wrote in support: "McFarland, whose queries are so innocently put their point hardly becomes apparent until the last word, scores again." From this point on in the hearings, the Arizona senator began to work for concrete evidence like the viewing of the films themselves.[26]

Senator Nye proved equally vulnerable on points raised during the afternoon session. Introducing a Wall Street report, he contended that motion picture profits were in a one-to-one ratio with earnings made from British sales and, that therefore the industry depended on British success in the war to ensure profit. The implication was not lost on McFarland, who endorsed the right of American citizens to aid a country supporting their financial interests. On charges that the U.S. government demanded the production of propaganda pictures, Nye, under McFarland's questioning, would not reveal his "excellent foundation" for the testimony. He stated it was the duty of the committee and not himself to establish the facts. After Wendell Willkie offered to produce the cost sheets for all pictures under discussion, Nye claimed these were juggled to make propaganda films look profitable. Pressed on this matter by McFarland, he refused to name his "reputable industry source."[27]

The first day's investigation proved significant in illuminating patterns and characteristics that would remain prominent through the conclusion of the hearings. These included a silenced, frustrated Willkie who, nevertheless, made his presence felt; the overbearing attitude of the isolationists; and the obstinancy of Senator McFarland, who remained determined to get at the facts. He commented to the press:

"While a Senator ought to kinda take it easy at first, see what's what and everything, I couldn't very well just sit there and let that kind of testimony be accepted. Wasn't facts at all. Just hearsay and what Senator Nye thinks about movies personally." Willkie quipped, "Looks to me like we got a Will Rogers in the house."[28]

Much of the nation's and the film industry's press relished the dramatic stance of the freshman lawmaker and the lines that had been drawn between the isolationists and McFarland. *Variety* described him: "A big slow drawling Arizonan, impish eyes lurking behind a bulldog face unexpectedly provided the answer to the film industry's prayer." It depicted Nye's speech as a "rambling anti-Semitic tirade," and reported that "the more Nye bristled, the more Mac mowed him down. . . . The North Dakota isolationist was tossed around at intervals by Senator McFarland who accused him of trying to gag everybody with ideas different from his." After objecting to both Willkie's exclusion from participation and the necessity to place senators under oath, McFarland had successfully challenged Nye on at least five major issues and, according to the press, had won the first round.[29]

The testimony of the next three days proved repetitious and insignificant. Champ Clark, the second day's witness, reiterated the charges of propagandizing and monopoly, but under McFarland's questioning, admitted to having seen none of the movies being investigated. Again Wendell Willkie asked for permission to call and examine witnesses. Senator McFarland backed him, stating, "I'm a pretty good Democrat, and I don't want to have to defend a Republican like Mr. Willkie when he's here to defend himself." Their efforts were to no avail as once more D. Worth Clark's gavel pounded down the request.[30]

As testimony proceeded, Champ Clark astoundingly insinuated that the propagandists wanted not only to abandon U.S. neutrality but also to foreswear independence and reunite with Great Britain. Moreover, he identified freedom of speech with access to the instruments for its dissemination, implying that politicians were jealous of the screen as a medium and the screenwriter as a commentator. An amused McFarland, using old courtroom skills, easily labled this testimony as hearsay in a performance the *Hollywood Reporter* termed "a circus that's been struck by a hurricane."[31]

The press delved a bit deeper into the Arizona senator's background after the second day's work. Referred to as an expected nonentity, he was now represented as a sports not a movie fan and a "champion of old-time Americanism," who believed that "The power of inquiry is limited by the Constitution." "You don't think we can go out here," he asked, "and inquire into the lives of people, if we can show no worth-while and legal purpose." The *Reporter* noticed that "an embarrassed wet blanket falls upon the committee whenever Senator McFarland mentions the Constitution and the legality of inquiry. . . . His easy personality disguises an aggressive willingness to tie into anyone who would curtail the Bill of Rights." The *Christian Science Monitor* took the inquiry to task, charging a clever plan to set up a stacked isolationist grand jury and maintaining that the investigation was born in subterfuge.[32]

Senator McFarland opened the hearings the third day by repeating his charges of hearsay and time wasting and the desirability of seeing the films. On the stand sat the economist John T. Flynn, a fallen-away New Dealer, who had at least seen the films. He expanded the list of those he found questionable to thirty-nine, stepped up the attack on the newsreels, criticized Charlie Chaplin, and generally echoed previous testimony. McFarland aroused Flynn's ire by noting that the German-American Bund had advised its members to join America First, and the meeting devolved into sarcasm and displays of temper.[33]

On day four Jimmie Fidler inadvertently undermined the isolationists' credibility by accusing motion picture producers of trying to influence movie critics, intimidate newspaper gossip columnists, and stifle radio comment. Fidler, whose column appeared in 140 newspapers and who had formerly broadcast over CBS, failed to substantiate his all-encompassing charges. Instead, much to the chagrin of the isolationists, he chose to digress into a criticism of actress Alice Faye, who had allegedly been dissatisfied with a dress purchased from a shop owned by Fidler's wife. An amused McFarland cynically commented, "We seem to have arrived at the real issue now." When Fidler persisted, Mac admonished "I think I've got about as deep as I want into this dress issue," changing the topic from Fidler's accusations to Fidler himself by referring to a CBS statement alleging that Fidler's radio program had brought the network endless legal difficulties as he had "destroyed values and reputations in order to build up a big audience."[34]

An Oklahoma newspaper, watching its first native-born U.S. senator with interest, put the issue in humorous perspective:

> Jimmie Fidler was investigated because his wife sold Alice Faye a gown alleged to have come apart. Fidler is a Hollywood commentator. Just about that time Fidler had a fight with Errol Flynn in which Fidler's wife joined, using a fork, which Flynn says was a social error because it was the wrong fork. Anyhow, it made Flynn's ear bleed. They have an especially cataclysmic drink in Hollywood called a zombie, and it is expected that there were a few zombies around at the time. Errol Flynn is Irish, and he likes to fight once in a while. Oh yes, Walter Winchell is another commentator and he is against Hitler. Hitler is against Winchell, so that makes it even. Wendell Willkie ran for President in 1940. Willkie lives at Elwood, Ind. His grandfather was born in Germany, as was the grandfather of King George of England. Willkie defends Hollywood against Senator Clark. All this sounds somewhat confused. It is true, but so is the investigation of Hollywood.[35]

Chairman Clark brought the four-day prosecuting stage to a conclusion by hinting at a conspiracy of the nation's newspaper columnists and the film industry to malign the investigation. McFarland responded by objecting strenuously to both the chair's criticism of the press and the lethargy of the subcommittee's progress, referring to the lack of accomplishment, the absence of real evidence, and the frustration of not seeing the actual films. He drew applause by stating "we had better be careful and not have the burning of the books Germany had in 1933. That was the beginning of dictatorship there."[36] The prosecution stage of the investigation now closed, and the hearings recessed until September 23.

Both sides took advantage of the recess to catch their breath and regroup. Senator McFarland flew off to deliver an anti-isolationist speech in Cleveland amidst approbation and further conjecture on his previously unknown status from *Life* and *Time*. The magazines now compared him more than favorably with his Arizona predecessor the "silver-tongued orator" Henry Ashurst. Those who had been shocked at McFarland's 1940 victory now spoke of "horse sense" having triumphed over one "to whom a neatly turned epigram was more cherished than a slice of political pork."[37]

Senator Nye and his cohorts were busy as well. At an America First rally in Des Moines, Iowa, aviator Charles Lindbergh charged that the "three most important groups . . . pressing the country toward war are the British, the Jewish, and the Roosevelt administration." Although Lindbergh was widely vilified for his remarks, Nye jumped to his defense, thereby further undermining the isolationist cause in the eyes of the public. Undaunted, Nye vowed that he would seek to broaden the investigation of Hollywood based on "tips" he had received from within the industry.[38]

The gamut of German-American publications also supported the isolationists as did radio priest Father Coughlin's *Social Justice*. Coughlin struck particularly hard at the B'nai B'rith's Anti-Defamation League, and the National Council of Christians and Jews which he accused of warmongering. He also lashed out at Wendell Willkie for garnering money and publicity, and turning the investigation into a "Keystone Comedy." In Coughlin's eyes, the Jews themselves were the "authors of the Jewish question," and he pointed accusing fingers at Jewish appointees in the Roosevelt administration.[39]

In the wake of such isolationist assaults on Hollywood, powerful allies such as the AFL, the CIO, the Jewish War Veterans, and Freedom Inc. rallied in defense of the motion picture producers. AFL Secretary-Treasurer John J. Stanley wrote to Vice President Henry Wallace, charging the investigators with anti-Semitism and urging him to "repudiate and condemn this subcommittee and to use your influence to halt its shameful activities." The Council of Actors Equity also joined the fray, denouncing the proceedings as an immediate threat to free thought and speech. Even President Roosevelt sided with the film community, ridiculing charges of propaganda and emphatically denying that the government exerted any pressure on movie producers.[40]

National publications continued to take advantage of the recess to lambaste the hearings. *Life* called them "Washington's funniest political circus of the year" and accused Burton K. Wheeler and a coterie of isolationists with setting up a "kangoroo court in which to accuse, judge, and condemn the Administration's foreign policy." *Life* also chastised the isolationists for attempting "to divide the American people into discordant racial and religious groups." *Time* quoted Senator Nye as singling out four foreign-born Jews as the major Hollywood propagandists. The magazine also ironically praised Senator McFarland in the context of freedom of speech as "working on Nye like a censor working on *Lady Chatterly's Lover*."[41] Stimulated by the reporting, whether pro or anti-isolationist, much of the nation eagerly awaited the resumption of the hearings.

When the committee reconvened with the Hollywood producers on the stand, Senator Charles W. Tobey assumed the role of prime inquisitor, but McFarland continued to probe for a more concrete basis for investigation. Louis de Rochemont, producer of the newsreel series *March of Time*, offered to produce six members of the Norwegian Air Force to testify to the veracity of the newsreel and other pictures dealing with their plight with the Nazis. McFarland urged hearing this firsthand testimony rather than continuing "futile" hearings. Chairman Clark suggested to the impatient senator that if he felt he was wasting time, he did not have to attend. The obstinate Arizonan demurred: "As long as you keep investigating, I'll be around here doing my duty." He held his own meeting with the flyers on the evening of September 25 at the Carlton Hotel, where they assured him that the movies were, indeed, too mild in their depictions of German atrocity.[42]

After Nicholas Schenck of Loew's Inc. gave two days of inconclusive testimony, Harry M. Warner took the stand, and the president of Warner Bros. came prepared. He received permission to make his opening statement without interruption and responded in the negative to all four charges as he perceived them. His films did not incite war intervention but dealt with current affairs. They were not inaccurate but depicted the world as it was. The films did not violate the public's viewing wishes, for profits spoke otherwise. And the government did not order their production, although he was proud to cooperate voluntarily with national defense efforts.[43]

Warner's description of the rise of Warner Bros. from its beginning in 1906 as a family nickelodeon business in western Pennsylvania to its present position as a leading West Coast motion-picture studio evoked the American ideal of individual enterprise coupled with opportunity. Production policy was based strictly on marketability, accuracy and realism, and variety according to Warner, and during the preceding two-and-one-half years, only seven of 140 Warner productions had dealt with the situation in Europe. One of them proved particularly relevant to the present hearings.[44]

Confessions of a Nazi Spy had returned a profit and even garnered acclaim from German-American citizens' organizations, but isolationists now found it objectionable. Their attack backfired, however, when it was discovered to their huge embarrassment that Nye had roundly approved the film at a private showing on May 11, 1939: "The picture is exceedingly good. The cast is exceptionally fine. The plot may or may not be exaggerated but is one that ought to be with every patriotic American. As for myself, I hope there may be more pictures of a kind dealing with propaganda emanating from all foreign lands."[45]

At the end of Warner's effective testimony Senator Tobey introduced charges that would hasten the heated denouement of the investigation by claiming that the British Purchasing Commission based in Washington, D.C., refused to hire Jews, Irish, and Germans. These charges served as McFarland's focus during day eight.[46]

When the final day of the hearings began, McFarland rose to the challenge by stating that the British Embassy denied to him any hiring discrimination, and he accused Tobey of the sole purpose "to create prejudice against the British Empire and our own government . . . after Congress has voted to give aid." Warming to the fight he further charged the subcommittee with overstepping the bounds of its authority and suggested that the proceedings be themselves investigated by both the Senate and the House Committee on Un-American Activities. Exclaiming, "I do not like it, I tell you right now. No, I do not like it and I'm going to fight it." As worked up as the mild-mannered Mac ever got, he continued: "You have a right to ask questions, but I am going to object any time you ask such questions. I am one person who believes in the policies of Franklin D. Roosevelt, and I do not want to sit there and hear them challenged in speeches made by you, Senator Tobey, or the chairman of this subcommittee, questioning his Americanism." He then startled the assembled with his next statement:

> . . . the time has come when I feel I must challenge you, Mr. Chairman, and any other member of this subcommittee, to take the matter before the United States Senate and find out whether they want a committee which is to pass upon the way the investigation should be made. . . . I venture to say that if the questions were presented on the floor of the United States Senate, you would not get 18 votes. . . . I challenge you here and I will challenge you there.

Clark replied, "I think people never holler unless they are pretty badly hurt." In response, McFarland rejoindered: "You are the one who is going to be hurt before this whole thing is over." A round of applause followed this exclamation.[47]

After this flare-up, the day's witnesses seemed perfunctory, for in suggesting a committee to investigate the investigating subcommittee, McFarland had severely undermined the credibility of the hearings. Darryl F. Zanuck spoke at length, and Barney Balaban spoke briefly. When finished, the two film executives left the courtroom amidst further applause.[48]

Senator Tobey's surprise witnesses to support his discrimination charges fared much worse. McFarland questioned the three employment agency clerks whom Tobey obviously had not screened and quickly revealed their allegations as being based on hearsay. McFarland objected to such "absurdly irrelevant testimony" and walked out of the meetings for the first time, but not before chairman Clark uttered a veiled threat that Senator Nye would "take care of him" on the senate floor. Clark closed the hearings by scheduling a one-week recess and promising that the subcommittee would view the films when it reconvened.[49]

All of the principals of the investigation kept active and highly visible during the recess. In a radio address, D. Worth Clark said sufficient evidence existed to support the monopoly charge, but he remained undecided on the propaganda issue. The relegation of this originally emphasized charge to secondary consideration was significant in clarifying the isolationists' determination to come away with at least some kind of victory even if they could not prove instigation toward war. Senator Nye spoke at length in the Senate, while Senator Wheeler carried his isolationist program on a two-month barnstorming tour of the West. In Phoenix and Tucson, Wheeler praised former Senator Ashurst in speeches and ignored McFarland, although privately, he categorized him as merely Willkie's pre-briefed mouthpiece. McFarland responded, "They [his own questions] were not suggested by anyone. I was in the dark as to what those who introduced the resolution were trying to accomplish and my questions were along the line of trying to ascertain their aims and desires."[50]

The press continued to seek out and publish material on the now well-known freshman senator, but his real reward came when the hearings were postponed indefinitely on October 9, 1941, the senator's forty-seventh birthday. The immediate reason for this action was the continued absence of Washington State's Homer Bone and the temporary in-state duties of Senators Tobey and Brooks, but the actual reason was the continued escalation of support for the interventionist position, concomitant with the erosion of the isolationist stance, conditions undoubtedly aided by the astute questioning and determination of Ernest McFarland. The hearings were irrevocably cancelled after the December 7 attack on Pearl Harbor.[51]

As the motion-picture hearings faded into the background, international issues again came to the fore. Despite his aversion to communism, McFarland supported extending Lend-Lease to Russia, then undergoing a severe beating from Hitler's armies and urgently in need of financial assistance for military supplies. In Des Moines, Iowa, on October 23, he stated:

> I want to make it clear right now that I do not like the communist form of government. . . . But I recognize the right of Russia to maintain any type of government she desires . . . without interference from Hitler. . . . Germany wants Russia's resources to use against Britain and against us if Britain falls.

The second Lend-Lease Act passed Congress on November 6, appropriating one billion dollars in aid to the beleagured Soviet Union.[52]

Far more controversy surrounded amending the Neutrality Act of 1937, then in effect. The administration wanted to permit U.S. merchantmen more flexibility on the high seas by allowing them to travel in combat zones, trade in belligerent ports, and bear arms, all prohibited under the older act. The House passed a bill permitting the arming of ships but refused the administration's other requests. Senate hearings resulted in a proposal allowing ships to enter war zones and belligerent ports.

The ensuing floor fight became quite heated with Vice President Henry Wallace having to rap repeatedly for order. Champ Clark led isolationist opposition, still formidable before Pearl Harbor, in attempting to proscribe the bill. Stating that the older provisions played too much into Hitler's hand by allowing him to call the shots and define combat areas, McFarland voted against all opposition proposals and for the final measure, which passed 50 to 37. He added that he would "always have a guilty conscience if he were to vote against the bill and deny the mariner's this right of self-defense."[53]

At the beginning of December, with Congress in recess, the senator returned to Arizona for the holiday season and a rest from congressional duties. While there, he expressed relief that national policy was finally and definitively established by the Lend-Lease Acts and the full neutrality revisions. He also allowed that "We should take a firm stand with Japan," which continued its aggressive incursions in Southeast Asia, China, and Indonesia. Only a few days later, on December 7, the Japanese struck Pearl Harbor, and Senator McFarland immediately flew back to Washington where, on December 8, 1941, he was the only member of the Arizona delegation present to vote for the state of war declaration against Japan. He did so with his young daughter Jewell in attendance in the gallery, encouraging her presence at the momentous occasion.[54]

Years later, he stated that the tension of voting to commit the nation to war was the greatest he had ever experienced. This personal tension and pressure increased immeasurably when shortly after Pearl Harbor, his wife Edna suffered severe complications in Phoenix during late pregnancy. She was hospitalized and yet another McFarland baby died. Doctors feared for her life, but she recovered, assisted by sympathy extended from an unexpected source. British Prime Minister Winston Churchill had arrived in Washington on December 22 to confer with Roosevelt and address a joint session of Congress.

After a luncheon speech, which he, in part, devoted to reflections on his American mother, Churchill was introduced to the disconsolate freshman senator. On being told by the senate secretary of Edna McFarland's serious illness, the prime minister went immediately to the phone and contacted the incapacitated and very surprised woman. He spoke briefly: "I am glad to be with your husband, Mrs. McFarland, and I am glad to speak to you personally. I hope you will soon be well." The Senator brightened enough to state his certainty that her recovery would now be "doubly fast," and the press wrote of Churchill's memories of one and sympathies for another American woman.[55]

Churchill's mission also reflected well on the despondent senator, for the prime minister assisted in drafting the United Nations Charter signed by twenty-six nations on January 1, 1942. This reaffirmed the principles of the Atlantic Charter, all of which had been addressed in Congress for the first time the previous July by Senator McFarland. Still, it remained an extremely trying time for the new senator personally and professionally, and he frequently numbered among the company of the Senate's heavier drinkers, not a small group, particularly during these troubled times. Thus the First Session of the Seventy-seventh Congress ended on January 2, 1942, amidst announcements of the fall of Manila to the Japanese. Congress did not adjourn but only went into recess, acknowledging the immense responsibilities to be borne by its members in the months and years ahead.[56]

This initial year of national service proved eventful for Senator Ernest McFarland. He had clearly established himself as an active pro-administration senator with a liberal outlook and the capability of working effectively with conservatives. In domestic affairs he strongly advanced the interests of his state, particularly concerning water. In foreign affairs he had the distinction of being the first senator to address planning for wartime goals, the peace, and postwar affairs. His impartial and strong-willed conduct during the film probe afforded him the unique opportunity to acquire exposure far exceeding the norm for a previously nationally-unknown freshman senator. Even the serious illness of his wife led to positive national exposure as a result of Winston Churchill's timely interest. The *New York Post* stated that McFarland had attracted "more favorable attention from the country than has fallen to the lot of any first-year senator in years." The *Washington Evening Star* concurred: "He has stamped himself as a senator to be reckoned with. He is no show-off. No deliberate stealer of the spotlight." *Esquire* even conjectured in a full length article that the Arizonan was, indeed, prime presidential material.[57]

Carl Hayden frequently distinguished between showhorse and workhorse senators. McFarland stood at a crossroads where he could be either striving for the limelight and a perhaps more celebrated and publicly-recognized career, or adhering to his natural inclination to unobtrusively plug away until jobs were completed. It would be to the satisfaction of armed forces veterans, southwestern water users, and his colleagues that he continued on the latter course.

CHAPTER FIVE

WARTIME SENATOR
1942-1945

AFTER YEARS OF SPECULATION AND DEBATE between isolationists and interventionists concerning U.S. foreign policy, the aggressor nations, Japan and Germany, determined the course of the World War and the eventual entry of the United States. American direction had already been implemented by President Roosevelt with adjustments of the neutrality acts, cash and carry, destroyers for bases, peacetime conscription, and finally Lend-Lease and armed ships and sailors in the North Atlantic. All were brought on largely by Hitler's conquests and mounting threat to the Western world, and all were designed to assist Great Britain while still maintaining precarious American neutrality.

It took only the fatal decision of the Japanese military hierarchy to attack Pearl Harbor and Germany's subsequent declaration of war against the United States to touch off a single minded national purpose that had not been rivaled since the American Revolution. Senator McFarland referred to Pearl Harbor as "the most treacherous and dastardly assault ever made by one nation upon another, surpassing even Hitler in cowardice and depravity." The nation now addressed itself to the problem at hand and began to shrug off whatever lethargy remained from the isolationist-influenced prewar years.[1]

These problems proved immense. Although FDR's mind was prepared for war, the nation's economy lagged. Conversion of production to wartime footing remained essential and the cooperation of labor necessary. The thorny complexities of production and labor posed immediate concern to all on Capitol Hill including McFarland, who found himself out of step with a growing majority opinion restrictive to labor. This, however, was just part of the learning process as he acquired valuable experience and self-definition.

On March 24, 1942, Senator McFarland held the floor for a lengthy time speaking on these issues and claiming the existence of an organized campaign to "high pressure Congress into passing vicious anti-labor legislation," outlawing strikes and repealing or suspending wage and hour laws. He indicated that most mail to his office supported this type of legislation and referred to press and radio reports of 119 key strikes in the first two months of the year and two million man-hours lost in the single month of February 1942.

McFarland labeled these figures "entirely inaccurate" and countered with his own statistics provided by the War Production Board, showing only .003 percent man-hours lost, no strikes authorized by a major labor organization since war began, and that those that had occurred were carried out against the advice and policy and in spite of preventive efforts by organized labor. Backed by these findings, he urged that no anti-strike legislation be considered, for it was not only unnecessary, but un-American.

McFarland's constituent mail also spoke largely against overtime payment for work on Saturdays, Sundays, and holidays, and in excess of forty hours per week, arguing that this should be limited or abolished by legislation because it was unpatriotic for workers to demand overtime. Moreover, overtime added to defense expenditures and often deterred management from scheduling full production in order to avoid increased payment. Here, too, McFarland disagreed and instead recommended legislation that would limit war profits and set wage ceilings.

Congress studiously addressed these war-production and labor issues throughout the next year, the debates culminating in the Smith-Connally War Labor Disputes Act passed on June 25, 1943, legislation that McFarland opposed to little avail. The May strike of the United Mine Workers called by union leader John L. Lewis, had exacerbated the anti-labor feeling that this act embodied, and although the strike was called off after President Roosevelt threatened to take over the mines, the damage to organized labor remained, irreparably in public opinion and now via legislation.

While referring to Lewis as "a dark cloud facing the nation," McFarland still stood against Smith-Connally because of newly affixed amendments that prohibited political campaign contributions from a union, provided punishment for those who aided or encouraged a strike, and prohibited appeals beyond the War Labors Board. He commented, "Tell a laborer he cannot do something he wants to do and it makes him mad."[2]

President Roosevelt disliked the act as well, sending in a stern veto message that the bill contained provisions "which have no place in legislation to prevent strikes in wartime and which in fact would foment slowdowns and strikes." He asked instead for the authority to induct strikers for non-combat military service, in other words, to put them in uniform and right back on the job. Congress responded swiftly and with stunning effect. Within two hours of FDR's message, the legislators overrode the veto, the Senate voting 56 to 25 and the House 244 to 108. It marked Roosevelt's first major defeat on labor legislation.

Senator McFarland voted to sustain the veto with eighteen other liberal Democrats, five Republicans, and Wisconsin Progressive Robert LaFollette, Jr. Senator Carl Hayden and Arizona representatives John Murdock and newcomer Richard Harless voted with the majorities to override. With his unsuccessful pro-labor efforts of June 1941, his March 1942 speech, and his June 1943 vote, McFarland clearly showed himself to be on the side of the worker. In a state that was becoming more conservative and would adopt right-to-work and restrictive labor organization laws in 1946, the senator was drifting from many of his constituents on this issue. For the moment, the Arizona press and public largely expressed displeasure with Mac's stance.[3]

The public expressed more satisfaction with Senator McFarland's work furthering Arizona war production and the federal government's awarding of war contracts. Serving state interests in coordination with the nation's war effort proved his most important function during the first year of war, and Arizona performed superbly even with some well-defined problem areas like a labor shortage.

At the end of 1942, the War Department reported that of $120,571,300 of authorized construction in the state, $101,710,580 had been finished, a completion rate of over eighty-three percent. Much to the senator's satisfaction, the bulk of the construction involved air bases, such as Luke Field, whose training advantages he had supported and urged because of the favorable Arizona flying weather.

McFarland had also continued his encouragement of state mining enterprises working closely with the Reconstruction Finance Corporation (RFC) to obtain increased and quicker maintenance loans and premium payments for the mines and metals. Department of the Interior reports substantiated Arizona's efforts in mining, including a rank of first in copper production with thirty-four percent of the nation's total in 1941. Gold production stood second in importance with approximately three hundred thousand mined ounces per-year in 1941 and 1942, and the state ranked fourth in the nation in silver production with over seven million ounces annually amounting to eleven percent of the U.S. total. Two-thirds of the silver and forty-five percent of the gold were derived as by-products of copper mining, the three accounting for ninety percent of Arizona's mineral production.

The war years marked a transition for the state's manufacturing industry as well. Although no one could yet perceive the enormous economic impact that industry would have in the postwar era, civic, business, and political leaders consistently encouraged this growth. McFarland reported expansion in the manufacturing sector "most gratifying." Goodyear Rubber Company had enlarged its base from experimental projects to a large manufacturing plant, Goodyear Aircraft, employing 7,500 workers. The Aluminum Company of America (ALCOA) operated the largest aluminum plant in the nation just outside of Phoenix. Additionally, Consolidated Aircraft, Airesearch, Garrett Corporation, and Allison Steel were growing concerns as manufacturing gave the state a more balanced economy and moved upward towards its postwar position as the state's leading source of income.

McFarland also reported on military training in Arizona, where twenty-one civilian pilot schools complemented the numerous government bases. At this time, for security reasons, locations and statistical data were often withheld concerning the bases that thickly marked the state, but postwar figures verified over 145,000 trainees in Arizona during the war.[4]

Training was not an exclusive province of the military. Skilled men were needed for the burgeoning manufacturing establishments as well. By October 31, 1942, 11,373 civilian workers had been trained in aircraft maintenance in the state's twelve centers by the Program of Vocational Training. Ironically, the trainees were originally intended for placement in the aircraft industries of Los Angeles and San Diego and the Pacific Coast shipyards, but with the huge growth of in-state industry, workers no longer moved out-of-state.

The Department of Agriculture's reports to McFarland proved equally encouraging showing in excess of one hundred percent production of 1942 goals in cattle, eggs, oats, barley, hay, flax, and potatoes. Milk and corn surpassed ninety percent, and sorghum and wheat exceeded seventy-five percent of expectations.[5]

Cotton remained the most important agricultural product, and Arizona led the nation in long staple production even though farm labor remained in short supply throughout the war. Senator McFarland blamed this predicament on government bureaucracy and criticized the Farm Security Administration's insistence that pickers transported into the state at FSA expense be paid by the hour rather than by the pound. The FSA mandated a wage guarantee of thirty cents an hour. McFarland supported the time-honored Arizona system of pay-for-poundage. Under normal working conditions, he contended, this would enable the picker to earn four to eight dollars per day, while the lesser hourly pay would not guarantee adequate poundage. On a day that he was momentarily honored as acting-President of the Senate, Senator McFarland appealed to President Roosevelt, armed with a Carl Hayden telegram noting the "wholly impractical demand" of the FSA and complaints from the Arizona Cotton Growers Cooperative Association. Roosevelt, however, backed by the Departments of Agriculture, Navy, and War, and the War Manpower Commission, staunchly upheld the FSA plan. McFarland's ire became further aroused when the War Manpower Commission announced and then rescinded an order to put troops stationed in Arizona to work in the fields. Still Arizona Cotton Growers had the final word and rejected the FSA contract, while continuing to use hired braceros from Mexico, Japanese internees, Italian and German prisoners of war, and newly-resident black migrants from the Deep South.[6]

Arizonans also confronted a problem area with wartime rationing procedures. Governor Sidney Osborn protested against proposed gasoline rationing, holding that it would "virtually destroy a tremendous [tourist] business in Arizona and all of the Pacific Southwest." McFarland backed him up and attacked the point-rationing system on consumer and canned goods, stating that miners and cattlemen depended far more than most civilians on the latter. He appealed to reason, noting the "exceptional conditions existing in our state . . . sparse population . . . the great distances from farm or ranch to town and from town to regional supply centers and markets." The senator's protests did little to ameliorate the situation, and many Arizonans felt they had to bear wartime hardships in excess of elsewhere in the nation.[7]

Neither the state nor its senator, nor indeed the country, had much to be proud about concerning wartime treatment of the resident Japanese. President Roosevelt himself succumbed to feelings of fear and suspicion and on February 19, 1942, ordered the removal of one hundred ten thousand

Japanese-Americans from restricted areas in the West. The relocation was undertaken ostensibly to prevent potential race riots and acts of disloyalty and subversion. While all Japanese-Americans in California were forcibly removed, in Arizona, the arbitrariness of the decision was particularly noticeable. Highway 60 (Grand and Van Buren Avenues in Phoenix) marked the division between those to the south to be relocated and those to the north entitled to remain in their homes and retain their businesses. In many cases the two disparate and fated groups lived within a few hundred feet of each other. Ultimately, two internment camps were established in Arizona: the Poston Center near Parker on the Colorado River and the Gila River Center in Bapchule south of Phoenix.

With the removal, Arizonans, particularly farmers, politicians, and the Washington delegation, all expressed concern about the possibility of postwar settlement of former non-resident Japanese-Americans within the state. Although the War Relocation Authority doubted that this migration would evolve, in-state skepticism remained high. Farmers feared that newly resident Japanese might dominate the postwar agriculture industry by expanding cooperatives operating at the relocation centers into large enterprises that could acquire and lease land for farming purposes. The Arizona Corporation Commission, for this reason, delayed articles of incorporation for the Japanese-organized Gila River Cooperative Industries. Additional paranoia existed because of the nature of Japanese-American farming. The internees were not bulk agricultural farmers, but rather "truck gardeners" producing foodstuffs that the press noted could be "fixed and annihilate the valley overnight if they had a mind to." Governor Osborn pushed through restrictive laws requiring persons with any business dealings (food production and marketing in particular) with Japanese farmers to file public notice of such transactions. The law also intended to discourage postwar Japanese settlement, and in Governor Osborn's words, keep Arizona from becoming a "dumping ground for enemy aliens."

When Senator McFarland came to the state in June

1943 to investigate these conditions and suspicions, he found "the feeling against the Japanese in Arizona very high." He also revised some old widely held beliefs and uncovered some new problems in his inspection of the camps. Arizona state administrators recognized the agricultural skills of Japanese-Americans and hoped they would be able to influence the near-by Indians on the Gila River Reservation to become better farmers. McFarland, however, expressed disappointment with the low agricultural production of relocation centers. In fact, he maintained that the Japanese had "muffed a golden opportunity" to contribute one hundred percent to effective food production and cotton-picking and thus prove their loyalty. The senator found that "The Japanese are working neither sufficient hours nor in sufficient numbers to get maximum production from the fertile land on which they are established." He lamented that farm machinery stood idle at 4:00 P.M. and that those Japanese who did work normally put in only thirty-five hours per week and should contribute "at least 48."

McFarland and thousands of other Americans cannot be exonerated by wartime exigencies from the shortsightedness that precluded them from seeing that the bulk of Japanese-Americans were already loyal and that it was the shabby treatment they received from their adopted country that cut deeply into productive and constructive efforts. This entire internment experience carried on a lesson unlearned and centuries old, dating from the subjugation of the American Indian. Home is where the heart is and when the home is taken, the spirit is broken.

The inspection of the camps convinced McFarland that the integration of loyal and suspected disloyal Japanese severely handicapped the operation of the camps. He took definite action on this situation later in the year when on December 17, he and Senator Thomas Stewart (D-TN) introduced a bill to provide for the expatriation (postwar deportation) of citizens of the United States who indicated allegiance and fidelity to a foreign country. Speaking in the Senate, he specifically referred to a question submitted to internees by the War Relocation Authority: "Will you swear unqualified allegiance to the United

States of America and foreswear any form of allegiance or obedience to the Japanese Emperor or any other foreign government, power, or organization?" Among males, seventeen years and older, 4,850 of 19,979 (twenty-five percent) replied in the negative. Among females of like age, 1,487 of 18,406 (eight percent) responded negatively. Concluding, "We cannot afford to allow these people to continue to enjoy the blessing of our great nation," McFarland displayed the dark suspicion endemic to much of the nation. The bill, however, died in committee.[8]

Later in the same summer that he inspected the Japanese relocation centers, Senator McFarland began a project that was to bring both him and Congress recognition of a much more salutary nature, the Servicemen's Readjustment Act of 1944, the famous GI Bill of Rights. As a veteran of World War I and a lifetime member of the American Legion, concern for the welfare of veterans came naturally to Ernest McFarland. Too, he well remembered that he owed his life to a team of Navy doctors at the Great Lakes School in 1918.

The work that emerged from McFarland and many others over the course of the next months ranks with the most significant ever produced by Congress. The GI Bill, continuing to expand enrollment to this day, has served in excess of thirty million veterans and their families and has continued the great tradition of American attention to education. Indeed, some American and world historians believe the bill has marked a watershed in U.S. history in providing for the future training, businesses, and homes for the professional and white and blue collar workers of the nation in the booming postwar years that achieved worldwide American industrial and professional dominance.[9]

Mac personally understood the problems that World War I vets faced. As one of them, he had come to Arizona in 1919 jobless and lacking funds. He quickly rectified his situation by entering law study and practice and then county and state politics. But for many others, the problems just would not go away, not even after a decade, and then the Great Depression exacerbated the grievous situation. Nineteen thirty-two's futile

Bonus March and Anacostia Flats encampment along the Potomac River in Washington, D.C., sadly and ineffectively protested un-kept congressional promises concerning veterans' bonuses and welfare. This embarrassing spectacle symbolized national failure as regular army soldiers, commanded by General Douglas MacArthur and directed on site by Major Dwight Eisenhower, scattered with tear gas and clubbed rifles many who had put their lives on the line along the Western Front fourteen years before. Now, ten years later McFarland stood among those whose thoughts immediately turned to preventing a similar postwar catastrophe. Certain specific issues, and indeed phobias, could be isolated concerning the problem of postwar demobilization. Most obvious was the "Depression Psychosis . . . part of the intellectual setting for the period." Simply stated, this constituted a fear of massive postwar unemployment. Unemployment had stood at twenty-five percent at the onset of the Roosevelt administration in 1933. By the advent of World War II, it still hovered dangerously in the double digits. Would not the return of ten to twelve million veterans grossly inflate prewar unemployment conditions? Moreover, massive lay-offs were to be expected as postwar production normally lagged behind that of wartime.[10]

Fear also played a part. Was it not the rank and file of unemployed veterans who led the march on Washington in 1932? Indeed, in Europe, throughout the 1920s and 1930s, idle veterans had contributed greatly to the immense political instability and the rise of fascism. Certainly, among many circles, a fear of violence existed as well. Perhaps Columbia University sociologist Willard Waller best summed up this anxiety in his work *The Veteran Returns*:

> Give the GIs a chance to have a stake in the society. Lack of a stake in the social order makes the veterans dangerous. They have been trained in the use of violence, want action, and cannot wait for long political discussions. They are also accustomed to organized effort. All these factors can make them politically dangerous.[11]

In a similar speech American Legion National Commander Warren Atherton more than implied this threat, stating: "[The veterans] will be a potent force for good or evil in the years to come. They can make our country or break it. They can restore democracy or scrap it." Past National Commander Harry Colmery saw "troublous times ahead. . . . After the last war, except for England, this is the only country where the men who wore uniforms did not overthrow the government, on either side of the conflict." Acknowledging this possibility, Columbia University set up a special task force to deal specifically with a study of potential violence. Thus, it was that negative anxiety as well as positive beneficence provided motivation for readjustment legislation.[12]

In addition to potential psycho-physical and economic repurcussions, there existed socio-political ramifications and stigmas to be addressed. Many congressmen expressed determination to combat any extension of federal New Deal largesse, while others just as ardently viewed veterans' benefits as an excellent arena to further experiment along such lines. Vice President Henry Wallace, for one, recommended government entry into the education arena, and not just for veterans, in his book *Sixty Million Jobs*, exclaiming: "This is a shocking statement to make, I know, but the United States, considering her material wealth, is one of the most backward nations in education in the world."[13]

Tangential to this type of polarization stood the ideal of exclusivity or favoritism towards the veteran. Ever since the post-Revolution era Order of *Cincinnatus*, the question of privileged status and special treatment for the veteran returned with each large mobilization. Certainly, to many, the concept struck against the very grain of democracy. Soldiers, after all, were just doing their job as any mechanic or farmer would. None of these matters were easily compromised or dismissed as national leaders in education, business, and politics readied themselves to address the situation.

Ernest McFarland numbered among many who carefully studied postwar readjustment. As early as April 1942, he had begun exploring the possibilities of assisting returning soldiers in opening small business enterprises, and by the following year his ideas had congealed into an all-encompassing plan. He first presented his program at the twenty-fifth Annual Convention of the Arizona American Legion held in Phoenix at the Hotel Westward Ho in August 1943. As the featured speaker of the opening session, the third-year U.S. senator asked the convention for support of his intended three-point congressional bill. Section one called for a bonus to be paid returning soldiers of $1.00 or $1.25 per day, served on this side of the Atlantic or "Over There" respectively, with ceilings of $500 and $625, twice the amount paid to WWI veterans.[14]

Second, McFarland advocated unfettered monthly financial assistance, an outright grant, not a loan, for any veteran wanting to return to high school, college, or vocational school. His third point included providing low-interest, long-term loans for down payments on homes, farms, or businesses via a government bond. McFarland asked for the convention's affirmation before he introduced legislation in the Senate, and it was quickly forthcoming. The Ernest A. Love Legion Post of Prescott sponsored a resolution supporting all of McFarland's points, and the convention unanimously adopted the proposal.

Armed with this vote of confidence, McFarland returned to Washington for a fall session of conferring with other government leaders and representatives of veterans' organizations who were developing similar contingency plans. These included President Roosevelt himself, who as early as July 1943 had addressed the issue during a radio broadcast, fireside chat. Original American Legion National Commander, Bennett "Champ" Clark, prepared to pave the way in the Senate as head of the Finance Subcommittee of Military Affairs, which would conduct hearings on monetary arrangements. In the House, Democratic Congressman John Rankin of Mississippi and Republican Congresswomen Edith Nourse Rogers of Massachusetts readied themselves for parallel supportive roles. Lobbying groups also kept active, the key among them being the National Legislative Committee of the American Legion directed by Francis M. Sullivan and overseen by Warren Atherton.

McFarland had first conferred with Commander Atherton in August when they agreed to work closely together in preparing legislation. However, after the Legion's September national convention, the organization took the precaution of drafting its own an inclusive Omnibus Bill covering several readjustment points such as hospitalization, unemployment insurance, and mustering-out pay. Indeed, at this point, McFarland constituted only one of many wheels turning in the nation's capital, not all of them coordinated or complementary. Besides the president, various legislators, and the Legion, three agencies had submitted lengthy reports on veterans readjustment in 1943. These included the Postwar Manpower Conference, the Armed Forces Committee on Post-War Educational Opportunities for Service Personnel, and the United States Office of Education. Together, they recommended education of some type to be a central focus of any readjustment plan. After all, the lowering of the draft age even before entry into the war to include eighteen- and nineteen-year olds had so obviously cut into ongoing educational programs and future educational opportunities. In their recommendations, these groups drew on prior World War I readjustment plans of Great Britain and especially Canada and even programs from states like North Dakota and particularly Wisconsin.[15] Now the time had arrived to coordinate the efforts of these various individuals and agencies -- a formidable task, but one particularly suited to the talents of McFarland, a man becoming increasingly known for his skills at negotiation, compromise, and, if necessary, cloakroom arm-twisting techniques.

By the time President Roosevelt endorsed the Legion's Omnibus Bill, S.1617, on October 27, McFarland had already detected shortcomings concerning higher education and loans and had begun working closely with Warren Atherton's special committee of veterans and educational leaders to strengthen the legislation. As the representative of the Senate, he never missed a conference meeting with members of the Legion, the Veterans of Foreign Wars (VFW), Disabled American Veterans (DAV), the Veterans Administration (VA), and various presidents of colleges and universities. He also routinely appeared before Champ Clark's subcommittee affirming that veterans actually would and could avail themselves of higher educational opportunities. Many doubted their interests and abilities in the academic sector.[16]

To advance his ideas McFarland, on October 29, 1943, introduced his first bill for the GIs, S.1495, cosponsored by the junior Democratic senator from South Carolina, Burnet R. Maybank. The bill suggested amending the Legion's Omnibus Bill by adding to and strengthening the educational and loan provisions. On November 3, Democratic Senator Elbert Thomas of Utah also introduced a bill specifically dealing with education. While this effort sparked additional forum for debate, McFarland worked more closely with the Legion, and his suggestions ultimately were those that were incorporated in the bill.[17]

On November 5, McFarland addressed a nationwide audience over the NBC radio network, summarizing his bill. He noted particular changes emphasizing especially his proposal to double bonus limits to $1,000 - $1,250, and he had expanded and specifically defined the options and use for non-bonus funds. A bond issued by the government could be redeemable within three to ten years with interest, or, if the veteran needed living expenses while pursuing an education, he could receive monthly payments of one hundred dollars, while books and tuition would remain a free benefit under the education section of the bill. Additionally, the veteran could apply the full amount of a government loan as an immediate down payment on a home, farm, or small business. Finally, the bill provided for an automatic three-month furlough with full pay immediately upon discharge as a form of severance bonus. McFarland concluded his address by commenting on the finances involved. At one thousand dollars per eleven million veterans, eleven billion would be the total cost to the government. He surmised:

Sure, this is a lot of money, but it is just part of the

cost of the war. . . . The war has already cost $254 billion. . . . It is our belief that we should take care of our veterans when they come home, not 10 years after the war. The stark tragedy of Anacostia Flats must not be relived--we must face this problem today. Let's send them this news overseas as an inspiration.

Walter Winchell, referring to the bill as "constructive," numbered among the many who responded with appreciation to McFarland's radio suggestions.[18]

It was too late during the First Session of the Seventy-eighth Congress for the Legion bill or McFarland's education and loan proposals to be given final consideration or reach a floor vote, but they laid the foundations for the major work of 1944. The more immediate issue as the year drew to a close proved to be the mustering out bonus. Majority Leader Alben Barkley had a bill pending for a three hundred dollar bonus when on December 1, Warren Atherton with McFarland's support, appeared before the Senate Military Affairs Committee asking for at least five hundred. A compromise was reached providing five hundred dollars for eighteen months service overseas, four hundred for twelve to eighteen months, three hundred for less than a year overseas, and two hundred for less than a year in the United States. On December 24, the Senate unanimously passed this "Christmas present."

The Christmas bonus faced a more controversial fate in the House where Barkley's fellow Kentucky Democrat, Representative Andrew Jackson May, chair of the House Military Affairs Committee, refused to act on the proposal, much to the dismay of servicemen, congressmen, and ordinary citizens alike. Intentionally slowing down the deliberation process, May left the capital for his home in Prestonburg for the holidays and to attend the funeral of a nephew who had died in a plane crash. Upon returning on January 11, his committee reported out a bill for a three hundred dollar maximum bonus. This appeared as inadequate to most, but an expected four hundred dollar compromise would be acceptable. This did not occur as the House stood firm for the lower provisions of one hundred dollars for all veterans with sixty days service, two hundred for those above sixty days in the U.S., and three hundred for those above sixty days overseas. The House also cut one billion dollars out of the bill while at the same time appropriating $1.35 billion to the United Nations Relief and Rehabilitation Administration (UNRRA), causing one congressman to comment, "we've taken money from the pockets of our fighting men so that UNRRA can play Santa Claus to the world."

The significance of the bonus controversy lay in revealing a small, but very stern opposition to the GI Bill in Congress. This caused McFarland, Atherton, Colmery, Clark and others to bear down harder in their work. The opposition feared that unemployment provisions would be taken advantage of by "the lazy and chiselley types of veterans." Underlying this remained the always-present rancor of a solid bloc of Americans to anything hinting of handouts or worse—socialism. One member rose in the House and stated, "America's boys didn't go to war for money—for dollars! They went out for patriotism. And America is grateful to them. Why, when a boy dies, America gives him a flag to drape over his coffin."[19]

While a flag and a coffin might seem to be enough for some, others were more specific in their objections. Republican Senator Robert Taft of Ohio stood against "utopian" planning. Congressman Everett Dirkson (R-IL) joined him in opposing New Deal type national planning, exclaiming "Gabriel had blown his fiscal horn." Others grew wary of veterans' education being placed in the hands of "crack pot, longhaired professors and radicals." Even advocate John Rankin seemed caught in the middle, worrying about overeducation, undertraining, and channeling "the nation's heroes into colleges and there subjecting them to the tainted theories of sociologists." He exclaimed "I would rather send my child to a red schoolhouse than to a red school teacher." Conversely, "double-dyed New Dealer" Senator Claude Pepper presaged liberal discontent objecting to limiting the number of veterans eligible for benefits.[20]

Ultimately, the mustering out pay-bonus issue was excised from the main bill and decided with a separate piece of legislation using the House figures. President Roosevelt signed this bill on February 3. Although, the amount stipulated fell short of that desired by the Senate, the isolation and solution of the bonus issue paved the way for more liberal and quicker consideration of the other portions of the veterans' program.

During the bonus uncertainty of December and January, McFarland kept busy with a specialized interest, tax exemption for playing cards shipped overseas to servicemen. He had already in 1942 successfully pushed through free postage for overseas soldiers, so he knew the legislative terrain. The Legion's Francis Sullivan, acknowledging McFarland's influence and interest, wrote the senator asking for his support in obtaining appropriate legislation. Mac responded promptly in introducing an amendment to the Revenue Act of 1943 at the opening of the new session of Congress. The amendment passed the same day and the bill later became law on February 25, 1944. More momentous matters loomed near, however, as congressional activity resumed in 1944.[21]

In the face of indecisiveness and potentially growing opposition, the Legion hammered out revisions and improvements on the Omnibus Bill with Harry Colmery taking the lead in jelling the ideas of McFarland and Atherton, who emotionally spoke of America's "lost battalion" — disabled veterans who received no aid while their claims were adjudicated. An unlikely ally emerged with the anti-New Deal Hearst press, which now championed quick action and an end to the "WASTE OF TIME . . . . There is nothing to DEBATE about, nothing to BARGAIN about [newspaper capitals]:

> Republics are proverbaly ungrateful. "But this great and once rich republic is peculiarly and especially ungrateful. It fights its wars with children mainly — in violation of its pledges — and then when it has mutilated or blinded them, refuses to care for them adequately, or even to try to rehabilitate them and make their lives more endurable and useful."[22]

On January 12, 1944, the same day that Hearst railed against debate and bargaining, a new Omnibus Bill was introduced in the Senate (the House on January 10), and hearings began immediately. McFarland was not among the eight senators who directly sponsored the bill at this time. Showing nonpartisanship, these included Democrats Champ Clark, David I. Walsh (MA), Walter F. George (GA) and Scott Lucas (IL), and Republicans Wayland Brooks, Owen Brewster (ME), Chan Gurney (SD), and Arthur Vandenberg (MI). In the House, Representatives John Rankin and Edith Nourse Rogers introduced the legislation. At this time, the Legion referred to the bill as "for GI Joe and GI Jane." This title quickly segued into the more media-effective and famous GI Bill of Rights.[23]

Then on January 28, Senator McFarland, for himself and Maybank, introduced an amendment to the bill that embodied his educational and loan provisions. McFarland wrote the amendment "with the approval and at the instance of the National Legislative Committee of the American Legion," and it essentially embodied the same provisions as S.1495 of the past October which had itself been based on the original recommendations from the Arizona Legion convention of the previous August. Speaking on the senate floor, McFarland eloquently warned of "unrest among them [the veterans] when they return from the holes, swamps, and deserts":

> Many will have given the best years of their lives. They have left good homes to fight beasts on the other side under the most trying conditions. Their mental and physical strength has been taxed to the uttermost. We cannot expect them to return and take up just where they left off -- whether it was at school or at work.[24]

After introducing the amendment, McFarland continued to meet with senators and veteran leaders as well as representatives of the Association of Land Grant Colleges, the National Educational Association, the American Council on Education, the Federal Housing Administration, and spokesmen for real estate, building and loan, banking, and other financial institutions. Concurrent with these activities and debate on the bill, McFarland continued to act as spokesman for the Legion before Champ Clark's subcommittee. Furthermore, he functioned as the major "arm twister" in lining up support from those groups, particularly the VFW, who stood opposed or lukewarm towards the bill.

The VFW represented opposition from an unlikely source, and it did not stand alone as other veterans organizations surprisingly came out against the bill as well. In a letter of February 16, 1944, to Champ Clark, the VFW, DAV, the Regular Veterans Association, and the Military Order of the Purple Heart expressed their negative views on the bill. Although these organizations claimed a combined membership of 555,000, only a third of that of the Legion, their views, particularly those of the first two, had to be respected. Essentially, the DAV worried that sufficient treatment for the disabled veteran might be sacrificed for general GI benefits and wanted some guarantees for disabled servicemen. The VFW, on the other hand, seemed fixated on public relations rather than substance. It resented its minor role in the initial drafting process. Being eclipsed by the Legion would threaten its membership appeal to returning veterans. Eventually, the VFW offered its support when it negotiated five hundred million dollars to be guaranteed the Veteran's Administration to proceed with an adequate hospitalization program.[25]

McFarland, Clark, and Colmery worked overtime to bring these recalcitrant organizations around to a supportive or at least non-obstructive role, and their efforts reached fruition on March 24, when the revised bill, S.1767, the Servicemen's Readjustment Act of 1944, including McFarland's amendment, passed the Senate by a unanimous vote. By this time, a total of eighty-two senators, McFarland among them, had listed their names as sponsors of the GI Bill of Rights.

Both Senator Clark and the Legion singled out McFarland for commendation for his work, Clark stating that "he has been most helpful in conference and in attending hearings of the committee, and many features of the bill he proposed previously are embodied in the measure now being considered" — deserved praise, indeed, for Mac had attended all the hearings and executive sessions as well as drafting the many provisions. Legion Commander Warren Atherton and Francis M. Sullivan wrote that McFarland's action had earned him "the undying gratitude of every man and woman who is serving in this war." The letter continued, "you have also rendered a distinct service to our nation because through this legislation with its educational provision and other features, you have ensured America against a serious national loss of skills and potential leadership."[26]

In further recognition of his contributions, the Legion, in April, selected McFarland along with Harry Colmery to appear on national radio to discuss the provisions of the bill. During the transcription, Colmery highlighted Titles II and III, the educational and home-business loan sections written by McFarland, as the most important sections of the bill. The senator then outlined them as follows: the educational title allowed every veteran with six or more months service to continue schooling with up to five hundred dollars per year tuition expenses and a subsistence allowance of fifty per month with an additional twenty-five if there were any dependents. If the veteran completed the first year successfully, he or she could continue schooling for a time period equal to service in the armed forces, less the qualifying six months. The veteran could attend an academic or vocational institution of his or her choice. McFarland considered the loan provisions "the very meat of the rehabilitation program," and explained that every veteran could borrow one thousand dollars from the government interest-free for the first year and at three percent thereafter for down payments on homes, farms, businesses, and any necessary equipment.[27]

The GI Bill passed the House of Representatives on May 18, 1944, also by unanimous vote, 387 to 0. The conferees of the two chambers now met and by June 8 had agreed completely on those sections encompassing all of Senator McFarland's work. Agreement soon was reached on medical and pensions benefits, but veterans' placement provided the final obstacle. The Senate desired placement to be implemented by the United States Employment Service with control exercised by a board chaired by the Administrator of Veterans' Affairs. The House wanted complete control through the VA. With Legion backing, the senate version prevailed when ill Democratic Representative John Gibson, whose proxy had not been accepted by the House Conference Committee, was raced to the capital from his Georgia home by police car and plane with the tie-breaking vote, thus precluding a potential year-long wait or complete loss of legislation. Gibson's conferee vote fell on June 10, the Senate approved on June 12, the House on June 13, and President Roosevelt signed the measure on June 22. The Serviceman's Readjustment Act of 1944 — the famous GI Bill of Rights--became the law of the land.[28]

Credit for the passage of this significant legislation belonged to many. President Roosevelt suggested and consistently endorsed veterans' legislation, and the American public added its voice to his. Warren Atherton, Francis Sullivan, and Harry Colmery spearheaded the efforts of the American Legion, the single most important operative organization in securing the bill. In the House, a cautious John Rankin, supported by Edith Nourse Rogers, who may well be called the Mother of the GI Bill, led the way. In the Senate, Champ Clark directed the legislative intricacies and committee hearings, and both Senators McFarland and Thomas worked overtime on the educational terms. Additionally, McFarland authored the major loan provisions, acted as the main liaison between the Legion and the Senate, and served as troubleshooter with the other veterans' organizations. Indeed, McFarland, as a "Father of the GI Bill" played an extraordinary role, central to the bill's passage.

In the aftermath of the signing of the GI Bill, Senator McFarland found himself in great demand as a speaker. He appeared at organizational meetings throughout the nation, on Mutual Broadcasting's *The American Forum of the Air*, and with Champ Clark in an episode of the newsreel *March of Time*, which NBC created to highlight the color and excitement of the bill's route to passage. A pleased and satisfied senator spoke before the 1944 Arizona American Legion convention in Tucson. He complimented the organization for being a major catalyst the previous year in beginning action on veterans' legislation and stated that it had "every reason to be proud of the part it has played in this great drama." In detailing his activity on the bill, he emphasized his "assumption that we were trying to help the returned veteran help himself."[29]

In a related statement the senator cautioned the public that its role in accepting, implementing, and guarding the intentions and values of the GI Bill now became paramount:

> The GI Bill of Rights is the biggest piece of legislation of its kind that has ever been drafted and passed by this or any other Congress. Now that the law has been written, the next step is its administration and its acceptance by the country. The attitude of the various groups and individuals who come into contact with the applicants for these benefits must be a sympathetic one. There are those who will seek to feather their own nests at the expense of the veterans. Some of these vultures have already appeared upon the horizon. It is possible that the law will have to be amended to forestall their aims. This can and should be done if necessary.[30]

McFarland expressed particular concern with the relation of small business and veterans in the country, hoping that returning veterans would be able to enter this arena as viable components and not just inexperienced entrepreneurs to be taken advantage of or ignored. Gradually Mac changed his speech focus from the actual drama of legislating the GI Bill to this new area of concern.

In a frequently delivered speech entitled "Small Business, the Necessity for Its Preservation, and its Relation to the Rehabilitation of Returning Servicemen," McFarland linked small business with "the roots of our life ideals" and "preservation of independence and self-reliance," where the middle class entrepreneurs, including farmers, were both capitalists and laborers. He warned of "large enterprises where cold calculation takes the place of warm human sympathies, and the large groups absorb the small local enterprise whose owner knew his customers personally and well." Mac criticized "the huge impersonal corporation" and the "very real gap" existing between the owner and both the employee and the customer. At the same time, however, he likened small business to a "valuable training ground" for developing larger entrepreneurs and he cited their responsibility for acknowledging this symbiotic relationship. McFarland concluded by emphasizing community responsibility as well in maintaining an equable business environment, one in which the veteran would fully participate and not be unfairly shut out.[31]

Community responsibility for guaranteeing the salient points of the GI Bill emerged as a consistent theme among experts. On January 2, 1945, NBC's *American Forum* featured such a panel to a nationwide audience discussing the topic, "How Adequate Is the GI Bill of Rights?" Senator McFarland, listed as the bill's co-author and sponsor spoke first, joined by sociologist Willard Waller, psychiatrist Lawrence S. Kubie, and veteran Lee Garling on the panel chaired by Selective Service Director Major General Lewis B. Hershey. All members steadfastly agreed on the matter of public and community responsibility for fairly implementing the legislative provisions.

As the discussion unfolded, McFarland assumed the defensive, while his panel colleagues pointed out their perceptions of the bill's shortcomings. These were both germane and in some cases overly meticulous. Waller worried primarily about the huge task of administration and was generally supportive as was veteran Garling whose primary concern involved the bureaucratic red tape that the veteran would have to cut through in order to obtain benefits. Kubie condemned the lack of sufficient psychiatric provisions and postgraduate training for veterans. Throughout, McFarland insisted on public, community, and business responsibility for a fair shake, while adding two important dimensions to the discussion. In noting that loopholes existed in some of the clauses and that they could be stretched or contracted, he emphasized the importance of a liberal interpretation and administration of the law. While strongly defending the final bill, McFarland acknowledged that it could and should be slightly amended, "I am not saying that this bill is perfect, but it is the best we could get at the time." He continued work to fine-tune the bill in subsequent sessions.[32]

The landmark legislation provided a socio-economic safety valve that forever altered the concept of adult education in the United States. The innovative American concept, which the GI Bill stood within -- that of freely available education -- thus continued to evolve forward from the seventeenth-century Puritan era into the mid-twentieth century and beyond.

Moreover, the bill altered forever the face of the American landscape by catalyzing the greatest housing construction boom in history. Throughout the nation, GIs returned to their families or started new ones while entering the work force or attending schools, millions of them and their dependents living in homes made affordable by the legislation.[33]

Senator Ernest McFarland stood in the very first ranks of the planners and expeditors of this measure. In particular, he attended to the intricacies of the bill's visionary and far-reaching education and home and business loan sections. Moreover, he acted as the main liaison between the Legion and the Senate, and troubleshooter-extraordinaire with the other veterans organizations. Years later, he became known as "the Father of the GI Bill." Indeed, he deserved to be ranked at the very top among the many "Fathers" of this seminal legislation, and he himself, later in life, emphatically stated, "I did more on the bill than anyone else." And if McFarland had done nothing else in his lengthy career, his work on the GI Bill alone ensured him recognition as a great and caring public servant.[34]

Along with veterans' affairs, McFarland distinguished himself as an emerging expert in communications, a field of dramatically increasing importance and rapidly expanding technology during the war years. It had only been two decades since the advent of commercial radio, and television lingered in its developmental stage. Burton K. Wheeler's Interstate Commerce Committee had already begun studying communications on the national level in 1939 with investigations of the telegraph industry. With the outbreak of war that year in Europe and the United States' increased involvement with and indeed construction of international communications facilities, the industry had expanded significantly. It would provide a proper venue for some of McFarland's most important work, and this experience tendered him knowledge applicable to his successful post-senate career as founder, president, and chairman of the board of the Arizona Television Company, KTVK-TV (Phoenix, Channel 3).

In 1941, however, communications constituted an area that did not attract the attention and interest of many prominent senators. It was to McFarland's good fortune that Senator Wheeler looked to his first term colleague to play a large role with communications investigations and legislation. At this time the nation's major telegraph companies, Western Union and Postal, faced a serious decline. Postal operated at a loss of over four million dollars in 1938 and Western Union's return rate on investment had declined from 8.1 percent in 1926 to less than one percent in 1938. The investigations had begun in 1939 and were intended to determine causes and propose remedies for the decline. As the inquiry continued in 1942, McFarland chaired the investigating subcommittee. The testimony of fifty-one witnesses isolated one major cause, technological competition from telephone, radio, teletype, and airmail. Moreover, the two major telegraph companies competed not only with each other but with the communications systems of the United States Army and Navy as well.

McFarland favored the remedy of merging Postal and Western Union and, with ranking Republican committee member Wallace White of Maine, introduced a merger bill in June 1942, which passed the Senate but was too late to get through the House during the Seventy-seventh Congress. McFarland

and White then went to work at the beginning of the Seventy-eighth Congress and reintroduced the bill. The major obstacle at this time proved to be Ohio Senator Robert A. Taft, "Mr. Republican," who felt the bill to be inordinately favorable to labor. On the senate floor, Mac explained that Taft's objections concerned provisions necessary to protect the senior telegraphic workers from the constant employee turnover brought on by the war. The argument proved persuasive. Taft's amendment failed, and the bill passed by a 70 to 10 margin including Mac's liberal clauses for labor. It passed the House with minor amendments and President Roosevelt signed the merger on March 6, 1943.[35]

McFarland had proven successful, and quickly so, in handling this, his first major legislative assignment, a success that was very apparent to committee chair Burton K. Wheeler, who harbored no ill feelings over his self-destructive appointment of the Arizonan to the film investigation in 1941. When Wheeler shouldered another important assignment in early 1945, he unhesitatingly went to Mac for work that was international in scope and ultimately led to one of McFarland's closest legislative defeats.

On February 20, 1945, McFarland issued a statement that included Wheeler's request asking him to coordinate a congressional inquiry designed to formulate a postwar policy for international communications. The letter stated in part, "It is essential that American international communications keep pace with the preeminent position that this nation will occupy in the postwar world. . . . It is important that a decision on communications policy shall have been reached before final worldwide peace agreements are made." Specifically, Wheeler wanted background on how to lower international communications rates, encourage a greater exchange of information among nations, and what type of communications system would best serve the nation's interest. The latter area embraced questions of public or private ownership and regulation. Wheeler indicated he had chosen McFarland for the job directly as a result of his successful work on the telegraph merger bill.

McFarland's statement accompanying the Wheeler letter revealed some strong preconceptions. The Arizonan emphasized freedom of the press and free exchange of news, noting that these would assist decisively in removing causes of war — everyone's ultimate objective. The key to this lay in lower and more equitable communications rates. He criticized the fact that American newspapers and press associations had to pay higher transmission fees than those of other countries. He stated that before making free press demands at the peace table, U.S. negotiators had to formulate specific policy that would adequately represent America's interests as well as international harmony. He hammered home an essential point:

> The plain fact is that we have no such policy and never have had. It is surprising and shocking to those who talk about the greatness of the United States, but there is no denial that a nation which is the richest, most powerful and greatest industrially and commercially, and thus most concerned with foreign trade, has been and is now a third-rate power in communications.

This constituted the problem as McFarland saw it, and he indicated that he would rely on a war-developed national resource to effect a solution; namely the use of the Armed Forces communications systems, the largest in the world.[36]

In the midst of communications brainstorming, McFarland became among the first in Washington to know of President Roosevelt's death in Warm Springs, Georgia on April 12, 1945. As he attempted to get through to Florida on a constituent call, he was informed that the lines were tied up in preparation for an announcement of FDR's death. At approximately the same moment, Mac had a "habitual social appointment," probably for a drink and some talk with Sam Rayburn. Harry Truman usually attended as well. Mac hurriedly walked over to the Speaker's office, arriving just as Truman did, the vice president upon entering being told that the White House, knowing where Truman usually was at that hour, was on the line trying to get in touch. When he hung up the phone, the vice president told the group that he'd been asked to come to the White House. The next call informed Rayburn's office of what McFarland already suspected: that the president was dead. This misfortune would shift the currents of fate in McFarland's career, as he would soon work in a much closer and more influential capacity with FDR's successor.[37]

Truman, who had said of the vice presidency that "he had no more use for that job than a hog for a saddle," now found himself at the nation's helm as a president that was not particularly well informed at that time even though it was fairly common knowledge that Truman would eventually become president. According to McFarland, "There was one thing I never understood. After he became V. P., I observed he was not taken into the inner circle at the White House. I never knew why the President didn't better prepare him for possible services as President."[38]

When World War II in Europe ended a few weeks after FDR's death, the secretive peace negotiations provided additional fodder for McFarland's free-information cannon. He condemned ongoing military censorship regarding the negotiations, stating that the military badly mishandled the surrender story, a fact proven by the German public's knowledge of the terms of surrender before the American soldiers were aware of them. This issue supported the senator's advice to free the sources of information, and he urged the lifting of censorship controls immediately now that hostilities were ended. He specified that, indeed, the war had been fought for freedom of speech and press, among other things, and he cautioned military authorities to be more aware of their role as servants of the people and civilian authorities, who had already gone on record in support of a worldwide free press.[39]

McFarland, who wanted a closer look at conditions in Europe, now went personally to new President Truman from whom he requested executive authorization for Burton K. Wheeler to appoint an Interstate Commerce Subcommittee to investigate communications in the European and

Mediterranean Theaters of war. Truman and McFarland had been close associates from their Senate days and were to become increasingly reliant upon each other as their Washington careers progressed. Both were cut out of the same homespun cloth, and they had adjacent desks during the Seventy-eighth Congress of 1943-44. Truman-McFarland parallels scarcely stopped there. Both had experienced a rural, prairie upbringing; both were veterans of World War I; both had risen to become thirty-second degree Masons; and both had engaged in the legislative and judicial branches of government during their political evolution; and like Truman as president in 1945, McFarland would go on later to serve in an executive capacity as governor of Arizona in 1955. Now after Henry Wallace had been shunted aside as vice president in the 1944 campaign, Harry had assumed the presidency, and Mac quickly exploited his connection. Truman agreed immediately to McFarland's request and instructed Wheeler to appoint the subcommittee: Republican Senators Albert W. Hawkes of New Jersey and Homer Capehart of Indiana, along with Wheeler and McFarland. Mac ranked as the most important man of the group, the only holdover from previous communications assignments, and the instigator of the investigation.

As news of the final German defeat spread throughout Washington and the nation, Senator McFarland made preparations to become among the first civilian authorities of the victorious United States to visit the war-torn European Theater of operations. Japan still fought on, but the end appeared inevitable and hopefully near. Americans looked back on the three-and-one-half years of war with pain and grief, but with pride in the tremendous accomplishment under conditions of duress. Mac stood large among them, most importantly regarding his work on veterans' affairs. Now he stood on the brink of significant international activity as the war drew to a close.

CHAPTER SIX

POSTWAR PROBLEMS
TRIUMPHS AND TRAVELS
1945-1946

ON MAY 14, 1945, JUST DAYS AFTER THE German surrender had been ratified on May 9, Senator McFarland accompanied by Senators Wheeler, Hawkes, and Capehart left
Washington for London, commencing a month-long, sixteen
thousand mile trip that ultimately proved eventful on political,
economic, social, and cultural levels. In London, McFarland
renewed his acquaintance with Winston Churchill, still Prime
Minister (of the all Conservative "Caretaker" government), who
entertained the group in the gardens at 10 Downing Street.
Undoubtedly, the garden conversation covered plans for the
allied troops to implement the occupation of Germany.
Churchill had been bombarding Truman with cables indicating
his concern that Stalin would bite off any ground relinquished
by western allies as the United States transferred troops to the
Pacific and the British and Canadians scaled back their numbers. Truman, however, had expressed his intentions to stand by
the Yalta agreement and withdraw to the lines prescribed therein. The worried Churchill began using the famous "Iron
Curtain" phrase during these crucial days at war's end. The
committee then embarked on its main assignment to inspect
British and American communications installations. McFarland
reported on the inferiority of British equipment and after touring the devastated areas of London, observed that physically, the
city was "in surprisingly good shape."

The committee moved on to France on May 19 to continue inspections of the war-ravaged continent amidst luncheons with ambassadors and dinner engagements with high-ranking generals. In Rheims, McFarland met with General Dwight D. Eisenhower where they spoke casually of his presidential possibilities for 1948. Mac related he hoped he would never have to run against Ike whom he considered a consummate political type. Confronted with the suggestion, Eisenhower demurred at this time, unwilling to contemplate changing his military to a political role. Returning that day to LeHavre, Mac visited with recently released prisoners of war including five Arizona soldiers. The senator noted that while France had endured less physical destruction than many countries, it continued to suffer critically from inflation and a lack of transportation and fuel.

On May 22, the group flew into Weisbaden, Germany, where it finally saw close up the devastation of war, eliciting McFarland's comment:

> A visit to Germany is the best education in the world
> to those who may be cool toward taking action to pre-
> vent another war. Germany is the testimonial and the
> proof of what could happen to the United States if we
> should become involved in another war.

He described Frankfurt, Munich, Darmstadt, and Salzburg as "flat, desolate heaps of rubble. They were shells." In Augsburg, McFarland met with fellow Arizonan and Seventh Army Commander Lt. General A. M. Patch, who related how he required German civilians to bury the dead and clean up internment camps.

General Maxwell Taylor, Commander of the 101st Airborne, greeted the senators with an honor guard at Berchtesgarden and accompanied them on a tour that included Hitler's mountain retreat and underground apartments at Eagle's Nest, and Hermann Goering's special train and collection of looted art treasures. Most telling was the visit to the Dachau Concentration Camp where they viewed the tragic results of internment. McFarland saw men "who had been starved to the extent they had lost their minds and great numbers sick with typhus and tuberculosis," commenting that "the accounts you have read and seen of these conditions have not been exaggerated."

On May 29, the subcommittee arrived in Italy, "the sick man of Europe, war-weary, poverty-stricken, overpopulated, desperate, looking for a way out of the morass that its strutting dictator led it into." While constantly inspecting communications installations, the group augmented the tour with memorial services in Anzio, a visit to Capri, and in Naples, meeting with Fifth Army Commander Lt. General J. T. McNarney; Mediterranean Naval Commander, Rear Admiral William L. Glassford; and Supreme Commander of the Mediterranean Theater, British Field Marshall H. L. G. Alexander. The party then spent several days in Rome where on Sunday, June 3, Pope Pius XII granted the senators an audience. McFarland termed the Pope "one of the best-informed persons in Europe," while cautioning that Italy, more than any other country, must be propped up by occupational military forces, particularly because of the strength of the Italian Communist party.[1]

Now that the European phase of the war had been successfully concluded and the Soviet and American forces were not confronting shared enemies in the field, anti-communist feelings once more began to emerge among many U.S. leaders and servicemen. In Rome at a Red Cross club, the four senators contributed to this development before an audience of 250 GIs. Senator Wheeler opened the evening with a three-minute anti-Russian speech that convinced many present of the inevitability of war between the Western Allies and the Soviet Union. The discussion then opened up to the GIs, who complained about the present ineffectiveness of American aid to Italy in comparison to Russia's successful application of communist ideology. At one point a corporal demanded that the U.S government should step in more firmly and that the soldiers, having "done as much fighting as anybody else, ought to have as much to say about the world." Concerning the Russians, the GI continued, "Is it better to dodge the fight and do it later, or fight it out now? I have a son of my own and I'd rather finish this up myself than have him have to do it when he grows up."

Senator Hawkes then asked for a show of hands among the gathered soldiers to divine their fighting intentions. McFarland, who had been silent, knew that President Truman had requested and received a promise from the committee to make no controversial statements to the press. This situation had gone too far, and the Arizonan promptly sidetracked the show of hands and steered the discussion to safer ground. Afterward, Senator Wheeler who, like many, shared a deep aversion bordering on paranoia to alleged communists, claimed the questions were planted by "a couple of Commies--you know, you can spot them in an audience right away." McFarland's level head, however, was not enough to offset the acute embarrassment to the dignitaries as reported in the press. When asked her opinion of the senators, a teenaged Italian girl summed it up for reporters: "They're dumb."[2]

On June 6, the group proceeded to the British communications center on the island of Malta and then to Athens -- in McFarland's words, a place of "poverty, inflation, and war-torn economy with the government drifting toward the left." Then the senators took in Cairo, which presented a deceptive picture of a gay well-lit urban metropolis. Behind the facade, however, McFarland recognized "the poverty and degradation of centuries of virtual slavery" that still existed — "men working for 28 cents a day with farming methods the same as those used in the time of Christ." He sensed a danger that the war had gravely depleted the middle class, leaving "no leavening group to take up the slack in the economy and wealth in the hands of the few." He did not find it at all surprising, under the circumstances, that the propaganda of communism appealed to the multitudes of the poor who were ripe for a change. Again, he warned that "with the exception of German militarism, every cause of war that existed before the war exists today: poverty, degradation, economic rivalry, hatred, and fear."[3]

When Majority Leader Barkley called for the senators to come home for pressing legislative business and cancelled a scheduled trip into the oil-rich Arabian countries, the senators returned with one-day inspection stops at Tel Aviv, Tripoli, Casablanca, the Azores, and Bermuda, landing in Washington on June 14.

After the committee met with Harry Truman to give its report, the president etched his deprecatingly humorous impression of the meeting in his diary

> I saw Sens. Wheeler, McFarland, Hawkes and Capehart. They'd been overseas, had seen Germany, France, Italy--and knew all the answers. Smart men I'd say. Since Julius Caesar such men as Charlemagne, Richelieu, Charles V, Francis I, the great King Henry IV of France, Frederick Barbarossa, to name a few, and Woodrow Wilson and Fran [sic] Roosevelt have had remedies and still couldn't solve the problem. Maybe these historical characters didn't have the brains and background of the four "able senators."
>
> Anyway their song was that France would go Communistic, so would Germany, Italy and the Scandinavians, and there was grave doubt about England staying sane. The Pope, they said, was blue as indigo about the situation. All of 'em except McFarland assured me that the European world is at an end and that Russia is a big bad wolf. Europe has passed out so often in the last 2000 years--and has come back, better or worse than ever, whichever pleases the fancy, that I'm not impressed with cursory glances of oratorical members of the famous "Cave of the Winds" on Capitol Hill. I've been there myself and have been through crisis after crisis in each of which the country surely would disintegrate (and it never did) [so] that "Senatorial Alarm" doesn't much alarm me.
>
> My good isolationist friend Wheeler is a natural purveyor of bad news. Capehart is a promoter gone political. Hawkes is an honest man with a good Chamber of Commerce mind and my Arizona friend is really worried but is an optimist and of all four I think most anxious to help me win a peace.[4]

The "Arizona friend" was here somewhat guilty by association in Truman's mind with three senators who had given him trouble in the past and would do so again in the future. But the president saw that McFarland disagreed with and qualified his powerful chairman's opinions and those of the two minority members. Mac retained the president's confidence as future events would indicate.

Upon his return to the states in July, McFarland continued to focus on international affairs, notably the decisions on the collective security organization, the United Nations. Throughout the war years he had tried to imagine the shape that postwar security ought to take. He had been the first member of the Senate to broach the subject back in July 1941 and in 1943 had supported the resolution of Senator Tom Connally (D-TX) to set up and join such an organization. At that time, McFarland spoke in the Senate about the principles and machinery of the organization, while expressing hope for close postwar cooperation "if possible with Russia and China."[5]

The United Nations Treaty now went to the Senate in June 1945, and, after a month-long debate, the upper house ratified it by a vote of 89 to 2. Senator McFarland received commendation for his work during the debates for looking beyond the UN's initial San Francisco Charter itself to the task of ensuring peace by removing causes of war. Progressive Senator Robert LaFollette's Wisconsin newspaper headlined a story, "The Simple Truth:"

In all the torrent of Senatorial oratory on the United Nations Charter, the speech of Senator Ernest McFarland stands out almost alone as an example of sound common sense. The senator said he was proud to vote for the charter 'as a step in the right direction' — and then proceeded to get at the heart of the issue.[6]

The "heart of the issue" recognized that despite the crushing of German militarism, all other causes of war remained as McFarland had warned during the European inspection tour: "The charter is no panacea, no cure-all medicine, no guaranty that once it is adopted we shall have peace everywhere at once." LaFollette concluded, "Sen. McFarland's speech was not headline stuff, of course. It was too sensible for that, but it comes closer to expressing the simple truth of the charter than all the oratory that made Page One."[7]

After the ratification and the conclusion of the war in the Pacific, McFarland turned his attention to ideas that had coalesced during his European trip. He exuded a sense of urgency, stating that the nation's postwar stature presented the greatest opportunity in history to influence democratic changes in worldwide government. Free expression of ideas and unhampered transmission of news via an integrated communications system constituted the key factors in McFarland's mind. These should be included in any sweeping peace treaty and be logistically based on the clearly superior installations and air transport systems built and operated by the U.S. Armed Forces around the world. The military foundation would provide the tangible communication capability during a transition-transfer period over to civilian and commercial control. Referring to the $460 million paid by American taxpayers for these international facilities, he stated it would be a "colossal blunder" to give away or "junk" our hard won rights. Linking communications to broader economic and social issues, he warned against complacency in a world where people work for a wage of six to thirty cents for a day of fourteen to sixteen hours and where "standards of living are so low that the average dog in any American household has better food and more adequate shelter than millions of men, women and children."[8]

McFarland began to put his communications ideas into legislative motion early in 1946 in his only major attempt to influence the course of foreign affairs, and one bound for defeat, but not without a lengthy nonpartisan battle. On February 7, he espoused his theory with an amendment to the proposed postwar loan of $3.75 billion to Great Britain to supplant the terminated Lend-Lease Act provisions.

In discussing this British loan, McFarland urged that all

such transactions by the United States government be conducted on as strict a business basis as possible. In order to implement his communications network plan, he specifically advised that three contingencies be placed on sanctioning the loan: 1) the United States should have permanent right to military, air, and naval bases then held under ninety-nine-year leases from Great Britain and that all restrictions on their commercial use should be removed; 2) commercial use should be permitted on all other U.S.-built but nonleased bases in the British Empire (notably in New Zealand and Australia); and 3) Great Britain should make every effort commensurate with postwar financial stability to repay previous indebtedness to the United States. The latter clause referred mainly to the unpaid World War I debt of approximately $4.33 billion in principal and $1.125 billion in interest. He backed these stipulations by stressing the extraordinary financial commitments already made by the U.S.: twenty-five billion dollars in Lend-Lease aid and a binding agreement to make available six billion of U.S. monies to the World Bank newly established by the Breton Woods agreement, funds earmarked specifically for rebuilding the devastated nations of Europe. Canadian wartime munitions chief, W. F. Drysdale, agreed saying that the British-U.S. debt should be directly repaid by allowing permanent American use of the bases. Moreover, McFarland recommended more government loans to American citizens who might need postwar help in establishing businesses instead of further loans to Great Britain, concluding, "I cannot for the life of me see any merit in extending a loan to a foreign nation at a rate half of what we charge an American veteran unless we are to receive benefits that make up the difference."[9]

Opposition to the McFarland amendment developed quickly. The Truman administration wanted an unfettered $3.75 billion loan and had the allegiance of Majority Leader Barkley and the party organization. Secretary of the Treasury Fred Vinson and Undersecretary of State William L. Clayton added their voices in support. Many editorials further stressed that the McFarland-type ideology was too militaristic. The

Arizonan countered that peace, not militarism was the issue. Peacetime commercial communications and transportation interests stood paramount in his mind to ensure freedom of information and peace, and that, in any case, the atomic age had considerably lessoned the military value of these bases.[10]

Southern Democrats split on the McFarland amendment, some expressing concern over the possibility of revived competition in the cotton industry emanating from British interests in Egypt and India. John Ellender of Louisiana supported by Colorado's Ed Johnson said the United States was "trying to revive a dead horse," in assisting Great Britain. In disagreeing with this viewpoint, Senators Burnet Maybank of South Carolina and Mississippi's James Eastland drew the return fire of formidable Republican Robert Taft who supported Mac. The nonpartisan alignment held true to Arizona as well with Senator Hayden opposed to McFarland and Representatives Harless in support and Murdock uncommitted. Wheeler and Republicans Hawkes and Capehart, who had accompanied McFarland on the European tour, supported the amendment, while New England Republicans Wallace White and George Aiken, who had participated on earlier communications committees, opposed. White's Maine colleague, Republican Senator Ralph Brewster was in support and predicted that the British would prove "fairly generous."[11]

McFarland's team appeared to get a boost in late April when Iceland absolutely refused to lease any bases to the United States. Democrats Johnson and Thomas Stewart of Tennessee waved a warning flag here. Senator Warren Magnuson (D-WA) and Republican Representative Bertrand Gearhart of California picked up the signal and noted "definite indications that future American control will be contested" in New Zealand, Australia, Christmas Island, Canton, and the Caribbean. Magnuson was backed by his powerful Naval Committee colleagues, Democrats Richard Russell of Georgia and Millard Tydings of Maryland. All McFarland supporters, they collectively denied charges that the United States was thinking in terms of empire.[12]

After three weeks of lively debate on the British loan,

Republican Senators Alexander Smith of New Jersey and Joseph Bell of Minnesota threatened to invoke cloture in order to bypass an implied filibuster by McFarland's supporters, something Mac denied. The Senate voted on May 8, 1946, the results showing a narrow administration victory for a clean no-strings loan. The McFarland amendment went down to defeat 45 to 40; twenty Republicans, nineteen Democrats and the Progressive LaFollette in support; and twenty-eight Democrats and seventeen Republicans opposed. Examination of the roll call confounds speculation as to where McFarland's efforts might be placed on a liberal-conservative plane. Republican rebels like William Langer (ND) and Henrik Shipstead (MN) joined fellow party conservatives like Taft and Capehart in support of Mac. The Democratic South split as did former isolationist senators. At heart lay one's perceptions on what commitments the United States had made during the war and what compensation the country might expect in return. This foreign policy defeat for McFarland only served to increase his stature as an active senator who could command significant support from colleagues on both sides of the aisle. He did not, however, return to the foreign policy arena with any frequency in the future.[13]

The British loan defeat also proved beneficial to McFarland in providing a hard lesson in steering bills to success. He undoubtedly took some votes for granted — that of Carl Hayden, for example, who supported the president. He neglected talking to each senator as he should have. From this time on, he "spaded the garden much more thoroughly," and as senator and later majority leader and governor "could pick up a bill at any time and tell how a vote would go in the Senate, House, or state legislature." His assistant, Roland Bibolet, never knew him to miss.[14]

After the war ended, Senator McFarland continued to address issues that had drawn his attention during the conflict, although in those years, they had been subordinated to the war effort. Now, with the termination of hostilities, congressmen were free to increase their efforts in areas of personal and state interest. McFarland built on the foundation of already accomplished wartime activity and proved constructive on several issues. Under terms of the Surplus Property Act of 1944, he negotiated the government's transferal of Davis-Monthan Air Base to the City of Tucson for commercial purposes, lowering the usage price from an initial $150,000 to a no-cost agreement for the city to provide upkeep and return it, if necessary, to the government in the future. He also worked successfully for the retention of active military centers at Luke Airfield and Fort Huachuca, and, keeping industrial considerations in mind, he made certain that ALCOA's facilities, scheduled for dismantling and removal to the East, were retained for eventual takeover by Reynolds Aluminum Company. Mac adamantly held that Arizona not be subject to the colonial theory that the West must remain in "agricultural feudalism."[15]

Other patterns of McFarland's legislative ethic continued to emerge during the postwar years, most continuing to reflect his Rooseveltian liberalism. Concerning Social Security, he worked to increase the scale of payments commensurate with the cost of living, to eliminate the "need clause" which restricted payments to only those in need, and to curtail state and federal investigations into the private lives of welfare recipients. In 1946, he successfully obtained legislation for an immediate increase of five dollars-per-month to the aged and blind and three dollars-per-month to their dependents, his first of three such bills to become law. Speaking in the Senate, Mac asserted:

> that the old people of this country are its forgotten people. . . . We seem to have money to establish international banks, to aid the hungry and homeless in every nation of the world. We seem to have money to lend billions to foreign nations. I have not opposed any of these programs thus far, but I earnestly most strongly believe that we have as great an obligation to our own people — particularly to older citizens and our children who do not have the means to maintain themselves in comfortable circumstances.[16]

Along similar lines in 1944, McFarland had helped extend school lunch programs for two years. When this time expired, he worked to continue the program further and to defeat two amendments by Robert A. Taft that would cut the program by $42.5 million and eliminate nutritional training programs and equipment purchases. Turning to other social legislation, McFarland used his position on the Judiciary Committee to support the Equal Rights Amendment for women, but it continued its lengthy history of failure to pass. Reflecting his southern heritage, he did not, however, vote for the elimination of poll-tax voting requirements, siding with southern senators and the majority in a 44-36 count, even though he had reported favorably on the poll tax elimination during committee reports.[17]

In early 1946, McFarland again confronted Taft in a role reversal involving national housing as proposed in the Wagner-Taft-Ellender bill. Cautious about Taft's proposals in support of limited public housing and concerned that it might be expanded at the expense of low-cost, privately-owned homes for veterans, Mac succeeded in pushing through an amendment that had the effect of making the subsequent program one of private rather than federal building. He tells of joking with Taft about the Republican's support of public housing while he was looking out for private interests. Taft replied that he had always been supportive of "slum clearance." The two struck up a cordial relationship that would become more significant when McFarland assumed the majority leadership in 1951. Taft, who often supported Arizona mining interests, referred to McFarland as the "copper, lead, and zinc man."[18]

During the waning days of his first term, McFarland's mother Keziah passed away on December 8, 1945. Her death was particularly troublesome to Ernest, for it resulted from complications from a fall and broken hip she sustained after insisting on seeing him off at the Phoenix airport. Upon hearing of her injury, he immediately returned home, but she passed on soon after. Just the previous October he had also lost his older brother Forrest. While these family deaths deeply affected McFarland, he continually pressed his work on, notably in the area of Arizona water interests versus those of California.

Senator McFarland's background as a student of water law at Stanford, counsel for the San Carlos Irrigation and Reclamation District, superior court judge, and owner of two Pinal County farms well suited him for his upcoming leadership role in bringing Colorado River water to central Arizona. The Colorado River Compact had been drawn up in 1922, and even then as a beginning lawyer, McFarland had been consulted on the legal intricacies of the draft. The Arizona Legislature refused to ratify this pact until its water claims were properly adjudicated to the state's satisfaction. Thus began the contest between California and Arizona over Colorado River use, a contest that was not decided until 1968 when the Central Arizona Project (CAP) bill became law.

During the war years, Mac had kept as active as possible in preparing for the time when the Senate could devote increased attention to water issues and by 1944, he had concentrated water affairs into his own hands as chair of an Irrigation and Reclamation subcommittee. That summer, he had held hearings in Phoenix regarding the southwestern water situation. Specifically, the committee then examined Bureau of Reclamation reports on the three proposed routes (one to be chosen) to carry water from the Colorado River to central Arizona: a high dam at Marble Gorge and a 139-mile tunnel to be constructed at a cost of $487 million; a high dam at Bridge Canyon (preferred by McFarland) with an all-gravity 72-mile tunnel and 82-mile canal to be built for $325 million; or a pumping station to lift the water 1,040 feet out of Lake Havasu (formed by the already operating Parker Dam) and into 212 miles of canals at a cost of $134 million. All was contingent on the availability of 2.8 million annual acre-feet of water, a figure that California disputed. By obtaining the water via congressional legislation, Arizona hoped to open up one-half million acres of new land and supplement the state's .325 million acres already under irrigation.[19]

During these 1944 Phoenix hearings, the uncertain

nature of state Democratic party politics had manifested itself, some local papers suggesting that Senator McFarland appeared "apprehensive" about Governor Osborn's possible threat to his senate seat in 1946. These reporters termed the meetings "superfluous" and charged the senator with trying to "wear away" Osborn's "glory" by taking "some credit for the Colorado River."

The governor may have agreed with this representation, for he chose not to attend the hearings, though invited by McFarland. In a letter released to the press and sent to Lin B. Orme, president of the Salt River Valley Water Users' Association, Osborn stated, "I am rather inclined to believe the hearings can be of no great value." Orme was known as an Osborn Democrat as was Senator Carl Hayden, who more correctly stood "senior" to the governor. Orme headed the old water users' association that dealt only with the Salt River watershed including the Verde but not the Gila of which the Salt is a tributary, and there existed some suspicion that the organization constituted an impediment to CAP plans, a conjecture that Orme denied at that time. McFarland had handled the hearings judiciously and by their conclusion, his critics admitted there was no "playing politics" and "no little amount of benefit." By giving Arizona farmers a strong voice at the hearings, Mac had solidified his position as the state's water leader.[20]

Early in 1945, the Mexican Water Treaty had come up for consideration by the Senate, and McFarland played a prominent role in behind-the-scenes negotiating. At issue lay Mexico's concern for the lack of Colorado River water for its use and Texas's desire for more water from the Rio Grande River, which formed a lengthy part of the international boundary. Mexico decided to tie the two rivers together to strengthen its position, and ultimately it was agreed that Mexico would receive 1.5 million annual acre-feet of Colorado River water. California felt this was far too much and stipulated six hundred thousand as an adequate figure. Arizona's concern involved two issues: assuring that the Gila River system, flowing almost entirely within the state, was not to be tapped for Mexico and to insure the ratification of the treaty in order to expedite development under the terms of the Colorado River Compact, which Arizona had only just recently signed on February 24, 1944. It had been necessary for the state to sign in order to guarantee its allotment under the compact's terms. California, which received 4.4 million annual acre-feet under the compact, objected to Arizona's 2.8 million because it doubted that the Colorado could regularly produce the 8.7 million acre-feet necessary to fulfill the quotas of both states and Mexico.

The Mexican Water Treaty also served as a divisive issue within Arizona. Lin B. Orme sounded a different note than the unity he had urged the previous summer. Claiming ideas of bringing additional water into central Arizona were "chimerical and fantastic" based on "his practical experience," he opposed ratification as a threat to the existing Salt River Project. The head of the Salt River Valley Water Users' Association claimed the International Boundary Commission could tap into Arizona water anywhere it chose, particularly the developed Salt. CAP supporters, of course, desired ratification so it could commence with construction as soon as legislation passed.

Furthermore, the Arizona Central Trades and Labor Council, with AFL advice, came out against the treaty. Organized labor claimed inadequate protection for American workers, because, under the treaty's terms, immigration and tariff laws could be waived enhancing the danger of importation of Mexican workers and materials. The council followed the AFL's advice even though it suspected that water enemy California's labor leaders had "wined and dined" the national AFL into advising that Arizona labor should oppose the treaty.[21]

Senator McFarland worked hard to assuage the fears of labor and the Salt River Association and engaged in floor debate to further explicate his views on use of the Colorado River. He claimed "this relation between water and our economy is already hanging by too narrow a thread; cut it only by the slightest amount and our agriculture will not be able to support our cities and our towns." He felt that no other river-basin state could make more profitable use of the river than Arizona. To substantiate his state's claim to 2.8 million acre-feet, he provided the following data:

1. Total drainage, Colorado River Basin: 242,000 sq. miles
   a) Mexico - 2,000
   b) California - 4,000
   c) Nevada - 12,000
   d) Wyoming - 19,000
   e) New Mexico - 23,000
   f) Colorado - 39,000
   g) Utah - 40,000
   h) Arizona - 103,000
      (43% of total; 90% of state is within the basin)

2. Colorado River flows:
   a) 245 miles through Colorado
   b) 285 miles through Utah
   c) 292 miles through Arizona
   d) 145 miles as Arizona-Nevada boundary
   e) 235 miles as Arizona-California boundary
   f) 16 miles as Arizona-Mexico boundary
      (Arizona total, 688 miles; California, 235)

He concluded, "This fact, coupled with the larger water basin in Arizona certainly gives Arizona a greater right to the waters."[22]

The Senate ratified the Mexican Water Treaty by a 76-10 vote on April 18, 1945, six days after the death of President Roosevelt and partly as a tribute to his Good Neighbor Policy. The treaty was very favorable to the United States, and its ratification now paved the way for Arizona's attempt to obtain legislation for funding and construction of the Central Arizona Project.

Senator McFarland went right to work, but matters of reports, hearings, and legislation took a great deal of time, particularly when opposed by the powerful State of California. One year after his subcommittee hearings in Phoenix, he presented its final report to the Senate, recommending additional water for three major purposes: to supplement the current operating supply, to replenish and buildup groundwater tables, and to develop new areas of land for irrigation. The report drew no final conclusion as to which of the three routes should be chosen, but McFarland made it quite clear that he felt the compact's stipulated 2.8 million annual acre-feet was, even so, an insufficient amount.[23]

Later in September 1946, speaking before a packed gallery of the Arizona House, McFarland summed up the state's situation as the "fight of its life" demanding cooperation and unity on all fronts: the governor, the legislature, state officials, citizens, and the Washington, D.C. delegation. He concluded, "We have come to the end of the easy road in this development. Now the hardest part is ahead. We have come to the forks and we must all travel one road together."[24]

Senator McFarland picked up a sought-after ally in late October when new Secretary of the Interior Julius A. Krug accompanied by Reclamation Commissioner Michael W. Strauss visited Arizona for a six-day trip. Just a month earlier the secretary had been in the state and, accompanied by McFarland, became the first cabinet member to visit the Navajo Indian Reservation since the tribe's subjugation eighty-one years earlier. At this time McFarland requested Krug to later return to the state and personally examine water and mining areas and, of course, to lend support in the ongoing 1946 political campaign.[25]

McFarland took time off from his campaign activities, while still remaining in the public eye, and again traveled with the secretary. The two officials attended the decennial celebration for Boulder Dam and then proceeded down the Colorado to inspect three other dams, Davis (under construction), Parker, and Imperial. By this time changes had been made in projections for future dams. Sites at Marble Gorge and Glen Canyon had been abandoned, while Bridge Canyon remained preferred with its all-gravity route. In fact, a one hundred mile long tunnel had been approved by the Reclamation Bureau to launch the project. No one at this time seemed overly impressed with the cheapest and ultimately approved route from Parker Dam and Lake Havasu.

Krug was favorably impressed with Arizona and its leaders. He noted "no semblance of such horribly frustrated chatter like where are we going?' in Arizona; the people have the leadership and know-how to make possible the state's further development." He commented on the abundance of "pressing needs" throughout the nation and that since the government would go bankrupt financing them all, personal inspections, such as his, were necessary. He saw Arizona in national terms as a key part of the nation's postwar economic development and assured audiences that Arizona "must have" supplemental water from the Colorado. He concluded by urging in-state unity and stated, "If your Senator McFarland can convince Congress of your needs as thoroughly as he did Mr. Strauss and myself, you won't have any difficulties." McFarland called Krug's visit "the greatest boost in recent years" for the prospects of Arizona's development and prosperity.[26]

Although incumbent Senator McFarland easily gained renomination and re-election, the 1946 campaign did have its moments of drama. The senator turned down lifetime security in order to run. A moderate liberal, he faced a challenge for one of the few time times in his career, from elements of the left, both obscure and specific. For the second straight senatorial campaign, mainstream Arizona labor withheld its support from him for intangible reasons, and finally, there appeared to be an erosion of support for him even among the veterans for whom he had done so much. These developments never constituted serious threats, but they did cause anxiety for a time in the senator's camp.

On March 11, 1946, Senator McFarland received a letter from President Truman offering him a lifetime appointment as Judge of the U.S. District Court at Tucson replacing retiring Judge Albert M. Sames, a Republican appointed by former President Herbert Hoover. Stating "your judicial experience ably qualifies you for the important post," the president concluded his letter:

I did want you to know, however, that I hope you will decide to stay in the Senate. The next few years, I believe, will be one of the most important periods in American history, and your continuance in the Senate will give your services to the Nation as well as to your state.[27]

With re-election expected and Truman's endorsement in writing, it is understandable why the fifty-one year old senator turned down the judicial appointment. He made the letter public stating he "should see those years through in the Senate." However, privately, McFarland admitted to "tossing and turning" for several nights over the difficulty of this decision, for he was quite certain that the appointment would surely end up with a U.S. Supreme Court seat in the future. McFarland then, with Senator Hayden's concurrence, recommended the appointment go to his close friend Howard Speakman of Phoenix, whom he felt was eminently qualified and "one of the best trial judges in Arizona." Truman nominated Speakman the next day and quick confirmation followed.[28]

On the same day as the president's letter, *Life Magazine* featured McFarland along with other incumbent senators running for re-election. The pictorial noted the senator's birth "in a one-room cabin," and that he had "been a hard-working Senator, who is capable of growing." Both the *Life* article and his rejection of a lifetime appointment kept the senator in the forefront of the news before the official April 18 announcement of his candidacy.[29]

Harry Jones Valentine of Phoenix presented the Democratic challenge in the primaries. A lawyer and twenty-five-year Arizona resident, Valentine had been a two-term state legislator, one-term state veterans service officer, and former school trustee. Additionally, he was a World War I veteran and member of the DAV and American Legion and an ex-coal miner who had been active in the United Mine Workers of America. Valentine's platform stressed more benefits for veterans, quicker action on developing the Colorado River, and stockpiling of

Arizona metals. He sounded a libertarian call by emphasizing individual freedom as "sacred" and protected by the Constitution, and exclaiming "the least governed are the best governed." Given McFarland's experience and commendable record of achievement and the similarity of Valentine's three basic planks to his own wider program, there seemed little reason for concern for the incumbent. He felt confident but the system called for opposition. Some came from an improbable source.[30]

W. B. Williamson, Sr., a Phoenix World War I veteran, had done roadwork for and supported McFarland during the 1940 campaign. After several years of moving from job to job, in 1946 he had embarked on a project as editor and publisher of the newly founded weekly newspaper *Veterans' News and Views*. In a cover letter of April 26 addressed "Dear Comrade," he stated, "I wish to call your attention to the Candidacy of our Comrade and Friend, Mr. Harry J. Valentine. . . . Please get behind him and use your influence with your comrades and friends. We must send him to the United States Senate." Campaign headquarters forwarded a copy of the letter to McFarland marked "Mac, I thought you would enjoy seeing this."[31]

Not amused, the senator fired back a letter to campaign assistant Jack Murphy expressing concern and hurt, "not because I feel I am in any danger of being defeated but because I have always regarded Bill as one of my very close personal friends." After a phone call from Murphy, Williamson sent McFarland the first of a series of long rambling letters about his past disappointments and hardships, many of which he blamed on the senator's perceived lack of patronage toward him. These letters were lengthy, conversational, informal, and bantering. They also revealed a strong underlying sense of bitterness, self-importance, and insecurity.

Most importantly, Williamson's correspondence caused McFarland headquarters a short period of severe anxiety by claiming a "strong sentiment" against the incumbent among veterans in northern Arizona because of his association with "big brass." Furthermore, Williamson predicted only a fifty-fifty chance of Mac's re-election, stressing that "your enemies (old Ashurst friends) who died hard were busy at home spreading poison," and cautioning that the "Osborn crowd are doing their best to cut down your vote all they can."

The latter assertion contained enough potential truth to cause some trepidation. Osborn had long coveted a U.S. Senate seat but had backed off in the face of McFarland's superior first-term record and considering his own popularity and power-base at the state capital. Moreover, a lingering illness continued to plague the governor.

However, Williamson ultimately protested too much. By insinuating that McFarland had offended veterans by supporting the British Loan, he raised serious questions about his credibility. The senator, while not against a loan to Great Britain, had been the leader of the opposition against a "no strings attached" provision. Concern over Williamson's allegations and switch of loyalty began to abate, while from Washington, the senator wrote him kind and supportive letters. With his contrary position no longer acknowledged, Williamson soon fell back into the McFarland camp while still stressing his importance in eccentric letters:

> Let me know if you want me to get out in the sticks again in your behalf. . . . [lacking funds] I'll take my cot and sleep out in the desert. . . . I can stop in the desert, take a sand bath, change to better clothes and hit a town and look almost like a gentleman . . . and meet the boys on an equal footing. That's what it takes to get votes with vets. They are rough and like other rough guys, the heat, cold, etc., don't bother me much and those trips whet up my appetite and keep my old pump ticking regular.[32]

The Williamson issue kept McFarland headquarters alert for any other divisive or strange campaign situations, and one soon emerged. Eight representatives of the Railway Trainmen, three of the CIO, and four members of the AFL met in Phoenix on June 20 and 21 to qualify and recommend candidates for the July 16 primaries. The joint committee threw its support behind Valentine with only two AFL representatives dissenting among the fifteen delegates. These two objected to the haste and "hit and miss manner that the committee had arrived at their decision," against McFarland and incumbent Congressman Richard Harless; in protest, the AFL removed its name from the final anti-McFarland recommendation.[33]

Indisputably, McFarland had proved an ardent labor supporter as his past record indicated: he had voted against the Smith-Connally Act and to uphold Roosevelt's veto of the same; he had authored the labor provisions of the telegraph merger act, regarded as among "the most liberal," and just in the past weeks he had voted against President Truman's clause to draft workers into the army in the Emergency Labor Bill. Plausible explanations for labor's opposition existed, however: the more overtly leftist stance of Valentine, a possible push from Governor Osborn whom labor did endorse, McFarland's support of using Mexican braceros in the cotton fields, and the most likely reason — his failure to openly oppose the controversial "right to work" amendment, which proposed to ban the closed union shop. Neither did McFarland back this amendment. He did, however, recognize the right of a state to pass such legislation and held that the will of the majority should prevail. Thus the pro-labor senator in his second party primary was once more denied its in-state support although the AFL abstained from giving Valentine an outright endorsement.[34]

This disappointment did not slow down McFarland's momentum, as other organizations rallied behind him, notably the national branches of AMVETS and the American Legion. McFarland returned to campaign for himself across the state, and, in a series of personal appearances and radio addresses, he emphasized his past record concerning national defense, agriculture, mining, veterans, labor, social security, and irrigation and reclamation. Valentine could do little to oppose this record of experience and accomplishment.[35]

Indications of cracks in the McFarland infrastructure notwithstanding, the July 16 primary election returns clearly showed the continuing confidence the Democrats of Arizona placed in their incumbent senator. Ernest McFarland defeated Harry Valentine by a near four-to-one margin with 61,287 votes to 15,818, easily sweeping every county. Incumbent U.S. Representative Richard F. Harless defeated his opponent Albert H. Mackenzie by a two-to-one margin of 51,873 to 24,520, and Representative John Murdock ran unopposed.[36]

The November 5 general election pitted McFarland against Republican Ward S. Powers of Phoenix, a ticket filler whose low profile further hindered his already slim chances. The campaign, however, excited a modicum of interest in the nation's capital where Democrats looked with some trepidation toward the off-year elections. The party commended McFarland's "political and economic sagacity . . . a byword both among his colleagues in the Senate and in the press gallery," and regarded him as a "fearless antagonist" with "more concrete accomplishments to his credit than most veteran legislators," and as "the successor to Jimmy Byrnes in ability to get things done."[37]

Senator McFarland kept in direct touch with Washington during the campaign, phoning President Truman to urge stabilization of cotton prices and wiring the Renconstruction Finance Corporation to protest against the government's recently disclosed purchase of foreign copper at $0.16/lb. while paying only $0.14 3/8 to major Arizona producers. Clearly perturbed, the "copper, lead, and zinc" man's protests enhanced his popularity still further in the mining state. Moreover, Secretary of the Interior Julius Krug's second visit and his ringing endorsement had considerable positive impact.[38]

McFarland's campaign efforts paid off in a decisive 80,415 to 35,022 defeat of Powers. Representatives Harless and Murdock won by two-to-one margins, while Governor Osborn prevailed 73,595 to 48,867. Voters approved the right-to-work amendment 54,237 to 41,401. More importantly, McFarland led the way for the Democrats to carry Arizona, the party's only far western success in 1946, the year of the election of the noteworthy Eightieth "Do Nothing" Congress. The Republicans won control of both houses for the first time in sixteen years, and California, Oregon, Washington, Nevada, Utah, and Idaho all went to the GOP. Undersecretary of the Interior Oscar Chapman wrote:

> Among all the bad news . . . I congratulate the people of Arizona on their good sense in sending you back to represent them. All good liberals and Democrats should congratulate them that they did so.

Similarly Senator Glenn H. Taylor (D-ID) wired:

> It was very good to learn that you breasted the landslide. Your election not only assures the American people of another vote in their behalf, it also assures us progressives of another great and able leader on the floor and in committees.[39]

With the election now settled in his favor, Senator McFarland prepared to embark on a new and important assignment. His experience with communications development and the postwar European trip led to his being designated to head a senatorial committee to investigate military communications installations in the Pacific region. This lengthy trip would carry to the end of the year, at which time he would return to Washington and take his seat in the new Eightieth Congress. As 1946 closed, Ernest McFarland's career continued on the rise. He had a very successful first term behind him, having demonstrated his ability to work productively with more moderate and conservative members of Congress as well as liberals. As he accrued more power and prestige during his second term, which would culminate in his selection as majority leader, he would tend increasingly towards a more moderate stance and cooperation with conservative elements. These alignments would provide the conscience liberal some difficulty, and he would, at times, be criticized from both left and right before ultimately falling in the Republican sweep of 1952.

PART III

UNITED STATES SENATE SECOND TERM *1947-1952*

CHAPTER SEVEN

THE REPUBLICAN
EIGHTIETH CONGRESS
1947-48

AFTER HIS RE-ELECTION AND BEFORE THE COMMENCE-MENT of the new Republican Congress in 1947, Ernest McFarland turned to an assignment of surveying various Navy and Army communications installations in the recent Pacific Theater of war "in connection with the eventual drafting of favorable legislation for the United States." Certainly, the senator intended to bring American international communication status into parity with the enormous wartime efforts at construction. The area under consideration stretched over immense distances, but McFarland, accompanied by political advisor and friend Ralph Watkins, Sr., and a military party of nine, was the only senator assigned to the task.[1]

The group departed for Hawaii in mid-November 1946, and after visiting there, island-hopped from Guam and Saipan to Tokyo. McFarland urged that these small Pacific Islands, along with Iwo Jima and Okinawa, be retained for purposes of defense and communications, noting the United States' noncommercial motive and the responsibility of the country to bring stability to the lives of the natives, many of whom actively cooperated with the Allies during the war.

In Tokyo, Senator McFarland met with General Douglas MacArthur, who confirmed his suspicions that the communications systems in the Pacific were now much more "broken up" and inefficient than during wartime. For his part, McFarland acknowledged the fine job the general was doing,

149

noting that he had "the respect of the Japanese people," and the cooperation of Japanese officialdom, most of which was held over from wartime service — far different from the situation in Germany where "the existing government was destroyed." Candidly, Mac related of the "show" that MacArthur put on for guests, who had to "walk a mile" through a huge, palatial room to where the commander's desk sat at the end. Then, in the midst of the audience, MacArthur's wife "rushed and gushed in and kissed the general and then left. On cue!"[2]

Before departing Japan, the senator's six-day inspection tour included visits to Kyoto and Nagoya, aerial surveys of devastated atom bomb targets Hiroshima and Nagasaki, and observations of the ongoing war crimes trials.[3]

In Shanghai, China, his next destination, McFarland witnessed a riot over inflationary measures and listened to reports of poverty, graft, corruption, and political unrest throughout the land. He discussed these problems with Special Envoy George Marshall in Nanking, concluding that the general "was doing as well as anyone could have done under conditions there." Conditions were indeed bad, and McFarland singled out political and social factionalism for censure, along with "key money" — prices of up to three thousand dollars for merely obtaining a key to an apartment prior to renting. He also visited Madame and Generalissimo Chiang-Kai-shek in Nanking before moving on to Tientsin, Tsingtao, and Peiping [Beijing]. Throughout these tours, McFarland stressed that China's future demanded the development of a well-balanced export trade, which would be tied to U.S. friendship and control of superior communications and transportation facilities, systems, and installations.[4]

In similar fashion, the party continued its airborne tour to Siam, New Guinea, the Philippines, and Australia, confirming enroute General MacArthur's prior warning of dangerous flying circumstances due to deterioration of equipment and poor maintenance on the part of assisted countries such as Australia. Mac further rankled Australians by singling out their country as a unique example of where "a freeflow of American news does not exist in a friendly nation," and censuring its lack of reciprocity in obtaining Australian news for the U.S. He later summed up his observations:

> The Senate should know that in the last stages of the war, this nation owned and operated the finest, fastest, and most modern communications system ever known in the world, built at enormous cost in blood and money. It included the finest worldwide airways communications service possible. That system is largely gone; junked, torn up, stolen, sold as surplus, given away. At the height of the war, it was relatively safe to fly. . . . Today, it has become dangerous. . . .[5]

Upon returning to the United States on December 15 after a month and fifteen thousand miles of traveling, McFarland rested for a couple weeks in Florence before the Eightieth Congress convened. After the holidays, he directed the preparation of a report drawn from the trip, beginning with recommending geographic expansion and commercial merger of existing communications systems to reach full potential in the Pacific. Distinguishing between commercial facilities "for profit" and military facilities, "for control," he stipulated that business operations should effect a "high degree of coordination" with the non-competitive military, while avoiding unnecessary duplication.

The report contained negative observations on Hawaii, which Mac considered overbuilt, yet afflicted with a personnel shortage due to demobilization, particularly among those well qualified and highly trained. He next turned to air transportation, communication, and navigation, especially urging the repair of the existing marginal and submarginal safety conditions which he blamed on lack of qualified personnel. Again he distinguished between civil and military systems urging military control of all those west of Hawaii, with civil agencies operating east of the islands.

Finally, McFarland said that China and the Philippines were "so rudimentary and uncertain as to constitute a menace to safety of life and a heavy drawback to reliable commercial business expansion." He recommended establishing reliable agreements with any "new governments which may come into power; making sure these various government personnel were trained along American lines;" promoting electronics and communications education; arranging for the manufacture and installation of American equipment; and finally overcoming "the understandable lack of enthusiasm on the part of American capital to invest in expensive foreign installations without security."[6]

Senator McFarland now had added Pacific and Asian information to that gathered in Europe, Africa, and the Middle East in 1945, and the domestic work of his earlier years in the Senate. Armed with this information and now acknowledged as the Senate's foremost communications expert, he began further research on amending the old Communications Act of 1934. These changes, mostly of a domestic nature, occupied him for the remainder of his senate career culminating in his new Communications Act of 1952.

Back in Washington, McFarland busied himself preparing for the first Republican-controlled Congress since 1930 and one in which he would suffer scrapes and bruises as well as gain a few successes as it ran its two-year course. Whether with success or failure, his work affirmed his reputation of being among the very busiest senators.

A typical day on Capitol Hill bore this out. Senator McFarland arrived at the Senate Office Building at 8:45 A.M. after a one-half hour drive from his Windom Place, N.W., home, then held appointments with visitors, lobbyists, officials, and other politicians or read and replied to constituents' mail during the early morning. This proved an arduous but thorough task as McFarland, influenced by his legal training, chose to carefully read and sign all letters, which numbered over a thousand per month, instead of delegating the work to secretaries.

At 10:00 A.M., the senator hurried off to committee meetings, in 1947 either Interstate Commerce or Public Lands. In fact, keeping Arizona interests at heart, McFarland relinquished his second-ranking Democrat position on the Judiciary Committee in order to sit at the bottom of seniority on Public Lands, a shift also caused by the Congressional Reorganization Act of 1946, which lowered senators' committee loads from four to two. He also gave up a high position on the Banking and Currency Committee.

After taking a twenty-minute lunch in the Capitol restaurant (usually the famous senate navy bean soup), Mac would arrive in the Senate Chambers sometime between 11:00 A.M. and 12:30 P.M., depending on committee requirements. Here, he became noted for regular attendance and attentiveness, later factors in his choice as majority leader. Known as a "strong and silent" type, he, like colleague Hayden, spoke infrequently but effectively.

Senate activity normally concluded at 5:30 P.M., unless recessed for a night session, when Mac would drive himself home. He reserved the evenings for analysis of legislation and spending at least one hour reading Arizona papers to keep abreast of home events. As far as dinners and social functions were concerned, McFarland tried to confine his attentions to visiting Arizonans or leaders of veterans' organizations. After accompanying the senator on a day's routine activity, a Tucson correspondent summarized, "This skeleton is fairly typical of the days of work. It hasn't the glamour of the playboys and it doesn't make the headlines, but it is the backbone routine of days in Congress. It omits the headaches, heartaches, triumphs and defeats, which all members suffer or enjoy." Administrative assistant Roland Bibolet has noted that Saturdays, always, were workdays — a day when visiting constituents would more easily get Mac's ear, and Sundays, a workday too, even if only to prepare for Monday's onslaught of the week's regular activities. Only at home could Mac get away from the work — to an extent — and enjoy Edna's company and the relaxing antics of their cocker spaniel, who would "salute" for a tidbit.[7]

The first major issue taken up by the Eightieth Congress concerned the restrictive labor provisions of the proposed Taft-Hartley legislation. The bill allowed the government to impose an eighty-day "cooling off" period on strikers in key industries, ended the practice of employers being required to collect union dues, required unions to disclose all financial practices, imposed a loyalty oath on union officials, and precluded union check-off contributions to political campaigns. Most importantly, it outlawed the "closed shop," whereby unions could mandate employment of only union members, a system that Arizonans had clearly condemned in their approval of an "open shop" by voting for a "right to work" amendment in the 1946 elections. The pro-labor McFarland opposed Taft-Hartley stubbornly and was thus out of step with public opinion. He did not stand alone, however, as the state's entire delegation, Hayden, John Murdock, and Richard Harless, opposed Taft-Hartley as well.

After the bill passed Congress, President Truman vetoed it only to see his veto overridden by both houses. McFarland again voted with the minority to sustain the president's veto, stating that the bill "encourages disputes and lawsuits . . . and will create strife instead of preventing it."[8]

Significantly, McFarland's opposition to Taft-Hartley revealed the presence of a potentially strong public opposition to him in Arizona. Heretofore, he had usually fronted a constituency united behind his actions and opinions, but subtle changes were occurring in the political atmosphere of Arizona — changes that did not bode well for the senator's political future. In 1946, Indianapolis newspaper magnate Eugene Pulliam purchased both Phoenix dailies, the *Arizona Republic* and the evening *Phoenix Gazette*. The new publisher began to offer the public an alternative political direction to the usual patterns espoused by the long entrenched Democratic party. From his pulpit of power and persuasion, Pulliam espoused the philosophy of conservative midwestern Republicanism as best represented by Ohioan Robert Taft. Moreover, in postwar America, a massive population migration began from east to west, many from the midwestern states moving to sunbelt Arizona. It was this growing constituency led by the intrepid Pulliam press with whom McFarland fell out of step. His opposition to Taft-Hartley gave the earliest definite indication of the emerging gap between the senator and a major new bloc of Arizona voters.

Throughout the entire Taft-Hartley saga, from debate to conferencing to passage to veto to veto override, the Arizona press expressed its opinion that the state's delegation should align itself with the mandate of the people, which had been clearly indicated in the previous election. When McFarland and the delegation did not comply, Pulliam heaped on criticism terming them "yes men" who always followed Truman, and highlighting the significant fact that the four Arizonans were among only 108 members of Congress who sided against the majority of 399. This gave rise to a questioning of the dele-gates' future effectiveness in Washington if they were so out of sync with the prevailing mood of both their Arizona con-stituency and the Eightieth Congress. Arizona was the only state in the nation whose full delegation opposed the majority. What would happen now in terms of committee consideration of Arizona's interests? Would the state be given a fair shake or be spurned and punished by new Republican committee chairs and leaders? It was a germane question even if the delegation's influence, particularly that of Hayden and McFarland, did not suffer measurably. Indicative of their continued effectiveness was the McFarland-led passage of the Wellton-Mohawk Reclamation Project. Still, the senator faced pressure, and in the face of escalating criticism from the press, he stated simply, "I followed the dictates of my conscience as to what was best for our country. That is the only rule I know to follow. I am sure no one would expect me to do otherwise."[9]

Closer to the senator's interest during this second term lay the priority issue of water, primarily getting the Central Arizona Project (CAP) through Congress, thereby guaranteeing Arizona's water claims against those of California whose dra-matic growth threatened upsetting an equable balance of Colorado River water distribution.

Major obstacles faced McFarland and Hayden, foremost being the adamant determination of California to limit Arizona to as small a portion of the river as possible. This effort stemmed from California's insistence that the Gila River's 2.2 million acre-feet of water should be included in Arizona's stipulated 2.8 million acre-feet annual allocation of the Colorado, and that the water could be better used by its own exploding population.

Moreover, California had a potential ally in Colorado strongman Eugene Millikin, who chaired the Republican-dominated Public Lands Subcommittee in 1947. Millikin also headed the Senate Finance Committee, which faced appropriation problems, and it was widely believed that in the interests of fiscal conservatism, the Eightieth Congress would cut back on reclamation projects. Budget cutting could help California in its opposition to CAP.

McFarland also had to dispose of a second water bill, the Wellton-Mohawk Project upon which hearings had been held during the 1946 session. This effort foreshadowed the CAP fight and suggested a microcosm of Arizona and California strategy and tactics.[10]

The project was divided into the Yuma Mesa and Wellton-Mohawk sections, and McFarland's bill intended to shift acreage for irrigation from the former, where the soil was too sandy, to the latter which was fertile but had been long deprived of adequate water due to upstream storage dams and wells cutting off the river underflow. Yuma Mesa's 159,000 irrigated acres would be reduced by about half, while 75,000 acres would be added to the Wellton-Mohawk Valley Irrigation District.

Subcommittee hearings commenced in April with California initially agreeing to the bill as long as it kept Arizona's allotment to the six hundred thousand acre-feet limitation of Colorado minus Gila water (2.8 - 2.2 = .6 million). California's underlying motive hoped to get Congress to precisely stipulate this six hundred thousand limitation figure for the entire state in the new bill.

Pressure slowly began to build between McFarland and his California counterpart, Democrat Sheridan Downey who, besides the limitation, demanded delay and extension of the hearings and a firm definition of consumptive use as the amount of water used minus return flow. Limitation and definition would commit CAP to California's specifications, and delay and extension would allow the larger state to further prepare its demand for Supreme Court adjudication of the entire Colorado River issue. This, in turn, could delay or preclude hearings on CAP during the session and allow California to introduce testimony, which would not have to be reintroduced if and when CAP hearings were held in the future.[11]

McFarland, attempting at the same time to keep the hearings rolling and accommodate California's aggressive stance, offered amendments specifying only a three hundred thousand acre-feet limitation and a reduction in substituted acreage at Yuma Mesa from seventy-five to forty thousand. Though California witnesses appeared unimpressed, McFarland proved successful in his battle for Wellton-Mohawk. On June 9, the amended bill was reported out of subcommittee as approved without a dissenting vote. The bill then passed the Senate on June 16, and attention turned to the House, where Arizona's Congressman John Murdock discarded his own bill, adopted McFarland's, and finagled passage by July 25. President Truman, declaring he was "not in favor of cutting reclamation projects as seemed the tendency of a Republican economy-minded majority," signed the bill on July 30, phoning McFarland congratulations. The *Yuma Sun* enthusiastically reported that "Cynical, blase Washington has rarely seen the sight of tall Arizonans whooping and slapping their thighs. Senators McFarland and Hayden and Congressmen Murdock and Harless were beside themselves with joy." The project has proved a great success over the decades, and in later years, McFarland claimed it was among those of which he was most proud. Indeed, the success served to buoy the confidence of the Arizona delegation as it looked to the larger issue of the Central Arizona Project, but this hope proved misleading.[12]

Everyone in Washington, D.C., Arizona, and California knew that the fight for Wellton-Mohawk was just a staging ground for tactics and strategy concerning the larger issue of the Central Arizona Project. Preparations for both expediting and defeating this legislation had been underway since Senator McFarland had introduced S.B. 433 on January 29, 1947. This bill called for construction of the proposed Bridge Canyon Dam route to the center of the state via an all-gravity canal and tunnel system.

Considering the large expense of this undertaking, the Bureau of Reclamation recommended the alternative and cheaper route of pumping and channeling water from Lake Havasu at Parker Dam via a proposed Granite Reef Aqueduct to central Arizona. McFarland then redrew the bill and introduced S. 1175 on April 28, with these recommendations included, along with the construction of Bridge Canyon Dam to provide power for the Parker pumping station. The amount of water to be transported was specified at 1.2 million acre-feet per annum, a figure arrived at in logical fashion: 2.8 million acre-feet (2.2 belonging to the Gila) as allocated by the Colorado River Compact, minus .6 million of the Gila-Wellton-Mohawk Project, minus 1 million of usage of the Gila River, equaling 1.2 million acre-feet. Cost estimates for the entire project fell between $.5 and $.6 billion and the amount of acreage to be irrigated approximated 750,000. After considerable delay, hearings on S.1175, the Central Arizona Project bill, were scheduled to begin on June 23, 1947, with Senator Millikin's subcommittee assigned to undertake the task. Sitting with the chairman were Republican Senators Zales Ecton (MT) and Arthur V. Watkins (UT) along with Democrats Carl Hatch (NM) and Joseph O'Mahoney (WY).[13]

Senator McFarland presented the opening statement, painting a dark picture of abandoned farms and impoverished cities:

> Arizona's economy rests largely upon the welfare of its farmers and the productivity of its lands. Reduce the water supply and you inevitably reduce the tillable land. The bond between water and our economy has already shrunk to a thread too slender. Cut the supply of water by only the slightest amount, and

our agriculture will not be able to support our cities and towns. I cannot over-dramatize the situation. Failure to obtain additional water will compel Arizona to reduce its present cultivated acreage and its present agricultural population; this, in turn, will likewise affect the cities and towns, which have grown, particularly during and since World War II.[14]

Indeed, a major part of Arizona's strategy strove to emphasize the dangers imminent in the threat of drought, along with the project's financial feasibility and the noncompetitive nature of the crops produced in the area compared with those grown in California.

Senator Downey rose to California's defense by disputing Arizona's numbers and definitions and even claiming that atomic power might well render hydroelectric power extinct or uneconomic, a prospect that Atomic Energy Commission Chair David Lilienthal admitted was doubtful.[15]

The Arizona press made much of this developing "verbal slugging match" between Senators McFarland and Downey, giving the advantage to the Arizonan's experience with water affairs, a view that seemed borne out as McFarland gathered considerable backing. Downey, aware of these sentiments, resorted to tactics that would prevent the bill from reaching the floor, and after Arizona's many and varied witnesses had completed testimony, the California senator revealed his intentions of introducing a suit by California against the United States forcing the U.S. Supreme Court to adjudicate interstate rights to the Colorado River once and for all.

This move was not unexpected, though greatly feared by McFarland as an effective delaying tactic that could take years before a decision. McFarland emphasized urgency and raised the specter of the depopulation of the state: "The people must know if they must move out of Arizona." The scare tactic proved effective as Chairman Milliken, affected by McFarland's picture of imminent peril, required the hearings to continue "because of the emergency" in Arizona, stating "we will go forward as rapidly as possible. I want action here."[16]

California witnesses now took the stand and argued about the scarcity of water, the potential shortchanging of Mexico, and the resultant responsibility for making up the deficiency cast on all Upper and Lower Basin states. Not only could this cause a tangled domestic web, but it also threatened an international Gordian knot.

Senator Downey lined up some neighborly allies as he continued in his effort to obtain Supreme Court adjudication. Both Nevada senators, Democrat Pat McCarran and Republican George Malone proved sympathetic, the former, with the Californian, introducing S.J.R. 145 on July 3, 1947. This McCarran-Downey Resolution requested the U.S. Attorney General to sue the Colorado River Basin states to allow final adjudication of water rights by the Supreme Court. Downey also requested that the resolution be referred to the Judiciary Committee where California held important influence.[17]

Downey's request set up the next contest, for Arizona wanted the resolution referred to the Public Lands Committee where it had more influence. Only one westerner, ex-chair McCarran himself, sat on Judiciary, while westerners were liberally appointed to Public Lands. McFarland believed that eastern states would lean more toward California's position and also might hedge at contributing to a western project with their tax dollars.

Carl Hayden lent his formidable prestige and seniority to the fight against this referral. When President Pro Tem Arthur Vandenberg (R-MI) assigned S.J.R. 145 to Judiciary, Hayden appealed immediately and forced a debate. Hayden, the senate rules expert, then sent a letter to every senator setting forth the legal reasons why the resolution belonged in Public Lands, while McFarland prepared a brochure of similar arguments to be placed on each senator's desk at the debate. They acquired Republican support from Public Lands Chairman Hugh Butler of Nebraska and Senator Millikin, and made the key point that the adjudication issue was already in front of Public Lands where Senator McCarran himself had placed it in evidence. The McFarland-Hayden tandem emerged victorious by 41 to 35, a personal triumph for the senior Arizona senator whose appeal required all other pending matters to be set aside. It marked the first time in over six years that the Senate's presiding officer had been overruled on an important parliamentary question.

Yet, it was a hollow victory due to subsequent House action where California ran a parallel strategy to that of the Senate. On July 12, the Subcommittee on Irrigation adopted the recommendation that Arizona-California water difficulties should be adjusted by court actions. Hearings in the Senate on the McCarran-Downey Resolution were then scheduled for the 1948 session of the Eightieth Congress.[18]

In the aftermath of 1947 CAP activities and with court adjudication appearing probable, some of the pro-Arizona feeling of the administration seemed to dissipate. Secretary of the Interior Julius Krug, Budget Director James E. Webb, and Bureau of Reclamation Director Michael Strauss all spoke favorably of court adjudication. Moreover, Interior had a dim view of Arizona's lack of a groundwater code, and recommended state legislative attention to the matter.[19]

During the fall of 1947, Arizona had the opportunity to present again its position before these government officials. Phoenix hosted the National Reclamation Association's annual convention during the last days of October concurrent with a recess meeting of the Public Lands Committee, many members being in attendance at the convention. Senator McFarland pointed out the irony of California's quest for more water when its Salton Sea wasted enough "to supply central Arizona every year." The senator had undertaken his own inspection of that desolate area a week earlier fighting his way through the thick scrub growth that bordered the sea to get a firsthand picture of over 1.1 million acre-feet of unused water flowing annually into the Gulf of California. Still the 150-square-mile body of water itself was maintaining a constant level, which would actually require 1.5 million acre-feet to even offset evaporation. Furthermore, the water was not contaminated as reported, containing only 1,462 to 1,480 parts-per-million of soluble salts. Phoenix drinking water tested at fourteen hundred to two thousand parts-per-million, and McFarland stated that some Arizona farmers were irrigating with water testing at six thousand parts and "glad to get it." As the senator dumped sand out of his shoe, he lamented California's desire to put "our" water on such land, and facetiously refuted that state's claim to put water where it would do the most good:

> If California really wants to do that, she will not advocate putting it on sandy Imperial Valley Lands that require a minimum of 10 acre-feet a year as she is doing. There will be no return flow from these lands because the water will go on into the Salton Sea and become unfit for any use.
>
> Arizona already has shown her willingness to put the water where it will do the most good by eliminating part of the Yuma Mesa project where water consumption was high and transferring that water to other lands where the amount required is low.[20]

At the convention, McFarland appeared as a featured speaker, and attempted to place CAP in national and even global perspective. Evoking historian Frederick Jackson Turner and his famous "Frontier Thesis," Mac stated that "America's power grew from homesteading her frontiers, but now the only frontier left is that which can be developed as reclamation projects in the West." He stressed reclamation's importance to the economy of the world and American capabilities to assist poorer nations as well. He identified as warning signs other nations that had failed due to limited acreage, a situation, he added, that was responsible for Japanese aggression in the past war. The senator concluded "When the U.S. must import more food than we export, then we are on our way to a fall." Impressed, Krug, Strauss, and committee chair Hugh Butler expressed favorable opinions on Arizona's viewpoint by the end of the meetings.[21]

Immediately after the convention adjourned,

McFarland, accompanied by Senators Butler and Watkins, toured the Indian reservation areas of northeastern Arizona. It proved a sad trip over endless miles of dusty, rutted roads in a bleak November, while observing desolate Navajo shepherds and their scattered hogans and the slightly better off Hopi in their aged mesa homes of a thousand years. At issue lay the need for increased tribal education and Social Security and the coordination and ratio of federal and state governments in this relief. McFarland believed that the United States should shoulder a greater burden in assisting Arizona, whose Indian population and reservation acreage far exceeded any other state in the Union.

After visiting such ancient Hopi villages as Oraibi, Walpi, and Hotevilla, the senators proceeded on to the relatively more modern towns of Ganado and Window Rock on the surrounding Navajo Reservation. Malnutrition was everywhere. *Phoenix Gazette* correspondent Ben Avery vividly described the tour:

> The Senatorial party already had heard and read the Navajo problem -- they went to the reservation to see with their own eyes.
>
> Shortly after they entered the reservation near Cameron they passed a grandmother herding a small flock of sheep; a mile farther they spied the hogan off on a wind-swept flat, and followed a rough wagon trail to it.
>
> The earth was barren around it —not even a tin can, a piece of paper; just a crazily leaning wagon of ancient vintage and a summer shelter where the mother had set up her loom and started to weave a rug.
>
> The cold wind whistled around the lonely hogan; just a wisp of smoke emerged from the nearest wood; the door, about two feet wide by four feet high, was fastened tight.
>
> Three United States senators, bundled in topcoats, huddled against the hogan out of the wind, rapped on the door, and called: "Hello, can we see you a minute? Can we come in?"

No response came from inside the hogan, and they finally gave up; wandered around the bare dooryard.

Finally, just as they were preparing to leave, the door opened a crack for the black eyes of a child of seven or eight, then the tousled head appeared, and the wind swung the door back.

Two children, both of school age out nearly 50 miles from the nearest school at Tuba City, crowded around the door. Stooping down, the senators tried to talk with the mother inside, but she could not understand English. The only food in sight — and there was no place to hide even a straw — was a half dozen ears of corn.

A few sheepskins lay on the dirt floor for beds, a fire smoldered in the center, and a few blackened pots near the door were all the hogan contained.

Except a grandmother, a mother, father and two children who existed there.

Death hovered as near as if this lonely hogan was a gas chamber — but starvation is much slower.[22]

Prospects were more than gloomy. Aging Senator Butler, himself from a sodhouse on the windswept plains of Nebraska, declared it doubtful that many of the predicted deaths could be avoided. Relief could not be arranged soon enough for those in the worst shape.

The whole scenario indicated the huge cultural gap and lack of understanding on the part of the Washington party -- no interpreters, lack of adequate prearrangement, all indicating the necessity of reinvigorating a program which, under John Collier, had made some strides during the Roosevelt administration, but had been interrupted by the war.

After the revelatory trip, Senator McFarland formed an advisory committee to work towards solution of the intricate social and economic problems on the reservations. These efforts pointed ultimately towards his Navajo-Hopi Rehabilitation Act of 1950, which would attempt a comprehensive solution to the Indians' problems with roads, education, and welfare.

Indeed, as the Arizona congressional delegation announced its plans for the Eightieth Congress's Second Session in early January, they highlighted Indian relief measures along with the Central Arizona Project and tax revisions favorable to small business. All of these efforts were killed with the dominant Republicans voting almost unanimously against them. They would have to await the Eighty-first Congress for action. Senator McFarland did, however, achieve congressional success with another Social Security raise similar to that of 1946 when he again sponsored legislation raising by five dollars-per-month, payments to the blind, elderly, and disabled along with three dollars-per-month to their dependents. His strategy concerning Social Security involved asking for small incremental increases with enough frequency to ensure adequate consideration for passage. This McFarland raise, attached as an amendment to a larger comprehensive social security bill, passed the Senate and the House, only to be vetoed by President Truman for technical problems in other parts of the bill. McFarland successfully led the fight to override the president's veto in the Senate by a vote of 65-12, his amendment providing the determining factor in this crucial vote. The House also voted to override, and the bill, including McFarland's raises, became public law on June 14, 1948.[23]

Unquestionably, the overriding concern for the Eightieth Congress involved foreign, not domestic affairs, and in this arena Ernest McFarland's attitude toward the emerging Cold War evolved as a mixture of distrust of the Soviet Union and fiscal conservatism in terms of foreign aid. Speaking in support of implementing universal military training, he cautioned against rapid disarmament "before we know what is happening behind the iron curtain." Furthermore, he again emphasized that all the causes of war still existed.

In urging the United States to take the lead in restoring and maintaining stability in world affairs, he strongly favored the concept of foreign aid but recommended a three-point program as a caution against overspending: 1) make sure England produces adequate coal for itself; 2) allow Europe to solve its own internal problems to the greatest extent possible; and 3) give highest priority to the solution of America's problems. He distrusted Britain's Labour party and particularly its design to nationalize all key industries. McFarland pointedly urged that no American dollars be made available to expedite Labour's policies. In urging self-help upon European nations, particularly Great Britain, McFarland continued the protective instinct that had surfaced in the British loan fight.[24]

In the 1947 session, McFarland had voted for the Truman Doctrine relief measure of four hundred million dollars to Greece and Turkey as well as $350 million for other war-devastated countries. Later in the session, however, he began to retrench after learning of the broad intentions of the Marshall Plan. He voted for an amendment to slash aid for Italy, France, and Austria from $597 to $300 million, but the amendment failed.[25]

When the Marshall Plan came before Congress in March 1948, proposing $5.3 billion in aid to war-devastated Europe, Republican Senator Robert A. Taft proposed a reduction of almost twenty-five percent to $4 billion. McFarland concurred and voted for the Taft amendment, which was rejected 56 to 31. He was one of eight Democrats and twenty-three Republicans voting with Taft. McFarland did vote for passage of the final plan, in the full amount of $5.3 billion, which passed 69-17 with four Democrats and thirteen Republicans against.[26]

Later he spoke of his concerns: "I unhesitatingly stand on my record as a supporter of the Marshall Plan, but it does not require running a gravy train. . . . We cannot ourselves remain a strong nation if we pour out unlimited amounts of money to other nations. Our role should be one of giving them opportunities to get back on their feet and technical aid in doing so." Furthermore, he felt that other countries, even Germany, whose governments were ravished by the war, should be given priority treatment over England, where the government remained intact and functioning. Ever distrustful of the Labour government's nationalization programs, he wanted to see results from that

country's own initiative before heavy American financial commitment, but a tight austerity program was even then underway.
He also spoke out against Britain's socialized medicine program,
calling it, a bit prematurely, "not a solution to health and hospital problems."[27]

During this same session of the Eightieth Congress,
McFarland turned his attention to a bipartisan effort urging
reform within the United Nations. On April 12, 1948, along
with five other Democrats and ten Republicans, he cosponsored
Senate Concurrent Resolution 50, the so-called ABC Plan, to
amend the United Nation's Charter. The three-part resolution
called for: 1) elimination of the "veto by a permanent [or tem-
porary] member of the Security Council in matters of aggression, armament for aggression, and admission to U.N. membership;" 2) establishment of "an effective world peace force";
and 3) "prevention of armament aggression," and establishment
of "quotas on armaments." The plan mandated international
control of atomic weapons. Production of such material would
be limited and "each nation subject to inspection by committee
as to its production."

This effort resulted in part from the Soviet Union's
obstructive use of the veto power in the Security Council, and
specifically called for reduction of Security Council members
from eleven to ten - two each from the United States, Russia,
and Great Britain, one each from France and China, and two
selected on a rotating basis from other nations. McFarland stated that this provision would prevent six small nations from out-
voting the five permanent members, currently possible with five
permanent and six rotating votes.

Establishment of a world police force under the plan
specified the foundation of an "international contingent" limited to twenty percent of the combined armed forces of the
world. This international army and its armaments would not be
drawn from any of the permanent members of the Security
Council (U.S., U.S.S.R., Great Britain, France, China), and
these "Big Five" nations were also to be limited to twenty percent each of the combined world forces. Thus, said McFarland,

"if Russia decides to ignore the ultimatum of the United Nations, four-fifths of the world's armed power would be available for use against her to force her compliance. While in effect it would force a showdown with Russia, it would not close the door to her participation in the U.N. in the future even if she decides to drop out of the organization now." The amendment failed to pass, undoubtedly deemed as too threatening to a potential cooperative relationship with Russia.[28]

While foreign policy dominated the Second Session of the Eightieth Congress, McFarland continued to nudge the Senate toward passage of the Central Arizona Project, a task of little immediate promise. CAP historian Richard Johnson later wrote that "At the beginning of 1948 it was difficult for any Arizonan to be optimistic about the Central Arizona Project." The latest Bureau of Reclamation report on CAP was in, raising the price tag from $.6 to $.7 billion, and Interior Secretary Krug had not yet approved it. Hearings on the McCarran-Downey Resolution to adjudicate CAP were as yet unscheduled, and important legislation like the Marshall Plan demanded priority. McFarland nevertheless hoped that he could dispose of hearings on the resolution and move directly to hearings on CAP by May 1, before other major legislation intervened or Congress adjourned as scheduled in early summer for the national conventions.[29]

In the meantime, he waited for publication and distribution of the previous year's hearings and for Secretary Krug's feasibility report, both of which would take time for committee members and witnesses to digest. While waiting, McFarland and Hayden contended that the California Imperial Valley Water District attempted to sell more than four times the amount of Colorado River water to Mexico than the 1.5 million acre-feet alloted by the Mexican Water Treaty. This indicated not only a surplus of water in the state, but also internal state competition with less well-endowed water districts. Quick appeals by the Arizona senators to Secretary of State George Marshall aborted these California-Mexico negotiations.[30]

The most important early 1948 activity concerning CAP had already taken place in Phoenix where the Arizona Legislature tried to adopt a state groundwater code as recommended by Washington. This proved to be no light undertaking for a group described as "gamboling into history as one of the most tumbling, fumbling, and boondoggling lawmaking bodies in the legislative history of the state." After several unsuccessful attempts at passage, most of the state's water experts left town and ended up in Washington, D.C., preparing for upcoming senate hearings on CAP. At this point, Senator McFarland played the key role in drafting a code that would both please Secretary Krug and pass the legislature. After forty-one days and two special sessions, the legislature adopted a groundwater code that controlled drilling at elevations up to 2,100 feet.[31]

McFarland proved unable to short circuit hearings on the McCarran-Downey Resolution, and they began on May 10. Mac delivered a five thousand word brief, declaring once again that the Gila River flowed almost entirely in Arizona and therefore could not be deducted from Arizona's amount of 2.8 million acre-feet of Colorado River water. Stating "California's waste actually is more than the Central Arizona Project's need," he charged that state with "distorting the intent of both Congress and the original Colorado River Compact and attempting to conjure a manufactured need for water into a vested right." McFarland also lined up helpful witnesses from New Mexico, Wyoming, Utah, and Colorado, and all parties waited anxiously for Krug's report. The secretary, however, "did not want to take sides," and for a short while the report was said to be "missing." Pressured by Subcommittee Chairman Millikin, he produced the report on May 13, and recommended for immediate approval of CAP and against the plan to tie up future development with a lawsuit. The Justice Department also reported unfavorably on the lawsuit resolution because, in its opinion, no justiciable issue existed.[32]

However, committees in both the House and the Senate took no further action on the McCarran-Downey

Resolution, and the Eightieth Congress ended with Arizona, the Upper Basin states, and the Interior Department aligned against California. For this, Senator McFarland expressed satisfaction, but the resolution remained pending, and he had not been able to obtain hearings on the primary CAP bill, S.1175, during the second session. All bills and resolutions would have to be reintroduced, but Senator McFarland would continue to shoulder the burden of the fight for CAP, a fact that water historian Richard Johnson acknowledged: "the water bills fight fell upon the shoulders of Senator McFarland because of Senator Hayden's responsibilities in the Appropriations Committee." McFarland himself wrote: "I do not want to detract in any way from the important position Carl Hayden took in this fight . . . but he insisted I take the lead." Mac was already laying plans to do so when, just before the Democratic Convention, he obtained a "sneak preview" of the party platform, which advocated "regional development of rivers for irrigation purposes."[33] A confident senator then turned his attentions to the impending presidential campaign, which threatened to be a vicious one.

During 1948, Senator McFarland determinedly supported Harry Truman's candidacy, traveling and speaking in New England, Virginia Beach, and Norfolk, as well as Arizona. He criticized old friend and former Secretary of Commerce Henry Wallace's decision to bolt the party and run for president from his own ultra-liberal Progressive party, noting that, his chances were dim: "He is making a terrible mistake and will be surprised at how few followers he has — he won't get anywhere." On Truman: "He is a straightforward, honest, sincere, hardworking, conscientious man whom history will recognize did a great job at a difficult hour."[34]

Truman's operatives had clinched the nomination long before the Democratic party convened in mid-July in Philadelphia, but there was widespread conjecture on who would emerge as the candidate for vice president. Momentum here visibly gravitated toward the distinguished former majority and present minority leader, Alben Barkley, who hopefully could best unite northern and southern interests, being a liberal from Kentucky. Strong interest also existed in the possibility of a candidate from the Far West, which had gone unrepresented thus far in high executive nominations, with Wyoming's Joseph O'Mahoney being the favorite. By this time, Senator McFarland's reputation was such that he could, without reservation, be nominated as a "favorite son" candidate by the State of Arizona, and this possibility appeared to be in the works. When O'Mahoney withdrew his name from consideration, sentiment for McFarland's nomination increased. A minimum of six western states including Oklahoma supported him, but McFarland declined "in recognition of the fine services of Alben Barkley," who received the nomination.[35]

The 1948 convention was unique in being the first covered by television. T.V. sets were in place throughout the Capitol Building, and trains ran up and back to Philadelphia on the hour. Roland Bibolet recalls once "fruitlessly" looking for Mac all over the senate wing, only to observe him in the City of Brotherly Love on T.V. Mac had been called up to replace Barkley on the podium for an afternoon and had hopped a train without informing his staff! The convention was also disappointingly attended, in part because of the immense heat compounded by the lack of air conditioning. The temperature at the rostrum topped off at ninety-three degrees. Those delegates and hangers-on in attendance watched enthralled as sweaty T.V. crews wrestled with their novel equipment. "One Democrat after another submitted to pancake make-up and eye shadow. . . . Several women addressed the convention wearing brown lipstick . . . told it would look better on black and white home screens."[36]

In September, McFarland accompanied the president on the Arizona segment of his noted "whistlestop" campaign, which altogether covered over 21,000 miles. Boarding the presidential car, the Magellan, at Yuma and riding the rails of the Southern Pacific, the dignitaries traveled the four and one-half hour desert trip to Phoenix, where Mac was pleased to present the president to a crowd of seven thousand. In his 10:30 P.M. speech, Truman intoned "God help the country if the

Republicans continue in control of Congress." He also expressed support of CAP referring to recently released positive reports by the Bureau of the Budget and the Department of the Interior, both of which recommended passage. A happy McFarland disembarked here, while the president carried on to Tucson and the long haul for El Paso in the morning.[37]

Similar campaign efforts throughout America paid off for Truman in perhaps the most stunning upset in presidential election history because of the three-way Democratic party split. As Franklin Roosevelt had in 1944, he too triumphed over Republican nominee, Governor Thomas Dewey of New York. With the election of Democratic majorities in both houses of Congress, the era of the "Do Nothing Congress," as Truman had termed it, had come to an end. The Eighty-first presaged good fortune for McFarland, Hayden, and Arizona, for they had help keep their state in the Democratic column. Hayden rose to the ranking position on the Appropriations Committee and *de facto* chair due to the ill health of Tennessee's Kenneth McKellar. He also became chairman of the Rules Committee. Senator McFarland became ranking member of Interstate Commerce and increased his subcommittee strength in Interior and Indian Affairs.

CHAPTER EIGHT

THE EIGHTY-FIRST CONGRESS
1949-1950

After two years of frustrating effort, Arizona and California once again prepared to do battle over the Central Arizona Project in the Democrat-controlled Eighty-first Congress. Senators McFarland and Hayden looked forward to the 1949 session with eagerness and more optimism than 1947-48. Described by the press as a "powerpack team," they had the Department of the Interior's positive recommendation along with the support of the four Upper Colorado River Basin states. McFarland introduced the newly numbered CAP bill, S.75, early in the session. Immediately thereafter, California introduced S.J.4, replacing the McCarran-Downey Resolution.[1]

Senator McFarland had little difficulty in setting the hearings on both bills once again in the Committee on Interior and Insular Affairs rather than Judiciary. Since the Interior Subcommittee on Irrigation had already heard full testimony on CAP during the Eightieth Congress, Mac was able to skip that phase this time around and schedule hearings before the full Interior Committee. Not only was this a time saving maneuver, but with his own membership on this committee and his friendship with many Western members including new Chairman Joseph O'Mahoney of Wyoming, McFarland could to a substantial degree control the proceedings. Arizona optimism, however, dissipated because of actions of President Truman, who on February 7, wrote Budget Director Frank Pace that "authorization of the Central Arizona Project is not in accord with his reclamation program at this time," or until legal rights to the river are determined and the seventy-eight year repayment clause is reconsidered.[2]

While Californians applauded the president's apparent reversal of position, McFarland determinedly sought to speak to Truman personally. New Arizona Governor Daniel Garvey backed him up, wiring the president:

> All Arizona is shocked and surprised at action of the bureau of the budget in accepting, apparently without investigation . . . unjustifiable attacks on Central Arizona Project and reporting adversely thereon in your name. Respectfully request adverse report to be held in abeyance. . . .[3]

Senator McFarland obtained an appointment with President Truman the next day, and accompanied by Carl Hayden, the junior senator asked the president to reconsider his statement. He expounded upon the economic feasibility of the project and certified that the seventy-eight year repayment was neither unusual nor long, but facilitative of payment. Furthermore he reiterated that Congress could handle the job of adjudication and the Supreme Court need not be involved. Truman said little, except that he would review his report.[4]

Within a week, however, the visit to Truman proved worthwhile. On February 15, Budget Director Pace wrote Senator O'Mahoney that "if Congress should decide Arizona is entitled to the Colorado River water she claims, the president would consider legislation authorizing the Central Arizona Project." It marked another significant reversal by the president; as McFarland asserted: "The [first] Pace letter badly needed clarification. This [second letter] means that we are now working on the project bill and not any report. Arizona has maintained that Congress has the jurisdiction to determine the merits of the water dispute, and this backs us up."[5]

After Chairman O'Mahoney set a guaranteed date of March 21 for opening the hearings, California struck back as

Senator Downey recommended removing Reclamation Commissioner Michael Strauss from office. Strauss had definitely leaned toward Arizona on the water issue, particularly since the state's adoption of the groundwater code that he had so strongly advocated. Now Downey charged him with "loose, inaccurate, and dishonest testimony in recent hearings," as well as incompetence. Senator McFarland rose to the director's defense claiming the removal would be "unconstitutional," and in committee, Carl Hayden challenged Downey on his interpretation of the rules. Pressured by the two Arizonans, the California senator backed down. Moreover, Arizona received another positive sign before the hearings opened when the Justice and Interior Departments and the Director of the Budget submitted their final reports, all opposing California's move for Supreme Court adjudication "except as a last resort."[6]

Senator McFarland opened the S.75 CAP hearings on March 21 with an hour-long statement which emphasized immediate and urgent need, financial feasibility, availability of water, and the delaying tactics of California. Without introducing any new ideas, Mac summarized all the testimony presented during the previous Congress.

The next day, however, McFarland did file new material supportive of Arizona — the Doane Report, an independent agricultural analysis that certified the project as economically sound. The fifty-one page document stressed farmers' ability to pay the irrigation charges and the large indirect economic benefits, especially to Los Angeles, through preservation of Arizona's food production. Moreover, the report interjected a new issue, terming CAP of potential value to national defense in terms of food production, strategic location, and power generated by a Bridge Canyon Dam for southwestern industries.

In California's opening statement both Senators Downey and Republican William Knowland attacked the Arizona position for the old reason of availability of water. Also the state water attorney presented the case supporting Supreme Court adjudication since S.J. 4 was being considered jointly by the committee.[7]

The hearings continued in a sometimes confusing, usually acrimonious, and often dilatory fashion for twenty days strung out over three months and yielding nearly one thousand pages of testimony. Chairman O'Mahoney "in great disgust" claimed "Any pride I might have had as a committee chairman presiding at a formal hearing has gone right out the window." He attempted closed hearings for a spell, but it was not the audience fighting; the disruptive combatants remained present. Then O'Mahoney tried to curtail debate and limit the proceedings to straight testimony, but as the press reported "He might as well have been talking to the fountain in the park."[8]

In truth, the heated exchanges were most often precipitated by either California's overly defensive position or the state's highhanded tactics when on the offensive. This was clearly apparent when, late in the hearings, O'Mahoney angrily chastised Senator Downey, telling him he was:

Arguing with the witness, trying to get him to reach a different conclusion than that shown in his printed report approving the Central Arizona Project.

Trying to make a mathematically impossible set of figures seem logical.

Exhausting the patience of the committee to the point where members are refusing to attend meetings.

Using purely dilatory procedure, to no profit gained by anybody — trying the patience of everyone in the senate committee.[9]

Sentiment in both committee and Congress had been clearly moving in Arizona's direction, and a letter from Senators McFarland and Hayden assisted this momentum. Sent to every senator, the letter played upon the emergency theme: "Without water from the Colorado River, Arizona is doomed to wither away to the point of disaster. This is a crisis for our state." A booklet entitled "Arizona, An Adventure in Irrigation," written by publicist Stephen Shadegg accompanied the letter. The hearings, however, remained inconclusive as they continued into April, May, and June. Other developments, however, forecast Arizona's success. The State Department issued its final directive against the sale of Colorado River water to Mexico by private companies in California, and the CIO announced its support of CAP, partly offsetting the AFL's opposition which had been proclaimed earlier in the year.[10]

While prospects for CAP remained favorable in the Senate, a tough battle was shaping up in the House. Arizona's John Murdock again presided over the Subcommittee on Irrigation and Reclamation; however, unlike in the Senate, hearings on S.J.4 were held before the House Judiciary Committee. McFarland testified again, repeating his opening statement in front of Murdock's panel, and at least on one occasion, he testified in front of all three congressional committees on the same day. The House matched the Senate in terms of the hostility between the two parties. McFarland, himself, became involved right after delivering Arizona's opening statement. William S. Peterson of the Los Angeles Power and Water Department challenged the senator with "Why don't you damned fools read a little further?" McFarland, who had been grabbed by Peterson, retorted "Don't call me a damned fool or I'll knock your block off" as he shook himself free of the detaining hand. Peterson tried to apologize, but Mac turned abruptly down the hall at which point Peterson attempted to grasp his hand. McFarland half-heartedly accepted it. By the time he reached his office a couple hours later a written apology from the Los Angeles official awaited him. The senator, who had been visibly angered, stated to his aides, "As far as I'm concerned, the incident is ended. Don't you think that's the sportsmanlike attitude in view of his written apology?" Chairman Murdock was less sanguine: "Senator McFarland has done a masterful job for us, and he certainly had done nothing to merit anything other than the completely gentlemanly treatment, which he himself always accords others." With tabloid aggression, the *Arizona News* reported: "McFarland, a World War I U.S. Navy enlistee, runs a tractor and does considerable plowing on his farm. . . . This corner picks the senator."[11]

While McFarland, labeled in the press as "the generalissimo of Arizona water strategy," always held the spotlight during the CAP hearings, Senator Hayden, too, had his moment when, in an extremely rare appearance for him, he testified in front of the senate committee. The "almost unprecedented" presence of the thirty-seven year congressman drew a record turnout of reporters and public witnesses. He did not disappoint Arizona supporters, and forecast the future in confident terms: "The Central Arizona Project is going to pass Congress, because Congress never fails to succor a distressed civilization." He rehashed the decades-long battle for Colorado River waters, all of which he had witnessed from the vantage point of Capitol Hill. Smoking an ever present cigar, the senator reached back into the past to the times when he and former Senator Henry Ashurst had fought noted California progressive Hiram Johnson over the river. At that time, he said none would have believed California's claim that Arizona did not control the Gila River, and he likened the current California actions to the "Politburo in Moscow." Hayden's appearance continued to certify the favorable approbation that Arizona maintained from press, public, and politicians.[12]

Throughout the hearings, Senators Clinton Anderson (D-NM) and McFarland made attempts at compromise that California rejected. When it became clear, as the hearings continued well into June, that more efforts at compromise had to be made, Colorado Judge Clifford Stone, McFarland, and O'Mahoney joined with ranking Republican Eugene Millikin to draft an amendment to S.75 stating that if the bill passed, no money for construction would be appropriated for a period of six months after passage, and, if a suit against Arizona were filed within that time, no appropriations would be made until the suit had been resolved. While the California senators objected to the measure because it necessitated passage of CAP, the amendment passed in late June, and S.75 was reported favorably out of committee on July 1, 1949, by a vote of nine to three. In this vote of all western senators, Senators Downey and Nevada's Malone and McCarran opposed. Forging alliances well, Democratic senators McFarland, O'Mahoney (WY), Robert

Kerr (OK), James Murray (MT), Clinton Anderson (NM), and Republicans Hugh Butler (NB), Zales Ecton (MT), and Arthur Watkins (UT) supported Arizona. In the House, subcommittee hearings on CAP had ended on June 7 with no action taken except the defeat, by a vote of twelve to three, of a motion to implement Supreme Court adjudication. The House Judiciary Committee made no decision on S.J.4, and no further action developed on S.75 in the initial session of the Eighty-first Congress. Arizonans, particularly in the Senate, looked forward to the next session and what appeared to be the imminent passage of the Central Arizona Project.[13]

Although McFarland spent most of his time during 1949 on CAP efforts, he continued to attempt to assist Arizona's Indians alleviate problems concerning social welfare, education, medicine, and transportation on the reservations. Senator O'Mahoney, who also chaired the Indian Affairs Committee, appointed McFarland, Clinton Anderson and Arthur Watkins to a subcommittee to determine long range plans and appropriations for Navajo and Hopi rehabilitation, with a target figure of ninety million dollars over a ten-year period.

When confronted with this long-term figure, House representatives objected, cutting ten of twenty million dollars allocated for road building as well as halving appropriations for telephone, radio, and common service facilities to $750,000. Senator McFarland chaired the conferees between House and Senate and criticized this move: "the roads were the very core of the rehabilitation program." Though extensive appropriations for educational and medical facilities remained, their effectiveness would be significantly reduced by cutting road funding in half. His arguments proved persuasive, and the conferees restored the ten million for roads while retaining the other reductions. The total figure was now $88.57 million as resubmitted to Congress, in truth a small amount when considering the breadth of the people and the land. At the same time Mac pushed through legislation to protect the Red Rock country around Sedona, Arizona.[14]

As the bill awaited further action later in the session, Mac turned his attention to communications legislation. McFarland had become convinced that procedure involving the Federal Communications Commission (FCC) should be streamlined and modified in the interests of efficiency as a first step in improving communication law because all subsequent adjustments and approvals would have to go through the FCC. With this in mind, he introduced a communications improvement bill in May 1949, with the intention of removing ambiguities, defining administrative and legal procedures, separating the prosecuting and judicial functions of the commission, and providing for more effective and speedy handling of cases.

As hearings on the bill were being held, McFarland received unified approval for his efforts by all members of the broadcasting industry who testified, and the bill was voted unanimously out of the Interstate Commerce Committee. Members of the FCC, however, objected to some proposed changes and limitations in their powers, and Mac continued to work throughout the summer on fine-tuning his measure before presenting it to the full Senate.[15]

McFarland considered the most important adjustment to be a guarantee to provide applicants for FCC licenses with access to information on all other parties who had an interest or objections because the FCC had frequently upheld applications without notification of these types of extraneous reasons. The proposal worked in reverse as well with all applicants having to conform to access of information. As finalized, the bill required an agreement, the "McFarland Letter," to be signed by all three parties involved, the applicants, those who held objections, and the FCC. Mac, himself, had to subscribe to the terms of the letter a few years later when making application for the Arizona Television Company.

McFarland expressed deep concern that FCC commissioners sometimes maintained too intimate connections with the affairs of companies doing business with the FCC, and his new provision stated that no commissioners, during their tenure, could engage in any business with any organization con-

trolled by the FCC. With these matters settled, the bill awaited further action in the next Congress.[16]

Mac's careful, judicious work including revising the
Communications Act was appreciated beyond the Senate and
led to something of a "favorite son" endorsement for the
Supreme Court in 1949 when Justice Frank Murphy died.
Arizona Governor Dan Garvey added his voice to those of many
prominent Arizonans in urging President Truman to make the
appointment. Garvey rejected local insinuations that he might
then run for McFarland's senate seat and wrote the president,
"Senator McFarland is not only an eminent and capable lawyer,
but he has an outstanding legal and judicial record here at home
and many years of valuable experience in Arizona's courts. His
appointment would receive hearty approval throughout the
West."

While McFarland appreciated this warm approval, he
expressed priority for other pursuits, notably his genuine concern for the Central Arizona Project and foreign affairs. This
led him to value his growing leadership role in the Senate over
a career as a Supreme Court justice. The *Maricopa Democrat*
concurred: "Mac certainly deserves recognition, but we can't
spare him from the Senate." Truman quickly put an end to the
matter selecting Attorney General Thomas C. Clark of Texas
for the vacancy.[17]

During this Eighty-first Congress, Senator McFarland
mitigated his stance for fiscal conservatism in foreign aid. He
voted against amendments to reduce the Marshall Plan by fifteen and ten percent in 1949, the latter reduction a bipartisan
effort by Robert Taft and Democrat Richard Russell of Georgia,
the leaders of the emerging Republican-Southern Democrat
coalition, which would come to plague President Truman. The
amendment was similar in scope and intent to the previous
year's measure, which McFarland had supported, but he had
changed his viewpoint. He did support, however, an amendment by Republican maverick William Langer of North Dakota
that would proscribe aid to any country that dismantled any
peacetime industries in Germany or received such dismantled

equipment. Since Russia, which was openly dismantling German factories, was not receiving Marshall Plan assistance, this amendment really targeted Great Britain and France, which were covertly removing some machinery. Here once again, McFarland supported the priority of German rebuilding, but the amendment was defeated 66-13 with seven Republicans and six Democrats in support.

In July 1949, Senator McFarland voted for the formation of the North Atlantic Treaty Organization (NATO), which facilitated military security among member nations. Requiring a two-thirds majority, NATO passed 82-13. The senator voted against all restrictions on American involvement with NATO concerning conveying atomic information or bombs or requiring additional congressional approval to implement military action.[18]

In the fall of 1949, McFarland got involved with the controversy over the renomination of Leland Olds for a third term on the Federal Power Commission. The senator stood uneasily with those who contradicted the Democratic party and Truman line by opposing the nomination. Olds had originally been successfully nominated for the position by President Franklin Roosevelt in 1939 and again in 1944, but now in the Cold War era and without his protector FDR, he faced serious criticism of his past leftist tendencies. President Truman submitted his nomination to the Senate Interstate Commerce Committee for the term running through 1954, and an investigating subcommittee gathered to consider Olds's status. The intrepid freshman senator from Texas, Lyndon Baines Johnson, chaired the subcommittee and immediately revealed not only his organizational skill but also his intentions regarding Olds. In choosing the subcommittee, Johnson stacked the deck against the nominee appointing Republicans Homer Capehart, John Bricker (OH), and Clyde Reed (KS) along with Democrats Herbert R. O'Conor (MD), Ed Johnson (CO), and McFarland. All were considered "rabidly anti-red," perhaps least of all McFarland who did express "a rather affectionate attitude" toward the curmudgeonly, scholarly Olds. Yet "wild goose talk about commissions interfering with private business proliferated." In any case, Johnson's appointments anticipated a unanimous vote against Olds, which would in turn preclude confirmation by the full committee, because the subcommittee, alone, numbered a majority.

The hearings concentrated extensively on articles and speeches by Olds dating back to 1926, when he was a self-pro-claimed leftist politician. In 1926 he had written: "A new age is being born which will succeed capitalist political democracy. The new age is being ushered in by revolutions in Russia, Italy, Mexico, Turkey, and China." Confronted with this document and others written for the labor news service, Federated Press, and the leftist *Daily Worker*, Olds admitted "they were radical," and he "probably [had] advocated public ownership of electric utilities at the time they were written." He told the committee that he had written the articles "to shock people into changing over from the irresponsible enterprise system of the early 1920s to something like the present system." He had, however, since "changed his mind and rejected the approach of Karl Marx . . . because I felt the road to harmony must recognize spiritual val-ues and that ambition for power was an unwholesome influence in human affairs."

Olds's defense did not impress the subcommittee whose members used the popular hyperbole of the day reflecting the growing fear of the Soviet menace and its intention to commu-nize the world. Reed said the hearings indicated that he was "a full-fledged, first class communist." Upon learning of these early articles, plus a speaking engagement with Communist party leader Earl Browder, McFarland expressed "shock beyond words, and at one point the sturdy Arizonan rose to his feet and departed . . . apparently not wanting to hear any more. Whatever hesitance he may have had at this time about joining the rising public clamor to purge government and society of dangerous leftists and communist dupes was brushed aside by pure grassroots politics in this matter, for he had been been asked by the Arizona Power Commission to oppose the nomi-nation. Rumors in the Arizona press stated that if the nominee were rejected, the post would go to an Arizonan.

The testimony of Democratic Representative John Lyle of Texas proved most damaging to Olds, who, Lyle claimed, "loudly praised Lenin's system and foresaw its installation here, urged readers to enroll in communist training courses, wrote of the decay of the church, sneered at the Fourth of July, and denounced the private enterprise system." During Lyle's testimony, McFarland did try to urge some consideration for Olds, repeatedly objecting to the incessant interruptions of the nominee's own statement. Amidst interruptions from Capehart and particularly Lyndon Johnson, Mac demanded some respect for the candidate: "Mr. Chairman, may I suggest that the testimony offered here this morning has been of such a serious nature that I personally feel Mr. Olds should be given the opportunity to make his statement without interruption."

The beleagured nominee did retain important defenders including President Truman, other Federal Power Commission members, the CIO's United Autoworkers, and the National Farmers Union. Moreover, his two previous nominations and his decade of experience held to his advantage. The subcommittee felt otherwise, however, and repudiated the nomination as expected unanimously. The full committee followed with a nine to two rejection, and on October 13, the Senate denied Truman his reappointment with a 53-15 vote. The entire Olds affair provided an early indication of the nation's second Red Scare. The ideological climate had changed radically from the wartime alliance with Russia to the Cold War hostility of 1949.[19]

Truman and McFarland ended up on opposite sides, too, when the president vetoed the Navaho-Hopi Rehabilitation Act. On October 3, 1949, the House unanimously approved McFarland's bill. Four hours later it passed the Senate by voice vote, the ease of passage considered surprising because of objections to Section 9 of the bill. Written in part by McFarland during the conference session, this section clearly established the federal government's prime responsibility for Indian welfare in the states of Arizona and New Mexico, where the Indian population was so much greater than in other states in the Union. The two states would benefit immensely being required to contribute no more than ten percent of the total instead of matching federal funds. The major objections had not been addressed, however, to this part of Section 9, but rather to the so-called Fernandez amendment which called for the application of state law (with some specific exemptions) to reservation lands, to run concurrently with federal and tribal law. Congressman Antonio M. Fernandez (D-NM) also attempted to make clear that no treaties, water rights, or educational arrangements could be tampered with by the states. Nor would tribes be subject to state taxes. These guarantees came to nothing, however, as prestigious ex-Commissioner of Indian Affairs John Collier joined with the American Civil Liberties Union in opposing the perceived threat of state imposition. President Truman agreed with Collier's argument and vetoed the bill on October 17, on the grounds that "the section, which would subject the reservations to state laws, contained a serious threat to basic Indian rights."

Senator McFarland quickly attempted to adjust to the setback by eliminating the Fernandez amendment, allowing the bill to be reported unanimously out of committee. He then rushed the bill to the senate floor where it passed by voice vote in less than five minutes. His strategy to eliminate the objectionable amendment rather than attempt a time-consuming and less certain override failed, however, when the House rejected the bill by a single vote.

The Navajo-Hopi Rehabilitation Act eventually passed Congress early the next session on April 19, 1950, without any further changes in its terms. The final act, a modernized step in Indian legislation implementing plans that had been recommended for over twenty years, appropriated twenty million dollars for roads and trails, ten million for soil conservation and range improvement, and twenty-five million for education out of the total approved of $88.57 million. In recognition of his legislative victory and services and of the responsibility they entailed, McFarland was then appointed to the Joint Committee

on Navajo-Hopi Rehabilitation, the so-called "watch dog" committee. This measure to assist Native Americans rivaled the
Wellton-Mohawk Act in terms of personal satisfaction for the
senator. According to Roland Bibolet, Mac believed "this was
what Christianity was all about."[20]

As the 1950 congressional session began, McFarland
once again focused upon the Central Arizona Project bill. With
S.75 out of committee, the second session of Congress would
assuredly bring the measure to the full Senate for debate. In
spite of California's delaying tactics, Illinois Democrat Scott
Lucas, who had replaced Vice President Barkley as majority
leader set February 6 as the opening date for debate.[21]

Arizona lobbied by distributing to each senator a new
booklet prepared by the Central Arizona Project Association
entitled "This Is the Truth About CAP," a point-by-point refutation "The Nation's Most Fantastic Project," a pamphlet from
the past spring. Letters exchanged between the leading senators
closely indicated the position of the two sides. McFarland
wrote William Knowland:

It [S. 75] is a rescue bill to provide supplemental
water for 725,000 acres of land in Central Arizona
owned by 30,000 farmers. . . . The bill would save the
economy of Arizona. The costs of the works to be
used solely for the diversion of water would be approximately $267,000,000. The remainder of the project is
needed for . . . hydroelectric energy. . . . The report
by the Bureau of Reclamation shows that it is engi-
neeringly and economically feasible and that its tangible benefits would exceed the total cost in a ratio of
1.63 to 1.

Sheridan Downey's language in a letter to McFarland
ridiculed Arizona's claims:

Here in one sentence is my view of S.75: The proposed Central Arizona Project would use water of
doubtful ownership, lift it nearly twice as high as the

Washington Monument, convey it farther than from Washington to New York, require Federal appropriations of more than a billion dollars, to irrigate 200,000 acres of privately-owned, war-boom desert land, that could not, and would not, be required to repay any of the construction costs, and would raise crops which are now surplus and subsidized by the Government.[22]

On the opening day of debate amidst a Senate Chamber with giant California posters criticizing CAP, McFarland began with a two-hour statement summarizing the project's positive points and the controversy to date. He had worked diligently during the previous weeks in distilling the 250,000 words of supportive testimony into ten thousand-words, even declining an invitation to the social event of the Washington season, a reception for Vice President Alben Barkley and his new bride. The preparation paid off.

As he spoke, McFarland calmly endured the ebb and flow of senators entering and leaving the chambers, interruptive quorum calls and questions from California delegates, and speeches by CAP opponents, Maryland Democrat Millard Tydings and Nevadan George Malone, who attempted to steer the subject into other areas. Malone spoke "on scores of subjects as he rambled on for more than five hours." McFarland patiently endured these distractions and resuming his speech as the day neared closing, he drew once more on the theme of desperation and emergency with words that could scarcely be called measured:

> To preserve and maintain the rewards of this monumental struggle, we are now in mortal necessity of a supply of water wherewith to supplement such inadequate stores as nature and terrain have made available, which stores are depleted to an extremely critical point. . . . Practically all of the farmers of the state would in time become bankrupt and those dependent on them would be unable to pay their portion of the bonded indebtedness of the schools and other

improvements built on the present economy. It would mean that thousands of people would leave their homes, and this would affect the bankers and businessmen and breakdown the whole economy of the State of Arizona.

Arizona would go out of the market for manufactured goods, its income tax payments would dwindle to nothing, and perhaps a quarter-of-a-million people would have to leave the state. Observers in Washington "labeled McFarland's final plea to his colleagues as the finest speech of his senatorial career."[23]

Senator Downey responded the next day when any excitement over the CAP debate had dissipated. He spoke only for the record as McFarland, Hayden, and Knowland were his lone auditors. Downey made the usual arguments summing up his state's case against CAP, but under the circumstances, he lamented the lack of a larger audience and acknowledged McFarland's effective speech of the previous day: "The distinguished junior senator from Arizona almost had his audience weeping on the senate floor — and when he can cause a senator to weep, he certainly must be eloquent."[24] The same four senators were the only ones present for the third day's debate, but even McFarland and Hayden were absent as California's opposition carried on yet another day. Downey never lost his sense of humor, though, exclaiming that the Senate would be a good place for Hamlet to deliver his soliloquy. After four days, California's position faltered badly as Nevada's McCarran and Majority Leader Lucas indicated they were in favor of the project, and Lucas set February 21 as the date for the final vote.[25]

As expected, California made a desperate last effort, offering over two-dozen amendments to the bill and then moving that S.75 be sent back to committee. McFarland and Hayden had already sent precautionary telegrams to every senator, and supporters responded by rejecting four amendments brought up as test votes. These collectively called for limiting the repayment period to between fifty and sixty years and requiring irrigators to pay for at least twenty-five percent of the construction required for the irrigation parts of the project.

California did not request a vote on the other twenty-three amendments, and the motion to refer the bill back to committee fell 56-30.[26]

Finally S.75, the CAP bill itself, came to a vote and passed easily 55-28. The vote split along party lines to an extent with forty-one Democrats supportive (Downey and easterners Byrd, Douglas, O'Conor, and Tydings in opposition), twenty-three Republicans opposing and fourteen in favor.[27]

The *Los Angeles Herald Express* headlined the "Biggest Steal in U.S. History: Colorado River flow taken from Cal. cities to spread on desert." The Chamber of Commerce echoed McFarland's predictions of emergency, except in reverse: "The future of the fastest growing metropolitan area in the United States is jeopardized." Arizona papers, on the other hand, were ecstatic and singled out McFarland's "generalship" for praise.[28]

After directing CAP and the Navajo-Hopi Rehabilitation Act to passage early in the session, McFarland concentrated on the senate effort to investigate and curb organized crime. Tennessee Democrat Estes Kefauver provided the initial impetus to proceed with the investigation. He assembled a special committee to do so, but Interstate Commerce decided to hold its own inquiry, and McFarland assumed the chair of the investigating subcommittee.

McFarland focused on interstate transportation of gambling and horseracing bookmaking information via telephone, telegraph, radio, and news media, while Attorney General J. Howard McGrath, supported by the president, directed efforts towards proscribing such activity by legislation. McFarland also garnered testimony from city representatives of New York, Los Angeles, Detroit, Miami, Baltimore, Denver, and New Orleans. But it was the appearance of alleged and well-known gambling figures that most attracted the attention of public and committee. The "near legendary" figure, Frank Costello of Brooklyn, seemed able to slide consistently off the committee's hook in terms of direct implication with illegal activities. Costello's colleague, Frank Erickson fared much worse, and acknowledged violations that brought him an income of up to one hundred thousand dollars per year.[29]

Yet, for all of the media excitement, the committee accomplished little during the two weeks of testimony, except for providing a body of information for Kefauver's group, which absorbed these efforts the next year. Senator McFarland was considered a logical choice to sit on the Kefauver committee, but he declined the role, stating he had devoted "enough time to the subject already." Mac thus missed an opportunity to spend some time in the media limelight provided the Kefauver group in 1951. There was other work to be done, however, that he obviously felt should be given priority, especially since he had just assumed additional responsibilities as the third-ranking senate Democrat.

In March, McFarland had been appointed chair of a committee of twelve to control and monitor senate floor activity in the frequent absence of Majority Leader Scott Lucas and Whip Francis Myers of Pennsylvania, both engaged in their campaign efforts of 1950. As chair, McFarland usually found it easier to monitor the floor himself rather than rely on the intangibles of directing eleven other busy senators to this task. In such a role, he controlled the floor activities for much of the session, and his successful work at this job provided significant criteria for his own elevation to the top position of majority leader the next year.[30]

McFarland accepted the floor leader job during most trying times. On June 27, 1950, the communist armies of North Korea struck into the Republic of South Korea precipitating the three-year Korean War. McFarland as *de facto* leader met with Truman and General Omar Bradley that day at the Blair House where he supported all necessary emergency measures and recommendations to expedite the defense against this aggression. He continued to do so during the next Congress as official majority leader. At another meeting of the president, the general, and the Big Four (vice president, House majority leader, Speaker of the House, and Senate majority leader), McFarland stood witness to Bradley's caution on escalation.

The chief of staff related on the threat of China's entry before the fact: ". . . the communists would come down. They'd come down in China, and we'd have the wrong war in the wrong place at the wrong time. We would win, but then the Russians would come in about that time." Mac himself seemed less worried. During the later 1950 elections, he spoke briefly about the war in terms of "partisan issues in this campaign:"

> . . . a large number of our Republican friends are attempting to scuttle this government's non-partisan program on foreign issues. They point to the Korean situation and assert that we should have been better prepared. Everyone knows that the Korean War was Russian inspired. We might as well realize that the Russians are cold-blooded realists, not fools. They will not foment a war where we are militarily prepared. If we had ten divisions and adequate supplies in Korea, a war would have been touched off in Iran, Indo-China, or by some Russian satellite. Everyone knows that it is physically, economically, and financially impossible to have adequate troops and supplies on every front simultaneously. The Korean War is being brought to a successful close; the war issue is fast going out the window.

This speech indicates shortsightedness concerning the progress of the war, the nature of Russia's involvement, and the conditions elsewhere in the world. Such shortsightedness was endemic in 1950 among politicians and soldiers alike.[31] After all, Russia, which could have vetoed any UN action in Korea, remained boycotting the Security Council meetings in protest of the exclusion of Communist China from the United Nations.

The 1950 session also saw the beginnings of McCarthyism and the government's reaction to charges from Wisconsin Republican Senator Joe McCarthy of being "soft on communism." Congress answered these charges during a wartime emergency by tightening security and surveillance with the controversial Internal Security Act of 1950 introduced by Nevada Democrat Pat McCarran. This legislation called for establishment of a Subversive Activities Control Board, registration of communist-controlled organizations, denial of certain privileges to members of such organizations, and provision for internment of subversives during a national emergency. The Truman administration became the target of many McCarthyite charges, but the president himself remained dead-set against the measure for being too threatening to civil liberties. In the absence of Senators Lucas and Myers, McFarland, going with majority will, acted as leader during the passage of the bill over President Truman's veto.

In trying to strengthen his veto position, Truman conferred with Senators Hubert Humphrey (D-MN) who supported him, Dennis Chavez (D-NM), who promised and delivered his support against overriding the veto, and McFarland. Senator McFarland had no positive commitment to the bill, but he knew a vote to override would strengthen him in Arizona. He did, however, promise to support the president if his vote might be crucial to the outcome. It would not be, and McFarland numbered among those who bowed to home-state pressures and political expediency and voted against the president on September 23, 57 to 10, with forty-five votes required to override. The defeat was considered a severe and humiliating one for the president and, in part, was attributed to a lack of leadership in the Senate. It is true that Mac here played politics at the expense of principle. But to be fair to the acting-majority leader, he was in a sense a victim of the time and circumstance of Lucas and Myers's absence and subject to the passions and pressure evoked by escalating McCarthyism. But Mac would go only so far with the Wisconsin demagogue.[32]

Senator McFarland was well aware of the administration's predicament and the power of McCarthy's charges of communist influence in the State Department. He had "to utilize every effort to prevent passage of a resolution condemning Secretary [of State Dean] Acheson and had to make the strongest arguments that this type of thing was Republican politics." The sophisticated Acheson had drawn criticism not only for his urbane manner but more importantly for having drawn a perimeter of American defense obligations that did not include Korea.

Further testimony to the powerful influence of McCarthyism surfaced with 1950 Republican victories over Majority Leader Lucas and Whip Myers as well as Maryland Democrat Millard Tydings who during 1950 had led a thorough investigation that condemned McCarthy's charges as exaggerated and unsubstantiated. As the new majority leader, McFarland would act more aggressively against the Wisconsin senator during 1951 and 1952, a stance which unfortunately would redound to Mac's disadvantage in the upcoming 1952 election.

The November defeat of both Lucas and Myers precipitated Capitol Hill speculation over just who would succeed to Democratic leadership in the Senate. McFarland gave this little thought returning to Arizona for a congressional respite. Here he received the news that CAP had once again failed to reach the House floor for a vote, having died in John Murdock's committee. Once again the water legislation would have to await a new Congress — and a Senate that awaited new leadership.

CHAPTER NINE

MAJORITY LEADER
EIGHTY-SECOND CONGRESS
FIRST SESSION
1951

ON JANUARY 2, 1951, DEMOCRATIC COLLEAGUES elected Ernest McFarland Majority Leader of the United States Senate. His selection constituted a logical outcome of the balance of power as it existed in the Senate at the beginning of the new Eighty-second Congress. The Democrats held a majority of only two, and within that majority, the conservative wing dominated, capably led by Georgia's Richard Russell, the kingpin of the Democrats and the strongest of the Senate's legendary "inner club." His Republican counterpart Ohio Republican Robert Taft complemented Russell; the two senators frequently cooperated realizing that the fine art of legislating involved more compromise and concession rather than pursuing one's ideals, liberal or conservative, to the bitter end. Idealistic "ultras" could cause excitement in committee and on the floor, but they proved largely ineffective in expediting the legislative process. McFarland had gained a reputation as one skillful at negotiation and compromise, familiarly known in senate lingo as "horsetrading or scratching each other's back."[1]

After Scott Lucas's McCarthy-influenced November defeat at the hands of Republican Everett Dirksen, many senators and D.C. observers considered the job of majority leader a distinguished but thankless and potentially dangerous task. The

inability to pass Fair Deal legislation in the previous, more liberal Congress had disheartened Democrats, especially moderates and liberals, who now came into the new Congress with low
expectations. Their slim majority, the pressures of the six-
month-old Korean War, and the rising tide of McCarthyism
meant that the Fair Deal platform of 1948 would be supplanted
by new divisive issues. Achievement of harmony would require
a new coalition and cooperation from all parts of the Senate.
Russell loomed as the key operative and king-maker.

With this in mind, one of the talented "Class of '48,"
New Mexico Democrat Clinton Anderson, hatched the idea of
maneuvering Russell into the position of leadership. If anyone
could weather the pressures of the times, it would be the unassailable Georgian, who, like McFarland, was up for re-election
in 1952. Anderson suggested that President Truman fly in the
White House plane, *The Sacred Cow*, down to Georgia to make
Russell an offer he could not personally refuse. Truman was
skeptical of Anderson because of his former secretary of agriculture's "jumping ship" and leaving the Cabinet to run for the
Senate in 1948. This occurred at a time when the president's
fortunes looked bleak, and Truman resented the defection.
Furthermore, Truman was preoccupied with war emergencies,
and he did not take Anderson's advice and instead dispatched
close aid Clark Clifford to see Russell privately. Clifford's offer,
the Georgian could and did refuse, being perfectly satisfied with
the publicly unrecognized substance of power. Too, he was
preparing for a 1952 run at the presidential nomination and
senate leadership might preclude this. Russell demurred,
specifically stating to Alabama Senator John Sparkman "to have
a southerner as Majority Leader would cause criticism of his
acts to fall upon the South as a whole." Instead, he chose to dictate his own choice as leader, someone who would not threaten
southern interests. [2]

Russell , with full realization that Mac could endanger
his career, as had Lucas, now turned to McFarland as his personal choice, in hopes that his recognized administrative, legislative, and compromising skills would forestall future political

opposition in Arizona by adding to an already distinguished career.

Other practical reasons existed for Russell's tagging McFarland. The Arizonan, of southern background but lacking a significant African American constituency and interested in obtaining support for his state's development (notably CAP), had supported Russell's 1949 slowdown on civil rights legislation when it appeared that the congressional mood remained unsuited for this step. Moreover, as several senators pointed out McFarland had the floor experience necessary for a leader because of his interim work in the absence of Lucas.[3]

Russell guaranteed southern support, while Carl Hayden and Senator Robert S. Kerr (D-OK), another of the distinguished "Class of '48" began rounding up western votes for McFarland. At the Democratic party caucus of January 2, 1951, Mac, who had expressed mild disinterest in the position, consented to a draft against the advice of some including Senator Anderson who, reversing his position on Russell, cited the danger of the position and catered to the liberal momentum. In fact, Anderson later claimed McFarland grew angry over his suggestion to withdraw. In any case, Carl Hayden, seconded by Colorado's Edwin Johnson, nominated Mac and he replied "If the majority of the Democrats want me, I'll take it." The White House did nothing to counter this apparent conservative tactic of using a cooperative moderate, but at the last moment, liberal Democrats led by Paul Douglas of Illinois rallied behind the candidacy of Wyoming's Joseph O'Mahoney. Douglas warned, to little avail, against bowing to the "oil and gas crowd, notably Johnson and oilman Kerr" and against impending defeat in 1952. A third faction candidacy for Sparkman, attempting to deflect votes from McFarland, never materialized as Sparkman, too, feared the danger of the position. The caucas elected Mac 30 to 19, and at O'Mahoney's request, voiced unanimity in the decision.[4]

McFarland later wrote in his autobiography that he was elected "without the support of the president," although he also stated that he did not think O'Mahoney had formal support either. This is unlikely because the White House sent administrative assistant Donald S. Dawson to persuade Clinton Anderson and Connecticut Senator Brien McMahon to launch a drive for O'Mahoney in what Douglas referred to as a "fight for the soul of the Democratic party." McMahon held a dinner party for sixteen so-called "safe" liberal senators where O'Mahoney announced his candidacy. Carl Hayden countered this with a press release implying a doublecross and stating the certainty of McFarland's election.[5]

In this tangled web, Truman's precise role remains unclear. McFarland also later wrote that he "got the impression that President Truman had been privately for me." The background support for O'Mahoney notwithstanding, this assertion may have held a germ of truth. Truman's program had failed with the liberal Lucas. Perhaps the president preferred McFarland over O'Mahoney, thus appearing more accommodating to Russell in hopes that a partial Fair Deal might slip through. The president had been a good friend for years and sent a letter of congratulations. The next day, calling the new majority leader to his office, he expressed confidence in his abilities and told him not to worry about the criticism circulating around the Capital, some of it predicting a repeat of the Eightieth "Do Nothing" Congress.[6]

The next item of business for the Democrats was to decide upon an assistant majority leader or whip. Liberals made another effort to influence this selection, but both McMahon and Sparkman declined the nomination. Attempting to continue expanding his own growing influence, Oklahoman Robert Kerr suggested Clinton Anderson, but "the ailing New Mexico millionaire would have sooner taken a job digging Kerr's oil wells." Kerr, who would have taken the position himself, next turned to yet another member of the "Class of '48," fellow oil supporter Lyndon Baines Johnson of Texas, known to covet the role to increase his own influence. Russell, aware of objections of geographic imbalance threw his support behind Johnson, nominated him, and the two upcoming senators approached McFarland who would have the final say. After a two hour meeting with the two, Mac chose Johnson and LBJ, at age 42, entered upon the path to senate leadership that would lead first to political acclaim as history's strongest majority leader and ultimately to crafting the Great Society as president. According to McFarland: "I found him [LBJ] energetic. Some of them [liberals] would have liked to have traded Lyndon off for their own man, and Lyndon was willing to step aside. But I said no. We really didn't have much trouble."[7]

While McFarland expressed gratitude for the high honor, Hubert Humphrey and Paul Douglas (both "Class of '48") admitted that the Fair Deal was already a dead issue, Humphrey adding "McFarland's a good man. We'll all support him." However, the *New York Times* summarized, "The Democrats' choice of Senators McFarland and Johnson . . . put the day-by-day command of the Senate in the hands of the men temperamentally more allied to the conservative wing of the party than to the Truman wing." Indeed criticism mounted, particularly with the announcement of Lyndon Johnson's selection as whip or assistant majority leader. Columnist Lowell Mellet in the *Washington Star* specifically termed Mac:

> an amiable inoffensive genuinely likeable ex-judge. He is everybody's friend. But he is no leader; during his ten years in the Senate, he has just gone along . . . content to be led. The country is crying out for leadership. . . . This is a time of crisis in our country's and the world's history. How well our country meets the crisis will depend greatly on the United States Senate, and that will depend on how well the Senate is led. So it is proposed that it shall not be led at all.[8]

This harsh estimate of McFarland brashly ignored Mac's consummate first term efforts: singular work on the Hollywood film probe, executing the merger of Western Union and Postal Telegraph, and most importantly drafting the free education benefits and the home and business loan sections of the famous GI Bill of Rights. During his second term, McFarland's work lay more in the direction of his state's water interests, but he still remained an acknowledged expert in areas of communications, veterans' affairs, and water. Unfortunately for future assessment, Mellet's negative view would become an unfair rule of thumb, one that would be adopted by future historians, notably Robert Caro. This criticism came in early January 1951, and, alas, McFarland was being condemned before he started.

The position to which Ernest McFarland ascended had existed only a relatively short time in the 160-year history of the Senate although there had been natural leaders and presidential favorites since Jefferson's time. The official office dated from 1920 when Oscar W. Underwood of Alabama was designated the Democratic party leader in the Senate, in his case minority leader. Underwood served in this capacity for the Democrats until 1923 when Joseph T. Robinson of Arkansas succeeded him, serving still in the minority. With the election of Franklin Roosevelt in 1932, Robinson became the first Democratic majority leader, serving from 1933 until his death in 1937. Alben Barkley succeeded him and served until 1949, with two years (1947-49) of the Eightieth Congress in the minority. When Barkley became vice president in 1949, Scott Lucas took over and served from 1949 until 1951. Upon Lucas's defeat by Everett Dirksen, Senator McFarland became the fourth majority and fifth party leader. Like Robinson, Barkley, and Lucas, he had served precisely ten years in the Senate before his selection, yet, at age 56, remained youthful enough to carry the physical burdens of the job.[9]

Certain emoluments beyond prestige went with the additional burden. Under the Senate Reorganization Act of 1946, the majority leader could virtually control the legislative calendar, and the position enjoyed increased funding and a large office, siderooms, and foyer in the Capitol Building itself as well as the normal rooms in the Senate Office Building. In the Senate Chambers, McFarland occupied one of two front-row center-aisle seats. Opposite him sat the Republican minority leader, Kenneth S. Wherry of Nebraska, during the first session of 1951 and Styles Bridges of New Hampshire in 1952. Unlike Lucas. who constantly bickered with Wherry, Mac cultivated a harmonious relationship with the Republican leader.[10]

Much more important than the technical provisions and

requirements of office were the majority leaders's relationships with the two branches of government to which he felt personally responsible: the legislative and the executive. Regarding this, Senator McFarland later stated in his autobiography:

> My official relationship with the president was based on two broad concepts -- my responsibility as majority leader and my duties in that post and my personal views as senator. . . . It was my duty to convey what I deemed to be the views of both the majority and minority members of that body. I did this even when it did not coincide with the viewpoint of the president. I was of the opinion that the president was entitled to this information. . . . I also deemed it my duty to convey to the Democrats . . . the president's views. . . . I tried to fulfill the double duty.

The tabloid *Newsweek* concurred with McFarland's approach: "He doesn't hesitate to tell Mr. Truman – politely but firmly – that certain bills or appointments don't have a chance. He won't push for doomed legislation simply to make a record. Therein lies the secret of McFarland's effectiveness, a point even liberals concede."[11]

Barkley and Lucas stressed supporting the executive and Lucas kept in constant touch with the White House over direct telephone, a connection that McFarland used sparingly. Relying on his personal friendship and trust with Truman, Mac demurred on a direct line, preferring the long mile between the White House and the Hill. "It was not too far for the Senate's ambassador to travel." Mac later stressed that when Barkley had frequently supported forlorn Truman amendments, both offices of majority leader and president appeared weak; therefore he would avoid that predicament.[12]

Party allegiance of senate members proved more important than the leader's preference for representing the legislature or the executive. In the Eighty-second Congress, the Democrats held the barest possible majority of 49 to 47, down from the previous majority of twelve, and it was certain that several

Democrats had not voted for Truman in 1948. Some went for Progressive Henry Wallace, while others deviated to States' Rights-Dixiecrat Strom Thurmond. This meant that the Democrats frequently could not raise a true majority, and McFarland often had to work the other (Republican) side of the aisle. The press considered his job the "toughest job in the United States Capital -- majority leader of the Senate without a majority to follow him . . . a party that is split down the middle over domestic issues but clings rather closely together in support of the Truman administration's foreign program." Highlighting the lack of a true majority loomed the ever-strengthening coalition of Republicans and Southern Democrats, which could effectively stymie any proposed bill at will. Indeed, Mac faced a formidable challenge in expediting legislation.[13]

In further defining the party leader's role, political affiliation was important relative to that of the president. The easiest leadership job is that of minority leader with a president of the opposite party, a situation where leadership's role concerns monitoring rather than expediting legislation. The next easiest task is that of a majority leader with a president of the same party who is not legislatively aggressive, a situation enjoyed by Senators Taft and Knowland under Eisenhower during the upcoming Eighty-third Congress. Not unlike this relationship in terms of difficulty is the tandem of a majority leader with a president of the opposite party such as Lyndon Johnson was to experience under Eisenhower from 1955 to 1961. Here the role is to both to monitor and compromise legislative activity so it may be expedited by the full Senate.

The situation of a majority leader with a president of the same party is more difficult because the essential task is fulfilling the executive's legislative program to the fullest extent possible. There are two variations here. The easiest is leadership under a popular, aggressive president with a strong majority such as Joseph T. Robinson enjoyed under Franklin Roosevelt. Here, leadership's power is essentially derivative because the prestige of the president affords the leader great leverage.

The most difficult position of leadership is that of

majority leader with a slim majority and a president who is leg-islatively aggressive without being able to muster popular sup-port for his program. This was precisely McFarland's position and similar to Scott Lucas's, although Lucas had enjoyed a majority of 54 to 42.[14]

In one respect, the pressures proved to be somewhat less for McFarland than for Lucas because Truman's Fair Deal domestic program was essentially dead, as Senator Douglas had lamented, by the time Mac took the reigns of leadership, so he should not be held responsible for its demise. With the nar-rowest of majorities, McFarland could not be expected to achieve legislative miracles. Offsetting this also stood the dire challenge of the ongoing Korean War. Momentum here had turned drastically against the forces of the United Nations after initial successes of the fall of 1950. As of late November 1950, Chinese and North Korean troops were marching steadily southward, driving UN forces before them. Reversing the ini-tiative and bringing the war to a satisfactory conclusion was the major challenge facing the Eighty-second Congress. As he led the Senate into its first session, the question loomed: could McFarland bring a degree of order to the potential chaos.[15]

On January 3, 1951, Vice President Alben Barkley gaveled the Senate into session in the redecorated Senate Chambers. Majority Leader McFarland then escorted Carl Hayden to be sworn in, as his fellow Arizonan at the same time concluded his fourth decade in Congress and commenced his fifth term in the Senate.

Immediately after the swearing in ceremonies "the edu-cation of Ernest McFarland," as the press termed it, began. The majority leader motioned to adjourn, and, as was customary, dis-pense with senate business until after the president's State of the Union Address which was scheduled later than normal for the following Monday, January 8. "Mr. Republican" Bob Taft, wishing to embarass the president, immediately challenged the motion, objecting to Truman's delaying his speech, and the Senate then agreed to reconvene instead on Friday, January 5, when senators would be able to enter preliminary comments into the record.

McFarland recognized Taft's design and humorously stated at Friday's session that the Senator from Ohio should be able to tell the president what he thinks he "should place in his message to Congress." Taft may have outfoxed McFarland for he proceded to set forth the Republican philosophy on U.S. foreign policy. Truman was not amused by Taft's maneuver or by Mac's alleged gullibility in letting Taft sound off. In reality, however, Truman bore some responsibility for the matter too, for he had first broken with precedent by not scheduling his address at the usual time right after the opening of Congress. Yet this incident coupled with Mac's hesitancy when first addressing the press as majority leader – he deferred to House Majority Leader John McCormack on one occasion – further garnished his initial reputation as a leader with little potenial.[16]

The next Monday, January 8, in his address, the president aggressively focused on the communist threat, which he perceived to be both in Korea and emanating from the Soviet Union. He asserted that the only realistic road to peace lay in facing the Soviets with force and that the defense of Europe was the best defense of the United States. He intended to ask for huge increases in taxes and universal military training. On January 11, McFarland supported these views in his first major address as majority leader urging bipartisan foreign policy and American reinforcement of NATO forces in Europe, the first issue of immediate concern to the new Congress. In his speech entitled "The Need for Unity and Cooperation in the Present Crisis," the new majority leader pled for and urged a unified stance behind the president: I am asking that my colleagues unite . . . make clear by their every action and every word that all of us have a single overriding objective. . . . Remember that there are no aisles separarting Democrats and Reublicans in the ships at sea, in the aircraft aloft, in the marching regiments." This aptly named "Defense Congress" would bear out the integrity and success of McFarland's efforts at unity. While domestic issues continued to be divisive, the Senate contributed to the overall bipartisan foreign policy recommended by Truman and backed and implemented by McFarland.[17]

As forces marshalled for debate on "troops to Europe," McFarland settled into his meetings and committee routines during January wearing several hats as perhaps the third most powerful man in Washington behind the president and speaker of the house.. On the 8th, weekly gatherings of the president and the "Big Four" began with Truman, McFarland, Barkley, House Speaker Sam Rayburn, and House Majority Leader John McCormack in attendance, frequently joined by Chief of Staff Omar Bradley who kept them apprised of Korean developments. McFarland also chaired and met weekly with the Policy Committee, for which he meticulously appointed "friends of Mac." On a monthly basis he called for both dinner gatherings of the Democratic committee chairmen and informal luncheons with all freshman senators. As majority leader, he also chaired the Steering Committee, which assigned all other senate committee appointments, and the Democratic Caucus which chose the whip and various senate secretaries and the sergeant-at-arms. In addition to all this, the majority leader functioned as a "sort of godfather to ninety-five prima donnas on either side of the aisle." Roland Bibolet referred to this "most onerous duty" as "wet-nursing . . . extending every courtesy, catering to their wishes, arranging for their absences," which reached epidemic proportions.

All of these tasks were associated with the office of majority leader, and Mac refused to divide responsibilities as did the Republicans, citing precedence and avoidance of signs of weakness. Moreover, McFarland could have chosen to resign from but continued to sit on his regular committees. Maintaining that his first duty was to his state, he held on to the second and third-ranking positions on Interstate Commerce and Interior. Likewise, McFarland who rarely ever spoke at length, now further confined his oratory to Arizona interests and the most important policy statements. "I always found it easy to get a good speaker when I needed one" among the profuse senate orators. He did, of course, remain constantly on the senate floor, and with typical courtesy he would never interrupt a senator's speech. Nor would he ever ask a senator to vote against his own convictions.[18]

McFarland's daily routine mandated a full schedule beginning with making and fielding phone calls before and during breakfast. He then joined chauffer Norman Edwards, "a joy to have around," for the thirty-minute limousine drive to the Capitol during which he perused Washington and Arizona newspapers before arriving by 9:00 A.M. After directing attention to office mail and phone messages until 10:00 A.M., he would leave for committee meetings or Monday's "Big Four" conferences. McFarland reached the floor by 11:55 A.M. for a five-minute daily press conference before the session opened at noon. Sessions normally ran until 5:00 or 7:00 P.M., and frequently later during the summer. With the exception of a brief lunch, usually of the famous senate navy bean soup, Mac remained on the floor constantly monitoring the legislative process. He regarded floor duty as imperative because as chairman of both the Majority Policy and Steering Committees, it was his task to determine the order in which bills were brought up and to prevent party strategy from being "stymied by Republican party parliamentary legerdemain." *Phoenix Gazette* journalist, John Kamps, accompanied McFarland on one or more of his typical days later in the session and offered other observations on Mac's role and demeanor:

> To the tourists, McFarland probably doesn't look much like one of the most influential men in the Senate. They don't see a table-pounding orator. They see a stocky, ruddy, round-faced, grey-haired man of 57 in a conservative suit affably circulating around the chamber talking with other members. . . .
> McFarland's easy-going manner is in sharp contrast to [Republican minority leader] Wherry's aggressive demeanor. If McFarland has a temper, he keeps it well-hidden. The timetable life he has been living since last January has left him unruffled.

The timetable life, according to assistant Roland Bibolet, included "endless work sessions, late hours; we usually reached home at 10-11 PM." Bibolet would call Edna upon Mac's departure for home. She would reply "Thank God," and he "Amen."[19]

Majority Whip Lyndon Johnson was of great assistance "collecting senators from corridors, dining rooms, and other places" as well as consolidating his own connections, which would be of immense value in his own later career as majority leader. Fellow Texan Bibolet recalls that Mac and the rising Johnson established a "very close and friendly relationship. The families were friends. They conferred quite often and constantly. McFarland had a little avuncular feeling for Johnson. He was older. He was more mature . . . . McFarland had a fatherly interest in him."

Concerning LBJ's regard for Mac, Bibolet further recalls "I know he loved him a great deal and felt very close to him." McFarland held Johnson's political skills in high esteem, particularly his "deep feeling for mankind." He thus gave LBJ full rein as whip, telling wife Edna, "I'm as high up in office as I ever want to be. Now we have some here that I would like to push forward and give them opportunities. I'm going to let them take the lead in certain things." He referred, of course, to LBJ: "I let him go ahead."[20]

Thus, as January 1951 closed, McFarland had begun to settle into the routine as majority leader. A capable administrator, he plied these new and unpredictable waters with skill. His calm and unflappable demeanor proved an asset as expected. He took the positive with the negative in equal stride, acknowledging the trust that the Senate had placed in him. Yet he remained aware that his selection as leader was a controversial one and not totally indicative of the strength and unity he so urged within his party.

Concern over foreign policy during the Cold War in Europe and the hot version in Korea engendered what press and politicians alike referred to as the "Great Debate" of 1951. War, whether hot or cold, always scrambles American politics. In December 1950, for example, both Democrat Joseph Kennedy and Republican Herbert Hoover attacked President Truman's growing troop commitment in Korea, while Secretary of State Dean Acheson and future Republican Secretary John Foster Dulles supported Truman. On most critical diplomatic issues during the whole course of the Cold War, the president could rely upon bipartisan support. But there was an unspoken understanding that partisanship ought not be totally extinguished from the "Great Debate." After all, constituents had to be assured that their congressmen were truly representing them, that "their" party was worthy. Early in 1951, Taft and Minority Leader Wherry criticized Truman for committing too many troops to NATO in Europe and questioned whether Congress had sufficient control over such forces.

Senator McFarland formally entered the debate with his first national broadcast as majority leader on February 10, 1951. Speaking at a Raleigh, North Carolina, Jefferson-Jackson Day Dinner, he staunchly upheld Truman's policy in Korea and NATO Commander Dwight Eisenhower's recommendation for a strong additional deployment of American troops in Europe. At the same time, he ribbed isolationist Taft as among the "timid men suddenly become military strategists."

Floor debate on NATO troops continued through the remainder of February and all of March with the majority leader constantly trying to drive the Senate to a quick, supportive decision for the president - not an easy task. Noting Eisenhower's dismay about not getting additional troops, on March 6, McFarland called for action on the "troops-to-Europe" resolution, which he had cosponsored, noting Eisenhower's handicap at the delay. Two weeks later he was sounding the same note as Eisenhower for the second time sent word that his mission was being hampered by Senate inaction."[21]

By this time, Senator Taft had been drawn into a supportive position for sending four divisions to NATO, but the problems were thorny indeed. McFarland outlined them: 1) should the United States require Europe to make firm commitments to bear a proper share of NATO defense before sending troops; 2) should a cap be placed on the number of troops assigned to NATO; 3) does the president, as commander-in-chief have the constitutional power to send troops to NATO on his own initiative; and 4) what kind of consultation and cooperation should be required between the executive and congressional branches of government in the conduct of just these troops or the whole Cold War. Hoping to reach general concord and cut through minor disagreements, he pointed to European assurances given in conference and directly to Eisenhower, and to NATO's agreement that the Joint Chiefs of Staff had to certify the Allies' intentions before American troops could be committed. On point two, McFarland cautioned that a limitation could hurt European morale. Therefore, Congress should compromise on the side of safety -- in other words, no limitation. On the issues of constitutionality and executive power, he cited the fact that Congress had ratified NATO and had long held to the tradition of unfettered executive action in potential emergency situations. He insisted that Cold War Europe fall within this definition. Concerning the final point of congressional-executive cooperation, McFarland pointed out that the president would be required to consult with appropriate congressional committees before dispatching additional troops beyond the four divisions in question.[22]

A significant block of conservative Republicans failed to see the logic of McFarland's assertions as the Senate considered the troop resolution on April 2. Senator Karl Mundt (R-SD) offered an amendment calling for congressional approval before sending even the designated four divisions. This was defeated by a 52 to 29 vote. Next Senator John W. Bricker (R-OH) proposed to send the troops resolution back to committee in hopes that further congressional control could be exerted upon the president.

Bricker's proposal aroused McFarland's ire and, controlling the floor, he declared recommitment would be hailed "as a victory by the Kremlin, a direct slap at Eisenhower, a vote of no confidence in our historic friend France," and that it had already been reported unanimously out of committee. The leader found support from the other side of the aisle from

Massachusetts Republican Henry Cabot Lodge: "If we recommit we are in effect saying Eisenhower come home." The Bricker motion went down to defeat 56 to 31. Then on April 4, 1951, Congress adopted the resolution to send the four divisions to Eisenhower, adding to the two already present in Europe. McFarland stated for national television, "The Senate notified the world that we will not repeat the mistakes we made in the 1930s when isolationism in America led Hitler to believe he could conquer Europe while the U.S.A. looked the other way."[23]

Immediately after passage of the "Troops for Europe" Resolution, the nation struggled with the news of President Truman's relieving General Douglas MacArthur of the Far Eastern command, including Korea. McFarland made the initial moves to orchestrate senate reaction to the controversial ousting. On April 11, the dismissal date, he released the following statement:

> In a time of crisis, the necessity of changing Commanders in a vital military mission is most unfortunate. But international unity at such a time far outweighs sympathetic consideration for even a great General. No one can deny that the allied world was falling apart over the confusion of conflicting statements from Korea. Our nation has become the greatest and freest on earth because it was founded on the principle of government by and for the people. The civilian - not the military - must be the source of final authority or we would have fallen under military dictatorship long ago. When military officers attempt to make non-military decisions outside of their authority, a grave danger to our form of government immediately arises. General George McClellan was removed from his command in the Union Army during the Civil War for his refusal to carry out the President's orders. When an American General takes steps which high military leaders believe might plunge us into a Third World War, alienate our allies, involve us in an endless struggle throughout Asia, and precipitate a

global conflict for which we are not yet prepared, they
have no choice except his removal.[24]

  Specifically, MacArthur had been relieved of command
for going over the executive's head once too often. The general had made offers of armistice negotiations without clearance
and had issued a public anti-administration statement through
the auspices of House Minority Leader Joseph W. Martin (R-
MA). The statement included a recommendation to use
Formosan troops against the Chinese, an idea strictly opposed
by Truman, who did not want to risk further geographic escalation that might induce Russia to join in and perhaps lead to a
third world war. Vague but startling allusions to the use of
small but strategically placed nuclear weapons also gave concern
to the man who by fate's dictum had invented the game.
  Senator McFarland fully supported the president's
action. When Michigan Republican Homer Ferguson proposed sending a senate committee to Tokyo to give the general
a hearing on his foreign policy views, McFarland effectively
resisted, stating MacArthur himself would resent such intrusion
and that it would cause psychological problems and create propaganda opportunities for the enemy. McFarland also went on
record as opposing the general's desire to emphasize Asia over
Europe in the fight against communism.[25]
  The majority leader shouldered the burden of senate
communication with the president during this crisis for about a
week, before requesting Senator Russell and others to return to
Washington and take part in the discussions. During this time,
McFarland received "backdoor" access to the White House in
order to avoid publicity. He was privy to the president's
thoughts as the MacArthur drama began to unravel. Upon the
general's return, Truman urged McFarland to extend to him
every courtesy, and the majority leader rode with the general
and House Minority Leader Martin in an open car parade to
give his farewell address to the joint session of Congress on
April 19. The senator did not find this ride particularly enjoyable. To him, it had the appearance that Congress was confer-

ring recognition upon MacArthur and thus stood in agreement with the general's previous statements. The president, however, reassured McFarland. Truman's political instinct indicated that the general had again overstepped himself by hurrying to Washington with speaking stops only in New York, and San Francisco, whereas he should have slowly crossed the country arousing people to his support. "Now he is through," the president summarized.[26]

Although true, it was not quite that simple. A week after MacArthur's speech, Minority Leader Wherry introduced a resolution leading to an investigation of the firing by two senate committees: Armed Services, chaired by Richard Russell, and Foreign Policy chaired by Tom Connally of Texas. Majority Whip Lyndon Johnson also sat on Armed Services and kept McFarland apprised of the inner workings of the committee hearings.

A major issue arose over whether the hearings should be open to the public or not. Republican leadership supported public testimony, while Russell and many Democrats opposed, preferring the hearings to remain closed in the interest of national security. Another tangible purpose was to foreclose on the opportunity for Republican's to capitalize on MacArthur's popularity, which would be enhanced with public hearings. Russell and his committee voted unanimously not only to keep the hearings closed but also to bar noncommittee senators in the interest of a truly bipartisan effort. At first, McFarland did not agree with these approaches, but he definitely changed his mind, perhaps after being persuaded by Russell or learning that the Soviet press was on standby to fully cover the hearings if they were open. The hearings ran from May 3 to June 27 and affirmed President Truman's action as appropriate, given MacArthur's insubordination, thus confirming civilian authority as superior to that of the military. Nevertheless, It represented a time of public hysteria as Washington, D.C., almost ground to a halt and mail piled up in the Senate Post Office like "great snow banks."[27]

*   *   *

As the Korean War continued to involve increasing numbers of U.S. servicemen, Senator McFarland worked to extend GI Bill benefits by coauthoring and sponsoring the Korean GI Bill of Rights. Customarily this bill would have to go through hearings before the Finance Committee, but an isolated incident in Arizona served to bring the matter to full senate attention. In early May 1951, the Tucson Veterans Hospital denied Korean combat veteran David R. Arellano treatment for non-combat related throat cancer. In doing so, the VA did not recognize the Korean conflict as an official war and considered Arellano in fact merely a peacetime soldier. He resorted to a public hospital for treatment.

The serviceman's plight received national media coverage bringing immediate results concerning McFarland's bill. President Truman urged the House and Senate to provide appropriate legislation, and with the bipartisan backing of Senators Taft and Walter George of Georgia, the Finance Committee waived hearings. On May 10, Senate Joint Resolution 72, the Korean GI Bill, passed both the Senate and House by voice vote. President Truman signed it into law on May 11.

The bill provided Korean War veterans medical, hospital, domiciliary, and burial benefits, and compensation and pensions for veterans and their dependents. It fell short of the 1944 bill's sweeping education, housing, and business assistance provisions that McFarland had authored, but he continued to work for further extensions and higher compensation under the new law.[28]

Later in the session McFarland again distinguished himself in the veterans' interest, this time standing against the administration. Truman had vetoed H.B. 3193 which provided totally disabled veterans of World Wars I and II the same $120 - per-month given the dwindling number of similar Spanish-American War veterans. In the Senate, McFarland played the major role in the successful effort to override, and on September 25, 1951, American Legion National Commander Erle Cock, Jr. conveyed the thanks of three million legionnaires

214 — ERNEST W. MCFARLAND

over "the important role you played in the enactment over the
President's veto."[29]

Senator McFarland also supported what he termed
"emergency legislation" concerning military training and conscription to back up the wartime demands. By mid-June, the
Universal Military Training and Service Act had been signed
and passed, extending Selective Service to 1955, requiring registration of all males of eighteen, lowering induction age from
nineteen to eighteen and one-half (instead of the initially
requested eighteen) and lengthening service from twenty-one to
twenty-four months. It did not require universal military training but provided for the creation of a commission to report to
Congress on the subject.[30]

Although McFarland's duties as leader cut down considerably on personally-sponsored legislation, he did achieve
notable success in areas other than veterans' benefits such as
senate passage for the second time of the Central Arizona
Project. However, after success in the Senate and failure in the
House in 1950, these subsequent efforts in the Eighty-second
Congress were in reality foredoomed.

Attention focused on the House where hearings began
in February 1951 and dragged on into April. McFarland made
many trips to the offices of committee members, but to no avail.
On April 18, Murdock's recalcitrant committee voted 16 to 8
that consideration of CAP legislation be postponed until the
Lower Colorado waters were adjudicated or agreed upon by
other means.

As majority leader, McFarland tried to control scheduling for one last desperate effort to see passage of CAP during this Congress. He introduced S.75 early in the session,
and the Senate skipped hearings this time and concentrated on
floor debate from May 28 through June 6. Once again the
Senate voted favorably on CAP, 50 to 28, with eighteen
abstaining or absent. This automatically sent S.75 over to the
House, but Arizona's forlorn hope that it would be considered
in spite of the House committee's decision to postpone did not
materialize."[31]

* * *

Civil rights in America remained an unsolved problem during the Truman years. The president had early on taken the initiative by desegregating the armed forces by executive order and establishing a government task force to investigate civil rights, but his civil rights plank of the 1948 Democratic platform (written by then-Minneapolis Mayor Hubert Humphrey), had fallen flat. The Eighty-first Congress, under liberal Democratic leadership, simply did not take up the call. Humphrey, Paul Douglas, and other liberals acknowledged that the Fair Deal's commitment to civil rights was withering. McFarland brought nothing to the fray to encourage civil rights advocates who were dismayed when he and Lyndon Johnson were selected by the southern bloc to lead the Senate. If anything, the Eighty-second Congress lost ground as it battled over cloture procedure and never got into the substance of civil rights reform. The NAACP denounced the new leadership duo; the Afro-American termed them part of an "unholy alliance;" and black Democratic Congressman Adam Clayton Powell of Harlem stridently announced, "There will be no civil rights in this session of Congress."[32]

The new majority leader tried to keep a positive approach, expressing optimism that civil rights could advance even with the Democratic split between liberal North and conservative South. McFarland cited both national defense and domestic economy as factors bringing the disparate wings together and noted progress made in the South where two states had recently abolished the poll tax. He did not, however, "want to give the impression that the civil rights problem has been solved."[33]

The major civil rights issue in 1951 concerned the establishment of a Fair Employment Practices Commission (FEPC), but neither the liberals in Congress nor the president pressed aggressively for legislation. Although McFarland insisted that potential measures be considered in committee by the Senate, nothing ever reached the floor. Nor was there any real effort to liberalize the controversial Hayden-Wherry Resolution which controlled debate. The best Congress could do was authorize coinage of fifty-cent pieces commemorating the lives of Booker T. Washington and George Washington Carver. For many, this was more an insult than a tribute.[34]

The Hayden-Wherry Resolution required two-thirds of the whole Senate to invoke cloture in dealing with filibustering. This unlimited debate along with negotiation, trade-offs, and compromise, provided one of many keys to the legislative process in the Senate. Filibuster provided the weapon to force these others, and it constituted a powerful threat indeed in the hands of Russell's minority bloc of southern senators.

There always existed, however, a large body of senators who desired to adopt cloture rules for limitation of debate, but the Senate as a whole, aware of its unique and privileged status, was reluctant to establish tight "gag" rules. A first effort at limitation occured in 1917, when Rule XXII stipulated that (a quorum of 49 senators being established) upon the motion of 16 (one-sixth) senators to close debate, cloture must be voted upon on the following day. If two-thirds of the senators voting upheld cloture, then members were limited to one hour apiece of final debate before the matter had to be brought to a vote.

A second stage came in 1948, when Senator Russell made a hair-splitting point of order that said Rule XXII could be applied only to debate on consideration of a bill, not on the motion to finalize said measure, in effect restoring unlimited debate. President Pro Tem Arthur Vandenberg (R-MI) held the chair and in the spirit of strict parliamentary procedure, accepted this nullification of Rule XXII.

The majority of the Senate, including McFarland, found this unsatisfactory, and the search began for ways to circumvent the ruling. In 1949 Republican Minority Leader Kenneth Wherry and Democratic Chairman of the Rules Committee Carl Hayden offered an amendment that reiterated the old rule adding debate on a motion as well as a measure to be subject to cloture upon the vote of two-thirds of the members present. The more pertinent issue here concerned the desire of many to have cloture invoked by less than two-thirds, even by a simple majority.

Advocates of this approach, however, proved unaggressive, much to the disgust of pro-civil rights organizations. Majority Leader Scott Lucas supported majority cloture but equivocated on the issue when pressured with problems of southern resistance and legislative priorities, supporting the latter.

Nor did the White House exert pressure. In February 1949, both A. Philip Randolph and Walter White, Executive Secretary of the NAACP, directly appealed to President Truman to support cloture by a simple majority. The president did venture his support, but the statement elicited cries of "conspiracy" from Russell, causing Lucas to attempt to maintain some harmony by supporting the Hayden-Wherry Resolution which would have weakened Rule XXII. Even so, southern members threatened to filibuster for the Vandenberg rulings. They cared not for cloture at all whether it was two-thirds of the entire membership or of those present, or by a simple majority.

One other course of action remained open to those favoring cloture: a new ruling from the chair -- in this case, Vice President Alben Barkley -- could overturn the Vandenberg ruling. With White House urging, Lucas began rounding up signatures (seventeen Democrats and sixteen Republicans) supportive of a Barkley ruling to allow cloture on a motion as well as a measure. He presented it to the chair on March 10, 1949.

Barkley ruled favorably on the petition, thus reversing Vandenberg's decision of a year earlier. Senator Russell immediately appealed the chair's ruling, and on the following day, the Senate overturned the vice president's ruling, 46 to 41, a blow for the administration and all civil rights advocates. Twenty-three Republicans joined with twenty southern and three western Democrats to maintain unlimited debate. The western senators were Pat McCarran of Nevada and Arizona's Hayden and McFarland. Had they gone the other way, it would have been 44 to 43 to limit debate.

The vote on the Barkley ruling proved significant in emphasizing the long struggle civil rights advocates faced in the legislative process. It became obvious that most southern bloc Democrats and Republicans, primarily concerned with economic conservatism and a bipartisan foreign policy, were more than willing to jettison civil rights in order to maintain the GOP-Southern Democratic alliance. Moreover, geography was a factor, for western senators like McFarland were not responsible to a sizable African American constituency and could vote with disregard for the issue and confine their attention solely to state interests. Southerners were adept at encouraging this lack of concern by granting legislative favors to the West in other areas.

In the aftermath of the defeat of the Barkley ruling, the Hayden-Wherry Resolution was adjusted to southern favor. Although the resolution did sanction cloture on motions as well as substantive measures, it required a two-thirds vote of the entire Senate (64), rather than just those present on the floor. On March 17, this new resolution was voted in by 63 to 23, with only fifteen Democrats and eight Republicans holding out against it. Roy Wilkins of the NAACP called the new ruling "a permanent roadblock to civil-rights legislation." As it turned out, he was incorrect, but it did erect a roadblock that would preclude strong legislation for fifteen years.[35]

Ernest McFarland later in his autobiography discussed these events in terms of senate privilege and uniqueness, minority rights, and the spirit of compromise and conciliation. Drawing on arguments of other Democratic senators with whom he agreed, McFarland cited Hayden, Walter George of Georgia, and Democrat Spessard Holland of Florida. Hayden spoke adamantly on the uniqueness of the Senate, stating, "It is a continuing body. Being solely responsible to the voters in their own states, tenure of office of senators has no direct relation to the will of the majority of voters throughout the nation." Senator George voiced his position:

> The Senate is a distinct institution within itself. It is not a body which expires. Its primary and main function, indeed in certain important matters, partakes of conference and negotiation between sovereignties. If we adopt outright majority rule in the United States Senate, it will be easily possible to change the form and substance of the government within ten years.

The McFarlands in Oklahoma 1909:
front L-R, William, Carl, Keziah;
rear L-R, Etta Pearl, Forrest, Ernest
at age 15.

Ernest at East Central Normal
School, Ada, Oklahoma;
1914, age 20.

Ernest at Great Lakes
Naval Base, Illinois;
1918, age 24.

From the Oklahoma prairies and streams, McFarland gazes into his future in far western Arizona; May, 1919.

Arizona's youngest county attorney in Florence, Pinal Co., 1925–31.

Ernest and Claire McFarland on board for Europe, Summer, 1929. After the loss of three children, Claire died in December 1930.

Superior Court Judge McFarland presides over his last jury trial at Pinal County Courthouse, 1940.

Edna, Jewell on horse, and Ernest McFarland at Florence home shortly before 1940 U. S. Senate campaign.

Mac in 1941, freshman Senator, defender of Hollywood film industry.

In the gardens of 10 Downing Street, London: L-R; Senator Albert Hawkes, Prime Minister Winston Churchill, Senator Burton K. Wheeler, McFarland, Ambassador John Winant, and Senator Homer Capehart.

Mac was, perhaps, the most widely traveled U. S. Senator during his 12 year tenure; here relaxing with paper on flight to Europe, May 1945.

Mac waits his turn as Ike addresses Arizona GIs going to mess near Rheims, France. McFarland and his Interstate Commerce Committee colleagues were among the first to visit war torn Europe immediately after the German surrender in May 1945.

The father of the "GI Bill," Mac wrote the free education and home and business loan sections of the landmark legislation.

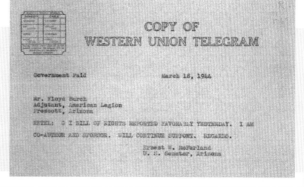

COPY OF
WESTERN UNION TELEGRAM

Government Paid   March 16, 1944

Mr. Floyd Burch
Adjutant, American Legion
Prescott, Arizona

HOTEL: G I BILL OF RIGHTS REPORTED FAVORABLY YESTERDAY. I AM
CO-AUTHOR AND SPONSOR. WILL CONTINUE SUPPORT. REGARDS.

                                    Ernest W. McFarland
                                    U. S. Senator, Arizona

With Italian dignitaries at the Vatican, preparing for an audience with Pope Pius XII: McFarland and Wheeler at front left; Hawkes and Capehart, 2nd and 4th from left in back between guards.

Jewell, Mac, and Edna in portrait for *Life* magazine article on 1946 campaign.

A victorious Mac looks forward to a second term.

With friend and advisor Ralph Watkins, Sr., Mac scrutinizes statue of Buddha in Japan on an Asian trip investigating communications.

Mac guffaws at joke as special ambassador to China, George Marshall, looks on at McFarland's right hand.

Chiang-Kai-shek greets Mac in Peking, December 1946.

Surrounded by guests, the Arizona Washington delegation sits, L–R: Congressman
Richard Harless, Senator Carl Hayden, McFarland, and Congressman John
Murdock, in Hayden's office.

1948 whistlestop campaign in
Phoenix – with Bess and
Harry Truman and McFarland;
Governor Dan Garvey at far
left.

The Colorado River Basin showing
Arizona'a predominance in square
miles; prepared for CAP hearings.

The U. S. Senate "Class of 1948" brought
in Mac's old school buddy, Oklahoma
Senator Robert S. Kerr, as well as Lyndon
Johnson and Hubert Humphrey.

"They want to irrigate this?" Mac dumps sand from shoe near California's Salton Sea. Mac directed passage of CAP in the U. S. Senate in both 1950 and 1951, but it failed to pass the House and only became law in 1968.

McFarland, 2nd from left, and Hayden, 4th from right, host a mostly Native American group on the Capitol steps. Mac wrote the innovative Navajo-Hopi Rehabilitation Act of 1950 for the nation's largest Indian population.

The Big Four consider a presidential joke, L–R: Speaker of the House Sam Rayburn, President Harry Truman, Senate Majority Leader Ernest McFarland, House Majority Leader John McCormack, and Vice President Alben Barkley.

Outgoing Majority Leader Scott Lucas congratulates incoming floor leader McFarland and Whip Lyndon Johnson, January 1951.

Senator Holland quoted columnist David Lawrence who echoed both John C. Calhoun's and Alexander Hamilton's concern for minority rights:

> This issue goes deeper, however, than civil rights and racial problems. It goes to the heart of minority rights on all questions. The right of unlimited debate has kept the Senate from becoming a rubber stamp for the Executive on matters of domestic as well as foreign policy. An intolerant majority can ride roughshod over the rights of the minority. In the Senate, it has been possible for unlimited debate to be checked only by the processes of public opinion.

Backed by such reasoning, McFarland largely dropped personal feeling in favor of senate tradition. He did not wear his heart on his sleeve realizing effectiveness lay elsewhere, and this did not redound to the benefit of civil rights during his two years at the senate's helm. He stated: "There were reforms which I felt were necessary and desirable, particularly on equal rights." His task as leader was to find out how and when such reform could be accomplished. With the ongoing threat of filibuster, he knew that compromise was absolutely necessary for reform. "I therefore set out to see just what could be done to take some definite steps in that regard," first approaching Senator Russell on FEPC and anti-poll tax legislation, and notifying him that ultimately it would be passed, so "it would be better for both sides if it were passed then."

Russell expressed willingness to go along with an amendment to eliminate the poll tax and would support an FEPC as long as it could not exact severe employer penalties. McFarland then conferred with Paul Douglas of the liberal faction. This group hoped for an act of Congress, not a constitutional amendment, on the poll tax, and insisted on stiff penalties for FEPC violations. Douglas would not accept the McFarland compromise of less severe penalties. Russell, became angered by the result and promised McFarland "he would never go that far again." He did, however, in the LBJ years, when the type of compromise Mac originally recommended was finally adopted.

Senator McFarland also agreed that the Hayden-Wherry Resolution on cloture by two-thirds of the full Senate should have been modified along the lines of the later 1975 change which allowed cloture by a vote of three-fifths of the full membership. He knew, however, that this change "would not have been made at that time," and referred to understandable priorities: "We had a war to win. It was our first duty to win with a loss of as few lives as possible." Furthermore, the Republican-Southern Democrat coalition had to be acknowledged, and the Republicans were far more interested in lower taxes, than in civil rights. Finally, the turgid atmosphere of the entire McCarthy era mandated avoidance of liberal issues, which included civil rights. Any direction of liberal social reform appeared to many as analogous to an implicit support of socialism, or indeed, communism. Given all of these constraints, McFarland was fortunate even to push through Social Security increases.

The senator lamented the uncompromising posture taken by the two wings of the Democratic party. "Years were lost, and progress was delayed by this action. With the study and full information on the problem . . . we would have been about twelve years ahead on this important question" of civil rights.[36] True to the spirit of his words, McFarland later as governor implemented an FEPC at the state level in 1955.

As the fiscal year 1951 drew to a close at June's end, Majority Leader McFarland evaluated the progress thus far of the first session, framing his report in terms of what had been accomplished in spite of major delaying factors that lifted three months out of the legislative calendar. These delays encompassed the time-consuming committee hearings and prolonged debate on three major issues: seven weeks of hearings and ten days of debate on long-range universal military training, a month of hearings and two weeks of debate on sending American troops to Europe during peacetime, and finally the MacArthur controversy requiring eight weeks of hearings.

In spite of these impeding factors, McFarland proudly pointed to "major legislation:" sending troops to Europe and extension of selective service as well as resolving to bar Communist China from the United Nations; extending the Reciprocal Trade Agreements Act; authorizing increased naval construction including a super-aircraft carrier; providing a short-term loan to India to provide grain to feed its impoverished people; extending benefits to Korean veterans; passing nine appropriation bills; reorganizing the RFC; and extending the Defense Production Act. The majority leader concluded by characterizing the record as strengthening the country domestically while at the same time "coping with the most critical international problems in the entire history of our republic."[37]

Much work remained, however, for the Eighty-second Congress. At McFarland's suggestion, the party caucus unanimously renounced summer vacation plans and determined to remain in continuous session until October if necessary. "Must legislation" included all new appropriation bills for the next fiscal year; $8.5 billion in foreign aid; and a tax boost bill similar to the $7.2 billion measure already passed by the House.

This legislative agenda proved formidable, and McFarland was forced to act as a martinet in keeping his colleagues attentive to the business at hand. The press variously referred to his tactics as "cracking the whip, riding herd, or reading the riot act," over, on, and to his colleagues. He deplored absenteeism and claimed his ambitious schedule could be met "if senators will make their time available to the Senate rather than the Senate's trying to accommodate the wishes of individual senators.."

Unfortunately, McFarland's remonstrations met with little success. According to historian Robert Caro, "the number of senators on the floor – for years so disgracefully small – grew smaller." Mac targeted "useless quorum calls" as "wasting the equivalent of one day a week. It's got to stop." He lamented, "We'll be here until Christmas," and pled with senators "to stop talking and start voting so we can get out of here."

Consequently, criticism of leadership heaped up as some

termed Mac "simply ineffectual" and stated "he was no leader at all." Other carping also seems unjustified in condemning positive characteristics indicated by Mac's statements "I just try to get along with people," and "I'll never ask you to vote against your convictions." According to some, these rather gracious comments indicated his inability to "get tough," although aforementioned press quotes belied this. In any case, according to Roland Bibolet, Mac's own convictions were designed to bring "uneasy unity" and develop "friendship and trust in a shattered Senate enduring terrible times; the worst it had ever gone through with no majority" and the specter of Joe McCarthy, who "few would stand up to." Although Caro claims there was "nothing Mac could do about" senate chaos, time would prove otherwise. On his own initiative, Mac did not ask others to do what he himself could not, hoping to lead by example. An end-of-session Republican check revealed that Senator McFarland had been present for all 202 roll call votes during the first session. Overall Bibolet summarizes that the Senate desperately needed a man like McFarland to surmount the monumental challenges. Whereas Barkley had been distant and Lucas too tightly wound, Mac presented his laid back, country boy demeanor, which, perhaps, was the only type that could work in the cauldron of prima donnas. His loyal assistant aptly termed McFarland "a senator's senator."[38]

As Congress struggled throughout the summer with its legislative agenda, the volatile element of McCarthyism escalated in the Senate Chambers. Wisconsin Republican Senator Joseph McCarthy had begun to cast serious aspersions against the loyalty of State Department officials early in the 1950 campaign, and those who opposed the ungrounded claims found themselves politically endangered. Millard Tydings, who had led the investigations of the McCarthy charges and found them empty, was defeated at the polls by his Republican opponent. So too had Scott Lucas been defeated, in part because of his criticism of McCarthy, as the public embraced the sensational charges. Now the new majority leader found himself unable to remain silent in the face of the pervasive negativity of the

"Tailgunner's" persuasive wrath.

During August 1951, McFarland had several encounters with the acerbic Republican, and, along with Republican Margaret Chase Smith of Maine, stood among the first senators to rebuke him officially, thus incurring McCarthy's lasting enmity, a factor of significance in the upcoming 1952 election. On August 9, the usually mild-mannered majority leader "tore into" the Wisconsin senator as McCarthy again attacked supposedly disloyal state department employees. The "enraged" McFarland "bitterly condemned McCarthy as a character assassin" declaring "When the name of any member of the Senate becomes an adjective for mudslinging, we have come a far way from the traditions of those great men who preceded us here." He likened McCarthy's statements to "smirking piety, self-righteousness, and political inference and innuendo." In typically reckless style, McCarthy countered that the majority leader and others were converting the Democrats into "a party of Communists and crooks." McFarland thus enlisted in the small but growing ranks of senators who wished to bring McCarthy down. His staff began conferring with liberal Democrat William Benton of Connecticut, who was eager either to expel or more probably censure the offensive senator.

Mac lavishly dealt criticism on other McCarthy supporters: "The echo of McFarland's booming baritone had hardly faded when he was at it again denouncing Republican tactics in caustic language," the objects of his wrath this time being conservatives Homer Capehart of Indiana and John Bricker of Ohio, who claimed the president had moved "Pendergast [machine] politics to the national level." Mac irately responded "No living man can on his oath aver that Harry Truman is anything but a personally honest, incorruptible man and president — and history will claim that. Conjecture arose over the new aggressive manner evidenced by the majority leader. Some felt that he was overly defensive and sensitive to charges that Truman lacked a strong leader in the Senate. McFarland responded that it was the correct "psychological time" to strike back at McCarthy's allegations and that although he did not

224 — Ernest W. McFarland

believe in "popping off" every time the opposition disturbed him, he would redirect the membership away from mudslinging rhetoric and back to the legislative task at hand. Actually McFarland regarded McCarthy as "really a likeable fellow," but he wished it would just "blow itself out." Mac desired to avoid giving McCarthy the publicity that a censure effort might create. He favored the silent treatment and avoidance of debate, but this was not to be. McCarthyism escalated even after McFarland had left the Senate.[39]

With such distractions, Mac's legislative agenda proceeded slowly, and not until October 8 did foreign aid pass and then only after being scaled down from 8.5 to 7.5 billion dollars. The Senate also finally approved the Japanese Treaty in September, and McFarland played a prominent role in organizing and encouraging steps toward this formal peace. In the August edition of *Cosmopolitan* magazine, he had set forth a six-point plan calling for a special conference of the heads of all nations and adoption of the following steps: 1) denunciation of aggressive war as a crime against humanity; 2) establishment of an armament program for all nations for police purposes only; 3) removal of all barriers to the free flow of communications and news, exchange of ideas, and travel among nations; 4) operation of all atomic energy plants under international supervision for the peaceful production of power; 5) dissolution of subversive organizations; and 6) conclusion of peace treaties with Japan, Germany and Austria that would insure the establishment of free government in each by secret ballot.[40]

During the summer and fall of 1951, Majority Leader McFarland broadcast a regular weekly radio report from the Shoreham Hotel to the people of Arizona presenting a cross-section analysis of current issues. Lasting for over two months, McFarland interviewed a special guest each week, commencing on August 10 with Richard Russell. Unquestionably the key man of this session, Russell had conducted hearings on the three major issues of troops in Europe, military training, and the MacArthur controversy. On the air, he explicated the Truman hardline Cold War position, emphasized a global approach to foreign policy, and criticized MacArthur for his limited single-theater view.

McFarland agreed, and along with his guest expressed disappointment over not attaining required universal military training. Russell also offered that McFarland had been cast into the most difficult majority leadership in his nineteen-year tenure, due to both the close party balance and the great issues at hand, and that he knew of no man in his "entire acquaintance in the Congress who could have done better in the face of greater difficulties."

McFarland also emphasized foreign affairs as radio host to Speaker of the House Sam Rayburn, General Omar N. Bradley, diplomat Averell Harriman, and Connecticut Senator Brien McMahon. On August 30, Rayburn agreed with the majority leader's assessment of the Eighty-second as the "defense" Congress, and defended the fifty-six billion dollar defense appropriation, adding that a third world war would be far more expensive.

On September 20, General Bradley speaking on war technology warned of the danger of complacency about American superiority in weapons and equipment. He, too, emphasized the success of Truman's Cold War foreign policy by couching the relief of Greece, the Berlin airlift, and the Korean conflict in terms of avoiding a "titanic holocaust."

On October 5, Senator McMahon, Chairman of the Joint Congressional Committee on Atomic Energy, advocated increasing reliance on atomic capabilities to serve the goal of maintaining "fewer men under arms." McFarland agreed but questioned whether the technical information was yet available to determine the feasibility of McMahon's plan. Ultimately, this direction would be implemented in the post-1952 era of Eisenhower's military "New Look" nuclear reliance.

On October 11, Averell Harriman commented on the ongoing dispute between the Mossadegh government of Iran and the Anglo-Iran Oil Company over the country's attempt to nationalize the oil industry. Harriman had recently acted as mediator between the two sides and expressed hope that an agreement could be reached that would insure more involvement and financial remuneration for Iran, but not without the necessary cooperation and assistance of British oil experts. This issue, too, would spill over into the Eisenhower era when the Central Intelligence Agency assisted in overthrowing Mossadegh returning the Shah of Iran to power.

Senator McFarland also turned to Arizona affairs during the broadcasts. When senatorial investigations of the RFC started, its new director, Stuart Symington, emphasized the success of small business loans in Arizona; McFarland, who designed the broadcast to highlight RFC credibility at a time when the agency was undergoing intense and damaging scrutiny, was delighted with the political pitch to his constituents. Senator Edwin C. Johnson discussed Social Security and Indians and credited McFarland with being the "sparkplug" in obtaining all social security increases since his tenure began. He praised the Navajo-Hopi Rehabilitation Act, which enabled these tribes to receive social security benefits ninety-four percent paid by the federal government. McFarland, who wanted to extend benefits to other tribes, explained that Arizona contained two-thirds of the reservation land in the country, land which brought in no tax revenue and to draw Indian benefits from state taxpayers would be unfair. The federal government should bear responsibility here and in other states as well. Colorado's Johnson heartily agreed, closing with the observation that McFarland was "the best majority leader since I've been a member of the Senate," a period that encompassed the tenures of Barkley, Lucas, and Republican Kenneth Wherry.

On October 19, McFarland's long-time Oklahoma friend Senator Robert Kerr spoke on the subject of taxes from his vantage point as member of the Senate Finance Committee. Even in the face of rising Cold War taxes, he insisted that real income was also on the rise. Spinning off a barrage of statistics, Kerr proclaimed national per capita productive capacity to be 3.5 times that of Europe. McFarland added that Americans had put the "nightmare" of the 1932 depression in the past and had largely forgotten the conditions which existed in 1940. Both senators expressed complete optimism with the evolving consumer culture and termed as "gloom peddlers" those who charged that inflation threatened America's postwar prosperity.[41]

Hopeful predictions of winding up the First Session of the Eighty-second Congress by late September proved to be errant. By the middle of October, the foreign aid bill had been dispensed with, but defense appropriations for the 1951-52 fiscal year and a revenue bill raising excise, corporate, and personal income tax rates were still pending.

With McFarland keeping the pressure on, the "must legislation" did get pushed through in the final days. The Senate joined in appropriating fifty-seven billion dollars for the Department of Defense on October 12. The revenue bill passed by voice vote on October 18, passed the House the next day, and was signed on October 20. On October 19, the last actual working day of Congress, Senator McFarland also secured passage of two additional bills providing increased salary for federal postal employees and retirement benefits for railroad workers, both organizations long-time supporters of McFarland.

On October 20, the Senate met for the last time for the formality of adjournment and recognition of its leaders, in reality something of a polite custom. The majority leader received many tributes from the floor complimenting his service and indicating both nonpartisanship and a non-ideological bias. Southern Democrats were in the forefront with Richard Russell once again acknowledging "Not in my time has any man been confronted by more difficult problems. He has an understanding . . . and perseverance . . . to make a magnificent record of service." Lister Hill, of Alabama echoed Russell, "I have never known a time where the majority leader carried such great burdens or had such a difficult task," in commending McFarland's "patience, demeanor, and character." John McClellan of Arkansas proclaimed, "You have been patient, courageous, helpful, and a genuine leader."

Southwestern senators joined in with Dennis Chavez of New Mexico commenting on leadership that had been "patriotic, loyal, and in every sense American, and all of it under very trying circumstances." Robert Kerr of Oklahoma effusively praised both the leader and the whip, Lyndon Johnson of Texas, who himself stated:

> I have been rather closely associated with the junior Senator from Arizona from early in the morning until late in the evening. I have always found him to be a fair, patient, tolerant Senator and a very able leader. This session of Congress has been one of the most significant, in my judgment, in the history of the Republic ... because of the type of legislation we have considered and enacted rather than for the quantity that has been passed. I think the quality ... is largely the result of the counsel, leadership, and assistance of the great majority leader. . . .

Frequent opponents, liberal Democrats from the northeastern United States, added their congratulations. Herbert H. Lehman of New York expressed admiration for McFarland's "fine and helpful manner. . . . There has never been a time . . . when the country was faced with so many serious problems." Rhode Island Senators Theodore H. Green and John Pastore voiced their respect, the latter hoping that "he will come back and give to the country the quality of leadership he has heretofore furnished."

Republicans, too, joined in the tributes. Speaking for Minority Leader Wherry, who was ill, Leverett Saltonstall of Massachusetts proclaimed, "I know he [Wherry] would say that it is easy to work with him, that he is courteous, fair, and temperate in his dealings with us on this side of the aisle." Homer Ferguson of Michigan added, "The majority leader has a very difficult position. He fills it very ably and with great distinction. I know I speak for all members of the minority in expressing affectionate appreciation of the courtesies he extends to us daily." Forgetting earlier differences, Homer Capehart of

Indiana summed up the Republican view: "If there has to be a Democrat as majority leader, I hope it will always be McFarland."

McFarland responded to the accolades by thanking everyone from Vice President Barkley and Whip LBJ to the pageboys and reporters. He singled out Harry Truman for his praise and concluded: "This Congress will go down in history as a national defense Congress [which] has done more than has any so-called peacetime Congress . . . for the defense of the United States of America . . . more to bring about eventual peace in a troubled world." Then Barkley officially adjourned the Senate's 1951 session.[42]

McFarland's own later positive assessment of the year's work rested on fairly solid ground. There is a problematical twist to a fair evaluation of the session, however, and his entire majority leadership. McFarland was criticized from both the left and right. Future historians, such as Robert Caro with the benefit of hindsight, have lamented his inability to initiate a more definite and liberal domestic program. To be fair, however, liberal Democratic senators like Humphrey were not critical and along with President Truman himself, realized that the Korean conflict demanded priority. This was, in fact, done as the domestic program was intentionally tied to the defense effort.[43] It would be more logical to criticize former Majority Leader Scott Lucas along these lines, for he was both of Truman's liberal persuasion, enjoyed a larger majority, and remained unhindered by the Korean crisis until very late in his term when he spent much of his time campaigning leaving McFarland to tend to the floor.

McFarland also had to endure the constant barbs of Republicans who were opposed to the supposedly bipartisan foreign policy. Walking the middle road between the two positions, it is to McFarland's credit that so much major legislation passed, so many major investigations and hearings successfully concluded, and the reality of a truly necessary and bipartisan foreign policy achieved. The defense appropriations bills, the Mutual Security Act expediting foreign aid, the Revenue Act providing high taxes for defense purposes, the changes in selective service and the defense production regulations can only be termed major and necessary pieces of work. McFarland guided these through and, at the same time, achieved a commendable legislative record in his own right sponsoring the Korean GI Bill, working for labor benefits, and steering social security increases and the Central Arizona Project through the Senate. Throughout these efforts, the *Arizona Republic* noted that the "usually silent, calm mannered man . . . proceeded to exercise one of his greatest talents – that of compromise maker. His praises on this score are sung by politicians wherever they assemble."[44]

After nearly ten months of continuous legislative session and major hearings, the Senate adjourned. The "defense" Congress had mounted a tremendous effort producing viable results in enduring the crisis of a change in military leadership, stabilizing the hot war in Korea (which had been running against UN forces in January 1951), and easing the international tensions of the Cold War with a strong show of support for and confidence in members of NATO. Majority Leader McFarland had kept the Senate on an even keel in the face of enormous responsibility and controversy. Indeed, he had kept order under the threat of potential chaos.

CHAPTER TEN

MAJORITY LEADER
EIGHTY-SECOND CONGRESS
SECOND SESSION
1952

AFTER A TWO AND ONE-HALF MONTH BREAK, the Eighty-second Congress resumed on January 8, 1952. The first session had been long and grueling, and Majority Leader McFarland called for a "short and snappy second." House Speaker Sam Rayburn expressed hope that Congress would finish its task before the July 7 opening of the major party conventions. This Congress, therefore, got off to a quick start with a specific adjournment date in mind and ultimately would contrast significantly with the domestic acrimony and the drawn out "great debate" on foreign policy of 1951.[1]

Unlike the previous year, President Truman presented his State of the Union Address on the opening day of Congress. He commended past efforts in lending economic assistance to Europe and halting communism in Asia, even though the Korean War still raged. He expressed concern, however, lest such efforts of bipartisanship lag and urged increasing and continued vigilance in foreign affairs.

Turning to domestic concerns, the president recommended direct attention to defense production, support of sound stabilization policies, and passage of Fair Deal measures improving farm production, housing, workers' conditions, and education, health, and Social Security services. Generally, he toned down Fair Deal emphasis and only mildly backed action on civil rights.[2]

Majority Leader McFarland reinforced the president's address the next day and detailed his own personal interests. Calling the message "constructive and forthright," he applauded the call for increased defense measures, particularly a larger Air Force. Construction and expansion of air bases could redound to Arizona's interest. Similarly, he agreed with Truman's advocating further development of natural resources where Arizona's contributions could be significant in mining and agriculture. He naturally expressed satisfaction with the president's call for increases in Social Security and extending benefits to veterans. It is notable that McFarland's vocal support was not rubber-stamping the vision of a popular president, but took nerve in light of Truman's fading approval ratings. McFarland did not try to distance himself from this situation which would only grow worse.[3]

On January 16 and 21, President Truman submitted his economic report and budget message to Congress. The former called for renewal of the Defense Production Act, continued military and economic aid to free nations, and tax rate increases along with elimination of certain tax loopholes. Finance Committee Chairman Walter George (D-GA) immediately opposed the tax recommendations. Truman's "price of peace" budget message met similar criticism from another Democrat, Senator Harry Byrd of Virginia, who proposed an $8.5 billion dollar slash from the $85.4 billion total. It is ironic that senators such as George, Byrd, and particularly Russell, who had all worked to give Mac the majority leadership, often took that majority away by siding with the Republicans against the president.

The budget, the largest proposed expenditure since World War II, alloted more than seventy-five percent to national security including the Korean "police action," atomic weapons, and the rearming of Europe. Historian Herbert Feis called it, "Not mutual trust, but mutual terror." Truman himself recognized the imbalance in stating "It is my hope . . . that we can some day cast off the heavy burden of armaments and devote our full energies to fighting the only war in which all mankind can be victorious -- the war against poverty, disease, and human misery."[4]

McFarland and the committee agreed with Senators George and Byrd that it would be "extremely unlikely" for Congress to authorize any federal tax increases; therefore, reductions in appropriations would be the only way to achieve a balanced budget. Furthermore, the only place where these reductions could be made were the Defense Department and/or the Mutual Security Program. McFarland's Majority Policy Committee recommended that the Appropriations and Armed Services Committees make a special study to cut defense spending, and that the Foreign Relations and Armed Services Committees hold mutual security aid down to $6.9 billion, a minimum of $1 billion below that requested. Congress expected the allies to pick up the slack.

Turning to domestic affairs, the committee urged quick extension of the Defense Production Act without amendment. Sensitive to McCarthy-era criticism, leadership espoused to root out corruption whether in public office or in private activities, while Democratic senators themselves would "measure up to the highest code of dignity and decency."

The Democratic statement continued by promising to seek a swift conclusion to the Korean conflict, to fight inflation by the extension of necessary economic controls, and to achieve greater efficiency in the operation of government. Mindful of election-year vicissitudes, leadership placed "the welfare of our country above the political advantage of any party," yet would "fight hard to win the national election," without stooping to "back-alley methods of mudslinging, distorting facts or vilifying opponents."[5]

Senator McFarland had set his own agenda of legislative priorities as well, advocating not only increased social security benefits and further extension of educational benefits and housing and business loan measures under the Korean GI Bill, but also interests unique to his state, such as additional benefits for Arizona Indian tribes. The senator also hoped for passage in the House of the Central Arizona Project bill, which had now twice gone through the Senate under his guidance. The majority leader looked ahead to an intense five-month schedule if he were to meet his self-prescribed deadline of early July.[6]

Numerous aspects of the session caused great concern. For one, Congress operated under the continued pall and duress of controversial investigations of government figures and organizations. An inquiry into Attorney General J. Howard McGrath's management of the Justice Department conducted by Truman-appointee and Republican Newbold Morris resulted in the firing of McGrath and the ruin of Morris. The House conducted this affair as well as scrutiny of the Bureau of Internal Revenue over alleged tax scandals. Moreover, there were highly visible, perpetual, endless, interminable, ceaseless investigations conducted by the House Un-American Activities Committee, seemingly discerning pernicious communist influence everywhere from pulpits and boardrooms to the UN and philanthropic organizations, not to mention everywhere within the government. Not to be outdone by the lower body, Pat McCarran's Senate Internal Security Subcommittee competed in the witch hunt with investigations of U.S.- China policy and subversion in the United Nations. McCarthyism gained momentum as the Eighty-second Congress wore on.[7]

McFarland only indirectly participated in these activities, but the questionable status of the Reconstruction Finance Corporation hit close to home, having long been favored by Mac for its assistance to small businesses in Arizona. It, however, also served larger operations as well and stood suspect of favoritism. Mac disdained suspicion and denied having ever influenced anyone on behalf of an RFC loan, stating his files "were open to anybody." Assistant Roland Bibolet remembers a reporter showing up at the Senate Office Building, claiming "I'm anybody. I want to see your RFC files." From the floor of the Senate, Mac phoned "Let him see it." The reporter found no evidence of influence peddling and, in fact, determined that most cases coming through McFarland's office were turned down. In this effort to abolish and redistribute the functions of the RFC, McFarland supported its continuance and with such a precarious situation had to tread softly yet work hard to allow the RFC to survive by the final 39-36 vote.[8]

The question of control of tideland oil deposits off coastal submerged lands led to a very unusual situation for the majority leader. On March 7, 1952, McFarland offered a resolution "to protect the interests of the U.S. in the oil and gas deposits on submerged lands in the continental shelf." State or federal regulation and ownership of these deposits provided the forum for debate. Texas Democrat Tom Connally first amended the resolution and then fellow coastal Senator Spessard Holland of Florida joined, until it "completely revised the McFarland resolution and gave to the states complete control of waters up to three miles beyond their shorelines." The amendment passed and Mac promptly voted against his own amended resolution which had now changed beyond recognition.

McFarland fell on the losing side here as the resolution passed both the Senate 50 to 35 and the House 265 to 109. In general, conservative Southern senators, mostly from states with shoreline, supported the resolution as did Republicans. Twenty-six Republicans, including Taft, favored the measure along with twenty-four Democrats including Russell. Eleven Republicans opposed, as did twenty-four Democrats. Lyndon Johnson found himself in an uncomfortable and potentially embarrassing situation here as the whip opposing the administration line, but with the Texas coastline in his home base, he had little choice. Mac understood and "let him run with it," although he continued to support the president. In the end, victory for shoreline Democrats and Republicans disappeared, however, when President Truman vetoed the bill, stating "it makes a gift of immensely valuable resources, which belong to the whole nation." LBJ, Connally, House Speaker Sam Rayburn, and others, such as oil magnate Bob Kerr expressed dismay and assumed that the veto confirmed "the Truman Administration is determined to ride roughshod over the rights of the states." Much to McFarland's satisfaction and scheduling control, Congress failed to take action to override the veto. It was left to the Eisenhower administration to later turn these deposits over to the states.

This tidelands oil situation revealed a murkier area in the McFarland-LBJ relationship. While the senate whip managed to avoid much of the leadership criticism that attached most frequently to the majority leader alone, there were times when LBJ was "not a good assistant." When oil loomed as an issue, Johnson would demur on persuasive manipulation on other issues of those senators upon whom he depended for state-controlled offshore deposits. Drew Pearson wrote, "he has adopted a policy of antagonizing no one – a policy which has won him the nickname 'lying down Lyndon.'" Roland Biblolet concurs that Johnson biographers have exaggerated his efficiency and cast him in too positive a light. He too can bear some of the responsibility for senate absenteeism and scheduling difficulties. In retrospect, it became apparent to these writers that if anything went wrong, it was laid on the shoulders of McFarland, while that which was right was attributed to Johnson. There is a discrepancy here, which can in part be charged to LBJ's magnetism, personal interest in oil, and rising in the Senate. Yet, McFarland rarely criticized his younger protegee and, as with all of his colleagues, cultivated a harmonious relationship. While later and with hindsight, McFarland claims to have taken LBJ "reluctantly" in some cases, there existed enduring mutual respect. When Biblolet left Johnson's staff to work with McFarland when he became governor, LBJ sent him a letter: "I have never known a man for whom I had more real affection and respect than Ernest McFarland," and in later years, Mac was a frequent visitor at the Johnson White House. Moreover, Johnson benefited from his tenure with McFarland, inheriting Mac's good points at negotiation, compromise, and earthiness, while adding his own sharp edge to these.[9]

Senator McFarland, too, sometimes turned against the administration line, such as taking a more conservative stance on immigration law. Introduced by Nevada's McCarran, the Immigration and Nationality Act of 1952 superseded all previous legislation in these areas. The bill removed racial bars to naturalization, granted quotas to each of the "free" nations of Asia, allowed American female citizens to bring in alien husbands outside of quota restrictions, and gave alien husbands of resident woman aliens preferred quota status. This constituted the liberal side of the bill. On the other hand, it also retained the controversial 1924 national origins quota system that favored northern and western over southern and Eastern Europe. It also provided for stiffer penalties, including deportation, for aliens convicted of criminal violations and contained measures to control domestic communism.

Liberals like Hubert Humphrey and President Truman urged a relaxation of the strict features of the act including larger quotas for southeastern Europeans and the capacity to transfer the often unused quotas of northwestern Europe to areas suffering intense war refugee problems. These suggestions failed, and the bill passed the Senate by voice vote and the House 206 to 68.

President Truman vetoed the act to the satisfaction of civil rights activists, claiming it was "worse than the infamous Alien Act of 1798." Not impressed, Congress voted to override 278-113 in the House, seventeen more than necessary, and 57 to 26 in the Senate, just one more than necessary. The vote cut across party lines with twenty-five Democrats and thirty-two Republicans for override and eighteen Democrats and eight Republicans standing by the president.[10]

Immigration and civil rights historians considered the vote "ugly and reactionary and a major embarrassment. A switch of two votes would have made the difference. It was therefore infuriating that Majority Leader McFarland and Majority Whip Lyndon Johnson voted against the president." Pulliam's pro-Republican Phoenix newspapers felt differently and commended McFarland and his colleague Senator Hayden, who had also voted to override: "Mr. Truman was obviously very wrong, indeed, to have such faithful Democratic wheel horses balk. . . . The new independence [of McFarland and Hayden] is deserving of praise."[11]

The issue of Mexican nationals in the U.S. workforce, whether they be legally hired braceros or illegal, undocumented immigrants, also overlapped into the civil rights arena during this busy month of March. McFarland found himself in a tight place stuck between his traditionally supportive constituents. Organized labor legitimately felt threatened by Mexican labor, which worked at far cheaper rates than American. Southwestern farmers defended the practice of hiring Mexicans because "American workers were unreliable . . . sometimes deserted the fields at harvest time . . . might even strike when crops were ripe . . . tantamount to un-Americanism . . . disliked stoop labor . . . and Mexicans were more productive anyway." Arizona farmers backed up their contention by noting that WWII veterans lacked motivation to work; they could toil in the fields for a ten-hour day, seven-day week for $17.50 or join the "52-20 Club" and receive a year's compensation at $20 per week without working at all. New Mexico Senator Clinton Anderson lamented the "alacrity with which immigration authorities were returning wetbacks to Mexico," thus decreasing what he felt constituted necessary labor. By 1950, the number of workers returned across the Rio Grande had reached a half-million annually.

After a year of investigations and recommendations on the problem, President Truman determined to side with the AFL, the CIO, and Mexican-American groups who complained that braceros and illegal workers depressed wages for American Hispanic and black minorities. Senator McFarland faced the expiration of the authorized bracero program in 1952 (ongoing since World War II) and Truman's threat not to renew it unless something were done about illegal workers. At the president's request, McFarland presented him with the so-called "wetback bill" which, signed into law, made it a "felony to employ or harbor illegal immigrants, and authorized immigration agents to search factories and fields without a warrant." McFarland thus sided with the administration and labor and against the position of Arizona's large farmers.[12]

Regarding other issues, McFarland initially did not side

with the administration over the president's action in the steel strike in spring 1952. He did, however, return to support the president in the later stages of the controversy, thus siding with conservative members of the Senate at first and ending in support of the liberal position which, however, ultimately failed.

On March 20, steel companies refused to abide by a Wage Mediation Board award of higher wages to workers without a rise in steel prices and the workers walked out. President Truman invoked emergency powers and used troops to seize the mills without invoking the Taft-Hartley Act, which critics sarcastically reminded Truman was designed specifically to ameliorate such situations. Republicans nationwide and the Pulliam press in Arizona decried his act as favoritism to the workers. Taft-Hartley would have kept them on the job by imposing an injunction mandating another eighty days cooling-off period without pay changes. Steel owners appealed directly to the U.S. Supreme Court to rule on the procedure.

Senator McFarland came out against Truman's move claiming, "I would never use inherent [emergency] powers of the Constitution when express legislative powers [Taft-Hartley] are available." This could be perceived as distancing himself from the executive decision, but in reality, the majority leader was going by the book. Thus, the Senate censured the seizure, 44 to 31, denying funding to facilitate it; Mac voted with the majority stating that it was "a clear encroachment upon the duties and responsibilities [the appeal to be decided] of the judicial branch."[13]

The court ruled that Truman's seizure exceeded authority except under express congressional legislation, and the president turned the steel companies back to the owners. The workers, who had stayed on the job under the direction of the federal secretary of commerce, now struck in earnest, and the president tried to obtain the legislation to again seize and operate the mills.

Although McFarland had opposed Truman earlier when the workers did remain on the job under federal supervision, now that the work had halted entirely, he supported the president, stating "Congress ought to pass a seizure bill and get the steel mills back to work." Indeed, there existed a possibility of a national emergency if the Korean War were to escalate or if hostilities broke out elsewhere. "We should not take a chance," intoned McFarland. Aligned with his opinion were such liberal Democrats as Estes Kefauver.

Conservative party members led by Virginia's Harry Byrd and Senator Taft's Republicans opposed, however. First they voted 49 to 30 to "request" [a stronger word] rather than "recommend" the president to invoke Taft-Hartley. The next day, June 11, the Senate voted 54 to 26 to deny the president's request to seize the mills. In both cases, Senator McFarland voted with the minority in upholding the position of labor and President Truman. Ultimately the strike ended on July 24, with Truman's intervention and mediation towards a $.16-per-hour wage hike, and a $5.20-per-ton price increase, and a modified closed shop. Fortunately, no emergency situation arose.[14]

Members of the Eighty-second Congress vigorously contested financing mutual security and foreign aid. In March, President Truman sent Congress a special message requesting $7.9 billion in foreign aid appropriations for the upcoming fiscal year. Senator Connally "lashed out in angry protest against the size of the program," stating "the United States can't go on forever appropriating large sums of money and was under no obligation to do so." Senator Taft backed him, advocating a cut of $1.9 billion. Opposed stood Mutual Security Administrator Averell Harriman, who felt Truman's request was "on the low side," and General Eisenhower, who allowed that "any cuts greater than a billion dollars would endanger the proposed military build-up and security of the United States." Senate and House committees did cut this $1 billion, but with Taft-supporters in control in the House, another $726.5 million was cut. The measure passed the lower chambers 245 to 110, slashing aid to just under $6.2 billion.

In the Senate, the Taft faction, led also by Senator William Knowland of California, proposed that a further one billion dollars be cut in addition to the already accepted one billion depletion. This measure failed 35 to 27, but the Senate then trimmed two hundred million making the total reduction $1.2 billion. Conferees eventually reached a figure for foreign aid of $6,447,730,750, and this bill passed slashing about $1.5 billion from Truman's original request. The bill constituted a defeat for both liberal Truman Democrats and moderate Eisenhower Republicans.[15]

Senator McFarland was definitely on the losing side, although, as majority leader, he had to enter into the spirit of negotiation and compromise demanded for the passage of appropriations and other legislation. In keeping with both the Majority Policy Committee Report and his own concern for adequate foreign aid, he voted against all the original cuts but for the final bill.

As the session wore on, the ominous reality and responsibility of the upcoming campaign intruded on McFarland's schedule. In mid-April, Senator McFarland returned to Arizona to address the Western Political Science Association in Tucson. In his speech, he commented that "Senate playboys gradually disappear." Supporters of his election opponent, Barry Goldwater, immediately jumped on this statement as a veiled reference to their candidate. McFarland advocates countered by pointing to a March 19 speech by Goldwater. Urging party militancy, he stated that "Senator McFarland formerly was a clean, honest American but had now succumbed to political pressure and condoned dishonest government," in reference to the scandals, however minor, of the Truman Administration.[16]

As the style of vindictive campaign rhetoric evolved, its character could be accredited, in part, to a coup staged by the challenger, Goldwater, in acquiring the services of Stephen Shadegg as his campaign manager. Carl Hayden, who had employed Shadegg for his 1950 campaign, recommended him to McFarland in 1952 as a speechwriter. Shadegg's asking price was too high and, in any case, Mac was a hands-on campaigner who would have found it very difficult to hand over major responsibility to someone outside his circle. So Shadegg determined to work for Goldwater instead. His apostasy, in retrospect, simply illustrated Arizona's growing ties to Republican influence. As the South began in the late 1940s to shift from exclusive Democratic to Republican allegiances, and this change gained momentum in the 1950s, and reached Arizona where the crossovers were scornfully known by loyal Demcrats as Pintos, so designated for their "spotty" character (a Pinto is a horse of many colors). The term Pinto Democrat was used derisively by party regulars throughout the 1960s as Arizona completed the shift to Rebublican dominance; along the way, Pintos often joined coalitions with Republicans, which heightened the contempt regular Democrats had for their former brethren. Most of the new Republicans were actually non-southern transplants (largely from the Midwest and California) in the the explosively-growing state, but enough were Pintos to feed the everlasting resentment of loyal Democrats.

The most prominent Pinto of 1952 was not Shadegg, but Lewis W. Douglas. A Democrat of unsurpassed prestige and well-connected to copper and business interests, he had represented the state for three non-consecutive terms dating back to 1922 in Congress; then he became President Roosevelt's budget director from 1933-36 before disagreements in policy catalyzed his resignation. He then served as ambassador to Great Britain under Truman from 1948 to 1951. In Tucson, on May 3, the distinguished Arizonan initiated a sweeping indictment of the Democratic party, which he felt "had departed from the faith of its fathers but still has an honorable roll to play if it avoids the whole variety of cheap, claptrap political paraphernalia which has made politics in this country increasingly sordid." Douglas later telegraphed McFarland:

> My dear Mac: Because of my personal friendship with you, I think it only courteous to tell you that for reasons which you may not understand, but which are very persuasive to me, I am going to support Barry Goldwater. It was not an easy decision to make. I hope at least that it will not mar our friendship.

The Pulliam press applauded Douglas' speech as "a masterful analysis of our political system and the perilous by-road from which America has turned."[17]

Returning to Washington D.C. with mixed feelings, McFarland put the election aside for a moment and set his sights on securing legislation in areas of high personal interest; namely, Social Security and veterans' benefits. He had twice successfully led the fight for increased Social Security benefits, in 1946 and 1948, and after seeing his requested amount cut by approximately one-third, his third effort passed the Senate in the 1951 session only to die in the House. Now, on May 12, 1952, he began to lobby once again for passage of his full 1951 request for $5 per month increases for the aged, blind, and disabled, and $3 per month for their dependent children. He stated to the Senate:

> You and I know that these people do not even have the everyday things which most of us consider necessities. They have no money to buy luxuries. In fact, they consider themselves fortunate if they have a roof over their heads. . . . I know how proud they are and how reluctant to ask for help. They have no organized lobby and are dependent on us. . . . The majority do not write; they just pray that somehow the suffering of their remaining years will be alleviated. . . . This is not going to be the salvation. It is not a King's ransom. The Consumer Price index has moved up 17.2 points [since the last increase in 1948] while the federal contribution . . . has remained virtually the same. How anyone could object to it, I cannot understand. Those who do not wish to take care of these needy persons can always find some excuse and usually do."

Off-the-record, he criticized Senator Taft's opposition and further stated "I care not about the authorship of this measure [his amendment]. I want some results." President Truman then entered the fray blaming Republican "scare tactics" when the measure was initially defeated. He termed present benefits "Plain inadequate. . . ." The bill finally passed on June 26, and marked Mac's tactic of asking for small amounts on frequent occasions, in confidence of obtaining something at least part of the time. He alone sponsored the only three increases for the aged, blind, and disabled during his senate years 1941-53.[18]

Senator McFarland also found time away from his majority leadership duties to continue his efforts on behalf of veterans. On May 19, Senator Lister Hill of Alabama introduced for himself and the majority leader S.3199, the Veterans Readjustment Assistance Act of 1952. The bill provided "vocational readjustment and restoration of lost educational opportunities" to armed forces personnel serving on or after June 27, 1950, the date of the commencement of the Korean conflict. A similar bill was reported successfully out of committee in the House and in total, some three dozen veterans' benefits bills were introduced in the 1952 session as the legislators all now willingly recognized the immensity of the Korean conflict, which had been raging for two years.

McFarland did not get everything he wanted, but the final 1952 legislation that passed constituted a great improvement on the limited 1951 Korean GI Bill. Besides increasing existing benefits, the updated measure provided educational aid paid directly to the veteran for tuition, books, miscellaneous education expenses, and personal subsistence payments. It was estimated that the program would cost one billion dollars a year, and more than three million people would be directly compensated. Moreover, the benefits were made available to personnel whether they had served in Korea or elsewhere. Veterans of peacetime service (non-Korea) would be paid at eighty percent the rate for wartime. President Truman signed the bill into law on May 23, 1952. This revised Korean GI Bill along with the Communications Act of 1952 marked McFarland's last major legislation in the U.S. Senate.[19]

As the session neared its end, the majority leader turned his attention to state interests. In a rather unique effort, he obtained the silver service of the battleship U.S.S. *Arizona* for the state capitol's museum in 1952. Initially told by Navy officials that such a service did not exist, McFarland insisted to the contrary. He pushed the investigation, which revealed the silver had been removed from the ship before Pearl Harbor and then reassigned to the U.S.S. *Tucson* after the *Arizona* was sunk in the Japanese attack of December 7, 1941. It remained with the *Tucson* until that ship was decommissioned in 1949, when the service was reassigned to the U.S.S. *Adirondack*. The silver, which had been purchased with contributions from the people of the state, was formally donated at the 1919 commissioning of the *Arizona* and had since been acknowledged as the "finest" in the Navy. It now seemed to have found an appropriate home, for the *Adirondack*, stationed in the Mediterranean, served as flagship of the Commander-in-Chief, Allied Forces, Southern Europe. Nevertheless, McFarland pointed out that the *Arizona* had never been decommissioned, remaining a memorial with a twenty-four hour honor guard. Under Navy rules, silver could be removed only from a decommissioned ship, and McFarland obtained legislation to expedite the return. The Navy agreed, ordering the silver set home in July 1952, where it has remained on display in the Capitol Building in Phoenix.[20]

Senator McFarland proved less fortunate in his efforts to obtain a U.S. national military cemetery for the state. Arizona veterans' organizations and Governor Howard Pyle requested such action, and the senator introduced a bill to authorize the Army to acquire an appropriate site. The Army expressed agreement noting that the state's veteran population of 72,000 warranted free interment benefits and that the nearest national cemeteries were in San Diego, Santa Fe, Fort Bliss, Texas, and Fort Logan, Colorado, all four to six hundred miles away. Unfortunately, Arizona Congressman John Murdock and Mac's own timetable combined to defeat his bill. After passing the Senate unanimously, Lloyd Bentsen's (D-TX) House Interior Subcommittee appproved the measure but, ironically, Interior Chairman Murdock held up final approval. Murdock spoke of numerous complaints from private cemetery associations and opponents over high maintenance costs and wasting the taxpayers' money. Murdock also stated that many national cemetery bills stood before Arizona's on the calendar, and he may also have wanted to avoid appearing biased, for his own son had died in the war. Time ran out, and the bill died in the House.[21]

It proved necessary for McFarland to put CAP on a back burner during all of this session activity. Ultimately California's successful obstructionism coupled with the ongoing emergency of the Korean War and mounting domestic problems of the Truman administration led McFarland to abandon efforts at congressional passage of CAP during the second session. Later in the year, on August 13, 1952, Arizona resorted to the only recourse left to it: filing suit in the U.S. Supreme Court against California for adjudication of the waters of the Colorado River, ironically reversing roles and implementing the unsuccessful move California had earlier attempted with such determination. The battle for CAP had entered a new stage, and congressional legislation for the project would not be re-introduced for another twelve years.

With CAP sidelined, McFarland's primary state concern during 1952 looked to continuing and upgrading assistance to Arizona's Indian population. In this endeavor, he met with a mixture of success and failure. Upon requesting $6.5 million for construction of roads, schools, and irrigation facilities for both the Navajo and Papago, he stated on June 25, 1952:

> The federal government has not done the right thing by the Indians. Had we rehabilitated the Indian years ago, he would have already been assimilated into the life of the white people and would have been treated as one of them. But what did we do? We sent the Navajo, Hopi, and Papago Indians out to the desert where, as a matter of fact, they were prisoners, because they were not permitted to leave the reservation.
> There are approximately 25,000 Navajo children of school age. Of this number, 15,000 are without school facilities. The Navajos made a splendid record in World War II. They fought for their country, and they should not be deprived of the privilege of sending their children to school. We send money overseas to rehabilitate foreign nations, but we whittle down appropriations designed to take care of the Indians

who are good citizens and all they want is good substantial buildings and an opportunity for their children
to attend schools.

In view of cultural plurality, McFarland's phrasing and
ideas on assimilation today, seem old fashioned, but he truly
held the Indians' interest at heart. Press reports continued,
"The McFarland amendment, which won such sympathy, it
even surprised its author . . . [was approved] by a whopping 49
to 29 . . . [and] was practically the only increase adopted by the
Senate in passing a $567 million bill for the operation of the
Interior Department starting July." High hopes led to great disappointment, however, as the conference committee wiped out
the amendment entirely.[22]

McFarland's long-range planning under the neglected
Navajo-Hopi Rehabilitation Act and new measures for the
Papago also met with mixed results. Traditional liberal but
perennial fiscal conservative Senator Paul Douglas opposed
and desired to cut eight million dollars from the $51 million
appropriations bill for Indians. Douglas contended that the
Indian Bureau's maintenance of one employee for every thirty
Indians was excessive and that Indian schools were "fancy,
flossy places." He based this conclusion on having visited only
the Phoenix Indian School, admittedly a beautiful facility, but
hardly representative of Indian schools throughout Arizona
and the West in general. Douglas' effort, however, failed by a
decisive voice vote.

A very high percentage of the Indian budget was earmarked for Arizona construction under the Navajo-Hopi
Rehabilitation Act, and the House had already cut the overall
total from thirty million to less than five million dollars.
Appropriations Chair Hayden supported McFarland and
Arizona's Indians by restoring twenty million, specifying twelve
to fifteen for Arizona use. The final appropriations as passed by
Congress for the fiscal year beginning July 1, 1952, alloted
$10.5 million for construction of roads, schools, hospitals, and
other projects on the Navajo-Hopi Reservation and a one mil-

lion dollar loan for reservation businesses. Additionally, a fund of three hundred thousand dollars continued payments to indigent Indians other than the Navajo and Hopi. New Mexico Senator Dennis Chavez termed McFarland's "Watchdog" committee efforts on behalf of Indians "tireless. . . . If these Indian citizens had as ardent champions in the other House of Congress . . . a more rosy future would lie ahead of them."[23]

As McFarland worked to end the session by the scheduled time, he realized that some of his goals, including major parts of the Fair Deal, would fail. Doomed were statehood bills for Alaska and Hawaii. Purportedly, Republicans awaited a GOP administration to gain credit for new state admissions as they did under Eisenhower in 1959. The road to statehood had already been paved, and with only minimal support, the territories would have been admitted under Truman.

A bill to begin cooperative construction with Canada on the St. Lawrence Seaway, which McFarland, Truman, and Taft supported, failed, being sent back to committee by a 43-40 vote. Opposed were seaboard senators, whether from the South or Northeast, who feared a loss of trade to the inland states to be tapped by the seaway. Finally, Fair Deal programs for civil rights, national health insurance, agriculture, and revising the Taft-Hartley Act were scuttled. To repeat, however, much of the proposed Fair Deal legislation had met defeat before McFarland had assumed leadership.[24]

McFarland closed senate proceedings by the stipulated time, July 7, 1952, the final days again highlighted by the traditional tributes to the majority leader. Fellow Democrats were effusive in their praise, Herbert O'Conor of Maryland speaking of Mac's "fairness and valuable ability to work out satisfactory agreements on controversial matters." Liberal Senator Herbert H. Lehman of New York, who had often criticized Mac, alluded to serious difficulties and many differences that had been ironed out, some with the House as well as in the Senate, due to "the patience and great degree of skill with which the majority leader has handled affairs." Emphasizing Mac's courtesy, consideration, and engaging personality, Tennessee's aging Kenneth

McKellar stated, "During the long time I have been in the Senate, I do not think we have ever had a leader who has been more successful than the senator from Arizona."

While these colleagues spoke in general terms, others were specific in their praise for McFarland. Colorado's Edwin Johnson outlined Mac's role in representing his state: "a majority leader who never forgot that second responsibility. It has been closer to his heart than the honor he has achieved in the [majority leader] role more in the country's eye." New Mexico's Dennis Chavez again highlighted McFarland's consideration of Indians: "Indeed in him they have a friend," while Nevada's Pat McCarran related his concern for mining interests, emphasizing McFarland's "consistency and diligence." Hubert Humphrey praised the majority leader's work on attaining civilian control of atomic energy: "great leadership in guiding us through the settlement of a most vital problem." Washington's Senator Warren Magnuson selected Social Security as an area for praising McFarland, whose "success in obtaining assistance for these people represents one of the greatest accomplishments in this field in the history of the Senate. They could not have a finer champion or friend." Perhaps most significant were the words of Alabama's Lister Hill who drew attention to McFarland's successful efforts on behalf of veterans.

> In this field, the activities of the majority leader, the junior senator from Arizona, have been outstanding. He has sponsored and fought for the veterans not only of his own state but of the nation. . . . He has been farseeing and aggressive. Few in Congress, I believe, have a finer record of helping the men and women of the armed services, past and present, than Senator McFarland.

From the Republican side of the aisle, New Jersey's H. Alexander Smith spoke of "the fine service which the majority leader has rendered to all of us . . . his uniform courtesy and assistance." Senator Styles Bridges had replaced Senator Wherry who had died just before the session, as minority leader.

From his vantage point of the front-row, center-aisle chair directly opposite McFarland's, he spoke for the record: "I appreciate the excellent judgment of the Democrats in selecting Ernest McFarland as their leader because of his fairness, impartiality, courtesy, and kindness."

On July 5, Whip Lyndon Johnson made the longest and most complimentary statement concerning McFarland's work, submitting to the *Congressional Record* the more than sixty measures that McFarland had introduced during his twelve-year career and that had gone on to pass the Senate or become public law: (see Appendix II; over forty became law.)

> Mr. President, as the majority whip of the Senate, I take this opportunity to extend my heartiest congratulations to Senator McFarland for the extremely able manner in which he has performed his duties as majority leader during the Eighty-second Congress.
>
> Senator McFarland has occupied a difficult position, and has acquitted himself well. He has brought to his post of leadership ability, talent, conscientiousness, honesty, and a spirit of co-operation which have made him liked on both sides of the aisle.
>
> His outstanding characteristic, however, is that he trusts the Senate. He trusts the Senate, and the Senate trusts him.
>
> He is not one to block the will of the Senate. He is not a man who seeks to defeat legislation by indirect processes and by foreclosing opportunities to debate and vote.
>
> He believes in the democratic method, and he believes that the Senate is the sole judge of its own destiny.
>
> To my mind, this mutual trust between the Senate and Senator McFarland is the true source of his success as majority leader. He has faced up to the issues and because he has, he has helped to save our position of world leadership.
>
> When efforts were made to whittle away at the defenses of our lives and liberties, he took a courageous, forthright stand. I believe that the Senate recognized his courage and his forthrightness, and that

they were the basic factors in rescuing our military preparedness.

I spent a quiet evening in my home the other night, with the Speaker of the House [Sam Rayburn] -- the distinguished and able gentleman from my own State of Texas. The Speaker is rounding out his fourth decade in the House. He has served as Speaker longer than any other man in history. As he looked back over the years, he told me that there has never before been better co-operation, and greater trust, between the two branches of Congress. He said that co-operation and trust exist because Ernest McFarland is one of the ablest, one of the most genuine, one of the finest men he has ever known.

The people of the United States owe a deep debt of gratitude to Arizona for the quality of the Senators it sends to Washington.

Except for the long, hard hours and the fine states-manship that Ernest McFarland has put into his task, many legislative problems of the Senate would never have been solved.

We of the Southwest know that there is a great day in the offing for our part of the country. We know that there are new economic empires to be built, new resources to be tapped, new industries to spring from our vast lands. But for the people of Arizona, that day has dawned already in the Senate. With Ernest McFarland as majority leader and Carl Hayden as the ranking member of the Senate Appropriations Committee, they are assured of the finest representa-tion that they can obtain.

No state--great or small, rich or poor-- has sent better men to Washington than has Arizona. The people of that State are to be congratulated for their wise selection. The Nation has been enriched.

On July 7, Vice President Alben Barkley, a four-decade veteran presiding, included the following among his closing statements:

I know something about the obligations, burdens, and responsibilities of the majority leader. I wish to

> say that not since I have been in the Senate has there been a majority leader who has worked more diligently, more conscientiously and more successfully to accomplish the purposes of the Senate than has the Senator from Arizona (Mr. McFarland). It has been a pleasure for me as Vice President to work with him and to give him any assistance within my power.

One does have to acknowledge that such complimentary, concluding remarks as these were often more form than content and indicative of a "club" mentality, but in McFarland's case they, too, were sincere and deserved. Thus, the Eighty-second Congress came to a close as many of the senators, including the majority leader returned to their home states to prepare for the upcoming 1952 elections.[25]

To assess accurately Ernest McFarland's majority leadership, one must consider the priorities of the nation during the years 1951 and 1952. Without question, those priorities lay in the area of foreign affairs. The Korean War was only six months old and going against the U.S. when he assumed the position, and the ongoing challenges of the Cold War continued in Europe while polticians and constituents alike attempted to learn to live with the bomb. It is not without some irony that McFarland, who was considered most informed on a broad range of domestic issues, was thrust into leadership during these times of foreign crisis. Faced with this challenge, he acquitted himself well by keeping the Senate on line toward a largely harmonious and bipartisan foreign policy. His skill at assuaging tempers and smoothing ruffled feathers was notable, and even in the acrimonious setting of the McCarthy era, he was able to work effectively through negotiation and compromise.

Unfortunately for McFarland's record, foreign demands engendered domestic sacrifices. Harry Truman's Fair Deal remained in abeyance as it had for the two years of Scott Lucas's leadership. McFarland must be held partially responsible for this along with Truman, Humphrey, and Douglas who were at the mercy of the Republican-Southern Democrat coalition stubbornly and skillfully led by Taft and Russell.

Yet, McFarland, too, emerged as partially responsible for many of the important changes in Social Security and veterans' benefits. He also effectively represented the interests of his state. This domestic credibility, coupled with the fact of increased stability in foreign affairs by 1952's end, redounds to his credit. The Korean War settled into a less combative period, and negotiations leading to the armistice of June 1953 had begun. In Europe, economic and political tensions had abated, somewhat, from previous conditions.

The United States embarked on a postwar path of free world leadership during the Truman era, all predicated on the containment of communism. The national commitment that he helped engender deepened in the passing decades until by the late 1960s, Truman's hard line foreign policy enabled him to become something of a conservative Republican hero. Although his Fair Deal had faded from the national memory, much had been implemented by LBJ's Great Society programs, and he stood as the foremost architect of America's worldwide anti-communist stance. As one of architect Truman's most conspicuous contractors, Mac's role, however, was quickly forgotten. He lived to see Truman lionized, and must have deeply felt the lack of recognition beyond the immediate circle of family and close political associates. Yet, the majority leader acted as an enabler and expediter as the government machine kept its course. McFarland is to be commended for his facilitative and contributory role during this two-year period, one that presented great challenges that he largely overcame. He had, in fact, brought order to a chaotic Senate.

PART IV

THE GUBERNATORIAL YEARS
1952-1958

CHAPTER ELEVEN

VICTORY FROM DEFEAT
THE ELECTIONS OF
1952 AND *1954*

THE REPUBLICAN PARTY LOOKED FORWARD to the elections of 1952 with optimism at both the national and state levels. President Harry Truman's popularity languished over the conduct of the Korean War, the firing of General Douglas MacArthur, domestic scandals, and economic problems. Aspiring Republican presidential candidates took advantage of 1952 "Lincoln Day" speeches to voice their criticism of the president. In Denver, former Minnesota Governor Harold Stassen called for "ending seven years of mismanaged Missouri misrule;" in Seattle, Ohio Senator Robert M. Taft, as had MacArthur, recommended the use of Chiang Kai-shek's Formosan troops against the North Koreans; and California Governor Earl Warren, speaking in Boston, urged Republicans to give leadership to "a bewildered nation."[1]

Republican expectations extended to gaining control of Congress as well, particularly the Senate. The GOP then held forty-six seats to a majority fifty for the Democrats. There were thirty-five to be contested in the November general elections, and if the GOP could gain three, it would capture the majority. Strategists set about the task of successfully achieving this end, and targeted Majority Leader McFarland for defeat.

Indeed, GOP confidence ran high in Arizona as the state moved toward two-party status for the first time since 1930 when the last Republican governor occupied the statehouse.

First-term Governor Howard Pyle now spearheaded this Republican resurgence along with the enormous public influence and backroom power wielded by newspaper magnate Eugene Pulliam, publisher of both Phoenix dailies, the *Arizona Republic* and the *Phoenix Gazette*. Supporting these men stood the popular one-term city councilman, department store owner, and photographer, Barry Goldwater, who had managed Pyle's 1950 gubernatorial campaign.

Pulliam waded into the upcoming political fracas with his shirt sleeves rolled up. His editorials celebrated the advantages of a two-party state and provided specific directions for changing political affiliation. He applauded the presidential candidates and Republican generals, stating "MacArthur has made the greatest contribution of any man in our time to Christian civilization," and "there is no greater advocate of freedom nor more violent opponent of communism than Eisenhower."[2]

Prominent national Republicans descended on Arizona fanning the partisan fires. Among them, Albert B. Hermann, campaign director for the Republican National Committee, called control of the Senate a "chief objective" for which the "Southwest holds the key." Pennsylvania Senator James H. Duff spoke in support of the Central Arizona Project in an attempt to erode some of Senator McFarland's well-established recognition in this area, and "Mr. Republican," Bob Taft, came into town to speak for his presidential interests and those of his party. Taft's opposition to water projects, however, worked against him, and Eugene Pulliam endorsed Eisenhower. Barry Goldwater echoed the publisher and, virtually unopposed, laid claim to the Republican nomination for the Senate.[3]

Goldwater, like his publisher-mentor, came out swinging. He accused McFarland of failing to represent the state, and noting his recent opposition to Truman's takeover of the steel industry, he charged that, "We find McFarland attempting to loosen from his neck the terrific weight of Truman." Pulliam backed Goldwater up, speaking oddly against the "creeping, galloping socialism" of the steel takeover.[4]

Republicans passed out more ammunition when the chairman of the Republican National Committee, Gay G. Gabrielson, appeared in Phoenix outlining five major complaints against the Democrats:

> 1) corruption in high places; 2) the attempt to socialize the United States; 3) the disgraceful infiltration of government by Communists; 4) high taxes and high prices; and 5) the fumbling indecisive foreign policy that is taking American blood in an undeclared Korean War that we refuse to try to win and can't afford to lose. . . . He [McFarland] is the Senate spokesman for the Truman New Deal-Fair Deal crowd. They have used him to defend their pitiful record. We are counting on every Republican as well as Independents and thoughtful Democrats to see to it that Goldwater is sent to the Senate.[5]

Too, the underlying defections of influential Democrats Lewis Douglas and Goldwater's manager Stephen Shadegg had further darkened the Democratic horizon. Yet, McFarland, the entrenched majority leader, remained confident of his chances against an upstart in national politics and pleased with support from labor organizations like The Brotherhood of Railway Clerks:

> Here in Arizona we are collecting such residents as Eugene C. Pulliam, publisher . . . also of the *Indianapolis Star*. These men and more like them who have migrated here with ways and plenty of means are working their puppets into City, County, and State Offices. They are so bold now that they are going to try and put one of their kind in the U.S. Senate in place of Senator McFarland. A Mr. Goldwater by name. He is just a tool in the hands of the sacred few.[6]

With the arrival of summer, attention turned away from state primary election preparations to the national conventions, both held in Chicago in July, with the Republicans commencing first. This foot race had dwindled to the expected two,

Eisenhower and Taft, with the ever-popular "Ike" prevailing. The GOP honored Howard Pyle as Arizona's first governor to speak before a major party convention, and the enthusiastic crowd warmly received this symbol of the resurgent Republican potential in the West. Pyle, an experienced radio personality, appealed to the assembled, stressing that the GOP constituted "the last hope of what is left of the free world." In the wake of the convention, Pulliam press support went out to even the thirty-nine year-old vice presidential nominee, Richard M. Nixon of California. Nixon had long been an inveterate enemy of Arizona water projects, but the editorials stated that, "The Hisshunter will help Ike. He is the one who can best dramatize the issue of Communist infiltration on the homefront. This fact, it seems to us is more important than Mr. Nixon's opposition to the Central Arizona Project."[7]

The Democratic Convention, which convened two weeks later, evolved as a more tangled matter after President Truman had earlier declined re-nomination. Vice President Alben Barkley, diplomat Averell Harriman, and Senators Estes Kefauver, Richard Russell, and Robert Kerr all were making the run. Movements for Speaker of the House Sam Rayburn and Illinois Governor Adlai Stevenson were also afoot. Surely Mac regarded this list with pride; all were cherished associates and friends and in his view deserving of high political recognition. He had served with Barkley and Rayburn on the "Big 4," known Kerr since youth, been supported by Russell for majority leader, and worked closely with Kefauver during the crime investigations. Averell Harriman had appeared on his radio show in the fall of 1951, as had Barkley, Rayburn, Russell and Kerr. Only Stevenson was somewhat out of Mac's loop. It would be a hard choice for Mac, one that might complicate his role as senate leader, perhaps even tarnish a friendship.

With Truman out of the race, the nomination was still undertimined when the convention opened. Majority Leader McFarland remauned silent on his choice while presiding with gavel in hand several times at the podium. His professional instincts as a party leader recommended a non-committal stance, although it is probable that he would like to have seen his fellow southerner-southwesterner and old college mate, Bob Kerr get the nod. In any case, Mac had his own campaign to worry about. President Harry Truman, however, did not remain silent, and ultimately his support and persuasion proved enough to bring the liberal Stevenson the hard won nomination. Mac then rallied behind the nominee, and Stevenson returned the favor by later campaigning in Arizona for his own and McFarland's ticket.[8]

After the conventions closed, the Arizona primary campaign escalated. Barry Goldwater had assiduously kept up his attack on his opponent while attempting to drum up support, some from unlikely sources. He criticized the deficit spending program of the "Truman socialistic left-wing crowd," and even entered an inner Democratic sanctum by attempting to garner the support of labor, addressing the AFL's Tucson Central Trades Council. The appearance served one ulterior purpose only, to garner press coverage from the Pulliam dailies, as the bid did not succeed and labor did not deliver. Yet, campaign manager Stephen Shadegg's strategy was sound. Goldwater, who had backed the successful "Right-to-Work" initiative in 1946, here spoke in support of the Taft-Hartley Act, both anti-organized labor positions. Goldwater's stance in addressing these issues in front of a traditionally critical audience had a positive effect. Hailed by the press as a gutsy, forlorn-hope mission, it could easily be construed by the public as an heroic assault and psychological victory for Goldwater.[9]

The McFarland-for-Senate machine officially swung into action on July 25 in his hometown Florence. In an impassioned opening salvo, he stated:

> In Congress, there is no substitute for experience. It would be unfair to our people and to the vital federal programs that affect our prosperity and growth if I were to relinquish to other states my seniority on committees controlling irrigation, reclamation, Indians, public lands, mines, and rail and air transportation. One who has such seniority and who also

holds such positions as chairman of the majority, chairman of the steering committee and Majority Leader is far more effective in helping to solve the legislative and federal administrative problems for the people of his state.

He continued by referring to Senator Lyndon Johnson's recent speech where the majority whip gave tribute to Mac's legislative efforts, and to House Speaker Sam Rayburn's statement that "there has never before been better cooperation and greater trust between the two branches of Congress."[10]

Indeed, "Speaker Sam" was coming to Arizona to boost Senator McFarland's campaign drive, and "McFarland Day" at Casa Grande on August 22 proved a gala affair. Gene Autry opened the proceedings singing some cowboy songs, one of which, "Cool Water," he dedicated to the senator. Then "Mr. Democrat" Rayburn took the stand applauding the honoree's record and experience: "If McFarland can't bring water to Arizona, no one can." Indeed, just recently Secretary of the Interior Oscar Chapman approved a right-of-way for canal construction from the Colorado River at Parker Dam to the Salt and Verde River confluence outside of Phoenix, a major water victory for the state engineered by Democrats.[11]

A few days later, Barry Goldwater appeared unimpressed by this. In an aggressive Tucson speech, he declaimed: "The world's richest cowboy singer from California came over and told you how to vote, and Harry Truman sent the gentleman from Bonham, Texas, out here to tell you to be sure and vote for Harry's personal spokesman. If I couldn't find anybody in Arizona to say a few kind words about me, I would stay out of the state." He also slighted the lack of an invocation at the Democratic rally stating, "The New Deal Party doesn't think God is necessary."[12]

The ensuing September 9 primary elections held no surprises. Senator McFarland, running unopposed, polled 108,992 Democratic votes, while Barry Goldwater received 33,460 from the Republicans, outdistancing his nearest rival eleven to one. It would now be his goal to obtain the votes of conservative and fence-sitting Pinto Democrats as well as to lure more voters out to the polls.[13]

A post-primary poll of approximately 2,500, or one percent of the state's registered voters, showed McFarland leading Goldwater by only forty-nine to forty-five percent despite a significant registration advantage for the Democrats. Clearly, many Pintos and Independents were leaning toward Goldwater, but his tally lagged far behind the preference indicated for Eisenhower, who received 58.5 percent. Goldwater, who drew support from professional, managerial, white collar, and female voters (his department stores featured conveniently-timed women's clothing sales) led in Phoenix but trailed in Tucson. McFarland's support came from farm and industry workers, the unemployed, and the retired.[14]

Barry Goldwater eagerly strove to narrow the gap and formally opened his campaign for the United States Senate in the old territorial capital and Goldwater family seat of Prescott on September 18. Campaign manager Shadegg maintained that this address was crucial to the final election outcome. The challenger referred to a speech where McFarland allegedly claimed he was one of the "four most powerful men in Washington." Goldwater then proceeded to ask if McFarland would therefore "accept 25 percent of the responsibility" for the various perceived misconducts of the Truman administration.

Later, Goldwater deviated from his prepared text referring to another alleged McFarland statement that the Korean War was "cheap, because we're killing nine Chinese for every American." Shadegg related "the statement had shocked and sickened Barry, who now shared the callous pronouncement with every Arizona citizen within the sound of a radio loudspeaker with the fighting rage of a man who has suddenly seen something dear and cherished pushed into the gutter." Goldwater concluded:

> I challenge the junior senator from Arizona to find anywhere within the borders of this state or within the borders of the United States, a single mother or father

who counts our casualties as cheap -- who'd be willing to exchange the life of one American for the nine Communists or 900 Red Communists, or 9,000,000 Communists.[15]

Ernest McFarland marshalled his forces for the general election campaign by assembling some "big guns" among Democrats. He received immediate post-primary support from presidential nominee Adlai Stevenson, who arrived in Phoenix on September 12, accompanied by Senator Hayden. Additional support included October appearances by fellow senators Estes Kefauver, Robert Kerr, and Lister Hill. Moreover, the national media joined in, and *Fortune* magazine, disregarding the closing gap, recognized McFarland's political clout, terming Republican chances "poor."

What Goldwater is up against now is the prestige and importance of McFarland, the veteran incumbent, member of the powerful Interior and Insular Affairs and Interstate and Foreign Commerce committees. Substituting Goldwater for McFarland would wipe out 12 years of Arizona Senate seniority which has produced many political plums.[16]

Challenger Goldwater argued against this stance, emphasizing the anti-Democratic "K^{1}C^2" theme of Korea, corruption, and communism. Surprisingly, he picked up additional support from a source that had historically been committed to the Democrats. The *Arizona Daily Star*, Tucson's largest paper, endorsed the Eisenhower-Pyle-Goldwater ticket citing the Democrats' fault for allowing the nation to enter three wars and stating "Senator McFarland should be retired."[17]

Goldwater, too, acquired prestigious campaign assistance on October 10, when Dwight Eisenhower campaigned in Phoenix and again on October 19, when Wisconsin Senator Joe McCarthy, still smarting from Mac's rebuke of a year earlier, brought his acerbic show to Tucson. In a typical performance, the self-styled "tailgunner" appeared on stage with a briefcase, continually withdrawing and replacing several "transcripts of testimony" alledgedly injurious to Democratic candidates and McFarland. Throughout this speech and with mock ingenius-ness, he "simulated absent-mindedness" and mixed up the first and last names of Adlai Stevenson and Alger Hiss. He described the Democratic organization as "dominated by Communists and Communist sympathizers, and having reached a point of almost complete moral degeneration," adding "McFarland has never raised a voice against Communism," a ridiculous, yet effective charge in the politically rabid climate of the day.[18]

In an effort to regain momentum, Senator McFarland revealed contributions to Goldwater of "thousands of dollars from Midwestern and Eastern politicians and a four thousand dollar contribution from Texas oil baron H.L. Hunt," with other Lone Star oilmen further sweetening the pot. Ultimately Goldwater outspent McFarland two-to-one, with fifty percent of his money coming from out-of-state. Mac also lashed out at the Pulliam press for lack of fair or sufficient front-page cover-age for Democratic candidates. As an example, he referred to a recent Adlai Stevenson speech under an Associated Press byline. It had been carried in full by the Republican *Los Angeles Examiner*, but the local *Republic* had deleted thirteen of eighteen column inches, including three paragraphs on Stevenson's explanation of his involvement with the Hiss case and his con-currence with the jury's decision of guilt.[19]

Goldwater found another soft spot in the Democratic armor when he charged abuse of senatorial mailing privileges. Terming the Democratic party as "stolen and corrupted by pinkos and phonies, crooks and cronies," he asked for an inves-tigation of McFarland's use of his own and Senator Lyndon Johnson's franking privileges. The senate whip had given per-mission for this use, and the majority leader had mailed out his voting record, as read into the *Congressional Record* by LBJ. The challenger also continually kept the spotlight on Korea as the war no one wanted to win. He also echoed MacArthur in advo-cating the use of Chiang Kai-shek's Chinese troops from Formosa and dismissed Democratic claims of stopping communism as ludicrous since the party could not even stop communism in the halls of Congress.[20]

McFarland turned attention from some of this criticism by noting his successes in veterans, water, communications, and Social Security legislation. Remaining confident until the end, some contend he did not campaign with his usual ardor during the final two weeks, while Barry Goldwater rapidly closed the diminishing gap and continued to build upon his long-growing momentum. This has been attributed not only to McFarland's late relaxation, a fact which Goldwater has suggested, but also to the proliferation of Burma-Shave style signs that mushroomed along the state's highways, bringing the message home: "Mac's for Harry, Harry's all through, you be for Barry, 'cause Barry's for you, Goldwater, for Senate." Roland Bibolet, however contends the signs meant little; the opposition of the Pulliam Press meant everything.[21]

The aggressive 1952 Republican campaign paid off for Barry Goldwater in Arizona and Dwight Eisenhower in the nation. Incumbent Senator and Majority Leader Ernest McFarland went down to a narrow defeat by 6,725 votes, the final tally at 132,063 to 125,338. Without question Goldwater rode Eisenhower's coattails to victory, for the popular "Ike" easily captured Arizona by more than forty-four thousand votes, 58.4 percent, far above Goldwater's 51.4 margin.

For the only time since 1920, Arizona had elected a Republican senator and governor. Howard Pyle scored even better than Eisenhower racking up a a sixty to forty percent victory, a gap of nearly fifty-three thousand. Newcomer John Rhodes fashioned a second upset over sixteen-year Democratic incumbent John Murdock by a margin of nearly ten-thousand votes for the U.S. House, and the incumbent Democratic attorney general went down to defeat by eighteen-thousand votes.[22]

Barry Goldwater's edge numbered the smallest of all the major candidates; thus, he stood as the one who most truly benefited from a number of factors including the nationwide Republican landslide and, most notably, McFarland's alleged overconfidence and the switchover of Pintos. During the primaries, approximately one hundred-five thousand Democrats and thirty-five thousand Republicans went to the polls, a total of one hundred-forty thousand registered voters. The apathy of the primaries was eclipsed by the immediacy of the general elections as eighty-one percent of the state's voters turned out, a total of 267,325, nearly doubling the primary vote. Somewhere the challenger managed to pick up close to one hundred thousand more tallies than in the primaries while the incumbent garnered only twenty thousand additional votes, a five-fold margin for Goldwater. Without question, a tremendous amount of the additional Republican vote came from crossover urban Democrats. Although Goldwater took only five of fourteen counties, he prevailed in the major cities of Phoenix, as expected, and Tucson where he had trailed only a few weeks before.[23]

Well-defined and observable factors influenced and substantiated the upset. Eisenhower's popularity was even eclipsed by that of Governor Pyle, giving the Republicans a very strong one-two punch with which to protect weaker candidates like Goldwater. McFarland remained tied to the sinking image of Truman and the relatively unknown Stevenson. Goldwater was himself very well known and popular in the cities as a civic leader and merchant. But his wide visibility in rural Arizona, too, was never acknowledged by Mac's political advisors. Goldwater had traveled all corners of the state in the 1940s taking and showing his masterful photographs of marvelous Arizona scenes, especially of Indians and the Grand Canyon. These trips, in fact, had made Goldwater a well-known and appreciated state figure long before 1952. Mac and the Democrats simply remained unaware of his stature and continued throughout the campaign to treat him as a political unknown. McFarland had never resided in either Phoenix or Tucson, and while now extremely well known, was only solidly entrenched in the state's extensive but under populated rural areas. He also had a down-home, country persona that clashed with the more urbane and sophisticated styles of Goldwater, Pyle, and a newly emerging Southwest. Moreover, the handsome Goldwater enjoyed the flashy image of a sportsman and a

"World War II fighter pilot," although he never saw action.

The major newspapers, particularly the Pulliam press, were responsible for emphasizing these qualities and constantly alerting the public to perceived Democratic deficiencies. No major newspaper supported McFarland, and he was kept on the defensive on the issues. Goldwater benefited significantly from the cooperative unity of the Republican party, and local appearances by Eisenhower, Taft, and McCarthy. Finally, Goldwater was greatly assisted by superior party organization and strategy in the hands of campaign manager Stephen Shadegg who emerged as a master political strategist and tactician. Mac's loyal assistant, Roland Bibolet, termed the campaign:

> a heartbreaker. McFarland was very much a methodical person and Goldwater was not. The Goldwater campaign was very bombastic, and he had the trends of the times with him; he was running with Eisenhower and against Truman. I think what really defeated McFarland was the absolute opposition of the two daily papers in Phoenix. . . . Those papers would really go after him hammer and tongs. . . . Goldwater was able to brand him as Truman's errand boy. But he wasn't an errand boy. He stood up many times to Truman and he was very much of an independent in his voting.

Too, finances proved a factor, and the well-endowed Goldwater lavishly outspent Mac under Shadegg's watchful eye. Bibolet also added money as a major Goldwater advantage, along with the Pulliam press and Ike's coattails. For his own estimate, Goldwater said:

> I had no business beating Ernest McFarland, and I knew that from the day I started, but old Mac just thought he had it in the bag and just didn't come home [enough]. I could never been elected if it hadn't been for Democrats. . . . I'd still be selling pants. [24]

Conversely, McFarland did not benefit as expected from the support of Democratic leaders and had to face the growing divisiveness between the Pintos and old-liners of his own party. Therefore, Republicans benefited from Democratic desertions, not to mention the rapidly growing influx of new residents into the state, most coming from the Republican Midwest. And, finally, McFarland seemed tied to a political campaign strategy fast becoming obsolete. While Goldwater addressed the countryside in absentia with his Burma Shave signs, he personally concentrated on the more populated urban areas. McFarland campaigned in the time-honored Democratic tradition wearing out shoe leather in all fourteen counties accompanied by a large entourage. These rural people did not desert him, but many among the growing urban population did.[25]

In every respect, the election represented the end of one political era and the beginning of another; henceforth, Arizona would be a two-party state. The immediate effects of the change included the loss of an enormous amount of influence in both houses of Congress and an alignment with more conservative eastern and urban groups favoring issues of economy, tax revision, and reduced foreign aid.[26] The repercussions of the 1952 Arizona Senate campaign were indeed far reaching, for in commencing the end of Democratic and rural dominance in Arizona state politics, the 1952 campaign was a harbinger of a new conservative and urban Republican agenda in the politically changing West.

Ernest McFarland was rumored to be very bitter about this particular campaign. If so, he remained quiet and kept it out of the press. In any case, he himself stood partly at fault due to overconfidence and the lack of a more direct, aggressive, and forward-looking campaign. Those close to him noted a feeling of guilt as well that emerged in a fashion that could relate to his religious upbringing on the Oklahoma prairies, for Mac gave up drinking alcoholic beverages, a pleasure that he had long enjoyed and, like many congressmen, sometimes abused, for the next two decades. There existed no apparent physical reasons for this decision.[27]

A great disappointment to Mac, yes, but the senator most assuredly knew that the election of 1952 could in no way detract from the exemplorary record he had fashioned for himself over his challenging years on Capitol Hill and in Arizona, in Europe, and in Asia—a record built on dedicated hard work.

While McFarland's untimely upset marked the close of his senate career, his duties as majority leader of that powerful body were not quite over. Perhaps as a final gesture of appreciation for his work and in recognition of his ambassadorship skills, the Senate dispatched the majority leader on an around-the-world goodwill tour lasting six weeks -- truly a mark of endurance for the early 1950s. Edna McFarland accompanied her husband on this remarkable trip.

On November 20, 1952, two weeks after the election, the trip commenced with a Washington, D.C., to New York to London flight via Shannon, Ireland, and proceeded on to the Scandinavian capitals of Copenhagen, Oslo, and Stockholm (a visit to Helsinki being cancelled due to inclement weather) before arriving in Germany on November 26. Visits to Frankfurt, Berlin, and Bonn preceded others to Geneva and Brussels. From December 1 to 7, he and Edna enjoyed some of the great capitals of Europe: Paris, Madrid, and (via Lisbon and Algiers) Rome, before heading east to Istanbul and Athens. On December 9, the McFarland entourage left Europe for Africa and the Middle East, stopping in Cairo, Jerusalem, Beirut, Damascus, Baghdad, Karachi, and Calcutta. By December 19, the tour reached the Far East, flying the fastest civilian transportation extant, the British Comet jet, which cut normal commercial flying time in half. Stopovers included Bangkok, Singapore, Hong Kong, and, arriving at 5:00 A.M. Christmas Day, Tokyo. Here, the senator made hasty changes in plans and, leaving Edna in the Japanese capital, flew to Korea to observe General Matthew Ridgeway's battle lines from a helicopter and have Christmas dinner with frontline GIs.

Although the harsh climatic, diplomatic, political, and military conditions may have proved depressing to the dinner parties involved, perhaps a glimmer of hope could be detected in both the eyes of the GIs holding expectations that the fighting would soon end and in those of McFarland who might have anticipated with some relief the less pressured life of a civilian attorney. He assuredly did not anticipate at that time the renewal of his political fortunes, which would be launched before the next year ended. From Korea, he rejoined his wife for several days in Tokyo before heading on to Honolulu, Los Angeles, a brief stopover in Phoenix, and a December 31 flight to Washington, D.C., thus completing a six-week circumnavigation of the globe that included thirty countries.

Along with honoring the outgoing majority leader and his wife, the trip had functional aspects. Besides serving as a goodwill ambassador, Mac also appraised postwar rehabilitation under the Marshall and other plans. Additionally, he again inspected various communications facilities as he had in 1945 and 1946. He also greeted many old friends who now resided abroad and made special arrangements for meeting with Arizona servicemen stationed around the world. Underlying the entire trip lay the constant theme of maintaining a vigilant eye on global communist activity.

Speaking briefly in Honolulu on the return trip, McFarland summarized his major observations of his voyage, which he termed a "study." He expressed satisfaction with the "pride" of the English people who did not want theirs to be regarded as a "give me" nation, and he cautioned against the overbearing attitudes of "ugly" American officials and civilians. McFarland regarded the Scandinavian countries as a single economic unit with Sweden, like fellow WWII neutral Switzerland, by far the best off, not only for avoiding the war, but also for instituting a "welfare state par excellence" of income redistribution via taxation and social welfare rather than nationalization of the means of production.

Turning to continental Europe, McFarland spoke of East Germany, which had undergone intense rioting in 1952 that had been harshly quashed by Soviet force. A decade before the erection of Khrushchev's Berlin Wall, Mac witnessed refugee camps in West Berlin handling a daily influx of five hundred people from the East fleeing Stalin's ruthless policies. He quoted an

272 — ERNEST W. MCFARLAND

old German friend: "You need have no fear of [West] Germany going Communistic as the refugees have educated the people as to what Communism is like."

In France, McFarland observed another example of a regulated economy, the "lack of stable government and inflation," and, perhaps ignoring his own advice regarding being overbearing, asked of a prominent French businessman, "Why is it that your country, once so proud and able to cope with any situation now finds herself in the situation she is in today?" The reply was simply and dramatically put: "We lost one million men in World War I and over a million in World War II -- it took the cream -- we no longer have the men with the guts it takes to solve these problems." McFarland then summed up war-torn Europe as "anxious about what the United States may do. They were afraid of a new policy that might involve them in a third world war."

McFarland considered Spain primitive by mid-twentieth-century standards, and in Italy he noted "problems in combating Communism, though our aid has materially helped the people." In Egypt, citizens already questioned which side the U.S. would be on in their fight with Britain over control of the Suez Canal. They blamed the British for a depression because of their refusal to buy Egyptian cotton over the canal dispute. McFarland isolated the major problem in the Near East as the conflict between four-year-old Israel and the neighboring Arab countries. Boundary disputes led to the first Arab-Israeli War in 1947 after which Israel refused to give up gains. The Arab nations flatly held the United States to account. Senator Guy Gillette (D-IA) accompanied McFarland to Israel and commented "the big thing was for all of us first to work against the common enemy, the Communists," to which Arab dignitaries replied that "Israel was their real enemy, not Russia; that we [the U.S.] talk about Russia being so bad, but that it hasn't been long since the United States was in bed with her."

In Jordan, McFarland spoke to a soldier of Palestinian background and asked if he felt this were his home. He replied "that it was not; that his home was in Palestine; that it had always been his home and that they would return, whether it be in a day, a year, or a hundred years -- it still would be his home," words of significance five decades later. The senator urged a firm UN hand and equity to both sides to solve the major problems of assuaging extreme nationalism and developing resources.

McFarland thought Pakistan "friendly" but India "indescribably impoverished." He had a better chance to see much of this country, flying over cotton irrigation projects in a small plane, and taking a train to the interior to visit Edna McFarland's sister, a missionary in charge of a small school.

Close attention to communism occupied the travelers' thoughts in the Far East. In Bangkok, McFarland observed "the people there did not seem to be much worried about the communists taking over their country. I suppose they have become accustomed to the threat." In Singapore, he detected little alarm over communist infiltration, which he deemed "natural" because of geographic location. In Hong Kong, the senator saw the people "living in fear that a third world war would break out" and they expected that their city would be the first to fall to the communists. He further observed "the Chinese people were dissatisfied with the Communist party rule, but were afraid to act and would not do so unless they had some assurance of help from the United States because otherwise they felt they would lose and be put to death." British businessmen threatened to stop trading with the communists and withdraw the attention given previously to Chiang Kai-shek's government.

McFarland avoided saying anything in Hawaii about the Korean trip because the war was still going on. He concluded by recognizing the great strides to recovery that had been made in Japan and the happiness and gratefulness of the Japanese people for U.S. assistance. The Japanese, he noted, seemed to take naturally to American style, liberty, and economic enterprise, but he added "the one difficult thing for them to understand is why we now want them to rearm when at first we talked so much against militarism."[28]

Immediately after returning to Washington, D.C., Majority Leader McFarland performed his last formal duty in

closing the old Eighty-second Congress and turning the reins of
senate party leadership over to Lyndon Johnson. Mac did what
he could to obtain this position for LBJ, calling all but two
unspecified senators. Johnson aggressively pursued Mac's
approbation and that of others such as newly elected John
Kennedy to assume the party leader position, but it was "a natural step, a natural progression" according to Roland Bibolet,
who would now continue as Johnson's administrative assistant as
he had been Mac's: "During the two years he [LBJ] had certainly gotten his feet warm in all the shoes that he would have
to wear." Years later McFarland confirmed: "Lyndon Johnson
doesn't leave any stones unturned. The night that I was defeated - as soon as I was defeated, he called me up and had me call
my friends boosting him. He doesn't give you any time to lick
your wounds." Bibolet put the changeover in other perspec-
tives: "The phone was ringing five minutes after the defeat
became apparent. . . . He called Senator McFarland expressing
his deep regret. In Washington, the body wasn't cold before
people are applying for the suite of rooms. There used to be an
old saying: "If you come in and find me slumped over my desk,
with a coronary, don't send for the doctor. Ask for the room."
This aggressiveness can be qualified, however, as Bibolet further
explained: "After McFarland's defeat, I know he used to talk
with McFarland on the phone quite a bit, getting his advice . . .
and because he felt kindly toward him . . . that although you
have been defeated, you're still a valued person and we love you
very much in the Senate." Johnson now took over this role acting in the minority for the new Congress, while Robert Taft
became the Republican majority leader.[29]

Although no one realized it at the time, McFarland, by
turning the leadership over to LBJ, initiated a trend in the
Democratic party that would continue to the end of the twentieth century – a trend that he, himself, had started. For eighteen
years, since the accession to the presidency by Franklin
Roosevelt, the characteristic party direction had been liberalism
as manifested by FDR, his successor Truman, vice President
Barkley, and culminating in the failed majority leadership of

Scott Lucas. With McFarland's leadership, the party line shifted to the center appealing, at times, to either the left or the
right. LBJ, at first surprisingly to his fellow southerners, continued this direction working effectively with Eisenhower while,
at the same time, being attentive to civil rights. Jack Kennedy
followed suit; feared as a liberal by the right, he was more conservative than thought with his mixed message on McCarthy
and his vacillation on labor activism. Moreover, he evidenced
reluctance on civil rights, the very area that Johnson excelled in
while precariously keeping the allegiance of powerful opposite
pole southerners like Russell and liberal Claude Pepper. The
longest serving (1961-77) majority leader, Mike Mansfield of
Montana, also fit in with this description with his questioning of
Vietnam, and Hubert Humphrey was jockeyed from his usual
liberal position into the center, particularly by the election of
1968 when he was torn between the positions of Lyndon
Johnson and the Robert Kennedy-Eugene McCarthy left. In
the late 1970s, Jimmy Carter paid obeisance to moderation, and
as late as the 1990s Bill Clinton, while initially mapping out a
liberal direction, was forced to a centrist stance by the Newt
Gingrich Republican Congress. All of these trends necessitated
negotiation and compromise and then more compromise, characteristics manifested first in the postwar era by Ernest
McFarland who, rather than catering to either the right or the
left, tried, with some success, to bring them together.

In reflecting upon Ernest McFarland's senate career, it
can be seen that it followed three distinct trends. Domestically,
he espoused a New Deal-Fair Deal liberalism that encompassed
pro-labor and Social Security views, but excluded civil rights. In
terms of foreign policy, he adhered to FDR's wartime preparedness and Truman's hardline Cold War stance along with moderate fiscal conservatism concerning foreign aid. Third, he gave
priority to Arizona interests as frequently as possible, avowing
that a senator held equal responsibility for his state as well as his
nation. Within each of these areas, McFarland proved adapt-
able and not bound by self-imposed definition. He was not a
strict ideologue but took long-range views that emphasized

negotiation, compromise, and a meeting of minds expressing different viewpoints.

By the end of his first term, McFarland had established himself as a moderate-to-liberal in domestic affairs. He supported labor consistently, voting against the restrictive measures in the wartime Smith-Connally Act. Likewise, during the Republican-controlled Eightieth Congress, he stood strongly against the Taft-Hartley Act voting against the bill and to sustain President Truman's veto, both 1947 efforts to no avail. He did, however, acknowledge majority will and held that voters in the 1946 Arizona elections had the right to support "right-to-work," anti-closed-shop legislation if they so chose.

McFarland ardently supported Social Security legislation and in 1946, forced through the first of his three increased-benefits bills. Others followed in 1948 and 1952, and collectively these were the only increases to pass Congress and become law during his twelve-year tenure, 1941-53. In the face of conservative opposition, he planned his social security strategy well, asking for small increases that he knew would be difficult for Congress to deny, and then asking for them frequently.

Senator McFarland did not limit his humanitarian intentions to the elderly, disabled, and poor, but stood strongly for the veteran as well in some of the most significant legislation ever passed by Congress. The GI Bill of Rights, a landmark work, once and for all established the government's responsibility towards the nation's servicemen. In authoring the education provisions and home and small business loan sections of the 1944 bill, McFarland contributed its most important and lasting features. In 1951 and 1952 he led the drive to extend similar benefits with the Korean GI Bill. In the process, he set precedents in veterans' legislation for years to come that served the later needs of both Vietnam era and peacetime servicemen that last to this day.

Communications, along with veterans' affairs and water, constituted one of three areas in which McFarland was the acknowledged expert in the Senate. Domestically, he always emphasized efficiency and serving the public's need and interests. His 1943 bill merging Postal Telegraph with Western Union substantiated these goals. Throughout his senate career, and particularly in 1949, he worked to improve the Communications Act of 1934, which established the nature of regulatory control between the federal government and the private sector. His revisions here were noteworthy and capped his senate years with their passage into law in July 1952.

Communications expertise quite naturally led to McFarland's increased involvement in foreign affairs, particularly concerning postwar planning. His primary goal was the enhancement of guaranteed world peace by ensuring smooth international communications involving parity of access to and distribution of worldwide information for the United States. Most importantly, he desired increased U.S. control, ownership, and maintenance of international communications facilities constructed during the war at American expense by American labor.

With these goals in mind McFarland embarked on international tours of Europe and the Mid-East in 1945 and Asia and the Pacific in 1946, conferring with Winston Churchill, Dwight Eisenhower, Douglas MacArthur, and George Marshall along the way, as well as Pope Pius XII and Chiang Kai-shek. His efforts proved disappointing as indicated by the narrow defeat (45 to 40) of his amendment to the 1946 British Loan, which was intended to implement an increased American role in postwar communications. Similarly, McFarland advised caution, efficiency, and a good return on the investment for U.S. foreign aid. He by no means supported the isolationist budget-cutting approach of Senator Robert Taft, but Mac did like to trim the edges and ensure just compensation and recognition of U.S. interests by those countries that we assisted.

The British loan amendment and communications efforts constituted McFarland's major attempts to influence U.S. foreign policy. One failed and the other had limitations, but both expressed his abiding concern for the strength of and respect due his nation. He was not nationalistically narrow visioned, however, and participated eagerly in planning for the United Nations. In July 1941, Mac became the first senator to address the issue of postwar communications and security arrangements, and he continued to present cogent ideas in this area on into his second term.

Despite his interest in foreign affairs, McFarland remained more attuned to domestic concerns, particularly those of Arizona. Here, the workhorse senator proved himself forceful and reliable. He and Hayden engineered the highest per-capita government appropriations of any state in the Union during McFarland's years in office.[30] His watchful eye cleared the way for federal financial infusions and legislation supportive of Arizona's basic interests in agriculture, mining, and range use. He facilitated the move of wartime industry to Arizona and helped it remain after the war ended. Similarly, his efforts established the state as a pre-eminent wartime training area, particularly for the Air Corps, and these facilities remained active in the postwar years. Finally, with the Navajo-Hopi Rehabilitation Act, McFarland riveted attention on guaranteeing federal responsibility for Arizona's Indian population, the largest in the nation.

The enormous effort to bring Colorado River water to Arizona to expand the state's agricultural capabilities consumed more of McFarland's senate time than any other single issue. He was instrumental in designing the Mexican Water Treaty of 1945, and, in 1947, he obtained legislation authorizing the Wellton-Mohawk Project. With McFarland designing and implementing Arizona's water strategy, he twice led the Central Arizona Project to senate passage in 1950 and 1951. Although CAP remained blocked in the House, these efforts from 1947 to 1952 proved to be fundamental building blocks along the road to success for CAP in 1968.

McFarland's record for his first ten years in the Senate proved productive concerning water, veterans, communications, Social Security, postwar planning, and state interests. His skills at negotiation, compromise, and the backroom work that so often went unrecognized by the public were widely appreciated by his colleagues, whose respect led to his selection as majority leader in 1951. These two years of leadership, however, proved difficult for McFarland, and they provided fodder for Shadegg's attack upon him during the fateful 1952 election. He carried some wounds from these years for the rest of his life. And, indeed, his career has been measured more by the alleged failures of his party leadership than by the substantial legislative achievements that he engineered during his twelve years in the Senate. Just as playwriters and scriptwriters distort history with false accounts serving their agenda, so too have Shadegg's misrepresentations of McFarland's career been passed on to later generations. It is time to set the record straight. Passions have cooled in the decades since Mac strode the senate floor; the cold dispassionate light of history can now be focused upon his career. Shadegg emerges as a master political strategist who cared more for victory than truth (and who would be welcomed in either party today!), and McFarland is seen as one of the most significant senators of his time. A few corrections to Shadegg's account are in order.

President Truman envisioned a return to Franklin Roosevelt's liberal social policies after the war's end, and he hoped to have more success in their implementation than FDR had during the immediate prewar years. In this he was to be sorely disappointed. Truman's Fair Deal faced the same opposition that hindered Roosevelt, the Republican-southern Democrat coalition, and, in the Eightieth Congress, the Republicans held the majority. When Truman was elected in his own right in 1948, the Democrats recaptured the majority in the Senate, 54-42, and in the House, 263-171. This marked Truman's only viable chance to see his program pass, but the opposition coalition could still muster a majority to prevent executive success. Liberal Majority Leader Scott Lucas was supported by such prominent senators as Paul Douglas and Hubert Humphrey. Yet all three acknowledged the Fair Deal dead in the water by 1951 when McFarland succeeded to the leadership upon Lucas' McCarthy-influenced 1950 defeat.

McFarland's leadership was doomed from the outset with respect to advancing the Fair Deal as he had a majority of only two as compared to Lucas's twelve. Moreover, he had to face the full force of McCarthy era animosity, a constant threat that McFarland did his best to dispel. Finally, the Korean War, which ran throughout his tenure as leader, demanded priority over domestic issues. McCarthyism, Korea, and the smallest of majorities precluded passage of a liberal program that had already been rejected during a period of liberal strength.

An upsurge of conservatism dominated American politics during the early 1950s, and McFarland's surprising defeat at the hands of Barry Goldwater constituted just one of many results of this trend. Yet assuredly Mac could look back with great satisfaction at a senate career that, although cut relatively short at two terms, was manifestly more productive than that of many who served far longer. This was the essence of Ernest McFarland's senate work and legacy: productivity. Appropriately labled a workhorse, he was much more than that, being a politician of unusual ability who could both design and implement significant legislation, while at the same time bringing those of varying viewpoints together through negotiation and compromise. Negotiation and compromise—design and implementation of legislation -- these mark the full complement of skills of a progressive and constructive United States Senator.[31]

When Ernest McFarland addressed his future possibilities after the 1952 defeat, he quite naturally turned to communications. In January 1953, three major companies, RCA, Western Union, and American Cable and Radio Corp., a subsidiary of ITT (International Telephone and Telegraph), offered to retain McFarland for the balance of the year as legal counsel and legislative advisor concerning their mutual interests. The contract stipulated a salary of thirty thousand dollars per year plus twelve thousand in expenses, the forty-two thousand total being almost thrice the sum McFarland had earned per year as a senator.

Specifically, McFarland would be charged with investigating international merger possibilities among the three companies and ITT. Based on findings during his senate work, the companies believed they were subject to price discrimination by foreign businesses. A merger might solve this. Since the job could perhaps be involved with legislative recommendations, laws required McFarland to register as a lobbyist with Congress, and few eyebrows were raised when he did so in April. The choice was a logical one since McFarland had expedited the merger of Western Union and Postal Telegraph Companies and, as recent chair of the Interstate and Foreign Commerce Committee's communications subcommittee, had written the Comunications Act of 1952, revising the original act of 1934.

Over the course of the year, McFarland recognized that neither the congressional nor the communications unions' mood favored the possibility of monopoly, and the participants themselves could not agree on the division of control and power in the proposed conglomerate. Merger, thus, was not immediately feasible. However, Mac's return to the communications arena proved far more significant in a personal way, for it laid the groundwork for his own entry into the television field, a venture that would retain his closest personal attention and participation over the next three decades.[32]

Television was a dynamic and growing field in 1953, perhaps the most significant domestic development in the United States during the entire decade of the 1950s. McFarland prepared his plans well to begin operations in the business, commencing with a partnership formed with three close friends: former 1946 campaign manager Ralph Watkins, of Buckeye, Leon Nowell of Coolidge, Florence's neighboring town, and Edmund Cooper of Phoenix, who also maintained a residence in Washington, D.C.

McFarland formally joined the operation in May 1953 when a corporation replaced the partnership with Mac subscribing to forty percent of the stock of the new Arizona Television Company. Watkins and Nowell retained twenty percent, Cooper ten percent, and various others the remaining ten percent. The corporation was capitalized at seven hundred thousand dollars, of which a half million was subscribed. Spokesman Watkins stated that the group expected to "build the finest television station in America and pioneer color television in Arizona." The trail had been broken, but obstacles remained in the new company's path.

On May 30 Arizona Television Company filed an application with the FCC for Channel 3, the last remaining channel open in the Phoenix area. However, another group, Phoenix radio station KTAR, had applied for the highly-desired low number designation five years earlier, only to have consideration of its application halted by an FCC freeze on new channels during the Korean War. Now that the freeze had ended in late 1952, both groups competed for the channel. KTAR, having filed so much in advance, expressed surprise at Arizona Television's move. Before the sudden filing, KTAR had been expected to be granted its application within a short time. Now the "early-bird" KTAR faced a formidable adversary.

In challenging for Channel 3, McFarland used all of his power, influence, and know-how in order to achieve his goal; he had plenty of all three, and it had been Mac as senator in June 1952, who had pushed the FCC to permit live television into the Phoenix market, allowing the rising city to join sixty-five others across the nation being served by 107 video outlets.

The former senate communications expert had the support of Hollywood, which had favored him ever since his role in the 1941 film probe. His friendship with Lyndon Johnson also proved invaluable. The new Democratic minority leader, himself, had become involved with television through his wife Lady Bird's family and interests. As McFarland had, in all probability, advised on LBJ's efforts at that time, now Johnson could assuage any potential Republican opposition in the Senate and use his harmonious relationship with President Eisenhower and the executive office. "Speaker Sam" Rayburn provided Mac the same advantage in the House. Too, McFarland could call upon the popularity and appeal of good friend entertainer Gene Autry who also counted as a member of the Phoenix media scene. In 1953, his Maricopa Broadcasting Company began operation on Channel 10 in which Autry held fifty percent. In 1954, he took over the other half, most assuredly with

McFarland's support. Despite all of these connections, the bottom line for Arizona Television's ultimately successful effort lay in its local ownership, for KTAR Radio was controlled by out-of-town interests.[33]

KTAR executives soon understood that their chances for FCC authorization were quickly diminishing, and by April 1954, the group purchased Channel 12 operating out of Mesa, thus clearing the way for McFarland's approval. On May 20, the FCC dismissed KTAR's application for Channel 3 while considering the new purchase, and on June 11, Arizona Television received FCC authorization. The only negative FCC vote came from Commissioner Frieda B. Hennock, who claimed her dissent lay in general principle, not a specific complaint against Arizona Television. She felt that the freeze on TV applications should remain intact until procedural problems with the opening of the ultra high frequency (UHF) range had been solved.[34]

Network affiliation presented the next question for Arizona Television. Initially, McFarland favored going with one of the two proven major networks, NBC, presided over by David Sarnoff whom Mac knew well, or CBS, each by 1955 possessing approximately 150 outlets. Ultimately, however, and prodded by competition from Gene Autry's new station which went with CBS, Channel 3 opted for the less secure but more exciting venture of joining new network ABC. The American Broadcasting Company only had about forty outlets, and adding the Phoenix area, proved among its coups in establishing credibility and near parity over the next decade.[35]

The FCC required that station construction begin within sixty days and reach completion within six months of its approval. The McFarland group complied, building the new station at 16th Street and Osborn Road in Phoenix and erecting a one hundred-foot, twenty thousand dollar tower on South Mountain overlooking the rapidly growing desert city. Two years of planning and realization came to fruition on February 28, 1955, when KTVK Television signed on the air at five o'clock in the afternoon as three thousand invited dignitaries, entertainers, and congratulators from all over the state poured into the studios, accompanied by wives, children, and even horses. The next day, the ABC Network kicked in with its then-short programming of four hours including *Cavalcade America*, *The U.S. Steel Hour*, *The Voice of Firestone*, and *The Adventures of Ozzie and Harriet*. KTVK-TV filled in the remaining on-air fourteen hours with local programming, films, news, and live shows. The station provided McFarland with an avocation, recognition, and a political forum for the next three decades.[36]

While engaging in these communications projects, McFarland, urged on by Arizona friends, kept in mind a return to the political arena by seeking the Democratic nomination for state governor against Republican incumbent Howard Pyle. Pyle, a long-term Tempe resident, radio personality, and a well-known World War II reporter from the Pacific not (Ernie Pyle), had led the statewide Republican party revival beginning with his 1950 victory for governor over Ana Frohmiller. Frohmiller, the state treasurer, took for granted her excellent chances in the heretofore one-party state, did not campaign rigorously, and lost her chance to become one of the first female heads-of-state in the nation. She lost by only three thousand votes, and Pyle went on to a second-term victory in the general Republican sweep of 1952 which brought in Goldwater and Arizona's first GOP representative, John Rhodes. Now, in the summer of 1953, McFarland's attention was grasped by an unusual Pyle maneuver that would hasten his decision to enter the race -- the infamous Short Creek Raid.

Short Creek, a Mormon enclave, lay in the Arizona Strip, a desolate, nearly unaccessible country north of the Grand Canyon, adjacent to Utah's southern border. Larger than Connecticut, Rhode Island, and Maryland combined, its five million acres provided home for only 700 people, many of whom lived in that ramshackle community. In this neglected outpost, Governor Pyle found "insurrection . . . of the foulest conspiracy . . . the production of white slaves . . . the cooperative enterprise of five or six coldly, calculating men." In other words, Pyle's surreptitious investigators uncovered concrete evidence of polygamy as practiced by old-time unrepentant Mormons.[37]

As the governor, in an official radio address, continued to list his charges and complaints, including statutory rape, adultery, and bigamy, the state police assisted by the National Guard and squads of social workers, staged a pre-dawn raid that nabbed the miscreants. The national media covered the raid as a bizarre spectacle, and ridiculed Arizona's law enforcement agencies for "capturing" a small, isolated community of people who kept their odd, harmless practices to themselves.

As Mormon warning signals exploded, over one hundred state police, "armed to the teeth," rushed the community, lights flashing and sirens wailing at 4:02 A.M., July 26, to find most of the local citizenry gathered singing hymns in the schoolyard, standing beneath the American flag. The raid netted thirty-four men, fifty women, and 263 dependent children. All of the men and six of the women were jailed in Kingman, the county seat over four hundred road miles away southwest of and around the Grand Canyon, while most of the children were distributed among foster homes and childcare centers throughout the state.[38]

Negative repercussions erupted around the nation. *Time* termed the operation "a love nest raid . . . conducted with the ponderous secrecy of an elephant sneaking across a skating rink." ABC reported "the war in Korea is off for the time-being, but to make up for it we had an insurrection in Arizona." Gene Pulliam's *Republic*, in many respects the engineer of Republican resurgence did not spare the lash either, calling the raid "a cloak and dagger script -- typical of Hollywood's worst . . . that would have made the Keystone Cops green with envy . . . a humiliation and an insurrection with diapers and volleyballs." Going further, the paper joined citizens in noting the resemblance to "the hated police state, the Gestapo, Hitlerism, and the doings of Joe Stalin." While LDS Church leaders in Salt Lake City disavowed the actions of its errant members and termed the raid "within the province of the authorities," those who had experienced the governor's wrath directly protested "the colossal conspiracy of aggregated press and propaganda machinery set up for a planned political parade," not to mention "the stench of tobacco smoke and the more intolerable intrusion, influences of people of vile lives, prejudiced minds and evil intents [the police]."[39]

With Governor Pyle under direct fire from the media and even Republican regulars, McFarland advocated a return to "normalcy" stealing GOP cant from the 1920s. He had only to gain the full-hearted support of his wife, Edna, who had provided much of the organizational balance to control and channel her husband's enormous energies. She brought cohesion, inspiration, comfort, and now, having been through defeat, solace as well. She would have been perfectly content to step out of the political light and into an equally viable but less visible life as wife of a communications and water law expert and advisor, and Pinal County farmer. He would not make the move without her full cooperation, and she turned for advice to those friends she knew well, the Democratic senatorial wives in Washington, D.C. Not long before, Edna had been a leader of this group which did everything from roll bandages for the Red Cross to host fancy luncheons in the Senate Office Building. Now she listened as her dear old friends advised her to support Mac's new run, the very counsel she probably yearned for. She had enjoyed the public life, and as he was about to enter his seventh decade, he was the obvious choice to lead the Democratic party's resurgence in Arizona. The McFarlands stood ready to re-enter the political arena.[40]

McFarland announced his candidacy on June 4, 1954, stressing his intention to expedite harmony between the executive office and both houses of the legislature, something that had frequently been lacking with Governor Pyle. Mac hoped to have no competition for the Democratic nomination, but in this he was frustrated. State senators Jim Smith and William F. Kimball also announced, the former, however, withdrawing very early in the race in favor of McFarland.[41]

Kimball, known as the "Dean" of the state senate, presented competition that could not be easily overlooked. A fourteen-year veteran of the upper house and the majority leader, he proclaimed that his knowledge of the inner workings of state government superseded McFarland's federal expertise in importance. Nevertheless, McFarland decided to largely ignore Kimball during the primary campaign and concentrate on Pyle.[42]

For his part, the incumbent manifested a testiness and anxiety over facing such a formidable opponent as McFarland, whom he referred to as "the great I am." His railings at old New Dealers and Fair Dealers and influence of corruption among labor bosses all became tinged with a cliched hysteria that was losing its appeal as the McCarthy hearings in Washington began to reduce the "tailgunner" to the pathetic drunken figure that he was shortly to become. On occasion, Pyle lost his temper on the stump when challenged by McFarland, particularly over Pyle's efforts to make elective offices appointive.[43]

Kimball proved largely ineffective in defining issues or stepping into the light shed by the two better-known candidates. The best he could come up with was suggesting that both were really lining up for the 1956 U.S. Senate race against Carl Hayden. McFarland never for a moment considered challenging Hayden; he would have rather swum to the bottom of the sea, but he did, of course, always hold Goldwater and 1958 in his sights. Voters flocked to the primaries on September 7, and when the votes had been tabulated, Arizona Democrats indicated their preference for McFarland by a three-to-one margin. National papers referred to his victory as a "spectacular political comeback, surprising even his most optimistic supporters." Kimball wired, "the Arizona voters have not only spoken, they have shouted — congratulations."[44]

McFarland and Pyle, who had been unopposed in the primaries, now readied themselves for the final race to the general elections in which voters could stretch the boundaries of party allegiance, a factor of growing political significance in Arizona. Already a victim of the party realignment that was convulsing the Arizona political scene, McFarland worried about Pintos and new Republicans. Would 1954 produce apostates with the clout of Lewis Douglas and Stephen Shadegg? A "Democrats for Pyle" organization emerged early. It supported Pyle's contention of corrupt labor bosses having influence over Democratic candidates and added the charge of Communist influence as well in advertisements purchased in the Pulliam press. Mac kept an assured public face but was not certain he could stand fast against the rising Republican tide. With less than full confidence, he decided to focus upon how Pyle and the new Republicans had failed to attend to the traditional Arizona concerns that were his strength.[45]

As the campaign progressed, McFarland concentrated on traditional issues welfare, water, and highways, as well as Pyle's efforts to reorganize government into a more appointive system. The challenger pointed to lack of Republican attention to highway and water needs and harassment and discrimination against welfare recipients via constant checks and unfair liens on their property. Mac correctly noted the loss of influence and effort from Pyle's statehouse to Washington, D.C., where Senator Goldwater waffled in his support of aging Carl Hayden. When Vice President Nixon arrived in state to campaign for Pyle, McFarland effectively used Nixon's and Senate Majority Leader Knowland's staunch opposition to Arizona water projects to offset any campaign advantage to Pyle. Too, Mac added that the Republican-controlled Congress overrode Hayden's influence and did not bend to Goldwater-Rhodes efforts which, in any case, were levied with far less strength than previous Democratic efforts.[46]

To counter Nixon's visit, McFarland lined up a formidable array of Democrats including Senators Hayden and Chavez of neighboring New Mexico and Minority Leader Lyndon Johnson, as well as Adlai Stevenson and Governor-elect Edmund Muskie of Maine. Other Washington friends appeared to help. LBJ "lent" Roland Bibolet back to McFarland for five months of campaigning, and former (and future) U.S. Senate Sergeant-at-Arms, Arizonan Joe Duke, managed the campaign efforts. In fact, after the voting, Bibolet left Johnson

in January 1955 to officially rejoin McFarland for the gubernatorial years. They all brought focus to Mac who continued his
scrupulous networking of the state and grassroots contact with
the man on the street, in the shop or mine, on the farm, in barbershops and bars. In fact, Governor Pyle backed off somewhat
from the Republican tradition of urban campaigning with his
"walkathons" up and down both sides of streets to counteract
Mac's "handshaking and shoe-leather" technique for which he
had long been recognized.[47]

As the general election date of November 2 neared,
polls continued to forecast a tight race - one that could not be
called. Indeed, polls of various types had played an active part
in the political maneuvers. To begin with, McFarland distrusted early predictions that Pyle would triumph in largely
Mormon Mesa by a four-to-one margin. This did not jibe with
the Mormon community's aggreavment over the Short Creek
episode. Mac gambled that if the Mesa polls could be so far off,
others probably were too. Furthermore, he believed he could
lose urban Phoenix-Maricopa County by five thousand votes
and still win the election. Other later polls indicated that Mac
might be right as some of them showed him with a slim lead.[48]

On October 23, the major Arizona Poll indicated a margin for Pyle of 47.2 to 43.5 percent, with nine percent undecided. Pyle's advantage was credited to the urban areas: a fifty to
forty percent lead in Phoenix-Maricopa County and a forty-
nine to forty-two percent advantage in Tuscon-Pima County.
The poll also indicated substantial preference for Pyle in the
women's vote, 49.7 to 40.5 percent. Could it be that Goldwater
Department Store clothing sales were kicking in as they had in
1952? Overall, McFarland showed a 46.4 to 45.1 advantage
among males.[49]

As the election approached, McFarland made a last-
minute check on his calculations and predicted victory by fifteen
thousand votes. At the same time, Las Vegas gamblers closed
their bets at six-to-five, Pyle. It was the old political warhorse,
however, who had it right in what proved to be a Democratic
cruise. Mac defeated Pyle 122,235 to 111,399, a margin of

nearly eleven thousand. Democrat Stewart Udall easily won his congressional district, while John Rhodes fashioned the only major Republican win in his return to the House for a second term.[50]

Pyle lost eleven of fourteen counties, while taking the Phoenix-Tucson urban enclaves and Goldwater's home base Yavapai County by a hairsbreadth. He wired the governor-elect "Congratulations, Arizona deserves the best, and I'm sure you'll do your best." McFarland expressed "humility and profound thanks."[51]

Analysis of the 1954 election held that the Democratic "silent" vote of farmers, miners, and workers had been decisive even though facing what appeared to be negative prospects. McFarland himself later stated, "I thought the biggest assistance I had was that the estimated polls gave Pyle the edge," thus encouraging apathetic, overconfident Republicans and Pintos to stay at home on election day. Republican apologists blamed "with certainty" the negative effects of the Short Creek raid, but, Pyle felt the raid was not the determining factor in a loss by such a margin. He was probably correct, though it certainly cost him votes.[52]

Emboldened with his victorious return to the political field, Ernest McFarland, who had judicial experience in county politics and legislative renown at the national level, now took on executive responsibilities at the helm of the state. He determined to do so with liberal aplomb, and he certainly could not have realized it at the time, but the governor's mantle would be his second crown on his way to becoming that rare public servant to have reached the top rung in all three branches of government.

CHAPTER TWELVE

ARIZONA'S TENTH GOVERNOR
FIRST TERM SUCCESSES
1955-1956

A WINTER SHOWER THREATENED PHOENIX ON JANUARY 3, 1955, as Ernest McFarland prepared for his inauguration as the state's tenth governor. Mac dressed resplendently in a blue suit and blue and red tie, omitting only bright yellow, the state's third color. He and Edna awaited their ride to the capitol from their new home at 306 West Royal Palm Lane. Seated with old Oklahoma friends, the Homer Bishops, who had made the trip from Seminole, they chatted quietly and a bit anxiously as well. Already forty-five minutes late for informal preliminaries, the governor-elect, borrowing from Abraham Lincoln, quipped "they can't begin the inauguration without us."

The delay was occasioned by events in hometown Florence. There, daughter Jewell and son-in-law Del Lewis, who managed Mac's nearby cotton farms, prepared for the sixty-mile drive to pick up the executive couple and escort them to the capitol grounds. Not far along the way, however, Del turned good samaritan, stopping to assist a stalled car carrying members of Florence Boy Scout Troop 21. Since McFarland was the first elected governor from Pinal County, the county seat troop had been chosen as the honor guard for the festivities. Scouts and scoutmasters squeezed into the Lewis's car and sped on their way to Phoenix. By the time Del got Mac and Edna there, they had missed the joint concert put on by bands from the University of Arizona (Tucson), Arizona State College

291

(Tempe), and Arizona State College of Northern Arizona (Flagstaff). Nevertheless, the party arrived in time for the scheduled noon beginning.[1]

The flag bedecked platform overlooked the palm-lined east grounds of the old copper-domed building, where over two thousand people awaited. Dignitaries filled the stage, including three ex-Democratic governors Rawghlie Stanford (1937-39), Bob Jones (1939-41), and Dan Garvey (1947-51) and the Arizona Supreme Court, including long-time friend, Justice Fred Struckmeyer. Newly elected Attorney General Robert Morrison and State Auditor Jewell W. Jordan were joined by foreign guests Ignacio Soto, the Governor of Sonora, Mexico, and his son Luis, as well as Edna and Jewell. Conspicuously absent was recently defeated Howard Pyle, who had hurriedly gone to Washington to join newly elected President Eisenhower as an administrative worker and later the nation's highway safety representative.

Dr. J.N. Harber, McFarland's recent campaign manager and new head of the state Democratic party organization, welcomed the audience. The Thunderbird Post American Legion Drill Team presented the colors; the massed bands blared the National Anthem; McFarland's minister Dr. Charles Kendall of Phoenix Central Methodist gave the invocation, and then Mac stood to take the oath administered by Chief Justice Arthur T. LaPrade.

In his first inaugural address, McFarland spoke of "a profound sense of humility . . . an honor . . . a call to service . . . measured only by the quality of service rendered," and of his choice by the people as a vehicle or "instrumentality to accomplish certain purposes . . . responsive to their will." Then, in a customarily short ten-minute speech, he outlined his basic intentions for the next two years.

First, the new governor highlighted Arizona's perennial problem of aid to schools as the state's population sped toward one million, with student attendance expected to grow accordingly: "We must project and make plans for the future." Next he called up another perennial: Arizona's and his own persistent quest for obtaining the waters of the Colorado for irrigation and reclamation purposes.

McFarland did not elaborate on these, but moved on to a statement of purpose "not to burden the legislature with a program that would not possibly be enacted in a sixty-day session." This assurance was based on past experience of legislative logjams. Indeed, Governor Pyle's programs had placed such a burden on legislators that the last session had lasted ninety days, thirty beyond the prescribed limit. Mac intended to avoid such slow waters.

McFarland then added a third goal - efficiency in government. This area required "immediate improvement" since the state was burdened with "hundreds of boards and commissions, the terms of the members of which are so staggered that an incoming governor has the responsibility without full authority . . . to remove many who may not be . . . in accord." He then concluded with "a greater sense of inspiration, ambition, and hope . . . the possibilities of one state are just awakening . . . we have only begun to grow. Let us remember these sacred words -- `Where there is no vision, the people perish.'"[2]

After Bishop Gerche gave the benediction, the new governor left the platform to host a public reception in the rotunda. The bands played on, and in twenty minutes the rains came down. Hundreds hurried into the building where office seekers already lurked (and would remain until the last day four years later). Moving through the decorated rotunda, the crowds climbed to the second-floor office where Roland Bibolet had arranged dozens of vases of flowers. Bibolet remembers the mid-1950s governor's suite as "really primitive," with a reception area, the main office with fireplace, a small work room with a walk-in safe, and a tiny office made from a blocked off corridor for the assistant: "It was like a fishbowl." Reporters used to loiter around the area because even from the outside one could clearly hear phone and personal conversations. Too, the governor enjoyed no private restroom but had to use the "gents" public room where, of course, he could be easily buttonholed by anyone seeking his ear.

Small quarters, however, did not dissuade governor and guests from enjoying themselves on this inaugural day. These expectant Arizonans, in the crowd and at home, awaited satisfied, knowing that since Sidney Osborn, they had not had a man of such experience and prestige in the executive office. Those who knew politics wondered whether McFarland would be able to lead the legislature, the historically stronger governmental branch. The legislature had long been dominated by the stodgy, conservative Democrats of the Senate, but a new group of liberal Democrats had assumed power in the House. Which way would the new governor go?[3]

On January 10, one week after the inauguration, Governor McFarland dispelled any doubt of his direction in his message to the Twenty-second Legislature. The address substantiated that he would align with the new House majority of liberal Democrats and use them as the wedge to force cooperation with the minority Republicans and the Senate, which itself sported a new face, having been expanded from nineteen to twenty-eight, two senators for each county.

The governor recommended a twelve-point program with aid to education heading the list. Specifically, he requested raising the ADA (average daily attendance allocation) to a minimum of $175 per pupil. It had stood at $115 since 1947. This could be accomplished by cooperation at the state and county levels via an equalization of taxes, with the broader tax base of the state taking the strain off of counties and school districts. He challenged the legislature to have an appropriate bill on his desk within ten working days. Warning of the rapid growth in school population, he urged taxation on a "current basis" of adjustment to new numbers every quarter, not every year.

McFarland next turned to public welfare, calling for the "immediate liberalization of the law, so that the recipients of assistance grants will not continue to be harassed by perpetual routine checks and re-checks." Furthermore, he emphasized that state welfare funds had decreased 1.5 percent in the past five years, despite the cost-of-living increase. Mac wanted financial limitations raised and financial reports eliminated including the home-lien clause, whereby owners could lose their small estates. Noting work already in progress, he then added health to his education and welfare themes.

McFarland next addressed his desire for increased efficiency in government, both on the job and in cost cutting. Again he spoke of the numerous boards, staggered terms, and the potential lack of sympathy for his program and "the people." When he concluded, "I may find it necessary to submit some recommendations," press and politicians alike took it as a show of strength and determination from the traditionally weaker governor's office - a warning that "heads might roll."

The next several recommendations concerned perennial Arizona taxation problems, the most important being the establishment of a use tax. This marked the sixth time that such a tax had been requested, the first occurring in 1943. Arizona was in danger of losing new and incoming industry because of peculiarities in state tax laws. Businesses were required to pay a two percent sales tax on material sold to the federal government, and many balked at this assessment. Indeed, among the forty-eight states, only Illinois employed a similar tax. If this sales tax were eliminated, a use tax could be levied to make up for lost revenue. This tax proposed to curtail out-of-state purchases of products available in state.

Mac also called for equalization of property valuations among counties to produce more equitable distribution of the tax load. He promised that increased government efficiency and expansion of industry, new and old, would provide enough revenues to forego the need for further tax increases.

McFarland extended his progressive agenda with a broad call for action on several other fronts: increased funding for highways and exploration of new ways and means for highway safety to mitigate the "appalling toll of four hundred deaths" the previous year; heightened awareness of and legislation to curb juvenile delinquency; establishment of an independent department of labor (Arizona was the only state without one); an amendment to allow exchange of teachers with foreign nations (Arizona was the only state not participating in the U.S. State Department's Fulbright program); a state office building to be erected in Tucson; and finally, the deferral of studies for a new capitol building until the next year.

The new governor then briefly referred to general plans for reform in other areas including dairy, livestock, agriculture, and, of course, water. Mac finally closed by claiming he would always be available to people who could help him identify and solve Arizona's problems. He hoped this open-door policy would help overcome legislative reluctance to change, move with the times, or modernize Arizona, and speed up the process so his program could be enacted in a sixty-day session. Although the press called the recommended program "short," it was comprehensive and ambitious, and it remained to be seen how the ever-changing and irascible Arizona Legislature would view it.[4]

Historically, in Arizona politics, the legislature dominated the governor's office, and certain interest groups, notably mining, dominated the legislature, particularly in the Senate. Now, with a constitutional amendment approved in 1953, reapportionment of senate seats attempted to keep pace with the changing face of the state. Previously, with a Senate of nineteen members, the four mining counties of Pima, Cochise, Yavapai, and Gila composed a bloc of eight votes, and together with the single votes of heavily mined Pinal and Greenlee had been able to control the upper house on critical issues. Traditionally, this scheme led to a conservative posture against higher appropriations and taxes. Now the realignment gave each county two seats, increasing the total to twenty-eight in an attempt at a more flexible political environment. Still, the Senate stood as a conservative bastion dominated by mining and cattle, with utilities interests even stronger after World War II. Labor in Arizona did not possess the matching power as it often did in national politics.[5]

The House of Representatives, too, had long been dominated by conservatives, Pinto Democrats, and a small but increasing number of Republicans. Now, however, for the first time, the liberal group managed to grab the majority bloc with the election of House Speaker Harry Ruppelius of Maricopa County besting by forty-nine to thirty-one the minority bloc under Charles O. Bloomquist of Cochise.

Phoenix Gazette political columnist Bill Turnbow, writer of the "Under the Capitol Dome" column, predicted "history in one category -- cordial relations," between the two houses, and on the "$64 question" of how McFarland would fare with the legislature, he stated "the governor who has an affable and cooperative mood will get along better than some of his predecessors." Speaker Ruppelius agreed that the governor "didn't saddle us with a big unwieldy program." Ominously, however, Bloomquist and Senate President Clarence Carpenter (D-Gila) had no comment to offer on Mac's program. Nor did, the "bitter" Bloomquist supporters extend the usual courtesy applause to Ruppelius as he assumed the speaker's chair.[6]

Although Tucson's *Arizona Daily Star* referred to McFarland's program as "sane and sensible," opposition to parts of it began to develop immediately. Ironically, the legislature moved ahead of the governor in one area; rain brought leaks in both chambers, causing legislative leaders to dispute Mac's recommendation to put off capitol construction plans until the next year. The governor also had to denounce persistent rumors that "heads would roll" in personnel shakeups in government agencies. Too, opposition quickly arose toward the proposed labor department and, as the session continued, to a previously unrequested one-cent increase in the gasoline levy that seemed to contradict McFarland's original commitment not to raise taxes. The school aid bill quickly incited a three-sided struggle with Mac staying with his original figure of $175, the House settling on $165, and the Senate holding out for $150.[7]

Disappointingly, by the end of the normal sixty-day session on March 10, little of substance had been accomplished. The Arizona legislature then went into its "inevitable" overtime at a cost of four thousand dollars per day, for although the legislators went unsalaried for this period, they did receive a per diem. Still, much had been accomplished in the two months, and certain bills concerning health measures, equal employment opportunity, and even school aid seemed on the verge of acceptance. Indeed, a small but vocal liberal minority in the Senate had begun to assert itself. Aligned with the House majority, the new coalition had some success.[8]

An initial break occurred just after mid-March when Governor McFarland signed the Equal Public Employment Opportunities Act. School desegregation had already occurred during the previous administration after the Supreme Court's landmark decision, *Brown v. the Board of Education*. Now, this act continued to keep Arizona in the mainstream of civil rights progress as it emerged in mid-decade. The act outlawed discrimination because of race, religion, color, or national origin, in public employment, a broad category encompassing but not limited to the state, counties, cities, towns, municipal corporations, school districts, and public educational institutions. The penalty, in retrospect, appears relatively light -- up to five hundred dollars for a misdemeanor charge, but it did more than keep pace with national efforts and included regulation of employment activities such as advertising, promotions and raises, demotions and transfers, layoffs or terminations, pay scale and any other form of compensation. The employer, too, received protection by the stipulation that a public job is not a gift, but "based upon a bona-fide occupational qualification."[9]

Once this law had passed, however, the legislature fell to unproductive bickering -- press, public, and politicians alike all questioned the lack of progress. Senate veteran Tom Collins (D-Pima) declared the legislature more hopelessly deadlocked "than he had ever known." Columnists blamed "pressure brought by the mines, railroads, and other big interests to avoid passage of anything that in any way raise their taxes." At day seventy-five, the *Gazette* noted "confusion . . . dodging . . . repetition of its do-nothing forerunners" and suggested, "the most constructive thing the legislature can do is adjourn. . . ." Less question existed over the governor's program than the process which drew increasing skepticism. Old McFarland aid, George Bideaux, perhaps summed it up best: "The whole business revolved around the ill feeling that exists between the majority and the minority in the house and each division goes out of its way to cause embarrassment to the other."[10]

At the center of the deadlock stood the all important school-aid bill over which the two houses continued to battle and blame each other for legislative intransigence. After the House lowered McFarland's requested figure from $175 to $165, the Senate held out for $150. The House rejected this low figure by a disturbingly close vote of 37-34, indicating weakness in the liberal infrastructure. The Senate then compromised at $155, but inserted a repealer clause to be in effect after two years and threw out the current basis formula for figuring the ADA. A new compromise conference agreed with the new figure, but threw out the repealer and non-current basis provisions. To "statehouse balcony railbirds" this appeared a viable compromise, but the House held out for $157.50, a figure reluctantly accepted by the governor.

Everyone, it seemed, maintained a stubborn stance - mining interests, the Senate, and even the governor. The House took the brunt of press displeasure, however, being termed "more like a temperamental, intolerant, unorganized French parliament . . . an amorphous, leaderless semi-mob." The usually supportive *Arizona Daily Star* sounded like the *Republic*, intoning, "the self-styled `liberals' fight among themselves and are rapidly proving their unfitness to govern. They are making democracy a synonym for irresponsibility and incompetence." Speaker Ruppelius was widely blamed for losing control when confronted with those who coveted his position. The press called for McFarland to bring together the leaders: "It is the governor's majority that is conducting itself in such a reprehensible way."

McFarland did just that, but secretly. After trying to remain above the fray, he plunged in and called Ruppelius and Democratic Senate President Clarence Carpenter together and threatened to call a second special session to deal with educational aid later in the year (a first had already been set to re-codify Arizona laws). The ploy worked and the legislature accepted Mac's $157.50 figure with no repealer but also with no current basis. Under tax-sharing, the counties would raise $30.50 and the state contribute $127.[11]

The hands-on governor continued to confer openly with not only the two leaders, but endlessly hour after hour with many legislative members of both houses. Mac kept a Bible open on his desk and referred to it for guidance if appropriate. Once in frustration he proclaimed, "maybe we can find the answer in here," whereupon young Jewish member Harry Ackerman quipped, "Let's hope the answer is in the Old Testament, Governor." The humor broke the tension if not the logjam.[12]

With the ADA issue resolved and tempers quieted, the legislative snarl unraveled and the legislature adjourned following an eighty-four day session. The proceedings ended on a bright note with the passage of a long-sought tuberculosis-control bill. Many observers, too, had lost sight of the fact that much of Mac's program had passed before the controversial school-aid bill. In appreciation, Governor McFarland briefly addressed a joint-session just before final adjournment. The time stood at 2:50 A.M., April 4, the end of an eighteen-hour day, as he expressed pride in the completion of most of his program, particularly in areas of health, education, and welfare.[13]

As the second longest legislative session in Arizona history adjourned, Mac wished the 108 legislators well as they returned to their own interests. Finally, he could indulge himself by looking closely into the operation of his new TV station, whose grand opening in March had almost escaped his attention as the explosive capitol scene, coupled with time-consuming administrative chores, had kept him immersed in state affairs, with little time for family or business. At the station, he took pleasure in some of the simple things like arranging airtime for a special Easter Seals program featuring Hollywood's newest superstar, Marlon Brando, joining the fight against TB. It fit in nicely with Mac's own executive program.[14]

With this first session, Governor McFarland's initial effort at executing the state's direction fashioned a record that proved far more positive than negative, even though it had last-ed overly long and did not achieve all that he called for. A total of 504 measures were considered with 144 passed. In evaluat-ing the governor's effectiveness in working constructively with the legislature, one must refer back to McFarland's message of January 10.

The school aid bill, considered of primary importance, proved a success in raising allotments per pupil to $157.50 from $115. True, McFarland did not receive the requested $175; nor did he get the taxation placed on a current basis, meaning that for the time being rich and poor districts would fare equally in improvement. The bottom line, however, lay in acknowledging the first raise in aid in eight long years of population growth -- a raise of well over thirty-three percent.

Concerning the governor's request for liberalization of the welfare laws, although the Senate blocked increased welfare payments, new measures did eliminate quarterly reports of earnings which Mac considered harassment of recipients. Moreover, the lien clause, which usually caused the loss of homes and estate property of elderly recipients, was also elimi-nated.

In respect to health legislation, in the waning moments of the session, the tuberculosis bill was rammed through, pro-viding $325,000 for treatment of the states five hundred known cases and $75,000 for families of afflicted breadwinners. The *Phoenix Gazette* called the act "a milestone for the state." Thus, in the areas of health, education, and welfare, the backbone of McFarland's new liberal program, he accomplished a great deal.

The legislature also acted positively on other recom-mendations, passing a constitutional amendment to be present-ed to the people on allowing Fulbright exchanges with foreign teachers. Although the Senate held out for immediate con-struction, the House accepted Mac's recommendation to put over for a time authorization of a new capitol building. The legislation also authorized McFarland to appoint a commission to study his request for a state office building in Tucson. Finally, the Equal Employment Opportunities Act certainly marked a progressive direction in state government civil rights.

In other areas, McFarland's success proved far more sketchy and the roles of both houses questionable. The biggest defeat appeared to be the denial of the requested department of labor. Passed by the House, the measure died in the Senate Planning and Development Committee. However, the inability to create this department was somewhat offset by an increase in unemployment benefits and an extension of the period of eligibility.

Taxation emerged as another area of mixed accomplishment, with little done in vaguely defined studies of equalization of tax valuation and withholding tax provisions. Most importantly, McFarland's specific request for a use tax, though passing the House, failed in the Senate. Too, the gas tax, unmentioned in the original message to the legislature, went down to defeat, perhaps for that very reason. The gas tax would have been put toward highway improvements, so action in this area, too, fell by the wayside. Here, the House provided additional deterrents with five bills never getting out of committee.

Similarly, no legislation passed to deter juvenile delinquency, although four thousand dollars was provided Arizona State College at Tempe to conduct a course for state officials dealing with children.

Additionally, and as critically noted by small farming communities throughout the state, no new measures were undertaken, at this time, to bring water to central Arizona. Finally, in the matter of efficiency in government, there were no major shake-ups even though the legislature cut over one million dollars from budget requests; the final budget of forty-nine million dollars was the highest in Arizona history.[15]

Both houses, particularly the Senate, deserved critical scrutiny in the evaluation of the legislative record. The increase in the number of senators from nineteen to twenty-eight appeared to change neither the character nor the control of that body. Only with aid to the public schools did it evidence any McFarland liberalism. Otherwise, it stood stubbornly with the House minority against his program stopping the use and gas taxes and the proposed labor department and holding down appropriations elsewhere.[16]

The Senate's role was to be expected, but the House also held up highway bills, exhibited lack of leadership at times and most negatively, manifested a minority, which, once entrenched, exhibited a tendency toward "needling" and jealously with "little influence on anyone."[17]

Shortcomings notwithstanding, the state and Tucson papers in particular, labeled the session's record a success, "a good one . . . a pretty competent job." McFarland emerged even better in evaluations faring "very well," as the "newsboys' favorite politico." Only the Pulliam press expressed "distaste," emphasizing the extended time, no highway measures, and no use tax, and angrily maintaining, "this legislature didn't do a lot more than it did do." The record spoke otherwise, although much remained unfinished. As McFarland turned his attention to other aspects of a governor's role, he kept the to be done list prominent in the back of his mind.[18]

"Other aspects" of a governor's job comprised a broadly diversified regimen, ranging from the humorous to serious, the mundane to spectacle. Mac crowned cotton maids and beauty queens, cut ribbons, threw out first balls at Little League play-offs, hosted the Governor's Ball, proclaimed prayers for Ike, who lay sick with heart disease, rode in parades, and attended county fairs throughout the state. At the Arizona State Fair in Phoenix, he played second fiddle to special guest, "Superman," between attending burro and dog races and pinning ribbons on sheep, hogs, and cows. Nearly all of the governor's appearances involved speechmaking, and Mac's small staff and even Edna at times would work on these until the wee hours. Always, Mac would take a prepared speech and tear it apart and reassemble it to his liking. Roland Bibolet related that time, distance, and even costume always presented problems:

A 7:00 A.M. informal breakfast speech (shirt-sleeves) in downtown Phoenix; an 11:00 A.M. parade to lead, mounted (in boots), in Buckeye; a 3:00 P.M. chamber of commerce meeting in Casa Grande (business suit); and a formal dinner in Phoenix at 7:00 P.M. (black tie). I remember dashing him around while he changed uniforms in my front seat—'McFarland's dressing room,' he used to call it. And while traveling thus, he used to write his speech verbally.

However lighthearted these responsibilities were, still Mac and staff had to be aware of the baleful gaze of the Pulliam press always looking over their shoulder. Bibolet explained "We always knew whatever was done there would be adverse criticism. And the press's influence was profound."[19]

McFarland also found time to joust humorously with his native Sooner state and endure jibes of a more plangent nature from faraway Connecticut. One of the lesser known pieces of legislation that passed during the previous session allowed movie firms to enter and film in Arizona without being subject to Arizona's withholding taxes. Representative Robert Hathaway of Santa Cruz County sponsored a bill hoping to lure more films after the state gained some recognition by providing the setting for Rodger's and Hammerstein's *Oklahoma!* Oklahoma's Governor Raymond Gary grew so enamored of the midwestern flavor of the prairie around Patagonia that he devilishly claimed it by raising the Okie flag. "Possible mob violence" was avoided when a *quid pro quo* exchange for one thousand acres of Oklahoma oil country was proposed -- the Greater Seminole Field and Earlsboro were mentioned -- when the question of population transplantation precluded all activity. It seems the Okies were unwilling to be removed from the source of their "white corn licker" in exchange for "Mexican tequila and other assorted skull-busters."[20]

A more serious interstate matter arose in the aftermath of New England summer floods that immobilized industry there. McFarland, in an uncharacteristically thoughtless manner, passed on to Chairman Stanley Womer of the Arizona

Development Board, "a very fine idea," an ill-considered suggestion of the Mohave County Chamber of Commerce that those crippled New England firms be urged to relocate in Arizona which would offer many inducements to make the move agreeable and profitable. Connecticut Governor Abraham Ribicoff cried foul -- that Arizona acted as a "flood vulture." An embarrassed governor was constrained to wire an apology to Ribicoff explaining, "Arizona would never hit a man when he's down," and that the state would give Connecticut assistance to recover. As the press played up the double take, the proposed delegation to Connecticut to implement the idea was scrapped. It is possible, indeed probable, that Womer, a holdover Pyle appointee, leaked the "fine idea" to the Pulliam press to further embarrass the governor. In any case, it was an egregious error.[21]

Other issues caused the governor minor problems as well. The Pulliam press twisted the knife with an extradition case involving former California politician William Bonelli, which gave rise to speculation of favoritism when McFarland refused to extradite, and Bonelli later fled to Mexico. An ongoing probe into the allegedly inefficient operation of the state mental hospital caused concern because of its closed "star chamber" hearings. The *Republic* claimed that secrecy, aloofness, and inaccessibility extended even to the governor's office as well. Always searching for ways to chastise Democrats, the paper started a minor smear campaign incorrectly tagging McFarland with misappropriating funds to obtain a new Cadillac while, in reality, he still used one left over from Pyle's office. A four thousand dollar cash shortage surfaced in a state labor agency dating back to 1948 and extending to July 1955; of course this occurred largely before McFarland's administration and it was his investigator who located the shortage. Furthermore, a serious drought gripped Arizona, and press complaints continued regarding lack of action on the use tax or funding for highway construction and safety. Finally, in what may have been customary from old Ashurst-Goldwater environs, Flagstaff officials slighted McFarland by not introducing him to a crowd at a July 4 festival.[22]

Amidst all of this minor, but still negative, rancor, McFarland must have been pleased with the radio remarks of Republican Jack Williams. The popular broadcaster devoted an entire program to the governor on July 29, and since the prominent Williams went on to become mayor of Phoenix and later Arizona's thirteenth governor, his words commending Mac's water efforts bear attention:

> ... you can't kiss off the fact that although Governor McFarland affects a Will Rogerish, whimsical sort of character, he moves steadily toward an objective and appears to get there much to the surprise of all concerned. You can define smart in many ways ... slick, shrewd, canny ... and then 'McFarland's Way. ...' He has moved in the forefront of great endeavor. ... McFarland ran the shrewdest, smartest political race that I have ever seen run in this state [against Pyle]. All of which leads me to say tonight, that I think when the history of Arizona is written, Governor McFarland may loom larger on its political horizon than any other name. ... If he isn't smart, then I'd like to be whatever he is.[23]

Summer 1955 work was not all fending off critical jibes and slurs; much constructive effort progressed on issues, both new and unresolved. Mac initiated further studies on highway problems and juvenile delinquency. He continued to urge stronger consideration of both the use tax and a state department of labor, and beneath both admonitions there lay the unstated gubernatorial threat of calling a special session of the legislature if necessary. He also tackled the problem of ongoing drought by officially requesting rail and trucking companies to provide lower rates for stockmen to ship livestock elsewhere where adequate feed was available, and he requested and received one million dollars of federal aid.[24]

Most importantly, and with the major assistance of Congressman Stewart Udall, McFarland attempted to bring the

Colorado River water problem into clearer focus. At the congressman's insistence that the Central Arizona Project would never have a chance of passing in the House of Representatives, McFarland and Udall suggested that the state prepare to act independently and find the means to build the project itself. Wayne Aiken, chair of the Arizona Interstate Stream Commission was appointed to front a CAP committee to study and make recommendations on the question, and McFarland, at one point, even suggested that prison labor be used to begin clearing a CAP right-of-way to demonstrate some progress. Organized labor, however, put this idea to the sword. While little came of any of these plans, it is also true that no help came out of Washington where Goldwater and Hayden effected little cooperation as the junior senator busily chased communists, too absorbed to do anything waterwise.[25]

A major factor in the "go it alone" strategy was the ponderous pace of the Supreme Court case which Arizona had initiated against California in 1952 and had now been underway for nearly four years. California employed considerable talent at delaying tactics, and it fell to that state's advantage to avoid a resolution of the case, thereby precluding federally assisted construction of CAP.

Arizona government machinery geared up for full operation when, on October 24, Governor McFarland called for the anticipated special session to revise the state's law code. The last time such a session had been summoned fell in 1928 under Governor George W. P. Hunt, and preparations had been ongoing for this over the past four years, during which time a commission had studied and made recommendations on the proposed re-codification. The governor requested the legislature to "convene in the spirit of restricting business to the recommendations of the Code Commission." He warned that if the revision did not proceed efficiently and at sufficient pace, other important needs, such as the use tax, could intervene and necessitate an additional special session for further consideration of both the code revision and any new immediate issue.

Though the revisions in the code were in the spirit of modernization and not intended to be substantive unless absolutely necessary, the session, limited by the constitution to twenty days, promised to be an arduous one. Longer hours than normal would certainly be required to check the 5,142 pages of the new code. Furthermore, with friction between the House and Senate and within the House between its majority and minority factions, the possibility of new problems and frustrations could not be ignored.

Governor McFarland's message to the special session proved ambivalent in suggesting both restriction of concentration to the code revision and implicitly threatening the possibility of additional session time and other issues to consider. The legislature responded accordingly when both houses indicated different procedures to accomplish the task. The Senate decided to expedite the revision as quickly as possible by accepting the work of the Code Commission as "substantially correct" and correcting any mistakes later. Chief Justice Arthur LaPrade strongly backed this decision, saying that while the newly-printed revision marked "the greatest piece of work ever done in this state," the House's desire to send it back to committees to be studied with possible substantive revisions would interminably and needlessly slow down the process: "How the Hell do I know if it's right. To find out, I would have to hire twenty-five lawyers and . . . another four years to check it," LaPrade exclaimed in frustration. The House listened and budged a little, limiting committee consideration to ten days, and at McFarland's suggestion, holding back on substantive changes in favor of language clarity.[26]

McFarland played an interesting role in the revision. As an ex-legislator he explicitly deferred to legislative prerogatives of working disagreements out internally. Now as an executive, the governor kept his distance. At the same time, however, McFarland as an ex-superior court judge and proficient lawyer expected speedy and efficient adoption of the code, as well as quality in content. Another significant factor of McFarland's implementation was having the new code written and expressed in "laymen's" language, so everyone could understand the meaning of the law. At his instigation, this was finally accomplished when the entire new code, subject to constitutional requirement, was verbally read in the legislature, an arduous task requiring the timesaving maneuver of having portions of the five thousand-plus pages read simultaneously by the legislators. As the fifty-four members read for two hours, the noise could be easily heard in the governor's office a floor below.[27]

As the first special session, as both feared and anticipated, segued into a second in late November, McFarland also acted decisively on other issues that continually reared their heads. An unusual example that occupied McFarland's attention as the year waned concerned creating a seaport access to the Gulf of California in the vicinity of Yuma, Arizona. The same type of imagination had proved successful with the special relationship of Houston, the largest and most prosperous Texas city, and its fifty-mile distant Port of Houston. Although the Gulf of California scarcely sat astride such traveled sea lanes as the Gulf of Mexico, perhaps some similar magic could make a successful outlet for agricultural goods in Arizona's desert southwest.

McFarland closely studied the old Gadsden Purchase Treaty of 1854 that had brought in the southern quarter of the state from Mexico. Even though the true mouth of the Colorado River lay in Mexico about seventy miles below Yuma, the treaty guaranteed that "the vessels and citizens of the United States shall at all times have free and unlimited passage [by the gulf and river] . . . to and from their possessions situated north of the boundary. . . ."

The governor then appointed a five-man Port Authority Board to study the possibility. Mexican planners and engineers also became involved as the proposed port could perhaps be in Mexico with American use guaranteed by the 1854 treaty. As old-timers recalled the times when profitable steamboats plied the river, these experts drew up feasibility studies.[28]

When it came to practical application of Colorado River waters, however, the major focus continued to be the ongoing

battle between California and Arizona over the Central Arizona
Project. Fresh from advocating increased attention to state
funding for the project, Governor McFarland, undoubtedly the
leading figure in Arizona's quest for the water over the past
decade, prepared once again to enter the trenches -- this time in
front of the United States Supreme Court.

The case of *Arizona v. California* had entered a stage
where California desired to have the four upper basin states of
Utah, New Mexico, Wyoming, and Colorado enjoined in the
suit, reasoning that these states, too, had a germane interest in
the outcome. In reality, this procedure could threaten to extend
the case many years beyond one restricted to just the two main
contenders (Nevada had taken California's side). This delaying
tactic, of course, was specifically designed by California, for as
long as the case remained in court it could continue drawing
water as usual. Arizona, however, could not commence construction of the Central Arizona Project, whether a federal or
state project, until the Supreme Court resolved the legal issues.

The case had been placed in the hands of Special Master
George L. Haight who, the past February, had held hearings on
the issue in Phoenix. At that time, Haight had recommended
against California's request. Haight died shortly after this ruling and before California could file a formal objection to his
report. The Supreme Court then appointed a new Special
Master, Simon H. Rifkind, to continue consideration of the
case. Rifkind held the position that California's objection must
be heard and ruled upon by the full U.S. Supreme Court in
Washington, D.C. It was at this stage that Governor
McFarland officially entered the proceedings.

The Arizona Interstate Stream Commission requested
that McFarland involve himself directly with the pending hearing because of his position, prestige, and experience.
Representatives of the upper basin states, as well as Arizona
watermen, held a strategy session at the old Hay-Adams Hotel
in Washington, where they determined that the governor
should make the final summary and "personal" plea to the
nation's highest bench.[29]

McFarland traveled to the capital and stayed at the Hay-Adams with *Phoenix Gazette* reporter Ben Avery. The two had struck up a cordial relationship and often traveled together, McFarland frequently requesting his company from *Gazette* publisher Eugene Pulliam, who always acquiesced. Roland Bibolet termed this a "good cop-bad cop" relationship, with Avery the good and Pulliam the bad, in efforts to obtain information for GOP strategists. Certainly this mutual arrangement allowed the inveterate Republican publisher to obtain an insider's eye to the governor's affairs, but at the same time, McFarland could obtain a forum for his views in the paper through journalist Avery, a lifetime Democrat.

Avery later related the governor's careful preparation for his appearance before the Supreme Court. McFarland stayed up until 4:00 A.M. the night before, meticulously organizing, checking, and rechecking his thoughts before committing them first to paper and then, pacing the room, to memory, casting the crumpled pages into the wastebasket. He felt it extremely important to appear without notes or brief.[30]

The late night hours of preparation paid profitable dividends on December 8 before Chief Justice Earl Warren's court. Warren, the former California governor had disqualified himself and left the courtroom during the hearings. Eight justices, here listed in descending seniority, remained: Hugo Black (AL), Stanley Reed (KY), Felix Frankfurter (MA), William O. Douglas (CN), Harold H. Burton (OH), Thomas C. Clark (TX), Sherman Minton (IN), and John Harlan (NY).

Young Phoenix attorney John Frank began the proceedings, arguing against the California motion to add the Upper Basin states to the suit. Frank, McFarland's special advisor on Colorado River matters, acquitted himself well in stipulating that Arizona only sought to divide lower basin waters, the upper basin's having already been divided by the 1922 Colorado River Compact. He then gave way to Hatfield Chilson of Loveland, Colorado, who argued the upper basin states' collective resistance to being California's straw men, stating, "If we had a real stake in this lawsuit, we would not have to be forced to get in -

- we would be clamoring to get in."

Governor McFarland took the remaining time to make his final plea and summary. In his argument, he noted the three years already spent on the issue and predicted another fifteen would be added if the four additional states became involved, during which time "the economy of Arizona will be ruined." He then related the legislative history of CAP in the U.S. Senate, highlighting California's delaying tactics as they had then occurred and likening the current issue as "simply more of the same."

In the face of the skilled arguments of Arizona's three representatives, California's Northcutt Ely and Nevada's W.T. Mathews made little headway with their argument supporting inclusion of the upper basin based on confusing interpretations of federal water claims in that area and federal obligations to Mexico. Frank effectively parried the argument.[31]

The hearing was held on a Thursday, and everyone expressed shock by the speed with which the Supreme Court rendered its decision. Expected to take until as long as January 12, 1956, the court on Monday announced a five-to-three vote (Warren, of California, abstaining) in favor of Arizona. The dissenting justices included northeasterners, Frankfurter, Burton, and Harlan. Connecticut's Douglas joined midwesterner Minton, Texan Clark, and the two southerners Reed and Black, in supporting Arizona, and backing up the late Special Master George Haight.[32]

His unprecedented appearance and the positive decision marked a significant victory for an elated McFarland, who had fought for the project since his early senate years. Though he certainly enjoyed the public acclaim heaped on him, Mac characteristically shared credit with others, singling out the less visible J.H. "Hub" Moeur, who had presided as chief counsel for the state stream commission, which had designed Arizona's strategy. Commission Chairman Wayne Aiken credited McFarland, stating the case was "expertly argued." New Mexico Senator Clinton Anderson wired the governor: "Congratulations on the magnificent job. . . . I am persuaded

that the fine decision rendered was influenced in no small measure by your outstanding argument and newsmen who heard the
entire proceedings were lavish to me in their praise of your
great effort."[33]

California governor, Goodwin Knight, indicated bitterness as well as disappointment in charging U.S. Attorney
General Herbert Brownell of "favoritism by not choosing sides
. . . . If Brownell, politically astute as he is, played politics, he
picked the weaker team. California's future is threatened dangerously." Knight and the rest of the state could commiserate
that the case was far from over. Arizona had broken up a massive potential logjam, but still had to win title to the water.[34]

To top off a successful week in Washington, D.C.,
Governor Mac, on his way back to Arizona, stopped off in
Bonham, Texas for the groundbreaking ceremony for Sam
Rayburn's $492,000 library. McFarland and Avery were the
only non-Texans in a large throng ranging from the state's
wealthiest citizens to local dirt farmers. Rayburn had completed twenty-two consecutive terms in the House and would go on
for three more, and McFarland commended "Speaker Sam" to
the crowd for "the benefit of his wisdom . . . during the most
trying times of our history [both world wars]. You are honoring
one of our greatest men, not only of Texas, but of the United
States and the World." Then the two "outsiders" departed for
their home state, where the governor would become immediately embroiled in the legislature's second special use tax session, where he once again would prove the significant factor in
the outcome.[35]

In terms of long-range planning, Governor McFarland
called the second special session of the Twenty-second
Legislature to deal with impediments to the future of industrial
expansion in Arizona. It would rank among the stormiest and
ultimately most significant in the state's history. And it would
redound positively to McFarland's reputation as an executive.

Specifically, Arizona law placed a two percent sales tax
on products manufactured in the state and sold to the federal

government. Unlike Arizona, California, where no such tax existed, had long been successful in luring new industry to that state. The problem in eliminating the tax lay in finding means to make up for lost revenue to the state. AFL and CIO leaders suggested levying a "use tax" as a replacement, taxing in-state purchasers of out-of-state products. Civic and business leaders supported labor in noting the sales-tax threat to industrial development. Sperry-Rand Corporation provided immediate and sharp focus on the issue by making known its desire to locate a plant in Arizona. It, however, remained suspicious, wary, and put off by the existence of the sales tax, for much of its production was earmarked for the federal government's defense program. Moreover, the giant corporation, desiring the tax's repeal, had to know by December 16, or it would in all probability locate elsewhere.[36]

On November 29, McFarland had already called the second special session into action, recommending both repeal of the two percent sales tax and institution of the use tax. He asked that the legislators conclude their business successfully by December 15 in time for a positive consideration by an unnamed large corporation, obviously Sperry-Rand. Now after deplaning from Washington and Texas, McFarland eagerly sought news on legislative activity and plans. Only a few days remained before Sperry-Rand's deadline.[37]

Legislative action had been vigorous but non-productive. The Senate originated and passed a bill eliminating the sales tax, and that same evening the House passed a similar bill, 51-16, but containing two amendments introduced by long-term water activist Sidney Kartus. The first and most controversial raised all in-state sales tax rates to two percent, in order to increase revenue by an estimated eight million dollars per year. Previously, sales tax rates had varied from a quarter to two percent. This raise would hit the mines and utilities hardest. The second amendment took some of the increased revenue back by exempting foods and medicines from the tax, decreasing revenue by four million per year. A third, non-Kartus, amendment limited the exemption to primarily defense industries.[38]

The next day, Tuesday, the Senate rejected the amended bill by a vote of 20 to 7. Committees immediately formed in both houses to work out a compromise, but as the midnight, December 15 deadline neared, little had been accomplished as Senate and House negatively jockeyed for position to see who would get the blame for the failure. The final conference meeting extended on past midnight and into the late morning hours, as Governor McFarland patiently and hopefully waited at his desk until 5:00 A.M. The House ultimately agreed to drop Kartus' controversial amendments, but the Senate held firm for its unfettered bill with blanket exemptions.

The governor then made an unexpected appearance at 2:00 P.M. Friday to recommend a recess stating, "tempers were understandably short and it would be unwise to resume deliberating until everyone got some rest." He also made it clear that in order for a use tax to pass, for which there existed general agreement, the sales-tax repeal must accompany it or he would use the veto. Informed of the deadlock, representatives of Sperry-Rand, on the afternoon of Friday the 16th, said that the company would look elsewhere for a site. So after thirty-six hours of deliberation, the legislature adjourned for the weekend as McFarland attempted to smooth out the animosities, if not the differences. He gained a modicum of success when he called Sperry-Rand, which then held out the possibility of reconsideration if a favorable bill were passed very quickly.[39]

Accordingly, on Monday, December 19, Governor McFarland called an unusual joint session during which he forcefully recommended compromise and action. He advised accepting the house version of the bill exempting only defense sales to the government from the two percent tax, but lowering the tax on remaining goods from two to one percent. He also extended the definition of manufacturer exemptions, and in a nod to the Senate, he further recommended that its use tax bill be accepted. Here, the Senate's version had slightly modified the House-originated bill by limiting the use tax only to goods not obtainable in Arizona.[40]

The House accepted the compromise that same

evening, while the Senate waited until the next day, but clearly aggressive leadership and action had effectively solved the legislative crisis. A triumphant Governor McFarland signed the two bills into law on Wednesday as Sperry-Rand confirmed its move to Arizona with plans to build a plant employing up to five thousand people and later construction of a research center. McFarland always included this breaking of the deadlock as the most satisfying moment of his executive years.[41]

The first session now took a deserved Christmas break before reconvening briefly in early January for a third special session to tie up the loose ends of the revised law code. This necessitated the repeal of all existing laws enacted since statehood before the longest bill in legislative history at two million words and 5,142 pages could be signed by Governor McFarland on January 9, 1956.[42]

This same day marked the start of the second session of the Twenty-second Legislature with Governor McFarland's message to the jointly assembled houses. In a lengthy speech, he reviewed some of the successes and all of what he felt were shortcomings of the past regular session, stating "promises have not been fully met." These faults were now to be rectified, and included, most obviously, a "full-fledged independent department of labor." While McFarland's concern with highway construction and safety held over from before he, immediately this time, called for an increase in the gasoline tax from five to six cents per gallon to expedite attention to these areas. Similarly, he recommended creation of a State Planning Board to handle layover issues like a new capitol building and a state office building in Tucson. He also urged forming a State Parks and Recreation Commission and a State Surplus Property Board to distribute surplus government property to public institutions such as schools and hospitals.

The governor then turned to political issues of salaries and particularly the length of terms of office, urging a major change from two to four years for county and state officials. In so doing, he stressed the inability of elected officials to get programs rolling before facing another election every two years. He countered this, however, by cautioning against machine politics and urging a limit for the governor's office of one four-year term. Moreover, in recommending moderate salary increases to meet the increased cost of living, he specifically exempted his own office and suggested these issues be settled via a referendum in the fall elections.[43]

The lengthy message also stressed the need for Arizona to continue to make its own preparations for financing and building the Central Arizona Project and to continue to address problems in agriculture, air pollution, and juvenile delinquency. Likewise, in the next week's budget address to the Legislature, McFarland continued to emphasize attention to efficiency in spending. After his office had completed an extensive study of each government department, McFarland lowered by four million dollars the overall requested amount in arriving at a yearly budget of sixty-seven million dollars, only a one percent increase over the previous year, but still the largest in state history.[44]

With legislative direction and the budget set by Governor McFarland, the Twenty-second Legislature looked toward a smooth-running session, avoiding the factionalism of 1955. Such, however, was not to be the case. In fact, the second session went on to prove more frustrating, tiresome, and longer than the previous year and with little to recommend itself.

After the requisite sixty days of legislative activity had passed, the only major part of the governor's program that had been signed into law created the Arizona Surplus Property Board on March 5. The usual Arizona anti-union sentiment held up the labor bill even though the unions disclaimed either its design or benefits, stating unorganized labor would be the major beneficiary. The proposed gas tax increase became bogged down in senate committee. Parks and recreation languished in joint conference. While the capitol roof continued to leak, creation of a State Planning Board became mired down in arguments over whether to repair the building or move the whole government to Papago Park. Newer controversies arose as well, such as changing the name and status of Arizona State

College at Tempe to Arizona State University. Besides the Surplus Property Board, only in the area of water did McFarland appear to be making tenuous progress.[45]

On February 22, the governor had made a surprise appearance before a joint meeting of the House and Senate to present a program under which the state could move independently in bringing Colorado River water to central Arizona. In a concise presentation, McFarland gave the history and his analysis of the water controversy dating back to 1922. Although he had been involved throughout the three-plus decades, very few in the legislature had similar involvement. Now the younger members listened attentively as the man probably more familiar with the issue than any other single person gave his views which, according to the press, were masterful and stimulating.

Thematically, he linked power and water via the Arizona Power Authority: "Our power and water programs are inseparable. The same dams must serve both our power and water needs and the power must aid in the progress of irrigation." He recommended legislation broadening the responsibility of the power authority to include dam construction, but restricting it concerning construction of aqueducts, canals, and laterals.[46]

Within a week, the Senate Committee on Agriculture and Irrigation responded with a bill creating a State Bureau of Reclamation out of the Arizona Power Authority. Opposition, however, began to coalesce around the Yuma area where the Wellton-Mohawk Project had been in operation for several years. Yumans required reassurance that their interests would be protected in the advent of the larger CAP. Even though McFarland and CAP President Wayne Aiken anticipated this and flew immediately to Yuma to assuage concerns, the bill continued to be hotly debated as the regular sixty-day session drew to a close. Once again, with redundant certainty, the legislature shifted gears into overtime.[47]

Passage of the water bill, the major goal of the overtime session, depended on convincing Senate Majority Leader Harold Giss of Yuma that the bill did not violate the prior rights of Wellton-Mohawk. A men's clothing store owner, Giss had developed into a great power in the Senate. A tireless worker, he closely studied every bill, and although he normally sided with the conservative bloc, he was always straight up-front with McFarland. Now, as he examined a measure affecting his home district, he made it clear that his regional population did not oppose the intent of the bill, but that prior rights should be specifically spelled out. Aiken and John Frank backed McFarland, warning that Arizona, via active legislative work on CAP, must show California that it must have and could implement increased Colorado River water use in order to expedite its chances in the ongoing lawsuit.[48]

The House, where Maricopa County and central Arizona held a decided population advantage, passed the bill 61 to 11 on March 26, but Giss and the Senate remained in further debate and consideration. Governor McFarland, who had "hesitated to inject myself too far in any legislative matter," now stepped up the pressure, firing off letters to legislative leaders and adding the gas tax to his concern for the water bill. He requested immediate action.[49]

By the second week in April when the session had reached a new record length, a compromise bill emerged specifically restricting any Arizona Power Commission planning to waters "not already in use." The bill passed the House 64-6 and the Senate as well with only one vote against. The gas tax did not make it through, although underlying threats of a special session were dissipated in the wake of the water bill passage. Governor McFarland waited for six hours in his office as the final loose ends were tied up. Then, at 2:55 A.M., April 14, he entered the legislative chambers to deliver a short speech of thanks. Although certainly disappointed that major portions of his program had failed to pass, he accented the positive: "There has never been a legislature in Arizona history that has had more difficult or important questions. . . . You have worked hard." Indeed, the assembly had been working for six solid months, including the past special sessions. Now, as confetti streamed down from the galleries, the longest session to that time adjourned at ninety-seven days.[50]

Despite his syrupy valedictory, McFarland knew that his program had fared poorly in the session just concluded. It may have been his fresh memory of the bitterness that surfaced during the three special calls of the previous session that kept him from issuing a call now for action on the gas tax. The prior session had tested his mettle. The legislature had finally offered him a barely acceptable set of compromises. His reluctant approval did not close the open wounds all sides carried into the second session. It was an election year; rather than go through that torment again, he could be satisfied with the Surplus Property Board, the last-minute water bill, and the State Planning and Building Commission, which also eventually made it through the intricacies of passage. Too, the requested salary increases for officials at state and county levels were granted, including the governor's office which he had favored exempting. Final decision on this as well as four-year terms, however, had to be referred to the people at the next election, and the electorate rejected the recommendations at that time. Also, efforts to combat juvenile delinquency had been shored up by making parents responsible for up to five hundred dollars damage.[51]

Yet, the shortcomings loomed large: no gasoline tax for increased highway construction and safety, no parks and recreation board, and most importantly, according to the governor, no independent labor department.

These legislative failures had to be weighed against first session successes with increases in school aid, a liberalized welfare code, higher unemployment benefits, elimination of the sales tax and replacement by the use tax, and revision of the state law code. Certainly, Governor McFarland had both forced and influenced a liberal direction in the Twenty-second Legislature. The influence and particularly the force had waned during the recent session, but perhaps this was to be expected as the pivotal 1956 elections approached.[52]

Election sparring started early, soon after the legislature disbanded when Senator Goldwater arrived in Phoenix criticizing McFarland's efforts to obtain an Arizona town site controlling construction of the proposed Glen Canyon Dam. Terming the governor's efforts too slow in thwarting Utah's similar designs, he suggested Mac retire to practice law in Florence.[53]

Actually, McFarland had been working methodically and with purpose, or as he put it, "quietly and on a nonpartisan basis." The Glen Canyon site lay on the upper Colorado River entirely in Arizona, but only a half-dozen miles from the Utah border, so that state also wanted to reap the expected benefits from the location of the necessary construction town. But with the cooperation of the Navajo Tribal Council, which sanctioned the project on its reservation, the State Highway Department speedily authorized one hundred thousand dollars, and the U.S. Bureau of Indian Affairs provided machinery to quickly blaze a fifty-five-mile dirt road through the desert to the dam site. Arizona's grasping the initiative, at McFarland's suggestion, resulted in the favorable verdict of the U.S. Bureau of Reclamation to award the eventual town site of Page to Arizona. Logistically, the Page location lay seventy miles closer to the supply city of Flagstaff than the nearest railhead in Utah, and construction costs of $100,000-110,000 per mile were far cheaper than Utah's $250,000-300,000 through its rugged canyonlands territory. McFarland rode among the first to travel the new road that had been planned, financed, and built for early use within two weeks by the end of April.[54]

Arizona's labor establishment was pleased that a major construction project was about to begin and grateful that Mac had helped locate Page within Arizona. The governor, however, was still at cross purposes with labor over at least two matters. First marked his refusal to stand outright against Arizona's right to work laws. These laws, which banned the union closed shop, had been voted in by the state's electorate in 1946. At that time, McFarland claimed the majority had the right to initiate such laws as it desired. He now stated that right-to-work was "no issue" because it could not be put on the ballot at this late date (summer 1956) and in any case was the province of the people at-large in terms of changes, not the governor. Ultimately the AFL-CIO Committee on Political Education (COPE) endorsed McFarland with only the machinists union objecting. Second, the absence of a department of labor remained hanging fire.[55]

While Mac dealt with these issues amidst flights back and forth to San Francisco where the Arizona-California water trial had resumed, opposition began to emerge for the upcoming elections. In the Republican primaries, Phoenix's Horace B. Griffen, state advertising manager for the Pulliam press brushed aside lesser candidates, produce executive and former state senator O.V. Miller of Phoenix and businessman and failed state senate candidate Fred Trump of Tucson. Essentially Griffen represented Pulliam and embraced the forlorn hope mission of at least presenting Mac nominal competition so he would not run unopposed. Griffen, a lackluster, even boring, speaker was uncomfortable with the role thrust upon him and ultimately was delighted to return to the obscurity of his press job.[56]

Nevertheless, Griffen outlined the basic Republican platform as tax relief for the home-owner, protection from inefficient welfare expenditure, aid to schools based on need, not average daily attendance, and increased job placement due to merit and qualification. According to Griffen, Mac was deficient in all of these matters. Like McFarland, Griffen advocated a labor department and assurance of a Glen Canyon town site. He also expressed concern against the spread of venereal disease within the state, but was cautious enough not to blame the contagion on Mac.[57]

McFarland formally announced his candidacy for a second term on June 14. As a heavy favorite and running without opposition in the primaries, he spent the summer dealing with the Glen Canyon Dam, the San Francisco water trial, and lambasting the Eisenhower administration rather than his in-state opposition. In mid-August, he attended the Democratic National Convention in Chicago where he was flown in by the fast-moving LBJ's presidential aspirations. Honored by being tapped as temporary chairman of the convention, Mac briefly spelled Sam Rayburn at the podium; however, he proved unable to deliver for LBJ even with a last minute appeal to the Arizona delegation, which cast its votes for Adlai Stevenson. Stevenson prevailed, and consideration turned to the vice presidency. Here, as a gubernatorial candidate, Mac asked the Arizona delegation not to do the expected: as a matter of course, states with prominent governors or congressmen routinely placed their names in nomination for the veep position as favorite sons - planning to collect back home later with political favors. Ultimately, Tennessee's Estes Kefauver prevailed over John Fitzgerald Kennedy and received the nomination as Stevenson's running mate. Mac did later indicate that, in the event of a logjam, he was prepared to resume supporting Johnson who remained in the wings ever alert to move for the nomination if the occasion arose. LBJ would have to wait for another time.[58]

Returning to Arizona, McFarland finally cranked up his general election campaign after the Republican Griffen had triumphed over Miller and Trump in the September 12 primary. Shortly after the primary, the Democratic party issued its platform, calling for continued liberalization of welfare laws and attention to highway construction and safety, as well as increased aid to poor school districts. As expected, the platform included a labor department and continued vigilance over water affairs. The Democrats issued a new call for a civil rights - human relations plank eliminating all discrimination in public places. The platform also targeted Arizona's Indians for increased attention, while at the same time, Governor McFarland spoke against federal termination plans for ending assistance to Indian tribes.

The governor carried his campaign into the Arizona hinterlands throughout October, speaking in twenty-seven towns in thirty days, carrying the party message with specific reference to local issues and problems: mining in Globe, Miami, Superior, Clifton, and Morenci; agriculture in the Gila and Verde valleys; highway construction and improvement along the Route 66 towns; parks and recreation in the north; and increased aid to combat the ongoing drought in the ranching areas above the Mogollon Rim. As always, Mac reflected grassroots concern and extra hard work: "Foot-weary aides first estimated the governor walked 40 miles in his particular type of sidewalk campaigning, and they flatly refused to scale the figure down to 10 miles."[59]

As election day drew nearer, Mac concentrated more on the Phoenix-Tucson axis amidst visits from Democratic notables Stevenson, Kefauver, Rayburn, Johnson, and Stuart Symington. State polls indicated the governor running ahead of the popular Ike's lead of fifty-nine to thirty-six percent over Stevenson. Carl Hayden, aiming for his sixth term in the U.S. Senate, ran even stronger with 64.7 percent support compared to only 24.3 for his opponent Ross F. Jones. Hayden, McFarland, and Stewart Udall, running for his second term in Congress, all attended the colorful Democratic "Spectacular" at the Bali Hi Motel before moving on to the Shrine Auditorium to hear Pennsylvania strongman and Pittsburgh Mayor David Lawrence rouse the crowd in his address. There, the public -- at thirty-five dollars a ticket -- and dignitaries alike, sat back and enjoyed the special Democratic campaign film, *Seventeen Days to Victory*, which had been prepared by Hollywood writers Moss Hart, Alan Lerner, Herman Wouk, and Oscar Hammerstein II. The show featured Marlon Brando, Bette Davis, Harry Belafonte, Henry Fonda, and then-Democrat Frank Sinatra, while entrenched and emerging party symbols, Harry Truman, Eleanor Roosevelt, and John Kennedy delivered their political messages across the big screen. Unfortunately, the pageantry was swiftly ruined when state party chairman Dick Jenkins fell dead at the microphone during his address, in a tragedy reminiscent of the venerable Alben Barkley's death the past April.[60]

The campaign waged on ponderously in some aspects, desperately in others. Griffen continued to call out McFarland on the right-to-work issue, which could be a double-edged sword. If Mac openly supported it, labor votes would flee his camp if he stood against it, Pinto Democrats could be expected to flock to the GOP. Prudently, he avoided the issue.[61]

Then, in a move redolent of desperation, Griffen's colleagues at the Pulliam press gave it "the old college try," according to one political analyst, by linking McFarland to favoritism allegedly extended by the highway department to his KTVK-TV business partner Ralph Watkins. The press released just enough information to make it appear that the governor was linked with the extension of bidless contracts to another company Watkins controlled. As the *Arizona Daily Star* pointed out in chastising its rival press, this constituted an example of "when the truth can smear": telling only part of the story in order to make a legal operation seem illegal while demeaning an outsider in the process.[62]

The *Star*, which had endorsed Pyle in 1954, went on to endorse McFarland now in 1956, stating:

> He has earned it by the way he has conducted the affairs of our state. He has made a good governor. He has been progressive, but not extravagant. He has kept the affairs of state on an even keel and has maintained an era of good feeling among most of the people and most of the vested interests. . . . He has followed a policy of moderation that has gone as far as to leave people alone and work out their own lives. The results speak for themselves. The state has prospered. The people are prosperous, yet the state stands high in providing those social services that are necessary. . . .[63]

The *Glendale News* sounded an aggressive note in its support.

> For the first time in many years, Arizona has a governor who has consistently given his best. . . . No one with common sense can accuse him of being dishonest . . . . He is not that kind of man. His personal integrity has been a bulwark against the many selfish interests that have tried to infiltrate Arizona's economy. At no time in the state's history has its economic status been more sound. . . . Mac has not stooped to the level of his needlers and for that one thing alone, we are proud of him.[64]

On election day, November 6, Mac and Edna drove

down to Florence to cast their votes with Del and Jewell. The confident favorite son surveyed the scene of the Pinal County Courthouse where he had initiated his career in politics over three decades before, and this confidence proved justified as he swept to his then largest vote-count, 171,848 to 116,744, carrying all fourteen counties in the process.[65]

In the high-interest election with an eighty-one percent turnout, McFarland led all Democratic candidates, including Carl Hayden, who also fashioned an easy victory. Mac trailed Eisenhower, however, as the ever-popular Ike trounced Stevenson with 177,000 to 113,000 votes, Arizona continuing its then never-broken tradition of supporting every winning president since its admission to statehood. In the congressional elections, both incumbents retained their seats, Democrat Stewart Udall eighty-two to fifty-five thousand and Republican John Rhodes by a seventy-nine to sixty-five thousand margin. In contrast to Mac's garrulous backslapping, shoe-leather approach, Rhodes had proven the master of the tea party-morning coffee campaign style with small, intimate groups of the state's women.[66]

The victorious McFarland paid close attention to the make-up of the new legislature. The liberal faction had been decimated by conservative Democrats, and this did not bode well for the continuation of the governor's program. In fact, the conservative Democrats would no longer need Republican support, even though the latter's number had increased from 22 to 25 out of 108. Among the defeated liberals stood former Speaker of the House Harry Ruppelius, who received "the kiss of death," according to the Republican press, because of his ardent support for and from the unions.[67]

Indeed, the Pulliam press celebrated, "Reuther loses Arizona," referring to national labor leader and AFL-CIO President Walter Reuther, who had set up the committees on political education throughout the nation to pull through labor-endorsed candidates. Not only did Ruppelius's defeat indicate this, but so did John Rhodes's strong run against a formidable opponent, William Mahoney. Furthermore, "reflecting a com-

plete collapse of conservative [Democrat or Republican] political respect for organized labor," the new House stationary
would henceforth be printed by a non-union printer: "a long
time [had passed] before any such legislative affront to union
labor could have been seriously considered in Arizona."
Somehow McFarland had managed to avoid such entanglement,
but the message was clear: "In the Arizona elections, Mr.
Reuther was told where to go." Mac would not be so fortunate
in the future, because speculation widely held that Mac would
attempt to regain his senate seat from Barry Goldwater in 1958.
If so, he had indicated that he retained formidable support
among Arizonans, both conservative and liberal. For the time
being, however, McFarland, prepared for the more immediate
future, stating the second term "gives me time to finish the job."
All indications showed that the new Twenty-third Legislature
would not make it an easy task.[68]

CHAPTER THIRTEEN
—————

SECOND TERM TRIALS
1957-1958

GOVERNOR ERNEST MCFARLAND REQUESTED that his second inauguration be "simple, but impressive." No husky gun salutes punctuated the affair. Nor did jet planes race out of the sun as they had for Governor Dan Garvey in 1949. In fact, Mac demurred on writing invitations at all, just letting it be known that all were welcome or adding a memo to his Christmas cards of the month past, thus saving the government some money in the process.

Nature had its say as well at the January 7 inaugural with leaden and dripping skies that limited the attendance. In this respect, and along with the university and college bands and the Florence Boy Scout Honor Guard, the ceremony closely resembled that of two years before. Famous Arizona family names numbered among those in attendance as Evo De Concini presided and Chief Justice-select Levi S. Udall administered the oath in replacing ill Chief Justice Arthur T. LaPrade. Mac took the oath on a Bible opened to a marked passage: "It matters not who keepeth the city if the Lord keepeth not the city." The Bible given to him by local ministers was inscribed, "to a Christian Statesman." Former Governors Garvey, Stanford, and Jones once again attended, and again Howard Pyle was nowhere to be seen. Mexican Governors Alvaro Obregon of Sonora and Braulio Maldamacho of Baja California were honored guests.

In his second inaugural address, Governor McFarland set a goal for prosperity and happiness for all Arizonans with specific objectives being job security for all, equal opportunity for education, health and recreation, and proper care and security for the aged, blind, dependent, and handicapped. The address reflected the theme of simplicity in its brevity and scope and linked its objectives to development of natural resources. He did not give specifics, but everyone in attendance knew this meant water as well as the usual plant, animal, and mineral resources, not to mention tourist attractions. Briefly reiterating the efforts of his first term, McFarland left the rostrum to others; he engaged in no speculation over how effective he might be with the new, more conservative legislature, but newspapers, cloak-rooms, and water cooler scuttlebutt featured such musings.[1]

Veteran *Phoenix Gazette* political columnist Bill Turnbow predicted legislative harmony during the upcoming session, and new House Speaker W. L. "Tay" Cook (D-Cochise) apparently hoped so too, dropping by the governor's office unannounced for a friendly visit. Both Cook, who had replaced the defeated Harry Ruppelius as speaker, and returning Senate President Clarence Carpenter, were conservative. McFarland had worked closely with Ruppelius to push through as much of their liberal program as possible during the past two years. The new conservative Democratic House seemed to belie Turnbow's prediction. Still, he expected "certain approval" of a gasoline tax hike, but at the same time warned of potential House divi-siveness where "all chiefs, no Indians" prevailed.[2]

The next week Governor McFarland addressed the opening of the Twenty-third Legislature's First Session by reviewing exactly why everyone was there: "to communicate . . . the condition of the state and recommend such matters as . . . shall deem expedient. I want you to know I have a profound sense of my responsibility. I also recognize where my responsi-bility ends and that of the legislature begins." Certainly that statement, a double entendre, could be taken as a suggestion of gubernatorial cooperation or as a veiled threat to get to work, or as both.

In his opening, McFarland noted that statistics indicat-ed that the growth of state business had finally caught up with that of population: "We must continue to work . . . for more new industry to provide . . . our ever increasing population demands." He also enjoined the legislators in their work to "reflect the dignity and equality of all men. We should permit no discriminations of any nature."

Then the governor took on the basics, beginning with the old call for the ADA education assistance to be set on a current basis. For welfare, he reviewed his own successes of a decade before in the Senate, noted more recent federal increases, and urged the state to match them.

An avid traveler, whether it be by plane, train, ship, or automobile, McFarland had always grasped transportation, particularly highways, as a vital issue. Referring to Eisenhower's recent Interstate Highways Act, he warned that Arizona must either keep up with matching funds or, in any case, the state would be indirectly contributing to someone else's road building. Once again, he resurrected the last session's *bete noire* of a gasoline tax increase to finance essential highway construction. Too, McFarland continued his interest and experimentation with highway safety. His imaginative use of the National Guard to keep all available state vehicles constantly on patrol had reduced highway fatalities from 423 in 1954 to 361 in 1955. But with increased travel, the death count had risen to 484 in 1956. This record, McFarland exhorted "is of concern . . . and calls for action." He wanted to increase the highway patrol by twenty-five for safety purposes and use the expected fuel tax increase to assist road construction.

Once again, he reviewed past legislative shortcomings in calling for departments of Labor and State Parks. He wanted labor to be independent and work directly under the governor rather than under the Industrial Commission whose functions were "chiefly in another field and where there would exist conflicts of interest." Concerning parks, he warned, "the encroachment of civilization is rapidly restricting these natural areas." He added a recommendation for zoological gardens and wildlife protection as well.

Naturally McFarland continued to urge funding to continue the interminable water lawsuit with California. To the equally ongoing new capitol building controversy, he added a recommendation for a new stadium to be constructed at Arizona State College at Tempe, which, at this time, was still a college, not a university. He also hoped the stadium would serve as a state fairgrounds.

McFarland concluded his address by noting that although he had been criticized "because I've refrained in the past from getting rough with the legislature," he would keep it that way "in a spirit of harmony" and custom, and continue to leave his door open to everyone "regardless of party." Very few Republicans sat in the Twenty-third Legislature, but the crossover Pinto Democrats had grown considerably. Everyone, including the press, seemed to ignore this fact "in the spirit of harmony." The question remained: how long would the honeymoon continue?[3]

Mac deviated from the budgetary practices of his predecessors by endeavoring to take the mystery out of the budget and make it meaningful to both legislators and at least those citizens who made an effort to follow public affairs. In his budget message of January 21, he gave legislators a clear summary of where the money was expected to come from as well as where it was intended to go. To take the message, in a less comprehensive form, to the public, he created the special office of Budget Advisor, to which he appointed Jack Lynch who put the budget in approximate big figures that were easy to understand: twenty, seventeen, and sixteen million dollars respectively from sales, property, and income taxes. Miscellaneous fees and luxury taxes would bring in twelve million more, and the new use tax would raise only three-quarters of a million. On the outgoing side, education would consume thirty-five million with another seven million in capital for higher education, notably for junior college development and the proposed Tempe stadium. An even one million was earmarked for the Tucson state office building that had been given the go-ahead by the past legislature. Though this budget, in keeping with the continued population growth and economic expansion, again stood as the highest in state history, once again Mac decreased the recommended expenditures for his own executive office. Tucson's *Daily Star*, nearly always supportive of the governor, termed the preparatory work "excellent analysis" and congratulated McFarland and Lynch. Insiders, however, knew that the publicity and time spent would make this area suitable fodder for discontented legislators if the occasion should arise.[4]

The first legislative issue that evolved into controversy did not concern the budget proposals but revived the new capitol building debate. Five million dollars had already been allocated for this project, but the question of design remained a thorny issue. Architects did not assist in a harmonious solution and fell to bickering among themselves and submitting questionable designs. Initially the Associated Capitol Architects (ACA) presented a plan calling for an eighteen-story building. The State Planning and Building Commission lacked enthusiasm for this proposal, not because of the height, but the monotony. Terming the building "more like a Kansas grain elevator than a capitol," the planners also objected to placement of windows only on the north or "cool" side away from the sun.[5]

The architects submitted a revised draft the following week that the planners found acceptable. This placed windows on all sides, added two set back top stories to break the lines, and capped the skyscraper with a dome. Now skeptics referred to it as a derby hat on a telephone pole. The plan included three story wings at the base of the spire to house the legislative chambers, all at a price tag of just above $7.75 million.

The final obstacle to the start of construction was the legislature, which would have to appropriate the funds. But before this could happen, renowned architect and Arizona resident Frank Lloyd Wright called the ACA's plans "incompetent." Wright maintained a small, exclusive architectural center and winter home at Taliesin West under the slopes of the McDowell Mountains to the northeast of the city and, as the nation's most celebrated architect, commanded attention. He suggested using the coveted Papago Park area, a natural desert setting of rocky hills, great boulders, cactus, and other desert flora that lay a few miles directly east of the center of Phoenix, more-or-less between the smaller towns of Tempe and Scottsdale. In the early twentieth century it had been considered for a national park, but by 1957 had plummeted in status to being considered for a fairgrounds. Many hoped its natural setting would remain inviolate.[6]

Wright envisioned three separate buildings, one for each branch of government interlinked by a massive umbrella-like copper dome for shade and symbolic purposes. Through vast holes cut in the dome, Old Faithful-style fountains would spurt to the sky. This plan met much skepticism as well, some planners referring to it as the *Teahouse of the August Moon*, after the current Marlon Brando-Glenn Ford hit movie. Undoubtedly McFarland lacked enthusiasm too. The veteran water-man would not have appreciated such evaporative water waste in a desert setting. In later years, he vehemently opposed the geyser-like apparatus at Fountain Hills, which was promoted as the tallest in the world.[7]

The imperious, flamboyant Wright did not help his own cause either by talking down to the legislators, evading questions of finance, and avoiding suggestions of modification. Even his guise, a great flowing black cape, drew suspicion. Underlying these difficulties lurked the stipulation that if the capitol grounds were removed, the land would revert to families of the original donors of near half-century before. In any case, it proved a moot point, for the legislature rejected all ideas and refused to appropriate the funds. Nor did it permit further consideration of Papago Park for a fairgrounds.[8]

In other legislative affairs, it appeared that once again the gas tax and an independent labor department were destined to fail. Perhaps the powerful Highway Commission exerted too much pressure on sensitive legislators to match federal funding. Perhaps the idea of a department that dealt specifically with matters of hours, wages, mediation, strikes, and cooling off periods seemed too susceptible to potential union inroads and influence. In any case, any pre-session ardor cooled considerably for these executive requests. Too, Republican Senator Hi Corbett of Tucson kept up just enough strength to thwart Arizona State College at Tempe's designs to attain university status. A bill to this effect had passed the House the last session, and the Phoenix dailies stubbornly kept referring to the institution as Arizona State University - all to no avail. By February's end Governor McFarland had signed only two bills, one for the additional highway patrolmen and the other allocating funds for junior colleges. Some slim hope still remained for the current basis ADA for school aid and even the Yuma port bill, though the latter often drew as many chuckles as commendations. State parks had seen its way through the House and now awaited the Senate's decision.[9]

Problems arose between executive and legislature when McFarland came out strongly against a proposed fifty-percent increase in the state sales tax. Legislators wanted this item in order to lower property taxes, but drew Mac's displeasure with their intransigence elsewhere. Noting that food and medicine were included among taxable items, McFarland threatened to veto any such measure. In a letter to leaders Carpenter and Cook, he explained:

> I am unalterably opposed to such an increase. This is a tax on the working man who must spend a large portion of his income for food and medicine, of double that [tax] imposed on large industries. . . . The tax on food and medicine should be entirely eliminated.[10]

The state's small press like the *Mohave Miner* applauded McFarland's stance, but the Phoenix Pulliam press called it a political ploy for the 1958 elections when most expected the governor to run against Goldwater again for the U.S. Senate. Irked legislators threatened to cut out the one million dollar request for the Tucson state office building, and the schism did influence the legislature's denial of funding a new capitol building.[11]

As this session wound toward its sixty-day limit, passage of the State Parks Board measure provided Governor

McFarland his first major success. Most of the rest of his program awaited final action on the appropriations; current basis ADA, the Tucson building, and other requests were all destined to be decided in the furious bargaining of the last few days of the session. Both houses accepted the principle of current basis, but different formulas from each demanded conference committee amendments.[12]

The Senate approved McFarland's requests except for a fifty-percent reduction for the Tucson building and awaiting further conferences on the ADA. Unfortunately, the House devolved into slowdowns amidst constant bickering, and both legislative units seemed more intent on finishing up within the stipulated sixty days. If so, they proved successful.

Without passage of the school aid bill, which provided the last verbal sparring, the House adjourned at 12:26 A.M., March 15 - twenty-six minutes beyond the official limit. The Senate even outdid its tardy counterpart by the nineteenth-century tactic of stopping their official clock, *de jure*, at 11:59 p.m. while senators scurried to wrap up a few loose ends before adjourning *de facto* after midnight. Unfinished issues included House-Senate conference committees on school aid, which were purportedly ready for compromise. McFarland and these legislators expressed bewilderment and frustration.

McFarland appeared before the joint house members preceding their departure for home and "refrained from comment indicating he was not too happy with the results." He merely bid them goodnight and god speed and made no threatening overtures about calling a special session, though this step had been predicted by many. Perhaps, Mac did not want to stir the waters further than the lack of productivity had already done. Possibly, as some claimed, his mind already focused on the 1958 election, and he did not want to offend Democrats now whose unreserved support he would need eighteen months later. An overt chastisement of the legislature at this time could prove very counterproductive for the following session. In any case, he stayed his hand. Asked prior to the evening whether he would call a special session, Mac, ever the baseball fan, said he "never thinks about the second game until the first one was over." Well, the first game was now in the books, and it remained for future months to determine if his letting the session down easy would have positive results.[13]

Not surprisingly to some, incredibly to others, the Pulliam press and the quasi-conservative *Tucson Daily Citizen* celebrated the punctuality of adjournment. "A good record," a "pattern for legislative progress," and "a place of glory in Arizona political history," were among the accolades as the press casually dismissed the school aid failure while lamenting the rise of property taxes in lieu of the failed sales tax increase. Indeed, it had been twenty-five years since an Arizona legislature had completed its business within the established sixty days.[14]

This fact provided no consolation to McFarland who valued his program over punctuality. While Pulliam railed against the previous "do nothing legislature," Mac had only to glance at the tally sheet to see by the lack of productivity that the Twenty-second had been more productive than the Twenty-third, which, by his measures, had failed on several fronts; it failed to adapt current-basis ADA, to establish a Department of Labor, and to raise the gas tax, or increase welfare payments.

Governor McFarland had to be satisfied with continued appropriations for the California water fight, an increased number of highway patrolmen, and the creation of a State Parks Department. With this, Arizona no longer remained the only state in the union without a park system. Too, the legislature appropriated funds for construction of a new stadium at Arizona State-Tempe, but still withheld university status. Also, no funds were provided for a state government building in Tucson or a new building in the capitol spread in Phoenix. Mac's most significant victory, ironically, did not involve his program recommendations, but rather lay in beating back the Legislature's effort to increase the state sales tax.[15] In sum, the session was far less productive than the one of two years before.

Legislative shortcomings did not end Governor McFarland's problems as the year 1957 wore on. First, a shortage of forty-two thousand dollars was discovered in the Arizona Industrial Commission. Arizona's chief accountant reported that the deficit had occurred sometime between 1951 and 1955. The culprit was not a McFarland appointee, but as the incumbent governor he had to bear the brunt of the public's displeasure.[16]

Another unpleasantry, however, did touch his office directly when a four thousand dollar donation to his 1954 election campaign from the Western Teamsters Union surfaced. The donation had not been reported as required, nor was it known where or how the funds had been spent, only that they had been expended. The source of the discovery three years after the fact and with an election in the future served to heighten the drama and controversy.

In Washington, D.C., Arizona's junior-Senator Barry Goldwater sat as a member of the McClellan Committee investigating suspicious activities in the nation's major labor unions, notably the Teamsters. Though Goldwater would later embarrass himself in front of AFL-CIO President Walter Reuther, he unearthed some interesting information with the testimony of Frank W. Brewster, President of the Western Teamsters. Brewster confirmed the union's contributing four thousand dollars to McFarland's 1954 campaign, because Mac opposed the right-to-work law in Arizona. Certainly, Brewster said, "if the governor had not satisfied the union on that score, he never would have received the contribution." The funds had been earmarked "for education purposes" by the union to enlighten people about labor's negative views towards right-to-work legislation. Goldwater regarded this "confession from on high" as direct evidence of big labor's immoral intrusion into the Arizona public.[17]

McFarland denied ever receiving or knowing about the check, and he again stated he had taken no public stance on right-to-work, because in 1946, the people had already made their determination in support of the measure. Goldwater, however, possessed a photostat of the check written to the McFarland Campaign Committee and endorsed by campaign manager Joseph Duke. Duke, who had been U.S. Senate Sergeant-at-Arms during the last part of McFarland's tenure, had returned to the same position in 1955 with Democrats back in the majority and Lyndon Johnson as majority leader. McFarland could not recall the check, although second endorser John S. Turner, secretary of the campaign committee, recalled that it probably paid for advertising. If this was the case, the funds hadn't been used as the union intended - to educate the public against right-to-work; no such advertising appeared in 1954.[18]

The major problem for McFarland concerned the legal requirement that donations be reported as to how they were received and expended. He did, however, have his defense and defenders. Certainly, he was not held personally responsible for knowing where and to whence each of the contributions made out to the committee had come from and gone. Arizona Democratic National Committeeman Steve Langmade made the most stirring defense by dragging Goldwater into the play. Langmade claimed that in 1952 Goldwater had personally received enormous sums from out-of-state Texas oilmen that went unreported by his campaign committee. This came at a time when Congress readied itself to consider turning over offshore tidelands oil to the states for private development, a measure Mac opposed. Langmade's real focus was ethical:

> We might suggest as a political philosophy that campaign contributions from labor, the man who earns his bread by the sweat of his brow might well be approved as a matter of ethics while contributions from special interests having a stake in legislation pending before Congress, should be condemned.[19]

The Pulliam press hammered away at the oversight, noting it constituted a punishable misdemeanor. Bill Turnbow's column speculated that the expose caused "state house railbirds — all Democrats — to take a dim view of Mr. McFarland's chances to return to the United States Senate." Conversely the supportive *Arizona Daily Star* exonerated McFarland and placed

340 — Ernest W. McFarland

blame on the committee, while pointing out that the union itself had reported the oversight. This fact contradicted Washington's McClellan Committee, which held that unions habitually destroyed such records. Furthermore, the *Star* continued, this was just an attempt to smear Mac with a link to the Teamster's current plight — a political ploy. Turnbow and Pulliam's charges had signaled the start of the 1958 campaign. Too, the Tucson paper upheld the right of out-of-state labor to contribute to campaigns just as out-of-state oilmen could and did.[20] As spring turned to summer, the issue faded. In any case the statute of limitations had run out at one-year on the now three-year-old event. The whole scenario, however, did foreshadow the urgency of the upcoming 1958 campaign.

Immediately following this ordeal, Governor McFarland had to face the continuing wrath of the Pulliam press as Turnbow complained that on March 21, he received a "bitter tongue lashing" from the governor who was "visibly on edge" since the Teamster's testimony. According to Turnbow, McFarland invited him into his office to relate a "little human interest story." In reality, Turnbow said the governor wanted an opportunity to voice his displeasure with recent reporting: "He got flushed and mad and said the reason why was some of the things I had been writing about him." Turnbow asked what things, but McFarland did not specify, while noting "my people don't think you have been so friendly. . . . You don't have any friends, but I have a lot of friends." Although Turnbow did not mention it, the press played upon his known heart condition, and stated "he was so shaken by the unexpected outburst . . . that Secretary of State Wesley Bolin assisted him back to the capitol press room." There, Turnbow lay down, drank some water and then rejected offers of assistance and drove home alone.

According to McFarland, the affair was "all in jest. . . . There was nothing to it. I was just kidding Bill." The governor did explain that he evidenced displeasure at Turnbow's "Under the Capitol Dome" column specifically and not just the *Gazette's* editorializing, but that "If a fellow can't kid somebody about gigging him, this country has come to a pretty state. I have always regarded Bill as a close friend." Indeed, the veteran reporter, if not the *Gazette* in general, had been customarily supportive of McFarland's programs and activities, but Turnbow called this incident "more like a tirade than a joke."[21]

The *Gazette* castigated McFarland as having "gone to far" with "inexcusable" conduct and alleging that another veteran reporter, Claiborne Nicholls, had been subject to the same "veiled threats" from the governor on the same day.[22]

McFarland had his defenders, one among whom wrote the paper that "the four-thousand dollar labor contribution, the root of the problem, paled in comparison to a man [Goldwater] who took five times that much from some rich oilmen in Texas in 1952." The writer brought up the common accusation against the Pulliam press of printing the truth "only so far as it suited your purpose. . . . There are labor unions here in the state, but it could not possibly help the state for Mr. Goldwater to help the Texas oilmen." Supporters aside, McFarland assuredly winced after reading the rural-based *Holbook Tribune's* comment that "His political chances in Arizona from now on are worth about a plugged nickel. . . ."[23]

When Bill Turnbow died just over three months later, it is likely that the public remembered the incident to McFarland's further discredit. Pulliam may have had ulterior motives in not immediately reporting McFarland's statement of regret over the reporter's death. The paper did publish statements by Republicans Goldwater, Congressman John Rhodes, Republican state chairman Richard Kleindienst, Howard Pyle, Phoenix Mayor Jack Williams, *Tucson Daily Citizen* publisher Clarence Kelland, and Democrats Carl Hayden, Stewart Udall, Stephen Langmade, and Justice Arthur T. LaPrade. The exclusion of McFarland from the report was never explained.[24]

In retrospect, McFarland's actions that March day were probably meant, not as a joke, but as a real conveyance of displeasure, or as a later supportive comment stated, "he offends people at the strangest times and for the strangest reasons." In all probability, McFarland grew very upset over Turnbow's statement, just days earlier, that Democrats "took a dim view of

Mr. McFarland's chance to return to the United States Senate." The human interest story of the governor's "almost" spilling a bottle of ink over a ready-to-be-signed bill just does not ring as the type of item to request the veteran reporter's presence. Both McFarland and Pulliam were named as honorary pallbearers when Turnbow laid in state under the capitol dome, roles which they repeated just days later when Justice LaPrade, too, was accorded the same honor, having died on June 30.[25]

As 1957 continued, McFarland dealt with isolated events as they arose, sometimes successfully, sometimes less so. Just after the Turnbow debacle, a satisfied governor acknowledged Arizona's designation as the winner of the Glen Canyon Dam town site, as ordered by Secretary of the Interior Fred A. Seaton. The town was to be named after former Reclamation Commissioner John C. Page. McFarland's work had been crucial in obtaining this selection.[26]

The capitol design question continued as a distinguished citizens' group supporting Frank Lloyd Wright attempted to get his plan referred to the ballot where presumably it would win strong public approval. Critics of Wright continued to belittle his efforts calling his proposal "a huge merry-go-round" and logistically complaining of lack of office space for lesser government workers than the three branches and their staffs. When he first entered the fray, Wright's views, largely because of his immense reputation, had broad support. Legislators, though, came slowly to favor a competing design, one with two new wings flanking a remodeled central structure. As both Wright and skyscraper enthusiasts continued to agitate, the wing compromise prevailed, and McFarland broke ground for the new additions on July 31.[27]

The Colorado River water trial with California also continued to draw McFarland's close attention as it entered its second year in San Francisco before Special Master, Judge Simon Rifkind. In August 1957, Arizona hired not only a new chief lawyer, Mark Wilmer, but also employed a new strategy. As McFarland sat by his side in San Francisco's old Federal Post

Office Building, Wilmer upped the ante on Arizona's claim to Colorado River water from 2.8 million acre-feet including the Gila River to 2.8 million plus the Gila's one million acre-feet for a total 3.8 million. Wilmer anchored his argument on legal right to water based on previous agreement instead of equitable right to the water based on potential use. California consistently had been claiming that Arizona could not even use the 2.8 million and that California, of course, could always use more. McFarland later maintained that this new strategy was not a "departure" from the state's old position, but rather a "clarification" of it. "We have always contended that we have been entitled to all the water from the Gila River plus 2.8 million acre-feet of mainstream water."[28]

In his many appearances in San Francisco and the home state, Mac also habitually hit at California's delaying tactics, such as a July attempt by Los Angeles Power and Water to obtain permission to build its own Bridge Canyon Dam. Calling the dam, which would be entirely within Arizona's borders, "a raid on the state's natural resources," he noted that Arizona had long before applied for the site in its CAP plans and, in any case, Los Angeles already received the bulk of the water and power generated by Hoover Dam. The affair certainly had all the appearances of a delaying tactic.[29]

In between water conferences and trial appearances, McFarland found time to participate in the dedication ceremonies for the now finished Sam Rayburn Memorial Library in Bonham, Texas, where he had attended the cornerstone ceremony two years earlier. The Tennessee-born Texan, who had been speaker of the House longer than anyone in history, had sent his old "Big Four" colleagues a personal invitation, but McFarland had not been able to make a formal reply pending gubernatorial duties. He arrived unannounced just before the dedication and had barely taken his seat when Rayburn surprised Mac and asked him to give a short speech and introduce former President Harry Truman. The press reported that Mac received thunderous applause from ten thousand Texans, including Majority Leader Lyndon Johnson and Supreme

Court Justice Tom Clark, as he reminisced about his and Rayburn's days on the "Big Four."[30]

When the governor returned from the Rayburn ceremonies, he found his state the subject of favorable national exposure and scrutiny. The *U.S. News and World Report* issue of October 11 singled out Arizona as one of three "boom states" along with New Mexico and Nevada, with Arizona growing fastest. The article, which McFarland had contributed to in a lengthy interview, provided a detailed mid-decade sketch of the growing state which until World War II had been something of a secret to the rest of the nation.

Population had recently surpassed the one million mark, a trifle less than the combined population of the other two states. The biggest boost had been provided by aircraft and electronics industries, which before the war had contributed one percent of the state's total wages and salaries. Now that figure stood in excess of twenty percent. In a ten-year period, personal income had increased 171.4 percent, more than double the national figure of 84.6. Old industry such as cattle ranching, farming, and tourism still maintained a strong presence. Tourism, alone, generated two hundred million dollars annually. Other ten-year figures showed the federal payroll up two hundred percent, employment up overall 73.2 percent - led by manufacturing at 160.3, trades 73.7, and construction 89.5. Only mining showed a loss with employment down 4.2 percent, but, as McFarland pointed out, Arizona still led the nation in copper production.

The governor also pointed to health, retirement, and the lure of the Southwest to soldiers stationed there during the war as reasons for the leap in population. Climate, of course, played a role too, "We don't dress up much." said Governor Mac who cryptically credited this fact to "Western spirit," most likely meaning individualism. Warming to the interview he applauded "the highest per capita swimming pools of any state," continuing "We have more sports and luxury cars here than about any other place. . . . If you come to Arizona, you can't leave the desert and if you drink the waters of the Hassayampa River . . . you'll never tell the truth again. Of course, there's seldom any water in the Hassayampa." Concluding, he waxed eloquent about the state he oversaw:

> The desert gives you a sense of getting away. . . . We feel nearer to nature. The countryside is just like nature built it. The long distance views of desert mountains backed by higher mountains with snow on them, with the nearby vistas of cactus-covered flat lands, just give you a satisfied feeling. Many people who have never been here think of a desert as a large flat land covered with sand. The desert in our state is a mass of growth - all of which blooms at some time of the year. Beginning in March, there are unbelievable brilliant masses of color in the desert from blooming desert plants, and all year around there are plants or shrubs or trees that are blooming. So, to see the desert you have to be out in it once a week all the year around. After one of our infrequent rains, it sprouts out with new growth and blossoms.[31]

As 1957 waned, Governor McFarland could look back on a tough year at the office. His recommendations had been unevenly disposed of by the legislature. He had been subject again and again to the vituperations of the Pulliam press over allegations founded and unfounded. He had perhaps embarrassed himself with the Turnbow incident, but he had distinguished himself elsewhere. He had as yet made no formal mention of his intentions for the off-year elections of 1958, but his path was fairly clear. When asked if he would consider running for the Senate, Representative Stewart Udall, known to desire advancement, said he would not oppose McFarland: "I don't want to stand in front of a truck." Columnists concurred, noting that the contest would be clear cut: "Goldwater has aligned himself with the GOP right wing including the late Senator Joseph R. McCarthy. . . . McFarland is a liberal of sufficient moderation to command southern support." The road back to Washington beckoned; Mac would have to go through Senator Goldwater, but the first matter at hand required setting the state back on his path during the Second Session of the Twenty-third Legislature.[32]

Ernest McFarland began 1958 - his last in the governor's office as he alone knew with surety - by turning to an old Arizona interest, mining. Not much had been said or done for the mines in the postwar era; the Jerome Phelps-Dodge operation had shut down in 1955, and employment and production across the state were sagging. In a letter addressed to the forty-seven other state governors (with added emphasis in those to the Rocky Mountain states), he decried the inadequacy of current protective tariff arrangements and urged their strengthening.

He sought a way to protect American producers against the declining prices of copper in the market. Declining prices brought declining profits, and that bothered officers and stock-holders, but Mac's main concern was that under the circum-stance, miners' wages could not keep up with inflation, particu-larly hurting Arizona where twenty percent of the work force engaged in some facet of copper production. The root of the problem, he traced to cheap foreign labor, then at two dollars a day in Chile and only fifty cents per day in Guatemala.

Within a week McFarland received announcements of support from twelve governors including Earl Long of Louisiana, Edmund Muskie of Maine, Orval Faubus of Arkansas, William Quinn of Hawaii, and Abraham Ribicoff of Connecticut, all non-mining states. It remained to be seen if Mac could prod the federal government into a more protective stance.[33]

With this positive opening step for the new calendar year, Mac turned his attention to the upcoming legislative ses-sion keeping in mind his unannounced candidacy for the U.S. Senate in the fall. He initially resolved not to ask for too much in new areas of legislation, but rather to stick well within the parameters already established over his past three years in office.

He resurrected the unfinished parts of his earlier leg-islative programs, emphasizing the creation of departments of labor and agriculture, continued funding for the Colorado River water court case, increased unemployment and welfare benefits, and more highway patrolmen. All this he hoped to achieve without a property tax increase. He did not request a gas tax increase either, although he said he would favor it if presented the opportunity.

Calling again for aid to schools based on a current daily basis, a measure that would increase costs by two million dollars, public and legislators alike wondered where the money would come from in the absence of increased gas and property taxes. The answer lay in the new part of McFarland's program, an increase in luxury taxes on cigarettes and alcoholic beverages. He also asked for a new measure mandating a five-day workweek for all state and county employees, to keep them at parity with private sector employees.[34]

Coupled with his budget message of the following week, McFarland's new program seemed one of economy, or as the favorable press termed it "holding the line." Legislative leaders and members received the recommendations with "a fair amount of enthusiasm."[35]

Surprisingly, McFarland, within a month, appeared to be behind a move to alter his "hold the line" edict by resurrecting the one-cent gas tax increase. He did so in the interest of relieving unemployment, which had risen from seven to thirteen thousand over the preceding twelve months. According to the governor, highway projects requiring labor sat on the shelf ready to go if funds could be raised. He related to the press "It might stop this unemployment trend . . . the worst situation since I have been governor. . . . People call me over the phone at home, in the office, anywhere - see me personally on the street, they tell me their families are hungry. They have to have food and they have to have work. This is one of the most distressing things that can happen."[36]

McFarland agreed that he had backed off from holding the line but had adapted to the new situation: "I had made the appeal last year and the year before [for gas tax]. I didn't see any use in repeating myself over and over again. . . . This unemployment situation gave me a new approach. Otherwise my suggestion is the same." He did, however, qualify his recommendation to an extent, suggesting a two-year trial run.[37]

The governor laid the blame for unemployment squarely on the Eisenhower Administration's "tight money, high interest" policy, and voiced additional concern for copper miners undergoing cutbacks in working hours and purchasing power. A few days later the rising star of the Democratic party, Senator John F. Kennedy of Massachusetts, appeared in the state, complaining that the recession had reached a "crisis" stage with Ike doing "too little, too late." He added that Governor McFarland could assuredly regain his senate seat if he so desired. Mac also kept the pressure on to gain federal aid for the copper miners, noting the rapid price drop from forty-six to twenty-five cents per pound. He wrote directly to the three most powerful Democrats in Washington, sending the Arizona Legislature's memorial to former Big Four colleagues, Speaker Sam Rayburn and John McCormack and his former assistant, Senate Majority Leader Lyndon Johnson. The memorial requested restoration of the four-cent tariff on foreign copper.[38]

McFarland next considered the idea of a rejuvenated sales tax raise, although, like the gas tax, he did not specifically recommend it. Moderating his previous opposition, he did say that he would not stand in its way if such legislation was newly proposed and if it did exempt food and medicine. The increase, though, had to be tied to school aid if he were to fully endorse it, particularly since his efforts to base the ADA on a current basis were still making little headway with the legislators.[39]

As the final week of the session approached, other parts of McFarland's program were also faring badly. The House had already blocked an unemployment benefit bill, some said in retaliation for the governor's turnaround on the gas tax. The luxury tax, too, remained held up in committee.[40]

Facing the legislature's aversion to any tax increases of whatever nature, McFarland decided upon a flank attack - he would come to the fray from the side of the people. It was not his program but the commonweal that was being denied. He would not "club the legislature into acting," but he would take private satisfaction if a bit of guilt spurred them on. Seeking a bully pulpit and knowing the media would carry his message to every corner of the state, Mac addressed a joint session and invoked the people's right to know where their representatives stood and demanded that the issues not be bottled up in committee. He implored the public officials to face their responsibility and act on the current basis-ADA, increased gas tax, increased aid for welfare and unemployment, and a rise in the luxury tax. He noted that a mere increase of two cents on a pack of cigarettes would produce $2.5 million, enough to cover the costs of placing education aid on a current basis, "the minimum that should be done for education in this state." A similar increase on liquor would provide welfare funds for the aged, infirm, blind, and dependents, while the gas tax could provide jobs for the unemployed by expediting highway construction. Finally, in a manner of compromise, he suggested the legislators could, if they wished, make the increases effective for the second half of the upcoming year, not at the beginning. He concluded his "11th hour appeal:"

> I must say to you in all frankness that I think there are certain things that the legislature owes the people. I say this to you in all kindness. I have been in the position in which you find yourselves today. . . . I have seen recommendations of the chief executive . . . voted down. As a matter of fact, I have helped vote some down. But at least they were presented for debate and vote. They were killed, not by being buried in committee, but by a vote on the floor.[41]

The reaction to McFarland's appeal appeared largely positive. The supportive *Daily Star* described the message as "timely . . . temperate in tone . . . modest in requests." Senate President Carpenter announced a series of caucuses to fully consider the message after which the Labor and Management Committee recommended passage of the unemployment benefits increase. Minority leader David H. Palmer (D-Yavapai) called the education legislation "long overdue."

Leaders in the House also voiced satisfaction, Floor Leader L.S. Adams (D-Maricopa) calling the speech "excellent," and Appropriations Committee Chair Robert W. Prochnow (D-Coconino) indicated, "we will have to raise more money and there is no reason why we cannot do this." Perhaps Democratic Senator Wilford R. Richardson of Graham County best summed up the optimism coupled with the predicament of the bottling up in committees:

> I have felt a weakness in this legislature in that regard. There is an apparent willingness among too many legislators to allow members of one committee - as few as five persons and in some cases just a strong chairman - to smother bills. . . . This is done even when members themselves may admit that the bills might pass if they ever reached the floor.[42]

Richardson's reference to a chairman obviously meant Yuma Democrat Ray Thompson who oversaw the Senate Revenue and Finance Committee. This year marked the third consecutive session that Thompson had effectively opposed the gas-tax raise. "He had squatters rights on the issue." The "gaunt and grey haired, small, wirey, and tough," senator depicted the increase as unnecessary at this time: "The facts supplied by the Highway Commission don't dictate the increase now." Thompson had the power, if he could resist the pressure, to thwart the bill by simply not convening the committee "until he had found more information." He had successfully used this tactic two years previously and it appeared that he might be doing so again. Clearly, a power struggle loomed for the gas tax component of McFarland's program.[43]

In one other area, unemployment benefits, the governor's appeal succeeded. The bill to raise the compensation from thirty to thirty-five dollars-per-week passed before session's end. Two more days of overtime, however, brought no further results, even under Mac's slightly veiled threat of calling a special session. Mac simply could not overcome the legislators' reluctance to pass measures, which entailed tax raises - it was an election year.[44]

McFarland was not willing, though, to bow to legislative reluctance, so he made good his threat to call on a special session and summoned legislators back to the capital on March 18. He backed the call by noting a rise in unemployment from 13,000 to 16,900 within the past month. In all probability, he also reflected on the success of his special session three years earlier. Several legislators resented being called back so soon; Mac should have allowed time for heated feelings to cool. But the coming election meant that Mac could not delay into the fall as he had done in 1955. He had had enough of excuses and tender psyches; it was time for action. His anxieties were mounting.

Accordingly, Mac made specific recommendations that were both redundant and germane: l) match the federal government in aiding the aged, blind, and dependents - "rather than pass on these increases to our needy citizens, the state has used those federal funds to reduce its own participation;" 2) increase the fuel tax by one cent to fund highway construction and provide employment; 3) set aid to public schools on an average daily attendance on a current basis; and 4) base the funding cost for the ADA switch to current basis on an increase in luxury taxes on tobacco and alcohol; this provision alone, was new. The summons also restricted the legislature's attention solely to these issues. He concluded his exhortation: Vote the legislation up or down; if you express your views on the floor of the legislature, the people will respect you whether they agree with you or not, and you will thereby establish a record on which you can be judged.[45]

Reporters referred to "the new Governor McFarland - talking and looking like a man prepared to fight," obviously hinting back to the executive who previously had said he would not use a club. The lawmakers themselves split on the summons, some feeling it was a good political move, while others objected to the quickness of the call. Not only were many legislators exhausted but they "were at each other's throats." Conversely out-of-towners complimented the governor for not putting them at the inconvenience of giving up their temporary residences and being forced to move back at some later date. Constant, carping critic Republican House Leader John Haugh of Pima County questioned the wisdom of raising taxes during a recession when even the Congress was attempting to reduce them.[46]

Perhaps the most interesting analysis came from the *Republic's* Columbus Giragi who lamented that Mac had the high ground: "If they perform as he directed . . . he will bask in the glory of a successful mule skinner who got the load up the hill. If they fail to heed his plea, they could be classed as a bunch of stubborn and balky jackasses." Giragi, a former McFarland supporter who had turned away, went on to sarcastically congratulate the governor for outmaneuvering the legislature, which would, in any case, "put the political hay in his barn." Disgruntled or not, there existed an element of truth in what Giragi wrote.[47]

As the legislature, after a five-day lay-off, began its twenty-day special session, it appeared that the gas tax and welfare increase would pass, but luxury taxes seemed doomed, facing strong opposition from the tobacco and liquor interests. This shortcoming precluded the current-basis ADA unless another source of state income could be found. There was talk of resurrecting a sales tax increase in lieu of the luxury tax. But McFarland would have none of this, even if it did exempt food and medicine. The legislature had its chance during the regular session to work this route. Now he limited the special session to those areas he specified. After all, a strong recession existed, and it was an election year. An across-the-board sales tax raise would not stand up. It was the luxury tax or nothing. And nothing it was to be.[48]

Within a few days, unhappily for the governor, it appeared little could be done with the four-point program, even though fourteen bills were being prepared in the two houses. The legislative minority, Mac's firm majority from his first gubernatorial year, still stood ready and willing to stand behind the program, but proved unable to withstand the coalition of conservative and Pinto Democrats aligned with the Republicans and a few stubborn individuals who wanted no taxes whatsoever. The Senate stood ready to abandon the premises, while the House majority continued to maneuver for enough votes to adjourn.

Mac made one last-ditch effort to catalyze positive action by assembling newsmen to threaten yet another special session and by emphasizing the gas tax increase as the single most important agenda item. After all, it would improve the roads and create jobs. Everybody wanted that, the governor exclaimed, "I am receiving more fan mail, more letters, telegrams, and telephone calls . . . than anything since I've been governor." He also pointed out that the state stood to lose five million dollars by not matching a new Eisenhower emergency road building program and that Arizona lagged a cent behind its neighbors in New Mexico and Texas. Furthermore, the increase only meant approximately an extra ten dollars a year for those who drove ten-thousand miles, and that out-of-staters, tourists mostly, would pick up sixty percent of the tab.[49]

Unspoken threats of yet another special session irritated legislators and reminded old political reporters of the late Governor Osborn's 1947-48 tactics of calling seven straight special sessions to get what he wanted. But McFarland disavowed these intentions, claiming that to add to his already spoken calls and recommendations would be "gilding the lily," and that "My emotions, I think as you can observe are not those of anger." He did, however, truly express a desire for a vote on the issues - "a verdict . . . then I would be content in feeling that I had done my duty."[50]

It was not to be. On April 2, the legislature, termed gutless and ridiculous by many, adjourned without bringing any of McFarland's four points to a floor vote. Not only did nothing come to vote, but it also marked the first time in Arizona history that a special session had passed nothing. The reasons included the early call back from the regular session and the fact that all four points had already been considered and rejected. Addressing the adjournment, Governor McFarland adopted a tone reserved for recalcitrant children, but added "I don't think

I should spoil your Easter vacation by telling you exactly what my actions will be." In the meantime, Reg Manning published a political cartoon of the Easter Bunny regarding a large "Big Ol' Special Session Goose Egg," wisecracking "Th' Governor says th' Legislature did. The legislature says the Governor did! One thing is sure, I didn't lay it!"[51]

The *Arizona Daily Star* summed up the session:

> Governor McFarland, in any event, has made a sincere record of trying to help the schools, the aged, the unemployed, and the property taxpayers. The ruling majority of the Legislature has made a record of showing itself to be unduly sympathetic to the pleas of the liquor, cigarette, and trucking industries. His program has been a moderate one. He has not indulged in any questionable reforms to make the people bow down to an all-powerful governor as did his predecessor. He has never sought to take power away from the Legislature and duly elected officials as did his predecessor. He has not sought to revise the income tax laws, as did his predecessor, in such a way as to give new tax exemptions to mining companies and impose payroll deductions on all workers. He did do his best. . . .[52]

Legislators shuffled to avoid blame; no one, for example, wanted to be associated with a committee's spending over sixty hours on fish and game and only two on education. The *Tombstone Epitaph* regretted that the "the unfair part of it is that voters don't know which voters favored the governor's program and which opposed. The handful of bills . . . never got out of committee where the lawmakers could express the will of the people they represent."[53]

While legislators and public argued and scratched their heads, Arizona Employment Securities announced a record high unemployment of 18,750 workers, 6.9 percent of the state's total non-farm workforce. The figures were indisputable for the past six months: 7,050 - 8,450 - 10,750 - 13,100 - 16,900 - 18,750 for October through March.[54]

* * *

Governor McFarland's two administrations present an unusual schematic for the analysis of political scientists or historians. What started with great promise and success in 1955 ended with the "do-nothing" special session of 1958. Yet, enough had been accomplished in just the 1955 session of Mac's first term for historians now, if not political pundits then, to rank him as one of Arizona's most productive governors. Not many of the then-baby state's chief executives can match his achievements: as a health, education, and welfare governor, McFarland broke barriers nearly a decade old. Unemployment benefits rose, restrictive welfare stipulations disappeared, attention to physical and mental health care dramatically improved, and aid to public schools increased by thirty-three percent. Most important for the state's future was paving the way for high-technology industrial development by elimination of the sales tax on goods sold to the federal government. Industrial expansion led by Sperry Rand Corporation reached Arizona highs during McFarland's term.

Later sessions produced institutional successes by founding boards for surplus property, state parks, and planning and building. The latter commission oversaw the perplexing problem of the capitol design and facilitated a new stadium in Tempe and a new state office building in Tucson.

Throughout his tenure, Governor McFarland provided leadership for the ongoing Supreme Court fight with California over Colorado River water. He assured funding for the continued legal battle, designed legislation for an independent role for Arizona if federal interest waned, and constantly directed and oversaw legal preparations for the San Francisco trial before Special Master Rifkind. Most significantly, Mac took to the legal trenches himself in the unprecedented maneuver of successfully arguing a phase of the case before the United States Supreme Court in Washington. This move, alone, saved Arizona costly years of litigation.

When legislative situations called for firm leadership

and direction in the areas of Colorado River water and industrial expansion, he provided it. When the situation called for deference to legislative prerogatives and precedents, he willingly recognized these and did not become overly aggressive or shrill, even when things were not going his way. As in the U.S. Senate, he kept his poise. Too, one should not lose sight of the myriad of less acclaimed accomplishments of his administration. McFarland kept a watchful eye on agricultural conditions in the state, obtaining emergency federal assistance during drought, fighting a variety of bugs and beetles while at the same time controlling pesticides, regulating dairy products, and boosting county fairs - all via executive recommendation followed by legislative action.

Refusing to sanction an increase in salaries for state employees, he did work to bring them parity with the private sector by cutting the state workday from six to five days. He, himself, worked overtime using no executive office vacation time, thus continuing his "workhorse" tradition of senate days. Associates commonly asserted, "Mac did not drive men, but only himself, and others followed." Mac even fooled himself upon his installation of the five-day week. Forgetting that he had the day off that first Saturday, the governor showed up for work at 8:30 am wondering why no one was there and the lights were out. He called Roland Bibolet to find out what was going on, but even upon learning of the new scheduling, ordered Bibolet into work. A workaholic to the end, Mac spent several hours on the job that day. Someone who called the office at that time said the phone was answered by "some grumpy old man," perhaps a janitor, perhaps Mac. Even on the regular workdays, Mac remained after hours, finishing up the job. Once again, when Mac left the office, Roland would call Edna, "The governor has left the building." She would cry "Hallejuah," and Roland would add "Amen."[55]

McFarland supervised the status and name change of Arizona State College at Tempe to Arizona State University, when that became a reality in the general election of 1958 after an affirmative vote on a public initiative. He pushed through legislation protecting Indian art and craftmanship from intrusion by non-Indian sectors. Originality had to be certified by law. His attention to detail informed the time-consuming revision of the entire state law code, and Mac made sure the statutes were cast in understandable terms, palatable to public comprehension and not cryptic legalese. Finally, his concern for highway construction and safety resulted in less highway accidents and new and improved roads, notably Highway 93 from Wickenberg to Kingman and across the Navaho Reservation to Page, which in itself marked a McFarland success in beating Utah for the construction-site town serving the proposed Glen Canyon Dam.

But success and failure go hand in hand, and highways symbolized the executive quandry McFarland encountered in attempting to both improve roads and relieve growing unemployment. Over the course of all four years he unsuccessfully battled the legislature for a one-cent increase in the gas tax to expedite these goals. Similarly, his yearly recommendations for an independent department of labor failed, as did his equally consistent pleas for a current basis ADA, which died in the face of a legislative aversion to a rise in luxury taxes.

In dealing with these political battles, McFarland showed respect for the legislature, demanding the same in return. He employed the veto sparingly, using it only thirteen times in four years compared to former Governor Osborn's thirty-eight in seven. Seven of Mac's vetoes dealt directly with what he perceived as unsound policy. None of his vetoes were overridden. After calling three special sessions during his first year, one of which was pre-set (the revision of the law code), he did not call another until his fourth and final year. And while the final call proved an empty effort, the initial Twenty-second Legislature produced enduring measures in 1955.

Even more than Governor Osborn during the 1940s, McFarland faced the changing demographics of political Arizona. Not only were Republican numbers increasing, but the GOP increasingly found support from the escalating number of Pinto Democrats who crossed over political lines with alacrity to protect their interests - interests which more and more aligned with the GOP during the 1950s era of "I Like Ike." Nevertheless McFarland achieved a success rate of twenty percent on his specific regular session recommendations, compared to the aggressive Osborn's ten percent. McFarland's predecessor, Howard Pyle, fared at the high success rate of thirty-seven percent, proof in itself of the changing political attitudes. Yet, when legislators of McFarland's own liberal persuasion had taken control as the majority for the brief two-year period of his first term, he effectively led them to his administration's most positive achievements.[56]

Besides Colorado River matters, McFarland held efficiency in government as an area of strong personal interest - a field over which he could exert some direct control via setting the budget. As governor, he attended to budget matters with more care than his predecessors and left a legacy of continued direction. He became the first executive to distribute budget proposals, justifications, and procedures to the public, and he was the first to employ a budget officer. After he left office, this position was allowed to lapse during Republican successor Paul Fannin's three terms, although Fannin did request this function. Under his successor, Democrat Sam Goddard, the creation of a state finance office with a formal budget director became official.[57]

McFarland exerted efficient control to the degree possible with his many appointments. Here, he often acted independently of party or legislative recommendations, sometimes drawing their displeasure. However, his appointments were recognized by press and public alike in almost all cases as being expertly made and skillfully implemented. At ninety-eight percent, he maintained the highest confirmation percentage of any Arizona Governor except the three one-term executives of the 1930s (Moeur, Stanford, and Jones) who together made barely more than half of McFarland's 172, of which 169 were confirmed.

McFarland felt that his predecessors had a questionable record on both appointments and efficiency. The state constitution, itself, might have been the greatest impediment to efficiency - it was badly in need of modernization. Writing for the Bureau of Government Research at Arizona State University in 1964 on the office of governor, he advocated a "cabinet form of government in which the governor would have a head of each department with full authority, subject to the will of the governor." If that sounded too authoritarian, he clarified his stance by lamenting the system of holdover terms of appointive offices: a governor finds himself in the position of being charged with responsibility without having authority . . . each legislature whittles down the powers of governor until about all he has left is persuasion, and when persuasion can only be used on appointees of his predecessors, it is not very effective." Mac recommended staggered terms of appointees to always ensure a majority for the incumbent's appointments or more power available to his chosen [cabinet] department heads. In this same article, he continued to urge the creation of a budget department, which, in fact, did occur thereafter.[58]

McFarland, in all probability, found the executive office more challenging and frustrating than his former roles of U.S. senator and majority leader, which he had found more rewarding and satisfactory. Interestingly, at the end of his career, Mac said he most enjoyed the bench.

One thing is certain. When McFarland had a liberal majority to work with, his program went through and instituted significant change and progress. When the conservative bloc returned to the majority, his program bogged down. As governor, McFarland had far less consistent success than as senator. His senate efforts have been enduring - his executive efforts less so. He was bucking the rising tide conservatism, however, particularly in Arizona, and now he decided to return to the U.S. Senate, the scene of his greatest successes as a politician.

CHAPTER FOURTEEN

STYLE VERSUS SUBSTANCE
THE *1958* CAMPAIGN

NINETEEN FIFTY-EIGHT WOULD PROVE a crucial year in Ernest McFarland's political career as he made a determined effort to regain his senate seat from Barry Goldwater. Most knowledgeable political observers had long anticipated this competition between the flamboyant incumbent and the experienced challenger. In a very real sense, the campaign that emerged, one of the most controversial in senate history, pitted style versus substance — the style of the Goldwater personality against the substance of the McFarland record.

Initially, conditions appeared to favor McFarland. While Goldwater's national profile was rising among conservatives, he remained undistinguished within the Senate, and certainly possessed far less clout than McFarland a decade earlier. Again Senator Carl Hayden's descriptive terms "workhorse and showhorse" senators are germane. While McFarland had certified his reputation as a workhorse, Goldwater had been rapidly acquiring a reputation as a showhorse. Furthermore, he lacked the skills and connections to capably assist Hayden, particularly in water matters:

> Senator Goldwater brought . . . little help for the veteran Senator Hayden in Arizona's water fight . . . neither an attorney nor experienced in politics . . . he could not possibly fill McFarland's shoes . . . nor did he make the mistake of trying to do so in face of the personal alliances McFarland had built among his senate colleagues.[1]

361

The contestants differed in other respects as well. A pro-Goldwater Republican colleague observed, "Let's face it, legislating is not his strong point," and in a strangely ingratiating manner, Goldwater's own later campaign literature perhaps best explained his evolving style:

> No law bears his name. In an organization of men who have elevated compromise to an art, he has been loath to wheel and deal, to strike a bargain here to gain a point there. . . . His own party never accepted him as a spokesman. . . . He avoided cloakroom maneuvering. . . . Mr. Goldwater's impatience with the dreary routine of legislation is reflected in the layout of his Senate office . . . models of more than 70 airplanes, a transistor radio, a miniature TV, a photograph of Mrs. Goldwater dressed in black lace.

McFarland's own former senate office desk held a different aura; he, too, had a couple of models of then-new jets if one could locate them amidst piles of correspondence, analyses of pending legislation, directives to fellow senators, and the occasional Arizona artifact such as the stuffed Gila monster Mac had named Mussolini — "He's slow and dumb, but very poisonous."[2]

With his eye on broad national political currents, Goldwater never mustered even a fraction of the power that had enabled Mac to write and sponsor two GI Bills, three social security increases, the Navajo-Hopi Rehabilitation Act, the Communications Act of 1952, and CAP measures that had passed the Senate and laid the foundation for future efforts. Faced with the substance of the McFarland legislative record and floor leadership, Goldwater truly appeared threatened. Indeed, many in Arizona wanted to "Send Mac Back." Goldwater did, however, have two holdover advantages in the Pulliam press and Stephen Shadegg. These, coupled with his aggressive style and the labor issue to brutalize, provided him a unique opportunity of "politically dynamiting" the McFarland campaign and achieving victory.[3]

Goldwater had established an anti-organized labor reputation as a member of Arkansas Democrat Senator John McClellan's committee investigating "criminal or other improper activities in the field of labor-management relations." In particular he detested United Auto Workers leader Walter Reuther whom he termed "a liar and a more dangerous menace than the Sputniks or anything else Russia might do." Using Shadegg's planning and Pulliam's media muscle, Goldwater intended to attack the threat of big labor in Arizona and then stigmatize the scrupulous McFarland with his big labor support — it was 1952 all over again, guilt by association.

Reuther, another man of more substance than style, felt little intimidation from Goldwater's brash insinuations and charges of corruption at the hearings. In fact, the labor leader outdid the committee by ardently advocating the elimination of corruption in union leadership and engineering the removal of Teamster President Dave Beck and the AFL-CIO's expulsion of the same union under its new leader Jimmy Hoffa. More influential than Hoffa or Beck, and thus seen as a greater threat by Goldwater, Reuther seized the initiative during the hearings and lectured the young senator on fine points of the law regarding workers' rights to organize. Goldwater "lamely backed off" but not before warning "someday you and I are going to get together and lock horns." With the elections of 1958, that time had now come.[4]

Indeed, the link to McFarland had already been made the previous year with the exposure of the four thousand dollar Western Teamsters' contribution to the governor's 1954 campaign. Negatively enhanced by extensive Pulliam press coverage, the incident would be resurrected with telling and exaggerated effect in 1958.

Never one to let an opportunity to slam Mac get away, Pulliam in April set the tone for the vindictive campaign soon to open. Seizing upon U.S. Comptroller General Joseph Campbell's assertion that the San Carlos Irrigation and Reclamation District had been mismanaged from its birth in 1927, Pulliam now implied that Mac had personally profited from government favoritism. Campbell maintained that the federal government improperly paid much of the district's operating costs, thus inordinately favoring district farmers. Mac had purchased Pinal County land watered by the project in 1928 and now thirty years later was accused of unfair profiteering. For greater effect, the Pulliam press added his brother Carl as a beneficiary as well. A surprised governor responded, "I have never before been subjected to more vicious character assassination than was conceived in the headlines and stories . . . carried in the *Phoenix Gazette* and *Arizona Republic*. . . . This is an irresponsible political maneuver of the lowest form." Except for sour stories such as this, Mac never graced the front page of Pulliam's papers during the campaign. The few favorable McFarland references that Pulliam allowed to find print were buried in back pages. Roland Bibolet also has substantiated the pressure on the McFarland camp: "I recall we all lived in a fishbowl. We were constantly under kleig lights; we were exposed twenty-four hours a day. Conversely, Goldwater was totally protected. No matter what he said, did, or felt, the thing was completely sanitized by the time it became public or was buried, never to become public."[5]

Mac's friend in the Pulliam stable, Ben Avery, pointed out in a subsequent edition of the *Gazette* that San Carlos had long been a problem area for the government. The Indian population, which farmed half of the affected land, paid only maintenance and operation expenses, while the white population paid back the costs of the project's construction. Over the years the farmers, including the McFarland brothers, had made all the required payments on time, even when the project had gone dry as occurred twice in the 1950s. Avery continued to act as a friendly informant to Mac, but as Bibolet has pointed out, he was of the Pulliam camp and received only appropriate information to leak. "Perhaps Ben wasn't even aware of this. . . . He was totally over his head in big-time dirty tricks which were afoot."[6]

The *Arizona Daily Star* went Avery one better by emphasizing that all government projects allowed some degree of largesse for the landowners and that the Salt River Project in particular enjoyed much more than San Carlos. The article also pointed out that Barry Goldwater and his brother Bob numbered among those "favored" SRP landowners as did Gene Pulliam. In fact, the Salt River Power District enjoyed tax-free status while, as the *Star* pointed out, the similar Tucson Gas, Electric Light and Power Company paid 27.6 percent of its gross income in federal taxes. The *Star* concluded that McFarland would become a martyr and that Goldwater would beg to be rescued by his "friends."[7]

After weathering this smear attempt, McFarland's suspicion peaked a week later when Democratic National Committeeman Stephen Langmade decided to run for the Democratic nomination for the Senate. The young, conservative Democrat reflected the divisiveness of his party by decrying AFL-CIO Committee on Political Education (COPE) support of the governor. The Pulliam press immediately jumped on the possibilities, headlining "Demo chieftain regrets muscle-in by COPE," and Langmade in turn "played Goldwater's game, reinforcing the anti-COPE theme with telling blows." Setting himself in opposition to McFarland, Langmade charged that the governor had worked closely and made "several secret" deals with organized labor. This was a far cry from the previous year when he unreservedly defended McFarland's receiving the four thousand dollar COPE contribution.[8]

McFarland, who had not even officially announced his candidacy, made no initial comment, but as the primary campaign wore on, expressed disdain and regarded Langmade as a "strawman" candidate giving Pulliam a further excuse to continue his attacks upon Mac by "reporting" Langmade's remarks. The governor would choose to simply ignore the younger candidate in the primary campaign and focus on his major challenge with Goldwater.[9]

Indeed, Langmade highlighted McFarland's lack of an official announcement to run, exclaiming, "there has been reluctance on the governor's part. I understand that a poll is being taken and that, if it's favorable, he will run against

Goldwater." Furthermore, he emphasized that "the public is no longer interested in settling the personal feud between the Governor and the junior Senator," whom he would like to "return to his dry goods counter." COPE leaders later stated that the Democratic party itself "dealt us a death blow" referring to Langmade who, they claimed, went on to make his sound truck and other equipment available to the Republicans after his defeat in the primaries.

According to a later analysis of the campaign by political scientist Frank Jonas:

> Langmade may be taken as the prototype of the Democrat in Arizona who aided and abetted Goldwater's bid for re-election. Many of those found their way into, and allowed their names to be used by, the Democrats for Goldwater organizations, sponsored by the Republicans.

Indeed, it was rumored that Langmade had received seventy-five thousand dollars as his price for assisting the Republicans. Bibolet termed the turnabout "a real Judas-class betrayal."[10]

All of these events - resurrection of the four thousand dollar contribution, the charge of San Carlos favoritism, and Langmade's entrance into the race - occurred before McFarland officially announced his candidacy, but he was simply waiting for the appropriate moment. That moment came on May 10 at a supposedly nonpartisan testimonial dinner at the Shrine Auditorium honoring his thirty-five years in Arizona's public service. Upon his entrance and seating to the applause of fifteen hundred attendees, the MC drew Mac's attention to a vacant chair near him at the speaker's table. When the band struck up "A Pretty Girl is Like a Melody," in through the crowd scampered his first grandchild, three-year old Kara Lewis to take her place beside the proud grandparent.

More awaited the governor as dinner sponsors presented him with congratulatory messages from Adlai Stevenson, Eleanor Roosevelt, and J. Edgar Hoover, among others, and a pile of petitions urging him to run for the Senate. Former senate colleague, ex-Colorado governor, and current Arizona resident Edwin Johnson reminisced about their years together. Keynote speaker, Oklahoma Senator Mike Monroney, then stepped to the stand. The tall Sooner noted, "I started my career under Mac's leadership. . . . I learned the ABC's of water development from him. . . . I remember how brilliantly Mac not only authorized but engineered legislation that increased social security benefits . . . this was the same spirit that enabled him to sponsor and pass the GI Bill of Rights." Monroney then unveiled a larger than life photo-portrait of Mac seated at the governor's desk.

McFarland, who had indicated that he would make his intentions known by May 15, assuredly knew this was the precipitous moment. Not only was he the honoree, but the date marked the exact anniversary of his arrival in Arizona - thirty-nine years before. Accordingly, he stated "I will accept the challenge. I will run for the U.S. Senate," setting off a spirited old time demonstration to the tune of "Happy Days are Here Again."

Undoubtedly, this was Mac's high point of public acclaim to that stage in his career and he grasped it for the moment it represented. Rumors on the floor were suddenly dispelled; one being that President Eisenhower would provide a federal judicial appointment to preclude Mac's running against Goldwater; another reinforcing Langmade's earlier aspersions that Mac was just marking time until a poll could verify that he led Goldwater. McFarland responded: "I never have been much for polls."[11]

The die was now cast and the exuberance of the electoral announcement would segue into the grim reality of political warfare -a hard fought, trench battle, the likes of which had never been seen in Arizona before, or for that matter few places elsewhere.

The Pulliam press kept the heat on Mac regarding the San Carlos land and water issue. When the U.S. Comptroller-General halted subsidization of pumped irrigation water in favor of using profits to pay back the federal district, McFarland pointed to politics as the real issue: an effort by the Republican government to discredit him during the campaign year. He requested a federal investigation but was turned down, leading him to empathize with other district landowners who also were subject to criticism. The opposition press merely responded that Mac "didn't wear a martyr's crown with very much grace."[12]

Obversely, Tucson's *Daily Star* maintained its firm support of the governor in excerpting from his banquet speech: "I have never defamed the character of one individual in order to further my own gain and that I will never do." The *Star* termed this rather characteristic McFarland statement "uncommon . . . in setting a standard of conduct that should command respect." The *Star* endorsed his return to the Senate noting previous experience as majority leader and his "clean, economic, progressive" gubernatorial record: "an era of good feeling." When Republican State Chairman Richard Kleindienst attacked McFarland by questioning how he amassed his wealth, the *Star* called him "slanderous and libelous." Kleindienst questioned Mac's worth of one million dollars when his "only visible means" was government service, contrasting that with the fabrication that before his D.C. career, Mac had to "pass the hat" just to get transportation to Washington after his 1940 election victory. The *Star* called the implications "cowardly and false" and suggested Kleindeinst "hang his head in shame" while, at the same time warning that "more mud is to be thrown" from the Republican camp. The Republican chairman had obviously forgotten the growing worth of KTVK-TV.[13]

The race soon began to draw national attention with the *Saturday Evening Post* endorsing Goldwater as "the most aggressive, articulate, colorful, and possibly the most conservative conservative in the U.S. Senate."[14]

The article astutely pointed out that Goldwater gave the impression that he was running against United Auto Workers Leader Walter Reuther, and equally on target, claimed he needed "maturity" and the ability not to get so "riled" by adversaries. These observations pointed to the Goldwater-Reuther confrontation in the 1958 McClellan hearings when Reuther turned the tables on his hectoring interrogator. Despite these shortcomings, the weekly magazine pegged him the "Glittering Mr. Goldwater" in its endorsement.[15]

As the Goldwater-McFarland race warmed up, much of the public's attention also focused on the Democratic gubernatorial primary contest, the outcome of which would almost certainly reflect upon the senate battle. In this race, incumbent Attorney General Robert Morrison faced off with conservative Dick Searles. Many observers felt strongly that Searles more closely resembled a Republican and accordingly the Pulliam press threw its weight behind him. Both candidates had sketchy pasts, but Morrison took the worst of the press's lambasting, including a front page mug shot, because of a name change, bounced checks for which he was intermittently jailed, spousal desertion, and a failed marriage, all occurring in California during the 1930s. After moving to Arizona in 1936, he broke away from the destructive behavior of his youth by attending the University of Arizona Law School, being admitted to the bar, rising to Pima County Attorney and finally to attorney general during McFarland's two administrations. In defending himself from the exposure of his youthful past, Morrison frequently employed the term "Pulliamism" referring to the Phoenix newspapers tendency to "editorialize politically outside their editorial columns."[16]

Tucson's *Daily Star* rushed to Morrison's defense in a series of editorials disparaging its Phoenix counterparts. Moreover Lyall Dawkins, editor and publisher of the small *Buckeye Valley News*, wrote a piece "What Price Mud?" which, reprinted and widely circulated, became the clarion call of his campaign.[17]

Searles, too, was not immune to such propagandizing. The former undersecretary of the interior had been married four times and divorced three, a fact made much of by a full-page newspaper ad taken by Morrison's campaign committee. Meanwhile working in the background of the gubernatorial race stood little-known businessman Paul Fannin, the unopposed Republican candidate.[18]

McFarland faced no such problem with his overtaxed opponent Steven Langmade. Keeping his eyes on his major target Goldwater, Mac never acknowledged Langmade as a serious threat during the campaign. In fact, he did not engage him on any specific issues or differences, and rarely, if ever, mentioned his name. In late July, they did share the same platform addressing the Phoenix Women's Club. While Langmade employed the Republican tactic of challenging McFarland's fiscal dealings, both personal and regarding raises to his staff, as "disgraceful and unethical," Mac focused on "a clean [primary] campaign and that nothing will ensue that might hinder our effort to beat Barry Goldwater."[19]

On the offensive, Langmade challenged McFarland to open debate, offering the use of his private airplane and a pilot to transport him to debate sites. Mac brushed him aside, clearly regarding Langmade as insignificant, and something of a turncoat, while concentrating his attention on Goldwater.[20]

True to his objective, McFarland, from the outset of the primary campaign, had Goldwater in his sights. Citing the *Congressional Record*, he noted that Goldwater had missed voting on three amendments to a recent labor reform bill and then missed the vote on the full bill as well. In fact, the senator had missed fifteen of twenty roll call votes between June 17 and 20, including one that dealt with appropriations for work on the Gila River. Sam Rayburn joined in censuring Goldwater's lackadaisical performance, but the senator continued to claim, incorrectly, according to the record, that he had missed only one labor amendment vote, and he mixed up his stories on why he was not in attendance. Goldwater further underscored his displeasure with this negative scrutiny by calling the labor measure in question a "sweetheart" bill, lacking strength. Although this joust and parry may have been relatively insignificant as an isolated issue, it indicated the escalating harshness of the campaign.[21]

Goldwater turned the tables on McFarland just before the September primaries by censuring his apparent lack of support for the copper industry in 1949's Eighty-first Congress. According to Goldwater, McFarland had split with Carl Hayden on the vote, but Mac returned to the record to prove that he had, indeed, voted with Hayden and in support of the copper program that had proven successful. He demanded a retraction and an apology.[22]

No apology was forthcoming. Goldwater's campaign manager Stephen Shadegg advised this evasion, not wanting his candidate to be perceived as guilty of either ignorance or deceit. Goldwater neither confirmed nor denied the statement, and the silent Pulliam press allowed the matter to drop from public attention. In his later writings, Shadegg pointed out with pride that what matters is whether you win or lose, not how you play the game: "We didn't apologize, and we won."[23]

As the primary approached, the Pulliam press conceded the ineffectiveness of Langmade's candidacy and reported heavy support for McFarland in a poll of Maricopa County constituents. The press, however, did favor Searles over Morrison, and here the pollsters were surprised. With all votes tabulated, the slighted Morrison vindicated himself over the media-favored Searles by a count of 79,992 to 59,695 votes. Analysts have used this to note the apparent ineffectiveness of Pulliam propaganda, at least in this campaign, for Searles lost Maricopa County by 34,414 to 29,412 votes. He won in only four small counties and was trounced by a three-to-one margin in Pima.[24]

McFarland enjoyed a far easier contest besting Langmade 107,373 to 40,799 votes (44,892 to 19,955 in Maricopa) including a five-to-one pummeling in Pima-Tucson, 22,532 to 5,147. The 72.4 to 27.6 percent actually fell 2.3 points less than the press had predicted, while the press's error with Morrison-Searles amounted to a 9.5 percent turnaround in Morrison's favor.[25] With Republican John Rhodes and particularly Democrat Stewart Udall heavily favored to return to the House of Representatives, the public's interest now focused on McFarland-Goldwater and Morrison versus untested Republican Paul Fannin for governor.

Shortly after the primaries, national pollsters Louis Harris and Associates released their analysis of where the candidates stood. The group termed its results "operationally useful campaign documents that could help the contestants improve their positions." The poll included interviews with 718 voters between July 5 and August 5, and showed that McFarland continued to hold a slim forty-four to forty-two percent lead over Goldwater (with fourteen percent undecided) a point down from earlier results in February. Harris Associates characterized Mac as "a very well-liked, genial, warm man with a distinct common touch whose record has been good," while Goldwater drew the summary observation as "an independent, selfless, fearless man of high principle."

The poll made available quotations from several among those interviewed that reflected further upon the candidates, albeit in a confused, sometimes biased, often shallow context: a Republican housewife commented:

> I think Ernest McFarland is an ugly cuss, but he has an open countenance. . . . I believe he's done the very best job he could. . . . For instance, he wouldn't want something purple but if he felt enough of the people wanted it that way, that's the way he would go. That's terribly important right now. . . . Goldwater would do what he wanted regardless. . . . He appears to be a very selfish man who makes a lot of decisions from a personal point of view, rather than from a wide point of view. . . .

An independent Phoenix pharmacist appeared at cross-purposes mixing up Mac's acknowledged water expertise and Goldwater's aversion to liberalism in stating:

> Our biggest worry here . . . is the water shortage. . . . I wish Governor McFarland had exercised a little more initiative in this area . . . an in between governor, just average. . . . He's getting pretty old. I think Goldwater's a liberal . . . and he really gets around. He isn't like the Republican party, and that's why I'm for him.

A Democratic waitress cryptically mentioned:

I don't like Governor McFarland. I have met him several times and he isn't at all friendly or cordial, and he seems very self-centered. . . . Goldwater, on the other hand does have the people in mind and he works for the interest of the small businessman.

A rancher commented on Mac, "I've met him, very friendly fellow, seemed more like a country boy. I liked that quality in him," and a nurse expressed "I'd rate the job McFarland has done as only fair. . . . But he's the lessor of two evils, and I'll be voting for him. . . . Goldwater's views on labor are reactionary; so were his views on McCarthy." A city employee stated, "McFarland's kept his promises and seems to know what's bothering people. . . . Goldwater's a businessman, and that doesn't make me like him any better. . . . I hope the next Governor worries as much about industry as McFarland did. . . . I didn't even know Fannin was running for governor until you mentioned it."

The Harris poll also went to great lengths to highlight public perception of the major issues of the 1958 campaign, and clearly the economic recession loomed largest. The poll reported: "we have seen that on virtually every specific aspect of the recession that the overall issue is working for the Democrats." Specific aspects included higher prices, dwindling jobs, and the desire for increased Social Security. The poll suggested that McFarland should lean on his successful efforts to bring industry to Arizona: "This positive McFarland approach should be sharply contrasted with Republican inaction."

The issues of education and high federal and state taxes appeared to work for or against both parties equally, while declining interest in water favored Republican candidates, and increasing interest in roads and highways favored Democrats. The "right to work" labor problem, which had favored Goldwater now appeared to be evening out according to the poll.

Harris then contrasted the senatorial candidates in some detail, emphasizing their strengths. McFarland was depicted as an experienced statesman dedicated to the commonweal. The poll's official observation recommended Mac "put his marvelously sympathetic personality to work for him" and "draw attention to his `all my life' concern with improving the lot of `the little man' by way of sharpening the contrast between himself and `what have they [Goldwater's office] done in Washington . . . where is the concrete evidence of any concern?'"

However, the poll isolated "two strong assets in the Goldwater make-up that are lacking from McFarland's." The first was the public's perception of Goldwater as a leader despite the fact that he did not support a "single one of the causes that are important to people." The other was Goldwater's all-Arizona image. He was home grown and known across the state for his deep love of the land. Twenty-five percent of those interviewed volunteered, "Goldwater is for Arizona." Only one in ten offered a similar unsolicited evaluation of McFarland. The poll here credited Goldwater's overt pride in Arizona and his high visibility as politician, pilot, photographer, and merchandiser, while McFarland "is too frequently identified with the past."

Younger Arizonans, a growing segment of the Republican party, were slotted as particularly gravitating toward Goldwater, although McFarland retained the allegiance of younger blacks and Hispanics. In concluding, the Harris poll noted McFarland's growing slowly stronger while Goldwater had begun "to fray a little. . . . In short, McFarland may be on the edge of a breakthrough with votes. As we have shown, all of the recession issues work for him. The problem is to avoid being sidetracked from these major issues." Indeed this was the challenge. Ominously, the poll forecast the possibility, indeed the soundness, of a Republican attempt to "weaken the unassailable McFarland image" by attacking his gubernatorial running mate Robert Morrison.[26]

As he had six years previously, Barry Goldwater opened his 1958 senate campaign in home-base Prescott. Predictably he lashed out at McFarland's party loyalty in supporting New Deal and Fair Deal legislation. Conversely the incumbent denied that he acted as a "me too" Republican but rather stood against the party line when necessary. He concluded his address to the audience of five hundred by challenging McFarland to a debate on the major issues, which emphasized national rather than state concerns such as balancing the federal budget, cutting foreign aid and taxes, and building up the military.[27]

McFarland replied that he saw little use for debate when Goldwater continued to employ the "when did you stop beating your wife type of argument." He would, however, agree to debate on certain resolutions he suggested: that the Republican administration had caused a lowering of American prestige abroad, had been too favorable to big business, and had weakened national defense. The candidates later set an October 12 date for a televised debate on these and other issues.[28]

While Goldwater continued to tear down New and Fair Deal legislation and hammer away at the statewide presence of COPE, the Republican party was shaken by the September 22 resignation of Sherman Adams, President Eisenhower's major advisor. Adams had been linked to influence peddling and pressured by his own party colleagues to resign, a move with which Goldwater concurred.

Democrats took advantage of the issue by stepping up their campaign visibility. Former-president Truman barnstormed the West, slashing at Taft-Hartley, and Carl Hayden, at the state party convention on September 30, asked for the return of Mac to the Senate where both had cooperated so effectively in the past. He pointed proudly to water and airbase accomplishments, the Phoenix Veterans Hospital, noted Arizona's highest rank in the nation in per-capita appropriations during their joint twelve-year tenure, and lamented the lack of direction and assistance from incumbent Goldwater, who often cancelled out Hayden's vote in the Senate.

Mac followed with a hard-hitting speech, which was backed by supportive speeches by Congressman Stewart Udall and gubernatorial candidate Morrison. He promised a return to the bipartisan cooperation of the Truman era and praised the other approved platform planks including continued health, education, and welfare legislation, state departments of water resources conservation and labor, and equal pay rights for women performing equal work.[29]

In October, the escalating campaign began to draw increased national attention, mostly supportive of the charismatic Goldwater. Raymond Moley, writing in *Newsweek*, exaggerated the influence of national COPE workers, most of whom were just Arizona union members and their wives. Moley later admitted that he was a writer of opinion and not "purely objective," and he cited the importance of timing in his statements.[30]

Writing for a Texas paper, Holmes Alexander depicted Goldwater as "a handsome jet pilot who had energy and color and a stainless record" fighting "criminal elements of the underworld, goons, racketeers, and shady characters with skeletons in their closet." He tied these vague groups to "Gray Ghost" McFarland, "the grizzled governor of the laborite left."[31]

Pulliam made certain that Arizona voters were apprised of the views of these prominent national commentators by reproducing both columns in his Phoenix papers. Indeed, the Pulliam press outdid itself in favoring Republican candidates. McFarland came to regret the days when he found himself featured top-half, front-page, for he found that highly visible location only when Pulliam had negative "news" to report. Otherwise, he lingered below the fold or buried in the inside pages. McFarland campaign headquarters did a study comparing the *Republic* with Tucson's *Daily Star*, clearly showing the disparity between the bias of the former and the more judicious coverage of the latter.[32]

National papers were more even in their treatment; Doris Fleeson in the *Washington Evening Star*, termed both candidates virtuosos of campaigning. She described Goldwater as "intense and articulate, substitute a twin-engine beechcraft for a white horse," and on Mac, "an old pro, Arizona style, gets around by shank's mare, on horseback, and at the wheel of his own modest car to shake hands." As the governor stated, "You can't shake any hands in the clouds."[33]

Some papers clearly sided with Mac, the *Chicago Daily News* declaring the Goldwater-Reuther issue "nonsense" and further noting that "with regard to [correcting] abuses in labor, Reuther alone has done a hundred times more than a dozen Goldwaters." Mac also kept the Hayden-Goldwater disharmony issue alive by advertising the three hundred times when Goldwater voted opposite Hayden on such issues as turning tidelands oil deposits over to the states and allowing a raise in the price of natural gas, Hayden opposing both. The *Arizona Daily Star*, too, continued its support criticizing Goldwater's McCarthyism and linking him to the Jenner-Bricker" crowd, "absolutist thinkers who would burn down the barn to kill the rats."[34]

With three weeks to go in the race, the two candidates finally appeared face-to-face on October 12 in a televised debate sponsored by the Phoenix and Tucson Leagues of Women Voters. Expected verbal fireworks did not materialize as both candidates maneuvered with respectful decorum, while disagreeing on major issues such as foreign policy and the growing power of centralized government.

While Goldwater deplored Marshall Plan giveaways in foreign aid, McFarland advocated continuation, but only with increased monitoring and ongoing assessment. Furthermore, he declared that American prestige had dwindled to a low ebb under Secretary of State John Foster Dulles who scuttled the bipartisanship that had characterized Truman foreign policy.

Alleging that the central government was too powerful, Goldwater stood squarely against federal aid to education. Mac, on the other hand, saw it as an essential ingredient in America's response to Russia's 1957 launching of Sputnik - it would jump start the catch-up process.

The candidates naturally disagreed on recent and pending labor legislation, McFarland believing it adequate and Goldwater terming it too weak. Similarly both disagreed on the potential of Secretary of Agriculture Ezra Taft Benson's farm program. Regarding the Supreme Court, Goldwater urged higher qualification requirements, while Mac cautioned against any curbs against the court.

Concerning water, Goldwater maintained that present reclamation programs should be buttressed by ocean desalting.

McFarland, noting that he had been the first to investigate this potential technology while in the Senate, correctly stated that this variable was many, many years in the future. He recommended expansion of existing reclamation and irrigation programs with possible new additions relying, however, more on state rather than federal initiative.

On a few issues, the candidates appeared comfortable with the other's views. Both believed, at that particular time, that community initiative should take precedence over further government legislation concerning continued school integration. The problem here evolved out of the Supreme Court's *Brown vs Board of Education, Topeka* (1954). While the court overturned segregation in public education facilities at that time, it urged school integration "at all deliberate speed," a vague phrase that did little to hasten integration in the Deep South. Indeed, that very fall, Governor Orval Faubus of Arkansas had strongly but unsuccessfully resisted the injunction to integrate. While Arizona's school integration situation had been resolved promptly in 1954 after the court decision, the candidates now felt increased government pressure could be counterproductive and that community awareness must resolve the issue. Moreover, Goldwater concluded that the Supreme Court should be very careful about further "overstepping" state prerogatives.

Finally, both candidates agreed on federal and international or free world security programs. The decorum, however, broke down slightly at debate's end with Goldwater having won the coin flip for the final comment. As he criticized a recent Democratic ad censuring Republican inflation, the program closed with McFarland's voice "ringing over the moderator's in rebuttal."[35]

Within days, Goldwater aggressively challenged the governor to further debate, exclaiming he was tired of "boxing a ghost" and that Mac was "so ashamed of his actions that he won't discuss them." Mac may well have been something of a ghost, for Goldwater's belligerent critique of U.S. foreign policy sailed harmlessly over Mac's bow and hit the Eisenhower administration with a broadside for its handling of the Hungarian and Suez crises in 1956. Goldwater believed the U.S. should have sent arms to Hungary during its futile uprising against the Soviet Union and that the U.S. should have encouraged France and Great Britain to re-take the Suez Canal from Egypt rather than urging a cessation of hostilities as both Eisenhower and Khrushchev did. Mac rather enjoyed the discomfort Goldwater brought upon his own party and leader.[36]

McFarland endeavored to link his fortunes to Hayden's almost unchallenged reputation. Shadegg and Goldwater both recognized this as a dangerously potent coupling and played cautious. Even during the heat of the campaign, Goldwater carefully avoided directly attacking Hayden, whom he would soon recognize as Arizona's greatest asset in Washington. For his part, Hayden continued in his quiet manner to urge Arizonans to "Send Mac Back." McFarland's continued exploitation of Goldwater's opposing Hayden in hundreds of senate votes never took grip with the electorate.

During this post-debate week Governor McFarland and Edna had a narrow escape when their plane ran dangerously low of fuel just east of hometown Florence. The pilot had radioed Phoenix airport at 6:57 P.M. on October 19 that the plane, bound from Tucson, had only five minutes of fuel remaining. Radio contact was broken off at 7:03 when the pilot with some help from Mac, who knew the rather bumpy terrain, made a "dead stick" night landing in the cactus- studded desert. Mac hiked out about a mile and called for help from a restaurant on the Florence Highway. The sheriff's department towed the plane out to the highway, obtained additional fuel, cleared the road for takeoff, and saw the governor's party off after a couple hours delay and a light dinner. Mac characteristically laughed off the mishap, knowing that he had more immediate matters to address, notably the bombshell that the Pulliam press had exploded earlier that day.[37]

In that Sunday morning edition, Eugene Pulliam's *Arizona Republic* set the tone for the remainder of the campaign

- McFarland would be portrayed as a minion of corrupt labor. Shadegg directed the entire process, employing newspaperman Bert Fireman, as the liaison between his own and Pulliam's offices. Shadegg knew that all the complaints about labor influence in the Democratic party would not carry great weight unless an in-state villain could be found. As he expressed the situation: ". . . it would be harmful to cry wolf until we could name the wolf and print his picture." Shadegg found his "wolf" in COPE representative Al Green. He presented Green as a "notorious labor chieftain" with a photograph of him with state Democratic party chairman Joe Walton leaving a restaurant. The connection thus made, Shadegg could now cry "wolf," and publish pictures and articles from October 19 on throughout the campaign.[38]

After the fashion of its attack upon gubernatorial candidate Robert Morrison in the primary, the *Republic* also published police mug shots of Green from old arrests in 1941 and 1943. Indeed, Green had served six months for having hired men to throw hot creosote on nonunion-constructed housing, and he had later been arrested for brandishing a firearm in a threatening manner. Both California arrests had been made over fifteen years before, and quite probably the mug shots had been acquired by Shadegg via illegal means.[39]

After making the link of Green to Walton on what was purely a social luncheon with his wife in attendance, it only remained to tie COPE directly to McFarland via campaign funding. The key components in Shadegg's strategy would then all fall in place: Reuther, COPE, Green, Green's prior record, party chairman Walton, COPE contributions, and McFarland, by association somehow guilty for all the real and alleged transgressions of this "notorious" group. Shadegg knew from vast political experience that Arizonans viewed labor leaders with suspicion, and that guilt by association worked - Americans were at that very moment in the threatening calm between McCarthyism and the John Birch Society.

Goldwater had already been making the contribution connection in his speeches, using both the old four thousand dollar figure from 1954 and the absurdly unrealistic new figure of $450,000 that he stated had been allegedly set aside by Reuther and Teamsters leader Jimmy Hoffa to defeat him. "In his more politically sober statements," according to political scientist Frank Jonas, Goldwater chopped the figure down to a realistic fourteen thousand dollars. Of this total, one thousand had been contributed for McFarland's specific use.[40]

In McFarland's reaction to this pernicious set-up lay the seeds of his ruin in the upcoming election, now only two weeks away. Simply stated, Mac overreacted and went too far to the defensive. The day after the Green expose, he went on Channel 3 along with Joe Walton to denounce the smear and point to Gene Pulliam, not COPE, as the agent wanting to control Arizona politics, Walton terming Pulliam a "carpetbagger," and Mac labeling the entire effort a Pulliam "smokescreen."[41]

McFarland then made a huge mistake a few days later by denying he had received any contribution from COPE. By this time, Goldwater had placed the grossly exaggerated figure of $450,000 in the public's mind even though it was, in reality, one-thirtieth of that amount. He also continued to remind the public that Mac had overlooked another four thousand dollar contribution, neglecting to mention that this had occurred in 1954 and not during the current campaign. Thus confused by figures and dates, the public was adequately set up when Pulliam revealed the actual fourteen thousand marked for all Democratic candidates including one thousand dollars for McFarland. Mac thus repeated his mistake of four years earlier by defensively overreacting and claiming no contribution filed when, in fact, the small sum had been filed and given by constituents who regarded him the better candidate. In any case it is quite probable that he knew nothing directly about the money, for it never passed through his hands. The damage was done, however, as the Shadegg-Pulliam coup made McFarland appear something less than honest and perhaps worse, one of big labor's very own.[42]

Because of Shadegg's timing, McFarland proved unable to take advantage of his own discovery that Goldwater paid more for billboards alone than Mac's entire campaign cost. Pulliam's unconscienable manipulation of "news" was never more brazen than in this campaign. He censored Mac for labor's contribution to all Arizona Democratic candidates, but failed to note that Goldwater alone received ten times as much, almost entirely from out of state. Frank Jonas, in his masterful 1970 study, penetrated to the heart of this Shadegg-Pulliam strategy:

> What has made it bad per se for labor union members and garment workers to contribute to a candidate's campaign and what has not made it equally bad for the factory owners, their bosses, to do so defies all reason. Yet this is precisely the condition in American politics, and candidates can base and then win a campaign on the assumption that Republican sources for campaign funds are legitimate while Democratic sources are made to appear somewhat tainted.

In Pulliam's hands, labor money through its Committee on Political Education was disparaged while the American Medical Association through AMPAC (American Medical Political Action Committee) could distribute thousands to reinforce Republican propaganda against "creeping" socialism.[43]

McFarland found himself in still deeper water with the Pulliam press when he charged Goldwater with using the same techniques as his "old friend and teacher, the late Senator Joe McCarthy. . . . When you prove one of his charges false and back him into a corner, he merely makes a new false charge." The *Republic* quickly labeled this a smear on Goldwater, "a strange campaign against the memory of the Wisconsin senator." In McFarland's televised speech, he charged that both Goldwater and McCarthy received large contributions from Texas oilmen in return for voting to turn tidelands oil deposits over to the individual coastal states. In conclusion, he quipped that "Goldwater, without Reuther, would be as maladjusted as McCarthy without communists." The newspaper noted that master of ceremonies Morris Udall had to call Mac back to the podium and remind him to include this part of the speech.[44]

Indeed, the Pulliam press and Shadegg did play on McFarland's age (sixty-four) as being old by comparison to Goldwater's forty-nine. His "advanced" age was a campaign constant and offered by Shadegg as the probable excuse for McFarland's "confusing behavior." Jonas explains how the Pulliam-Shadegg tandem manipulated events to put Mac in the worst possible public light.

> In this period of American politics, if a nominee did not appear at a debate, even though he had not accepted an invitation to do so in the first place, he was accused of being afraid to debate his opponent.
>
> This technique was used particularly against McFarland. In his case, the opposition would either stack the panels when he was expected to be present, or it would not publish the invitation and probably not extend it to him clearly or in good time, when the place and date of the panel debates were announced. Then when McFarland did present a paper, the newspaper would ridicule his speaking style or the content of his speech while praising his opponent's presentation. On occasion they would note that McFarland had forgotten parts of his speech or had to be called back to finish reading a manuscript.

The technique proved particularly effective for Goldwater's final rally on election eve. No mention was made that McFarland may or may not have been invited to appear, but when he did not, the press vilified him as "Afraid of questions . . . Mac misses final rally." In reality, Shadegg knew beforehand that McFarland had a prior television commitment at the same hour, and he used this known scheduling conflict, with or without invitation, to the advantage of the Goldwater campaign.[45]

Shadegg had other interesting techniques in his anti-Democratic arsenal. The "lilacs and lace" approach involved interviewing Democratic housewives who registered concern over Attorney General Morrison's candidacy because of his record and marital background. A series of such pieces ran for a week late in the campaign, and although Mac had no such perceived deficiencies, he by implication became tied with his party colleague as tainted. Similarly, frequent letters to the editor were run from "concerned mothers" worrying over potential corrupt union influence.[46]

Pulliam also highlighted former Democrats who had turned Pinto. Columbus Giragi, himself a recent convert, placed Al Green among "invaders specifically trained at political brainwashing." In reality Green engaged in no propaganda activities such as radio broadcasts, television appearances, or speechmaking. Pinto efforts drew strength from supportive articles about Langmade's fear of COPE and timely reproductions of earlier national columns by Holmes Alexander, Victor Riesel, and others. Too, the powerful Lewis Douglas, after supporting McFarland in the two gubernatorial campaigns, again came out for Goldwater for the Senate as he had done in 1952. Douglas wrote McFarland of his "lasting friendship," "greatest sincerity" and "distressing dilemma," while arguing that Mac could not win. McFarland characteristically replied, "I have never been one who has tried to unduly influence a friend in regard to my candidacy for office. I accept my friends' decisions in this regard. I disagree with you when you say it is very doubtful as to whether I can win. This I fully expect to do."[47]

A "new politics" that was being pioneered by Shadegg and scores of political managers across the country in the post World War II era manifested itself in this campaign. Winning became all important, and with Machiavellian design, almost any means to that end were permissible. What came to be widely known as "dirty tricks" during the Watergate expose were foreshadowed by the schemes of Shadegg and his ilk. For example, when his covert phone taps on Green produced no useful tidbits, he simply accused the McFarland camp of tapping his own lines and then simply ignored the denial - the unproved charge was enough, especially when it got such broad and favorable media coverage as he could always rely upon from Pulliam.

Also, paranoia reared its head, generated by anonymous rumor mongers outside of either camp when, on October 24, the *Phoenix Gazette* reported that "vile and abusive phone calls poured into the home of Mrs. Baron Goldwater," the senator's mother. At least one of them reminded the listener of the fate of Victor Riesel, the columnist who had been blinded by acid after attacking waterfront rackets. Other calls suggested that Goldwater's private plane might be sabotaged, and at least two hinted at assassination plots. All of these reports remained unsubstantiated and, of course, none materialized. Shadegg, however, sought press coverage for many of them so Goldwater could be seen in a sympathetic role, the potential victim of evil people. It was no accident that some feelings of revulsion swept back over McFarland's campaign. The McFarland camp made no similar claims to receiving threats or sensing evidence of conspiracy until the final days. No one questioned Mac's plane literally running out of gas over the desert sixty miles short of the runway.[48]

The most important weapon against McFarland, however, was Barry Goldwater himself. The charismatic, handsome and relatively young politician nicely complemented, on the front lines, the behind-the-scenes string pulling of Stephen Shadegg and the manipulations of Pulliam. Goldwater's flashing style proved increasingly appealing and effectively over-shadowed McFarland's charges and record of substance. Posed "action" shots such as climbing in and out of jet cockpits received national coverage and fitted in with department store sales and housewife interviews.

In one particularly effective instance, Goldwater spoke at the Westward Ho in front of the Phoenix Junior Chamber of Commerce. On stage, an oversized seven by seven foot newspaper front page had been assembled in a standing position. The paper, *Labor's* Arizona edition, featured a large, prominent photograph of McFarland along with headlines supporting his return to Washington - all under the large print newspaper title *Labor*. At the appropriate moment of introduction, Goldwater dramatically burst through the assemblage ripping it, and symbolically its assertions, to shreds. The concomitant action shot of what became known as "the breakthrough" received enormous press play, once again providing, for free, heavy campaign propaganda for the senator. The appellation, the "Breakthrough," became juxtaposed in the public's mind with McFarland's biggest mistake - now known as the "Breakdown" — his denying any COPE contributions.[49]

Still, as late as the final week of the campaign, the updated Harris Poll predicted a Democratic sweep. The two and one-half to one Democratic edge in voter registration appeared insurmountable to the pollsters, although Goldwater had done just that six years earlier as an inexperienced challenger. The poll favored Mac by fifty-two to forty-eight percent and Morrison by an estimated fifty-six to fifty-nine percent over Fannin's forty-four to forty-one.[50]

McFarland, never particularly impressed by polls, issued a statement on October 31: "Warning: Beware of last-minute smears. . . . I disapprove as strongly of personal attacks on my opponent as I do of the personal attacks by my opponent and the Pulliam press against me." The governor's statement resulted from information he had received of the circulation of a leaflet that could be construed as an attempt by him to smear Goldwater. He reinforced his disavowal by notifying the Senate Subcommittee on Privileges and Elections and suggesting that an investigator be sent to Phoenix in the eventuality of smear complications. Mac was taking the correct steps to defuse this development, but little did he realize that this leaflet would create a roorback that would sound the death knell for his campaign.[51]

The infamous "Stalin" leaflet appeared in Phoenix on October 31 depicting a winking, pipe-smoking, grandfatherly Joseph Stalin looking over his shoulder proclaiming "Why not vote for Goldwater?" The lead paragraph stated: "Union lauds Goldwater. `Honest, Sincere' Miners say." The caption beneath the picture read, "Goldwater fully endorsed by Pulliamism and lauded by Mine-Mill-Smelter Union which was expelled from organized labor for Communist domination. Politics makes strange bedfellows." Republicans immediately blamed COPE and by implication McFarland. Pulliam pulled out all stops in headlining "Mac In Tears About Smears. What

Does He Say Of This?" Clearly the paper implied not only that McFarland sanctioned the flyer but also that he had taken a weak and inappropriate stance crying about earlier smears directed against him. Goldwater reacted quickly to the situation stating:

> From the inception of this campaign, there have been scurrilous rumors circulated by organized McFarland supporters. My family life, my business, my brother, my mother, and my personal actions have been smeared. I will not keep silent and accept this latest smear accusing me of being supported by communists.[52]

McFarland's reaction came in his telegram to Senator Theodore Green [D-RI], head of the Senate Subcommittee on Elections:[52]

> My opponents have deliberately circulated a phony attack on the Mine, Mill, and Smelters Union which is supporting me. They attempt to make it appear that this attack is coming from my own supporters. For the sake of decency . . . frauds must be traced to their perpetrators.

Shadegg called these claims "absurd and untrue" and referred to Mac's allegations of a reverse smear as "the act of a desperate man."

For its part COPE denied any involvement with the leaflet. K.S. Brown, Secretary of the Arizona AFL-CIO stated:

> We of Arizona COPE are shocked by the appearance of the hate handbill. . . . COPE had nothing to do with this scurrilous handbill which apparently is unsigned and printed without the union label. We have never put out any piece of literature that we have not been proud to sign . . . . We . . . have some serious differences of opinion with Senator Goldwater . . . . But we would never under any conceivable circumstances accuse him of being soft towards communism.

The distribution of the "Stalin" leaflet became of crucial significance, for, unsigned, it constituted illegal campaign propaganda. It had been individually placed in only a few areas in Phoenix and then left here and there in parking lots still tied in large bundles. Smaller bundles were widely placed in bus stops and elsewhere. Certainly the flyer was photocopied many times, and Shadegg also sent it to four or five hundred prime names on the Goldwater mailing list. He also supplied the handbill to the Pulliam press where the Sunday edition front-page treatment smashed McFarland's campaign with its statewide distribution.[53]

Governor McFarland alerted county sheriffs to track down the origins of the pamphlet and awaited the arrival of investigator James H. Duffy, Chief Counsel of the Senate Subcommittee on Privileges and Elections. Upon arrival, Duffy concentrated on the illegal further dissemination of the scurrilous leaflet. In an official statement, he exonerated McFarland and scolded Shadegg for sending it to Goldwater's leading contributors. Duffy's statement read: "I have conferred with representatives of both sides, and have found no concrete evidence to the effect that Governor McFarland or his opponent had anything to do with the leaflets. I have no direct evidence that Senator Goldwater printed the leaflets, but Mr. Stephen Shadegg . . . has admitted that he received four or five hundred copies . . . which he sent to everyone on the senator's mailing list."

Shadegg was the wrong man to target. He immediately, and again with effect, set the Pulliam press loose to discredit Duffy as a liar, Democrat henchman, and McFarland tool. Shadegg and Goldwater's administrative assistant accosted Duffy at 2:30 A.M. in his motel room. They insulted him and attempted to elicit a signed statement rebutting the earlier one. Duffy refused, claiming that Shadegg's proposed new statement contained misrepresentations and untruths.[54]

McFarland attempted to bring the drifting and confused public back into his camp. Appearing on his own Channel 3 on the evening of November 2, he castigated the "bitter campaign of untrue statements, smear and fear tactics," laying the blame at the feet of Eugene Pulliam. According to Mac, Shadegg and Pulliam seized upon the Stalin leaflet because they realized that Mac led Goldwater by at least fifteen thousand votes, so desperate action was called for in the last days of the campaign.

This episode served as a microcosm of the whole campaign. The Goldwater forces simply outmaneuvered the McFarland team from beginning to end. Shadegg knew how to conduct a bare-knuckled, media-centered campaign in which the old practices of gentlemanly conduct no longer applied, even though pious lip service was given to them. In 1964, Shadegg would collect all of his new notions of how to manage a campaign into a book that became the most popular political handbook of the times, *How to Win an Election: The Art of Political Victory*. Even with "modern" managers, there may have been no way for Mac to avoid taking at least a small hit from the Stalin leaflet. But Shadegg fully exploited an opportunity that even McFarland supporter Duffy said he [Shadegg] did not create, and Mac's campaign fell into fatal disorder while his managers looked on in disbelief and bewilderment.

Nevertheless, Mac continued his televised plea for reason; he drew on family, his past, and his religion. Whereas Goldwater had succeeded in generating sympathy by talking of threats against his family, the same approach failed when Mac spoke of the hardships for his wife Edna. While he, himself could "consider the source and proceed without personal animosity," he knew that "these insulting insinuations and smears have . . . injured her deeply."

Mac still lived in an earlier era. He used campaign tactics that had worked when Arizona was a tiny state in the 1920s and 1930s. But the postwar population explosion coupled with a communication revolution produced a new kind of political battleground that Mac never understood. This is especially ironic when placed against his vast expertise of the worldwide communications network developed by Great Britain and the United States during World War II. He knew the new technology and how it worked in coordinating huge operations. He was cognizant of every development in the new entertainment field of television, which he already knew from the inside as a successful businessman. How could a person of such knowledge and understanding not have a glimmer of what it all meant on the campaign trail? For Mac, the role of the media was to report after the fact what politicians said and did. Shadegg, years ahead of Marshall McLuhan, planned Goldwater's comments and activities as media events. McLuhan did not invent his great theme - "the media is the message" - he observed it in the work of people like Shadegg.

McFarland spoke of his farming background, his family's ability to overcome financial duress and provide him a quality education, his gaining the respect of Republicans as well as Democrats while in the Senate, and finally, echoing Emerson, of his spiritual anchoring:

> I have learned that in every man God gave a spark of the Divine. Although many times I have felt he has blessed me beyond measure with his inspiration, never have I felt that I alone enjoyed such blessings. The future of Arizona was born and is reborn every hour in the sweat and tears, in the hopes and ambitions, the industry and labor, in the faith and prayers of every Arizonan. We as leaders can serve in but small measure in forming their destinies. It is our duty to inspire every man and protect all that is virtuous. To paraphrase Shakespeare, if I steal a purse, I gain but trash. If I steal from you your good name, I gain a shrinking of the human soul.

Mac also invoked the Biblical commandment "Love thy neighbor as thyself," in referring to Pulliam's painting him "as something fantastically grotesque in public character." As for himself, he kept the commandment "indelibly imprinted in his mind that it might reflect on his every act" exclaiming: "We have always believed that this applied to our political opponents as well as to our friends and neighbors." He concluded his address, "These are my humble beliefs. These are the motivating influences of my public and private life. I shall never forsake them." Mac stood true to these words; Shadegg, unfortunately, beat him to pieces.[55]

McFarland's speech, though sincere and heartfelt, failed to ameliorate the growing momentum toward Goldwater. Perhaps his frequent appearances on Channel 3 and his admittedly labored, stogid speechmaking grew wearisome for the public. Certainly the flashy Goldwater used the television more effectively, even frequently - only three times but simultaneously with all the state's networks, including McFarland's station! In any event, McFarland's premonition about the Stalin leaflet proved correct. He stated much later that once he saw it at such a late date in the campaign, he knew he would not be able to overcome its adverse effect.[56]

Shadegg had already successfully crippled the McFarland campaign with the technique of political dynamiting via media exposure of COPE's Green and now his timely use of the leaflet sealed McFarland's fate. A later FBI investigation placed the leaflet's origin with two disgruntled California union men acting on their own, claiming they disliked COPE and McFarland. But they disliked Goldwater even more, and testified before being fined one thousand dollars by the court that this was an attempt to discredit that candidate as well as the Pulliam press. As such it totally backfired.[57]

Arizona voters chose Senator Goldwater over Governor McFarland by a vote of 164,593 to 129,030, a strong victory (fifty-six to forty-four percent) since the early odds were about even. Paul Fannin won the governor's chair in what could be considered an upset and, as expected, John Rhodes won for First District House representative. Only Stewart Udall in the House's Second District and Wade Church for attorney general won major offices for the Democrats.

The results were significant, for Goldwater was the only major Republican electoral success in the Far West in 1958, and the election gained him the national attention necessary to become the leader of the Republican conservative revolution that was to erupt. Indeed, with the deaths of Robert Taft in 1953 and Joe McCarthy in 1957, conservative Republicans had been in disarray. Former Senate Majority Leader William Knowland attempted to provide some leadership, but he, too, went down to defeat in his 1958 bid for California governor.

Democrats swept into office across the nation taking nine of ten senatorial seats in the West and nineteen of twenty-five nationwide. Incumbent Senators Chavez, Mansfield, and Jackson had been expected to succeed themselves, while other newcomers Ernest Greuning in Alaska, Frank Moss in Utah, Gale McGee in Wyoming, and Howard Cannon in Nevada won tough battles that stretched the Democratic margin in the Senate by thirteen seats, a record eclipsing the twelve-seat gain of 1932. The party also climbed from 235 to 280 representatives in the House. The McFarland defeat among these victories stood out "like a sore thumb" and became closely scrutinized in the aftermath.[58]

What made Goldwater different from defeated Republican incumbents Malone of Nevada, Watkins of Utah, and Barrett of Wyoming asked *The Saturday Evening Post*? As had Goldwater, the others had "stood on principle" and endured "all the rocks the AFL-CIO had to throw." Analysts strove to isolate the differences and generally came up with a variety of factors including Goldwater's personality, Shadegg's managerial skills, the theme of outside labor bosses, and most importantly the propagandizing of the Pulliam press.[59]

Indeed, Frank Jonas credits the press for facilitating the victory: ". . . Goldwater won because he threw as many rocks . . . he threw them harder and timed them better. He hit his target more frequently and more accurately. Furthermore, he had the strength of a monopolistic press behind him." The Pulliam press functioned as Goldwater's slingshot.

Larry Marton, secretary of the McFarland campaign, stated:

> When you have two newspapers such as Eugene Pulliam's . . . (whose combined circulation is greater

than all the other dailies in the state) emphasizing a given theme and carefully censoring out efforts to combat that theme, the situation is critical. I think it would be summed up that Arizona neither voted against McFarland or for Goldwater but rather against what was believed to be a monster labeled LABOR, a tribute to the effectiveness of the Pulliam press.

Mac, himself, stated "with everything else Goldwater could not have defeated me without the help of the Phoenix papers."[60]

It is arguable, however, that Goldwater did not throw "as many rocks" but many more, and that their accuracy did not refer to the truth of the aspersions against Mac, but to hitting the target where it was most painful. Along these lines, Jonas concluded his analysis of the campaign:

The nature of this particular printed page would seem unique. It consisted of two daily newspapers . . . with no competition . . . giving . . . all out support to one candidate . . . never overlooking a single opportunity to do so. In order to do this they employed many known propaganda devices and techniques. The result appeared to observers to be a perversion of the canons of good journalism and the ethics of a national honorary journalistic fraternity which the publisher, Eugene Pulliam, helped to found in his younger days. One might conclude that they turned their establishment into a giant public relations firm during a political campaign.[61]

Yet, it is too simple or easy to lay the cause of McFarland's defeat solely at the feet of the questionable and effective tactics of the Goldwater-Shadegg-Pulliam triumvirate. The large margin of victory would appear to indicate other reasons as well, and they can be found in the McFarland camp. While Goldwater's star had begun to shine in the nation due to his aggressive and controversial nature, McFarland, who had once gleamed brightly, now was fading after the 1952 defeat and four difficult years in the governor's office. He was termed, afterward, as a "weak candidate with an incompetent campaign" employing "the usual reticence," an "obstacle . . . weak and uncooperative," and "too much of a handicap." This handicap of un-cooperation referred to McFarland's becoming overly defensive upon being accused of benefiting from COPE contributions of $450,000. Mac's denial of receiving anything made him appear on the surface to be a liar. He had neither the political moxie nor the skill to minimize the damage once the truth came out that he had received a one thousand dollar contribution, which he may in fact have been unaware of at the time he made his denial. Shadegg, though, hesitated not one moment in his charge that Mac had received fourteen thousand dollars. Shadegg knew the charge was false, but it was not illegal; it was just another gambit in the new media-based politics that Mac and his managers simply did not understand.[62]

Despite the "aged grey ghost" and "weak" assertions, McFarland proved a formidable oponnent. The ex-majority leader and two-term governor who had broken the Republicans in 1954 could not be taken lightly with such vocal supporters as Truman, Rayburn, Johnson, Kerr, and Humphrey. That Goldwater's team realized this is strongly suggested by the stylized steps with which Shadegg, at every opportunity, assailed Mac. In the end it all worked. Goldwater, aided by the Pulliam press's exploitation of the labor issue and the Stalin leaflet, rode triumphantly back into the Senate on a white steed upon which he would soon charge to the forefront of the conservative revolution that would capture the Republican party after Nixon's defeat in 1960.

Richard Kleindienst, the state Republican chairman, attributed great significance to the handbill. Orien Fifer, managing editor of the *Republic* stated, "It was this article [on Green] and the Stalin leaflet that elected Goldwater . . . those two articles." Larry Marton felt the leaflet was "the straw that broke the camel's back" and "the most significant factor." Others held that the leaflet's effect was cumulative in adding to the Green article. After all, it was not promulgated by the

Goldwater headquarters, but as masters of the new politics, Shadegg knew how to exploit the opportunity. It was its subsequent use that altered the political balance and continued the momentum toward Goldwater in the closing hours of the campaign.

Others downplayed the leaflet, Bert Fireman maintaining that it was of very little significance. Stephen Langmade said it was not particularly important. Barry Goldwater, too, downgraded its effect. Perhaps there exists a pattern of understatement here between Fireman, who played the crucial role of liaison between Pulliam and Shadegg and Langmade who ran against the tide of his party's interests, and Goldwater who benefited significantly.[63]

There existed no such confusion in McFarland headquarters as to the negative effects. An election summary attributed the defeat to "the most effective job of journalistic brainwashing ever seen in Arizona." This analysis also asserted Goldwater's wealth as a key factor, particularly with his purchase of premium and simultaneous time on all eight Arizona television stations, thus ensuring a captive audience. McFarland could counter only with frequent broadcasts on his station and a one-time purchase of simultaneous time on only four stations.[64]

Excuses and analyses aside, it was over and McFarland could take small comfort in the defeat. It is difficult to discern which of the two Goldwater campaigns produced greater anguish for Mac. In the first, as the incumbent and standing majority leader of the United States Senate, he had been upset by such a narrow margin. In 1958, he dreamed understandably of returning to the scene of his greatest successes. This made defeat bitter, especially when he dwelled upon thoughts that his loss had been occasioned by a series of "dirty tricks."

But Mac, for the public ear, said little, remaining near mute as he had six years earlier. Letters of condolence that flowed in from across the nation said more. Washington columnist Drew Pearson wrote, "of all the election races in the nation, there were two that disappointed me terribly. One was yours and the other was that of my friend George Leader in

Pennsylvania. . . . I hate to see a man like you defeated, especially by a phony like Goldwater.[65] Stewart's younger brother, Morris Udall, wrote:

> While the verdict of the voters has been filed, I must say it is not my verdict. I have an abiding belief that time will show the fraud and deception which brought about this injustice. How intelligent people can reject your long record of distinguished public service for a glamour boy who has never accomplished anything constructive is utterly beyond my understanding. If it is of any consolation in this hour of disappointment, let me record one observer's belief that the history of this State will record you as one of its ablest servants. It was a real honor to play a small part in your campaign.[66]

Perhaps Mac's own administrative assistant, Roland Bibolet, best summed up the thoughts of thousands of McFarland supporters: "We rejoice in the fact that you always continue to grow in stature as a man, still a great title anywhere."[67]

McFarland expressed some of his own views on the election in a letter to the AFL-CIO national office:

> COPE was used as a whipping boy in Arizona. A plain endorsement of the AFL-CIO would have been much better. . . . COPE was pictured as something very terrible - controlled by unprincipled bosses from outside. . . . It is going to take labor . . . some time to overcome this hate, fear, and smear campaign. The success of these tactics . . . will cause them to use them again. . . . When it comes to using labor to defeat candidates by smearing methods upon labor, then I say we have reached an all-time low in the politics of our state. . . .[68]

The historiography of the 1958 election merits attention. Writing in both 1959 and a decade later, Frank Jonas reported the controversial events in detailed amazement and even a degree of approbation referring to McFarland's mediocre campaign and Shadegg's brilliance. After Mac's 1984 death and as late as Goldwater's retirement in 1987, Pulliam press accounts still spoke of McFarland's candidacy as "affable but uninspiring" while depicting Goldwater as "very charming, very charismatic, and very convincing." In April 1990, upon Shadegg's death, The *Phoenix Gazette* remarked that McFarland was "not a dynamic guy. He didn't have much charisma except with the good old boys. In contrast Goldwater had the charm, persuasive ability, and credibility."[69]

Shadegg wrote profusely about the events in the early 1960s *How to Win an Election* in a proud, almost haughty manner, but more recently in his mid-1980s *Arizona Politics*, one can detect a more defensive, even apologetic tone omitting many controversies held against the Goldwater camp while adding some heretofore unpublished information on alleged labor threats against Goldwater. Goldwater wrote briefly of his "convincing upset victories" in 1979's *With No Apologies*, an autobiography which Shadegg claims to have ghostwritten in its entirety. Feeling it necessary to write a second autobiography nine years later upon his retirement, the senator, with the assistance of journalist Jack Casselry, inexplicably confused the two elections attributing the Stalin leaflet to the 1952 instead of the 1958 campaign. Was he subconsciously suggesting the flyer was not that important?[70] It does resemble a Pulliam-Shadegg tactic.

In any case, the Arizona electorate made its choice, seemingly one of style over substance, but more profoundly it was the "new" politics over the old. Goldwater went on to establish the Senate's worst attendance record during his years, frequently voting against Arizona farm, labor, and water interests. Yet his style commanded national attention and catapulted him to political fame. Indeed, his effect on American politics proved enormous in carrying the spirit of Republican conservatism from the deaths and defeats of Taft, McCarthy, and Knowland in the 1950s to the ascendence of Ronald Reagan in the 1980s. Without Goldwater, there could have been no Reagan.

Although McFarland was never able to put the losses to Goldwater entirely out of mind, he did not allow those uneasy memories to cripple him intellectually. With his hand directly on the controls, his business engine prospered as never before, and in the middle of the 1960s, he would successfully re-enter the political arena with election to the Arizona Supreme Court. These successes dulled the sharp edges of the Goldwater charge that he was too old and run-down to get things done. At the ripe age of eighty-three, Mac, when asked about these rough campaigns, simply stated, "Some things are worse than losing an election."[71]

PART V

LATER ARIZONA YEARS
1959-1984

CHAPTER FIFTEEN

NEGOTIATING THE POLITICAL WILDERNESS *1959-1964*

As THE END OF THE DECADE APPROACHED Ernest McFarland found himself out of public office for only the third time since he entered politics in 1923. There were the four years in the early 1930s after the loss of his first family and the two years between the U.S. Senate and Arizona governor, 1953 and 1954 — altogether only six years out of thirty-six. But this particular hiatus "felt" different and not as welcoming. Certainly with two senate defeats behind him, he could not aspire to that position again. He could perhaps attempt to regain the governor's chair, but with the recent conservative drift, that position might serve up more anquish than he had an appetite for - memories of his exasperating battles with the leg- islature during his second administration continued to disturb him. Still, there existed talk of a gubernatorial race against Paul Fannin in 1960, but for now Mac remained totally silent on his future intentions.

He did, however, possess tremendous political acuity and ongoing influence. One did not just jump off the campaign train and come to a complete halt, even if in defeat. Scarcely hours after his concession, Mac received a conciliatory phone call from Harry Truman, to which he responded by letter on the predicament of the Democratic party in Arizona. Mac asked the former president for suggestions and perhaps an appearance at a revitalizing Democratic banquet — to be held, Mac suggest- ed, in no less than two weeks.[1]

Truman, however, was unable to participate in anything on such short notice, and no banquet occurred. Although he did not know what might come next, Mac kept his options open and refused to be exiled to the political wilderness. He was hopeful that he could play a meaningful role in a potential Lyndon Johnson presidential candidacy in 1960.

Democrats were eager to wrest the White House back from the Republicans in 1960 after eight years of Eisenhower. Candidates, particularly from the U.S. Senate, lined up to carry the party's banner. By mid-1959, three senators had announced for the Democratic presidential nomination: Hubert Humphrey of Minnesota, Stuart Symington of Missouri, and the youthful John Kennedy of Massachusetts. Two-time loser Adlai Stevenson still commanded a lot of influence and respect and lurked in the background, showing once again that when presidential fever gets in the system only embalming fluid can remove it. More speculation hovered around the possible candidacy of the most powerful senator of them all, Majority Leader Lyndon Johnson of Texas, who had yet to announce his position.

His former senate boss, Ernest McFarland, had no doubts on the matter: "Johnson said he's not going to run, but of course he will," he told the *Christian Science Monitor*. The *Congressional Quarterly* also interviewed Mac on the possibility, and to it he pointed out as proof the action of the Texas Legislature clearing the path for Johnson to run for both president and senator.[2]

The interviews in both journals took place at the 1959 Western States Democratic Conference in Denver and indicated McFarland still wielded influence in party politics in national and regional circles as well as the state level. Political pundits as often manufacture fancied scenarios as comment upon real ones, and at this time a few Arizona scribes began to speculate that McFarland really was preparing for another run for the governor's office. Mac had no comment, but said he would work hard for LBJ's presidential aspirations with whatever influence he possessed.[3]

Johnson considered Arizona important and relied on his

long association with both McFarland and Carl Hayden to line up the state's support should it become necessary for his unstated ambitions. The South was solid no more; civil rights had eroded all the old bonds. Johnson would have to pull off some sort of Houdini-like political illusion if he were to have any chance of capturing the Democratic nomination in 1960. He would have to shed his widely recognized image as a southerner to be able to appeal to moderates and liberals outside the South. But this had to be done without offending his southern constituency, which would simply reject him if he attached a northern or eastern label to his political views. Perhaps a western or southwestern label would permit him to court simultaneously a national following while appeasing his southern base. It seemed the only way to go. Therefore, the West and Arizona were critical to Johnson's political success. His unquestioned ability to work with Republicans as majority leader, as McFarland sometimes had, enhanced his reputation with all except his party's northern liberals. To assuage them, he agreeably continued to work for some kind of civil rights legislation, but this engendered the lasting enmity of conservative Republicans and jeopardized his standing with southern Democrats. Johnson's new persona, though, seemed to be working when Kentucky, a Democratic state from the Upper South, threw its support to him for the presidential nod.[4]

Testing the waters of the West, LBJ announced plans to come to Phoenix in December as the first speaker among a series of candidates at the Democratic Party Public Affairs Forum. McFarland stood as his number one booster hosting receptions before and after the presentation and sitting with Johnson at the speaker's table. Here the two received telegrams from Carl Hayden, who, unable to attend, referred to LBJ as "the wisest man I know" and to Mac as "the truest and noblest Roman of them all." In between accolades, Johnson "electrified the crowd" by departing from his prepared speech and criticizing not only the Republicans as expected but also those Democrats (northern liberals) who would not attempt harmony with the present administration and those who would oppose nonpartisan civil rights legislation (southern conservatives). Clearly LBJ was trying to accent both his western and his moderate roots. It appeared, at this time, that he had a hold on mainstream Arizona Democrats, particularly with Mac as his front man. There existed much opposition beneath the surface, however, as soon became apparent.[5]

According to the press, "the breach between conservative and liberal Democrats here figuratively is as wide as the Grand Canyon . . . as jagged and deep as crevices in Arizona's mountains." Amidst this divisiveness and the mercurial nature of politics, McFarland found himself in the unusual position of being grouped with the conservative camp, a far cry from his categorization while governor. National not state politics, however, here determined the labels, and LBJ was considered conservative; therefore, Mac was too. Other factors influencing these determinations included personal loyalty and friendship between Johnson and McFarland and Johnson's age and experience compared to other candidates.[6]

Younger Arizona "liberals" had gathered behind Congressman Stewart Udall in backing Senator Kennedy, who at that time led the national polls among Democrats. Some Udall followers worried that if LBJ obtained the nomination, McFarland would move in and "deal his old cronies" political plums, leaving the younger set out.[7]

While Kennedy led nationally, Johnson appeared to be gaining strength in the West early in the year. McFarland joined LBJ supporters Clinton Anderson, Bob Kerr, and Mike Mansfield at the Western Democratic Conference in Albuquerque. Here, nose counts indicated that Johnson had already wrapped up 169 of 361 western delegates, including twelve of Arizona's seventeen. This figure apparently left little room for the four other Democratic candidates, particularly in Arizona, where besides Kennedy, Symington had some support and Stevenson a little. Humphrey, who had vacationed in the state for a few days without campaigning, held none, it seemed, and focused on his West Virginia primary battle with Kennedy.[8]

One of the keys to Lyndon Johnson's acceptance hinged

on his efforts to push a modicum of civil rights legislation through the Senate. Using his tactical and organizational ability plus a bit of deception to get the legislation to a floor vote, Johnson succeeded in the spring of 1959 even when faced with the powerful Richard Russell declaration of "a plot to provoke race riots in the South." The passage of civil rights legislation enhanced Johnson's standing somewhat in the Northeast, but he needed the West far more, and John Kennedy was coming to town.[9]

On April 9, 1960, accompanied by Stewart Udall, Kennedy barnstormed Arizona for a single day beginning in Flagstaff, moving on to Tucson, and then to a quick stop in Yuma before addressing the Phoenix Press Club at the Hotel Westward Ho. Youngest brother Ted Kennedy had already been in the state stressing his brother's qualifications and hinting that he himself might be opening a law office in Arizona. Moreover, for more than a month, Democratic National Committeewoman Lisa Bronson of Sedona had been lining up the women's vote behind the young New Englander.

The groundwork was well laid, but its fulfillment remained up to Kennedy himself. He effervecsed and won roaring approval from all the crowds he faced. His personality and charisma drew the committed and curious to the hotel speech attended by fifteen hundred as compared to Johnson's largest crowd of eight hundred. Earlier in the day he drew twelve hundred at Flagstaff and six hundred at both Yuma and Tucson. The personality factor proved crucial, for if Kennedy had not quickly and effectively covered the state, Arizona would probably have continued its hard sail to Johnson. As it turned out, Kennedy not only halted LBJ's momentum, but became the sudden favorite among many of the state's regions and, importantly, its delegates.[10]

McFarland continued to push for Johnson knowing that much would be decided at the end of April state party convention. A number of crucial items were at stake. First, the fourteen county chairmen would choose the thirty-four delegates to the national convention in July, each delegate to possess one-half vote of Arizona's seventeen total. McFarland was chosen as an at-large delegate, not affiliated with a particular county. Then it had to be determined if the state delegation would be "unstructured" and not bound to a single candidate. Preliminary meetings of the county heads indicated preference for unstructured and unbound delegates. This stood against the wishes of the Kennedy camp, which had almost succeeded in binding the state, gaining commitments from twelve counties with only Maricopa (Phoenix) and McFarland's Pinal holding out.[11]

Serious problems faced the 446 delegates to the state convention, particularly regarding whether the two hundred members from Maricopa County would vote as a single bloc under the "unit" rule and thus dominate the convention. This approach would also work against Kennedy since his supporters had been unable to capture the party's endorsement there. However, Stephen Langmade, the conservative but young Democrat was lured into the Kennedy camp, and urged against the unit rule because it could freeze out the smaller counties which were already committed to Kennedy.[12]

Furthermore, there were individual positions to be decided including Langmade's as national Democratic committeeman. Both Udall and McFarland had withdrawn their names early from this race. Apparently, Mac had trouble finding statewide support, and Udall had thrown his name in only to help propel the Kennedy movement. McFarland then worked strongly against Langmade, well remembering the younger Democrat's challenging and suspicious activities in the 1958 campaign. Mac supported Jim McNulty of Bisbee for the position, and he pushed Mildred Larson, his former Washington secretary and wife of his KTVK-TV partner, for national committeewoman. In doing so, he worked against state chairman Joe Walton's candidacy, reasoning that if Larson, from Maricopa, were selected, the other national post should go to another county, hence to McNulty of Cochise. Frank Minarik of Tucson rounded out the challengers for this position.[13]

Finally, it remained to be determined who would chair

the national delegation to the Los Angeles convention. This depended wholly upon the delegation's preference for president. As the state convention drew near, this contest appeared to favor Stewart Udall, as Kennedy remained the frontrunner on the basis of his early April visit. Joe Walton estimated thirty-five percent for Kennedy, twenty-five percent for Johnson, fifteen for Symington and the rest uncommitted. A later questionnaire put out by Langmade on the convention's eve indicated a delegate count of Kennedy at fifty-eight, Symington thirty-eight, Johnson thirty-four, Humphrey seven, and Stevenson three.[14]

Johnson appeared to have peaked too soon while Kennedy's momentum increased. Just two days prior to the convention, however, Joe Walton received a telegram that presumably would turn the whole campaign around in Arizona and greatly please Ernest McFarland at the same time. Senior Senator Carl Hayden came out firmly for LBJ, wiring, "I am convinced that Lyndon Johnson has the best understanding of the problems that the people of Arizona have to contend with." The Pulliam press, which adamantly opposed Kennedy's purported liberal "socialist" program reported:

> The Hayden endorsement of Johnson carries much more weight than the Udall backing of Kennedy and is a definite personal rebuke to Udall, who has been assuming the leadership of the party in Arizona without official sanction. Udall's tie-up with the forces of Senator Kennedy has been described as an arrangement to further Udall's hope of inheriting Senator Hayden's mantle someday.[15]

A Reg Manning cartoon depicted Udall being blown off his Democrat mule by the cannonball of Hayden's endorsement, and the *Republic's* political column stated Hayden had "removed Udall's last chance" to take over as chair of the national convention delegation. An unnamed "high" Democrat, possibly McFarland, expressed the opinion that Udall had moved too fast and too provocatively instead of trying to "reason on Kennedy" and added that he had made the mistake of "trying to invade Maricopa County and tell the people here what to do." Others commented that Hayden had "cut Udall down to size."[16]

The Hayden (McFarland)-Udall squabble thus added to the tensions at the convention. Moreover, additional hackles were raised by both Johnson and Kennedy forces against supporters of Stuart Symington. Astutely, the Symington forces had arranged for their candidate, the third to officially address Arizonans, to present his public forum in the same hotel and on the evening of the state convention. Symington had been holding up surprisingly strong thus far without an appearance, and the opposition believed his timely appearance would influence crucial votes away from their candidates, Kennedy and Johnson. The fluctuating Symington represented a moderate stance between the supposed Kennedy liberalism and Johnson conservatism, but stood closer to LBJ. The volatile nature of politics is seen here again, or was it merely the shallowness of typical reporting, as McFarland, once feared as a liberal to many while governor, was now categorized as conservative. In reality it was a matter of personal friendship and loyalty and a firm belief that LBJ knew western interests better than the other candidates.[17]

The state Democratic convention on Saturday April 30 opened amidst "bedlam" at the Westward Ho. Only two minutes after the opening gavel, Chairman Walton had to call a lengthy recess to avert the confusion of noisy challenges and allow county delegations to plan further cohesive strategy. The Kennedy people used this time wisely; whereas LBJ had apparently recovered and regained the initiative with Carl Hayden's endorsement, things were not as they seemed. Now Udall and his colleagues aggressively matched the momentum from the Hayden-McFarland tandem again, and this time they would not relinquish it.[18]

The major issue among many revolved around whether Maricopa County would vote as a unit. If it did and could obtain thirty-two additional votes, it could control the proceedings. The unit vote would favor a Johnson-Symington coalition that could thwart Kennedy efforts. After Walton's recess, the Maricopa delegates caucused and voted for the unit rule, ninety-three to ninety-one, a victory for the Johnson backers. However, at the same time, Kennedy workers gathered up the county chairmen of the twelve Kennedy counties for a caucus. An earlier motion had passed empowering these county chairmen to write the rules for the convention, and now they did just that, proceeding to vote out the unit rule option. The chair for Maricopa and McFarland of Pinal, which still held out for Johnson, were not party to this decision, but the twelve present at the hastily assembled meeting constituted not only a quorum but a unanimous majority. Dismayed Maricopa delegates wandered back to their seats only to learn that Udall had grasped control of the convention. McFarland shared this disappointment but still held a faint hope that Johnson could prevail later in the campaign.[19]

The convention went on to certify the credentials of the thirty-four delegates chosen to go to Los Angeles with nineteen now committed to Kennedy and six strongly leaning that way. JFK was then assured a majority and the unit rule, still in effect for the national convention, could be binding for all Arizona delegates if adopted.[20]

The Pulliam press, well pleased with the confusion in Democratic ranks if not by the pro-Kennedy outcome, wildly speculated on how Udall was able to stage a coup that in effect could disenfranchise forty-seven percent of Arizona's votes, the Democrats of Maricopa County. The *Republic* again noted Ted Kennedy's preliminary trip to the state but emphasized the role of "Father Joe Kennedy, the Boston millionaire pouring money and promises into Arizona to win the votes for his son Jack." The press continued that the convention "has been unrivaled in bitterness and the amount of money spent. There have been reports of proxies being bought, of delegates being bribed" and "ugly reports of offers made to youth leaders to influence their votes at a mock convention." Though no further detail substantiated these reports, the paper did express fear that Udall would now control patronage and challenge Hayden for the Senate in 1962.[21]

Not everyone took the *Republic's* insinuations without question, and the Democratic *Tempe Daily News* took Pulliam to task noting that Democrats "choose" their candidates while Republicans "appoint" theirs and that "Pouring cash is a Republican pastime. Democrats are too broke. . . . It is the product of an inspired and controlled Republican press aided and abetted by a biased Republican columnist whose obvious assignment from the front office is to paint all things Democratic in mud-colored hues."[22]

Yet the *Republic* may have been close to the truth. Reprinting Drew Pearson's Washington column, the *Gazette* wrote of the Kennedy deal that "euchered" twenty-five of thirty-wo delegates from Johnson and elder statesmen Hayden and McFarland. Pearson claimed Kennedy, indeed, promised Udall support in a 1962 run against Hayden, speculating that the Mormon Udall, who ran poorly in Catholic precincts, could use the Kennedy influence profitably.[23]

The Udall-Kennedy forces swept others away as well. Whatever pre-arrangements Stephen Langmade had made with them disappeared, and Tucson's Frank Minarik became new national committeeman, further centralizing Democratic power in Udall's Pima County. McFarland did see his choice for national committeewoman, Mildred Larson, win, small consolation for the disarray of Johnson supporters. The Humphrey people, too, went over to Kennedy.[24]

Nevertheless, McFarland graciously praised Udall's victory on the floor as the convention neared conclusion. He did so to recommend harmony after what had been his party's most divisive day in state convention history. Furthermore, it being apparent that Udall would obviously become the chair of the national delegation, McFarland advised that Udall be permitted to name his own officers. Meeting three weeks later when these selections were made, the Udall forces, already dominant, declined this overt show of control and allowed the convention as a whole to choose, but their influence dictated choices. Udall

The Big Four outside the
White House, L-R: Barkley
Rayburn, McFarland,
McCormack.

President and floor leaders, L-R: Mac, LBJ, Truman, House Whip Percy
Priest and McCormack. Autographed to Mac by LBJ.

Mac and LBJ while
Majority Leader and Whip.

Mac flanked by the opposition:
Republican Senate Minority Leader
Kenneth Wherry and future
president Dwight Eisenhower.

Democratic Policy Committee, L-R: Joseph O'Mahoney, Lister Hill, McFarland, Barkley, Johnson, Earle Clements, Richard Russell, Jan. 9, 1952.

Predicting his future: McFarland's handwritten statement at closing of second session, 82nd Congress: July 7, 1952.

Mr. president it is always a bit difficult to make this last motion & it gives us happiness yet we are saddened by the fact that we are parting from our good friends [...] whom [ ] will not be back in the Senate with us at the next session.

After the November 1952 defeat, Mac was sent by the Senate on an around the world goodwill trip visiting 30 countries with Edna. Here he enjoys dinner with Arizona frontline GIs on a cold Christmas Day in Korea, 1952.

On the final leg of the trip, Mac and Edna visit the *U.S.S. Arizona* Memorial at Pearl Harbor, Hawaii.

Politics back in his blood, McFarland files gubernatorial nomination petitions, July 1954, with Rose Mofford, herself a governor over thirty years later.

McFarland presents innaugural address at the State Capital as Arizona's 10th Governor, Jan 3, 1955; at left front Edna and Ralph Watkins, Sr.; R–L: Jewell, former Gov. Bob Jones, Gov. Manual Soto from Sonora, Mexico, former Gov. Dan Garvey, Attorney General Robert Morrison, unknown, and future Gov. Wesley Bolin.

Mac also spent more time on his Florence farms; here with Del Lewis.

Temporarily out of politics McFarland founds KTVK-TV, channel 3, an ABC affiliate with minority partners, L-R: Ralph Watkins, Sr., Hank Larson,, Mac, Leon Nowell, 1953.

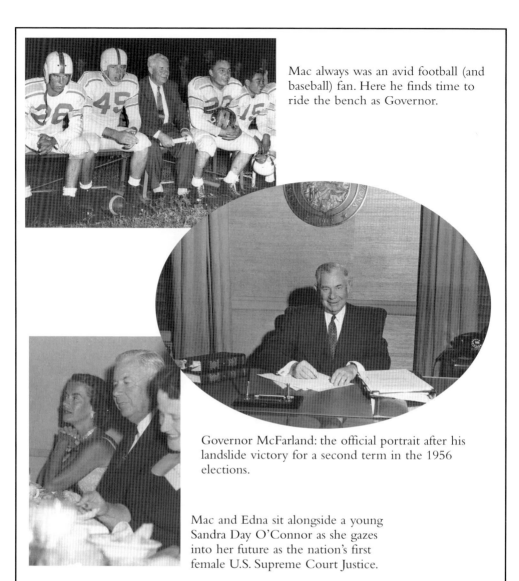

Mac always was an avid football (and baseball) fan. Here he finds time to ride the bench as Governor.

Governor McFarland: the official portrait after his landslide victory for a second term in the 1956 elections.

Mac and Edna sit alongside a young Sandra Day O'Connor as she gazes into her future as the nation's first female U.S. Supreme Court Justice.

Governor Mac hosts an eclectic group, L-R: daughter Jewell, actress Anne Baxter, actors Charlton Heston and Tom Tyron, Mrs. and Mr. Frank Lloyd Wright and McFarland, who did not approve of Wright's design for a new Capitol building in Papago Park.

Gov. Mac and old friend Gene Autry at Florence Parada.

Governor McFarland and Senator Hayden examine location of new townsite of Page, construction center for the Glen Canyon Dam, 1957.

McFarland gives high fives at his Hotel Westward Ho testimonial dinner, May, 10,1958, where he announced his candidacy for the U.S. Senate against Barry Goldwater.

Goldwater's victory allowed Mac more time as grandpa: L–R: Jewell, grandpa, grandchildren William and Kara Lewis, Edna, and Del Lewis.

Beauty shops, barber shops, bars, and bowling alleys; Mac campaigned in them all.

Mac visits Harry Truman at the Truman Library, Independence, Missouri as Ralph Watkins, Sr. looks on, summer 1964.

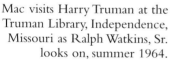

Mac kept his eyes on the political scene. Here, front and center, he leads the Arizona delegation at the 1964 Democratic party convention in San Francisco. Soon to be elected governor, Sam Goddard smiles broadly in back, third from right.

President Lyndon Johnson exuberantly greets old colleague McFarland, at left, back to camera at the convention. He will easily gain the nomination and triumph over Barry Goldwater in the 1964 elections.

While on the Supreme Court, McFarland served on the National Commission on the Causes and Prevention of Violence in America 1968-69; Here with LBJ in the oval office.

Chief Justice McFarland at center in 1968; at left Justices Charles Bernstein and Levi Udall, at right Justices Fred Struckmeyer, Jr., and Lorna Lockwood. Mac had now held his state's highest office in each branch of government, a feat unique in American political history.

Justice of the Arizona Supreme Court; McFarland was elected in his own right in the 1964 elections.

Mac retired to family, farm, law and TV work; here breaking ground for new addition at channel 3, L–R: Ralph Watkins, Jr., Del Lewis, Hank Larson, Mac, Leon Nowell, Roland Bibolet.

During a 1976 Bicentennial tour, Mac and Edna visit Senator Robert Byrd of West Virginia; then floor leader in the Senate, Byrd serves still today in 2003, serving over a half century on Capitol Hill and chasing Carl Hayden's 57 years.

1982, Stanford University, a smiling Mac at 88 years of age.

Poster board honoring Mac at his Oct. 9, 1971 retirement dinner.

became chair and his assistant W. P. Mahoney vice chair. Senator Hayden was recognized but relegated to the lesser position of honorary chair. Only crumbs remained for McFarland who became honorary assistant to the vice-chair (Mahoney), one position lower than former Governor Dan Garvey, a Kennedy man, who became honorary vice-chair. Joe Walton also was chastised and designated only honorary secretary.[25]

Arizona's unique standing of importance to Jack Kennedy emanated from a number of sources. Kennedy feared that if he did not obtain the nomination on the first ballot, his youth, religion, and other possible factors would severely inhibit his chances in later counts. He could not allow his perceived weaknesses and deficiencies to be ruminated upon at length on the Los Angeles convention floor. This would switch the tide to the more experienced, supposedly more moderate and less controversial LBJ. It was the first ballot or never. Arizona stood third in line behind Alabama and Alaska in the nominating order. Kennedy desperately needed an early indication flowing his way by having an early state defer to Massachusetts so his home state, thus altering the order, could place his name in nomination. Alabama would in no way defer to Kennedy or Massachusetts. It was believed that the new state Alaska was going to remain uncommitted in its first convention. Therefore it fell to Arizona if early Kennedy momentum was to succeed. Such a gesture would also appear to lock Arizona into the Kennedy column thereby diminishing LBJ's luster. Not only could Kennedy advance his own chances, but he could also deflate Johnson's by winning Arizona despite LBJ's support from venerable friends Hayden and McFarland. Hence the grand strategy evolved, put together in part by middle brother and campaign manager Robert Kennedy, implemented early on by Ted's state visits and Joe Kennedy's financial influence, and carried through by the personable candidate himself with Stewart Udall closely monitoring and manipulating behind the scenes. As the Hayden-McFarland people greeted LBJ at the front door, Udall and the brothers ushered JFK out the back with the prize in hand.

Though emphasizing harmony on the outside, McFarland continued to explore ways to assist Johnson on the inside. Mac believed that if the national convention could go to a second ballot, LBJ could gain the nomination. He urged that the delegation not commit to Kennedy as a unit (technically members were still uninstructed) and not to defer to Massachusetts. A further and logical strategic move would be for Arizona to place Carl Hayden's name into nomination as a "favorite son" for president, thus using up its potential first ballot impact for JFK and leaving an opening for LBJ on later ballots. McFarland worked to this end.

With the assistance of Yuma's Senator Harold Giss, Mac attempted to implement this strategy at the meeting of the national convention delegates three weeks after the state convention. Giss proposed that the honor of a favorite son presidential nomination be accorded Hayden. McFarland then urged concurrence, stating: "He knows more about the government than any member of Congress." Two state supreme court justices, M.T. Phelps and Charles Bernstein, also backed the move as did Barry Goldwater from his Republican vantage point: "If any man is entitled to designation as a favorite son, it is Carl Hayden, the Dean of the Senate." Indeed, Hayden was deserving having by that time served on Capitol Hill for forty-eight years, one year longer than Sam Rayburn, and having attended his first Democratic convention in 1904 as a territorial delegate.[26]

Udall, not in attendance, busied himself in Washington where he made frantic efforts "to persuade Hayden not to accept the honor if it were to be offered." He succeeded, however, as the Udall delegates held firm, voting against the Hayden-favorite son proposal nineteen to twelve. The *Republic*, always acknowledging Hayden's strength and popularity in the two-party state that it had helped to create, critically commented: "Arizona will not soon forget the arrogance of its youngest congressman . . . one man who apparently feels he must pay off a debt of some sort to the Kennedys."[27]

McFarland did not yet give up hope for Johnson's candidacy. Along with National Committeewoman Mildred Larson, television partner Ralph Watkins, Sr., and local developer Kemper Marley, Mac stood with eight Arizonans among one hundred eighty Americans contributing to full page ads for LBJ in major Washington papers. National columnist Holmes Alexander chose LBJ over JFK; in Texas, Sam Rayburn and John Connally continued to beat the bushes; and the Scripps-Howard newspaper chain endorsed Johnson. Clearly, the veteran Texan still had a chance at the convention if he could survive a first ballot rush for Kennedy.[28]

In Los Angeles delegates generally gathered into hotels by states, and tended to be noisy, brusque, and curiously garbed. The Arizona delegation, adorned with copper-colored cowboy hats, joined forty-nine others in old downtown Los Angeles. Kansans wore sunflowers, Michiganers green and white polka dot Soapy Williams neckties, and colorful Hawaiians sported leis. Others added an endless variety of colors and behavior to the massed conventioneers. The Arizonans lodged in the Mayan Hotel, while a few miles away, at the Biltmore convention site, swirling crowds, brass bands, and the media all competed for attention among the headquarters of the five major candidates: Kennedy, Johnson, Symington, Humphrey, and Stevenson.

On the eve of the convention the Arizona delegation stood at about twenty-three to eleven for Kennedy. With the delegates already committed to vote as a single unit, the big question loomed over whether they would do so on the first ballot. This appeared likely with the Hayden gambit out of the way, and if the delegation did so, it could defer to Massachusetts and expedite the early nomination of Jack Kennedy. Mac worked hard against this eventuality as the hours waned before nomination night.

The caucus vote of the Arizona delegates on whether to go for JFK on the first ballot or wait for developments was scheduled for 1:00 P.M. Monday, the opening day. In the meantime McFarland, along with two Johnson aides lodged near the Arizonans, kept the pressure on potential converts to LBJ and

414 — ERNEST W. MCFARLAND

especially on those who felt that Arizona might better serve themselves by being noncommittal at this stage. However, JFK, too, kept active, sending brother Ted and sister Eunice Shriver to the Mayan to continue building his case for first ballot unit support.[29]

At the afternoon meeting, proceedings went as expected with the delegation voting to go for Kennedy immediately. The proposal however stated that this support would be effective for all balloting beyond the first as well. To this, Mac strenuously objected, stating he would oppose this position from the main floor if necessary. His threat forced a compromise whereby the delegates agreed to hold a caucus between each ballot if called for. Udall noted that Mac had brought Johnson into a better position as a strong second choice. McFarland, sensing the inevitable but still retaining hope, stated LBJ "is a proven leader who has everything it takes to make a great president. He knows both foreign and domestic affairs and is a proven friend of Arizona." Mac scourged the gathered delegates for committing in advance and continued, "Johnson has voted for us up and down the line; never has he failed us. This is the first time that Arizona has failed to give him the recognition he so justly deserves." He declared, "Kennedy is a nice young man, but I can't cast my vote for him," adding, however, that he would later lend "enthusiastic support to Kennedy or any other candidate gaining the nomination."[30]

For some Arizonans, the reaction to the Kennedy dominance was very negative. While McFarland proved gracious, exclaiming, "I accept my defeats," state Senate Majority Leader Giss flatly declared "this thing is a steamroller." He joined faltering state chairman Joe Walton and others in worrying over the future of the Democratic party in the state: "The whole ticket will be damaged because Arizonans do not vote and think the way Kennedy votes and thinks." To these people, a 1960 Republican victory now appeared inevitable and the growing strength of the young liberal Tucsonan Udall dangerous. Specifically many felt that a Kennedy nomination would make it increasingly difficult for Democrats to gain election to state offices and that Udall could be charged with sacrificing the interests of his party for his own personal prestige. The Pulliam press concurred with this sentiment and editorialized so consistently as to break Udall's temper on the podium: "Pulliam will not dictate to Arizona Democrats on whom to vote for." The tension also escalated into shouting and near fisticuffs between Udall supporter Jim McNulty and *Republic* reporter Bernie Wynn all in front of television cameras. Tempers, indeed, were high. Here again, the mediating McFarland found himself outside his normal circle and among conservative Democrats and Pulliam supporters.[31]

On the national level, the Kennedy momentum did not let up, and he inexorably rolled toward the nomination. On Saturday, July 9, before the convention convened, he tallied an unofficial 546 of 761 necessary votes with Johnson at 235. On Sunday Governors Edmund G. Brown of California, Herschel C. Loveless of Iowa, and George Docking of Kansas declared for him, and most importantly, Chicago's Mayor Richard Daley "unwrapped his package" of 59.5 of 60 Illinois votes. On Monday, the convention's opening day, all eyes turned to Pennsylvania, knowing that if that rugged state of miners and steelworkers came out for JFK, the race was predictably over. Early in the day United States Steelworkers President David McDonald, who controlled about thirty votes, declared for Kennedy; then the powerful Mayor David Lawrence of Pittsburgh brought the Keystone State's Kennedy total votes up to sixty-four. The rush had now commenced and New York's commitment grew toward one hundred votes. When Humphrey released his votes to any favorite son, Kennedy dipped his net in here as well, bringing the official count by day's end to 688.5 to 304.5 for LBJ with 761 required.

Lyndon Johnson kept emphasizing in his speeches the importance of maturity, particularly regarding foreign affairs, as his main theme. He appeared to get a boost when Minnesota Senator Eugene McCarthy threw in his support, and not as many California votes materialized as JFK had hoped. McFarland, Kerr, Rayburn, Mike Mansfield, and Representative Daniel Inouye of Hawaii kept agitating as well, but it proved to no avail as Kennedy assembled the requisite 761 votes by Wednesday, the day of the nomination.[32]

In doing so, the Massachusetts senator had overcome great obstacles of age and religion and, indeed, he had turned his youthfulness and Catholicism to his advantage. Criticized for his wealth and his liberalism, here too he succeeded in turning the arrows directed against him. Financial resources proved a key factor in keeping the pressure on those with lukewarm or wavering support via constant vigilance and activity among his army of campaign workers. His suspected liberalism combined with youthful energy made him appear as a man of the hour ready to actualize Harry Truman's old Fair Deal and modernize America, particularly regarding the civil rights plank the convention had adopted. Finally, his family stood behind him as stalwarts brother Ted and sister Eunice scurrying effectively from delegation to delegation implementing the plan masterminded by brother Robert and the clan patriarch Joseph P. Kennedy, who was realizing his ambition of seeing a son head for the White House. Indeed, both Joe's and Robert's reputations served to complement that of the nominee. It was Kennedy's time and JFK grasped it with no intentions of letting go or allowing any weak links or deficiencies, personal or organizational, stand in his way.[33]

When the actual balloting began on the convention floor, a big surprise awaited Arizona, which luxuriated in its expectant role of throwing the nomination to Kennedy. Instead, Alaska, which had been expected to remain noncommittal as a proud and new state, yielded to Minnesota, which in turn passed to Massachusetts, prompting the home state's nomination and the climb to a first ballot victory. McFarland's hopes for a snafu during the first ballot were dashed and Arizonans disappointed in their seemingly lesser role than expected. However, both Mac and his state were important in the ultimate outcome. Obtaining Arizona, seemingly safe in Johnson's column and a symbol of the West and party moderation and conservatism, proved a key to JFK in exposing Johnson's vulnerability in his own back yard. Kennedy acknowledged Arizona's important contribution by inviting the delegation to his Biltmore headquarters and proferring his thanks. As for Mac, he turned his attention to the vice presidential contest where his unwavering support of LBJ would witness and indirectly influence an unexpected outcome.[34]

The day after Kennedy's nomination, the Arizonans caucused again to select their vice presidential candidate. The meeting also manifested an effort at harmony, McFarland leading the way stating, "We're Democrats and we will get a lot of pleasure out of getting behind Senator Kennedy." Harold Giss made a similar statement of unity. Concerning a vice presidential choice, Udall speculated that Johnson would be offered but refuse the position because of his responsibilities as majority leader. He had been informed by Johnson campaign manager, Senator Mike Mansfield, that such was the case. Although Udall stated that Johnson would naturally be the Arizonans' first choice for the second spot, the delegation did not consider his name, taking Mansfield's information as definitive. In a show of hands, the Arizona delegation indicated as its choice Stuart Symington by a two-to-one margin over Senator Henry Jackson of Washington. Hindering Symington's chances was the absence of fellow Missourian Harry Truman. The former president had allegedly indicated to his dissatisfaction that the entire convention had been "rigged" for Kennedy.[35]

Therefore, the Arizona team, along with just about everyone in Los Angeles, was taken aback when Kennedy announced Johnson as his choice for running mate. Bewildered Arizonans were informed of the decision by a reporter as they boarded the bus for the ride from the Mayan to the Biltmore. Mac himself was preparing to return home when called back. Quickly, the delegation's confusion dissipated as Harold Giss logically concluded the existence of a "dream team." No one was more shocked than McFarland, who expressed "particular happiness" that his long battle had yielded delicious secondary fruits. Mac claimed the choice "greatly strengthened" the ticket and that "Senator Johnson is a majority leader whether he be in the Senate or vice president of the U.S. He's that kind of man," the implication being that senate Democrats would look to LBJ for leadership whether he occupied the senate president's chair or the first row, center aisle seat. Furthermore, McFarland, still looking to his friend's future chances, added that the selection would demonstrably serve him well in the North votes that he would need when he made his own probable later run for the presidency.[36]

But Ernest McFarland's convention ordeal of hard work, disappointment, and reward was not yet over. Johnson had yet to be nominated and Mac would be the logical choice for one of the seconding speeches. Such was not to be, however, as Mac was forced to pay for his obstinate support for LBJ over JFK. The new nominee dispatched brother Ted to inform the loyal Stewart Udall that he had been selected to make the final seconding speech for LBJ. By the ordinary courtesies of politics, this honor should have been given McFarland, Johnson's personal friend and supporter, as representative of the key state of Arizona. Not being invited to speak could only be seen as a rebuke and intentional slight to the elder Democratic politician.[37]

Pennsylvania's David Lawrence nominated Johnson and followed the custom of leaving the nominee's name to last following the many lead-in encomiums. Then the house erupted into its second demonstration for the tall Texan. Seconding speeches followed from a quartet of governors representing the nation's varied regions: Luther Hodges of North Carolina, Abraham Ribicoff of Connecticut, Orville Freeman of Minnesota and Stephen McNichols of Colorado. Then representing the Southwest of Lyndon Johnson came Udall who, with little time to prepare a speech, abruptly guaranteed the support of his region to the man he had so recently worked so avidly against.[38]

Political columnist Virgil Hill painted a picture of McFarland and Udall:

> Far to the rear of the great hall, Ernest McFarland stood under balcony shadows while young Stewart

Udall facing dazzling lights spoke out. . . . Occasionally a sign bobbed along, "All the way with LBJ." McFarland had gone all the way until the road doubled back and was not invited to go those last few yards. . . . To an old political soldier abrupt about faces are not easy to execute. McFarland may find words to accept the situation. As he said after Lyndon Johnson went down before the smashing Kennedy attack, "I always accept my defeats." But still to be answered by Arizona Democrats as a whole is what they think of the Incredible Compromise made here at what Harry Truman warned would be a rigged convention.

After Udall finished, Johnson gained the nomination without even a formal roll call. Convention chairman, Florida Governor Leroy Collins, brought his gavel down amidst all the hoopla and simply said the necessary two-thirds voice vote had been obtained.[39]

Reactions to the Johnson nomination ranged from the effusive to the derogatory. Besides McFarland's positive accolades, Stewart Udall called the choice "not good, but great. . . . Johnson is the most qualified parliamentary leader of the present generation . . . and knows that legislation is the art of the possible." Conversely Barry Goldwater expressed alarm that the conservative LBJ would align with the liberal JFK, calling the action a "double cross of his friends" and a sell out of "his entire Democratic philosophy to the socialistic philosophy of Jack Kennedy. . . . He repudiated every single principal of conservatism." Some, including Republican National Chairman Senator Thruston B. Morton of Kentucky charged that the two lead Democrats had rigged the convention weeks in advance, and that caused Harry Truman to decline to attend. Others claimed LBJ had forced himself upon Kennedy much to the latter's surprise, and the *Arizona Republic* worriedly editorialized on the "oddest bedfellows," warning ominously, however, that LBJ had voted the liberal position fifty-four, sixty-seven, and fifty-eight percent in 1957, 1958, and 1959 respectively. The liberal Americans for Democratic action did not buy this line and condemned LBJ's inherent conservatism from oil and gas-rich and civil rights-poor Texas. Similarly, labor leaders worried over Johnson's support of Taft-Hartley.[40]

Aside from the applauders and critics, political analysts pointed to the balance of the ticket. Johnson provided not only geographical balance, but more importantly his selection deferred to an extent to southern feelings. *New York Times* columnist James Reston pointed out that contrary to some perceptions that LBJ was turning his back on the South by joining Kennedy, he was incorporating it into a hoped-for harmony among Democrats. The South had resented the civil rights plank and, with the liberals triumphant, feared ostracism from party policy. With Johnson's appointment liberal intent was seen as less threatening, more benign, and inclusive. Not only was LBJ one of the South's own (and also the West's), but he also possessed the necessary skills of negotiation and compromise, some in part inculcated by McFarland, to make the South more amenable to a progressive party direction. This is, in fact, what he would successfully do as president in 1964-65 with the Civil Rights and Voting Rights Acts.[41]

Still, the Kennedy-Johnson strategy of the amelioration of southern discontent would not bear fruit immediately, and only time would tell if it would be successful at all. This was made clear in convention meetings with Governors Lionel Vandiver of Georgia and Ernest Hollings of South Carolina who continued to be suspicious of Kennedy. Moreover, many analysts predicted a Kennedy defeat by a substantial margin under any circumstance. National columnist David Lawrence cited many factors including JFK's relative inexperience compared to Richard Nixon; a lack of desire for change throughout the country; the threat of the Democratic platform's "equal access" clause (in all areas of community life irrespective of race, religion, color, or natural origin) to businesses, small and large, and private clubs and schools, whether they be in the North or South. Finally Lawrence pointed to the unfortunate yet obvious threat of Kennedy's Catholic religion to his chances.[42]

Amidst all the positive and negative conjecture over the outcome, Arizonans left the Los Angeles convention with confidence in prospects ahead and satisfaction with the role the delegation had played. Even though the honor of deferring to Massachusetts to expedite the Kennedy nomination had failed to materialize, the delegation played a vital role. Udall supporters expressed satisfaction with both the prominence of their leader and the rumors that he might be appointed to the cabinet as secretary of the interior upon a Kennedy victory. For Ernest McFarland, the unexpected turn to Johnson for vice president meant that he would become a leading campaigner for the national ticket. If Kennedy had chosen another, Mac in all probability would have lingered on the fringes of the campaign. Now he would be engaged to employ his still significant influence.[43]

Accordingly, Mac and Senator Hayden formed the lead entourage accompanying Johnson's visit to the state in mid-September. Introduced by McFarland, LBJ spoke at Phoenix College, the Hotel Westward Ho, and on television, all the time blasting the Republican program and urging Arizona's conservative Democrats to stay in line behind federal aid for education and roads, health insurance for the aged, and a higher minimum wage. Stewart Udall joined the group the next day in Tucson. Even though this was Democratic country, few turned out to greet the nominee until Johnson hit the University of Arizona campus where over one thousand students gathered in enthusiastic support. In his Tucson address, Johnson focused mainly on the continuing Central Arizona Project battle in the courts and Republican presidential nominee Richard Nixon's steadfast opposition. At the close of the visit McFarland was named to the state Kennedy-Johnson committee headed by former governor and state supreme court justice Rawghlie Stanford.[44]

McFarland remained in the background when Jack Kennedy made his only campaign stop in Arizona only days before the election. He, like Nixon, spent only a few hours in Phoenix before moving on, and Udall and Hayden served as his support team. Perhaps the reason for such a short visit lay in the fact that most political observers felt that Arizona fell safely in Nixon's domain. The *New York Times* had reported so as early as September 15. Still, the day before the election, the Associated Press had Arizona's four electoral votes as a toss-up among the Western states, giving Nixon the ten combined votes of only Oregon, Idaho, and Utah, and Kennedy the thirty-eight of California, Nevada, and Alaska, with the remaining undecided.[45]

The *New York Times* proved more foresighted than the Associated Press as Richard Nixon swept to a Republican victory in Arizona over John Kennedy by 221,241 to 176,781 votes, or almost fifty-six to forty-four percent. This decisive victory in the state was largely attributed to the growing charisma and influence of Barry Goldwater. In fact, many already spoke of him as presidential material. Unarguably, his campaign presence was the major factor in allowing the Californian Nixon to so heavily overcome a voter registration that favored the Democrats, sixty-six to thirty-two percent. Pinto crossover voting continued to escalate.[46]

Yet JFK won the extremely close national election, and while Arizona had lost its political weather vane status in supporting a loser for the first time in a presidential race, it had been instrumental in the nomination process, playing a pivotal role in clinching the overall prize for Kennedy. Similarly, Ernest McFarland, in supporting a loser for the Democratic presidential nomination, contributed to Johnson's selection as the vice presidential candidate. In turn Johnson strengthened the national ticket and thus contributed to the close nationwide victory where any number of single factors, including Johnson's inclusion on the ballot, could be stipulated as the major determinant. Thus, with some degree of irony both Arizona and McFarland were links in the chain of Kennedy's victory. A final note on Arizona and the 1960 election came on December 6, when President-elect Kennedy named Stewart Udall as secretary of the interior. Udall, the first Arizonan to hold a Cabinet position, along with Johnson and Sam Rayburn, added another dimension to the West's growing influence in national politics, a tradition which Ernest McFarland helped further as majority leader. Now, with the election concluded, Arizona slipped back into its growing Republicanism, while Ernest McFarland returned to a political wilderness, densely inhabited, however, with television and law, farm and family.[47]

The six years from late 1958 to late 1964 marked the longest time period Ernest McFarland stood outside public office during his entire professional career. He did, however, have more than enough to occupy his attention, devoting about half his time to the television station and splitting the rest between the law office and farms. Of course, he tended to fit the family in as much as possible, particularly the growing group of grandchildren born to Del and Jewell Lewis.

Arizona Television Company, KTVK-TV, went through a series of significant developments in the early 1960s. Affiliated for a decade with the newest national network, ABC, Mac's Channel 3, like the network, struggled to keep abreast of financial and technological problems and advances, always operating in the red. Loyal workers helped Mac change the bottom line from red to black by the middle of the decade, and keep abreast technologically while doing so. Particularly important were the installation of videotape capability huge cumbersome machines at that time and the initial switchovers to color reproduction. Too, the company proved able to fend off continuing outside pressure to take over its ABC affiliation.

As president and chairman of the company, Mac exercised direct control over operations. It was an amicable situation all around, Mac mingling well with workers from electricians to studio hands or propping his feet up on his desk while dashing off exuberant, forceful calls to colleagues in Washington. Goldwater had sometimes charged in the campaigns of the 1950s that Mac had a "sweetheart" contract with his workers, but this was untrue. He could have hired nonunion labor in this open-shop state, but, always dedicated to the principle of organized labor, he hired union blue and white-collar help, paying a higher price in the process because unions drove hard bargains.

McFarland also performed some of his law work in the

TV studio offices, but his time at the bar lessened as the decade wore on. He did keep apprised of state legal developments and problems and at times offered advice on the Colorado River case with California. This lengthy ordeal finally came to an end in 1963, when the U.S. Supreme Court ruled in Arizona's favor eleven years after Mac, as majority leader, had initiated the suit in Washington. He could now look back with pride at laying much of the legislative foundation for the Central Arizona Project in his Washington years and for buttressing the legal work with his Supreme Court victory while governor in 1955. Still, another five years would elapse before the CAP bill became law in 1968.

McFarland also kept involved with his Florence law practice, although his partner of nearly four decades, Tom Fulbright, handled the bulk of the work, mostly routine cases dealing with daily lives in Pinal County. Mac advised on these, some of them involving farm problems of irrigation, pesticides, or other facets of agronomy.

Indeed, farming continued to be an outlet for relaxation and staying close to both his "home" community of Florence and to the land itself. Mac's farms had by now increased to four with the purchase from his brother Forrest's widow of six hundred acres on the Florence-Coolidge highway and the opening of a new tract for cultivation across the Gila River near "F" mountain. Mac had given the original farm on the old diversion dam road to Del and Jewell upon their wedding in 1952, and now Del oversaw all the Pinal County operations as well as learning the ropes at the Phoenix station.

On the farms, cotton provided the major cash crop augmented by barley and wheat. He did not run cattle as friend Gene Autry did in Pinal County, but insisted he had a "cotton ranch." Perhaps Mac did not want to bother with the cattleman rancher image as he was known to say "Something always seems to happen to a man when he climbs up on a horse. He thinks he's above everybody else and becomes a Republican." Nevertheless, he continued to expand his "cotton ranch" into other areas in the 1960s, notably table grape production, a venture that would finally turn profitable in the 1980s.[48]

Mac's dedication to the farms was almost compulsive. Whenever the law practice called him to Florence, he carved out time to visit at least one farm, and in the normal course of events, he spent Saturdays there, a program that Del Lewis follows to this day. While there, he would converse with Del and the foreman, check tractors and equipment for repairs, note available supplies, and perhaps look over the books a bit before getting on to the fun part out by pickup into the fields themselves to evaluate the various crops and irrigation ditches. On these occasions he would most frequently be accompanied by one or more of the grandchildren who at this time numbered three: Kara born in 1954, Bill in 1957, and John in 1960. Del and Jewell would have two more, Leah and Del, Jr. in 1966 and 1967 respectively. Mac also remained an avid sports fan in his later years, and sometimes Saturday mornings in Florence would be topped off with a sixty-mile excursion down to Tucson to catch the University of Arizona Wildcats football team in action and even an evening trip back to Tempe to see the Arizona State Sun Devils.

Mac stood as the central figure in the extended family, keeping close contact with brother Carl who still farmed in Coolidge, though limited by a serious back injury suffered in a private plane crash, and with his sister Pearl and her husband who still ran the lumber business. He was extremely close to Del and Jewell, always concerned for their interests, and Del responded in kind with hard work at the farms and learning the procedures of the television station. As her mother had before her, Jewell taught at Florence High School, while Edna ran the Phoenix home with no in-house domestic workers.

As they had since their departure from Washington in 1953, the McFarland's lived in their modest home at 306 West Royal Palm Lane in north central Phoenix. This included the gubernatorial years since Arizona had no executive mansion. After deeding the original Florence farm over to Del and Jewell, Mac continued a legal residence there with a trailer home at Florence Gardens north of the river to keep his hand (and vote) in local affairs.

Mac continued the frequent traveling he had enjoyed all his life, but with a different twist now. He and Edna would often fly the grandchildren to eastern vacation spots such as New York, Philadelphia, and of course Washington, taking in prominent historical sites when Mac would "lecture" to the children about the majesty of the American story. He cut down on international travel during those years, other than neighboring Mexico, where he would vacation and attend national presidential and state gubernatorial inaugurations with Edna, Del, and Jewell.

In sum, and with the exception of the 1960 campaign, these years provided McFarland with a much appreciated break from the political wars, a time to enjoy and further his other interests of family, farm, and television. He kept being mentioned, however, as a potential candidate for this or that position, and some friends urged him especially to challenge Governor Paul Fannin. He demurred, though, and Republican Fannin kept a tight hold on the gubernatorial office from 1958 to 1964. The relative stability of the Arizona political scene, however, fell apart in 1964 when Barry Goldwater announced his candidacy for the Republican nomination for president and, in turn, Paul Fannin decided to try for Goldwater's senate seat. The gubernatorial race stood wide open, but it was not the governor's chair that Mac decided to seek. The sour taste of his battles with the legislature remained. The situation clarified in early summer when state supreme court justice Renz Jennings resigned to run against Fannin for the United States Senate. Mac's mind now called back to the 1930s and its memories of his constructive days in judicial garb. The hectic events of the ensuing three decades blew away the realities of the Great Depression and left pleasant reflections on the dignity of the law. Jennings's resignation focused Mac's political antennae on the state supreme court.[49]

CHAPTER SIXTEEN

SUPREME COURT JUSTICE
1964-1967

NINETEEN SIXTY-FOUR PROVED TO BE A FAR DIFFER-
ENT presidential election year for Ernest McFarland than 1960
had been. Whereas the commencement of the Sixties had
marked his apparent demise in politics with a second senate
defeat behind him and the subsequent loss of party influence
and leadership, these drawbacks did not put the old political
warhorse down for good. The new election year differed not
only in that McFarland became an active competitor again at
age seventy, but also because of the ascendance of Lyndon
Johnson in the wake of the Kennedy assassination.

In 1964, there existed no question over who would gain
the Democratic nomination for the presidency. Lyndon
Johnson had grasped the reins of power and leadership in
November 1963 and had led a nation united in grief to resounding legislative activities in the following year, notably the Civil
Rights Act of 1964. Irritating disturbances like the Gulf of
Tonkin incident in August did nothing to deter or confuse
Johnson's bid for his own presidential term. In fact, the alleged
attack by North Vietnamese patrol boats on U. S. Navy destroyers presented LBJ with the opportunity to grasp more power
from a willing Congress, which turned over to Johnson a "blank
check" with which to combat communist aggression in South
Vietnam. Armed with this foreign policy mandate and a characteristically brilliant touch with domestic affairs, LBJ seemed
unassailable in 1964. Contributing to this scenario was the old-
style moderate-to-liberal Republican deference to the conserva-

427

tive wing of the party in nominating a weak presidential candidate, ironically McFarland's most formidable opponent of old political wars, Barry Goldwater. This time, the lamb Goldwater was to be sacrificed by his party to the lion of Lyndon Johnson's ambitious and powerful vision of a "Great Society" in America. Goldwater went on to defeat by the largest margin of the popular vote in American presidential history.

Likewise, no question arose over who would lead the Arizona Democratic delegation to the national convention in Atlantic City, Ernest McFarland being accorded the honor. The August convention held no nominating surprises like the previous one had, but Mac held much attention, nevertheless, because of his recent decision to run for election to the Arizona Supreme Court.[1]

Ironically, Barry Goldwater's decision to run for the presidency influenced McFarland's course. By vacating his senate seat, he left it open for new contenders, among whom stood Governor Paul Fannin for the Republicans. In late June, Supreme Court Justice Renz Jennings announced his resignation from the court in order to become the Democratic nominee for the Senate. At this point, McFarland, pressured by friends and still mentioned as a possible gubernatorial candidate, announced his intention to run for Jennings's vacant judgeship. On July 8, he made it official by filing his candidacy.[2]

Still called judge by hundreds of fellow lawyers, Mac expressed motivations that involved more than just pressure from acquaintances, however. He explained his decision in terms of realizing "boyhood dreams . . . opportunity to advance in the legal profession . . . an additional challenge for me to prove my qualifications." Furthermore, he added that he firmly believed in the election, not the appointment, of justices and with six years on the superior court bench, he had the same qualifications as his four opponents. He neglected to mention that that his experience began thirty years before, but did refer to his more recent political work as senator and governor, stating:

My chart has been the public. It then should be obvious that a person who has had legislative experience can be more effective should he attain the office of chief executive. Similarly, one who is fortunate enough to be honored by elevation to the highest court of his state is doubly blessed by having some experience with the everyday problems of those who petition the court.[3]

A most unusual campaign followed. Governor Fannin appointed Tucsonan Republican Edward W. Scruggs as interim justice to fill out Jennings's term, and Scruggs announced he would also contest the bench seat in the November elections. He quickly started his campaign by buying billboards and purchasing TV time, leaving Mac in the dust. Misinformed by friends, Mac was unable to purchase time even on his own station, and all billboard space had been reserved by other candidates. So, he resorted, yet again and for the last time, to automobile and shoe leather campaigning in the small and large towns across the state. This time, he traveled without the large entourage that accompanied him during the gubernatorial and senatorial years. In a remarkable effort, McFarland appeared in all significant state towns except Page and Bagdad, walking the streets, shaking hands, in and out of barbershops, groceries, laundramats, service stations, and bars, and extemporizing on park benches and under mainstreet shade trees.[4]

The Arizona voting populace was ready to welcome the old veteran back with open arms, and he triumphed over Scruggs by a vote of 199,494 to 135,468, the highest percentage for any opposed candidate in the election. His total marked the largest number of votes he had received in any election in his career. It was to be his thirteenth and last contest with ten victories in 1924, 1926, 1928, 1934, 1938, 1940, 1946, 1954, 1956, and 1964 standing against three losses in 1930, 1952, and 1958. When asked whether he would now like to be addressed as senator, governor, or Mr. Justice, he typically drawled "I'd just as soon be called Mac. You fellas get stuffier and stuffier as I get older." The press summarized his notable victory:

At seventy Mac is showing results of a lifetime

430 — Ernest W. McFarland

in the political arena. The brisk, sometimes hurried gait of other campaign years which saw him barnstorming the state is now a deliberate stroll. The handshake is still warm and transmits a sincere feeling of friendship, but is not the bonechrusher of the old days. But a few moments of conversation reveals, even to a stranger, that behind a pair of eyes whose sparkle belie their age, rests the same steel trap mind that, for almost half a century, has guided one of the State's most outstanding careers before the bar, at the polls, and on Capitol Hill.[5]

The 1964 election brought great satisfaction to McFarland in ways other than his own victory. To his delight, President Lyndon Johnson easily triumphed over Barry Goldwater. Mac, who campaigned with LBJ briefly in San Francisco, assuredly wished that Arizona had gone for Johnson, but the state remained loyal to its favorite son if only by the small margin of 242,535 to 237,753, votes, a 50.4 to 49.5 percent difference. Arizona was the only western state Goldwater captured to add to his small total from the Deep South. Like Eisenhower had, via his popularity, Goldwater by his conservatism was able to crack the "Solid South," winning in Louisiana, Alabama, Mississippi, South Carolina, and Georgia. Together with Arizona, these gave him 52 electoral votes to LBJ'S 486. The nation, however, preferred, by the largest popular vote margin in history (nearly sixty-one to thirty-nine percent), the prospect of LBJ's "political consensus" to Goldwater's "trigger-happy image in foreign affairs" and identification with such groups as the John Birch Society. A much anticipated pro-Goldwater white backlash failed to materialize.[6]

Also to McFarland's pleasure, the statehouse returned to Democratic hands for the first time since he himself had left six years before. Sam Goddard fought off Goldwater lieutenant Richard Kleindienst by a vote of 252,098 to 221,404. Also Morris Udall captured the Second District seat in the House for the third straight election and George Senner won his second victory in the new sparsely populated northern Third District.[7]

Republican victories included John Rhodes in the First District of Maricopa County for a seventh term and Governor Paul Fannin for Goldwater's vacated senate seat. Fannin defeated Carl Hayden's former administrative assistant, thirty-three-year-old Roy Elson by a relatively close vote of 241,089 to 227,712. The unassailable Hayden, of course, had been returned to the Senate for his seventh and final term in the 1962 elections with a surprisingly close victory over Republican dissident and arch-conservative Evan Mecham.[8]

On January 4, 1965, Ernest McFarland stood back on center stage in front of the old state capitol building. A decade after he had been inaugurated there as governor, he was administered the oath of office as associate justice of the Arizona Supreme Court by Chief Justice Jesse Udall. As the Arizona press proudly and uniformly declared, Mac had now achieved the political trifecta of having served in high-level positions in each branch of government, the legislative, executive, and now the judiciary. His Florence law partner of thirty years, Tom Fulbright, followed with complimentary remarks before Udall administered the oath to the judges of the newly formed Court of Appeals and incoming Governor Sam Goddard.[9] The Court of Appeals had been legislatively (not constitutionally) created, in part, to lighten the huge backlog of cases facing the Supreme Court, perhaps the single major problem facing the five justices.

McFarland joined a veteran group on the court, all of whom he had known for many years. Besides the chief justice, a Republican member of the venerable Udall family which McFarland had known since World War II days in Washington, Mac also traced his relations back several decades with the families of his other court colleagues, Fred Struckmeyer, Jr., and Lorna Lockwood. In both cases, he had worked closely with their parents, arguing cases before Lockwood's father back into the 1920s. Lorna, herself, had served as an assistant to Congressman Murdock in Washington and had, thus, worked with Mac on Central Arizona Project strategy. Struckmeyer, Sr., had been an attorney for Mac during the 1940 campaign and had successfully argued against his alleged ineligibility to run at that time. McFarland developed his closest personal relationship on the court with Fred Struckmeyer, Jr. Charles Bernstein, too, dated back to Mac's gubernatorial years when he served on the superior court.

The court's first matter of business required selection of a new chief justice for the year 1965. Following established rotation principles, the justices unanimously chose Lorna Lockwood for the position. By following precedent, the court also broke precedent, for Lockwood became the first female chief justice in the nation's history, 189 years as Udall pointed out. A former state legislator, assistant state's attorney, and superior court judge, she encompassed all the qualifications and experience necessary. Her major tasks, besides writing her own opinions, would be to assign individual cases to specific justices and to begin to integrate the new court of appeals into the state judicial system. Struckmeyer's selection as vice chief set him in rotation to become chief justice the following year.[10]

By early February, cases had been sorted out and assigned. McFarland's first opinion affirmed the conviction of Joe Lewis Curry for the illegal sale of narcotics, in this case marijuana. McFarland's first law clerk, John Moran, recalled that though it was a fairly routine case, it indicated at the outset Mac's "thoroughness in both research and writing." Moran noted that working with the new justice was more like having a partner than a boss as Mac often went to the law library himself to research (usually the clerk's job) and that he frequently worked overtime on Saturdays and Sundays, enjoying every minute of it.[11]

On February 25, McFarland wrote his first reversal in *State v. Kananen and Hill.* The defendants had been convicted of forgery by the Maricopa County Superior Court but appealed on the basis of evidence obtained by search without a warrant. In evidencing concern for defendants' rights, McFarland held that accompanying the officers to the alleged crime scene room hours after the arrest and while handcuffed failed to amount to "clear and positive evidence in unequivocal words" for proving consent. Mac's opinion set forth the rule for the future in Arizona in regard to admission of evidence in regard to search and seizure.[12]

McFarland did not concern himself so much with the accused's rights when the arrested party had a prior record and evidenced familiarity with police procedure and the rights guaranteed therein. In such a situation, McFarland's tenth opinion, *Arizona v. Miranda* on April 22, 1965, proved to be his most famous and most controversial, even to this day, in its eventual reversal by the United States Supreme Court in the landmark *Miranda v. Arizona.*

On June 20, 1963, the jury in Maricopa County Superior Court convicted Ernesto Miranda for a kidnapping and rape on March 3 of that year. The specific circumstances involved his abduction of an eighteen-year-old concession stand worker at the Paramount Theatre in downtown Phoenix. After she had taken the bus a mile or so to 7th St. and Marlette, Miranda abducted her as she began to walk home, forced her into the back seat of his car, tied her hands and ankles, and apparently threatened her with a knife (a "sharp thing to my neck"). He then drove her to the desert, only about twenty minutes away in those days, and undressed and forcibly raped her. The victim was fortunate, for Miranda then allowed her to redress and returned her to the vicinity of her home with the plea to pray for him.

Ten days later, during the ensuing investigation, the police apprehended Miranda and placed him in a lineup where the victim identified him. Afterward, the police interrogated Miranda and advised him of his rights to remain silent and not incriminate himself and that anything he said could be used against him. At this time, it was not guaranteed that the accused had a right to counsel unless he requested a lawyer to be present. Miranda made no such request and went on to volunteer an admission of guilt and sign a written statement to that effect. At the subsequent trial, his attorney offered no evidence in his defense, nor did he say that Miranda had been coerced to confess. He was convicted of rape.

After the trial, Miranda's lawyer Alvin Moore filed an appeal to the Arizona Supreme Court based on five major considerations: 1) denial of a motion to quash the information; 2) denial of a motion to dismiss because the case had not been brought to trial within sixty days; 3) the argument of the proposition of [the victim's] fear to the jury; 4) the admission of the confession of the defendant; and 5) lack of evidence to sustain the verdict.

As the justice assigned to the case, McFarland carefully, but rather easily, dispensed with all of the objections except the admission of the confession of the defendant. This clearly constituted the crux of the appeal, and Judge McFarland meticulously analyzed the matter, which ultimately took up twelve of the nineteen pages of his written opinion.

Concerning the other moves to dismiss, McFarland had linked quashing the information with arguing the proposition of fear. He ruled that the seriousness of the charges were sufficient to allow the information and that the prosecution's conclusion of fear and arguing that aspect to the jury was clearly upheld by the victim's testimony. Furthermore, the specific word "fear" had been struck from the record as requested by the defense before the official information upon which Miranda was tried was read to the jury.

The lack of evidence stipulation alleged that there existed no real proof that the victim had, in fact, resisted the sexual advances. McFarland could find no merit in this contention, referring to the victim's testimony of pushing, screaming, and "trying to get away," but he "was a lot stronger . . . and she could not do anything." Furthermore, as to the rape itself, the victim had testified to and the defendant had admitted to penetration. The foundation on which McFarland ruled maintained that those comprised the questions for the jury and that the jury had decided against the defendant. He concluded "where there is evidence to support a verdict, we will not disturb a finding of a jury."

McFarland dispensed with the sixty-day question by laying out a chronology that showed that the state was prevented from holding the trial on time because of delays occasioned by

Miranda's application for a sanity hearing. The original trial date lay well within the sixty-day stipulation when just one-week prior, Miranda made his application. The first new trial date also fell within the sixty days, but was again set back when one of the medical reports upholding Miranda's sanity was filed late. The trial was then held just two days after the pro-sanity ruling and only five days after the designated sixty. McFarland opined that the short delay had been due only to the defendant's late filing for a sanity hearing, and that the state had, in fact, done its part by allowing that hearing and then holding the trial as soon as possible thereafter. In drawing all of these conclusions, McFarland cited nine prior cases in the Arizona courts as precedents.

The crucial question again, was whether an admission of guilt could be accepted when given without a lawyer present. With a subconscious suspicion that he may be opening the door to one of the most notable criminal decisions ever handed down by the U.S. Supreme Court, Mac ruled that Miranda's signed confession was admissible as evidence. McFarland was fully aware that his decision was not quite in keeping with recent pronouncements of the U.S. Supreme Court decisions in *Gideon* and *Escobedo*; but he was also aware that it did not directly violate those new dicta which had turned on slightly different points of law. In *Gideon v. Wainright* (1963) and *Escobedo v. Illinois* (1964), both controversial decisions, Chief Justice Earl Warren's court came down on the side of protecting the accused's rights against aggressive police (i.e. society's or public) intrusion. In *Gideon*, the court ruled that the accused had the right to a lawyer even if unaffordable. In *Escobedo*, the court further clarified that the accused had the right to the presence of a lawyer, *if requested* (italics author's), while being interrogated.

McFarland distinguished *Miranda* from *Escobedo* because Miranda had not requested a lawyer while giving a voluntary statement, while Escobedo's request for one had been denied, even as his own lawyer sat elsewhere in the police offices. Furthermore, McFarland claimed that Miranda, who had a record of prior arrests and a conviction in California, was familiar with police and court procedure and knew his rights.

Indeed, he was read his rights to remain silent and against self-incrimination.

McFarland went beyond the differentiation with *Escobedo* in his ruling by noting that no objections had been previously raised on the voluntarism of the question and that there had been no request for a determination of the defendant's willingness outside of the hearing of the jury. Furthermore, the police had not threatened the defendant, nor had they offered immunity and, again, they had read the basic rights of the time such as those were understood by McFarland.

Justice McFarland also distinguished between investigative and accusatory stages of the police process. The questioning of Miranda stood within investigative procedure according to McFarland who continued: "We hold that only when the process shifts from the investigatory to the accusatory — when its focus is on the accused and its purpose is to elicit a confession — our advisory system begins to operate, and, under the circumstances here, the accused must be permitted to consult with his lawyer." This reasoning coupled with Miranda's not having requested or been denied counsel and his own prior courtroom experience disallowed the complaint.

McFarland acknowledged protection of individual rights by the Sixth and Fourteenth Amendments, but noted within that guaranteed context "there must be a balance between the competing interests of society and the rights of the individual. Society has the right of protection against those who roam the streets for the purpose of violating the law. . . ." Furthermore, "Each case must largely turn upon its own facts, and the court must examine all the circumstances. . . ." He concluded the opinion:

> The facts and circumstances in the instant case show that the statement [confession] was voluntary, made by the defendant of his own free will, that no threats or use of force or coercion [Miranda made no charge of these] or promise of immunity were made; and that he understood his legal right; and the statement might be used against him. Under such facts and circumstances we

hold that, notwithstanding the fact that he did not have an attorney at the time he made the statement . . . constitutional rights were not violated, and it was proper to admit the statement in evidence.

While he had referred to nine Arizona court cases in denying the defendant's objections in four of the five areas, for this particular section of the opinion, McFarland called upon over thirty cases for backup -- cases drawn from the U.S. Supreme Court and federal and state courts in Arizona, Pennsylvania, New York, Iowa, Nebraska, Illinois, California, Maryland, Nevada, and Washington. The Arizona Supreme Court held unanimously for McFarland's thoroughly drawn opinion.[13]

Approbation for McFarland's decision was soon forthcoming beyond his own concurring court justices. Many, particularly law enforcement officers and prosecuting attorneys in Arizona and throughout the nation, objected to the Supreme Court's protection of the accused. Maricopa County Attorney, Robert Corbin praised the decision for clarifying several foggy points of police procedure, most importantly that "Officers will no longer be required to advise a man of his right to counsel, but he will still be able to see a lawyer whenever he requests one." D. L. Green, Apache County Attorney wrote, "*Miranda* was one of the best opinions I have read in years. You have surely separated the wheat from the chaff and made a sensible distinction which we public prosecutors and peace officers can live with . . . particularly in these small counties where counsel isn't generally available for the defendant. . . ." Chief Judge Henry B. Stevens of the new Court of Appeals wrote the day after, "Thank you for an excellent and practical opinion."[14]

Mac's legal clerk, John Moran, seemed almost alone in his discomfort with the opinion. He had the gut feeling that a degree of coercion may have been employed in order to extract a confession. Nevertheless, Miranda had made no such accusation, and Moran observed that Mac, unlike with this case, normally "seemed to come down on the side of the individual and against the system. He was a pretty liberal man." He placed McFarland in the middle of a somewhat out of tune conservative court (Bernstein was considered the most liberal) during the liberal Warren era. McFarland, himself, did not fit the Warren mold for he was "a rather careful and strict constructionist who did not look upon the court as a vehicle to create new law, but rather to conserve and clarify already written law." He "interpreted" and did not "mold," and in his interpretations always searched for a "fence corner case" somewhere to tie things together. In this case, Mac had drawn on approximately forty other "fence corner cases." Nevertheless, Moran's concerns presaged a national reaction to the opinion that perhaps McFarland even anticipated, for he had written the case with great care and clarity and, as usual, "in readable form, in layman's language."[15]

On November 22, seven months to the day after McFarland's opinion, the U.S. Supreme Court announced it would review the decision in order to clarify the mixed messages emanating from the *Escobedo* decision of 1964. While *Escobedo* clearly stated that the accused had the right to counsel if requested, many states, like Arizona, had ruled strictly that the attorney's presence must be requested, otherwise it is not guaranteed. However, several other tribunals had ruled that the right to attorney is implicit at all stages whether or not requested. Such rulings had been made in California, Idaho, Massachusetts, Rhode Island, Tennessee, and Oregon. Clarification was, indeed, necessary.[16]

Another seven months elapsed before Chief Justice Earl Warren, on June 13, 1966, wrote the decision, upheld by a vote of six to three, that overturned McFarland's opinion in the landmark case, *Miranda v. Arizona*. Warren did not distinguish between investigatory and accusatory stages in his decision, merely stating that the accused has the right to counsel from the moment of apprehension and the accused must be so informed of this as well as the other basic rights against self-incrimination and to silence. Of course, Warren asserted that the accused could waive these rights as well, but the waiver must be made "voluntarily, knowingly, and intelligently." Throwing a spear at the Arizona courts, Warren described Miranda as "Mentally abnormal and thus unable to exercise his rights," although the actual sanity plea and upholding was never officially in question. This homegrown appeal was the work of two Phoenix attorneys, renowned legal scholar John Frank, who had helped with CAP, and courtroom dynamo John Flynn. In his best Irish manner, Flynn enthralled the court for thirty minutes with Frank's smooth words that were carefully designed to play upon and reinforce Warren's deep seated views that even dissolute characters like Miranda should be free of coercive government practices.[17] Justices John M. Harlan, Potter Stewart, and Byron R. White all dissented, while Tom C. Clark, Hugo L. Black, William O. Douglas, William J. Brennan, and Abe Fortas upheld the chief.

As with *Escobedo, Miranda* became instantly controversial. Justice White regretted that in some situations ". . . the Court's rule will return a killer, a rapist, or other criminal to the streets . . . to repeat his crime whenever it pleases him." New York Police Commissioner Howard R. Leary lamented "How far and how long are the rights of the accused to be considered, with little regard for the rights of the victim?" Civil libertarians, of course, applauded the decision and its famous "Miranda Card" dictum that the victim:

> has the right to remain silent, that anything he says can be used against him in a court of law, that he has the right to the presence of an attorney, and that if he cannot afford an attorney, one will be appointed for him prior to any questioning if he so desires.[18]

McFarland had already shown flexibility in these matters by the time of the U. S. Supreme Court *Miranda* ruling. In July 1965, he had upheld the convictions of two men in the Santa Cruz County Superior Court for the murder of Maurice Powell. The defendants, Ronald Goodyear and Steven Jackson, had appealed mainly on the basis of not being given separate trials. McFarland dismissed this by noting that court procedure had been meticulously adhered to. All references of the defendants to each other were struck, and the trial court explicitly instructed the jury as to whom the evidence applied. McFarland had disallowed the objections on other lesser grounds such as the introduction of "gruesome photographs" as well.[19]

Nevertheless, the case came back on re-appeal in April 1966, McFarland listened attentively to new objections, most importantly Goodyear's contention that not only was he denied counsel, but that he had been under the influence of phenobarbital and a tranquilizer at the time of his interrogation. Noting that these statements, occurring before the charge, had been included in the confession and had been admitted as evidence in the court case, McFarland overturned the convictions.[20]

While this reversal would be in keeping with the upcoming U.S. *Miranda* decision, controversy over the latter continued front and center in national and legal circles during McFarland's subsequent years on the court. J. Edward Lombard, Chief Judge of the U.S. Second Circuit Court of Appeals in New York, termed *Miranda* the imposition of a "constitutional strait jacket." Lombard spoke at the meeting of the California State Bar in September 1967 and castigated the higher court for resorting to inflexible decision-making procedure rather than the optional course of rule-making which would have set a specific (not immediate) date for concurrence and allowed for further airing of the views and experience of federal and state judges and law enforcement officials. Now, the ruling took immediate effect and could be changed only by constitutional amendment or superseding opinion. He dryly commented that the court could extricate itself from the "concrete in which it is embedded by a change of membership."[21]

The next year, 1968, McFarland attended the Conference of Chief Justices in Philadelphia where he listened as Governor Charles L. Terry, Jr., of Delaware lambasted *Miranda* for requiring law enforcement agencies "to fight by Marquis of Queensbury rules" while criminals could "butt, gouge, and bite." He claimed that trial judges believed that crucial cases had become "a gimmicky game of procedural button pushing, almost wholly divorced from a search for truth." He continued:

> It is strange that this court, which had been so con-
> scious of the social consequences of its decisions in
> other areas, should be so cavalier about the social con-
> sequences of its decisions in the field of criminal law.
> At a time when society is becoming incredibly com-
> plex and in light of an alarming rise in the crime rate,
> the Supreme Court majority has dismissed without
> any meaningful analysis the effects of its criminal
> decisions.

Terry singled out Justice Harlan's dissenting opinion, the governor stating: "Nothing in the letter or the spirit of the Constitution or in the precedents squares with the heavy-hand-ed and one-sided action that is precipitously taken by the court in the name of fulfilling its constitutional responsibilities." Terry further held that the court had to "totally torture consti-tutional history to justify its decision." Others frustratingly declaimed the decision as turning "loose upon society without punishment, murderers, rapists, and robbers," and unleashing further disrespect for the law.[22]

It is not known whether McFarland felt any relief at these later vestiges of support for his original position, but crit-icism and discontent, notwithstanding, the Supreme Court would stand by its decision and did just that as the decade ended. In the April 1969 case *Orozco v. Texas*, Justice Hugo Black, writing for the majority, extended the *Miranda* protec-tions to the accused when in custody at the police station or "otherwise deprived of his freedom of action in any way." This constituted a possible case where *Miranda* could be reinterpret-ed, but it was not. The Supreme Court overturned the convic-tion of *Orozco* on the technicality that without benefit of coun-sel while being questioned in his apartment, he led officers to the gun that proved to be the murder weapon. Having not brought Orozco to the station house, the police had not read him his rights, although one officer admitted that the accused was, in fact, under arrest the moment he had given his name.

Justices Warren, Douglas, Brennan, and newcomer Thurgood Marshall concurred with Black, while Justices Harlan, White, and Stewart dissented as they had with *Miranda*. Abe Fortas took no part in the decision. White employed the now familiar "constitutional straitjacket" phrase to describe the decision, while Harlan once again elaborated: "the passage of time has not made the Miranda case any more palatable to me . . . the constitutional condemnation of this perfectly understandable, sensible, proper, and, indeed, commendable piece of police work highlights the unsoundness of *Miranda*."

So *Miranda*, including McFarland's overturned opinion, became an integral part of American jurisprudence, though since Warren's departure from the court in 1969, Nixon's "law and order" presidency of the early 1970s, and particularly during the Reagan 1980s, interpretation and use of *Miranda* has been going more along the lines of McFarland's original intention. As Justice Struckmeyer has said, "*Miranda* was not a deterrent. It punishes the public. Recently the tide has been turning." Certainly McFarland treated the case on an individual basis regarding *Miranda*, a convicted felon familiar with police and court procedure. As Charles Meyers, former Dean of the Stanford Law School has stated, "McFarland had little tolerance for empty formalism. The issue for him was whether the defendant's statements were in fact voluntary, not when an attorney was made available." Legal assistant John Moran sheds additional light on the case, noting that while Mac normally strived for brevity, he "tried to do something of a dissertation" with *Miranda*, holding the attitude that "here's the law as it exists today." In this case, the law was then reinterpreted and changed for the future. Moran concluded, "I think he foresaw that it was an important decision."[24]

Miranda did not stand alone among McFarland decisions in being overturned by the U.S. Supreme Court. In the November 1965 case of *Lassen v. Arizona Highway Department*, the "Judge," as he was most frequently now called, ruled in favor of the highway department. In this opinion, he stood by

Arizona's historic practice of permitting state and county highway departments to build across state land, even if reserved for educational purposes, without paying for easements. This marked the third time that Arizona's high court had so ruled, the most recent case being the previous year. The court's stance held that "the construction of highways enhances the value of surrounding lands to such an extent that institutions which benefit from state lands suffer no losses by granting free rights of way." The Highway Department claimed that the principle involved followed that of the United States in making railroad grants and more recent easements with the emerging interstate highway system.

State Land Commissioner Obed M. Lassen, however, was determined to upset the traditional practice and accrue monies for the Arizona School Commission by bringing suit against the highway department. McFarland, backed by a unaimous court, ruled against him, but a challenge to Mac's decision was already in the making in Washington, D.C. where United States Solicitor General [in 1965] Thurgood Marshall had noted that Lassen's position was similar to cases pending in eight other western states. Marshall filed a brief asking that the U.S. Supreme Court reverse the Arizona decision although he did, in part, agree with McFarland's enhancement appraisal. Meeting a year later in November 1966, the Supreme Court overturned McFarland for the second (and last) time. In this case, McFarland again showed himself as a strict constructionist. He saw his role as clarifying and applying law, not making it. The Warren Court, on the other hand, continued in its role, begun with the *Brown v. Topeka Board of Education* civil rights case of 1954, of remaking America, even if upsetting older, traditional western law.[25]

In December 1965, McFarland handled another case that held the public's close attention, *City of Phoenix v. Phoenix Civic Auditorium and Convention Center Association.* In 1963, the city and the association had signed an agreement on how to build and finance the proposed downtown complex. The agreement stated that the city would purchase the land and then lease it to a competitive bidder who would agree to construct the complex. The lease would run for forty years after five of which the construction would be completed. Then, Phoenix would rent the center for thirty-five years in order to pay back the $8.75 million construction bill.

In his opinion, McFarland affirmed a declaratory judgment of the Maricopa County Superior Court, stating that the lease-buy back was in reality a purchase agreement that was unconstitutional (the city had asked the court to check the validity). The Arizona Constitution allowed up to four percent bonding on property valuation. Phoenix's stood at $532.5 million, so the city could bond up to $21.3 million. At this juncture, the city had already bonded $17.5 million, and the additional $8.75 million would put it over the constitutional limit. Mac knew this decision would be unpopular with Mayor Milt Graham and many of the city's leading citizens, but he rationalized that the constitution must not be circumvented:

> The people in framing the Constitution were undoubtedly of the opinion that constitutional safeguards against indebtedness were to the best interests of the economy of the state. . . . We cannot override these safeguards to meet the exigency of the situation. We cannot make constitutional limitations meaningless by judicial circumvention in order to assist the city . . . no matter how desirable it might be.

Judge Charles Bernstein alone dissented, terming the arrangement a lease and not a purchase agreement. McFarland and the other justices disagreed: "We must look to the transaction for what it is and not what it is called." He realized that "there were times when it was in the public interest for a city to exceed its constitutionally imposed debt ceilings," but the constitution had its purpose in the minds of its framers and "the remedy is a constitutional amendment."[26]

Another remedy did exist, however, for financing the convention complex, and McFarland affirmed it in March 1966. Actually, he ruled against an application for a re-hearing of the

December case, but in a supplemental opinion he cleared the way for the use of excise taxes drawn from motel-hotel income. This tax had been ruled legal the previous year and had never been appealed by the hoteliers. Now the extra monies would be put to good use in benefiting tourism by the construction of a convention complex. A satisfied Mayor Graham predicted the complex would be the "greatest single boost to the Valley since the expansion of Motorola."[27]

Between the two convention center decisions, the court had undergone its annual rotation. Fred Struckmeyer succeeded Lorna Lockwood as chief justice, while Charles Bernstein stood next in line assuming the vice chief position. The time also marked the end of the Appeals Court's first year of activity, and, although it had assisted the Supreme Court considerably, the backlog of cases remained great. Struckmeyer called for increasing the size of the Appeals Court and also bringing in qualified lawyers as judges *pro tempore* up to six months in lower courts to lighten the statewide load. Nevertheless, the Supreme Court more than pulled its own weight, some of which could be attributed to the addition of McFarland and his proven work ethic. The court produced 253 opinions compared to 177 issued in 1964. McFarland, as a freshman judge wrote forty-five of these, slightly less than twenty percent. His contributions would increase as the court years progressed.[28]

Throughout these first years on the high bench, shared work patterns, habits, relationships, and roles among the five justices began to define themselves. McFarland worked to others' exhaustion, arriving at the Capitol by 8:00 A.M. and staying on the job until "6:30 after the traffic slowed down." Legal aides and other justices never have disputed this figure, stating fourteen hours for Mac was commonplace. His closest friend and ally on the bench, Struckmeyer, termed him a classic workaholic whose relaxation was work and for whom relaxation grew tedious: "I couldn't imagine him weeding a flower bed. Work gave him happiness and health and in his seventies, he was in the prime of life . . . very healthy." Stuckmeyer continued, noting that with his high intelligence and ability to dig for information if not flowers, Mac normally kept ahead of the other justices and eventually strove to be first in number of opinions written -- quantity without sacrificing quality. A certain style of dominance emerged by working harder. Fourteen hours beat eight every time, and the more one put in, the more one knew about a case, and the less disagreement one faced. "Because of his preparedness, his views were accepted." Very rarely did another register a dissent to Mac's opinion, and none of his decisions were ever reversed by his own court. Ultimately, Struckmeyer termed Mac's perceived dominance as "force of character, ability to convince, and leadership."[29]

Mildred Hagerty, McFarland's judicial secretary has concurred: "We worked ourselves to death . . . more decisions than anyone else . . . real early to real late," all of this despite a disorganized desk that defied description. More importantly, Hagerty singled out his intensity, "He didn't spare himself." Noting characteristics that Mac had displayed since the Senate, she perceived him as driving himself while others followed his example. "He put so much of himself into everything that everyone felt they must do the same." Moreover, Mac exemplified "loyalty to his people and received loyalty from them."[30]

As a younger legal assistant, John Moran saw Mac from a different angle, noting that "there was nothing fancy about Mac . . . and little eloquence." Newcomers often expressed bewilderment at the common bumpkin image Mac portrayed and sometimes "criticized him behind his back," until they recognized the dedicated methodology behind his homespun mask. "The fact is, he understood the principles better than others." Moran also remembered Mac as a "twenty cup of coffee per day drinker and the blacker the better." He worked his law clerks hard, often on three, four, or five cases at once, and they wrote much, but he equally often accompanied them on their research excursions. Then he "slashed and burned" their written summaries to the point where they frequently had to swallow their pride. Moran, too, recalls the disorganized desk, reminiscent of the Senate, with piled, open books and strewn papers. Mac was prone, while answering the phone, to write one piece of information down on one envelope or scrap and another on whatever was available until bits of data on one subject became scattered incoherently over the expanse of his working area. Somehow Hagerty pulled it all together.

Through the frenetic casework activity, Moran never saw him get angry or upset, and he was always willing to listen. Ultimately he would sift information through his computer-like mind where it became imbued with the McFarland persona and "rural, humble Oklahoma" background. He expressed himself with warmth and simplicity and often in an anecdotal, storytelling fashion. To top it off, he was "a great reader."

Perhaps McFarland's intense dedication to his work grew, in part, to pick up the slack of his bench colleagues. Jesse Udall was older and not as sharp or active as he once had been. Lorna Lockwood at times seemed predisposed to luxuriate in the high honor and uniqueness of being the nation's only female chief justice, and Charles Bernstein, a "hail fellow—well met" seemed to overworked law clerks as a bit pushy in getting his own way and somewhat lax in his own contribution to the work schedule. Bernstein was the bench liberal while McFarland and his friend Struckmeyer stood between him and the conservative Lockwood and Republican Udall.[31]

Court routine orbited around the weekly Tuesday meetings where cases would be discussed. In the morning, the assembled justices would mount the stairs to the second story of the Capitol to the court's inner chamber, draw the shades, and sequester themselves. No one was admitted to these sessions where sometimes "heated arguments" occurred, the judges freely expressing opinions on everything "ranging from law, philosophy, and administration, right down to the purchases of office equipment." It was a close-knit group that McFarland clearly enjoyed.[32]

During the Supreme Court years, McFarland resumed the globe trotting activities that had been in abeyance since his senate period. The court normally recessed for eight weeks in July and August, and Mac took advantage of this respite to visit areas previously unseen, South America in 1966, Africa in 1969, and in 1967, another around-the-world tour that took in war-ravaged Vietnam and the Soviet Union.

In summer 1966, brother Carl and his wife Louise accompanied Mac and Edna south of the equator for the first time. Both official and personal interests surfaced during the trip, which began in Guatemala and proceeded on through Panama, Ecuador, Peru, Chile, Argentina, Uruguay, Brazil, and Venezuela before the return home—nine countries in thirty-two days.

McFarland invariably scrutinized housing and wage conditions for the working classes including farmers noting the usual absence of a middle class in these countries. For example, in Peru ten percent of the population lived on eighty percent of the land, and Latin American wages generally ran from one dollar for unskilled to two dollars for skilled labor per day. At the time, the minimum wage in the U.S. of $1.25 per hour mandated wages of, at the very least, ten dollars per day for the most unskilled workers.

Of course, U.S. ambassadors and lesser officials turned out as escorts and greeters, and whenever possible, which was often, McFarland fulfilled invitations from Latin American legislators and justices including the heads of the Guatemala Supreme Court and the Peruvian Senate. He also attended to U.S. organizations in the various countries, notably Peace Corps and Alliance for Progress offices.

Of personal interest, McFarland rigorously sought out television stations, always finding comparatively "crude" equipment, and he and Carl relished visits to farms, particularly the long staple cotton operators in Peru. Both McFarlands farmed long staple Arizona cotton in Pinal County, and both continued to await the hoped-for dramatic expansion of that industry in Arizona through legislation for the Central Arizona Project. (The U.S. Supreme Court had ruled for Arizona over California in the decade-long water case in 1963, but no legislation had yet been struck).

The travelers moved through an exotic third world of

banana groves, coffee trees, avacados, pineapples, corn and bean fields, beautiful lakes, and smoking volcanoes. Time and again, they would emerge into large modern cities that hid their poverty behind facades of the glittering modernity of casinos, nightclubs, pools, restaurants, bars, and luxury hotels. Their stops included Quito, Lima, Santiago, Buenos Aires, Montevideo, Rio de Janeiro, Sao Paulo, Caracas, and Brasilia newly rising out of the Amazonian rainforest.

Mac took it all in stride with his usual energy and interest, sometimes leaving the others behind exhausted. Frequently Carl, Edna, and Louise retired early and slept in late at their lodgings while Mac attended early morning meetings or late night festivities as an honored guest. Brother Carl was doubly inconvenienced by a painful back condition. In a recent small plane emergency landing similar to the one McFarland experienced while governor, Carl had landed hard in a cotton field, throwing his back permanently out of alignment. A lost bag containing his medicine for pain compounded the stress. Fatigue and high altitudes caused Mac to cancel the planned excursion to La Paz, the hemisphere's loftiest capitol city. The nation-hopping judge had planned to go on himself but demurred when retarded by his fellow travelers. Nevertheless, he took typical traveler's delight in flying over and observing a portion of the country and the grandeur of the high Andes. Similarly, Mac enjoyed Quito, on the equator, where the sun rose at 6:00 A.M. and set at 6:00 P.M. with precision. Whether strolling in the footsteps of the Incas, straddling the two hemispheres at the equator, or jawing with native street vendors or a businessman who sold "organs and locomotives," Mac thoroughly enjoyed the month-long excursion. He returned to the states filled with new knowledge and experience, invigorated, and eager to resume work.[33]

McFarland continued to churn out the opinions and finished the years 1966 and 1967 with forty-seven and forty-four respectively, a pace of about one-per-working week. He also continued to oversee the television station operation, although, as he had with the Florence farms, he turned increasing respon-

sibility over to Del Lewis. At one point in early 1967, he tested
the marketability of the station offering it for sale. Channel 3
was valued at $10 million as an ABC affiliate or $3 million as an
independent. McFarland's sales ardor cooled, however, and he
kept the station in local control allowing it to continue to grow
toward its $100 million-plus worth in the 1980s.[34]

Outside courtroom activities continued for the justices
as well. In late 1966, McFarland and colleagues broke ground
for the new College of Law at Arizona State University. Soon
after, in the court transistion, the judge was elevated up a notch
in court hierarchy assuming the vice chief position for 1967
while Charles Bernstein became chief justice. Mac would not
have to wait for the next year to become chief, however, for
Bernstein suffered a heart attack in July forcing McFarland into
the acting-chief position, assigning as well as writing cases for
the remainder of the year. Bernstein recovered well and
resumed his associate position on the bench in 1968.[35]

When McFarland had initially announced and campaigned for the Supreme Court in July 1964, Lyndon Johnson's
self-proclaimed Great Society seemed inexorably to be moving
ahead in areas of civil rights and economic and social legislation
intending to indeed make American quality of life better and
more available to all. McFarland watched with pride as his former senate protege pushed American liberalism forward, but an
invader had leapt upon the national host that same summer with
the Gulf of Tonkin incident in the waters off of divided
Vietnam. The perceived communist North Vietnamese aggression toward U.S. ships forced the president to assume the
responsibility of containment of communism just as had his
predecessors Truman, Eisenhower, and Kennedy. The dexter-
ous, convincing, manipulative LBJ could fashion guns and but-
ter both, and he would not be the first president to lose a war,
or so he claimed.

The escalation of the Vietnam conflict now just as
inevitably began to slowly bleed the Great Society dry. After
election in his own right in 1964, Johnson extended liberalism

with stronger civil rights legislation and constructive programs dealing with health, education, welfare, the environment, and poverty. By 1966 a peak had been reached in the flurry of legislation conceived by the "Fabulous 89th" Congress; then the responsibility of the undeclared war began to predominate. At the same time, during 1967, LBJ's image grew tarnished just as he was gearing up for the 1968 campaign. Many objected to the transference of federal priorities to Vietnam rather than domestic concerns. A growing number believed the war unworthy and perhaps unwinable, adding to their ranks throughout the increasingly divided United States, legions of youthful demonstrators marching and listening to the underground politics and protest music of Bob Dylan, the Beatles, Jimi Hendrix, and other members of a growing counterculture. A far greater number could not understand why the government did not prosecute the war more vigorously and to a quicker, successful conclusion. Some on both sides of the war issue began to suspect the existence of a credibility gap between statements of government intentions and accomplishments and reality.

LBJ compounded this confusion and division with his own idiosyncratic personality. His excesses of speech and behavior, such as holding his beagles up by their ears and proudly showing off his scars from recent operations, offended many. More important, as *Life* magazine pointed out, LBJ "fiercely tries to appear to be what he isn't and vice versa." A "wave of bitterness toward him is washing through the country — in part because of his own efforts to confuse and deceive people about himself and issues." Sage Walter Lippman encouraged the growing anti-Johnson cult: "The war in Vietnam can't be won. It would take a man of noble stature and of the highest moral courage to admit [that] fact about the war. There is no reason to think Mr. Johnson is such a man." LBJ supporters, including McFarland, who knew Johnsonian excesses firsthand, regarded with dismay the proliferation of detractors. They truly believed that he had fashioned an exceptional record in domestic legislation, but they also recognized it would be delusionary to think that Johnson was not in danger.[36]

As an old school armed services veteran of World War I and a government leader during World War II and Korea, Mac had no doubts where he stood on U.S. responsibility and capability. Speaking at Memorial Day services in 1967, he evoked former President Eisenhower's statement that if he were of age, he would enlist to fight in Vietnam. McFarland said that by this statement, Ike did enlist. While recognizing the right of dissidents to freedom of speech, he also urged "our right to remain silent if our utterances encourage the enemy." Now, with the Supreme Court break of summer 1967, McFarland determined to see Vietnam firsthand as part of a second circumnavigation of the globe that took in the Soviet Union and Eastern Europe as well.[37]

Leaving with Edna on July 29, McFarland was also accompanied by close friend Ralph Watkins, Sr., who had been on Mac's previous around-the-world tour fifteen years earlier. The price tag per individual ticket was $1,734. The group first visited all eight Hawaiian Islands where Mac attended a U.S. chief justices' conference. Then they went on to Fiji, New Zealand, the expanse of Australia from the Melbourne-Canberra-Sidney area to Brisbane and Darwin, and on to Singapore before touching down at the Saigon Airport on August 16. Saigon sat in the midst of the nationwide war zone where U.S. servicemen worked alongside the Army of the Republic of Vietnam (ARVN) against the National Liberation Front Viet Cong supported by Ho Chi Minh's North Vietnamese regular army. Among these combatants, millions of agrarian Buddhist peasants tried to eke out a living, as their ancestors had for a millennium, while maintaining a neutrality strongly threatened by the pulls of both warring factions. From their hotel balcony, the McFarlands and Watkins could hear the night bombings and observe the flashes and explosions of distant guns. Equipped with a recorder, Watkins taped a foreword to an account of the trip with the sounds of war providing background.

The next morning, McFarland and Watkins began their rounds with a briefing by Ambassador Ellsworth Bunker and meetings with General B. G. Gates and his staff of intelligence operations. As they began to piece together the situation in Vietnam, two major themes emerged: one, the pending elections of a new civilian government in the south, and second, concern over criticism, disunity, and racism in the United States.

The election routine was extremely complex. Eleven candidates from eleven different parties vied for the presidency while the Senate offered up sixty seats for which individual groups of ten candidates ran. There were forty-eight such groups, hence 480 candidates. In the House, one elected official would ultimately represent each bloc of fifty thousand in population. These blocs encompassed the hundreds of smaller hamlets, which elected their own counsels of from three to thirteen citizens. The hamlets provided the crux of many of the problems in Vietnam. In a strategic hamlet program, the U.S. assiduously tried to relocate these small population groups from the war zone and areas of potential Viet Cong influence. Thus, hundreds of thousands were being removed from homes and villages holding centuries of ancestral lineage. Once isolated and controlled, these peasants could participate in the election process. Those who refused to move or resisted could not vote. Cultural ties, notwithstanding, refusal or resistance also indicated implicit enemy status and influence and often led to destruction and death at the hands of U.S. search and destroy squads. Those who were elected in supposedly controlled areas often found themselves uncomfortably subject to Viet Cong infiltration, which, in turn, fostered American distrust and suspicion: "When they were elected, the Viet Cong would tell the people the elections were false, and those elected should be eliminated. One of the candidates running for chief of the hamlet said `I might be unlucky enough to be elected.'"

Complexities aside, however, the real power lay in the hands of the National Leadership Committee chaired by General Nguyen Van Thieu and overseen by the prime minister, General Nguyen Cao Ky, who together formed a military dictatorship that had maintained control since 1965 and which would remain predominant after the fall elections.

The South Vietnamese people took their elections seriously, however, and interest ran high with turnouts of eighty percent. The ever-inquisitive McFarland noted that in Saigon crowds numbering up to a million people thronged the streets just to watch election news and advertisements on one of eight hundred TV sets scattered throughout the city, often mounted on platforms so they could be seen by the public. A major question that loomed large in candidates' and voters' minds concerned the continued support of the United States, particularly in regard to disunity and protest then erupting in America. Not only were peace and anti-war protests and marches escalating, culminating in the moratorium at the Pentagon in October 1967, but racial strife continued unabated as well, Watts in the summer of 1965, Chicago in 1966, and now Newark and Detroit in the summer of 1967.

When visited, Gilbert Shinebaum, Secretary of the U.S. Embassy told McFarland:

> They're not quite sure the United States is the great democracy they've heard about. . . . They don't fully understand the riots. . . . It has lowered the prestige of the U.S. Local papers wonder. . . . This is not a white race here in Vietnam. This is very important to the Vietnam people - the importance of domination of the white race. They're concerned about our deep-seated feelings about other races.

Prior experience with the French exacerbated this suspicion of white dominance. Charles De Gaulle, in particular, was the butt of much joking and derision.

The Viet Cong, of course, used and exaggerated reports of American homeland disunity very effectively in undermining South Vietnamese confidence both in America's capabilities and intentions. The Saigon government and people found themselves in the awkward position of worrying over American commitment and over potential dominance and racism if that commitment were fulfilled. Noting the contradictory position, General Gates still claimed, "The Viet Cong are hurting [but] the difficulty that any part of the population has in standing up to the VC is the belief that we will stay with them. If we don't we'll let down all those people." Shinebaum added, "The Viet Cong are very subtle. They pass their propaganda by innuendo rather that direct statements." Gates certainly placed the U.S. dilemma in global perspective: "If we did pull out, as some would have us do. . . . We would lose all rights in the world. It would make it more likely that we would have a major war because it would increase the influence of the communist world. I would indicate that aggression does pay off. . . ." Typically Gates backed up his stance with the infamous and unsubstantiated body count of 4.9 Viet Cong to every one American killed in action.

Upon McFarland's inquiry into foreign aid in Vietnam, the embassy information officer stated that only nine percent of American dollars went to war while fifty-two percent dealt with economic stabilization, the most important U.S. goal. He outlined three further goals; the first concerned highway, airport, and port maintenance and repair coupled with care of the refugee population. The second goal targeted improvement in communication and understanding between the American and Vietnamese people, while the final goal, involving twenty-eight percent expenditures, dealt with healthcare, hospitalization, and medical training.

After two days of information-gathering in Saigon, McFarland and Watkins headed for the front lines, "Charlie territory," in a chopper armed with fifty-caliber machine guns but lacking doors, and flying seventy-five feet over jungle trees and thirty feet over rice paddies, causing Mac to remark "Looked a little as if they were trying to draw fire." The group landed in the lines of the First Division where they interviewed men from the enlisted ranks to the top. While there, and as gunfire chattered around the area, McFarland witnessed the defection of a Viet Cong officer who "fingered a woman who was an important cog in the area." The peasant woman was brought in and interrogated with her children, who were offered Cokes. She refused to talk and made her kids pour the soft drinks on the ground. Also during the visit, eighteen Viet Cong were captured. McFarland asked at what expense and effort and received the reply "three batteries and two hundred men to capture eighteen" of the original three hundred confronting VC. There were no U. S. casulties.

Officers peppered their talk with similar statistics showing the inordinate ratio of enemy to allied deaths and alluding to Viet Cong inability to fight on the offensive:

> In July they attacked 2 battalions on the 9th ARVN, 141st Viet Nam Army. That operation cost them 149 dead and the ARVN lost 18. In early August, [the] 165th attacked Ton Lee Chong forces camp, with 120 for 16 killed. Whenever they try an offensive operation . . . we have inflicted such staggering losses on them that they avoid them if they can.

Further conversation indicated U.S. competition with the ARVN body count. Replying to Watkins's question on normal "kill ratio," Colonel Frederick Araese stated "ten to one: In fact, if we have less than they [ARVN] at any time we're not pleased." He continued:

> At Ton Lee Chong we came in to help them, and the body count was about 120. They [ARVN] lost 18 dead, so they had a favorable ratio. The same thing at Kong Loy, 150 body count, and the dead was 15. We don't always do that well, U.S. forces as an average. We thought these were exceptional actions on the part of the VN.

The colonel concluded, "We're the richest army in the world. If we lack anything at all, we have it quicker than you can shake a stick. I don't know how any army could go into action any better equipped than we are." Furthermore, he stressed "These fine American boys are in water or mud above their knees sometimes, and have other discomforts, but they have a grin on their faces. Their morale is first class."

The interview with Colonel Araese then segued into defoliation or "jungle clearing." The 1st Division was slated to clear thirty thousand acres in the immediate area:

> You should see some of that. . . . We take away the
> hiding places and their base camps. This gets them off
> the back of the local people. . . . They can't get food.
> They have to go into a village and leave when we
> destroy their hiding places [presumably the villages].
> In villages, we can pick them off. If we get their lead-
> ers, they can't replace them. When we get their goon
> squad . . . we try to keep them down. . . . They're
> using water buffalo or elephants. Moving by night,
> they leave tracks, and our squads find them.

Asked if ARVN soldiers were employed on these operations, Araese replied "No, we use a 'copter called OH 13 [called
`Puff the Magic Dragon,' these gunships could fire 17,500
rounds of ammunition per minute]. Those pilots have a lot of
guts," referring to their low elevation flying. Having been
painted such a rosy picture, it is easy to see that McFarland, like
the great majority at that time in the United States, failed to
detect their own suspect optimism and the determination and
capability of the enemy.

Interview day at the front also happened to be "ice cream
day," something the military took very seriously: ". . . today's an
ice cream day and they're out in the jungle; we'll fly it in so the
men will have their ice cream. . . . Paper plates and plastic forks
- no dirty mess kits, etc. Darndest looking battlefront you ever
saw." With ice cream and Puff the Magic Dragons fighting a
demoralized enemy using elephants and water buffalos, it is no
wonder that the "richest army in the world" was confident. Few
could predict the impending turmoil of 1968 with the Tet
Offensive and LBJ's withdrawal from the presidential race. Still,
there were those such as Walter Lippman, Under Secretary of
State George Ball, Senators Wayne Morse and Ernest Gruening,
and even Omar Bradley who held grave concerns over the war.
McFarland was not among them. Buoyed by his visit to the
"Dog Face" infantry, he continued his investigation visiting with
air force mechanics and navy gunners while riding on patrol

boats in the Mekong Delta. The patriotic McFarland expressed doubt only in the division at home.

After the two days in the military sector, McFarland and Watkins attended a presidential press conference with the forty-four-year-old General Thieu who commented on a number of issues. Not surprisingly, he said he and General Ky had no intentions of resigning their positions of authority in the wake of the pending elections. He also noted his support of American bombing missions over Hanoi, and his regret of the depletion of draft-eligible men in the south. ARVN officials combed the small hamlets and villages, snatching up anyone eligible, much like old British Navy press gangs, and he wanted to lower the draft age from twenty to eighteen. After all, the North Vietnamese and Viet Cong were employing twelve-year-olds. On a suggestion relayed by Dwight Eisenhower that a declaration of war was important, Thieu cautioned "it would bring Russia and Red China into the war." The loquacious Thieu concluded on a light note suggesting that the French were negotiating with England to purchase Gibraltar, to be renamed the Gaulle Stone. On the French premier, himself, Thieu jested, De Gaulle was complaining over the price of his tombstone: "What? $5,000 for three days," indicating the certain expectation of a Christ-like ascension.

After five days in Vietnam, the McFarland party departed and continued the around-the-world trip, the itinerary for which reads like a lifetime of travels: Manila, Tapei, Hong Kong, Delhi, Agra, Moscow, Leningrad, Krasnodar, Kiev, Bucharest, Budapest, Prague, London, New York, Washington, D.C., and Phoenix. Unfortunately no notes exist for McFarland's visit to the Soviet bloc nations, although his files are crammed with communist literature including a singular booklet defending atheism.[38]

Upon his return to Phoenix, Judge Mac made his thoughts about the war known. Echoing General Gates, he stated, "the time is past for talking about whether or not we should be in Vietnam; unless we secure an honorable peace . . . this country will no longer be a leading power in the world. . . .

Let's get it over with and leave for future historians and politicians to talk about whether we should have been there after it's over." Mac made three points concerning the troops: they knew what they were fighting for, their morale was excellent, and they believed they were winning the war. He termed doves and pacifists, defeatists and their attitude of the impossibility of winning the war "globaloney," qualifying this statement with "the only weapon we need in Vietnam that we do not have presently is unity. Unity will end the war much sooner." He expressed particular concern over those in Congress, like Senator Thruston Morton (R-KY), who most recently had joined the ranks urging de-escalation, and he further urged Arizonans to start getting Christmas cards and presents out to the fighting servicemen. Evan Mecham, defeated by Hayden in 1962 for the Senate, editorialized in support of McFarland and administration policy: "And if someone tells you that President Johnson's policy is wrong, ask them if they would advcocate having thousands of drug-mad Asiatics engaging in Banzai charges against our thinly spread troops . . . as Soviet and Peking supplies move unhindered to the front." Mac's thoughts were more diplomatically couched, but no less impacted.[39]

When McFarland left war torn Vietnam, he proceeded on to the Soviet Union and Eastern Europe. Even without existing records or memoirs on this portion of the trip, it is certain that Mac returned from his second circumnavigation of the globe, a much more well informed citizen of the world. This would come at a time when his domestic responsibilities were to increase dramatically. He was due by the customary rotation to take over as official chief justice of the Arizona court and, with such battles as *Miranda* behind him, his indoctrination as acting chief for most of 1967, and his increasingly workaholic tendencies, he stood well prepared for the new challenge. Unbeknownst to him, however, President Johnson would call on his old friend and add to his tasks the following year by placing Mac on a heavily burdened committee to investigate violence in the United States, an investigation that would try McFarland's confidence and pride in the direction of his own country.

CHAPTER SEVENTEEN

CHIEF JUSTICE
1968-1970

WHEN THE SUPREME COURT TURNOVER FROM 1967 to 1968 brought in McFarland as chief justice, the ascension culminated his extraordinary career of holding his state's top positions in each branch of government. State newspapers immediately picked up on the unique accomplishment. Tucson's *Daily Star* found only Arthur Goldberg among comparable active politicians. The current ambassador to the United Nations had been in the executive branch as Secretary of Labor and in the judicial branch as a U.S. Supreme Court Justice, but he had no legislative experience, and his positions were appointive, whereas McFarland's were elective. Of course, many, including President Johnson, had held executive and legislative positions, but those with judicial experience were relatively few in number. Mac, too, was aware of the historic nature of his accomplishment, and he began to make a few inquiries into past civil servants who might have had similar career experience. Some did exist; Andrew Jackson had held a position in the Tennessee judicial system and had been both a U.S. senator and congressman and then president. Closer to the mark stood the late James Byrnes of South Carolina who had governed and been a U.S. senator, served a brief tenure on the U.S. Supreme Court, and had been secretary of state, again briefly. It is certain that no U. S. Senate majority leaders to this date in 2003 have held positions comparable to McFarland's as state governor and state supreme court chief justice.[1]

As chief justice, McFarland targeted cutting down the

461

backlog of court cases as the major goal. The prior year, even as acting chief and world traveler, Mac had written better than a case per active court week, forty-four total. For the next three years he would further step up his pace to nearly 1.5 cases per week finishing with sixty-five, sixty-six, and sixty-seven for 1968-70, the highest figures among the tribunal. During his first three years on the court, the new chief justice noted that the backlog had been cut down from 838 to 260. In his comments on being inaugurated as chief, McFarland recognized that Arizona did not stand alone with this problem. It was endemic throughout the nation's judicial systems from Baltimore and San Francisco where one normally waited two years between charge and trial to over three years in Connecticut to five years in Illinois. Texas possessed a Texas-sized backlog of 120,000—cases in all of its courts.[2]

Chief Justice Earl Warren recognized the backlog situation across the country and spoke about it during a February visit to Arizona. As guest of honor he presented the major speech at the dedication of Armstrong Hall, the home for the new Arizona State University Law School. The seventy-three year old McFarland introduced the seventy-six year old chief justice, the most influential Supreme Court leader since the days of John Marshall over 125 years before. In front of three thousand students, faculty, administrators, and dignitaries in ASU's Gammage Auditorium, Warren painted a negative picture of the state of judicial administration, terming it "a cruel joke perpetrated on this nation." He referred mainly to the average two-year backlog that existed throughout the nation and commiserated with those who might be innocent of crimes living under a cloud of suspicion, or worse, languishing in jail if unable to afford bail. He also expressed disdain for those guilty of crimes who could afford bail to remain on the streets and perhaps commit more mayhem in the interim. He did not acknowledge his own role in strengthening the accused's rights, which aggravated this very problem. This did not go unnoticed, however, to the small contingent of protesters gathered outside who objected to Warren's liberalization of the law not only in terms of *Miranda* and *Escobedo*, but also concerning such issues as striking down prayer in schools.[3]

McFarland's routine during his year as chief justice was augmented by other concerns such as the imminent passage of the Central Arizona Project into law and the presidential campaign of 1968. Concerning the latter, Mac began to withdraw from the active participation that had characterized previous elections. Although he continued to support Democratic candidates generously, never again would he actively engage as a leading Arizona convention delegate or take to the stump with his previous fervor. The physcological success of the coordinated Tet Offensive carried out by the Viet Cong and North Vietnamese in January and February 1968 coupled with the unabated growth and rancor of the antiwar movement caused Lyndon Johnson to withdraw from the race in March. McFarland's strong and active commitment to campaign politics rose and fell with LBJ's fortunes as evidenced by Mac's diminished role in Los Angeles in 1960 and his turnabout heading the state delegation in Atlantic City in 1964. Without the strong connection to the retiring president, McFarland removed himself from direct and immediate action. He did, however, support his old senate colleague, Hubert Humphrey, over Robert Kennedy just as he had LBJ over John Kennedy, and he generously donated to the Humphrey-Muskie ticket which came up short to old California nemesis and political Lazarus Richard Nixon.[4]

To McFarland, the failed candidacies of Johnson and soon Humphrey were brightened somewhat by the eventual success of the Central Arizona Project, which President Johnson finally signed into law on September 30, 1968. This brought to fruition efforts that had begun in the 1920s, and McFarland had been involved in nearly all stages since as a young attorney he had advised negotiators on the Colorado River Compact of 1922.

To review, Mac and Carl Hayden had pushed CAP through the Senate in 1950 and 1951 only to see it held up in the House. A decade long lawsuit ensued while the U.S.

Supreme Court adjudicated Arizona and California water rights. In 1955, McFarland, as governor, had successfully and personally argued an important segment of this case before the U. S. Supreme Court, which finally was decided in Arizona's favor in 1963. The legislative process then began anew, and by 1967 Senator Hayden had pushed the bill through the Senate, and in 1968, Republican Congressman John Rhodes worked assiduously to obtain the same result in the House. During the years of adjudication, the price authorized for CAP had risen from $.7 to $1.3 billion dollars. (by the time of its actual construction in the 1980s, costs neared four billion).

President Johnson invited Judge McFarland to attend the September 30 signing, but duties as chief justice kept him in Arizona. Thus Mac missed "one of the longest ceremonies for the signing of a bill yet seen," perhaps because the president, who had been in the middle of the fight while still favoring Arizona, was most satisfied to see the issue finally reconciled. A scarlet-clad U.S. Marine Band ensemble played softly in the White House foyer, before bursting into "Hail to the Chief" as Johnson entered the glittering East Room for the noonday signing. Over two hundred awaited him there as he related how he was cornered by Mac and Hayden on CAP from the moment he was sworn in as a senator in 1948.

Opening his official statement with "Next to the air we breathe, water is our most precious resource," LBJ then linked CAP to his overall environmental program, calling it "a landmark bill, a proud companion to the more than 250 conservation measures I have signed as president." As Johnson spoke, his wife Lady Bird looked on proudly. An influential environmentalist herself, she had vigorously opposed any new damming of the Colorado River in the Grand Canyon. In this stance, she was strongly backed by Sierra Club president, the powerful "Archdruid" David Brower, who also looked on with watchful eye.

President Johnson proclaimed the ceremony "Carl Hayden Day in the White House," and indeed it was. As Johnson finished the signing, he handed the single pen to the

ninety-year-old senator who realized the culmination of a lifelong dream. Hayden declared "Today is the high water mark of
my career," one that dated back fifty-six years to statehood in
1912 and further to territorial days. Arizona's entire congressional delegation numbered among the attendees, but Hayden
was uncharacteristically effusive in his praise for others' work,
singling out former Senator McFarland and the late
Congressman John Murdock for their work along with
Democratic Congressman Morris Udall and his own administrative assistant, Roy Elson. Representative John Rhodes was
the lone Republican congratulated by Hayden. Notably omitted were Republican Senator Paul Fannin, Republican
Congressman Sam Steiger, Democratic Secretary of the
Interior Stewart Udall, all in attendance, and Barry Goldwater.
Like McFarland, the out-of-office Barry Goldwater did not
attend the signing.[5]

Midway through his chief justice year, Ernest
McFarland accepted additional responsibilities as a member of
the thirteen-man National Commission on the Causes and
Prevention of Violence (NCCPV). President Johnson created
the commission by executive order on June 10, 1968, in the
wake of the incredibly escalating violence occurring in the
nation - violence book-ended by the assassination deaths of the
Kennedy brothers within a five-year period. Democratic presidential candidate Robert Kennedy had been shot and killed only
days earlier and only two months after the assassination of civil
rights leader Martin Luther King Jr. In the wake of the King
killing, violence born of the frustration and outrage of Black
America erupted in over one hundred American cities. The
inflamed nation eerily mirrored the similar conflagration of
more than one hundred South Vietnamese villages, towns, and
cities only two months before during the Tet Offensive. This
most tragic year had thus far symbolized destruction and death
in an increasingly controversial war and on the streets of domestic America—a nation, it seemed, permeated by violence of the
most astounding proportions both at home and abroad.

Moreover, just as the war had raged from 1964-68, so too had racial violence from the urban ghettos and hot black pavement of the North to the small towns and dusty red dirt roads of the rural South. And the assassinations had ranged from those on the fringes of mainstream American society like Black Muslim Malcolm X and American Nazi party leader George Lincoln Rockwell to the leader of the nation itself, John Fitzgerald Kennedy. Furthermore, the endemic violence was not confined to ghettos and leaders but had spilled over to college campuses and middle class America. Underlying the entire issue was the acknowledged fact that the United States produced the highest crime rate in the world whether it be with gun, knife, fist, or deceit. No other country compared.

Accordingly, Lyndon Johnson's executive directive read:

> My charge to you is simple and direct. I ask you to undertake a penetrating search for the causes and prevention of violence - a search into our national life, our past as well as our present, our traditions as well as our institutions, our culture, our customs, our laws.

Along with King and Robert Kennedy, his statement alluded to the four presidential assassinations, the deaths of civil rights activists Medgar Evers, Viola Luizzo, and three student workers in Freedom Summer 1964, and tabulated the murder count for each year since 1963: 8,500; 9,250; 9,850; 10,920; and 12,230 through 1967. He concluded by intimating that much of the blame for these deaths lay with the availability of firearms in America. Guns took the lives of an estimated 6,500 Americans annually as compared to thirty in England (less that 1/200th of the United States) and ninety-nine in Canada (1/65th).[6]

Johnson's appointments reflected both his deep concern for accomplishment in the investigations and diversity of membership. Dr. Milton Eisenhower, President Emeritus of Johns Hopkins University and brother of the former president, chaired the commission, which initially included nine members. Representing Congress were Democratic Senator Philip Hart of Michigan, Republican Senator Roman Hruska of Nebraska,

Democratic Congressman and House Majority Whip Hale Boggs of Louisiana, and Republican William McCulloch of Ohio. Chicago attorney Albert Jenner, Jr., and Archbishop of New York Terence Cardinal Cooke represented their fields. Black minority members included attorney and Ambassador to Luxembourg Patricia Roberts Harris of Howard University, also the only female, and United States District Court Judge A. Leon Higginbotham of Philadelphia, Pennsylvania. Eric Hoffer of San Francisco, listed as longshoreman, migratory worker, author and philosopher, rounded out the original choices as perhaps a nod to both the counterculture and intellectuals.[7]

During the next week, President Johnson decided to expand the commission by three to a total of twelve members plus Chairman Eisenhower. He included McFarland on this expanded list assuredly recalling earlier discussion with Mac in the Oval Office of the White House. Justice McFarland had visited there shortly after the King assassination when the city was engorged by rioting, flames in the ghetto areas, and national guard troops and tanks in the streets. At that time, McFarland remarked on the embarrassment to the capitol and that it should be a model city. The ensuing dialogue ranged from improved street lighting to Mac's suggestion that video cameras, not then in general use, be employed to film criminals during bank or public transportation robberies. He now found himself in a position to do something about it.[8]

Named with McFarland, the second judge chosen, was a second active attorney, Leon Jaworski, senior partner of a Houston law firm, president-elect of the American Bar Association, and special counsel to both the United States and Texas attorneys general. Dr. William Walter Menninger, staff psychiatrist of the Menninger Clinic of Topeka, Kansas, filled the final position and represented the medical community. Born in 1931 and at thirty-seven years old, Menninger was the commission's youngest member. Conversely, McFarland, at seventy-three years, was the oldest by seven years over Congressman McCulloch.

The task before the commission involved arduous work

over the next eighteen months. Initially, McFarland had hoped that the work could largely be accomplished during the Supreme Court's two-month summer recess. Such proved not the case, however, as meetings, hearings, workshops, retreats, and conferences continued through 1968 and on through the Nixon administration's first full year, ending finally in December 1969. The commission oversaw and assigned work to seven task forces dealing with protest, firearms, the media, violent crime, assassination, an overview of the tradition of violence in America, and a reconsideration of law and order. Thirty days of public hearings and most of the conferences were held in the fall of 1968. McFarland attended these on nearly every weekend, departing Phoenix after court business on Friday and returning late Saturday or most frequently on Sundays. The task forces, each involving a half-dozen or more professional researchers and dozens of aides, attempted to accomplish the most elaborate and comprehensive study of violence in America ever undertaken: "enough projects to launch a small university with a score of doctoral theses," all attempting to blend social science with legalistic reality and historical balance.[9]

A degree of revision proved necessary to attain proper historical perspective. In their investigation of the tradition of violence in America, the commissioners took issue with much recent historical interpretation, notably the consensus school of 1950s historians. Consensus interpretation depicted the two-century development of the United States in glowing fashion, emphasizing the positive significantly over the negative. For example, the consensus school luxuriated in its view of the relative absence of class conflict and strife in America. The second half of the Sixties belied this view. While Vietnam may have been the immediate cause of campus unrest, the outbreak of frustration in the African-American community had far deeper roots in the national past. Ironically, consensus historians generally applauded the "consensus conscious" LBJ. The leading accomplishment of the currently emerging New Left historians was to drive the consensus crowd from the historiographical forefront. As historical interpretative sands shifted in yet one more cycle, academicians of the New Left looked caustically on domestic racism and the nation's propensity to involve itself at such great depth in anti-communist efforts in foreign affairs. For this brief period, the violence commission aligned itself with the new critics of the national way, a way which so obviously encompassed violence in America. For McFarland—veteran, senator, governor, judge, lawyer, and farmer—the transistion to national critic did not come easy, and many of his statements continued to identify old and ancient villains as the perpetrators of contemporary violence. In speeches that autumn, he singled out the American Communist party, among others, for its contribution to national discord. Taking his lead from J. Edgar Hoover's September presentation to the commission, Mac cited the party's U.S. Secretary Gus Hall's claims that communists had infiltrated most college campuses dating back to 1964's Free Speech Movement in Berkeley. McFarland also noted the party's declared close involvement with anti-draft rallies and particularly the Students for a Democratic Society (SDS). Since the claims originated within the party itself, perhaps McFarland should have been aware of their potential inflation. Communists had, in fact, infiltrated the SDS, but they had never gained control. Here, Mac fell prey to the same theorizing that had entrapped many in the Cold War era: why blame someone else when the Communist party is available? In reality, the white, middle-class youth of collegiate America fashioned their own complaints, many of them legitimate. Communism had little influence on these middle class people who had been raised in suburban affluence in the height of the McCarthy years.

McFarland also credited communists with overwrought protest over "police brutality wherever possible in order to discredit law enforcement and to accentuate racial issues." Lumping the Student Non-Violent Coordinating Committee (SNCC) in with the communist-influenced organizations, Mac termed it "dedicated to the destruction of the United States."

True, SNCC had turned from pacifism to militancy as the Sixties wore on, but here again, McFarland chose to ignore the legitimacy of black complaints in favor of disparaging the group's apparent growing threat.

McFarland did not limit his complaint to organizations of the left, but also included those of the right in his condemnation of violence: the Ku Klux Klan, the American Nazi party, and the "superpatriot" Minutemen, self-proclaimed guerillas with "an obsession for weapons of all kinds." Too, McFarland went beyond ideological motivation to voice the commission's findings that causes of crime and violence were also "rooted in conditions and influences in contemporary life . . . poverty, inequality of employment opportunity, inferior housing, inadequate education, discrimination, and the breakdown of family life."[10]

During the first weekends of the commission's meetings, violence once again reared its head at the Democratic national convention in Chicago in August 1968. McFarland, who did not attend, watched with undisguised disgust as the television spilled out the drama of Mayor Richard J. Daley's police confrontation with the haplessly organized yippies, assorted other members of the counterculture, local street toughs, and hundreds of innocent victims guilty of only supporting the party's failed end-the-war plank. As the assembled taunted the police with the "whole world is watching" chant, the helmeted, masked troopers waded into the crowds with mace, gas, and clubs, brutally dispersing and arresting hundreds.

This marked another low point for the country in the pivotal year 1968. The NCCPV assigned Daniel Walker, president of the Chicago Crime Commission, to the task of investigating the Chicago rioting. The ensuing 364-page Walker Report placed the blame squarely on the shoulders of Mayor Daley and the police, terming the fracas a "police riot." The commission decided to release the report immediately upon its completion in December 1968, Milton Eisenhower commenting that although the report had not been fully reviewed, it was of immediate and widespread interest to the public. He continued: "not being fully reviewed . . . it carries neither the approval or the disapproval of the commission."[11]

The immediate release did not come with the approval of McFarland either. Mac voted against the release as premature, not having been thoroughly reviewed, and "largely a rehash of the charges and countercharges published in the newspapers and aired on the television." He continued, "the mere releasing of it would lend some authenticity to it in the eyes of the public." Although McFarland did not actually criticize the report, only its release, the Arizona press strongly condemned Walker's conclusions while supporting McFarland's stance. The press noted that since no deaths had occurred, the report's evidence of undue violence fell short and was, in fact, a part of a "nationwide effort to discredit police" and exonerate "the anarchists, hopheaded hippies, licentious Yippies, public lovemakers, feces throwers, and all of the other squalid nasties." Mayor Daley, of course, also objected to the findings noting that contrary to the report, he had disciplined (nine) of the officers in question. Opposition to the report notwithstanding, the judgment of time and history has sided with the conclusion of the original report, but the reaction to it did indicate the potential for division on the commission itself.[12]

As the commission meetings entered into a new year, 1969, and a new president, Richard Nixon, who extended its tenure, McFarland and the other twelve settled down for the long haul. Another full year would pass by before the group concluded its endeavors. No one, McFarland included, had thought it would be of such duration, but the commission's oldest member stood prepared for the task ahead, his workaholic tendencies only reinforced by the additional challenge.

Justice Struckmeyer recalled Mac's leaving the Arizona Supreme Court chambers on Friday evenings for the airport and the plane to Washington and then returning for the early Monday morning sessions with case opinions well advanced if not completed. Asked by Struckmeyer, why, with his heavy workload, he did not take the time to relax and rest on the plane, McFarland replied "At 30,000 feet, there was nothing to see out the windows, the magazines were out of date, and I was too old to look at the stewardesses." To top it off, during these years and lasting into the mid-1970s, Mac also had to fit in quarterly trips to San Francisco for board meetings of the Western Regional Savings and Loan Association. Struckmeyer here again expressed surprise that with McFarland, overwork did not induce increased tension, but rather seemed a form of relaxation. Working too hard remained a foreign concept to Mac.[13]

At times during his role as commissioner, McFarland took a special stance, or no stance, to the conclusions drawn. For example, being a television station owner, he divorced himself entirely from official participation in the media report. Off the record, he strongly backed the commission's conclusion on the overemphasis on violence in television and the movies: "The television industry has a definite duty to perform in improving the programming." On the report dealing with law enforcement, McFarland again supported the commission's findings but qualified his statement noting that most of the recommendations concerned urban situations unlike those that existed in Arizona: they "were directed primarily to large cities and adoption, therefore, should not be all inclusive but should be left up to local governments." Similarly, he fell short of full concurrence with conclusions regarding firearms. Joined by Hruska, Jaworski, and Boggs, McFarland held that control, though necessary, should be left to state regulation. Again, this, in part, deferred to the rural circumstance of certain states with perhaps a dash of western individualism thrown in: "each state should be permitted to determine for itself without additional restrictions from the federal government the system which best meets its needs to control."[14]

In its concluding days, the commission faced one more divisive issue, the sanction or censure of civil disobedience. By the slightest majority, seven to six, the vote condemned "massive civil disobedience as a tactic to change the law." McFarland sided with the majority for whom Leon Jaworski acted as spokesman: "We suggest that if in good faith the constitutionality of a statute . . . is to be challenged, it can be done effectively by one individual or a small group. While the judicial test is in progress, all other dissenters should abide by the law involved until it is declared unconstitutional." Both black members of the commission, Higgenbotham and Harris, dissented, Higgenbotham stating " if the idea . . . of everyone wait . . . had been applied . . . probably not one present major civil rights statute would have been enacted. I fear that the majority's position ignores the sad actual history of some of the most tragic `legal` repression of the civil rights of Negroes in this country." Chairman Eisenhower also stood with the minority but declined to issue a statement, not wanting to diffuse his authority and the harmony of the panel. Dr. Menninger, Senator Hart, and Terence Cardinal Cooke also dissented, while Congressman Boggs, Senator Hruska, Congressman McCulloch, Jenner, and Hoffer made up the rest of the majority. McCulloch had been a key Republican supporter of the Civil Rights Act of 1964 and the Voting Rights Act of 1965, both of which had been greatly influenced by civil disobedience.[15]

Two days after this divided report, the commission adjourned on December 10, 1969, after eighteen months of work. By the following April, its final recommendations were published in *To Establish Justice, To Ensure Domestic Tranquility*. It seemed a timely report as only days later, America's attention again turned to violence with the deaths of four students at Kent State University in Ohio and two at Jackson State College in Mississippi, perishing beneath the gunfire of national guard units. It was too late for these people, as the nation once again grappled with its violent image, but hopefully the conclusions could be put to positive effect in subsequent times. The major recommendations were comprehensive and included increasing welfare expenditures by twenty billion dollars immediately upon conclusion of the Vietnam War while maintaining postwar military expenses level even with an increasing GNP. Concerning violent crime, the commission advocated restrictive licensing of handguns and "further experimentation . . . [with] low cost drugs such as methadone . . . so that addicts are not compelled to resort to robbery and burglary." Too, McFarland supported substituting a misdemeanor violation for a felony concerning possession, but not sale, of marijuana. In the area of group violence, the commission called for both increased control over police action and more judicious reporting by the media. Recommendations for television entertainment included elimination of violence in children's cartoons and increased and permanent funding for the Public Broadcasting System to develop further educational and cultural programming then ignored by commercial networks. It is not a coincidence that shows like *Mr. Rogers* and *Sesame Street* began to flourish at this time. Concerning student unrest, the commission urged, "that the American people recognize that the campus is a mirror of the wider society and that their focus ought to be on the unfinished task of striving toward the goals of human life that all of us share and that young people admire and respect." The commission also recommended that the voting age be lowered to eighteen, which soon occurred by amendment to the Constitution in 1972.[16]

McFarland took more personal interest in the studies on assassination than the other areas. Recommendations here included his own input that more free television time be provided for campaign purposes, lessening the occasion for direct contact with large, potentially unmanageable crowds. Also, the news media was admonished to de-emphasize attention given to the personal lives of the president and first family.

Assassination, however, continued to plague the United States. By the time of the commission's study, McFarland had experienced the deaths of the Kennedys and King, and the attempted assassination of FDR in 1933 and Harry Truman in 1950. (Still to come during McFarland's lifetime were the shooting resulting in the paralysis of presidential candidate George Wallace in 1972, two assassination attempts on President Gerald Ford in 1976, and the wounding of President Ronald Reagan in 1981, not to mention the murder of musician John Lennon in 1980). Of all the underlying causes for these and other violent crimes, McFarland stressed the breakdown of family life resulting from poverty, inequality of employment, and consequent inferior housing. He urged adequate housing and particularly home-ownership, which he had supported actively since the GI Bill a quarter century before.[17]

Mac also stressed education, and here the commission made a full and unique recommendation contrasting with earlier consensus interpretation of history:

> . . . that the nation's schools emphasize in American history . . . the complexities and subtleties . . . shun the myths by which we have traditionally made supermen of presidents, founding fathers. . . ; and restore to history a full and frank picture of violence and unrest in America's past in the hope that children can be educated to repudiate violence and recognize its futility.

All told, the commission made eighty-one specific recommendations in the final ten task force reports.[18] On December 10, 1969, the commission disbanded and McFarland returned to Supreme Court work in his last full year as a public servant.

During his tenure on the NCCPV, McFarland managed to continue his globetrotting as well as his normal court duties. In late summer 1969, the Judge took time off from court and commission duties to tour the only major part of the world he had never visited — Africa. He had briefly been in Egypt and the north, but this time he took in sub-Saharan Africa, visiting nine countries, many of them newly emerging as their founding dates indicate: Nigeria-1963, Ghana-1960, Congo-1960, Zambia-1963, Tanzania-1964 (including the island of Zanzibar), and Kenya-1963. Only Rhodesia, founded in 1865 and the ancient kingdom of Ethiopia had national histories reaching deep into the past. This tour constituted McFarland's seventh and last major world trip after those of 1930 (Europe), 1945 (Europe), 1946 (Asia), 1952 (around the world, including wartime Korea), 1966 (South America), 1967 (around the world, including wartime Vietnam), and now 1969 (Africa).

The travel routine followed patterns of past adventures with unique Africanisms thrown in. Mac, who used to take, compile, and write up his own notes on trips, now consigned these duties to secretary Mildred Hagerty as he had Ralph Watkins on the Vietnam tour. The group was greeted and hosted by ambassadors and representatives—at times African, sometimes American. This depended somewhat on the political stability. In Nigeria, for example, American representatives had been withdrawn due to a recent military coup. In addition, usually hovering in the background and offering a form of stability and modern hospitality as respite from often primitive conditions were representatives of ITT.

Calling Africa the "last frontier" and "a dark continent, consisting of many more black people than white ones," and noting that "the origin of the Negro is as obscure as that of the Chinese," the trip journal reveals anticipation, nervousness, and ambiguity about this visit to unfamiliar lands and people. Hagerty meticulously investigated the history and politics of each country as well as its economic basis in products ranging from crops to flowers, from finished goods to raw minerals and tourism.

The threesome, including Edna, wove some common threads through these diverse countries. McFarland visited chief justices in Kenya, Ghana, and Tanzania, and judges in South Africa. ITT stood at hand and hosted in Kenya, Nigeria, South Africa, Rhodesia, and Ethiopia, while U.S. ambassadors attended to the group in Congo and Tanzania and a small state dinner was arranged in Rhodesia. The judge observed opposite extremes in apartheid South Africa and Rhodesia as contrasted to communist influenced Tanzania, which headquartered the "Black Conquest of Africa" movement. This group controlled the government and advocated two major goals: internal development and "liberation" of South Africa. Here the U.S. Peace Corps had been phased out and Russians, Chinese, and East Germans were prominent. Hagerty's perceptive eyes and ears collected information ranging from the fifty percent death rate among children under five to the absence of miniskirts (which abounded in Kenya). A brief excursion to the island of Zanzibar, "where actual abolishment of slavery wasn't until the

1900s," allowed McFarland and company to thrill to the Indian Ocean, "fish, dolphin, and shark jumping all over," as he had to the Pacific in the 1930s. They observed no draft animals of any kind in Ghana and Congo because of the deadly Tetsi fly infestation. Men carried supplies on their backs and pulled carts, and everywhere in Africa, mothers carried babies from turbans wrapped around their heads.

In Kenya the group was treated to its most frequent observations of animals in the wild: elephants, rhinos, zebra, giraffe, waterbuck, hartebeest, dik dik, impala, warthogs, baboons, bushback, and dozens of species of monkeys. Here, too, Hagerty's "earring thermometers" registered highs in the nineties. Crossing from Rhodesia to Zambia, the McFarlands observed Victoria Falls, "the largest curtain of falling water in the world." In Zambia, the group visited the native village of Chief Matumi, one of seventy-one villages he ruled with an iron hand and where he procured some of his many wives for a price of "ten cows each." In Ethiopia, Hagerty reported an alarming eighty percent rate of venereal disease but little insanity. And so it went from country to country.

Perhaps South Africa provided the most varied observations, Judge McFarland noting that both it and Rhodesia stood in disfavor with the United States because of their apartheid policies. He also remembered well that change took time, and it was only five years earlier that his own United States supported a racist system of segregation in the southern states. The contrasts here were striking. The McFarlands attended the "Miners' Dances at the Gold Mine thrown for five thousand Bantu miners, while the five hundred white employees danced separately. They also visited a diamond mine where one pound of the precious stone was extracted for each twenty million pounds of discarded dirt, an astounding ratio. Amidst the heavy Dutch influence and the near visible ghost of Cecil Rhodes, the travelers attended a Rotary International meeting, toured the home of golfer Gary Player, and noticed the near complete absence of television. McFarland also recognized South Africa as a "police state" where a person could be jailed as frequently as necessary for up to 180 days without being charged and where a "brainwashing" radio program called "Current Affairs" broadcast every morning at 7:30 A.M.

The trip concluded in Ethiopia where Haile Selassie still precariously clung to his near half-century of rule and where the McFarland's were wined and dined at 8,200 feet in Addis Ababa by both ITT and the American Embassy the last two days of their African sojourn. A weary judge and his wife and secretary then returned stateside where Mac would resume judicial duties on a changing Supreme Court.[19]

A major change had come to the court with the addition of Republican Judge Jack D. H. Hays. In the November 1968 elections, he had swept Charles Bernstein out of the position amidst controversial charges that the court harbored secret records. In a bid to enhance his election, Hays, of the Maricopa County Superior Court, challenged "talk about the great diligence and work of our Supreme Court." Appearing before the Yavapai County GOP Women's Club, he asked, "where are the statistics and reports to back it up?" Specifically he referred to the court's allegation that it had been working overtime, as it had, to cut down backlog cases. Hays termed these absent statistical reports "secret and not available to the public."[20]

There was some truth in Hays's allegation, but Chief Justice McFarland had attempted to dispell it. Apparently in 1967 and 1968, *Arizona Republic* reporters were denied seeing some requested records on the basis of their confidentiality. Now a letter from McFarland and Vice Chief Jesse Udall and an individual statement by Bernstein denied the allegations, McFarland stating, "I think they should be public. If you want to see them, I see no reason why you shouldn't have them." His letter said the records "are available and have always been available to the public during business hours." Still discrepancies existed with past requests, and now when reporters asked again to see the records, they were told that they had to be released by Chief Justice McFarland who was then in Washington.[21]

The entire matter blew over and in a sense was resolved

by Hays' victory over Bernstein. The issue had all the appearances of a typical Pulliam press ploy to disparage Democrats, and it is highly probable the press knew that McFarland was in Washington on violence commission business when his signature for release was required. To be fair, the *Republic* did print a later editorial stipulating that Arizona had kept much more current than other states, and that the "effort to discredit . . . has probably boomeranged." Yet planting these thoughts in the public mind could not help the liberal Bernstein and resembled Shadegg-style practices of earlier years. In any case, Hays gained election and had immediate impact on the court.[22]

Hays influenced an early 1969 case that cost Democratic State Auditor Jewell Jordan her position and eliminated the position as well. In late December 1968, Chief Justice McFarland wrote a three-two decision that allowed Jordan to retain her job—months later, that decision was reversed when Bernstein's aye was replaced by Hays's nay.

The matter concerned two amendments to the state constitution that were adopted in the fall election when Hays triumphed over Bernstein. One abolished the office of state auditor, presumably at the behest of Republican Governor Jack Williams who won a second term that fall. Williams had previously ousted one-term Democrat Sam Goddard in 1966. The second amendment extended from two to four years many state offices including those of governor and auditor.

McFarland, backed by Democrats Bernstein and Lockwood, found the two amendments in conflict. In such a case the Arizona Constitution requires the one with the most supportive votes to supersede the other. Here, the extension in office received 266,035 votes to 206,432 for that abolishing the auditor position. Moreover, Jordan, who had held office for eighteen years, ran unopposed on the ballot and received 275,954 votes.

While McFarland's opinion may have been technically defensible, it was also manifest that the large majority of Arizona voters did want to abolish the office of state auditor. Attorney General Gary Nelson, representing the state for Governor

Williams, had the case referred back to the Supreme Court knowing that the new vote of Justice Hays would overturn Mac's opinion. McFarland dissented "bitterly," being concerned with poor precedents being set: "no new arguments were made by the attorney general and the rehearing was based solely on the change in membership of the court." He was correct, but the protest was to no avail. It had all the appearances of a no win situation anyhow since the mandate of the people clearly wanted to abolish the position. It also appeared to be another set-up to embarrass sitting Democrats; such was Arizona politics.[23]

New Justice Hays had a further positive impact on the court in making the tribunes work all the harder. McFarland picked up on the challenge of Hays' work ethic, having already been used to overtime and extra exertion. In fact, the previous year 1968, before Hays's arrival, while chief justice, and while serving on the violence commission and federal loan board, marked Mac's highest single year so far for opinions - sixty-five in all; in 1969 and 1970, he topped that churning out sixty-six and sixty-seven. As stated earlier, Justice Struckmeyer had noted that Mac always worked to be ahead in numbers but never sacrificed quality for quantity. Hays ironically respected McFarland, though they sat at different political poles. He related Mac "dominated without dominating and he disagreed without being disagreeable."[24]

During his final court years, McFarland handled some important cases and wrote decisions of import and fairness. In June 1969, he wrote the final decision paving the way for the Phoenix Civic Center, a project for which he had written opinions in 1965 and 1966. In this instance, McFarland supported the Civic Center Corporation in enjoining the Maricopa County Superior Court from hearing further suits brought against it. This established once and for all the legitimacy of the agreement for Phoenix to use excise taxes and rentals from leasing the downtown auditorium in order to pay back construction costs. The Phoenix Civic Plaza Building Corporation could now call for bonds.[25]

In an earlier important case from December 1968,

McFarland had validated the procedure of plea-bargaining in *State v. Jennings*. In this case, the defendant pled not guilty to eight charges for which he had a prior record; then, after five of the charges were dropped, he pled guilty to those remaining. The legal question concerned acceptance of the guilty plea under these circumstances. McFarland opined, yes. According to Stanford Law School Dean, Charles Meyers, McFarland "openly confronted, discussed, and affirmed the practice of plea-bargaining, rather than evading the issue and leaving prosecutors and trial attorneys unsure of the constitutionality of the practice."[26]

Sometimes, McFarland's dissents were observed as more important in the legal world. In the 1970 case, *Streenz v. Streenz*, the court had legitimated the right of a minor child to sue the parents, thus overturning previous Arizona law. McFarland, supported by Jesse Udall, here upheld the integrity of family structure over the single child's rights, warning against adverse effects for overall family unity and society in general. Former legal aide John Flood termed this decision "a very humanitarian exposition of the relationship between the strict guidelines of the law and the personal feelings of every judge."[27]

In *Jarvis v. State Land Dept., City of Tucson* (1969), McFarland continued his half-century of water law interpretation, this time dealing with protection of scarce water resources from allocation by a city. He stipulated that water rights must be purchased in advance and not be compensated for later.[28]

McFarland put a new twist on freedom of speech, upholding the principle while contending that people also had a right to be free of its abuses in *Arizona v. Starsky* (1970). Additionally several of his cases helped shape definitions of legal insanity, while others dealt with aid to education, taxation policies, and insurance. Two of his final cases from October 1970 involving automobile insurance were widely published in legal circles throughout the nation, and overall his decisions were frequently cited in other opinions throughout the country.[29]

In the spring of 1970, Ernest McFarland had made the

decision to end his lengthy half-century career of public service. In his six years as justice and chief justice he had written over 320 opinions, some of national import, and easily the highest number among his colleagues during that time. Newspapers, including those that had worked strongly against him for much of his career, published accolades on his "graceful exit," both when the April announcement came out and in December immediately before his official January 4, 1971, resignation. Attorney W. Francis Wilson wrote, "You are indeed the greatest justice our court has ever known."[30]

McFarland accepted the encomiums with typical humility, noting that he was "leaving office, not retiring." He cited great satisfaction at having nearly eliminated the court's backlog of cases and putting it on a current basis, and looked forward to re-embracing his law practice, television responsibilities, and farm and family life. Asked by reporter Bernie Wynn the secret of his success, he replied, "I always make it a point to enjoy my work no matter what." Edna elaborated, "It's because he could never hold a grudge no matter what."[31]

As his departure from the court loomed near on New Year's Eve 1970, McFarland reflected on a variety of issues including the war still raging in Vietnam: "The United States always has had a way of solving its problems. Maybe the solutions weren't always 100 percent satisfactory, but . . . we always came out . . . on the right side. I feel that, God willing, we'll do it again." On law and order he thought campus unrest diminishing in the wake of the Kent and Jackson State killings in 1970, when hundreds of colleges ended their spring terms early in response to the tragedies. Mac believed and hoped "positive action" would take hold over unrest. He stressed individual effort over government aid and particularly opportunity for education to solve the nation's economic woes. Reflecting on his own career, he offered that "in order to succeed you either have got to be a little bit smarter or work a lot harder. . . . I always figured I wasn't smarter, so I always worked harder."[32]

Friends and colleagues would have agreed with this assessment, Mildred Hagerty remembering, "Mac didn't think or let on that he had a bright brain but his dedication, hard work, and loyalty were remarkable." Attorney Mark Wilmer when asked three words to describe McFarland, summed him up with "Humility, fairness, and integrity . . . absolute confidence and trust." John Moran regarded him as "in the August of his years with no more mountains to climb and no more political peaks to achieve . . . kind, gentlemanly, and he loved the law and loved and enjoyed people." Stanford Dean Charles Meyers wrote "To say Ernest W. McFarland has left a lasting mark on the interpretation and application of the law in Arizona is indeed an understatement. His well-reasoned opinions, personal integrity, and years of exemplary public service have set standards for all judges, lawyers, and politicians to ascribe to." Justice Struckmeyer said of his colleague and friend, "Mac was a man of firm convictions and from these he worked aggressively to accomplish goals; his outlooks and views and actions were reflections of his morals; he was fundamentally a person in touch with what the people ordinarily felt and their needs and that comes from his background." He concluded:

> He brought with him an awesome knowledge of government from the township level to the level of the Executive of the U.S. and all stops in between. . . . He could relate to the average citizen even in a complex legal case. . . . Mac was versatile - going from legal purist to a sympathetic and understanding jurist. He had an art - a feel for justice - not easily matched. The judicial system of the State of Arizona is fortunate that Mac passed our way.

Upon leaving public office for the last time, McFarland reflected: "You just have to keep going and that is what I hope to do."[33]

CHAPTER EIGHTEEN

THE AUTUMN
OF HIS YEARS
1971—1984

As Ernest W. McFarland looked forward to retirement from public life, he had no intention of slowing down. Rather he would concentrate on the private things that always stood in place behind his public duties: television, the law practice, and the farms. He had always embraced his family, but now there would be even more time for it, a pleasant prospect. Additionally, he began to take an active interest in history, both his own and that of his hometown Florence. At first, Mac barely broke stride after leaving the bench, engaging himself on these many fronts, but eventually as the 1970s closed, he faced and was tempered by the physical incapacities of old age and illness. McFarland's later years can be essentially divided in three; from 1971 to 1976, he continued an active constructive life, still contributing to society in a myriad of ways. From then until about 1981, however, his activity was seriously cut back after brain surgery in 1977. Still he maintained enough vigor and presence to write and publish his autobiography *Mac* in 1979. During the final years from 1982 to 1984, he steadily deteriorated, but for the most part he remained lucid and somewhat mobile with a wheelchair, while at the same time being essentially incapacitated and needing constant assistance. In his last months, he sometimes lost touch with his immediate surroundings, though these phases seldom persisted more than a few minutes.

McFarland's first major activities of the 1970s lay in reaping the rewards that awaited him in recognition on his lengthy public service. He did so with customary humility. Within weeks of his retirement party in the court chambers, his small hometown proposed to honor him with a name change from Florence to McFarland. The proposal, emanating from the chamber of commerce, noted the inappropriateness of the original name in the first place; in 1868, Territorial Governor Richard McCormack had been asked to assign a name to the small settlement that had been growing for two years on the banks of the Gila. He decided to name the village after his sister, who had recently died in Cincinnati, Ohio. She had never been to the West. Mac "scotched" the proposal, telling the chamber "Thanks, but forget it. Florence is a place rich in Arizona history." Indeed it was, and if the original name seemed detached, it had, at least, been the name now for over a century, and that alone in McFarland's mind would preclude the name change. He similarly stopped a real estate firm from naming a new subdivision McFarland Heights. He would eventually gain name recognition in his hometown, but it would be in his own fashion and at his own choosing.[1]

Casa Grande, the town where he had begun his law practice in 1920, too, rolled out the red carpet. At the Francisco Grande resort on February 17, over a hundred state and county officials honored him at a testimonial dinner, eliciting Congressman Morris Udall's comment: "There are few people who could bring so many prominent Democrats and Republicans into one room." Indeed, although Mac had worked strongly for Democratic candidate Raul Castro during the election of 1970, victorious Governor Jack Williams, now entering a third term, attended and was effusive in his praise. Messages from LBJ and Barry Goldwater adorned the affair.[2]

Just two weeks before, Udall had spoken in the House of Representatives on McFarland's retirement, calling it a "bittersweet occasion, well deserved, but much lamented." Udall read into the record excerpts from the *Phoenix Gazette*, the *Arizona Daily Star*, and the Florence *Blade-Reminder*, which looked forward to Mac's being around town more often where three more grandchildren had been added to the family of Del and Jewell Lewis.[3]

Mac did continue to maintain a residence in Florence and maintain a voice in town and Pinal County affairs. Never again, however, was he to be a county or at-large delegate to a national convention. The real draw for Mac in Florence was the farm and, of course, the children. By 1971, Kara was seventeen, Billy-fourteen, Johnny-eleven, Leah-five, and Del, Jr.-four. In these years before his surgery, he was an active grandpa, quickly learning to replace some of his former workaholic tendencies with more leisurely pursuits. The grandchildren fashioned much of this change as did frequent football game excursions to both Arizona State and the University of Arizona, sometimes two in one day. The farm, too, provided a relaxing, constructive, project. Every weekend he would drive down from Phoenix and the Royal Palm residence to once more go over the books and check the machinery with Del and then yet again head out to the fields of grapes, cotton, alfalfa, and wheat with a grandchild or two in tow.

McFarland kept his law practice active at his office in the television station at Sixteenth Street and Osborne. It was a truncated practice, however, as he concentrated mostly on advising for the station's legal affairs and drawing up wills and contracts for friends. Over time, uncashed checks gathered dust in his desk.

He came to his offices each weekday but concentrated more on station affairs than law, and KTVK-TV rapidly expanded during these years. As the ABC affiliate carved out a spot in Phoenix and moved up the ratings to eventual number one status, the operation expanded in many ways. The building grew larger with an added second story; in 1976, Arizona Television purchased a new half-million dollar transmitter, and by 1977, Mac had concentrated full control of the enterprise into the family. He had always controlled forty percent of the stock personally, but during these years, he bought the remainder from former partners Watkins, Nowell, Bibolet,

Cooper, and Larson. He paid high prices, added large insurance policies to the purchase, and only in the case of Larson was there some objection. Overall it was an amicable concentration with Del Lewis retaining his own smaller share.[4]

Along with his many other tributes, McFarland received recognition for his service to broadcasting in 1975 with the Copper Mike, awarded to an Arizonan who had made an outstanding contribution to broadcasting in the state. In 1970, the award had been given first to Governor Jack Williams, long a broadcaster for radio station KOY. Local television comedians Wallace and Ladmo and Pat McMahon had received the honor the year before Mac in 1974. Among others connected to broadcasting, Eugene Pulliam, publisher of the *Republic* and *Gazette* indirectly purveyed enough influence about the state to gain the award in 1973. Now the man who had been his foremost political enemy of the preceding three decades stood beside him. Surely McFarland, author of the Communications Act of 1952 and founder of a locally owned and operated television station, was deserving of this accolade, something that could not be said so much for Pulliam whose broadcast credentials were suspect. But, with Mac out of politics, and Pulliam mellowing with years, the two old combatants found it prudent to be mannerly and comfortable around each other. Indeed, McFarland's service to broadcasting and communications received national attention. Congratulatory telegrams arrived from Lady Bird Johnson, a communications mogul herself, John McCormack, and Milton Eisenhower and Leon Jaworski, colleagues on the violence commission. Jaworski, too, had recently been in the national spotlight for his role in directing the Watergate investigations, which resulted in President Richard Nixon's 1974 resignation. Arizona's first Hispanic governor, Raul Castro, whom McFarland had supported in 1974, also attended the ceremonies, which saw Mac review his career in communications from his initial efforts in the telegraph merger of 1943 to the present. The Copper Mike Award also marked a transition for Mac at the station. The day before, he had turned over the presidential reins of the company to Del Lewis. Mac remained chairman of the board, but his role in the day-to-day operations diminished to a degree.[5]

The 1975 Copper Mike just capped a continually growing list of awards dating back to 1971. When that year's "Greater Arizona" awards were handed out by Greater Arizona Savings and Loan, McFarland stood amongst an eclectic group of recipients which included comedian Dick Van Dyke, racecar driver Roger McClusky, Big Surf, "the world's first authentic inland surfing operation," and McCulloch Corporation which had brought the London Bridge to Lake Havasu stone by stone from its original Thames River moorings. A more unique award was earlier presented to Mac by the Arizona American Legion. Believing he was to be the keynote speaker for the 1971 annual convention in Yuma as he had been many times before, he found the tables turned as the Legion honored him as the first recipient of its new Distinguished Service Award. He used the occasion to tell the audience that his law and order and anti-violence stance stood firmly in line with that of the Nixon administration. On this occasion, he received telegrams from Nixon, Truman, and Johnson.[6]

McFarland also sounded a similar theme when interviewed by the *Tucson Daily Citizen*, but he hesitated to blame violence on a generation gap. Rather, he blamed this, the nation's worst problem as he saw it, on a "work" gap and overly permissive parents. He urged community programs as solutions.

In this first major interview after retirement, McFarland also expressed his preference for elective over appointive offices, including judges and justices. He believed that the proliferation of appointed boards and commissions indicated a second major problem in America, the growing movement of the government away from the electorate. Similarly, he deplored the spending of huge amounts of campaign money to get "amateurs" elected by "Madison Avenue Boys." As a career politician, he naturally resented negative stereotypes about his trade, choosing usually to counter them with Truman's motto that "a statesman is nothing but a dead politician."

Mac closed the interview with some conclusions on those

he had associated with, calling Truman an "affable man, but he was a practical politician, a professional in the best sense of the word." He termed LBJ, the hardest working president "partly because he was ambitious and a slave driver. But his record in domestic matters was unparalleled." Asked whom he considered the greatest senators, he rattled off the names of Republican Bob Taft and Democrats Tom Connally, Richard Russell, and Arizona's own Carl Hayden.[7]

As this first year of retirement wore on, Mac faced an upcoming seventy-seventh birthday, and big doings were scheduled. Governor Williams and Phoenix Mayor John Driggs both proclaimed October 9, 1971, "Ernest McFarland Appreciation Day," the first time the city had ever honored an individual. Co-chairmen Ralph Watkins and John Moran supervised the preparations for the dinner at Del Webb's Townhouse. Twelve hundred people showed up for the affair, setting up another Morris Udall quip that only Mac could draw that many on the same night the London Bridge was being "re-dedicated" at Lake Havasu.[8]

The governor, mayor, and the entire state supreme court turned out, as well as many legislators of both parties who came in response to an invitation from the state senate chambers by Yuma's Harold Giss. Prominent Arizonans decorated the honorary committee list: Sam Goddard, Howard Pyle, Dan Garvey, Evo DeConcini, Walter Bimson, Frank Snell, and Kemper Marley. Many former associates pitched in to make it a gala affair — Mildred Hagerty, Edna McDonald, and Tom Fulbright. The committees produced an opulent printed program containing a brief history and telegrams from President Nixon and former presidents Johnson and Truman, and KTVK-TV debuted a thirty-minute feature, *Arizona's Mac: A Tribute to Ernest W. McFarland*, drawn from news archives. As William Lawrence of ABC moderated, the twelve hundred enjoyed their prime rib and the evening unfolded as an enjoyable tribute. Throughout the festivities, additional telegrams were read from Barry Goldwater and Paul Fannin and Democrats Speaker of the House Carl Albert of Oklahoma and Senate Majority Leader Mike Mansfield of Montana. Hubert Humphrey wired "you will always be my leader," and Carl Hayden recalled his association as one of his richest and most rewarding. Fred Struckmeyer remembered, "Mac's car was usually there when I left the office. He fought hard for the poor and oppressed and usually won." Lorna Lockwood referred to him simply as "Mac the Great," and the normally antagonistic *Phoenix Gazette* uncharacteristically grouped Mac with its own state hall of fame — a select group limited to Hayden, George Hunt, Padre Kino, Zane Grey, World War I ace Frank Luke, Spanish-American War hero Bucky O'Neill, and now McFarland.

Finally Mac, himself, arose and gave his thanks while urging Arizonans to "help turn science and mankind away from destruction and on to a path of building a world for all." And, he concluded, "In the next ten years, I want to help you build a better and greater Arizona."

McFarland's initial spree of post-retirement rewards was topped off in May 1973 when Arizona State University awarded him an honorary doctorate. Mac, of course, had been instrumental when governor in supporting university status for the former Arizona State College at Tempe, and he obtained funding for construction of the original first level of Sun Devil Stadium. The ASU degree now joined that of the University of Arizona's honorary doctorate he had received in 1950 and his own degrees from East Central State College of Oklahoma, the University of Oklahoma, and two from Stanford. Honored along with McFarland was internationally known architect Paolo Soleri who, in his field of arcology or human ecology-urban development, was in the early construction stages of the experimental community Arcosanti midway between Phoenix and Flagstaff.[9]

Indeed, Mac paid close attention to furthering education in those institutions that had served him and also those of his state. In 1971-72, he played a twofold role in assisting his first alma mater, East Central in Ada, Oklahoma. Over the fifty-six years since Mac's graduation, East Central had risen from a two-year normal school to an emerging state university,

and in 1971, the college invited him to deliver the commencement address, while at the same time being honored with its
"Distinguished Alumnus" award, to be presented by the college
for the third time on the July 30, 1971. This was a summer ceremony restricted to about one hundred graduate students
receiving Master's degrees as well as an equal number of bachelor's recipients. The first awardee the previous summer had
been former Librarian of Congress Edmon Law, while at the
Spring 1971 commencement, Paul Hughes, a Phoenix television personality had been so honored. Ironically, Hughes
would later emcee McFarland's Copper Mike Award in 1975.[10]

In his address, McFarland blended historical analysis
and personal anecdote, urging his listeners to learn from past
successes and failures, to detect those of the present, and to better prepare for the future. He mixed innocent memories of the
stirrup-high prairie grasses of his Oklahoma youth with memories of experience drawn from World War II and Korea. He did
not mention the ongoing tragedy in Vietnam. He did, though,
draw on the violence report in urging youth to keep focused on
studies: "an idle brain is the devil's workshop."[11]

McFarland enjoyed himself immensely on this return
trip to his native state, revisiting Earlsboro and other ancient
haunts and old friends. Nineteen seventy-one marked a good
year for Mac's birthplace; Earlsboro's other nationally known
native by birth, Willie Stargell, led baseball's major leagues in
home runs and, along with Roberto Clemente, led the Pittsburgh
Pirates to victory in the World Series, activities that old baseball
fan McFarland certainly followed (see chap 1, note 6). After visiting Earlsboro, Mac presented the feature address at the annual
Old Settlers' Reunion in Seminole where he had "batched it" as
a high school junior in the early days of the twentieth century.
He renewed old acquaintances at the Petroleum Club in
Oklahoma City where he accompanied Oklahoma Governor J.
Howard Edmondson and Governor of Colorado John A. Love.
In these appearances and speeches, he stressed the future: "Our
lives have just begun. We will see many great things yet. We
have many things yet to do. . . . Let us never quit."[12]

For nearly a decade, East Central University had been planning for a health, physical education, and activities center on campus dedicated to the memory of Mac's old senate colleague and East Central classmate, Robert S. Kerr. Kerr had died in 1963, and since that time fundraising had proceeded for the one million dollar center. The fall after McFarland's visit, East Central President Stanley P. Wagner and Oklahoma City banker Jack Conn launched a drive to secure the final one hundred thousand dollars necessary for construction. The Kerr Foundation came up with a fifty thousand dollar challenge to be matched by alumni donors, and after "several" thousand dollars of small gifts had been received, Wagner appealed to McFarland for assistance, noting that East Central's status as a public, state institution appeared to have dried up additional donors. McFarland generously responded. Although, it is not known precisely how much he gave, his name was ultimately included in the half-dozen or so people who made a "special" contribution to the Robert S. Kerr Activities Center. Wagner wrote Mac that his contribution "restored my faith in mankind."[13]

A year later in 1972, McFarland also remembered the schools of his adopted state, the University of Arizona, Arizona State, Northern Arizona, and Grand Canyon College. To each, he presented an endowed scholarship of one hundred thousand dollars, the interest from which would be used to support new students annually. He presented similar gifts to Stanford University and the University of Oklahoma as well as contributing to a Stanford building campaign.[14] As Mac expressed satisfaction at his continuing role in education, he ruminated on even bigger plans for Stanford Law School, but developments in his old hometown Florence beckoned.

By the spring of 1974, the nation was starting to crank up for its bicentennial celebration of independence. Quite suddenly, communities across the land began to feel an exciting, vibrant sense of history. Old buildings came to be appreciated for their uniqueness or for how they symbolized the American dream. Local or nearby historic sites were tied into proud

American traditions of liberty, freedom, and prosperity. Florence was swept up in the excitement, and McFarland became interested in its efforts to reflect the spirit of the Bicentennial, an undertaking well suited to the leaders of one of the oldest Arizona towns. Mayor Joseph O'Betka had led the way in preparing for preservation and restoration efforts by hiring Harris Sobin and Associates of Tucson to conduct a historic study of the town's buildings, architecture, streets, and irrigation canals. Sobin, a professor at the University of Arizona, strongly confirmed Florence's historicity in his research, and O'Betka obtained additional funding from the National Endowment for the Humanities.

The original Pinal County Courthouse, constructed in 1877, stood as a centerpiece among several promising buildings in exemplifying the restorative potential of a Florence downtown historic district. Vacant since it had last served as a county welfare office in 1970, the building had been placed up for auction for restoration purposes only. It was to be condemned and demolished if no buyers could be found, but in 1972, the town entered into negotiations with Mildred Woodruff who agreed to purchase and restore the old courthouse for eight thousand dollars. Unfortunately, neither her well-intentioned plans nor her funding developed expeditiously, and in early 1974, the sale was invalidated and the building once again faced the auction block or demolition.[15]

At this stage, McFarland entered the picture. Having joined the Pinal County Historical Society shortly before, he certainly had heard of the preservation project and the building's plight. Mac began to envision the old structure as suitable for housing his own memorabilia, papers, and books, as well as other appropriate holdings.

At a July auction, McFarland stood as the sole bidder for the ninety-seven-year-old structure, offering the minimum eight thousand dollars (the appraised amount for the property) and paying one thousand dollars down. Although, he professed no immediate plan except for the effort to preserve and upgrade, he did say he did not want to found another museum to compete with the Pinal County Historical Society's new facility several blocks up Main Street. Indeed, for a long time, the old courthouse had itself served as the county history museum from 1952 to 1963, but it had a much older history than that. Built in 1877, the building had served as the courthouse until 1891, undoubtedly its most colorful historic period. Territorial judges decreed there and county jailers carried out their duties, including executions, in the courtyard where early prisoners were chained to a huge boulder before a proper jail was constructed. Even this new jail fell victim, though, to intrusion. In 1889, former Union Civil War spy Pauline Cushman assisted the jailer in successfully warding off a mob bent on lynching four inmates suspected of murder. In the same period, a couple of stagecoach robbers who killed a passenger in the nearby hills were not so lucky and were strung up from the jailhouse interior rafters by an enraged mob.

In 1891, the current Pinal County Courthouse opened its doors and it remains the oldest active public building in Arizona. At this juncture, the older courthouse commenced nearly a half-century as a hospital. Mac's own life had intertwined with this stage of the building's history in a sad traumatic way, for it was in this hospital that his three children and wife endured, suffered, and died in the tragic two-year period 1929-30, now a distant but still troubling memory. In 1939, the hospital closed with construction of a new facility, and the old building then became a nursing home for the elderly, continuing as such until these occupants, too, removed to more modern habitations. The period as historical museum and welfare office followed until the edifice closed in 1970. With Mac's purchase after four years of debilitating vacancy, restoration promised a new future. But it would not come easily; the tumbleweed and desert scrub-filled 125-foot lot and building with crumbling porch, disintegrating roof, cracked walls, and broken windows presented a formidable challenge to McFarland as he planned for its restoration.[16]

Barry Goldwater numbered among the first to applaud McFarland's efforts at historical preservation, sending congratulations and a one hundred dollar donation. Arizona newspapers joined with more praise when Mac finally decided upon the most prudent course to take regarding completion of the project.[17]

In December 1974, at a small ceremony attended by about forty people in front of the worn building, McFarland presented the deed to the property to Arizona State Parks Director Dennis McCarthy, an appropriate gift from the man who had himself been instrumental in founding the state park system seventeen years earlier in 1957. In turn, McCarthy presented Mac and Edna the Certificate of Entry for the building in the National Register of Historic Places. Mac now envisioned the new state park as a place not only to store and display the records and mementos of his own career but also to celebrate and symbolize Arizona's territorial days, commenting that the building "stands as an example of the ability and character of the people who built it.[18]

In transferring the historic site to state parks, McFarland backed up his gift with a trust fund established for future restoration and maintenance and to complement a federal preservation grant. With the fund and grant, McCarthy announced an eighteen-month reconstruction and stabilization plan to begin in February marking the county's centennial. McFarland also now began to piece together an advisory board, a private group to work in conjunction with state parks in making recommendations for the use of the new facility. The McFarland Historical State Park Advisory Committee (MHSPAC) counted among its original members Florence Mayor Joseph O'Betka, Pinal County Superior Court Judge T.J. Mahoney, Della Meadows of the Pinal County Historical Society, Arizona State University Professor of History William W. Phillips, Del and Jewell Lewis, and old friends and assistants Tony Jones, Roland Bibolet, Mildred Hagerty, and Edna McDonald. Soon the presidents of all three Arizona universities enrolled along with noted educator J. Wallace Sterling, Chancellor of Stanford University.[19]

McFarland State Park was off and running, and, as the restoration proceeded, the old building began to yield up new stories and interesting facets of the past. These ranged from the macabre, the suicide of seven Apache Indians in the jail, to the ministerial, the records of Florence's first Protestant services held in the courtroom. The building's roots could be traced to Florence's founder, Colonel Levi Ruggles. Ruggles, who surveyed and laid out the town site drew up the plans for the courthouse in 1877 for a fee of twenty-five dollars. Pinal County purchased the north end lot overlooking the distant Gila River for eleven hundred dollars and then accepted a construction bid for twenty-seven hundred dollars in November. By March of 1878, the entire structure was complete consisting of courtroom, jury room, sheriff's office, jail, and three other offices for the assessor, secretaries, and county clerk. The sprawling, covered porch, extending around all sides of the L-shaped building, was added later in the hospital era, at which time an extra front ward was added as well, along with a second story nurses quarters over the earlier jail. Such was the building that McFarland set out to restore, but it was not to be completed before major complications interrupted Mac's active retirement life.

In the mid-1970s, to most it seemed that Ernest McFarland was virtually indestructible. Upon reaching eighty years, he appeared healthy, robust, and at ease. And with an eye toward current clothing styles and a tincture of dye for the grey hair of three decades, he even appeared younger than years earlier. Retirement seemed most salubrious for the octagenerian, but reminders of mortality constantly loomed. Harry Truman, the president with whom he had worked most closely, passed away in 1971 at the age of ninety.

Closer to home, the most noted politician in the history of Arizona, Carl Hayden, died on January 25, 1972, at the age of ninety-four. Upon his 1969 retirement, Hayden had served the state as a legislator on Capitol Hill for a still-existing record fifty-seven years, a period of time beginning with Arizona statehood and encompassing forty-two years in the Senate and fifteen in the House. Perhaps his most productive years were the twelve spent at McFarland's side when the two obtained the highest per-capita appropriations of any state in the union and patiently forged Arizona's strategy to Colorado River water, Hayden's last great triumph achieved in September 1968.

Now McFarland joined dignitaries from all over the nation as twenty-five hundred gathered to honor Hayden in Arizona State University's Gammage Auditorium just blocks away from his birthplace in Tempe. A planeload arrived from Washington including Democratic Senators Frank Moss of Utah and Howard Cannon of Nevada. Old senate acquaintance Homer Ferguson of Michigan attended. Arizona Democrats paying respects included Congressman Morris Udall, former Governor Sam Goddard, State Supreme Court Justice Lorna Lockwood, Secretary of State Wesley Bolin, Hayden's former administrative assistant Roy Elson, and of course, McFarland, paying respects on behalf of himself and their mutual alma mater Stanford. The Republican party, in power both nationally and statewide, was as much in evidence with Senator Paul Fannin, Congressmen John Rhodes and Sam Steiger, Deputy Attorney General Richard Kleindienst, former Supreme Court Justice Jesse Udall, Governor Jack Williams, and publisher Eugene Pulliam. As the many gathered, Senator Goldwater "swooped down" on the ASU campus by helicopter to deliver a tearful tribute.

Former president, Lyndon Johnson, arrived at the auditorium with motorcycle escort to speak for fifteen minutes on the late senator who served as Maricopa County Sheriff when LBJ was born in 1909. Johnson termed Hayden "the nation's senator . . . the third senator from every state" and concluded "he stood tall and straight before many generations of his fellowmen," ending with a Texas tribute: "Now that he is gone, he leaves a lonesome spot against the sky."

After the ceremonies, McFarland joined his former whip in the Palm Garden of the Hayden home as he and LBJ "swapped" reminiscences of past decades. Twelve months later LBJ, too, was dead at the relatively young age of sixty-four. The next year Lewis Douglas, born the same year as McFarland, died and in 1976, Mac's old, mellowing rival Eugene Pulliam passed away. Too, McFarland's immediate family had dwindled, younger brother Carl dying in 1970 and Sister Etta Pearl in 1972. Mac and Edna, though, continued their active ways as their friends passed on.[20]

In the mid-1970s, McFarland, too, began to endure occasional physical discomforts, spells of unknown origin. At times he experienced sudden headaches and on occasion grew somewhat irascible, unusual for one who had handled senate and gubernatorial challenges with consistent calm demeanor. He found little rest and relief as the hours saved by scaling back television, law, and farm responsibilities were consumed in the Florence projects which Mac and Edna jointly oversaw. Their days remained full.[21]

When not engaged in these various enterprises, they continued to enjoy traveling although this, too, was cut back from globetrotting to visitations throughout the United States. Edna meticulously reported on these in her Christmas letters. In 1976, for example, she wrote of four lengthy journeys: Nebraska in February to visit a sick aunt; West Virginia in May to meet new U. S. Senate Majority Leader Robert C. Byrd and Governor-elect John D. Rockefeller, IV; and the bottom of the Grand Canyon at Havasupi Falls in June. Here the McFarlands helicoptered down to the canyon floor and back up after four days of camping. Later the same month, the couple found themselves in Newport, Rhode Island, to visit the mansions and view the Tall Ships before heading to Washington, D.C. celebrations at the Smithsonian and Kennedy Center. The McFarlands then toured Monticello and Williamsburg to cap off the Bicentennial. In the midst of the 1976 campaign, Mac and Edna also managed to meet Ted Kennedy and the surging Jimmy Carter. Edna felt "sorry" for President Gerald Ford but applauded the change from the "Nixon regime."[22]

Back to work the next year in March 1977, McFarland at eighty-two was honored by the Arizona Supreme Court, which requested him to sit in for absent Justice Jack Hays. The court selected McFarland to write the opinion for *Arizona v.*

Overton based on his previous experience in dealing with the question of sanity. This opinion again proved important in further clarifying the definition of sanity or insanity, and like many McFarland opinions, *Overton* became widely referred to.

In this instance, Herbert Overton was apprehended for the August 1965 murder of a Maricopa County Deputy Sheriff who had confronted him regarding failure to pay taxes on his vehicle. Overton, too, was shot but not seriously wounded in the confrontation. After the arrest, medical examiners found him mentally incompetent to stand trial. There the situation remained for nearly a decade until May 1975 when Overton was deemed competent. At this juncture, the Maricopa County Superior Court found him guilty of second-degree murder. Upon appeal, McFarland overturned this decision, terming Overton not sane at the time of the murder, based in part on the earlier testimony of the medical examiners.

In making this reversal, McFarland declared that to be sane, a person must know both the nature and quality of his act and that it was morally wrong at the time of action. In 1965, the three psychiatrists acting as medical examiners testified that while Overton did know the nature and quality of the act, he did not know that it was morally wrong because of his mental condition. One of these reaffirmed his views before McFarland, as did another deputy sheriff, who in attempting earlier to collect the back tax had reported that Overton appeared mentally disturbed because of his nervous, trembling appearance, and the very small amount of money involved. Moreover, Overton had informed the deputy that "the Lord told him" he did not have to pay.

However, other acquaintances of Overton and law enforcement officers testified that he indeed seemed sane in relating the tax situation and shooting to them. McFarland set the precedent in this case by acknowledging that a jury can accept testimony as to sanity from lay witnesses only if they had an association with the accused of both significant intimacy and duration. Indeed, he continued, if this proved the case, lay testimony could even be used by the state to rebuke expert testimony. But, in *Overton*, McFarland declared that young

Attorney General Bruce Babbitt had failed to establish that the witnesses' relationships with Overton were sufficiently intimate and enduring. Therefore, the testimony of the expert witnesses must be upheld and the accused exonerated of the murder charge by reason of insanity. All of the justices concurred with McFarland's ruling including old friend Fred Struckmeyer, the only justice along with Hays still remaining from McFarland's court years.[23]

After this case, his last ruling, McFarland exchanged his judicial gown for the businessman's gray flannels and saw to the consolidation of Channel 3 ownership solely in his family. In June, he obtained approval from the Federal Communications Commission to buy out his partners for $5.91 million. Then the McFarlands broke for summer vacation, this time traveling in "deluxe pick-up camper trailer," the better to scout about the Southwest. They worked the bugs out of the vehicle and their routine on a "shake-down" cruise to Organ Pipe National Monument on the Mexican border. They then took a lengthy tour of the canyonlands, national parks, and monuments of southern Utah.[24]

Mac enjoyed this trip just as he had others for the past fifty years, but unfortunately, it was his last time at the wheel, their last long vacation, for his health continued to deteriorate. The "spells" were occurring more frequently. The headaches worsened and he began to adapt a hobbling gait where his left foot would often drag behind as he walked. Not surprisingly, his temper grew shorter as these debilitating attacks increased and lasted even longer. He continued to work, but finally had to admit himself to St. Joseph's Hospital, "seriously ill" with pain and exhaustion on July 13, 1977. Doctors called for rest and comprehensive testing. Two weeks of rest helped, but his condition did not improve significantly. Then the test results revealed the existence of a brain tumor, necessitating major surgery. On July 28, surgeons removed a saucer-sized section of his skull, took out the tumor, and replaced the bone with a plastic plate. McFarland's constitution readily absorbed this shock at age eighty-two, the tumor was benign, and he began a steady recovery returning home by summer's end. But after effects lingered.[25]

The ordeal dramatically changed Mac in some respects, certainly transforming his physical appearance. He had finally become a fragile, old man, having lost a great deal of weight and becoming more stooped and slower in his already slow gait. He now employed a cane and no longer sought out the fashionable suits and ties that he had preferred in early retirement. Too, he no longer tinted his hair a shade more youthful, allowing a crop of grey to white hair to again crown his appearance. Mac had finally accepted aging. He had no choice. He no longer exuded the physical presence of the workaholic public servant of the past. Yet, he tried to bear his age and condition with distinction in the manner of the venerable old statesman that he was. Mac remained the active, interested participant-observer, one acquiring new and deserved honors of distinction. Not surprisingly, the older man accepted these with active grace and even continued old and entered into new projects.

Stanford University led the way in keeping attention on McFarland after his illness. On November 14, 1977, the *Stanford Law Review* and Law School honored its 1922 alumnus at a meeting of the Maricopa Bar Association in Phoenix. Walter F. Craig, class of 1934, and chief judge of the U.S. District Court of Arizona presided and termed Mac "in Herbert Hoover's words, an uncommon man." Law school Dean Charles Meyers went further praising McFarland as Stanford Law School's "most distinguished alumnus in public service" reflecting "the virtues of self-reliance, hard work, education, and the highest standards of personal conduct." *Law Review* editors unanimously voted to dedicate the current issue of the journal to him, the first time an alumnus had been so honored. Senior Robin Johanson pointed out that the recognition stood not only for Mac's noted career, but also for his avid interest in the work of the school, for the students in particular, and via his generous gifts to Stanford in the 1970s: "he has been and continues to be an example." The university also kept a close eye on prospects for acquiring McFarland's personal and public papers.[26]

Three weeks later, McFarland returned to Florence for the formal dedication of McFarland Historical State Park. The original eighteen-month restoration schedule had been met, and the dedication had just awaited Mac's recuperation so he could be present. On December 4, about two hundred people attended the ceremonies, which featured Stanford Chancellor J. Wallace Sterling as the major speaker. Mac, too, spoke and made a friendly gesture toward Mexico and Hispanics in thanking the audience and by recognizing "two great nations who helped build this town and state. . . ." Old state capitol acquaintance Rose Mofford, who had risen to secretary of state, also spoke. Mac's wife and family, children, and grandchildren accompanied him around the grounds, observing the re-plastered walls and the new roof as Park Ranger John Swearengin and assistant Katie Montano patiently explained the underpinnings of the foundation. Approximately forty thousand dollars had been expended in bringing the century-old building once again to life in preparation for the formal opening.[27]

Characteristically, preservation efforts divided the Florence community, and some residents bemoaned being told what to do with their property by outside experts from the University of Arizona Architecture School or the National Trust for Historic Preservation. As a public building, both formerly and currently, McFarland Park stood apart from the commotion while at the same time symbolizing the historical drift. At the center of the controversy stood the proposed zoning agreement, which would divide the town into three historic districts-commercial, residential, and transistional-between the two. Florence had long been an economically recessed area and many residents lived in trailer homes. New rules would eliminate replacements or additions, eventually ridding the area of trailers. This concerned only the historic area, however, but many believed this to be too large.[28]

McFarland threw his weight behind the history-oriented group, and indeed extended his interests beyond the park building to another structure, the John Clum House, about one hundred yards up a side alley from the park. With its sloped tin roof and thick adobe walls, it represented yet another style of territorial architecture vanishing from Arizona but still abundant in Florence. Mac bought the old home, refurbished it, in part with National Register funding, and planned it for practical and personal use. Mac and Edna still resided in Phoenix at their Royal Palm Lane home of over twenty years, but since Del Lewis had taken over the active presidency of the television station, he, Jewell, and their children not in college, had moved from the Florence farm to Mesa. The main farmhouse and its adjacent cottage house were now occupied by tenants who continued to work the farm. McFarland thus used the Clum House, as did Del and Jewell, as their Florence residence.

John Clum possessed his own unique niche in Arizona history. Born in 1851 and a Rutgers graduate, the young man came to the desert Southwest in the 1870s to act as agent to the Apache Indians on their desolate one-year-old reservation at San Carlos. Under the auspices of the Dutch Reformed Church, Clum proved an innovative agent, troublesome to the United States Army, which exerted nominal control. Among Clum's accomplishments was the organization of the Apache police, but when the army flexed its administrative muscles beyond Clum's tolerance, he resigned his position. He then studied law and after his admittance to the bar entered newspaper publishing, moving to Florence in October 1877 and founding the *Arizona Citizen*, Pinal County's first newspaper. In 1878, he built his home even as the old courthouse was being completed down the street. McFarland purchased it as both structures attained the century mark.

After spending just a brief time in Florence, Clum moved on with the paper to Tucson where it became Arizona's first daily. In 1880, he moved to Tombstone, then at the height of its reputation as a wide-open silver mining town. Here, he founded the famous *Tombstone Epitaph* and reported, in between stints as mayor, on such occurrences as the Earp-Clanton gunfight at the OK Corral. After leaving Arizona, he moved to California and then Alaska where he established the territory's first post office in 1898. He retired from the post office in 1911, and at age sixty took up with the Southern Pacific Railroad, traveling widely promoting tourism in the American West. Clum died back in Tucson in 1932.

Newspapers reported on the remarkable historical symbiosis of a venerable Arizonan of the 1970s restoring the home of a venerable Arizonan of the 1870s. At the dedication ceremonies for the park, the McFarlands and the Pinal County Historical Society formally opened the house with a tea. Next on the agenda, McFarland State Park was formally opened to the public in the spring of 1978 when Mac once again spoke at ceremonies presided over by new governor, Bruce Babbitt.[29]

Honors for McFarland continued after the park's dedication and opening. In May 1978, Arizona's Disabled American Veterans chapter decided to found a DAV Hall of Fame honoring those who had most contributed to veterans' betterment throughout the state and nation. The organization selected for its first inductee the "Father of the GI Bill," and Mac and Edna attended the ceremonies at the Yuma convention accompanied by youthful Democratic U.S. Senator Dennis DeConcini. Speaking without notes, Mac regaled the standing-room-only audience at the Stardust Hotel with his memories of the great bill and Senator Hayden. Mac cast his support behind DeConcini's controversial decision to cast the deciding vote in turning the Panama Canal over to the nation of Panama in 1999. Referring to DeConcini as a "workhorse," Mac employed the phrase often used to describe himself.[30]

As McFarland approached age eighty-four and continued as a newsmaker, the *Arizona Republic* decided to feature him in a lengthy interview-pictorial for its Sunday magazine, "Arizona." The article "Big Mac" was to be his last major public interview and merits examination. In it he continued to demonstrate a sharp mind, not hesitant in discoursing on past events, issues, and people.

The interview was held in the conference room at Channel 3 and began with recollections of Pearl Harbor, the Hollywood film probe, and the GI Bill for which Mac emphatically stated, "I did more on the bill than anyone else." Recalling Roosevelt as a "great fellow. He knew people and he knew how to get along," Mac brought up a tidbit on former Arizona Congresswoman Isabella Greenway who had been the bridesmaid at Franklin and Eleanor's wedding. When she did not support him for a third term, Roosevelt grew overly concerned and sought Mac's commiseration. On another occasion when Churchill complained in Mac's presence to the president about trouble with Free French Leader Charles DeGaulle, Mac piped up that since De Gaulle got his financial support from the U.S., Churchill no longer had to have any trouble if Roosevelt so desired. Roosevelt so desired and the complaints ceased.

Mac continued to express admiration for Harry Truman: "He was a fellow you couldn't keep from loving, but he wasn't as gruff as reporters pictured him." In fact, the only time he had ever heard Truman swear involved the occasion when his daughter Margaret drew fire from the press over her singing. Mac and Harry liked to share drinks together when they could during his presidency, but usually one or the other was too busy to socialize as much as in the old senate days.

McFarland clarified that he wanted Lyndon Johnson for the whip position while he was majority leader, preferring the ambitious Johnson to his old Oklahoma friend Bob Kerr: "I knew I could work better with Lyndon than Bob because old Bob wanted to do things just the way he wanted to do them all the time." Mac also recognized the Johnson zeal for power early on, stating he himself was "as high up as I want to be in public office," but "Lyndon aspired to be president, but would never admit it."

Mac conjured up his old favorite story about Eisenhower when the two flew to Rheims right after the European war ended. At the time, Ike professed to Mac no political ambition, but when he came back to the states to address a joint session of Congress, McFarland humorously referred to him as "the greatest politician in the United States." Fellow Democrat George Aiken of Vermont disagreed, telling Mac to "look at him [amidst cheers]; even his bald head's turning red, he's blushing so much," to which Mac countered "you think that's not good politics?"

Finishing his remarks on old associations with presidents and presidents-to be, McFarland had little to say about Nixon who had been a senator during Mac's two years as majority leader: "he didn't do much of anything I ever heard of." Kennedy, who did not overlap with Mac in the Senate, went unmentioned in the interview.

Finally, Mac concluded with reference to his two defeats by Barry Goldwater, remembering that in 1952, Pulliam and Shadegg had characterized a vote for McFarland as a vote for communism. Regarding the 1958 defeat, he recalled knowing immediately that he would be unable to overcome the negative impact of the Stalin pamphlet. But Mac did not let the past bother him: "When an election was over for me, it was over."[31]

As the 1970s drew to a close, McFarland had one more big project to wrap up, his own autobiography. In fact, he had been preparing for this since his court years, carefully gathering together his official and personal papers and placing them in storage at the television station. Now after the operation and with more time on his hands, he and Mildred Hagerty began to go over the material, refresh the memories, and put the work together. Convening at the station on a daily basis, Mildred would take down in shorthand Mac's reflections on his career. They then researched and produced documents to enhance and corroborate the text before Mildred typed the whole thing up into a loose-leaf manuscript.

Much of the work was accomplished by early 1979 when Mac's daughter Jewell, a schoolteacher, and his "adopted granddaughter" Pat Heck began to prepare the manuscript for publication. Problems arose at this time when University of Arizona and Stanford editors recommended extensive changes in text and style. In a quandry, Mac sought the advice of Stanford's J. Wallace Sterling who had read the entire manuscript and written the foreword. Sterling saw the real McFarland in the very informal and casual textual approach, and he urged him to make no changes and consider private publication. Mac opted for this course, and by Thanksgiving the 350-page autobiography was in the bookstores put together with private funding. Sterling's words in the foreword are notable: "He has moral courage and an innate sense of good humor and judgment. He possesses a natural humility, which has to be experienced to be believed, yet is in harmony with the range and quality of his achievements. His demeanor, his conversation, and his personal correspondence are redolent with a rare homespun flavor. . . ." The book's jacket was graced with notes from Governor Babbitt and then-current Senate Majority Leader Robert C. Byrd. Babbitt wrote:

> To me, the most revealing single test of a political leader is how he reacts to adversity. . . . When Mac upset Senator Henry Fountain Ashurst in 1940, that old showhorse, embittered by the voter ingratitude, turned his back on Arizona and lived out his days in isolation in Washington. When Mac was in turn defeated in the Republican landslide of 1952, he did just the opposite. Uncomplaining, he came back to Arizona and plunged into two productive decades of public service as Governor and Supreme Court Justice. . . . Mac is still working.

Senator Byrd summarized:

> Some philosophers have asserted that history is the result of the deeds of great men. The life and career of Ernest W. McFarland would appear almost an intentional verification of that hypothesis for he has been a central figure in some of the most significant political dramas of our era, and his influence has been a determinant of the course that many events have taken in the United States and Arizona. . . . The people owe Senator McFarland a genuine debt of gratitude and appreciation.

Such tributes aside, the text did lack both polish and structure, but no one ever claimed McFarland to be highly polished, and while the chronology frequently skipped from chapter to chapter, the topical arrangement appropriately reflected McFarland's priorities. Most notable was the lack of complaint or bitterness over even his major political disappointments. He did not mention the 1952 and 1958 campaigns at all, stating to *Republic* reporter Bernie Wynn "I have never defamed the character of one individual in order to further my own gain, and that I will never do." Wynn termed this attitude "almost novel among today's politicians." Privately he confided to Wynn that the Pulliam press opposition and particularly Stephen Shadegg's "falsifying" his voting record and "trying to pin false labels on him [the Stalin pamphlet]" cost him the 1958 election. But Mac did not linger over these setbacks in his autobiography. He also refused to emphasize some of his greater successes, scarcely mentioning his role in drafting the GI Bill.

Two areas, water and law, received considerable attention in the work reflecting McFarland's lifetime interests, while the entire book encompassed his political career which provided structure for his many contributions. The homespun textual delivery well reflects the life and philosophy of this man, and while the editors, publishers, and some scholars can disown the effort for its lack of polish or scholarly rigor, it remains an invaluable tool for the historian and an accurate reflection of McFarland's life's work. Appropriately, the volume was simply entitled *Mac: The Autobiography of Ernest W. McFarland.*[32]

In January 1980, Mac attended book-signing receptions at the Florence park and at the state capitol. Two hundred gathered in the old courthouse to hear Rose Mofford and Governor Babbitt speak in tribute. Official state balladeer, Dolan Ellis, strummed a guitar singing the old pearl "There's No Catfish in Ajo," while McFarland pinned on a fifty-year Knights of Pythias emblem awarded for the occasion. Mac then retired to the old judge's chambers where long lines waited for him to sign the book at his original senate desk, which had been relocated to the park. A few days later, Babbitt hosted again as Mac sat at his old governor's desk in the capitol building, signing for a new group in the restored governor's chambers. At this reception, Mac continued to badger the governor about establishing a saltwater seaport on the Colorado near Yuma.[33]

One final honor awaited Mac in 1980, when the Board of Trustees of Stanford University in June established the Ernest W. McFarland Professorship in the School of Law. Essentially, the endowed chair was a gift from McFarland that stretched back to his Arizona origins. Before going to California to prepare for law in the fall of 1919, Mac, with assistance from his World War I veteran status, had purchased a quarter section of land outside of Casa Grande, the site of his first law office. Over the intervening sixty years, Mac had never used the land referred to as his "jackrabbit farm." By 1980, he had completed the transaction, turning over the 160 acres, which had been appraised at one million dollars, to his alma mater. With this guaranteed backing, the trustees set up the chair and later sold the land for five million dollars. Stanford invited Mac up to Palo Alto for his last significant trip out of state. Edna, in ill health, did not accompany him this time. Once again Chancellor Sterling acknowledged him as "Stanford's Most Distinguished Living Alumnus in Public Service," an honor presented Mac on a Stanford scroll.[34]

As the media noted at these latest appearances, McFarland at eighty-five years was growing increasingly enfeebled although he remained mentally sharp as he would until his final illness. He finally had to give up driving after a 1980 fender-bender and by 1981, as he continued to fail physically, he resorted more and more to a wheelchair. Nurses played an increasingly important role in the daily lives of the McFarlands. Still Mac got around haltingly with nurse drivers and assistance. Although he could no longer attend Arizona and Arizona State football games in person, he could still appreciate drives to Florence and overnight stays in the Clum house, although Edna, failing even more severely did not join him there. Mac continued to monitor progress at the park where a library-archives building was under construction to the rear of the courthouse. Pushed around in his chair by Park Ranger Jerry Ravert, Mac supervised the placement of his books, papers, and memorabilia, the bulk of which was transferred from the TV station. A whole batch of old family papers was discovered in the attic of the Coolidge farmhouse owned by his late brother Carl's family, and these too were removed to Florence. By 1982, the archives building stood complete and open to the public. With over three hundred archival boxes of papers in the basement, a ground-level display floor and an upper-level research area and library (and new public restrooms), the facilities were state of the art. Greeting visitors just inside the entrance loomed an enormous magnified photograph (about four by seven feet) of Mac seated at the governor's desk, the same that had been unveiled for his 1958 senate campaign.

His collection had finally found an appropriate home, but not without some prior complications. Both Arizona State and the University of Arizona had vied for the McFarland Papers, and when Stanford, too, entered the fray, the competition became very spirited. Mac's designation as its law college's most distinguished living alumnus came up in the midst of this skirmish, but the papers' "Arizona" flavor ultimately overcame Stanford's enticing blandishments. Mac slowly became receptive to Arizona State University's overtures and looked forward to a meeting in the university library with President John Schwada, Archivist Charles Calley, and history professor Bill Phillips. The university already had the Hayden Papers, and the Arizona Historical Foundation, which is housed within the ASU Hayden Library, held the Goldwater Papers. The thought occasionally spilled out of Mac's mind during these times that his career and his papers deserved commensurate standing with Arizona's "two other" famous senators. ASU might be the place to secure that stature, three giants shoulder to shoulder.

Looking forward to bringing the paper problem to closure, Mac did a "slow burn" waiting for ASU president Schwada to arrive. When the minutes went well beyond an hour, Mac slowly raised himself out of his chair to his full height and indignantly said, "This place will never get my papers." He then tramped out of the office. Fortunately, historian Phillips convinced McFarland, at the very least, not to allow removal of his papers from the state. The idea of a small state-of-the-art archive at McFarland Historical State Park was hatched at this time. So, though tempted to put his papers elsewhere, Mac ultimately stuck with his original idea of housing his collections at Florence.[35]

McFarland realized a dream, a high point in his last years, when in 1982 he flew the length of the Central Arizona Project by helicopter. Sixty years after the idea had been broached with the Colorado Compact, the project had finished its construction stage. The waters of the Colorado remained to be tapped but the sinewy concrete aqueducts had been laid for hundreds of miles. Originating at the Parker Dam, the concrete water trough swept east skirting the Buckskin and Vulture Mountains and Wickenberg, passing Castle Hot Springs, then through north Phoenix and Scottsdale before leaning south to Florence and beyond to Tucson. Eventually the Phoenix to Florence segment would be christened the Fannin-McFarland Aqueduct, but that lay in the future, 1992. For now, as he flew over the dry canals and pumping stations, his mind overflowed with memories of the decades of planning, adjudicating, politicking, and legislating. They gave substance to the Salt River Project's motto that "Arizona Grows Where Water Flows." He clearly visualized in his mind's eye the flow that would come with the opening of the gates in 1985. These dry canals, which stretched beyond view, would glisten with flowing water. Mac could almost visualize his whole political career in this panoramic picture. Perhaps he ruminated on a Yuma seaport again as held the great Colorado in sight. Assuredly, he reflected silently, with pride in his own role in setting strategy to the water in the 1940s and arguing judiciously in the 1950s. He knew as his own time ran out, soon the waters' time would come and provide a fitting memorial to his work of a lifetime.[36]

In early 1983, Del and Jewell Lewis prevailed upon the elderly couple to leave their long-time Royal Palm residence and move close to the Lewises in South Mesa. They needed closer attention, and although the McFarlands never did hire live-in help, they now required around-the-clock assistance by nurses acting as cooks and maids in eight-hour shifts. Edna, in particular, failed rapidly and remained bedridden most of the time.

Mac, however, kept up appearances as best he could and did a commendable job at his eighty-ninth birthday, October 9, 1983. Professor Bill Phillips hosted the event with a special pig barbecue at his home, and the party provided an example of how Mac phased in and out in the last years. When Del wheeled him in, Mac did not seem to know where he was or why he was there. Phillips felt unrecognized. After fifteen minutes or so, two car loads of old chums from the Yuma area came. Something went "pop" in his mind. He was instantly alert and keen of memory. The stories flowed for the rest of the evening; he even took a second helping while talking affably with the guests before being whisked away by wheelchair to limousine to home. He also continued to go into the television station offices on a weekly basis early into the new year. The entire family joined Mac and Edna in their Mesa home for what became a last Christmas, gathering around the tree under which spread numerous presents.[37]

By February 1984, however, McFarland could no longer persist, and he applied to the FCC to transfer control of Channel 3 to Del Lewis. On February 29, transfer was granted, and soon after, Del and Jewell requested a court order that placed the McFarlands' assets in trust. Judge Robert Myers of the Maricopa County Superior Court so ordered based on their "inability to manage their financial affairs because of age and poor health." Edna was eighty at the time and not doing well, but Mac had already set up a trust for her continued care, which would be necessary as she lingered on until October 1992 when she died at age eighty-eight.[38]

McFarland resided at the unfamiliar Mesa home for another two months before a final illness fell upon him when on Tuesday, May 29, 1984, he was admitted to Good Samaritan Hospital with congestive heart failure. His condition remained fair for a few days, but on Sunday, Mac fell unconscious and was transferred to the critical care unit. McFarland never regained consciousness and at 4:00 P.M. Friday, June 8, he died "quietly" of respiratory failure. Del and Jewell were at his bedside while the older grandchildren waited nearby. Edna, remained bedridden at the Mesa home.[39]

News spread quickly throughout the city and the state, and by the end of the day's business hours, flags flew at half-staff. Governor Bruce Babbitt led the official remarks for the departed Mac: "Arizona today lost a piece of its history and its soul. Ernie McFarland represented the best of our tradition and heritage combined with a keen vision of Arizona's future. He cannot be replaced." Secretary of State Rose Mofford echoed his remarks: "Ernest W. McFarland was Arizona. I held his advice and counsel in the highest regard. I shall greatly miss his presence, as he was Arizona's past, present, and future."

The press sought out others in high position for comment on Mac's passing. Morris Udall referred to his "national and international reputation. He was a good man and loyal friend, and his life was full and rewarding." Older brother Stewart called him "a stalwart of the Democratic party . . . truly one of the big men of his generation." Perhaps the *Phoenix Gazette* said it best: "There will be few like Old Mac. Arizona is indeed fortunate he came this way. He gave the state much more than he ever took from it."[40]

On Monday, McFarland lay in state in the great hall of the capitol under the rotunda. Tourist patterns within the building were re-routed to make way for those who came to pay their respects. The antique clock of the hall museum was quiet and phones were unplugged and answered elsewhere in the building. The rotunda glowed from rose-hued lamps and emitted the fragrance of the many flowers contributed in sympathy. Two state policemen, in shifts, stood vigil, remaining at attention beside the casket from 9:00 A.M. to 4:00 P.M. An Arizona flag drapped the coffin, while a folded U.S. flag with its field of stars displayed rested next to Mac's head. The *Republic* recognized the old-timers who would turn out in respect and urged that younger Arizonans "who settled here to enjoy the fruits of the labors of pioneers such as Mac to enrich their souls taking a few minutes to pass by his bier and salute a man who gave so much to the lasting quality of Arizona."[41]

The next day on Tuesday June 11, the McFarland funeral took place at the Central United Methodist Church to which Mac had belonged since 1919 — sixty-five years. Dr. Lawrence Hinshaw, the senior minister, had known him for forty of these and recalled him in his address as "one who wanted to give more than he received," one who left a message: "Remember to dream large dreams and to give yourself to your dreams." Indeed, Mac gave to the end, and his service requested memorial contributions be given to either the state park or the McFarland Pioneer Chapel, an extensive side chapel he had donated to the Methodist Church. His contributions were ecumenical as the presence of Thomas O'Brien, Bishop of the Diocese of Phoenix, attested. Mac had done much for the diocese, and the bishop delivered the pastoral prayer.

Del Lewis and his three sons, John, Bill, and Del, Jr., acted as pallbearers, while five former governors served as honorary pallbearers; Howard Pyle, Paul Fannin, Sam Goddard, Jack Williams, and Raul Castro followed the casket to the alter. Joining them as designated honoraries were then-current Chief Justice William A. Holohan and Mac's old friend and former associate on Arizona's high bench, Fred Struckmeyer.

Governor Babbitt delivered the eulogy and reached back to his own childhood for words. He remembered meeting Mac at age seven when Senator McFarland reached down to shake hands "with a twinkle in his eye," and told the future governor not to think of him as a "high placed politician, but as a neighbor and friend." Babbitt continued, "I remembered about the humility and significant qualities of the man. . . . The real monuments to Mac lie in the hearts and minds of the tens of thousands of those who were touched by his generousity."[42]

The long funeral cortege then wound the miles through Phoenix to Greenwood Cemetery on West Van Buren for interment. High on the mausoleum wall, the inscription upon Mac's catafalque read "Senator, Governor, Judge — Servant of the People."

NOTES

CHAPTER 1

¹For McFarland Family background, see the Public and Personal Papers of Ernest W. McFarland (hereinafter MP), Subgroup VI, Personal, 1902-1985, Series 8, Family Records, 1902-1980, Subseries 3, Edna and Ernest McFarland Papers,1932-1980, Box 305, File 23 (hereinafter 305/23); McFarland Historical State Park Archives, Florence, Arizona. See also Ernest W. McFarland, *Mac: The Autobiography of Ernest W. McFarland* (Phoenix, Arizona: privately published, 1979) 2 (hereinafter cited as *Mac*) and James E. McMillan, "Ernest W. McFarland: Southwestern Progressive, The United States Senate Years, 1940-1952" (Ph.D. diss., Arizona State University, Tempe, 1990) 10. See also James E. McMillan, "First Sooner Senator: Ernest W. McFarland's Oklahoma Years," *The Chronicles of Oklahoma*, LXXII, no. 2. (Summer 1994):178-99.

²For the land openings in Oklahoma Territory, see Edwin C. McReynolds, *Oklahoma: A History of the Sooner State* (Norman: University of Oklahoma Press, 1954, 1964) 289-307. The Dawes Act precluded communal land holdings by tribes by allotting land to individual Indians in set amounts up to 160 acres per head of family. In this failed effort to assimilate the Indian into a white culture and agricultural economy, the lands remaining after allotment were turned over to the United States at an extremely low cost. Nationwide, 90,000,000 of 145,000,000 acres (more than 60 %) of former Indian lands reverted to the U.S. Government between 1887 and 1932. Most Indians became abused and apathetic victims of the act, while a small number were able to work the terms to their advantage.

³H. Wayne Morgan and Anne Hodges Morgan, *Oklahoma: A History* (New York: W. W. Norton and Co., 1977): 51.

⁴The photographs are in *Mac*, chapter 1.

⁵For Earlsboro history, see "Earlsboro" file, Santa Fe Museum, Pottawatomie County Historical Society, Shawnee, Oklahoma. Additional information on Earlsboro was provided through interviews in Earlsboro, May 24, 1990, between the author and Mr. Bruce Jenkins and Mr. and Mrs. John Permetter. For county history, see

517

Pottawatomie County, Oklahoma, History (Claremore, Oklahoma: Country Lane Press, 1987) and *Frontier Lore* (Shawnee, Oklahoma: Pottawatomie County Historical Society, 1975). See also Charles W. Mooney, *Localized History of Pottawatomie Co., Oklahoma to 1907* (Oklahoma City: privately published, 1971).

[6]Earlsboro's other most prominent citizen-by-birth is Hall of Fame baseball player Willie Stargell of the Pittsburgh Pirates. Stargell, born in 1941 in sight of the old McFarland homestead, was a descendent of Seminole freedmen. His grandfather Wil Stargel is listed among the pioneer Earlsboro black families of the 1890s. See Willie Stargell and Tom Bird, *Willie Stargell: An Autobiography* (New York: Harper and Row, 1984): 1-15, on Earlsboro's background regarding black families. Stargell died in 2001.

[7]On the later oil boom, see Louise Welsh, Willa Mae Townes, and John W. Morris, *A History of the Greater Seminole Oil Field* (Oklahoma City: Oklahoma Heritage Association, 1981).

[8]Thorpe was selected "American Athlete of the Half-Century" by the Associated Press in 1950 -- not bad, in the era of Ruth, Grange, DiMaggio, and Jesse Owens.

[9]MP, Series 7, Naval and Educational Records, (294/3). Okemah was the birthplace and childhood home of noted American folksinger and songwriter Woody Guthrie (1912-67) during these years.

[10]John A. Walker, ed., *The East Central Story: From Normal School to University, 1909-1984* (Ada, Oklahoma: East Central University Foundation, 1984): 6-14.

[11]On Kerr, see Anne Hodges Morgan, *Robert S. Kerr: The Senate Years* (Norman: University of Oklahoma Press, 1977). The textbooks are in MP, Series 7, Box 296.

[12]Both yearbook quotes are from the *Pesagi, 1915*, the East Central Normal School yearbook, in MP, Series 7, Box 295; interview, author and Delbert Lewis, February 22, 1990, Phoenix.

[13]On the Schoolton experience, see *Mac*, 13-15.

[14]John Gillespie and Dale Story, *A History of East Central State College, 1909-1949* (Ada, Oklahoma: republished privately, 1980).

[15]*Mac*, 15-16.

[16]*Mac*, 16.

[17]*The Sooner*, 83, University of Oklahoma yearbook, 1917, in MP, Series 7, Box 295; Roy Gittenger, *The University of Oklahoma, 1892-1942* (Norman: University of Oklahoma Press, 1942): 84. Monnett Hall today houses the Carl Albert Center for Congressional Research.

[18]For McFarland's navy experience and illness see MP, Series 8, Subseries 1, Keziah McFarland Collection, (298/6,7).

[19]Interview, Roland Bibolet, Nogales, Arizona, June 18, 1993.

Bibolet served as McFarland's administrative assistant in the Senate, 1944-53, and during the gubernatorial years, 1955-59.

CHAPTER 2

[1]McFarland discusses these years in *Mac*, Chapter 2, "Early Years in Arizona." Valley Bank became Valley National Bank and is today Bank One.

[2]MP, Box 298. The later quote is from an interview on August 27, 1957, for *U.S.News and World Report*, in MP 173/6. Parts of the interview appeared in the issue of October 11, 1957.

[3]On Arizona during the 1920s, see Jay Wagoner, *Arizona's Heritage* (Salt Lake City: Pereguine Smith Inc., 1977), Chapter 17, "Border Troubles, World War I, and the 1920s."

[4]*Mac*, 26-27. Late in his life, McFarland donated this land to Stanford University, which in turn sold it for several million dollars to set up the McFarland endowed professorship of law.

[5]Material concerning the Stanford years is contained in MP Box 296.

[6]Letters, undated and Mother's Day, 1920 and 1921, McFarland to Keziah McFarland, MP, Box 298.

[7]Letter, Mother's Day, 1920, *loc. cit.*; Mac 27-28.

[8]Letter, Mother's Day, 1920, *loc. cit.*

[9]Ibid.

[10]Letter, Mother's Day, 1921, *loc. cit.*

[11]*Mac*, 28.

[12]Wagoner, 328-37. On Hunt, see John S. Goff, *George W. P. Hunt*, (Cave Creek, Arizona: Black Mountain Press, 1987).

[13]E. W. McFarland, "The Operation of the Initiative and Referendum in California" (M.A. thesis, Stanford University, 1924), MP, Box 294.

[14]On Florence, see Ava S. Baldwin, "The History of Florence, Arizona, 1866-1940," (M.A. thesis, University of Arizona, 1941); Roger L. Nichols, "A Miniature Venice, Florence, Arizona, 1866-1910," *Journal of Arizona History* 16 (Winter 1975); Harris Sobin, *Florence Townsite, A. T.: the Final Report of the Florence Townsite Historical Study* (Tucson: Harris Sobin and Associates, 1977.

[15]*Mac*, 30-33; *Arizona Blade-Tribune* (Florence), weekly, September 1926 and 1928.

[16]Interviews in Florence with author and Billie Early, January 1990 and John Swearingen, February 1990.

[17]Della Meadows, *Where Two Are Gathered: Centennial History of the First Presbyterian Church, Florence* (Florence: Pinal County Historical Society, 1988).

[18]Information on Clare Collins is in MP, Box 302.

[19]*Mac,* 23; *Arizona Blade-Tribune,* February 15, 1929.

[20]Information and correspondence on this trip are in MP, Box 302 and *Mac,* 35-37. See also Frank E. Ross, "Arizona's U.S. Senator Is A Scholar of Wide Margins," in the *Arizona Republic* (hereinafter *AR*) December 15, 1940, written just after McFarland's election to the U.S. Senate.

[21]*Arizona Blade-Tribune,* February 21, 1930; Mac 32-33. Dugan was also found having sexual intercourse with a prison guard, information not used in the trial.

[22]*Arizona Blade-Tribune,* September 12, 1930; Mac, 33.

[23]*Arizona Blade-Tribune,* December 19, 26, 1930. McFarland's Oklahoma friend and future U.S. Senator, Robert S. Kerr experienced a similar family tragedy when he lost his first wife and three children to illness in a three-year span of the 1920s. See McMillan, "First Sooner Senator," and Morgan, *Kerr.*

[24]Swearingen interview.

CHAPTER 3

[1]See Wagoner, *Arizona,* Chapter 18, "Arizona in the Depression of the 1930s."

[2]Baldwin, "Florence," Chapter 6, "The Depression, 1929-1940."

[3]Interview, author and Del Lewis, Phoenix, Feb. 22, 1990.

[4]On the entire Winnie Ruth Judd case and aftermath, see J. Dwight Dobkins and Robert J. Hendricks, *Winnie Ruth Judd: The Trunk Murders* (New York: Grosset and Dunlap, 1973); Jana Bommersbach, *The Trunk Murderess, Winnie Ruth Judd: The Truth About an American Crime Legend Revealed at Last* (New York: Simon & Schuster, 1992).

[5]*Arizona Blade-Tribune,* April 21, 1933.

[6]*Mac,* 34, 35. While governor, McFarland received a thirty-seven page letter from Judd, that while again indicating her insanity, promised not to cause any trouble while he was in office. She made no escape attempts during this time. During her final years of parole appeals, Mac sat, an interested spectator, as Chief Justice of the Arizona Supreme Court. Judd died in 1998.

[7]See Rich Johnson, *The Central Arizona Project, 1918-68* (Tucson: University of Arizona Press, 1977): 13-20. See also Edwin Cole, *The Gila: River of the Southwest* (Lincoln: University of Nebraska Press, 1952): 364-65 and Gregory McNamee, *The Gila: the Life and Death of an American River* (New York: Orion Press, 1994).

[8]Baldwin, "Florence" 43-54; interview of Brock Ellis by KTVK-TV, Phoenix, 1984, on videotape *Mac* 18. Ellis was one of the Arizona law students who was permitted to use McFarland's Florence law office for training and advice. He became Pinal County Attorney in the late 1930s and remained a close associate of McFarland's. The Roosevelt Dam stood 284 feet high and formed a lake twenty-three miles long; the Coolidge, 259 feet, with a twenty-six-mile lake. Harold E. Fey and D'Arcy McNickle, *Indians and Other Americans: Two Ways of Life Meet* (News York: Harper & Row, Perennial Library edition, 1970): 43-45.

[9]*Arizona Blade-Tribune*, Sept. 14, 1934; *Mac*, 37.

[10]Ellis interview, video, *Mac* 18; *Mac*, 38-39.

[11]Ellis interview, video, *Mac* 18; *Mac*, 192-94.

[12]Ellis interview, video, *Mac* 18; MP, 304/1, 2, 3.

[13]Frank E. Ross, "Arizona's U.S. Senator Is a Scholar of Wide Horizons," AR, Dec. 15, 1940; interview with Billy Early, Florence, Arizona, January 1990.

[14]*Congressional Record* (hereinafter *CR*) June 15, 1940, and Scrapbook 4 (hereinafter SB 4) in MP; Subgroup I, U.S. Senate.

[15]Letter James M. Barnes to Henry F. Ashurst, Sept. 1, 1940, Henry Ashurst Papers, Box 1, Folder 5, University of Arizona Library, Special Collections.

[16]*The Messenger* (Phoenix), June 15, 1940, p. 2., MP, SB 2.

[17]*Mac*, 42; for McFarland's recollections of this campaign, see *Mac*, 42-49. For documents on all aspects of McFarland's senate career, see James E. McMillan ed., *The Ernest W. McFarland Papers: The United States Senate Years, 1940-1952* (Prescott, Arizona: Sharlot Hall Museum Press, 1995).

[18]*AR*, April 26, 1940 in MP, SB 11; *Mac*, 44.

[19]*AR*, August 8, 1940, in MP, SB 1; "Senator Henry F. Ashurst," MP, 290/6. This is a thirteen-page update on Ashurst for McFarland's campaign purposes.

[20]Senator Henry F. Ashurst, during senate speeches of June 24, 1939 and April 1, 1940 and *AR*, May 12, 1939. Ashurst venerated Burr who made similar statements regarding his activities in the election of 1800, the Hamilton duel, and the Burr Conspiracy.

[21]Ibid.

[22]*Mac*, 48; McFarland speech, Aug. 7, 1940 at Casa Grande, in MP, 131/8; *Mac*, 44; Ashurst's campaign expenses in Ashurst Papers,

Box 6, folder 11.

[23]*Mac*, 46-47, also *CR*, May 30 and June 15, 1940.

[24]Letters and enclosures, McFarland to C.H. Southworth, May 5; Mabel to McFarland, June 5; Lee to McFarland, June 25; McFarland to Guy Anderson, July 13; Frank L. Gegax to Jewett Shouse, no date; Shouse to Gegax, Aug. 9; all 1940, in MP, 131/3,4.

[25]MP, SB 1; *Casa Grande Dispatch*, July 26, 1940.

[26]Letter, McFarland to Phoenix Junior Chamber of Commerce, Aug. 25, 1940, MP, 131/5; *Phoenix Gazette* (hereinafter *PG*) Aug. 21, 1940 and undescribed newsclipping, MP, SB 1.

[27]Letter, Ashurst to Mayela McKinney, Aug. 28, 1940, Box 1, Folder 5, Ashurst Papers; *PG*, Aug. 21, 1940; undescribed newsclipping, MP, SB 1.

[28]*Labor* (Washington, D.C.), Sept. 3, 1940; *PG*, Sept. 5, 1940; undescribed newsclipping, MP, SB 1.

[29]*The Messenger*, June 15, 1940; MP, SB 1; *AR*, Aug. 31, 1940.

[30]*AR*, Sept. 1, 1940, and material in MP, SB 1.

[31]*PG*, Sept. 3, 1940; *AR*, Sept. 6, 1940; *Tucson Daily Citizen*, Sept. 4, 1940.

[32]*Casa Grande Dispatch*, Sept. 6, 1940; *Tucson Daily Citizen*, Sept. 4, 1940; "Primary Election Returns, State of Arizona," September 10, 1940, in MP, SB 1.

[33]All three telegrams, Western Union, Sept. 11, 1940, in MP, SB 1.

[34]All letters Sept. 11, 1940 except Goldwater, Sept. 25; in Ashurst Papers, Box 1, folder 5; Goldwater to Ashurst, Box 2, Folder 1. Ashurst here emulated Aaron Burr who had given perhaps the most famous farewell speech in senate history.

[35]*PG*, Oct. 4, 14, 1940; the McFarland-Hayden correspondence regarding this meeting is in MP, 39/1, 41/5, and 50/12. For Hayden's significant role in the development of the American West and particularly regarding water, see Ross R. Rice, *Carl Hayden: Builder of the American West* (Lanham, Maryland: University Press of America, 1994) and Jack August, *Vision in the Desert: Carl Hayden and the Hydropolitics of the American Southwest* (Fort Worth: Texas Christian University Press, 1999).

[36]*AR*, Oct. 5, 12, 24, 1940.

[37]Interview, author and Anthony O. Jones, Phoenix, Arizona, July 29, 1986.

[38]"General Election Returns, State of Arizona, November 5, 1940," in MP, SB 1.

CHAPTER 4

¹*Mac*, 50, 54; *CR*, 77th Congress, 1st Session, 83.

²Letters, McFarland to Carl Hayden, Nov. 8 and Dec. 2, 1940, MP, 50/12.

³Letters between Howard Speakman and McFarland, Feb. 12, 24, and March 8, 1941, MP, 159/9.

⁴Letter, McFarland to Franklin Roosevelt, January 25, 1941, Franklin Delano Roosevelt Library, Collection 59, Box 3; McFarland to Hayden, Nov. 28, 1940, and C. Emory Harrison to McFarland, Dec. 5, 1940, MP, 50/12.

⁵McFarland speech, Flagstaff, Arizona, Aug. 14, 1941, MP, 47/2.

⁶*CR*, 77th Congress, 1st Session, 255.

⁷Speech, Aug. 14, 1941, *loc. cit.*; McFarland's Voting Record, 77th Congress, 1st Session, MP, Box 12. For additional information on the Lend-Lease Act, see Warren F. Kimball, *The Most Unsordid Act: Lend-Lease, 1939-1941* (Baltimore: The Johns Hopkins University Press, 1969).

⁸McFarland speech, Phoenix, Arizona, March 29, 1941, in *Appendix to the Congressional Record, 77th Congress, A1698-9*; Lee read it into the Record on April 15, 1941.

⁹McFarland speech, Miami, Florida, June 14, 1941, in *Appendix to the Congressional Record, 77th Congress*, A3265-6.

¹⁰McFarland's Voting Record, *loc. cit.*

¹¹*CR*, 77th Congress, 1st Session, 6292-3.

¹²McFarland's Voting Record, *loc. cit.*; undescribed newsclippings, MP, SB 3.

¹³McFarland radio address, Feb. 8 1941, MP, 47/1; letters between Speakman and McFarland, Feb. 24, Mar. 8, 1941, MP, 159/9.

¹⁴*CR*, 77th Congress, 1st Session, 3392; *Mac*, 95-6.

¹⁵Undescribed newsclippings, April 1941, SB 3, MP. See also *Mac*, 58-59. Mac introduced his first bill in January 1941 to authorize the RFC to make loans to small mining operations, but if failed to pass.

¹⁶For detailed background on the issues and politics of water in the West, see Norris Hundley, *Water and the West* (Berkley: University of California Press, 1975), and Donald Worster, *Rivers of Empire* (New York: Pantheon Books, 1985). On the Colorado River, see Philip L. Fradkin, *A River No More* (Tucson: University of Arizona Press, 1984). See also Rich Johnson, *The Central Arizona Project, 1918-1968* (Tucson, University of Arizona Press, 1977) and John Terrell,

The War for the Colorado River, 2 vols. (Glendale, California, 1965).
    [17]McFarland speech, Phoenix, Arizona, Aug. 12, 1941, MP, 47/2.
    [18]*St. Louis Globe Democrat*, Aug. 2, 1941, in *Academy of Motion Picture Arts and Sciences Press Clipping File on the Senate Subcommittee War Film Hearings*, Volume 1, Aug. 1 through Oct. 15, 1941, Hollywood, California, "Build Up" p. A, MP, 14/15 (hereinafter referred to as AMPAS); Wayne S. Cole, *Senator Gerald P. Nye and American Foreign Relations* (Minneapolis: University of Minnesota Press, 1962) 176; and *Vital Speeches of the Day* 7: 720-23, Sept. 15, 1941. See also James E. McMillan, "McFarland and the Movies: The 1941 Senate Motion Picture Hearings," *Journal of Arizona History* 29 (Autumn 1988): 277-302.
    [19]*Mac*, 63-65.
    [20]G. Jowett, *Film: The Democratic Art* (Boston: Little, Brown & Co., 1976) 296-7 and Robert Sklar, *Movie Made America* (New York: Vantage Books, 1975), chapter 3.
    [21]Letter from Will Hayes, President of the Motion Picture Producers and Distributors Association to D.W. Clark in *AMPAS*, "Build Up" p. K; and *Hollywood Reporter*, Sept. 3, 1941, in *AMPAS*, "Build Up" p. P.
    [22]*Hollywood Reporter*, ibid.; Elwyn B. Robinson, *History of North Dakota* (Lincoln: University of Nebraska Press, 1966) 415-422.
    [23]*Hollywood Reporter*, Sept. 3, 1941, in "Just Before," pp. C-D, *AMPAS*. Willkie took pains to point out that *Escape*, one of the films under suspicion, had appeared in serial form in the *Saturday Evening Post* prior to its publication as a novel by Little, Brown and Company. It was a Book-of-the-Month Club selection, received favorable reviews in the press, and sold over 300,000 copies — all before it was filmed. Copies of Willkie's letter are also in U.S. Senate Committee on Interstate Commerce Hearings, *Propaganda in Motion Pictures* (1942) 18-22 (hereinafter referred to as *Hearings*) and Folder 10, Box 1B, McFarland Papers.
    [24]*Hollywood Reporter*, Sept. 3, 1941.
    [25]*Hearings*, 1-5, 8, 25-7, 32, 35, 60; and *New York Times*, Sept. 10, 1941; and *Variety* (Daily), Sept. 10 1941, both in *AMPAS*, "First Day" pp. A,B,E,F.
    [26]*Hearings*, 33-34, 57-60.
    [27]*Hearings*, 38,42. The report was made by Goodbody and Company.
    [28]Both quotes, *Los Angeles Examiner*, Sept. 14, 1941. In a summary statement placed in the records, Willkie called Nye the "star witness" for the industry.
    [29]*Variety*, Sept. 10, 1941, and *Hollywood Reporter*, Sept. 10, 1941,

in *AMPAS*, "First Day."

³⁰*Hearings*, 66,79-81, and *Hollywood Reporter*, Sept. 11, 1941, in *AMPAS*, "Second Day" pp. A,B.

³¹*The Hollywood Reporter*, ibid.

³²*The Hollywood Reporter*, ibid, and *The Christian Science Monitor*, Sept. 11, 1941, in *AMPAS*, "Second Day" p. J.

³³*Variety*, Sept. 11, 1941, in *AMPAS*, "Third Day" p. C, and *Hearings*, 89.

³⁴*Variety*, Sept. 16, 1941, in *AMPAS*, "Fourth Day" pp. A,B and *Hearings*, 154, 168, 192, 276. Fidler resisted attending the hearings but complied when told he would be served by a U.S. marshall.

³⁵The unidentified Oklahoma City newspaper is quoted in *Mac*, 61-2.

³⁶*Hearings*, 203-204.

³⁷*Life*, Sept. 22, 1941, 21-25; *Time*, Sept. 22, 1941 in MP, SB 3.

³⁸Cole, *Nye*, 190,195; *Los Angeles Examiner*, Sept. 17, 1941, in "Recess," C, *AMPAS*.

³⁹*Social Justice*, Sept. 22, 1941, in "Recess," Q-R;

⁴⁰Cole, *Nye*, 190, 195; *Hollywood Reporter* and *Los Angeles Examiner*, both Sept. 17, 1941, in "Recess," C-D, *AMPAS*.

⁴¹*Life*, Sept. 22, 1941, 21-25; and *Time*, Sept. 22, 1941, in MP, SB 3. *Hearings*, 384-385, 394-395.

⁴²*Hearings*, 290-291, and *Christian Science Monitor*, Sept. 24, 1941, in *AMPAS*, "Sixth Day" p. B. A lengthy transcription of McFarland's interview with the flyers is found in the McFarland Papers. By this stage of the investigation, even the Washington presses' society pages were commenting favorably on McFarland and predicting a quick end to the hearings. The society pages downplayed McFarland's "country" image, referring to him as "tall expansive, with a keen mind and a ready quip," in *Washington Times Herald*, Sept. 24, 1941, in "Sixth Day," G, *AMPAS*.

⁴³*Hearings*, 340-343.

⁴⁴*Hearings*, 346.

⁴⁵*Hearings*, 343; *Hollywood Reporter*, Sept. 26, 1941, and *Hollywood Citizen News*, Sept. 25, 1941, both in *AMPAS*, "Seventh Day" p. B.

⁴⁶*Hearings*, 384-5.

⁴⁷*Hearings*, 394-5.

⁴⁸*Hollywood Post*, Sept. 27, 1941 in *AMPAS*, "Day Eight," A,B,C.

⁴⁹*Hearings*, 409, 438-448.

⁵⁰*AMPAS*, "Second Recess" pp. DD, FF, EE; *Pittsburgh Post Gazette*, Oct. 13, 1941; and *New York Post*, Oct. 14, 1941. Senator Scott Lucas, who chaired the Audit and Control Committee, was urg-

ing Clark to bring the hearings to a hasty conclusion.

[51]Nye was speaking at Soldiers and Sailors Memorial Hall in Pittsburgh, Pa. when informed of Pearl Harbor. At first, he disclaimed the news as rumor, but as verification came in, he cut short his speech. See Cole, *Nye*, 198-201. Cole states that the onset of war relegated Nye to political oblivion: "the world had passed him by, and he faced the scorn, abuse, and political oblivion commonly reserved for leaders of lost causes."

[52]McFarland speech, Des Moines, Iowa, Oct. 23, 1941, MP, 47/1.

[53]Undescribed newsclippings, MP, SB 3; McFarland's Voting Record, 77th Congress, 1st Session, *loc. cit.*; McFarland speech, Baltimore, Maryland, Nov. 8, 1941, 47/1.

[54]Undescribed newsclippings, MP, SB 3; McFarland's Voting Record, 77th Congress, 1st Session, *loc. cit.* At the dedication of the Ernest McFarland Memorial, Wesley Bolin Plaza, State Capitol Grounds, Phoenix, Arizona, November 11, 1998, Jewell Lewis related this story of the war declaration, stating "Mac was so many things to so many people; to me he was just Dad." Other speakers included the author, Polly Rosenbaum, Rose Mofford, Roland Bibolet, Tom Smith, Del Lewis, and Bishop Thomas O'Brien.

[55]*AR* article, "Big Mac," August 13, 1978, MP, SB 1971-84.

[56]Undescribed newsclippings, MP, SB 3.

[57]*New York Post*, Oct. 14, 1941; *Washington Evening Star*, Oct. 9, 1941; *Esquire*, June 1942, 52, 156-58.

CHAPTER 5

[1]McFarland speeches, Denver, Colorado, February 23; Buffalo, New York, March 18; Easton, Pennsylvania, March 26, all 1942, MP, 47/3. For the homefront during World War II see John Morton Blum, *V for Victory: Politics and American Culture During World War II* (New York: Harcourt, Brace, Jovanovich, 1976). For wartime diplomacy, see Gaddis Smith, *American Diplomacy During World War II* (New York: John Wiley and Sons, 1965).

[2]*CR*, 77th Congress, 2d Session, 2857-8. For wartime congressional issues see Roland Young, *Congressional Politics in the Second World War* (New York: Columbia University Press, 1956).

[3]Ibid. Due to population growth, Arizona was awarded a second legislative district in 1942, essentially for Tucson and the southern part of the state. Democrat Richard Harless was the first representative

elected under the restructuring.

[4]Miscellaneous papers, MP, 129/3; Jay Wagoner, *Arizona*, 316-17. For a regional approach to World War II and the West, see Gerald Nash, *The American West Transformed: The Impact of the Second World War* (Bloomington: University of Indiana Press, 1985).

[5]Letter and enclosures, R.L. Webster, Assistant to the Secretary, Dept. of Agriculture, to McFarland, January 5, 1943, MP, 129/3.

[6]Letter, McFarland to Roosevelt, November 7, 1942; telegram, Hayden to McFarland, November 6, 1942; letter Roosevelt to McFarland, November 30, 1942; telegram from Claude Wickard, Secretary of Agriculture and Paul V. McNutt, Chairman, War Manpower Commission to H.S. Casey Abbott, President, Arizona Cotton Growers Cooperative Assoc., November 4, 1942; telegram, Robert P. Patterson, Undersecretary of War and James V. Forrestal, Undersecretary of the Navy to Abbott, November 5, 1942; all in Franklin Delano Roosevelt Papers, Collection 258, Box 4, Folder "Cotton, 1942-45," and undescribed newsclippings, November 1943, MP, SB 3.

[7]Letters, Osborn to McFarland, June 1, 1942 and McFarland to Osborn, June 8, 1942, MP, 159/8; undescribed newsclippings, MP, SB 3. McFarland did drive to work refusing to use senate limousines until majority leader.

[8]Wagoner, *Arizona's Heritage*, 320-24; *AR*, June 13, 1943; undescribed newsclippings, MP, SB 3; *CR*, December 17, 1943. For Japanese relocation throughout the West during World War II, see Roger Daniels, *Concentration Camps USA*. (Hinsdale, Illinois: Dryden Press, 1971).

[9]Interview, the author and Anthony O. Jones, June 21, 1987, Florence, Arizona. Jones was McFarland's administrative assistant for periods of the senator's first term, 1941-46. Peter F. Drucker credits the GI Bill with changing the United States to a "knowledge society" and effecting a new emphasis from Western to World civilization. See "The New Society of Organizations" in *Harvard Business Review*, Sept.-Oct. 1992, 95-105.

[10]Davis R.B. Ross, *Preparing for Ulysses: Politics and Veterans During World War Two* (New York: Columbia University Press, 1969) 34-5; James E. McMillan, "Father of the GI Bill: Ernest McFarland and Veterans' Legislation," *The Journal of Arizona History* (Winter 1994): 357-376.

[11]Keith W. Olson, *The GI Bill, the Veterans and the Colleges* (Lexington: the University Press of Kentucky, 1974) 4, 101; Willard Waller, *The Veteran Comes Back* (New York: Dryden Press, 1944) 185-88; Theodore R. Mosch, *The GI Bill: A Breakthrough in Educational and Social Policy in the United States* (Hicksville, New York: Exposition

Press, 1975) 9.

[12]Mosch *The GI Bill*, 26. The Atherton and Colmery quotes are from Olson, *The GI Bill*, 20.

[13]Henry A. Wallace, *Sixty Million Jobs* (New York: Simon and Schuster, 1945) in Mosch, *The GI Bill*, 6.

[14]Letter, Lucy Salamanca Morey to McFarland, April 29, 1942, MP, 13/4. Morey was Chief of Inquiry Section, Legislative Reference Service, Library of Congress. *Prescott Courier*, August 13, 1943; *Phoenix Gazette* and *Arizona Republic*, August 14, 1943; McFarland's entire speech was placed in the *CR*, 78th Congress, 1st Session, October 29, 1943, pp. 8885-6.

[15]Mosch, *The GI Bill*, 15-16, 27-8.

[16]*CR*, 78th Congress, 1st Session, October 29, 1943, 8882; "Statement Before the Senate Finance Committee," in MP, 6/106; *Mac*, 86-7; *AR*, "Big Mac," August 13, 1978. This is in the Sunday magazine *Arizona*, and is found in the McFarland Papers, Scrapbook, 1971-1984.

[17]*CR*, ibid.; Mosch, *The GI Bill*, pp. 32, 39. Thomas desired to include the Merchant Marine under the bill's terms as well as veterans. This met too much opposition and was later dropped.

[18]McFarland radio address, November 5, 1943, MP, 30/28. The address was placed by Maybank in the *Appendix to the CR*, 78th Congress, 4749-50. Letters, McFarland and Winchell, November 3, and 15, 1943, MP 6/106.

[19]David Camelon, "I Saw the G.I. Bill Written," *The American Legion Magazine*, September 1949, Part I, "The Fight for Mustering Out Pay," 48-50; see also Part II, "A Surprise Attack," October 1949, and Part III, "The Wild Ride From Georgia," November 1949. Parts II and III are on 18-19 and 51-57.

[20]Ross, *Ulysses*, 42-3, 63, 75, 96, 108.

[21]Letter, Francis M. Sullivan to McFarland, December 17, 1943, MP, 30/28; *CR*, 78th Congress, 2d Session, January 12, 1944, 122.

[22]Hearst's *The New York Journal American*, December 4, 1943, and January 12, 1944, in Ross, *Ulysses* 80-1.

[23]Ross, *Ulysses* 99.

[24]*CR*, 78th Congress, 2d Session, January 28, 1944, p. 858; undated press release of March 1944, MP 120/3.

[25]*Southwest Veteran* (magazine), March 11, 1944, vol. XVIII, no. 28, and press release, March 3, 1944, both MP, 127/1; undescribed newsclippings, March 1944, MP, Scrapbook 4.

[26]Bennett, "Champ" Clark III, "Statement Before the Finance Committee," MP, 47/4; *Prescott Courier*, March 14, 1944. The letter from the Legion was published in the *Phoenix Gazette*, April 5, 1944.

²⁷Radio Transcription, Station WRC, Washington, D.C., April 14, 1944, MP, 48/16.

²⁸Camelon, *loc. cit.*, Part III, "The Wild Ride from Georgia."

²⁹McFarland speech, Tucson, Arizona, August 1944, MP, 47/4.

³⁰McFarland statement, undated, MP, 48/16.

³¹McFarland speech, "Small Business: The Necessity for its Preservation and the Relation to the Rehabilitation of Returning Servicemen," MP, 48/16. The speech is dated 1944 and was given several times during the latter part of that year.

³²Panel discussion, "How Adequate Is the G.I. Bill of Rights?" presented January 2, 1945, by NBC's *American Forum*, transcription printed by Ramsdell Inc., Washington, D.C., MP, 47/5. The sixteen-year-old radio show emanated from the Shoreham Hotel.

³³The Land Ordinance of 1785 mandated public land be set aside for elementary and secondary schools. The Morrill Act of 1862 provided land and funding for agricultural and mining-engineering higher education. Implementation and updating of the GI Bill includes the Korean bill which McFarland cosponsored and coauthored (see Chapter 10), the Vietnam era bill, and the present Montgomery GI Bills. President Bill Clinton spoke hopefully in 1993 for a GI Bill for all Americans in his inaugural address.

³⁴*Arizona Republic* article, "Big Mac," August 13, 1978.

³⁵*Mac*, 74-76.

³⁶Letter, Burton K. Wheeler to McFarland, February 20, 1945 in MP, SB 3 and McFarland speech in U.S. Senate, February 22, 1945, CR, 79th Congress, 1st Session; *Washington Star*, February 21, 1945; *New York Times*, February 22, 1945.

³⁷MP, miscellaneous undescribed papers donated by Mildred Hagerty.

³⁸Ibid.

³⁹Undescribed newsclippings, MP, SB 3.

CHAPTER 6

¹Most of the information on the European tour is drawn from a McFarland speech draft of August 14, 1945, MP, 47/5. See also press release July 12, 1945, MP, 25/2; undescribed newsclippings, MP, SB 3. Germany surrendered on May 4; VE Day when hostilities officially ended fell on May 8; and the surrender was ratified on May 9.

²*New York Times*, June 5, 1945, *New York Herald Tribune*, June 6, 1945, *Washington Star*, June 6, 1945, *PG*, June 5, 1945; all MP, SB 3.

[3]McFarland speech draft, August 14, 1945, *loc. cit.*

[4]Robert Ferrell, *Off the Record: The Private Papers of Harry S. Truman* (New York: Harper and Row, 1980) 48-49.

[5]McFarland speech, U.S. Senate, *CR*, November 1, 1943, MP, 47/4.

[6]Robert M. LaFollette, "The Simple Truth," August 6, 1945, in *Mac*, 178-79.

[7]Ibid. and McFarland speech, U.S. Senate, July 24, 1945, *CR*, 79th Congress, 1st Session, 800.

[8]McFarland speech draft, August 14, 1945, and press release July 12, 1945, *loc. cit.*

[9]McFarland speech, U.S. Senate, *CR*, 79th Congress, 2d Session, April 29, 1946, 4180.

[10]*Washington Star*, April 30, 1946; *Los Angeles Examiner*, April 27, 1946; undescribed newsclippings of March 6, 1946, May 8, 9, 1946; all in MP, SB 6.

[11]*Washington Star*, April 30, 1946; *Mac*, 102-06.

[12]*Washington Star*, April 30, 1946; *Los Angeles Examiner*, April 27, 1946; *AR*, May 6, 1946; undescribed newsclipping, April 28, 1946; all in MP, SB 6.

[13]*Mac*, 106, 108; undescribed newsclippings, MP, SB 6.

[14]Letter, Roland Bibolet to author, Dec. 17, 1993. Bibolet started work for McFarland as administrative assistant on Nov. 1, 1944, and would continue until 1959, during McFarland's gubernatorial years with the exception of 1953-55 when Bibolet remained in Washington with minority leader Lyndon Johnson.

[15]*Mac*, 69; undescribed newsclippings, July 24 and August 3, 1945 in MP, SB 3; 1946 campaign pamphlet and "agriculture" file, MP, 12/1 and "money" file, MP, 12/7.

[16]1946 campaign pamphlet and "welfare" file, MP, 12/2; *CR*, 79th Congress, 2d Session, January 28, 1946, 449-50, June 14, 1946, 6934, 10421; 78th Congress, 1st Session, December 2, 1943, 10196.

[17]*Mac*, 69; *CR*, 78th Congress, 2d Session, May 28, 1943, 5017; 79th Congress, 2d Session, February 26, 1946, 57.

[18]*Mac*, 90; *CR*, 79th Congress, 2d Session, April 15, 1946, 9697-8; videotape *"Mac Remembered,"* McFarland State Park. With a majority of only two in the 1951-53 sessions, he would frequently have to "work the other side of the aisle," so good relations with the acknowledged Republican leader were to be valued.

[19]Undescribed newsclippings, August 1, 1944, MP, SB 3.

[20]Ibid. and *Arizona News*, August 4, 1944.

[21]*Mac*, 202-3; Fradkin, *A River No More*, 299-302; undescribed newsclippings, MP, SB 3.

[22]*CR*, 79th Congress, 1st Session, April 12, 1945, 3299.

[23]Undescribed newsclippings of August 29, 30, 1945, MP, SB 3.

[24]*PG*, August 8 and September 24, 1946; *AR*, September 24, 1946.

[25]*AR*, September 15, 1946. Krug had replaced FDR's Interior Secretary Harold Ickes in Truman's Cabinet.

[26]*AR*, October 23, 24, 1946; *Arizona Range News*, November 1, 1946; undescribed newsclippings, MP, SB 6.

[27]Letter, Truman to McFarland, March 11, 1946, MP, 133/15.

[28]*PG*, March 11, 12, 1946; *Prescott Courier*, March 11, 1946; undescribed newsclippings, MP, SB 4.

[29]*Life*, March 11, 1946; undescribed newsclippings of April 18, 1946, MP, SB 4.

[30]*Glendale News*, May 24, 1946; undescribed newsclippings, MP, SB 4.

[31]Williamson's letter and enclosure, unsigned, April 26, 1946, MP, 132/1.

[32]The Williamson-McFarland correspondence of April-July 1946 is found in MP, 132/1,2,5.

[33]Minutes, Arizona State Federation of Labor, June 20, 21, 1946, MP, 132/5.

[34]Campaign pamphlet, "An Unparalleled Record in the Interest of Our State," MP, 132/51.

[35]Ibid., letters from the organizations listed to McFarland of June 11, MP, 133/5; April 18 and June 12, MP, 132/2; July, 15, MP, 133/14; June 7, MP, 132/5, all 1946.

[36]Primary Election Returns, State of Arizona, July 16, 1946, MP, SB 6.

[37]Press release to *Southwestern Labor Record* and *Arizona Sun*, both October 17, 1946, MP, SB 4. Byrnes, like McFarland held a myriad of positions during his distinguished career as U.S. senator, U.S. secretary of state, U.S. Supreme Court justice, and governor of South Carolina.

[38]*Bisbee Daily Review*, October 11, 1946; *Phoenix Gazette*, October 15, 1946; AR, October 19, 1946, *Arizona Daily Star*, November 1, 3, 1946.

[39]Arizona General Election Returns, November 5, 1946; *Nogales International*, November 8, 1946; *Phoenix Gazette*, November 12, 1946, all in MP, SB 6; letters, Chapman to McFarland, November 7, and Taylor to McFarland, November 22, both 1946 and MP, 133/17.

CHAPTER 7

Because of the frequency of newspaper citings, abbreviations are used for the most prevelant publications: *Arizona Republic (AR)*, *Phoenix Gazette (PG)*, *Arizona Daily Star (ADS)*, and *Tucson Daily Citizen, (TDC)*.

[1]Letter, McFarland to Ruth B. Shipley, Dept. of State, November 2, 1946, MP, 146/5.

[2]*Mac* 78-9; undescribed newsclipping December 19, 1946, SB 6, MP; letter McFarland to George Marshall, December 3, 1946, MP, 146/20; letter, Roland Bibolet to author, December 17, 1993.

[3]Undescribed newsclipping, SB 6; "Itinerary for Japan," MP, 146/4.

[4]Undescribed newsclipping, ibid; speech, 25 September 1947, Florence, Arizona, MP, 47/6; undescribed newsclipping, SB 6. A picture of the visit with Chiang-Kai-shek is in *Mac*, 78.

[5]Speech, "Freedom of News in the World," dated only "1947," MP, 47/6.

[6]Memorandum, "Observations on Pacific and Far East Communications," Captain C.F. Horne, Deputy Chief of Communications, U.S. Navy, to McFarland, January 10, 1947, MP, 146/11. Horne accompanied McFarland on the trip.

[7]*ADS*, May 17, 1947; letter, Roland Bibolet to author, December 12, 1993.

[8]*ADS*, June 12, 1947.

[9]Undescribed newsclippings, May-August 1947, MP, SB 6.

[10]For the Wellton-Mohawk Project, see *Mac*, 203-205 and Rich Johnson, *The Central Arizona Project, 1918-68*; (Tuscon: The University of Arizona Press, 1977) 29-30, 35.

[11]*ADS*, April 9, 1947; undescribed newsclipping, MP, SB 6; *Prescott Courier*, April 9, 1947; PG, April 9, 1947.

[12]*PG*, April 14, 1947; undescribed newsclippings, MP, SB 6; *PG* and *AR*, June 9, 10, 1947; *Yuma Daily Sun*, July 23, 1947; *AR*, July 30, 1947.

[13]*PG*, May 2 and June 6, 1947. The original CAP bill, S.2346, had been introduced by McFarland on June 18, 1946, during the 79th Congress, but no hearings were held or action taken.

[14]"Opening Remarks in Support of S.1175," MP, 38/3; *Los Angeles Times*, June 23, 1947; undescribed newsclippings, MP, SB 6.

[15]*AR*, June 25, 1947.

[16]*PG*, June 27, 1947; letter Millikin to McFarland, June 21, 1947, MP, 34/3; *AR*, June 26, 1947; *ADS*, June 28, 1947.

[17]*TDC*, June 30, 1947.

[18]*PG*, July 1, 9, 1947; *AR*, July 7, 12, 1947; *CR*, 80th Congress, 1st Session, 8430, July 8, 1947.

[19]*AR*, August 19, 1947; *PG*, July 29, 1947.

[20]*AR*, October 24, 1947; undescribed newsclipping, MP, SB 6; letter, Bibolet to author, December 17, 1993.

[21]*AR* and *PG*, November 1, 1947.

[22]*AR*, November 2, 4, 1947. Both articles were written by Ben Avery, who continued to write for the *Republic* into the 1990s. Earlier *Republic* reporting on the Indians during the summer had received national publicity. Newspapermen from the *Denver Post*, the *Los Angeles Examiner*, and the *Albuquerque Tribune* as well as representatives of the Associated Press and a major newsreel, accompanied McFarland's party. Some remained to continue their investigation. *AR*, November 16, 20, and December 22, 1947, and January 7, 1948.

[23]*AR*, January 4, 1948. "The McFarland Record," 30-31, MP; CR, 80th Congress, 2d Session, March 19, 1948, 3249, 3261.

[24]"The McFarland Record," 42, MP; *CR*, 80th Congress, 2d Session, June 14, 1948; AR, June 5, 14, 1948; speech, August 7, 1947, Globe, Arizona, before the VFW's annual convention, MP, SB 6; speech, "Freedom of News in the World," *loc. cit.*; Speech, September 28, 1947, Florence, Arizona; undescribed newsclippings, both in MP, SB 6.

[25]McFarland's Voting Record, 1947, MP, 128/1.

[26]*CR*, 80th Congress, 2d Session, March 12, 13, 1948, 2792, 2878.

[27]*PG*, July 29, 1949; undescribed newsclippings, MP, SB 6. See also speeches "Dangers to American Democracy," April 10, 1948, and "A Party with a Great Record Worth Fighting For," June 7, 1948, both MP, 47/7.

[28]*CR*, ibid., April 13, 1948, 4299; undescribed newsclippings, MP, SB 6.

[29]For 1948 activity, concerning CAP, see Johnson, *Central Arizona Project* Chapter 2; on the hearings, specifically, see 49-51. See also U.S. Congress, Senate, 80th Congress, 2d Session Hearing Report. Committee on Interior and Insular Affairs. "Colorado River Water Rights." Washington, D.C., U.S. Government Printing Office, 1948.

[30]*Arizona Times*, March 11, 1947; *PG*, April 3, 1947, *AR*, April 4, 1947.

[31]*Johnson, Central Arizona Project*, 42-47.

[32]McFarland, "Statement in Opposition to S.J.R. 145," MP, 38/3; *AR*, May 10, 1948; *PG*, May 11, 12, 1948; Julius Krug, "Report of the Secretary of the Interior," in letter to Hugh Butler, May 13, 1948, MP, 37/2; *Los Angeles Times*, May 13, 1948; *AR*, May 13, 1948;

PG, May 14, 1948; *AR*, July 10, 1948; *AR*, September 17, 26, and December 7, 1948. Republican presidential candidate Thomas Dewey had also announced in favor of CAP.

[33]*Mac* 222; Johnson, *Central Arizona Project*, 30.

[34]Undescribed newsclippings, MP, SB 7. South Carolina Governor Strom Thurmond also led a break from the Democratic party by opposing the civil rights plank. He became the presidential nominee for the "Dixiecrats," the States Rights party.

[35]*Washington Post*, July 12, 1948; *AR*, July 13, 1948.

[36]Letter, Bibolet to author, December 17, 1993; David McCullough, *Truman* (New York: Simon and Schuster, 1992) 636.

[37]*PG*, September 23, and *TDC*, September 25, 1948. See McCullough, chapter 14 for details of the entire Whistlestop Campaign. See also Robert H. Ferrell, *Harry S. Truman: A Life* (Columbia: University of Missouri Press, 1994) chapter 13.

CHAPTER 8

[1]For 1949 CAP activity, see Johnson, chapter 3. On the Senate hearings, see specifically pps. 64-66. See also U.S. Congress, Senate, 81st Congress, 1st Session. Hearing Report. "The Central Arizona Project and Colorado River Water Rights." Washington, D.C.: U.S. Government Printing Office.

[2]Johnson, *Central Arizona Project*, 60; *PG*, February 7, 1949; *Arizona Times*, February 8, 1949.

[3]*AR* and *Arizona Times*, February 8, 1949; telegram, Garvey to Truman, February 8, 1949, MP, 35/8. Garvey, Arizona secretary of state during the Osborn administration, became acting governor upon Osborn's death in May 1948. After Arizona voters approved a succession amendment in November 1948, he was sworn in as governor.

[4]*AR* and *PG*, February 8, 1949; *PG*, February 9, 1949; undescribed newsclippings, MP, SB 7.

[5]Johnson, *Central Arizona Project*, 62-3; *Arizona Times* and, February 15, 1949.

[6]*AR*, March 3, 10, 18 and *PG*, March 3, 1949.

[7]*PG*, March 21, 22, 1949; *AR*, March 22, 1949; *PG*, March 23, 1949.

[8]*AR*, March 27, 1949.

[9]*AR*, May 1, 1949.

[10]*PG*, May 28, 1949; letter, McFarland and Carl Hayden to George W. Aiken, April 8, 1949, MP, 34/1.

[11]*PG*, May 30, 1949; *Arizona News*, April 1, 1949.

[12]*AR*, April 29, 1949.

[13]*Mac*, 209; *PG* April 9, June 20, 1949; *AR* June 10, 14, 1949; Johnson, 68-9.

[14]*PG*, August 25, 1949.

[15]*Mac*, 79-80.

[16]Ibid. and *PG*, August 10, 1949. See also *Broadcasting Magazine*, June 6, 27, August 15, 22, 29, September 19, 1949, and April 3, July 10, and August 14, 1950; *PG*, August, 10, 1949.

[17]*Mac*, 80-82.

[18]*Congressional Quarterly: Individual Voting Records, U.S. Senate*, 1949 (CQ News Features, Washington, D.C., 1950) 14-15.

[19]*Mac*, 184-85; *Washington Star*, September, 30, *Washington Post*, September 30, *PG*, September 30, October 4, 14, October, all 1949; Carl Hayden voted for confirmation of Olds. See also Robert Caro, *Lyndon Johnson: Master of the Senate*, (New York: Alfred A. Knopf, 2002) 254, 260-62, 274, 283.

[20]*PG*, October 3, 18, 1949; *AR*, October 4, 10, 18, 21, 28, 1949; *CR*, 81st Congress, 1st Session, October 17, 1949, 2d Session, April 19, 1950, 5410; "The McFarland Philosophy," 16, MP 140/40. For a positive assessment of McFarland's Navajo-Hopi Rehabilitation Act by Native American historian D'Arcy McNickle, see Harold Fey and D'Arcy McNickle, *Indians and Other Americans: Two Ways of Life Meet* (New York: Harper and Row, 1970) 182-88; letter, Roland Bibolet to author, December 17, 1993.

[21]Johnson, 70-1; *AR* and *PG*, January 25, 1950.

[22]*AR*, February 1, 1950; *PG*, February 2, 1950; "This Is the Truth About CAP," and "The Nation's Most Fantastic Project," MP, 35/9; letter, McFarland to William Knowland, February 2, 1950, MP, 35/11; letter, Sheridan Downey to McFarland, February 5, 1950, MP, 34/6.

[23]Johnson, *Central Arizona Project*, 70; *AR*, February 7, 1950; *PG*, February 13, 1950.

[24]*AR*, editorial, "An Orchid for McFarland," February 8, 1950.

[25]*AR*, February 9, 1950; *PG*, February 7, 10, 1950.

[26]Telegram, Hayden and McFarland to various senators, February 20, 1950, MP, 34/1; *Los Angeles Times*, February 22, 1950.

[27]*PG*, February 23, 1950; *ADS*, February 22, 1950; *Washington Post*, February 22, 1950.

[28]*Los Angeles Herald Express*, February 22, 1950; *PG*, February 22, 1950; *AR*, March 2, 1950.

[29]Undescribed newsclippings of April and May 1950, SB 7, MP; *AR*, March 23, April 5, 11, 1950; *Mac*, 109.

[30]Undescribed newsclippings of April and May 1950, MP, SB 7.

[31]"1950 Campaign Speech," n.d., MP, 47/8; interview of McFarland by Joe B. Frantz, Sky Harbor Airport, Phoenix, February 8, 1970, in Oral History Collection, Lyndon Baines Johnson Presidential Library, Austin, Texas; see also McCullough, 773-83.

[32]Alan D. Harper, *The Politics of Loyalty: The White House and the Communist Issue* (Westport, Connecticut: Greenwood Publishing, 1969) 160-61, 295-96.

CHAPTER 9

[1]George E. Reedy, *The U.S. Senate: Paralysis or a Search for Consensus?* (New York: Mentor Publications, 1986). For an analysis of the inner club and art of voting, see pages 26-29 and 47-55.

[2]Rowland Evans and Robert Novak, *Lyndon B. Johnson: The Exercise of Power* (New York, Signet Publications, 1966) 41-2; Clinton Anderson with Milton Viorst, *Outsider in the Senate: Senator Clinton Anderson's Memoirs* (New York: World Publishing, 1970) 108-111; letter, Roland Bibolet to author, December 13, 1993. The "Class of 48" consisted of those newly elected Democratic senators of that year who quickly gained prominence and recognition in senate affairs. These included former Secretary of Agriculture Clinton Anderson (NM), former Oklahoma governor (and McFarland's old normal school classmate) Robert S. Kerr (OK), former Congressman Lyndon Baines Johnson (TX), former Minneapolis Mayor Hubert Humphrey (MN), and economist Paul Douglas (IL). Russell quote from Caro, *Master of the Senate*, 364.

[3]*Mac*, 109-10; *Newsweek*, December 4, 1950, 16.

[4] Morgan, *Kerr*, 108-109; Alonzo Hamby, *Beyond the New Deal: Harry S. Truman and American Liberalism* (New York: Columbia University Press, 1973)441-42; *AR*, January 6, 1951. *U.S. News and World Report*, January 19, 1951, p. 31; Clinton Anderson, 108-111.

[5]*AR*, January 4, 1951; *New York Times*, January 3, 1951; *Newsweek*, December 25, 1950, p. 16.

[6]*Mac*, 115-16; letter, Truman to McFarland, January 3, 1951, MP, 51/3; Willard Shelton, "The Do-Less 82nd," *Nation*, January 6, 1951, 5-6; *AR*, January 6, 1951. Shelton's article was written December 29, 1951, in anticipation of McFarland's selection.

[7]Evans and Novak, *Lyndon B. Johnson* 42-3; *AR*, January 3, 6, 1951; Morgan, *Kerr*, 108-109; Clinton Anderson, 108-111; Roland Bibolet, interviewed by Michael L. Gillette, Los Angeles, California, May 14, 1980, in Oral History Collection, Lyndon Baines Johnson

Presidential Library, 2-3. For Johnson's choice as whip and a negative view of McFarland's capabilities, see Robert Dallek, *Lone Star Rising: Lyndon Johnson and His Times, 1908-1960* (New York: Oxford University Press, 1991) 389-90 and Caro, *Master of the Senate.*

[8]Hamby, *Truman*, 442; *New York Times* and *AR*, January 3, 1951; Mellet in Caro, *Master of the Senate*, 365.

[9]Floyd M. Riddick, *Majority and Minority Leaders of the Senate: History and Development of the Office of the Floor Leaders* (Washington, D.C., U.S. Government Printing Office, 1973) 2-3. Riddick was parliamentarian of the Senate. The article was prepared under the direction of Francis K. Valeo, Secretary of the Senate as a result of S.R. 151, August 2, 1973, introduced by Senators Mike Mansfield (majority leader, D-MT) and Hugh Scott (minority leader, R-PA). The article is in MP, 51/1; ibid., 4, 7-8; David B. Truman, *The Congressional Party: A Case Study* (New York, 1959) 112.

[10]Riddick, *Leaders*, 8-13; *Mac*, 111; Reedy, *Senate*, 20-22, 50; Roland Bibolet, phone interview, August 26, 2002.

[11]Riddick, *Leaders*, 10-15; *Mac*, 119; memorandum for Mrs. Carmen Dyches, "Work as Majority Leader," August 1951, MP, 51/1; *Mac*, 141.

[12]*Mac*, 120; *Newsweek* article of October 22, 1951.

[13]*Mac*, 124; *AR*, January 6, 1951.

[14]Ralph K. Huitt, "Senate Democratic Leadership," 4, 54. The paper was delivered at the 1960 Annual Meeting of the American Political Science Association in New York City. It is in MP, 51/1. See also *Mac*, 136-7.

[15]The phrase "he brought order to chaos," is Roland Bibolet's, interview, April 1990, Nogales, Arizona.

[16]*Mac*, 116-18; *CR*, 82d Congress, 1st Session, January 5, 1951, 4. Robert Caro is particularly harsh on McFarland's majority leadership, stating, "by the of end of the year he was a figure of ridicule in the Senate and in national publications as well." This is refuted in part by *Newsweek's* October 22 article (note 12) and by the assessment of the *Arizona Republic* of August 31, 1951 (note 44), and by Caro's questionable research on McFarland. The author did not avail himself of the McFarland Archives; he several times erroneously refers to Mac as "Bob" McFarland, even in the index where there is only one McFarland, and, in what could be construed as a Pulliam type typographical error, at one point allows a reference to "Boob" McFarland. For James McMillan's refutation of Caro's position, see "Order Amidst Chaos: U.S. Senate Majority Leader Ernest W. McFarland," presented at Arizona Historical Society Annual Meeting, Tempe, April 2003, in author's possession.

[17]Speech in *Mac*, 120-123.

[18]Letter, Roland Bibolet to author, December 17, 1993; "Reminiscences of Roland Bibolet," in MP, miscellaneous papers donated by Mildred Hagerty; CR, ibid., 46; AR, January 5, 6, 10, 14, 1951; *Encyclopedia Britannica Book of the Year 1952*, 702; *Mac*, 116-18, 120-24, 127-28; CR, 82d Congress, 1st Session, January 16, 1951, 323; *New York Times*, January 11, 12, 1951. The calendar of all Big Four meetings and guests is in the Papers of Matthew J. Connelly, Harry S. Truman Library. Unfortunately no minutes of these meetings exist; letter to author from Benedict K. Zobrist, Director, Harry S. Truman Library, Independence, Missouri, May 22, 1992. See also interview with Stephen J. Spingarn, March 20-29, 1967, Washington, D.C., in Oral History Collection, Harry S. Truman Library, pages 388-90.

[19]*PG*, October 15, 1951; letter, Roland Bibolet to author, Dec. 17, 1993.

[20]Roland Bibolet interview, Johnson Presidential Library, *loc. cit.*, p. 4; McFarland interview, Johnson Presidential Library, p. 10.

[21]*AR*, March 7, 1951; *New York Times*, March 21, 1951.

[22]Statement on "Troops to Europe Resolution," undated, MP, 48/18.

[23]*AR*, April 4, 1951; press release, April 2, 1951, both MP, 47/9; statement for NBC, April 4, 1951, MP, 49/21.

[24]Statement, April 11, 1951, MP, 47/9.

[25]*AR*, April 9, 1951; *New York Times*, April 7, 10, 1951; statement, April 8, 1951, MP, 49/7.6

[26]*Mac*, 144-46. A picture exists in the Douglas MacArthur Archives, Norfolk, Virginia, of McFarland accompanying MacArthur to the joint session in the open-air limousine. It is taken from a distance and the riders are not identified in the photo. House Minority Leader Joseph Martin rides beside MacArthur in the far back seat, while McFarland and House Majority Leader John McCormack ride in the middle seat.

[27]*AR*, April 25, 1951; *Mac*, 173; letter, Roland Bibolet to author, December 17, 1993; Ferrell, *Truman*, 330-36; McCullough, *Truman*, 840-52.

[28]Undescribed newsclippings, MP, 1/10.

[29]"The McFarland Philosophy," MP 140/40.

[30]*AR*, March 1, 1951.

[31]Johnson, *CAP*, 78-81, 98; *Mac*, 210.

[32]Donald R. McCoy and Richard Reuthen, *Quest and Response: Minority Rights and the Truman Administration* (Lawrence: University Press of Kansas, 1973) 285. A complete discussion of these events is found on pages 171-77.

[33]Interview of McFarland by Rose McKee of International News Service March 1951, distributed in October 1951, MP, 49/21.

[34]McCoy and Reuthen, *Quest and Response* 171-177, 287-88; Ferrell, *Truman*, 297-98.

[35]See *Mac*, chapter 12, "Senate Rules (Filibuster)," and page 169.

[36]Ibid.

[37]Statement, "The Record of the Senate," July 6, 1951, MP 47/9.

[38]*AR*, June 27, July 2, 15, August, 14, October 30, 1951; *New York Times*, July 29, 1951; Caro, *Master of the Senate*, 386-7; Roland Bibolet phone interview, August 26, 2002.

[39]Thomas C. Reeves, *The Life and Times of Joe McCarthy: A Biography* (New York: Stein and Day, 1982) 378-79, 400; letter, Roland Bibolet to author, December 1, 1988. *AR*, 21 and 31 August 1951; *New York Times*, 10 August 1951. McCarthy had written positively of McFarland (and Hayden) as among the top senators upon his elevation to the majority leadership. Now McCarthy became a bitter enemy of McFarland and influenced the upcoming 1952 elections; *Mac*, 138.

[40]*AR* and *New York Times*, both August 22, 1951; comment, "How Can We Assume Peace in Our Time," for *Cosmopolitan Magazine*, May 15, 1951, MP, 49/29; *AR*, August 16, 1951.

[41]All radio transcriptions are in MP, Box 49.

[42]"Tributes to Ernest W. McFarland, A Senator from the State of Arizona, in the Senate of the United States, October 20, 1951, Relative to His Record as Majority Leader of the Senate of the United States during the First Session of the Eighty-Second Congress," MP, 51/1.

[43]"Summary of the First Session of the 82nd Congress by the Honorable Ernest W. McFarland, Majority Leader, U.S. Senate," MP, 51/1. See also "Review of the Work of the First Session of the 82nd Congress by the Majority Leader," October 26, 1951, MP 51/8, and Ernest McFarland in the *Democratic Digest*, December 1951.

[44]*AR*, August 31, 1951 in *Mac*, 137.

CHAPTER 10

[1]*AR*, January 5, 1952.

[2] Harold Foote Gosnell, *Truman's Crises: A Political Biography of Harry S. Truman* (Westport, Connecticut: Greenwood Press, 1980) 490-91. The death of Senator Vandenberg in April 1951 caused concern for the continuation of the bipartisan foreign policy.

[3]Ernest McFarland, "Comment on the President's State of the

Union Message," January 9, 1952, MP, 51/8.

[4]Feis in Gosnell, *Truman's Crises*, 491-92; *Collier's Encyclopedia 1953 Yearbook* (New York: Crowell-Collier Publishing Co., 1953) 726; letter, Roland Bibolet to author, December 28, 1993.

[5]"Statement by the Democratic Majority of the Senate," and "Declaration of Democratic Principles by the Majority Members of the U.S. Senate," MP, 51/1.

[6]*AR*, January 1, 9, 1952.

[7]For a summary of these issues see *Colliers 1953*.

[8]Ibid., 728; Gosnell, *Truman's Crises*, 495.

[9]MP, 12/2; CR, 82nd Congress, 2d Session, March 7, 1952, 1962; *Colliers, 1953*, 728; Gosnell, *Truman's Crises*, 494; McFarland interview in Johnson Presidential Library, 16-17; Bibolet interview in Johnson Presidential Library; Pearson in Caro, *Master of the Senate*, 388; Roland Bibolet phone interview, August 26,2002. for a rare example of McFarland's criticizing Johnson, see *Mac*, 126-7; letter, Johnson to Bibolet, November, 24, 1954.

[10]Gosnell, *Truman's Crises*, 494; *Colliers*, ibid.; McCoy and Reuthen, *Quest and Response*; 301.

[11]McCoy and Reuthen, *Quest and Reponse*, 302; *AR*, June 28, 1952.

[12]McCoy and Reuthen, *Quest and Response*, 298-311.

[13]*AR*, April 22, 24, 1952. A preliminary injunction was granted to nullify the seizure on April 29. On June 2, the Supreme Court ruled the seizure unconstitutional. See also McCullough, *Truman*, 897-902; Ferrell, *Truman*, 370-75.

[14]Gosnell, *Truman's Crises*, 492-4; *PG*, June 10, 11, 1952. For LBJ's role in instituting the procedure of pairing to preclude further cuts, see Caro, 397-400.

[15]*Collier's, 1953*, 729.

[16]*AR*, May 1, and *PG*, May 3, 1952. McFarland's mid-April speech in Tucson was entitled "How Congress Works," MP, 48/19.

[17]*PG*, May 5, 10, and *AR*, May 4, 1952. For the entire text of Douglas's speech, see *AR*, May 5, 1952. Telegram, Lewis Douglas to McFarland, September 30, 1952, Lewis Douglas Papers, Box 308, File "McFarland 1952-58", University of Arizona Library Special Collections, Tucson. Subsequent correspondence between Douglas and McFarland indicated that Douglas favored McFarland's foreign policy views of extensive aid to allies over Goldwater's but favored Republican domestic policy, particularly fiscal. The latter outweighed the former. See letters between the two of October 15, 1956, May 5 and 26, and June 16, 1958, in Douglas Papers under McFarland. See also Robert Paul Browder and Thomas G. Smith, *Independent: A*

Biography of Lewis W. Douglas (New York: A.A. Knopf, 1986). The Pulliam reaction is in *AR*, May 5, 6, and *PG*, May 10, 1952.

[18]Reprinted material from *CR*, May 12, 1952, in MP, 48/17; legislative files, MP, 12/14: See also *CR*, 82d Congress, 2d Session, May 12, 1952, 5023, 5031, 5033; June 3, 1952, 6420; July 8, 1952, 9756; *PG*, May 6, 1952; *AR*, June 14, 1952.

[19]Letter, McFarland to Sidney B. Moeur, May 26, 1952, MP, 49/27. Hill was one of the dwindling number of Democratic liberals from the Deep South. Others who served with McFarland included John Sparkman of Alabama and Claude Pepper of Florida. Upper South liberals included Alben Barkley of Kentucky and Estes Kefauver of Tennessee.

[20]*Mac* 70-72; *AR*, June 8, 1952.

[21]*PG*, May 24 and June 10, 1952; *AR*, February 7, 1952.

[22]The McFarland Philosophy, 24, 27, 28, MP 140/40; *CR*, 82d Congress, 2d Session, June 25, 1952, 7974; *AR*, June 26, 1952.

[23]*PG*, June 25, 1952; *AR*, July 6, 1952; *CR*, 82d Congress, 2d Session; July 5, 1952, 9545-6.

[24]*Collier's*, 729-30.

[25]"Tributes to Ernest W. McFarland at the Closing of the 82nd Congress," MP, 51/1; *CR*, 82nd Congress, 2nd Session, July 5, 7, 1952. All tributes except Barkley's and Humphrey's, July 5. Over forty McFarland bills that passed the Senate became law. See appendix for McFarland legislation referred to by LBJ. Johnson succeeded McFarland as party leader in 1953. He was minority leader from 1953-1955. He was considered the Senate's most powerful majority leader from 1955 to 1961. Johnson then became vice president (1961-63) and president (1963-1969). Roland Bibolet served under Johnson from 1953-55 before returning to McFarland when he became governor in 1955.

CHAPTER 11

[1]*PG* February 13, 1952. For further information on politics and elections in the West and Arizona in particular, see Frank H. Jonas, ed., *Politics in the American West* (Salt Lake: University of Utah Press, 1969) chapters: Jonas, "The Western Scene," and Ross R. Rice, "Arizona: Politics in Transition," hereinafter Jonas-Rice; Hugh A. Bone, "Western Politics and the 1952 Elections," and Paul Kelso, "The 1952 Elections in Arizona," both in *Western Political Quarterly* 6

(March 1953) 93-102.

²*AR*, July 17, 1952. Dan Quayle, vice president during the Bush administration from 1989-93, is Eugene Pulliam's grandson.

³*AR* February 28, 29 and March 3, 8, 1952. It has been said that "In Arizona, water is politics." McFarland was an acknowledged legal and political expert in the area. For Goldwater's subsequent reputation in the field, including alleged ignorance of water issues, "mistakes" and "hypocrisy" concerning public versus private interests, see Jonas, *Politics*, 8, 13, and Jonas, "The Western Scene" *Western Political Quarterly* 18 (September 1964): 10.

⁴*AR* March 7-9 and *PG* March 17, 18, 21, 1952.

⁵*AR*, May 20, 1952. *PG*, March 17 and April 9 and *AR*, March 26, 1952.

⁶Letter, R.D. Grant to Hartmen Barber, April 22, 1952, enclosed in R.D. Grant to McFarland, May 9, 1952.

⁷*AR*, July 9, and *PG* July, 15, 1952. State Department employee Alger Hiss had been found guilty of perjury regarding his ties with the Communist party in the 1930s. Nixon had been one of his major adversaries in the court hearings.

⁸L.C. Smith and Jim Foster, "The People's Choice: Dwight Eisenhower," (unpublished manuscript at Arizona State University History Department, Tempe) 9-15; *PG*, July 21, 22 and *AR*, July 21, 24, 1952.

⁹*AR*, July 3, 10, and *PG*, July 2 and August 2, 1952.

¹⁰*Graham County Guardian*, July 25, 1952. This statement was not reported in the Phoenix papers; *Congressional Record*, July 5, 1952, 9591-3.

¹¹*Mesa Tribune*, August 22 and *AR*, August 23, 1952. Gene Autry, a good friend of McFarland, owned ranch land in Pinal County and shared a common communications interest as well, owning a radio station in Tucson, and later a TV station in Phoenix.

¹²*AR*, August 24, 28, 1952, and miscellaneous newsclippings in Scrapbook 11, MP. McFarland spoke before thirty-five hundred people at Casa Grande, Goldwater before one hundred in Tucson.

¹³Along with the Pinto threat, Arizona GOP supporters, *de facto* Republicans, would often register Democrat in order to participate in the primaries for offices that were consistently held by Democrats in the normally one-party state (Jonas-Rice, 48, 63). See *PG*, September 30, 1952 for the final primary results.

¹⁴*AR*, September 23, 1952.

¹⁵Stephen C. Shadegg, *Arizona Politics: The Struggle to End One-Party Rule* (Tempe: Arizona State University, 1986) 57-62. The entire text of Goldwater's speech, minus his *ad lib* conclusion is in *PG*, September 19, 1952.

[16]*Prescott Courier*, October 19, 1952; "Race for the Senate," *Fortune* 46 (October 1952) 121-125. This article was found in the Barry Goldwater Collections, Arizona Historical Foundation, Hayden Library, Arizona State University, Tempe, Scrapbook: Newspaper clippings of political activities, August-October 1952, number 9. Scrapbooks 7-10 cover the 1952 campaign and are similar in content to those in the McFarland collection. Goldwater's personal papers on the campaign are unavailable, lost, or unfound at the time of writing.

[17]*ADS*, October 7, 1952.

[18]*Prescott Courier*, October 19, 1952. The charge against McFarland was untrue. The majority leader was on record in opposition to the Communist party and system. See also letter from Roland Bibolet to the author, December 1, 1988. Goldwater had been friends with McCarthy for several years since the latter had frequently vacationed in Arizona. Later, during McCarthy's troubles with the Senate, Goldwater remained one of his few supporters.

[19]Smith-Foster, p. 19; *Tucson Daily Citizen*, October 21, *PG*, October 22, *Arizona Daily Star*, October 23, 1952; undescribed newsclipping, Scrapbook 13, MP. Post election research revealed that during the month preceeding the election, the *Phoenix Gazette* alloted 376 column-inches of front-page news space in stories, photographs, and headlines to the Republicans and 177 to the Democrats. Similar information is not readily available for the *Arizona Republic*, which had the larger circulation. See Nathan B. Blumberg, *One-Party Press?* (Lincoln: University of Nebraska Press, 1954) 47-49. The figures are somewhat distorted by Eisenhower's October visit. Stevenson's visit was in September.

[20]*CR*, July 5, 1952, 9591-3; *AR* and *PG*, October 9, 1952; Lyndon Johnson to clerk of the *Congressional Record*, September 15, 1952, in Lyndon Baines Johnson Papers, LBJA Congressional File, Container 48, E.W. McFarland folder, Lyndon Baines Johnson Library, Austin, Texas. In the wake of Goldwater's victory, he ceased to ask for an investigation.

[21]Kelso, "1952 Elections," 100-02. Dean Smith, *The Goldwater's of Arizona*, (Flagstaff: Northland Press, 1986) 199-201; Shadegg, *Arizona Politics* 56.

[22]Shadegg, *Arizona Politics*, 62-3; Kelso, "1952 Elections," 100-02; Bone, "1952 Elections," 95. The Republican party did capture a slim majority in both houses of Congress during the 1952 elections, 48-47 with one Independent in the Senate. Vice President Nixon would also have a crucial tie-breaking Republican vote if called upon. The Republicans also gained since 1950 in the Arizona House from 11 of 72 to 30 of 80, and in the Arizona Senate from zero to 4 of 28 (Jonas-Rice, 62).

[23]Kelso, "1952 Elections,"100-02. Besides Maricopa (Phoenix) and Pima (Tucson), Goldwater took Yavapai, Coconino, and Apache counties.

[24]Letter, Roland Bibolet to author, December 28, 1993; James W. Johnson, *Arizona Politicians: the Noble and the Notorious* (Tucson: University of Arizona Press, 2002) 79.

[25]For campaign styles in Arizona, see Jonas-Rice, 51. Republican election advantages continued in Arizona. Writing fifteen years later, political scientist Ross Rice summed these up: "1. A higher proportion of Republicans than Democrats go to the polls. 2. The ratio of registered voters between the parties has narrowed because of Republican migration from normally Republican strongholds in other states. 3. The economy attracts higher-paid professional and technical workers, plus retired persons, while minority-group, lower-paid, union workers find less promise. 4. There have been many attractive candidates who have escaped the rigors of intra-party primary battles. 5. There is superior party motivation of workers who seemingly thrive in their role of laboring for a minority party. 6. National attention was focused for a decade on the charismatic Barry Goldwater." See Jonas-Rice, 67.

[26]Kelso, "1952 Elections," 100-02. The Arizona population grew from 499,261 to 749,587 between 1940 and 1950, a rate of about fifty percent. Figures for registered voters in Arizona include the following: 1940 - 158,382 Democrats, 20,872 Republicans; 1950 - 225,191 Democrats, 50,191 Republicans; 1956 - 250,616 Democrats, 111,107 Republicans. Figures are not available for 1952. Figures for other U.S. Senate races in Arizona are as follows from David R. Berman, *Parties and Elections in Arizona, 1863-1984* (Morrison Institute of Public Policy, School of Public Affairs, Arizona State University, Tempe, 1985):

Year	Democrat		Republican	
1940	McFarland	101,495	I.A. Jennings	39,65
1944	Hayden	90,335	Fred W. Pickett	39,891

(Hayden had already been elected in 1926, 1932, and 1938)

1946	McFarland	80,415	Ward S. Powers	35,022
1950	Hayden	116,246	Bruce Brockett	68,846
1952	McFarland	125,388	Goldwater	132,063
1956	Hayden	170,816	Ross F. Jones	107,447

1958   McFarland   129,030   Goldwater   164,593

1962   Hayden   199,217   Evan Mecham   163,388
(This was Hayden's seventh consecutive, and final election to the Senate. He also served from 1912-27 in the House, a still-standing record 57 years on Capitol Hill, 1912-69.)

[27]Interview, Del Lewis, December 1990, Phoenix, Arizona.

[28]For the entire 1952 world trip, see MP, 147/30, with the exception of the itinerary which is found in 160/7.

[29]Letter, Roland Bibolet to author, December 28, 1993.

[30]McFarland campaign brochures, 1956 and 1958, in MP.

[31]McMillan, "McFarland: Senate Years," 468-475.

[32]Contract letter draft to McFarland, January 24, 1953, from David Sarnoff (Chairman of the Board, RCA), Ellery W. Stone (President, RCA), and Walter Marshall (President, Western Union); *Washington Daily News*, April 24, 1953; *ACA News*, December 1953; all in MP, 247/1; *Mac* 224-5. McFarland turned down a salaried job with the Central Arizona Project at this time and said he would work for CAP without compensation.

[33]*AR*, May 31, 1953; *PG*, May 30, 1953; *Arizona Free Press*, July 24; press release, June 9, 1952, from McFarland's office on Phoenix's admission to network service; all 1953 in MP 254/8.

[34]*AR*, May 27 and June 12, 1954; *PG*, May 27 and June 11, 1954; Federal Communications Commission Public Notice 7043, 11 June 1954, Report No. 800 and Dissenting Opinion of Commissioner Hennock; all in MP 254/8.

[35]Interview with Del Lewis, June 15, 1993, Phoenix, Arizona

[36]"Station West," KTVK-TV Newletter, vol.1, no. 1, Phoenix, Arizona, March 1964, in MP 254/8.

[37]Pyle polled twenty-nine percent of the overall vote in the 1950 primaries. On Short Creek, see MP, Subgroup II: Governor, Series Eight: Campaigns, Subseries One: 1954 Campaign, Box 187 on Pyle. See also Series Five: Press Releases and Newsclippings, 1954-58, Subseries Two, Scrapbooks (SB) 1954-58, SB 1, Campaign, Inauguaration, and First Term Governor, August 1954-May 1955. Clippings found therein on Short Creek include *AR* and *PG*, July 27, 28, 1953.

[38]Broadcast of Elmer Davis on ABC Radio, July 27, 1953 in MP 187/43.

[39]*AR* and *PG*, July 27, 28, 1953, SB I; Mormon Church publication *Truth* (December 1953) Vol. 19, No. 7, in MP, Box 187.

[40]*Mac* 228; interview with Del Lewis, June 15, 1993, Phoenix, Arizona.

[41]*Nogales International*, June 4, 1954; *PG*, July 1, 1954.

[42]Bill Turnbow's column, "Under the Capitol Dome," *PG*, July 1, 2, 20, 1953; *AR*, July 21, 1953, in MP, SB 1.

[43]*Arizona Free Press*, August 20, 1954; *AR* and *PG* August 16, 1954, in MP, SB 1.

[44]*PG*, December 6, 1952 and August 20, 1954; *Arizona Free Press*, August 20, 1953. Goldwater did advocate Pyle's running against Carl Hayden in 1956.

[45]*Miami Herald*, Fla. September 9, 1954; N. D. Houghton, "The 1954 Elections in Arizona" *Western Political Science Quarterly*, (March 1955.)

[46]California Republican William Knowland became majority leader after Taft's death in 1953. See also miscellaneous campaign newsclippings, MP, SB 1.

[47]*PG*, September 29 and *Arizona Daily Star*, October 11, 1954.

[48]*Mac*, 229-33.

[49]*AR*, October 31, 1954.

[50]*PG*, November 3; *Nogales International*, November 5; *Eloy Enterprise*, November 4; all 1954.

[51]*PG*, November 3, 1954.

[52]Shadegg, *Arizona Politics*, 71.

CHAPTER 12

[1]The McFarland Papers covering the gubernatorial years are less complete than those covering the Senate; therefore I have relied heavily on newspaper accounts of the day. Most of these clippings are located in MP, Subgroup II, "Governor," Subseries Two, Scrapbooks 1-8, 1954-58. When the date of the newsclipping is undescribed, it is identified by Scrapbook (SB). Otherwise, clippings are just identified by newspaper name and date.

See also Chapter 18 of *MAC*, entitled "First Term as Governor" and Jay Wagoner's *Arizona Heritage*, pages 356-58. A more recent description of these years is found in *Arizona's Governors, 1912-1990*, edited by Dr. John Meyers of Heritage Publishers Inc. of Phoenix. See also James Johnson, *Arizona Politicians: The Noble and the Notorious* (University of Arizona Press, Tucson: 2002). Of more assistance have been three lengthy documents from the McFarland Papers. "The Governor's Record" is thirty-eight page description of his first administration prepared for the 1956 campaign and found in Box 305,

File 23 (305/23). "Ernest W. McFarland's Record and Position," (197/1, 28 pages) and "The McFarland Philosophy," (140/40, 48 pages) were both drawn up for the 1958 U.S. Senate campaign and while covering his entire career were particularly valuable in examining his second administration.

As a wedding present, McFarland gave Del Lewis managerial operation of his Pinal County farms.

[2]*PG*, January 3, 1955; inaugural program and address, MP 165/14.

[3]Letter, Roland Bibolet to author, January 6, 1994.

[4]Message to the Twenty-second Legislature, First Session, State of Arizona, January 10, 1955, MP, 165/14; *PG*, January 10, 11, and *ADS*, January 10, all 1955.

[5]Jonas-Rice, *Politics in the American West*, 57-59, 63.

[6]*PG* and *TDC*, January 11, 1955.

[7]*ADS*, January 12, and February 19; *AR*, January 20, all 1955.

[8]*AR*, March 6, 1955.

[9]*Arizona Sun*, March 18, 1955.

[10]*TDC*, March 14; *ADS*, March 21; PG, March 26, all 1955; also George Bideaux's "Down in Cochise County," March 31, 1955.

[11]*PG*, March 21; *ADS*, March 28; *AR*, April 2, all 1955.

[12]*AR*, April 2, 1955; letter, Roland Bibolet to author, January 6, 1994.

[13]*Arizona Health Digest*, vol. 2, # 11, April 1955.

[14]Ibid. and *Arizona News*, April 8; *Holbrook Tribune News*, April 8; *TDC*, April 4; *PG* and *AR*, April 5; *ADS*, April 6, all 1955.

[15]*ADS*, April 11, 1955.

[16]*ADS*, April 9, 1955.

[17]*ADS*, April 6; *Arizona Free Press*, April 8; *AR*, April 4, all 1955.

[18]Ibid.

[19]Letter, Roland Bibolet to author, January 6, 1994.

[20]*AR*, April 25; *Nogales International*, August 19, both 1955.

[21]*Mesa Tribune*, September 1; *PG*, September 13, 20, all 1955; letter, Roland Bibolet to author, January 6, 1993.

[22]*AR*, June 13 and September 18, and miscellaneous newsclippings of April, all 1955, in MP, SB 2. In March 1987, Professor William Lyons of the History Department, Northern Arizona University, Flagstaff, related to the author that McFarland was ignored in a receiving line by local residents after giving a speech at the college during his gubernatorial administration.

[23]*Nogales International*, July 28, 1955, reprinted by the *Legislative Review* of September 13, 1955. Like Goldwater, the eclectic Williams had also been a supporter of Joe McCarthy. The water

issue Williams refers to is described in following paragraphs and concerns the state's acting independently in financial efforts for CAP.

[24]*ADS*, August 17 and *AR*, April 19, both 1955

[25]Johnson, *Central Arizona Project*, 102-3; The suggestion of acting independently also reflected back to the original ideas of Fred Colter, which continued to be verbalized by legislator Sidney Kartus; ADS, April 19 and August 5; *Mesa Tribune*, August 16; *AR*, July 1, 8; *Yuma Daily Sun*, July 1, all 1955; interview author and Wayne Aiken, Phoenix, June 16, 1993.

[26]"Statement and Proclamation to the Legislature," MP 165/15; *TDC*, October 25 and *ADS*, October 19, 21, 24, all 1955, and miscellaneous clippings, MP, SB 2.

[27]Wagner, *Arizona*, 357; letter, Roland Bibolet to author, January 6, 1994.

[28]Undescribed newsclippings, MP, SB 2.

[29]*PG*, December 6; *AR*, December 8, both 1955; interviews between author and Wayne Aiken, *loc.cit.*, and Ben Avery, Phoenix, June 15, 1993.

[30]Avery interview. For Avery's reflections upon McFarland's death, see *AR*, June 9, 1984.

[31]*AR* and *ADS*, both December 9, 1955.

[32]*TDC* and *PG*, both December 12, 1955.

[33]Wayne Aiken in *PG*, December 17, 1955; Clinton Anderson in *Yavapai Messenger*, December 15, 1955.

[34]Brown in *ADS*, December 13, 1955. It did take until 1968 for CAP to pass Congress; McFarland had predicted another 15 years, i.e., about 1971. The Supreme Court did rule in favor of Arizona in 1963.

[35]*AR*, December 12, 1955.

[36]*TDC*, November 23; *Mesa Tribune* and *PG*, both November 29, all 1955. A study by the Stanford Institute indicated that state revenues could amount to $.8 to $1.3 million by Sperry-Rand's employing three thousand workers.

[37]"Message to the Second Special Session of the Twenty-second Legislature," November 29, 1955, MP, 171/2.

[38]*TDC*, December 13, 1955.

[39]*PG*, December 13, 16; and *ADS*, December 16, all 1955.

[40]*PG*, December 19; and *AR*, December 22, both 1955.

[41]*TDC* and *AR*, both December 21, 1955; *Mac*, 247-8.

[42]*AR*, January 8, 1956.

[43]"Message to the Second Regular Session of the Twenty-second Legislature, January 9, 1956," MP 171/2. See also *PG* and *AR*, both January 10, 1956. By employing the National Guard to assist the Highway Patrol, highway deaths had decreased from 403 to 358 from

1954 to 1955 and from 55 to 28 over those consecutive Christmas holidays.

[44]"Budget Message to the Second Regular Session of the Twenty-second Legislature, January 16, 1956," MP, 165/3; *Mesa Tribune*, January 14, and *Douglas Dispatch*, January 16, both 1956.

[45]*Arizona News* February 24; *AR*, March 6; *PG*, March 10, all 1956.

[46]"Message to the Legislature, February 22, 1956," MP, 171/3; *ADS*, February 23, 1956.

[47]*AR* and *ADS*, both February 28, 1956; *Yuma Daily Sun*, March 8, 1956.

[48]*Mesa Tribune*, March 15, 1956.

[49]*Mesa Tribune*, March 30, 1956; rough draft of letter from McFarland to Harry Ruppelius and Clarence Carpenter in MP, 167/2.

[50]*Mesa Tribune*, April 11; *ADS*, April 12, 14; *PG*, April 13; *TDC*, April 14; *Yuma Daily Sun*, April 15, all 1956.

[51]*TDC*, April 13, 15; *ADS* and *AR*, both April 14, all 1956.

[52]"Record of the Twenty-second Legislature of the State of Arizona," in MP, 165/7.

[53]*AR*, April 29 and May 6; *ADS*, April 29, all 1956.

[54]Letters between McFarland and Carl Hayden of March 14, 27, 29, 1956, in MP; *Nogales International*, April 23; *AR*, April 24 and May 4, 5, all 1956.

[55]*PG*, July 30 and *AR*, July 29, both 1956.

[56]*AR* and miscellaneous newsclippings, all May 21, 1956 in MP, SB 3; letter, Roland Bibolet to author, January 6, 1994.

[57]Ibid.

[58]*TDC*, August 16, 1956. The speech critical of Eisenhower is in MP, 172/9; see also Caro, *Master of the Senate*, 813,818.

[59]*AR*, October 2, 1956; *ADS*, September 26, 1956. The election campaign intinerary is in MP. 184/4. The desegregation plank did not pass at this time.

[60]*PG*, October 16; *ADS*, October 14; *AR*, October 18, 21, all 1956.

[61]*TDC*, October 23, 1956.

[62]*AR*, October 21 and *ADS*, October 25, both 1956.

[63]*ADS*, October 26, 1956.

[64]*Glendale News*, November 2, 1956.

[65]*PG*, November 6, 1956.

[66]*PG*, November 8, 1956; Jonas-Rice, *Politics in the American West*, 51.

[67]N.D. Houghton, "The 1956 Election in Arizona," *Western Political Science Quarterly*, vol. 9, March 1956.

[68]Houghton, ibid.; *AR*, November 9, 1956.

CHAPTER 13

[1]Inaugural message, January 7, 1957, in MP, 165/2; *AR*, January 8, 1957; *PG*, December 20, 1956.

[2]*PG*, January 4, 14, 1957.

[3]"Message to the Twenty-third Legislature, First Session, State of Arizona, January 14, 1957," in MP, 165/2.

[4]"Budget message to the Twenty-third Legislature, First Session, January 21, 1957," MP, 165/4; *PG*, January 21, 1957; undescribed newsclipping from *ADS* in MP, SB 4.

[5]*PG* and *AR*, January 25; *PG*, January 21, all 1957.

[6]Undescribed newsclippings in MP, SB 4.

[7]*PG*, March 11, 1957.

[8]Letter, Roland Bibolet to author, January 6, 1994.

[9]*ADS*, February 1; *PG*, February 6, both 1957; undescribed newsclipping from *TDC* in SB 4. The federal government put up one hundred dollars for every six state dollars regarding construction of interstate highways and one hundred for every twenty-eight state dollars for other highway construction.

[10]Letter of March 4, 1957 in *Mojave Miner* of March 7, 1957. An undated newsclipping from the *Tombstone Epitaph* stated workers' sales tax increase would be from two to three percent, while the raise for industry would be from one to 1.5 percent.

[11]*AR*, March 7; *PG*, March 5, both 1957.

[12]*AR*, March 11, 1957.

[13]For all, see *TDC*, March 12 and *AR*, March 11, 13, 15 all 1957.

[14]*TDC* and *PG*, March 15; *PG* and *AR*, March 16, all 1957. Property taxes had gone up from twenty-five to thirty percent.

[15]*TDC*, ibid.

[16]*AR*, March 6, 1957.

[17]*PG*, March 16, 1957. Arkansas Democrat John McClellan chaired the committee.

[18]Ibid.

[19]*AR*, March 17, 1957.

[20]Undescribed Bill Turnbow column in *PG* in SB 4; *ADS*, March 19, 1957.

[21]*AR*, March 22, 1957.

[22]*PG*, March 22, 1957.

[23]All undescribed newsclippings in MP, SB 4, including undated letter to editor of *PG* and article in *Holbrook Tribune*.

[24]*AR*, June 29, 1957. McFarland was attending a governor's

conference in Williamsburg, Virginia, but distance did not preclude publication of statements of regret from Hayden, Rhodes, and Udall, all in Washington, D.C. McFarland's statement appeared on July 1 in the *TDC*. See also *Mac*, 270.

[25]Ibid.; *AR*, July 1 and *Winslow Mail*, May 17, both 1957.

[26]*AR*, March 23, 1957.

[27]*ADS*, April 14, July 8, 12; *PG*, June 1, 21, 25 and July 1, all 1957 and undescribed picture of July 31 groundbreaking in MP, SB, 7.

[28]Johnson, *Central Arizona Project*, 110-116; *PG*, August 5; *ADS*, August 8; *AR*, August 7 and October 2, all 1957.

[29]*AR*, July 16 and *PG*, October 24, 1957. Many of these issues were debated and discussed at the meeting of the National Reclamation Association held in Phoenix in November. Ironically, as plans evolved for the construction of Glen Canyon Dam, Mac and Arizona later sided with California in opposing federal plans to deplete Lake Mead behind Hoover Dam, in order to rapidly fill Lake Powell behind Glen Canyon.

[30]*Nogales International*, October 18; *ADS*, October 10, both 1957.

[31]Interview of McFarland by David Reed on August 29, 1957 in MP, 173/6 for the issue of *U.S. News and World Report*, October 11, 1957. See also *ADS* and *AR*, both October 18, 1957.

[32]Stewart Udall in *ADS* March 29; columnist Doris Fleeson in *Washington Star*, June 27 and *Los Angeles Examiner*, June 28, all 1957. McCarthy died of alcoholism in 1957.

[33]*Bisbee Daily Review*, January 5 ; *ADS*, January 9, both 1958.

[34]"Message to the Twenty-third Legislature, Second Session, State of Arizona," January 13, 1958, in MP, 165/2; *PG*, January 13, 1958. See also 1958 budget message, MP, 165/5.

[35]*PG*, January 13 and *ADS*, January 15, both 1958.

[36]Press conference February 18, 1958, MP, 173/6; *PG* and *TDC*, both February 19; *AR*, February 18; *ADS*, February 20, all 1958.

[37]Press conference, *loc. cit.*; *Arizona News* and *AR*, both February 21, 1958. The *Republic* supported the gas tax.

[38]Miscellaneous newsclippings, SB 7, MP; *ADS*, February 23, 1958.

[39]Press conference, February 21, 1958, MP, 173/6; *PG*, February 27, 1958.

[40]*TDC*, February 21, 1958.

[41]Miscellanious newsclippings of February 28 and March 4, 1958 in SB 7, MP.

[42]*ADS*, March 6 and *PG*, March 5, both 1958.

[43]*TDC*, March 6; *Mesa Tribune*, March 16, both 1958.

[44]*AR*, March 15 and *Douglas Dispatch*, March 16, both 1958.

[45]"Proclamation Calling a Special Session of the Twenty-third Legislature of the State of Arizona, March 18, 1958," MP, 165/5; *AR*, March 16, 1958.

[46]*AR*, March 16, 18; *ADS*, March 18, both 1958.

[47]*AR*, March 23, 1958.

[48]Press conference, March 24, 1958, MP, 173/6; *AR*, March 19, 1958.

[49]Press conferences, March 24, April 1, 3, 9 all 1958, MP, 173/6; *ADS*, March 29, 1958.

[50]Press conferences, ibid.

[51]*PG*, April 2, 3; cartoon in *AR*, April 5, all 1958

[52]*ADS*, April 6, 1958.

[53]*Tombstone Epitaph*, April 10, 1958.

[54]*AR*, April 7, 1958.

[55]Letter, Roland Bibolet to author, January 6, 1994.

[56]Roy D. Morey, *Politics and Legislation: The Office of Governor in Arizona*, Arizona Government Studies, Number 3, Institute of Government Research (Tucson: University of Arizona Press, 1965) 24-27, 35-39, 52-65, 86-87.

[57]John P. White, Leonard E. Goodall, Ernest W. McFarland, and Paul Fannin, *The Office of Governor in Arizona*, Bureau of Government Research, Public Affairs Series No. 7 (Tempe: Arizona State University, 1964) 11-12. See also Jonas-Rice, 65.

[58]Ibid.

CHAPTER 14

[1]Johnson, *Central Arizona Project*, 98. The title of this chapter is based on the paper "Style vs. Substance: The 1952 and 1958 McFarland-Goldwater U.S. Senate Campaigns," given by Dr. McMillan at the joint annual meeting of the Arizona and New Mexico Historical Societies, April 1990, Santa Fe, New Mexico.

[2]James M. Perry, *A Report in Depth on Barry Goldwater: A New Look at a Presidential Candidate* (Silver Spring, Maryland: *National Observer*, 1964) 64-77. This chapter, "The Lonely Position," was found in the Goldwater Papers, Arizona Historical Foundation, Arizona State University, Tempe. The Gila Monster resides today behind glass at McFarland State Park.

[3]Frank Jonas, ed., *Political Dynamiting* (Salt Lake City: University of Utah Press, 1970). Jonas coined the term "political dynamiting" for this work. The two chapters covering this campaign are "The Newspaper as a Giant Public Relations Firm in Politics," and

"The Unintentional Smear," pages 143-219, both written by Jonas and R. John Eyre.

[4]John Barnard, *Walter Reuther and the Rise of the Auto Workers* (Boston: Little-Brown, 1983) 164-5.

[5]*PG*, April 19; *AR*, April 20, 21; *TDC*, April 21, all 1958; letter, Roland Bibolet to author, July 24, 1994.

[6]*PG*, April 20, 1958; letter, Roland Bibolet to author, July 24, 1994.

[7]*ADS*, April 22, 1958.

[8]Jonas, 144.

[9]Miscellaneous undescribed newsclippings, 1958 campaign scrapbook 15, MP. See also *AR*, July 23, 1958. Scrapbooks 16 and 17 also cover the 1958 campaign. In the McFarland Papers, boxes 137-141 deal with this campaign, while boxes 142-144 deal specifically with Barry Goldwater.

[10]*AR*, May 8, 1958; Jonas, *Political Dynamiting*, 145, 177 (fn 6, 7); letter, Roland Bibolet to author, July 24, 1994.

[11]*ADS* and *AR*, May 11, 1958.

[12]*PG*, May 13, 1958

[13]*ADS*, May 14, 25, 27, 1958.

[14]*Saturday Evening Post*, June 7, 1958, p.38; *AR*, June 3, 1958.

[15]Ibid.; *Holbrook Tribune News*, June 6, 1958; Barnard, *Walter Reuther*, 164-5.

[16]*AR*, August 7, 8, 9, 10, 1958. Ben Avery, a Democrat who did not like Morrison, wrote this series. Jonas, *Political Dynamiting*, 145-6.

[17]*ADS*, August 17 and 19, 1958 with *Buckeye Valley News* in *ADS*, August 19.

[18]*PG*, miscellaneous clippings fron the week of August 31-September 6, 1958, in MP, SB 16.

[19]*AR* and *PG*, July 22, 1958.

[20]*AR*, July 23, 1958.

[21]*ADS*, August 3; *AR*, August 2 and 5; *PG*, August 4, all 1958.

[22]*AR*, September 6, 1958.

[23]Stephen Shadegg, *How to Win an Election: The Art of Poltical Victory* (New York: Taplinger, 1964).

[24]*TDC*, September 11, 1958; Ross Rice, "The 1958 Elections in Arizona," *Western Political Quarterly* 12 (March 1959): 266-75.

[25]*TDC*, September 11, 1958; *AR*, September 14, 1958. See Goldberg, *Goldwater*, 128-29 for national perspective.

[26]The Harris Poll was published in late August and is found in MP, 139/29. Interestingly it makes no mention of the Searles candidacy. See also Robert H. Goldberg, *Barry Goldwater* (New Haven: Yale University Press, 1995), 125.

[27]*Prescott Courier*, September 11, 1958. The entire speech of September 10 is found in MP, 142/5.

[28]Letter, McFarland to Goldwater of September 16, 1958, in MP, 142/6.

[29]*ADS* and *AR*, September 23 and *AR*, October 1, all 1958; 1958 campaign brochure in MP, miscellaneous collections; speech of September 23, 1958, in MP, 137/2. The Equal Rights Amendment for women (ERA) failed to pass. Just prior to the party meeting, McFarland had dedicated Arizona's first state park at Old Tubac, founded under the 1957 legislation.

[30]*AR*, October 10, 1958; *Newsweek*, October 13, 1958; Jonas, *Political Dynamiting*, 168, 180 (notes 49 and 50 in Jonas).

[31]*Amarillo Globe-Times*, August 1, 1958, in MP, 137/9 and *AR*, October 18, 1958; Jonas, *Political Dynamiting*, 169.

[32]Jonas, ibid.; MP 139/24.

[33]*Washington Evening Star*, October 1 and 22, 1958.

[34]*Chicago Daily News*, October 13; *Yuma Daily Sun*, October 12, 15, 16; *ADS*, October 5, all 1958. William E. Jenner and John W. Bricker were ultra-conservative Republican senators from Indiana and Ohio respectively. In 1958, Jenner retired and Bricker was defeated.

[35]*ADS* and *AR*, October 13, 1958. The actual argument on inflation concerned the price of beef. McFarland always seemed to have difficulty lining up the votes of cattle ranchers even though as a senator, he was responsible for much favorable legislation for them. He was in fact tied to Truman's price controls on beef.

[36]*AR* and *PG*, October 16, 1958.

[37]*ADS*, October 20, 1958.

[38]*AR*, October 19, 1958; Jonas, *Political Dynamiting*, 143-44; letter, Stephen Shadegg to Frank Jonas, December 18, 1958, p. 179, note 2. See also Stephen Shadegg, *Arizona Politics* in chapter 9, "Goldwater Again Defeats McFarland," pages 85-99. Journalist Fireman was also a historian who assisted Goldwater in founding the Arizona Historical Foundation. Fireman became its first director.

[39]*AR*, October 19, 1958; Jonas, *Political Dynamiting*, 147-50.

[40]Ibid., 163-66.

[41]Ibid.; McFarland-Walton speech, October 20, 1958, MP, 137/1.

[42]*PG*, October 28, AR, October 29, both 1958; Jonas, *Political Dynamiting*, 179, note 29; see also Stephen Shadegg's *Arizona Politics* and *Barry Goldwater: Freedom Is His Flight Plan* (New York: Fleet Publishing, 1962). In the latter, see chapters 15 and 16, "The 1958 Campaign: Fighting for Survival," and "Smear, Slander, Sabotage, and Victory," 207-32.

[43]Jonas, *Political Dynamiting*, 164-65, 179, note 36. Goldwater

reported contributions of $175,748.33 while McFarland reported contributions of $107,911.25.

[44]*AR*, October 31, 1958; Jonas, *Political Dynamiting*, 166.

[45]Ibid., 170-71.

[46]Ibid., 166-67, 172.

[47]Ibid., 144, 168; letters Douglas to McFarland, May 13, 1958, and McFarland to Douglas, May 26, 1958, Lewis Douglas, Box 308, File "McFarland, 1952-58," University of Arizona Library Special Collections, Tucson.   Giragi's speech appeared in *AR*, November 2, 1958.

[48]*PG*, October 24, 1958; Shadegg, *Arizona Politics*, 88-90. There evidently also were rumors of a pending divorce between the Goldwaters.

[49]*AR*, October 30, 1958; Jonas, *Political Dynamiting*, 175.

[50]*ADS*, October 24, 1958.

[51]Statement, October 31, 1958, MP, 137/2; Jonas, *Political Dynamiting*, 190; see Shadegg's books listed in note 42.

[52]Jonas, *Political Dynamiting*, 185; *AR*, November 1,2, 1958.

[53]Ibid.; telegram, McFarland to Green, November 1, 1958.

[54]Duffy's statement of November 3, 1958, MP, 138/19; Jonas, *Political Dynamiting*, 203.   The Stalin leaflet was not sent to the *Arizona Daily Star*, which supported McFarland, a fact noted in the issue of November 4, 1958. Duffy was a Democrat and he indicated to Shadegg that he hoped for a McFarland victory.

[55]KTVK-TV speech, November 2, 1958, MP, 137/4.

[56]"Big Mac" *AR*, Aug. 13, 1978, and Jonas, *Political Dynamiting*, 178 (note 24).

[57]Ibid., 208. Goldwater dropped interest in a post-election investigation of the leaflet.

[58]Jonas, "Western Politics," 241-42; Jonas, *Political Dynamiting* 173.

[59]*Saturday Evening Post*, January 10, 1959, 10; Jonas, "Western Politics," 242 and *Political Dynamiting* 174.

[60]Ibid., 175, 181, notes 64 and 65; letter Larry B. Marton to Frank Jonas, December 4, 1958; interview by Jonas of McFarland, June 16, 1959.

[61]Jonas, *Political Dynamiting*, 176.

[62]Jonas, "Western Politics," 243, 274.

[63]Jonas, *Political Dynamiting*, 205-07.

[64]"Arizona's 1958 Senatorial Campaign," MP, 139/23; Jonas, *Political Dynamiting* 178 (note 24).

[65]Letter, Drew Pearson to McFarland, November 25, 1958, MP 138/19.

[66]Letter, Morris Udall to McFarland, November 5, 1958, MP 138/19.

[67]Letter, Roland Bibolet to McFarland, November 7, 1958, MP 138/19.

[68]Letter, McFarland to James L. McDevitt, November 17, 1958, MP 138/19.

[69] Jonas, *Political Dynamiting* and "Western Politics," 243; *PG*, April 18, 1990; *AR*, January 18, 1987. A Pulliam press article in 1994 discussed major figures in Arizona politics and omitted McFarland while including everyone else imaginable. Was it an oversight or intentional? After receiving several letters regarding the omission, the columnist corrected the mistake. A recent article (2002) in the *Republic* listed McFarland as the fourth most important person in state history (as chosen by the paper) behind 1)Hayden, 2)Goldwater, and 3)Padre Kino. Another article in the state press listed his positive approval rating as 6th among about 20 names, but his name recognition was last at only 16 percent

[70]Shadegg's *Arizona Politics* and *Barry Goldwater: Freedom Is His Flight Plan*. See also Barry Goldwater, *With No Apologies*; Barry Goldwater with Jack Casserly *Goldwater* (New York: Doubleday, 1988). In the latter, the mistake on the Stalin leaflet being used in the 1952 campaign is on page 97. The 1958 election is covered in one sentence on page 117. See also Edwin McDowell, *Barry Goldwater: Portrait of an Arizonan* (Chicago: Henry Regnery Co., 1964) 134-38. More recent works include Lee Edwards, *Goldwater: The Man Who Made A Revolution* (Washington, D.C.: Regency Publishing, 1955). Robert Goldberg, *Barry Goldwater* (New Haven: Yale University press, 1955) and Peter Iverson, *Barry Goldwater: Native Arizonan* (Norman: University of Oklahoma Press, 1997).

[71]*AR*, August 13, 1978,"Big Mac." Barry Goldwater spoke at the dedication of the Fannin-McFarland segment of the Central Arizona Project in the fall of 1992. At that time he stated: "Mac was such a good man. I should never have beaten Mac." He repeated this remark as guest speaker at a McFarland memorial dinner at the Biltmore in Phoenix in November 1994. See also, Johnson, *Arizona Politicians*, 79.

CHAPTER 15

[1]Letter, McFarland to Truman, November 7, 1958, MP. Truman did come to Phoenix in January to speak in his party's behalf.

[2]Both quotes in *ADS*, June 1, 1959.

[3]Ibid.

[4]*ADS*, June 3 and *AR*, June 7, 1959. Democratic National Chairman Paul M. Butler, a Massachusetts Catholic, said the party would not nominate a southerner like Johnson because of the civil rights issue.

[5]*PG*, December 10 and 11, 1959.

[6]Ibid., April 9, 1960.

[7]*AR*, April 1, 1960. McFarland feared the reverse.

[8]*PG*, January 29, 1960. At this time, LBJ led in West Virginia according to Senator Robert Byrd. Ultimately Kennedy won this crucial primary.

[9]*AR*, February 16 and 27, 1960.

[10]*PG*, April 9 and *AR*, March 10 and April 14, 1960.

[11]Ibid., April 11 and *AR*, April 11 and 17, 1960.

[12]*AR*, April 29, 1960.

[13]Ibid., April 17 and 30, 1960.

[14]Ibid., April 11 and 29, 1960.

[15]Ibid., April 28, 1960.

[16]Ibid., April 29 and 30, 1960.

[17]*PG*, April 28, *AR*, April 30, 1960.

[18]Ibid., April 30, 1960.

[19]Ibid., April 30, *AR*, May 1, 1960.

[20]*AR*, May 1 and 6, 1960.

[21]Ibid., May 1, 1960.

[22]*Tempe Daily News*, May 2, 1960.

[23]Drew Pearson in *PG*, May 7, 1960.

[24]*AR*, May 1; *PG*, May 24, 1960; and undescribed newsclippings in MP, SB.

[25]*PG*, May 24, 1960, and undescribed newsclippings in MP, SB.

[26]*AR*, May 21-24 and *PG*, May 24, 1960; undescribed newsclippings in MP, SB. At this time, Goldwater also expressed hope for his own chances as a Republican presidential candidate as a favorite son.

[27]*AR*, May 24, 1960.

[28]Ibid., June 3, 4, 6; *PG*, May 24; Holmes Alexander in the *Los Angeles Times* of May 15; 1960.

[29]*ADS*, July 10 and *PG*, July 11, 1960.

[30]Ibid., July 10 and 11; *AR*, July 12 and 13, 1960.

[31]*PG*, July 12 and 13, *AR*, July 13, 1960.

[32]Ibid., July 11 and 14, 1960.

[33]Ibid., July 14, 1960.

[34]*AR*, July 17, *ADS*, July 15, 1960.

[35]*PG*, July 14 and 15, *ADS*, July 15, 1960.

³⁶*ADS*, July 15, 1960.
³⁷*PG*, July 15, 1960.
³⁸*ADS*, July 15 and *AR*, July 17, 1960.
³⁹Ibid., and *PG*, July 15, 1960.
⁴⁰Ibid., July 15 and 16; *AR*, July 16.
⁴¹Reston in *ADS*, July 15; *PG*, July 10, 1960.
⁴²Lawrence in *AR*, July 15; *ADS*, July 15, 1960.
⁴³*ADS*, July 16 and 17, 1960.
⁴⁴*PG*, September 15 and 20, *ADS*, September 16, 1960.
⁴⁵Totton J. Anderson, "The Political West in 1960," *Western Political Quarterly 13* (March 1960) 287-99; William L. Strauss, "The 1960 Election in Arizona," ibid. 305-308.
⁴⁶Ibid., 295, 305, 308.
⁴⁷Ibid., 289, 307. Idaho and Montana had also lost their "weather vane" status. Furthering western political influence at this time was the selection of Senator Henry Jackson of Washington State as national chairman of the Democratic Party. Additionally, Senator Mike Mansfield of Montana became the next Senate majority leader and would serve in that capacity from 1961 to 1977, the longest tenure in that position. Udall did win re-election to the House, 95,512 to 75,811 votes. He would resign, however, on being appointed secretary of the interior by President Kennedy, and his brother, the late Morris Udall, replaced him in the House. Udall served as secretary from 1961 to 1969, and Morris continued in the House from 1961 to 1991, including running for the Democratic presidential nomination in the 1976 primaries.
⁴⁸McFarland's quote on ranchers is drawn from August 1958 minutes from a campaign meeting of that year, found in MP.
⁴⁹Interview, Del Lewis, July 13, 1990, Phoenix, Arizona.

CHAPTER 16

¹MP, miscellaneous newsclippings, SB 1, Subgroup III, Supreme Court, Subseries Three, 1964-67. See *Mac*, Chap. 20.
²*ADS*, June 21, 1964, *AR*, July 9, 1964.
³*Mac*, 297-8; miscellaneous newsclippings in SB, 1964-67, MP.
⁴*Mac*, 298, Watkins article in *Buckeye Valley Journal Post*, January 21, 1965, SB, 1964-67, MP.
⁵*Evening American* November 23, 1964, in SB, 1964-67, MP.

⁶Ross Rice, "The 1964 Election in the West," *Western Political Quarterly*, 18 (June 1964): 431-38.

⁷Ibid., "The 1964 Election in Arizona," John P. White, 443-50;

⁸Ibid.

⁹Schedule of swearing in ceremony, MP, SB 1964-67.

¹⁰*Mac*, 298-300; newsclipping of January 12, 1965, in SB 1964-67.

¹¹Letter, John Moran to Dr. Charles J. Meyers, Dean of the Stanford Law School, June 30, 1978 in MP, unorganized papers donated by Mildred Hagerty; interview with John Moran, August 1994, Phoenix, Arizona; John Moran videotape, #15 Channel 3; see also Meyers's opinion of Mac's judicial work in *Mac* 304-07. *State v. Curry*, February 4, 1965 - 398 P. 2d 899, 97 Ariz. 191.

¹²*State v. Kananen*, February 25, 1965 - 399 P. 2d 426, 97 Ariz. 200; letter, Moran to Meyers, *loc. cit.*; newsclipping of March 2, 1965. in MP, SB 1964-67. Later legal aid, John Flood, noted that both the Curry and Kananen cases were among those McFarland decisions most cited in later court cases in Arizona and elsewhere.

¹³*98 Arizona Reports*, "401 P. 2d 721, *State of Arizona v. Ernest Arthur Miranda*, No. 1394, April 22, 1965," 18-37; newsclipping of April 27, 1965 in MP, SB 1964-67.

¹⁴*PG* 5/11/65; letter, Green to McFarland of May 18, 1965, and letter Stevens to McFarland, April 23, 1965, both in MP, SB 1964-67.

¹⁵Interview, John Moran, Phoenix, Arizona, August 1994; television video interview with John Moran, Channel 3, Mac # 15, June 1984, Phoenix, Arizona.

¹⁶*PG* and *AR*, Nov. 23, 1965. *Escobedo* was a 5-4 decision.

¹⁷*AR*, June 13, 1966.

¹⁸*Life*, June 24, 1966.

¹⁹*Phoenix Gazette Weekly*, July 27, 1965.

²⁰*State v. Goodyear*, July 19, 1965 - 403 P. 2d 397, 98 Ariz. 304; *State v. Goodyear*, April 22, 1966 - 413 P. 2d 566, 100 Ariz. 244; *Phoenix Gazette Weekly*, July 27, 1965; *AR* April 23, 1966.

²¹Undescribed newsclippings, MP, SB, 1964-67.

²²Address by Charles L Terry, Jr., Conference of Chief Justices, Philadelphia, Pa., July 31-August 3, 1968, in MP, SB 1968-70.

²³*Phoenix Gazette Weekly*, April 8, 1969, "Tribunal Rules Miranda Applies Wherever Subject Is Not Free," by Kenyon Roberts.

²⁴*Mac*, 305; Struckmeyer video interview, Channel 3, # 16, June 1984; interview, John Moran, August 1994, Phoenix, Arizona.

²⁵Ibid. Moran wrote the bulk of this opinion. *AR*, November

6, 1966; *PG* November 16, 1966; *State v. Lassen*, November 12, 1965
- 407 P. 2d 74, 99 Ariz. 161.

[26]*PG*, December 14, 1965; *AR*, December 14, 1965; *Mac* 305-
06; John Flood, "McFarland Landmark Cases," March 11, 1977, in
MP, unorganized papers donated by Mildred Hagerty. Flood, a former McFarland legal assistant, compiled this file at the request of
Charles Myers, Dean of the Stanford Law School, who had requested
to add commentary to McFarland's chapter 20 in *Mac* on the Supreme
Court.

[27]*PG*, March 8, 1966; undescribed newsclipping, MP, SB
1964-67.

[28]*PG*, January 4 and May 3, 1966.

[29]*Mac*, 301; Struckmeyer video interview #16, #17, Channel 3,
June 1984.

[30]Mildred Hagerty video interview #14, Channel 3, June
1984.

[31]Moran video interview #15, and personal interview, *loc. cit.*

[32]Ibid. and *Mac*, 303.

[33]MP 227/1; "Memorandum on Trip to South America,
August 1966," and itineraries. The memorandum leaves off after
Chile, omitting Argentina, Uraguay, Brazil, and Venezuela.

[34]"The Gallegher Report," New York, February 28, 1967,
MP, unorganized papers donated by Mildred Hagerty. The report was
a business report to advertising, marketing, and media executives. In
the late-1990s, Del and Jewell Lewis sold the station for well in excess
of 300 million dollars.

[35]*Arizona Weekly Gazette*, November 22, 1966, July 18, 1967.

[36]Lippman and *Life* in "LBJ Image Distorting His Worth," by
Peter Lisagor of the Chicago Daily News Service, in MP, undescribed
newsclippings.

[37]*PG*, May 30, 1967.

[38]"Vietnam, August — September, 1967," MP 228/1. This
report (twenty-one pages) on the trip was written by both McFarland
and Watkins, and much of it is transcription of tape-recorded interviews. There are no existing notes on the remainder of the world tour
after Vietnam.

[39]*Westside Daily American*, September 28, 30, October 1, 1967.
This was Evan Mecham's paper. *PG*, September 18, 1967.

CHAPTER 17

¹*ADS*, January 11, 1968; *PG*, January 5, 1968; miscellaneous letters in MP. Historian Bill Phillips ditributed over four thousand inquiries to attendees of the 1994 annual conference of the National Council for the Social Studies asking for contrary evidence regarding McFarland's unique service. Not a single rebuttal was returned.

²*PG*, January 2, 1968.

³*PG*, February 19, 26, 1968; *PG Weekly*, February 13, 1968; undescribed newsclippings, MP, SB, 1968-70.

⁴Letter, Hubert Humphrey to McFarland, November 2, 1968, in SB 1968-70.

⁵*AR*, October 1, 1968; *PG*, October 1, 1968; telegram, James R. Janes, Special Assistant to the President, to McFarland, September 27, 1968; see Johnson, *Central Arizona Project*, chapter 10. A portion of the CAP between Scottsdale and Florence is named the Fannin-McFarland Aqueduct.

⁶Statement by Lyndon Johnson to the National Commission on the Prevention of Violence in America and Executive order 11412 of June 10, 1968, in MP, box 223.

⁷The vitaes of the members are in MP box 223.

⁸*Mac* 309-10; press release of June 21, 1968, in MP box 223. Washington suffered $15 million damage, Chicago, $10 million, and Pittsburgh, Baltimore, and other cities over $1 million.

⁹National Commission on the Causes and Prevention of Violence. Final Report. *To Establish Justice, to Insure Domestic Tranquility* (Washington, D.C.: USGPO, 1969) (hereinafter cited as *To Establish Justice*); see James F. Short, Jr. and Marvin E. Wolfgang, Co-Directors of research for the twelve variously titled volumes of staff research reports in "Task Force Reports: preface," 305-310. The final report is based upon these twelve volumes.

¹⁰Speech, Veterans Day, November 11, 1968, Tucson, Arizona. Mac also spoke to the Arizona Masons on his 74th birthday, October 9, 1968, emphasizing Masonic contributions to U.S. history. McFarland was a 32nd degree Mason.

¹¹Statement of Milton Eisenhower, December 1, 1968, in MP; press release in University of Arizona special collections.

¹²*PG*, December 5, 12, 1968; *AR*, December 6, 1968; *ADS*, December 15, 1968; miscellaneous newsclippings in MP, SB 1968-70.

¹³*Mac*, 302-08; Struckmeyer video interview # 16, June 1984, Channel 3, Phoenix, Arizona.

¹⁴*To Establish Justice*, 144, 158, 176; PG, January 2, 1970.

[15]*PG*, December 8, 1969.

[16]*To Establish Justice*, 229-37.

[17]*Mac*, 317. The Charles Manson murders of the summer of 1969 also kept violence in America on the front pages.

[18]*To Establish Justice*, 232.

[19]African tour information is in MP 230/2. The African countries of Rhodesia and Congo are now Zimbabwe and Zaire respectively.

[20]*PG*, September 24, 1968; miscellaneous newsclippings of October 2 and 5, 1968 in MP, SB 1968-70.

[21]Letter McFarland and Udall to Mrs. Rachael G. Markham, President of Yavapai County Republican Women's Club, MP, SB 1968-70.

[22]*AR*, October 9, 1968.

[23]*PG*, December 31, 1968; *ADS*, January 1, 1969; miscellaneous newsclippings of February 1969 in MP, SB, 1968-70.

[24]Struckmeyer video interview #16 and 17, Channel 3, Phoenix, June 1984.

[25]*AR*, June 6, 1969; *Weekly Gazette*, June 10, 1969.

[26]*State v. Jennings*, December 11, 1968 - 448 P.2d 59, 104 Ariz. 3; *Mac* 305-6; miscellaneous newsclippings, MP, SB, 1968-70.

[27]*Streenz v. Streenz*, June 11, 1970 - 471 P. 2d 282, 106 Ariz. 86; *Mac*, 306; letter, John Flood to McFarland, April 26, 1978, in MP, Mildred Hagerty's unorganized papers.

[28]*Mac*, ibid.; John Flood letter, *loc. cit.*; *Jarvis v. State Land Dept., City of Tucson*.

[29]*Mac*, 306-07; *State v. Starsky*; Flood letter; letter from West Publishing Co. to McFarland, December 11, 1970 in MP, SB 1968-70. West published the two cases *Transportation Insurance Co. v. Wade*, October 8, 1970 - 475 P. 2d 253 and *Porter v.Empire Fire and Marine Inlurance Co.*, October 8, 1970 in "Judicial Highlights," a column published in the advance sheets of all "Reporters in the National Reporters System." See also *Sanders v. Folsum*, 1969 P. 2d 612; *Bacchus v. Farmers Insurance Group Exchange*, 475 P. 2d 264, 1970; "McFarland Landmark Cases" compiled March 11, 1977, and McFarland's most sheparded cases compiled by John Flood, both in MP, unorganized papers donated by Mildred Hagerty.

[30]*AR*, April 16 and 19, 1970; *PG*, April 16, 20, and December 25, 1970; *ADS*, April 19, 1970; letter, W. Francis Wilson to McFarland, June 11, 1970, in MP, SB 1068-70.

[31]*PG*, December 31, 1970.

[32]Ibid.

[33]Channel 3 interviews, June 1984, Phoenix, Arizona, Mildred Hagerty #14, John Moran #15, and Fred Struckmeyer #'s 16, 17; *Mac*, 307-08; *PG*, December 31, 1970. Perhaps Moran refers to the

"August of Mac's years" instead of the more usual September to indicate that he was still flourishing as in summer and going out on top.

CHAPTER 18

[1]*PG*, January 12, 1971; *AR*, January 1, 1971; *TDC*, March 1, 1971.

[2]*Casa Grande Dispatch*, February 22, 1971; letter Raul Castro to McFarland, MP.

[3]*CR*, Extensions of Remarks, February 5, 1971. Udall spoke of the 4th.

[4]Interview, Del Lewis, August 14, 1996, Phoenix.

[5]*AR*, November 15, 1975; miscellaneous newsclippings and speech of November 16, 1975; letter from John McCormack to McFarland, December 31, 1975, all MP, SB 1971-84.

[6]Miscellaneous newsclipping, MP, SB 1971-84; *PG*, June 26, 1971; *Arizona Blade Tribune*, July 1, 1971; *AR*, June 27, 1971.

[7]*TDC*, March 1, 1971.

[8]On the banquet, see "Ernest W. McFarland Appreciation Day" program, MP, SB 1971-84; *PG*, October 10, 1971; *AR*, October 9, 1971; *Mesa Tribune*, October 11, 1971; *ADS*, October 9, 1971. It was a $10 per plate dinner.

[9]*PG*, March 29, 1973.

[10]Interview, Del Lewis, August 14, 1996, *loc. cit.*; letters between McFarland and Stanley P. Wagner, President of East Central University of Oklahoma, April 29, May 1, June 29. all 1971, MP 294/9.

[11]Commencement address of July 30, 1971, MP, 294/9. The commencement program is also found here. See also McMillan, "First Sooner Senator," 197.

[12]Miscellaneous undated newsclippings, MP, 295/9; see also note 6, chapter 1.

[13]Letters, Wagner and McFarland, October 19, 1971 and Octber 20, 1972; *Daily Oklahoman*, October 8, 1971, all in MP, 294/9.

[14]Interview, Del Lewis, August 14, 1996, loc. cit.

[15]*Arizona Blade-Tribune*, May 2, 1974; *AR*, April 28, 1974, "Florence where time's been standing still." See Sobin study and Nichols, "Florence Townsite," note 14, chapter 2.

[16]Miscellaneous newsclippings of July 1974, MP, SB 1971-84.

[17]Letter, Goldwater to McFarland, July 24, 1974, MP, SB, 1971-84.

[18]*Tri Valley Dispatch*, January 1, 2, 1975; *Arizona Blade-Tribune*, January 2, 1975, and miscellaneous newsclippings of December 1974 in *AR*, January 2, 1975; *PG*, December 31, 1974.

[19]*PG*, December 31, 1974; *Tri Valley Dispatch*, January 1, 2, 1975.

[20]*AR*, January 30, 1972, March 8, 1974.

[21]Interview, Del Lewis, August 16, 1996, *loc. cit.*

[22]Christmas letter to "friends and relatives" from Edna McFarland of December 1976, in miscellaneous papers of Mildred Hagerty, MP.

[23]*Arizona v. Overton*, 114 Ariz. 553, 562, P. 2d 726 (1977), case of March 21, 1977. Chief Justice Cameron and later Chief Justice Gordon (1997) concurred. See also John Flood letter of April 26, 1978.

[24]Edna McFarland's Christmas letter of December 1977, *loc cit.*

[25]Interview, Del Lewis, August 16, 1996, *AR*, July 29, 1977; *ADS*, July 29, 1977; *PG*, August 8, 1977; miscellaneous newsclippings, MP, SB 1971-84.

[26]*Stanford Law Review*, vol. 29, no. 5, in MP, SB 1971-84.

[27]*Arizona Blade-Tribune*, December 8, 1977; miscellaneous newsclippings in MP, SB 1971-84. Mofford became the governor of Arizona in 1988 upon the impeachment and conviction of Evan Mecham.

[28]*PG*, March 28, 1978.

[29]On John Clum, miscellaneous newsclippings in MP, SB 1971-84.

[30]*PG*, April 24, 1978; *Yuma Daily Sun*, May 7, 1978; *AR*, April 22, 1978.

[31]"Big Mac" in "Arizona" magazine, *AR*, August 13, 1978.

[32]Bernie Wynn in *AR*, October 28, 1979; interview, Del Lewis, August 16, 1996, *loc. cit.*; *Mac*, "Foreword," vii-ix; the title of this chapter, "The Autumn of His Years," is from Sterling's "Foreword." The quotes of Governor Babbitt and Senator Byrd are on the jacket of *Mac*. As of this writing in 2003, Robert Byrd is serving a record eighth term as U. S. Senator having been elected in 1958 (Carl Hayden served seven terms in the Senate). Byrd served in the House from 1952-1958, and is thus entering his second half century of service on Capitol Hill and has a chance to bypass Hayden's record fifty-seven years including his fifteen years in the House.

[33]*AR*, January 16, June 8, 1980; miscellaneous newclippings of signings in MP, SB 1971-84. Video, *Mac Remembered*, produced by KTVK-TV, Channel 3, June 1984, upon McFarland's death, on display at McFarland State Park.

[34]Clippings from *Stanford Law Review* in MP, SB 1971-84.

McFarland was scheduled for the cover of the *Law Review* but was displaced when Idaho U. S. Senator Frank Church died. The Stanford plaque hangs at McFarland park.

[35]See McFarland Park history file at park headquarters; interview with Bill Phillips, May 24, 1990, Pinetop, Arizona. The archives and library building was officially dedicated on McFarland's birth date, October 9, 1987, with presentations by former governor Sam Goddard and Arizona State University historians Bill Phillips and Jim McMillan.

[36]Video, *Mac Remembered*, loc. cit.

[37]Interviews, Bill Phillips, May 24, 1990, and Del Lewis, August 16, 1996.

[38]*AR*, March 13, 1984.

[39]*AR*, June 4, 5, 9, 1984.

[40]*AR*, June 9, 1984; *Detroit Free Press*, June 9, 1984; *New York Times*, June 10, 1984; *PG*, June 9, 1984; *Washington Post*, June 9, 1984; *ADS*, June 12, 1984; *Scottsdale Progress*, June 11, 1984; miscellaneous newsclippings, MP, SB 1971-84.

[41]Ibid.; video, *Mac Remembered, loc. cit.*

[42]Hinshaw also recollected that schoolteacher Edna campaigned at his side and sometimes "corrected his English." Sadly, few state legislators attended the funeral. Representatives Polly Rosenbaum (D-Globe) and Betty Rockwell (R-Phoenix) did attend. Rosenbaum said, "that it is tragic," and planned to tell the legislators she was "chagrined by their absence." House Democrats had previously scheduled a session that day that conflicted with the 10:00 A.M. funeral; *AR*, June 13, 1984; miscellaneous newsclippings, MP, SB 1971-84. Reverend Hinshaw presided over the memorial service for McFarland's daughter Jewell on April 14, 2003, and her eulogy was delivered by Governor Janet Napolitano. Rosenbaum, in a 2002 poll taken by the *Arizona Republic*, picked McFarland as the most important figure in Arizona history. Overall, McFarland placed fourth in the poll behind Carl Hayden, Barry Goldwater, and Padre Kino, respectively. Polly Rosenbaum passed away in December 2003 at age one hundred and five years. She was defeated in 1996 after serving over four decades in the Arizona Legislature.

APPENDIX I

CHRONOLOGY

I. EARLY LIFE AND CAREER, 1894-1940

1894: Oct. 9:	Birth, near Earlsboro, Oklahoma.
1914:	Graduates, Earlsboro High School
1915:	Graduates East Central Normal School, Ada, Oklahoma.
1917:	Bachelors degree, University of Oklahoma at Norman.
1917-19:	United States Navy service/illness at Great Lakes Navy School, Ill.
1919 May:	Moves to Phoenix, Arizona and works briefly at Valley National Bank before enrolling at Stanford University in fall.
1921:	Admitted to Arizona Bar and opens practice in Casa Grande.
1922:	Juris Doctors degree, Stanford University; receives Masters of Arts in Political Science later in 1924.
1923:	Appointed Arizona Assistant Attorney General; serves until 1925.
1924:	Elected Pinal County Attorney; serves 1925-31; moves to Florence, Arizona; re-elected in 1926 and 1928.
1926 Jan. 1:	Marries Clare Collins.
1929 Feb.:	Loses newborn and two-year-old children to illness in two weeks.
1929 Aug.-Sept.:	Cruise to Europe via Panama Canal and Cuba with Clare. Returns via New York and transcontinental auto trip.
1930: Feb.:	Prosecutes and upholds sanity of Eva Dugan for execution.
1930: Nov.:	Defeated for Pinal County Superior Court Judge.
1930 Dec.:	Clare McFarland and child die in childbirth.
1931-34:	Private law practice; attorney for San Carlos Irrigation and Reclamation District; farmer;

	meets Edna Eveland Smith.
1933: April:	As Defense Attorney, upholds insanity of Winnie Ruth Judd allowing her to avoid execution.
1934: Nov.:	Elected Pinal County Superior Court Judge re-elected in 1938 and serves until Jan. 1941, when sworn in as a U. S. Senator.
1935-36:	Writes Gila Decree establishing water appropriation rights.
1939 June 1:	Marries Edna Smith in Tucson and adopts her daughter Jewell.
1940 Sept:	Defeats incumbent Senator Henry Fountain Ashurst in Democratic party primaries for U.S. Senate by 63,353 to 37,955 votes.
Nov.:	Wins U.S. Senate election in Arizona by landslide over Irving A. Jennings, 101,495 to 39,657.
1940 Dec.:	With Senator Carl Hayden,meets with President Franklin Roosevelt to discuss Arizona water issues.

II. U.S. SENATE: FIRST TERM, 1941-46

1941 Jan. 3:	Sworn in as a U.S. Senator.
Jan. 9:	Introduces first bill: S. 268, to authorize RFC loans to small mine operations; it fails to pass.
Mar. 8:	Lend-Lease passes Senate, 60-31.
July 24:	First major speech in Senate and first formal mention of postwar planning by a U.S. Senator.
Sept. 9-26:	Major role in Interstate Commerce Subcommittee's investigation of Hollywood film industry. Mac supports Hollywood successfully.
Dec. 7:	Japanese attack Pearl Harbor; McFarland only Arizonan in attendance to vote for state of war declaration. Daughter Jewell witnesses.
Dec.:	Meets Churchill, who phones Edna McFarland while she is recuperating from illness and premature loss of child.
1942 Mar.24:	Elucidates pro-labor philosophy in Senate.
July 9:	First bill to become law: S. 2599 compensates farm/range public land users for losses sustained for U.S. Armed Forces training purposes.
Aug.-Nov.:	Chairs Special Senate Elections Investigation Subcommittee.
Nov.:	Supports Arizona cotton growers against FDR in

		dispute over labor hiring practices. His efforts are unsuccessful.
1943	March 6:	McFarland's first major piece of legislation, a bill merging Postal Telegraph and Western Union, becomes law.
	June:	Visits to Arizona's Japanese-American Relocation/Internment Camps.
	June 25:	Smith-Connally Act passes over FDR veto; McFarland votes to sustain veto of restrictive labor law.
	Aug. 13:	Featured speaker at annual Arizona American Legion convention; outlines postwar plans for veterans.
	Oct. 29:	Introduces S. 1495 providing home and business loans and educational benefits for returning veterans.
1944	Jan. 28:	Adds S. 1495 as an amendment to American Legion's bill, S. 1767.
	Mar. 24:	Co-sponsors final GI Bill which includes S. 1495; passes Senate unanimously; later passes House unanimously on May 18.
	June 22:	FDR signs GI Bill after conference sessions.
	July 31:	Chairs Irrigation and Reclamation Subcommittee investigating water resources and use in the West; meetings begin in Phoenix.
1945	April 18:	Mexican Water Treaty ratified by Senate.
	May-June:	Immediately after the German surrender, McFarland chairs Interstate Commerce Subcommittee investigating postwar communications; inspection tour of Europe, North Africa, the Mediterranean, and the Near East. Meets with Churchill, Eisenhower, and Pope Pius XII.
	Sept. 2:	Japan surrenders, ending World War II.
1946	Mar. 11:	Declines President Truman's offer of lifetime appointment as Federal Judge in U.S. District Court of Tucson.
	May 8:	McFarland Amendment to British Loan defeated after extensive debate, 45 to 40.
	July 16:	Defeats Harry Valentine for Democratic nomination for U.S. Senate in primary election, 61,287 to 15,181.
	Aug, 10:	First McFarland-sponsored Social Security increase becomes law.
	Nov. 5:	Defeats Republican Ward S. Powers for U.S.

Senate, 80,415 to 35,022.

Nov.-Dec.: Mac the lone senator on inspection tour of Japan, China, Pacific Islands, Philippines, Australia, and Hawaii for postwar communications planning. Meets with MacArthur, Marshall, and Chiang Kai-shek.

III. U.S. SENATE: SECOND TERM, 1947-50

1947 April 23: Senate endorses Truman Doctrine, 67-23.

April 28: Introduces S. 1175, Central Arizona Project Bill (CAP).
April-June: Directs passage of Wellton-Mohawk Project; becomes law July 30.
June 23: Taft-Hartley passes over Truman veto; McFarland votes to uphold veto.
Nov.: National Reclamation Association meeting in Phoenix.
Dec.: Inspection tour of Navajo and Hopi Indian Reservations.
1948 March 14: Marshall Plan passes Senate.
April 12: Presents "ABC Plan" for United Nations; it is rejected.
April 28: Reintroduces S. 1175, CAP.
June 14: Obtains second increase in Social Security.
July: Declines overtures to be a "favorite son" western candidate for vice president; receives support for Supreme Court vacancy the next year.
1949 Feb. 7: Truman announces opposition to CAP.
Mar. 21: Hearings on CAP, now S. 75, begin; reported successfully out of committee July 1.
July 21: Senate ratifies NATO, 82-13.
Sept. 30: Votes against confirmation of Leland Olds for FPC.
Oct. 3: McFarland's Navajo-Hopi Rehabilitation Act passes Congress only to be held up by Truman veto and House failure to override.
1950 Feb. 21: CAP passes Senate, 55-28.
April 19: Navajo-Hopi Rehabilitation Act becomes law.
June 27: Korean War begins. McFarland as acting majority leader replacing Scott Lucas, meets with President Truman, General Bradley, and three other members of "Big Four": Rayburn,

Barkley, and McCormack.

Sept. 23: McCarran Act passes over Truman veto. McFarland as acting majority leader votes to override.

IV. MAJORITY LEADER, 1951-52

1951 Jan. 2: Selected majority leader 39-18 over Senator O'Mahoney. Lyndon Johnson chosen as assistant majority leader or whip.

April 4: Senate passes "Troops to Europe" Resolution co-sponsored by McFarland and sending four divisions to Eisenhower and NATO.

April 11: Supports Truman's firing of MacArthur; Senate hearings last through May and June.

May 10: Korean GI Bill passes without home-business-education benefits.

May 28: Central Arizona Project passes Senate for the second time, 50-28.

Aug. 9: Castigates Senator McCarthy on the senate floor, one of first to do so.

Oct. 20: Lengthy First Session of 82nd Congress ends.

1952 Mar. 7: Votes to retain offshore oil deposits for the nation, not the shoreline states. Supports Truman's veto which stands.

Mar. 20: Truman seizes steel mills; McFarland against seizure.

May 12: Introduces third Social Security increase; becomes law July 8.

May 19: Veterans Readjustment Assistance Act of 1952 passes, upgrading Korean GI Bill with McFarland's education benefits and home and business loan provisions.

June 16: Daughter Jewell marries Delbert Lewis in Florence. They will have five children: Kara, born April 1, 1954; William, September 24, 1957; John, May 9, 1960; Leah, July 18, 1966; and Delbert, Jr. May 3, 1967.

June 30: Votes for McCarran Immigration and Nationality Act.

July 7: Second Session, 82nd Congress closes as scheduled.

July 15: McFarland communications bill becomes law revising Communications Act of 1934.

Nov.:	Goldwater defeats McFarland 132,063 to 125,338.
Nov. 20- Dec. 31:	Around the world tour visiting 30 countries with Edna; spends Christmas with soldiers on Korean War front lines.

V. GUBERNATORIAL YEARS, 1953-58

1953:	Lawyer, Western Union; founds Arizona Television Company, Phoenix.
1953:	Governor Pyle orders Short Creek Raid on Mormon polygamists.
1954:	Defeats incumbent Howard Pyle for Arizona Governor, 122,235 to 111,399.
1955: Jan. 3:	Inauguration as Arizona's 10th governor.
Feb.-April:	Proposed health, education, welfare benefits pass Legislature.
Oct.:	Calls special session to revise entire Arizona law code.
Dec. 8:	Wins a section of the water case for Arizona over California in front of the U.S. Supreme Court keeping upper basin states from being enjoined in CAP lawsuit, thus saving time for Arizona.
Dec.:	Calls Special Session of Legislature to eliminate sales tax on products sold to Federal Government and instituting a use tax on products purchased from out of state. Opens the way for Sperry-Rand and other industry to enter state.
1956: Nov.:	Elected to second term as Arizona Governor over Horace B. Griffin, 171,848 to 116,744.
1957 Jan 7:	Inaugurated for second term.
Mar.:	Creates Arizona State Parks.
	Page selected by Bureau of Reclamation as construction site for Glen Canyon Dam over Utah site, a coup for McFarland.
July 31:	Groundbreaking for wings and tower sections of new capitol building.
1958 Mar.-April:	Special Legislative Sessions fail to produce
Nov. :	Defeated by Barry Goldwater in fourth attempt for the U.S. Senate, 164,593 to 129,030 in controversial campaign.

VI. LATER ARIZONA YEARS AND SUPREME COURT, 1959-1970

1959-64:	Private law practice, television, and farming interests.
1960:	Attends Democratic convention and unsuccessfully supports Lyndon Johnson's presidential bid for the party nomination against John F. Kennedy.
1963:	Arizona wins overall case against California in U. S. Supreme Court.
1964:	Leads Arizona delegation at Democratic convention in support of LBJ.
1964 Nov.:	Elected as Associate Justice, Arizona Supreme Court over incumbent Justice Edward Scruggs, 199,494 to 135,468.
1965 Jan. 4.:	Takes oath as associate justice from Chief Justice Jesse Udall.
April 22:	Writes *Arizona v. Miranda* decision, later overturned by U.S. Supreme Court in 1966 in famous *Miranda v. Arizona*.
1966:	Trip to South America with Edna and brother Carl and wife. Visits nine countries in thirty-two days.
1967 Jan.:	Selected by Arizona Supreme Court colleagues as vice chief justice; serves nearly full year as acting chief during the illness of Chief Justice Bernstein.
1967:	Visits Vietnam and tours front lines. Returns via Soviet Union and Eastern Europe.
1968 Jan:	Selected as Chief Justice, Arizona Supreme Court. Has now held state's highest positions in legislative, executive, and judicial branches of government, a feat unsurpassed in American politics.
1968 June:	President Johnson creates thirteen man National Commission on Causes and Prevention of Violence in America chaired by Milton Eisenhower; McFarland named as member and serves until December 1969.
1968 September:	President Johnson signs Central Arizona Project into law after U. S. Senate passage in 1967, and House passage in 1968. McFarland unable to attend signing ceremony due to court duties.
1969:	Visits Africa with Edna and secretary Mildred

| | Hagerty. Visits nine countries. |
| 1968-1970: | Sets record pace for court in writing over 60 cases per year, over 300 for his entire term. |

VII. RETIREMENT YEARS, 1971-1984

1971 Jan.:	Retires from Arizona Supreme Court and public life. Selected for Greater Arizona Award and American Legion's Distinguished Service Award.
July 30:	At East Central State University, his Oklahoma alma mater, he receives Distinguished Alumnus Award, speaks at summer commencement, and donates large unspecified sum to top off Robert S. Kerr Activities Center.
Oct. 9:	"McFarland Day" celebrated in Phoenix in honor of his public service career on his 77th birthday.
1972:	Establishes endowed scholarships at ASU, UA, NAU, Grand Canyon College (AZ), East Central State College (OK), and the University of Oklahoma.
1973:	Honorary Doctorate granted by ASU. Mac had earlier received one from UA upon his daughter Jewell's graduation in 1950.
1974:	Purchases old Pinal County Courthouse in 1974, and donates it and restoration and upkeep funds to Arizona State Parks System.
1975:	Awarded "Copper Mike" for distinguished service to communications in Arizona; remains Chairman and President of Arizona Television Company from 1971-84.
1977 Mar.:	Writes final judicial decision, *Overton v. Arizona*, as visiting justice for Arizona Supreme Court.
July 13:	Hospitalized for operation on benign brain tumor.
Nov.:	*Stanford Law Review* dedicated to McFarland.
Dec.:	Attends McFarland Historical State Park dedication in Florence. It opens to the public in spring 1978.
1978 May:	Selected to DAV Hall of Fame.
1979:	Autobiography, *Mac: The Autobiography of Ernest W. McFarland* published.
1980:	Designated as Stanford University Law School's "Most Distinguished Living Alumnus." Ernest

	W. McFarland Chair, an endowed professorship established at Stanford Law School facilitated by Mac's donation of old Casa Grande land.
1982:	Flies by helicopter the length of the yet dry Central Arizona Project.
1983 Oct. 9:	McFarland attends his 89th birthday and last celebration at Scottsdale home of historian W. W. Phillips.
1984:	Construction of Central Arizona Project completed from Colorado River to beyond Granite Reef Dam outside of Phoenix.
June 8:	McFarland dies of heart failure, Phoenix, Arizona. Lies in state under Capitol Dome and after services at Central Methodist is interred at Greenwood Memorial Cemetery. Governor Babbitt delivers eulogy.

POSTHUMOUS EVENTS, 1985-2004

1985:	Colorado River waters flow to Central Arizona as part of CAP goes into operation.
1987 Oct. 9:	Dedication of McFarland Library and Archives at the state park on 93rd anniversary of his birth. Speakers include former Governor Sam Goddard and historians Bill Phillips and James McMillan.
1992 Oct.:	Edna McFarland dies in Phoenix.
1993 Feb. 12:	Ceremony for naming the Fannin-McFarland Aqueduct of the Central Arizona Project with Barry Goldwater as featured speaker.
1994 Oct. 9:	Centennial of McFarland's birth celebrated at McFarland State Park.
Nov. 20:	Barry Goldwater and former Governor Rose Mofford speak at the Ernest W. McFarland Political Heritage Dinner at the Biltmore in Phoenix.
1995:	*Ernest W. McFarland: The United States Senate Papers, 1940-1952*, published by Sharlot Hall, edited by James E. McMillan, who had also published articles on McFarland in the 1988 and 1995 *Journal of Arizona History* and the 1995 *Chronicles of Oklahoma*.
1998 Nov.:	Dedication of McFarland Memorial at Wesley

	Bolin Plaza on State Capital grounds, Phoenix designed by artist Susan Schwarzenberg. Speakers include former Governor Mofford, Roland Bibolet, James McMillan, Polly Rosenbaum, and Del and Jewell Lewis.
1999 Nov.:	McFarland honored at Arizona State University West for 45th Anniversary of the GI Bill symposium. Governor Jane Hull and historian James McMillan speak.
2001:	Statue of McFarland dedicated in Mesa, Arizona, honoring his work on GI Bill.
2003 April 9:	McFarland's daughter, Jewell, dies in Phoenix. Services at Central Methodist Church, where eulogy is given by Governor Janet Napolitano; interment at Greenwood Memorial Cemetery.
2004 April:	Biography, *Ernest W. McFarland: Majority Leader of the United States Senate, Governor and Chief Justice of the State of Arizona*; published by Sharlot Hall Museum Press, Prescott, Arizona, and written by James E. McMillan.

APPENDIX II

McFARLAND'S U. S. SENATE SPONSORED
BILLS AND LAWS

(Read into the *Congressional Record* by Asst. Majority Leader Lyndon
Baines Johnson) July 5, 1952

Mr. President, the full measure of Senator McFarland's success
as legislator can best be demonstrated by the number of bills that have
gone through Congress bearing his name. Since he first came to the
Senate in 1940, he has been responsible for more than 60 measures
which became public laws or passed the Senate, through his sponsor-
ship or cosponsorship. Many of those measures are laws today, and the
Nation is benefited by them.

Mr. President, I ask unanimous consent that a tabulation of
those measures be printed at this point in the *Record* as a part of my
remarks.

Measures Introduced or Cosponsored by Senator McFarland
from 1941 to 1952 which became public law or passed the Senate.
[over 40 became public law]

Agriculture
1. To provide price supports for long staple cotton similar to
those for short staple cotton. Public Law 585 (H.R. 81220, Eighty-
second Congress, second session.
2. To prevent the entry into this country of certain mollusks
which spread a highly communicable disease among farm animals.
Public Law 152, Eighty-second Congress, first session.
3. To amend the Agricultural Adjustment Act to establish marketing quotas subject to vote by farmers. Public Law 272 (S. 1962),
Eighty-first Congress, first session.
4. To permit the Secretary of Agriculture to apply certain subsidy provisions to perennial agricultural crops such as citrus and to
encourage their export to ECA countries. Public Law 47
(S. 1209), Eighty-first Congress, first session.
5. To provide a revolving fund for the purchase of agricultural com-
modities such as waste cotton for processing and sale in occupied countries. Public Law 820 (S. 2376), Eightieth Congress, second session.

6. To provide for the construction and maintenance of the Western Land Boundary Fence project. Senate Joint Resolution 46, Eightieth Congress, first session, S. 1115, Eighty-first Congress, first session.

7. To increase subsidies paid by the Commodity Credit Corporation on lambs and livestock with corresponding decreases in any subsidy paid by the RFC. Public Law 164 (S. 1270), Seventy-ninth Congress, first session.

8. To encourage the growing of important war crops by preserving the acreage allotments of cotton, wheat, and peanuts which might otherwise be lost. Public Law 12 (S. 33), Seventy-ninth Congress, first session.

9. To provide for the deferment from military service of persons essentially engaged in agricultural occupations. (S. 729), Seventy-eighth Congress, first session.

10. To provide for payment of compensation to holders of grazing permits on public lands for losses sustained by reason of the use of such lands for war purposes. Public Law 663 (S. 2599), Seventy-seventh Congress, second session.

Irrigation and Reclamation

1. Obtained Senate approval of $125,000 for research to develop an inexpensive method for converting salt water into water which can be used for irrigation and domestic purposes. Eighty-second Congress, second session.

2. Central Arizona Project, S. 75, Eighty-second Congress, first session.

3. To protect the scenic beauty along the south approach highway to the Grand Canyon with the Kaibab National Forest. Public Law 77, Eighty-second Congress, first session.

4. To preserve the Gila Pueblo and make it an archeological laboratory. Public Law 254, Eighty-second Congress, first session.

5. Central Arizona project, S. 75, Eighty-first Congress, first session.

6. To authorize the withdrawal of public notices in the Yuma reclamation project to encourage the filing of water right applications. Public Law 383 (S. 1542), Eighty-first Congress, first session.

7. To allow water to be furnished to the Yuma auxiliary project through the works of the Gila project. Public Law 102 (S. 690), Eighty-first Congress, first session.

8. To grant consent of the United States to the upper Colorado River Basin compact. Public Law 37, Eighty-first Congress, first session.

9. To permit the disposal of withdrawn public tracts too small

to be classed as a farm unit under the Reclamation Act. S. 1543, Eighty-first Congress, first session.

10. To allow the San Carlos Irrigation and Drainage District to drill, equip and acquire wells for use on the district and for reimbursement. Public Law 10, Eightieth Congress, first session.

11. To provide for the creation of the Wellton-Mohawk irrigation district and the Yuma Mesa division of the Gila project. Public Law 272 (S. 483), Eightieth Congress, first session.

12. To amend the San Carlos Act with reference to repayment charges. Public Law 149, Seventy-ninth Congress, first session.

13. To provide for an investigation of hydroelectric power development and irrigation projects. Senate Resolution 304, Seventy-eighth Congress, second session.

14. To authorize construction of flood-control projects, including Holbrook project on the Little Colorado. Public Law 534 (H.R. 4485), Seventy-eighth Congress, second session.

15. To provide for an investigation of the supply and distribution of hydroelectric power. Senate Resolution 155, Seventy-eighth Congress, first session.

16. To provide for the acquisition of Indian lands required in connection with the construction, operation, and maintenance of transmission lines from Parker Dam power project. Public Law 764 (S. 2469), Seventy-seventh Congress, second session.

Social Security
1. Increase payments to aged persons and to the blind by $5 per month and to dependent children by $3 per month. Public Law 590 (H.R. 7800), Eighty-second Congress, second session.

2. Increased payments to the aged and to the blind by $5 per month and to the dependent children by $3 per month. Public Law 642 (H.J. Res. 296), Eightieth Congress, second session.

3. Increase old age assistance payments and blind persons' assistance by $5 per month and dependent children's assistance by $3 per month. Public Law 718, Seventy-ninth Congress, second session.

4. To prevent the earnings of aged persons from barring their old age assistance payments. (H.R. 1752), Seventy-ninth Congress, first session.

Veterans and Military Affairs
1. To establish national cemeteries in the State of Arizona. S. 2621, Eighty-second Congress, second session.

2. To provide educational and other readjustment benefits to the veterans of Armed Forces since beginning of the conflict in Korea. Public Law 550 (H.R. 7656; S. 3199), Eighty-second Congress, sec-

ond session.

3. To make bonus payments to members of the Armed Forces who engage in combat duty. Public Law 356 (H.R. 5715), Eighty- second Congress, second session.

4. To provide medical, hospital, and pension benefits to veterans of military service since beginning of Korean conflict. Public Law 28, Eighty-second Congress, first session.

5. To equalize the pay and retirement benefits of certain commissioned officers of the Coast Guard. S. 2477, Eighty-first Congress, first session.

6. To facilitate the retirement of those who were automatically transferred from the Customs Bureau to the Coast Guard. Public Law 308 (H.R. 1824), Eighty-first Congress, first session.

7. To incorporate the AMVETS, American Veterans of World War II. S. 2326, Seventy-ninth Congress, second session.

8. To provide allowances and educational benefits to all veterans of World War II. Public Law 268 (H.R. 3749), Seventy-ninth Congress, first session.

9. To provide for the readjustment of veterans of World War II to civilian life. Public Law 346 (S. 1767), Seventy-eighth Congress, second session.

10. To provide for a tax exemption on playing cards sent to servicemen outside the United States. Public Law 235 (H.R. 3687), Seventy-eighth Congress, second session.

11. To enable all members of the Armed Forces to send mail free of cost. Public Law 507 (S. 2208), Seventy-seventh Congress, second session.

Indians

1. To promote economic recovery of Papago Indians and the better utilization of the resources of the Papago, Gila Bend, and San Xavier Reservations. S. 107, Eighty-second Congress, second session.

2. Obtained Senate approval of an increase of $6,500,000 for road construction, schools, and irrigation facilities on the Papago and Navajo Reservations. (H.R. 7176), Eighty-second Congress, second session.

3. Obtained Senate approval of an increase of $200,000 for range water development on the Papago Indian Reservation. (H.R. 7176), Eighty-second Congress, second session.

4. To authorize necessary expenditures to be made by the Joint Committee on the Navajo-Hopi Indian Administration. Senate Concurrent Resolution 64, Eighty-second Congress, second session.

5. Obtained an increase of $250,000 in the appropriating for an additional water supply on the Navajo Reservation. Public Law

254 (H.R. 5630), Eighty-second Congress, first session.

6. To promote the rehabilitation of the Navajo and Hopi Indians and the further development of the resources on the reservations. S. 1407, Eighty-first Congress, first session.

Mining

1. Enabling the State of Arizona to make leases encouraging the further development of its oil and mineral resources. Public Law 44, Eighty-second Congress, first session.

2. To place a tax on the importation of foreign copper. Public Law 33 (S. 2022), Eighty-first Congress, first session.

3. To encourage and stimulate exploration for and conservation of strategic and critical ores, metals, and minerals. (S. 2105), Eighty-first Congress, first session.

4. To bring about the continued production of copper, lead, and zinc by continuing an effective subsidy program. Public Law 88 (S. 502), Seventy-ninth Congress, first session.

5. To authorize the Reconstruction Finance Corporation to make loans to those desiring to engage in producing minerals of value to the United States in time of war. (S. 381), Seventy-eighth Congress, first session.

Education

1. To make grants to the States for surveying their need for elementary and secondary school facilities and for emergency school construction in districts overburdened with enrollments resulting from defense activities. (S. 2317), Eighty-first Congress, first session.

2. To authorize the Secretary of the Interior to convey certain lands on the Gila reclamation project to the University of Arizona. Public Law 90 (S. 118), Seventy-ninth Congress, first session.

3. To extend the operation of the school-lunch program. Public Law 425 (H.R. 4278), Seventy-eighth Congress, second session.

Communications

1. To make the first major revisions in the Communications Act of 1934. Public Law 554 (S. 658), Eighty-second Congress, second session.

2. To amend the communications Act of 1934. S. 1973, Eighty-first Congress, first session.

3. Repeal of the Post Roads Act of 1866 to eliminate telegraph rate discriminations between the United States and private persons. Public Law 193 (S. 816), Eightieth Congress, first session.

4. To continue an investigation of international communications by wire and radio. Senate Resolution 24, Seventy-ninth

Congress, first session.

5. To permit consolidations and mergers between domestic telegraph carriers and between international telegraph carriers. Public Law 4, Seventy-eighth Congress, first session.

Transportation

1. To protect the scenic beauty along Oak Creek Canyon within the Coconino National Forest. Public Law 70 (S. 812), Eighty- first Congress, first session.

2. To amend the Transportation Act of 1940 with respect to the movement of Government traffic. Public Law 256, Seventy- ninth Congress, first session.

Miscellaneous

1. To extend the Special Committee To Investigate Senatorial Campaign Expenditures. Senate Resolution 5, Seventy-eighth Congress, first session.

2. To relieve barbers and beauty shops from the prohibitive burden of keeping books on purchase of supplies for purposes of the Revenue Act. Public Law 250 (H.R. 5417), Seventy-seventh Congress, first session.

BIBLIOGRAPHY

Manuscript Collections

Ashurst, Henry F. Papers, Special Collections, University of Arizona
Library, Tucson.

Douglas, Lewis W. Papers, Special Collections, University of Arizona
Library, Tucson.

Earlsboro File, Santa Fe Museum, Pottawatomie County Historical
Society, Shawnee, Oklahoma.

Goldwater, Barry M. Papers, Special Collections, Arizona Historical
Foundation, Charles Trumbull Hayden Library, Arizona State
University, Tempe.

Johnson, Lyndon Baines Papers, Lyndon Baines Johnson Library,
Austin, Texas.

MacArthur, Douglas Archives, Norfolk, Virginia.

McFarland, Ernest W. Papers, McFarland Historical State Park
Library and Archives, Florence, Arizona.

Roosevelt, Franklin Delano Papers, Franklin Delano Roosevelt
Library, Hyde Park, New York.

Truman, Harry S. Papers, Harry S. Truman Library, Independence,
Missouri.

Government Documents

Appendix to the Congressional Record. 1941-52. Washington, D.C.:
UUGPO, 1941-52.

Congressional Record. 1941-52. Washington, D.C.: USGPO, 1941-52.

National Commission on the Causes and Prevention of Violence.
Final report. *To Establish Justice, To Insure Domestic Tranquility
Washington, D.C., USGPO, 1969.*

Riddick, Floyd M. *Majority and Minority Leaders of the Senate: History
and Development of the Office of the Floor Leaders.* Washington,
D.C.: U.S. Government Printing Office, 1973.

U.S. Congress, Senate. Committee on Interstate Commerce.
Hearings on Propaganda in Motion Pictures. 77th Cong., lst sess.,
Washington, D.C.: U.S. Government Printing Office, 1942.

U.S. Congress, Senate. Committee on Irrigation and
Reclamation. *Hearings on Arizona Water Resources.* 78th Cong.,
2nd sess.,Washington, D.C.: U.S. Government Printing Office,
1944.

U.S. Congress, Senate. Committee on Foreign Relations. *Hearings on the Water Treaty With Mexico.* 79th Cong.,1st sess., Washington, D.C.: U.S. Government Printing Office, 1945.

U.S. Congress, House. Committee on Irrigation and Reclamation. *Hearings on Gila Project Reauthorization.* 79th Cong., 2nd sess., Washington, D.C.: U.S. Government Printing Office, 1946.

U.S. Congress, Senate. Subcommittee on Pubic Lands. *Hearings on Bridge Canyon Dam and Central Arizona Project.* 80th Cong., 1st sess., Washington, D.C.: U.S. Government Printing Office, 1947.

U.S. Congress, Senate. Committee on Interior and Insular Affairs. *Hearings on Colorado River Water Rights.* 80th Cong., 2nd sess., Washington, D.C.: U.S. Government Printing Office, 1948.

U.S. Congress, House. Subcommittee on Irrigation and Reclamation. *Hearings on Upper Colorado River Basin Compact.* 81st Cong., 1st sess., Washington, D.C.: U.S. Government Printing Office, 1949.

U.S. Congress, Senate. Committee on Interior and Insular Affairs. *Hearings on the Central Arizona Project and Colorado River Rights.* 81st Cong., 1st sess., Washington, D.C.: U.S. Government Printing Office, 1949.

U.S. Congress, House. Subcommittee on Irrigation and Reclamation. *Hearings on the Central Arizona Project.* 81st Cong., 1st sess., Washington, D.C.: U.S. Government Printing Office, 1949.

U.S. Congress, House. Committee on Interior and Insular Affairs. *Hearings on the Central Arizona Project.* 82nd Cong., 1st sess., Washington, D.C.: U.S. Government Printing Office, 1951.

Newspapers (National)

ACA News
Albuquerque Tribune
Amarillo Globe Times
Chicago Daily News
Christian Science Monitor (Boston)
Daily Oklahoman (Norman)
Denver Post
Detroit Free Press
Evening American
Hollywood Citizen News
Hollywood Post
Hollywood Reporter
Labor (Washington, D.C.)
Los Angeles Examiner
Los Angeles Herald Express
Los Angeles Herald Tribune

Los Angeles Times
Miami Herald
New York American
New York Herald Tribune
New York Post
New York Times
Pittsburgh Post Gazette
St. Louis Globe Democrat
Washington Daily News
Washington Evening Star
Washington Post
Washington Times
Variety (Hollywood)

Newspapers (Arizona)
Arizona Blade-Tribune (Florence)
Arizona Free Press
Arizona News (Phoenix)
Arizona Range News (Wilcox)
Arizona Republic (Phoenix)
Arizona Daily Star (Tucson)
Arizona Sun (Flagstaff)
Arizona Times
Arizona Weekly Gazette
Bisbee Daily Review
Buckeye Valley News
Casa Grande Dispatch
Douglas Daily Dispatch
Eloy Enterprise
Flagstaff Sun
Gilbert Enterprise
Glendale News
Graham County Guardian (Safford)
Holbrook Tribune News
Maricopa Democrat (Phoenix)
Mesa Tribune
Messenger (Phoenix)
Mojave Miner
Nogales International
Phoenix Gazette
Phoenix Sun
Prescott Courier
Scottsdale Progress
Southwest Labor Record (Phoenix)

Station West (KTVK-TV Newsletter, Phoenix)
Tempe Daily News
Tombstone Epitaph
Tri Valley Dispatch
Tucson Daily Citizen
Veterans News and Views (Phoenix)
Westside Daily American (Glendale)
Winslow Mail
Yavapai Messenger
Yuma Daily Sun

Books

Academy of Motion Picture Arts and Sciences Press Clipping File on the Senate Subcommittee War Film Hearings. Hollywood, California: 1941.

Anderson, Clinton and Milton Viorst. *Outsider in the Senate: Senator Clinton Anderson's Memoirs.* New York: World Publishing, 1970.

August, Jack *Vision in the Desert: Carl Hayden and the Hydropolitics of the American Southwest.* Fort Worth: Texas Christian University Press, 1999.

Baker, Richard Allan. *Conservation Politics: The Senate Career of Clinton P. Anderson.* Albuquerque: The University of New Mexico Press, 1985.

_____. *The Story of the United States Senate: A Bicentennial History.* Malabar, Florida: Robert E. Kreiger Publishing Co., 1985.

Barnard, John. *Walter Reuther and the Rise of the Auto Workers.* Boston: Little-Brown, 1983.

Bennett, Michael. *When Dreams Come True: The GI Bill and the Making of Modern America.* Washington D. C.: Brassey's Pub., 1996.

Berman, David R. *Parties and Elections in Arizona, 1863-1984.* Tempe: Arizona State University Morrison Institute of Public Policy, School of Public Affairs, 1985.

Bird, Tom and Willie Stargell. *Willie Stargell: An Autobiography.* New York: Harper and Row, 1984.

Blum, John Morton. *V for Victory: Politics and American Culture During World War II.* New York: Harcourt, Brace, Jovanovich, 1976.

Blumberg, Nathan B. *One Party Press.* Lincoln: University of Nebraska Press, 1954.

Bommersbach, Jana. *The Trunk Murderess, Winnie Ruth Judd:The Truth about an American Crime Legend Revealed at Last.* New York: Simon and Schuster, 1992.

Browder, Paul and Thomas G. Smith. *Independent: A Biography of Lewis W. Douglas.* New York: A.A. Knopf, 1986.

Caro, Robert. *Lyndon Johnson: Master of the Senate.* New York: Alfred

A. Knopf, 2002.

Cole, Edwin. *The Gila: River of the Southwest*. Lincoln: University of Nebraska Press, 1952.

Cole, Wayne S. *Gerald P. Nye and American Foreign Relations*. Minneapolis: University of Minnesota Press, 1962.

Collier's Encyclopedia Yearbook, 1953. New York: Crowell-Collier Publishing Co, 1953.

Conkin, Paul K. *Big Daddy from the Pedernales: Lyndon Baines Johnson*. Boston: Twayne Publishers, 1986.

Dallek, Robert. *Lone Star Rising: Lyndon Johnson and His Times*. New York: Oxford University Press, 1991.

Daniels, Roger. *Concentration Camps, U.S.A.* Hinsdale, Illinois: Dryden Press, 1971.

Dobkins, Dwight and Robert J. Hendricks. *Winnie Ruth Judd: The Trunk Murders*. New York: Grosset and Dunlap, 1973.

Donovan, Robert J. *Conflict and Crisis: The Presidency of Harry S. Truman, 1945-48*. New York: Norton, 1977.

_____. *Tumultuous Years: The Presidency of Harry S. Truman, 1949-53*. New York: Norton, 1982.

Edwards, Lee. *Goldwater: The Man Who Made a Revolution*. Washington, D.C.: Regnery Publishing, 1995.

Encyclopedia Britannica Book of the Year, 1952.

Etulain, Richard W. and Michael P. Malone, eds., *The American West: Historical Interpretations*. Albuquerque: University of New Mexico Press, 1989.

Evans, Rowland and Robert Novak. *Lyndon B. Johnson: The Exercise of Power*. New York: The New American Library, 1966.

Fannin, Paul and Leonard E. Goodall, Ernest W. McFarland, John P. White. *The Office of Governor in Arizona*. Tempe: Arizona State University Bureau of Government Research, Public Affairs Series No. 7, 1964.

Faulk, Odie. *Arizona: A Short History*. Norman: University of Oklahoma Press, 1970.

Ferrell, Robert H. *Harry S. Truman and the Modern American Presidency*. Boston: Little, Brown and Company, 1983.

_____. *Off the Record: The Private Papers of Harry S. Truman*. New York: Harper and Row, 1980.

Fey, Harold E. and D'Arcy McNickle. *Indians and Other Americans: Two Ways of Life Meet*. New York: Harper and Row, 1970.

Fireman, Bert M. *Arizona, Historical Land*. New York: A. A. Knopf, 1982.

Fradkin, Philip L. *A River No More: The Colorado River and the West*. Tucson: The University of Arizona Press, 1984.

Frontier Lore. Shawnee, Oklahoma: Pottawatomie County Historical

Society, 1975.

Gillespie, John and Dale Story. *A History of East Central State College, 1909-1949*. Ada, Oklahoma: pvt. repub. 1980.

Gittenger, Roy. *The University of Oklahoma, 1892-1942*. Norman: University of Oklahoma Press, 1942.

Goff, John S. *George W. P. Hunt*. Cave Creek, Arizona: Black Mountain Press, 1987.

Goldberg, Robert. *Barry Goldwater*. New Haven: Yale University Press, 1995.

Goldwater, Barry M. *The Conscience of a Conservative*. Shepardsville, Kentucky: Victor Publishing Co., Inc., 1960.

_____. *Freedom Is His Flight Plan*. New York: Fleet Publishing, 1962.

_____. *With No Apologies: The Personal and Political Memoirs of United States Senator Barry M. Goldwater*. New York: Morrow, 1979.

_____. with Jack Casserly. *Goldwater*. New York: Doubleday, 1988.

Gosnell, Harold Foote. *Truman's Crises: A Political Biography of Harry S. Truman*. Westport, Connecticut: Greenwood Press,1980.

Hamby, Alonzo L. *Beyond the New Deal: Harry S. Truman and American Liberalism*. New York: Columbia University Press, 1973.

Harper, Alan D. *The Politics of Loyalty: The White House and the Communist Issue, 1946-1952*. Westport, Connecticut: Greenwood Press, 1980.

Hechler, Ken. *Working With Truman: A Personal Memoir of the White House Years*. New York: Putnam, 1982.

Hundley, Norris. *Dividing the Waters: A Century of Controversy Between the United States and Mexico*. Berkeley: University of California Press, 1966.

_____. *Water and the West*. Berkeley: University of California Press, 1975.

Iverson, Peter, *Barry Goldwater: Native Arizonan*. Norman: University of Oklahoma Press, 1997.

Johnson, James W. *Arizona Politicians: The Noble and the Notorious*. Tucson: University of Arizona Press, 2002.

Johnson, Richard. *The Central Arizona Project, 1918-1968*. Tucson: The University of Arizona Press, 1977.

Jonas, Frank H., ed., *Political Dynamiting*. Salt Lake City: University of Utah Press, 1970.

_____, ed. *Politics in the American West*. Salt Lake City: University of Utah Press, 1969.

_____, ed. *Western Politics*. Salt Lake City: University of Utah Press, 1961.

Jowett, G. *Film: The Democratic Art.* Boston: Little Brown and Co., 1976.

Kimball, Warren F. *The Most Unsordid Act: Lend Lease, 1939-41.* Baltimore: Johns Hopkins University Press, 1969.

Labor's League for Political Education. *Voting Records for Senators and Representatives.* Washington, D.C.: Labor's League for Political Education of the American Federation of Labor, 1952.

Luckingham, Bradford. *Phoenix: The History of a Southwestern Metropolis.* Tucson: University of Arizona Press, 1989.

_____. *The Urban Southwest: A Profile History of Albuquerque, El Paso, Phoenix, Tucson.* El Paso, Texas: Texas Western Press, 1982.

Luey, Beth and Noel Stowe, eds., *Arizona at Seventy-Five: The Next Twenty-Five Years.* Tucson: University of Arizona Press, 1987.

MacNamee, Gregory. *The Gila: The Life and Death of an American River.* New York: Orion Press, 1994.

McCoy, Donald R. *The Presidency of Harry S. Truman.* Lawrence: University Press of Kansas, 1973.

_____. and Richard Reuthen. *Quest and Response: Minority Rights and the Truman Administration.* Lawrence: University Press of Kansas, 1973.

McCullough, David. *Truman.* New York: Simon and Schuster, 1992.

McDowell, Edwin. *Barry Goldwater: Portrait of an Arizonan.* Chicago: Regnery, 1964.

McFarland, Ernest W. *Mac: The Autobiography of Ernest W. McFarland.* Phoenix: Privately pvt. pub., 1979.

McMillan, James E., ed. *The Ernest W. McFarland Papers: The United States Senate Years, 1940-1952.* Prescott, Arizona: Sharlot Hall Museum Press, 1995.

McReynolds, Edwin C. *Oklahoma: A History of the Sooner State.* Norman: University of Oklahoma Press, 1954, 1964.

Malone, Michael P., ed., *Historians and the American West.* Lincoln: University of Nebraska Press, 1983.

Mann, Dean. *The Politics of Water in Arizona.* Tucson: The University of Arizona Press, 1963.

Meadows, Della. *Where Two Are Gathered: Centennial History of the First Presbyterian Church, Florence.* Florence, Arizona: Pinal County Historical Society, 1988.

Meyers, John, ed., *Arizona's Governors, 1912-1990.* Phoenix: Heritage Press, 1989.

Moley, Raymond, Jr. *The American Legion Story.* New York: Duell, Sloan, and Pearce, 1966.

Mooney, Charles W. *Localized History of Pottawatomie Co., Oklahoma to 1907.* Oklahoma City: Privately published, 1971.

Morey, Roy D. *Politics and Legislation: The Office of Governor in*

Arizona. Arizona Government Studies No.3 Institute of Goverment research.Tucson: University of Arizona Press, 1965.

Morgan, Anne Hodges. *Robert S. Kerr: The Senate Years*. Norman: University of Oklahoma Press, 1977.

Morgan, H. Wayne. *Oklahoma: A History*. New York, W. W. Norton and Co., 1977.

Morris, John W. and Willa Mae Townes and Louise Welsh. *A History of the Greater Seminole Oil Field*. Oklahoma City: Oklahoma Heritage Association, 1981.

Mosch, Theodore R. *The G.I. Bill: A Breakthrough in Educational and Social Policy in the United States*. Hicksville, New York: Exposition Press, 1975.

Nash, Gerald D. *The American West Transformed: The Impact of the Second World War*. Bloomington: University of Indiana Press, 1985.

_____. *The American West in the Twentieth Century: A Short History of an Urban Oasis*. Albuquerque: University of New Mexico Press, 1973.

Olsen, Keith W. *The G.I. Bill, the Veterans, and the Colleges*. Lexington: University Press of Kentucky, 1974.

Pesagi, 1915. East Central Normal School Yearbook. Ada, Oklahoma: East Central Normal School, 1915.

Poen, Monte, ed., *Letters Home by Harry Truman*. New York: G.P. Putnam's Sons, 1984.

Pottawatomie County, Oklahoma, History. Claremore, Oklahoma: Country Lane Press, 1987.

Powell, Lawrence Clark. *Arizona: A Bicentennial History*. New York: Norton, 1976.

Reedy, George E. *The U.S. Senate*. New York: NAL Penguin, Inc. 1988.

Reeves, Thomas C. *The Life and Times of Joe McCarthy: A Biography*. New York: Stein and Day, 1982

Rice, Ross R., ed., *An Annotated Bibliography of Arizona Politics and Government*. Tempe: Center for Public Affairs, Arizona State University, 1976.

_____. *Carl Hayden: Builder of the American West*. New York: University Press of America, 1994.

Robinson, Elwyn B. *History of North Dakota*. Lincoln: University of Nebraska Press, 1966.

Robinson, Michael E. *Water for the West: The Bureau of Reclamation, 1902-1977*. Chicago: Public Works Historical Society, 1979.

Ross, Davis R. B. *Preparing for Ulysses: Politics and Veterans During World War Two*. New York: Columbia University Press, 1969.

Shadegg, Stephen C. *Arizona Politics: The Struggle to End One Party*

Rule. Tempe: Arizona State University, 1986.

_____. *How to Win An Election: The Art of Political Victory.* New York: Taplinger Publishing Co., Inc., 1964.

Sklar, Robert. *Movie-Made America: A Cultural History of American Movies.* New York: Vantage Books, 1975.

Smith, Dean. *The Goldwaters of Arizona.* Flagstaff, Arizona: Northland Press, 1986.

Smith, Gaddis. *American Diplomacy During World War II.* New York: John Wiley and Sons, 1965.

Sobin, Harris. *Florence Townsite A.T.: The Final Report of the Florence Townsite Historical Study.* Tucson, Arizona: Harris Sobin and Associates, 1977.

The Sooner, 1917. University of Oklahoma Yearbook. Norman: University of Oklahoma, 1917

Terrell, John. *The War For the Colorado River,* 2 vols. Glendale, California: Arthur H. Clark, 1965.

New York: New York Times, Bantam Books, 1970.

Trimble, Marshall. *Arizona: A Panoramic History of a Frontier State.* Garden City, New York.: Doubleday, 1977.

_____. *Arizona: A Cavalcade of History.* Tucson: Treasure Chest Publications, 1989.

Truman, David B. *The Congressional Party: A Case Study.* New York: Wiley, 1959.

Truman, Harry S. and Robert H. Ferrell, eds., *The Autobiography of Harry S. Truman.* Boulder: Colorado Associated University Press, 1980.

Wagoner, Jay. *Arizona's Heritage.* Salt Lake City: Peregrine Smith, Inc., 1977.

Walker, John A., ed. *The East Central Story: From Normal School to University, 1909-1984.* Ada, Oklahoma: East Central University Foundation, 1984.

Wallace, Henry. *Sixty Million Jobs.* New York: Simon and Schuster, 1945.

Waller, Willard. *The Veteran Comes Back.* New York: Dryden Press, 1944.

Worster, Donald. *Rivers of Empire: Water, Aridity, and the Growth of the American West.* New York: Pantheon Books, 1985.

Young, Roland. *Congressional Politics in the Second World War.* New York: Columbia University Press, 1956.

Magazines and Periodicals
American Legion Magazine
Arizona Health Digest
Arizona Highways

Arizona Legionnaire
Arizona Reports
Broadcasting Magazine
Cosmopolitan
Democrat Digest
Esquire
Harvard Business Review
Journal of Arizona History
Life
Nation
National Oberver
Newsweek
Saturday Evening Post
Southwest Veterans Magazine
Stanford Law Review
Time
Truth (Mormon Church)
U.S. News and World Report
Vital Speeches of the Day
Western Political Quarterly

Articles

Anderson, Totton. "The Political West in 1960." *Western Political Quarterly* 13 (March 1960): 287-99.

"Big Mac." *Arizona Republic, Arizona Magazine*, August 13, 1978.

Bone, Hugh A. "Western Politics and the 1952 Elections." *Western Political Quarterly* 6 (March 1953): 93-102.

Camelon, David. "I Saw the G.I. Bill Written, Part I: The Fight for Mustering Out Pay." *The American Legion Magazine* 47 (September 1949): 1819, 48-57.

———. "I Saw the G.I. Bill Written, Part II: A Surprise Attack." *The American Legion Magazine* 47 (October 1949): 18-19, 51-57.

———. "I Saw the G.I. Bill Written, Part III: The Wild Ride From Georgia." *The American Legion Magazine* 47 (November 1949): 18-19, 51-57.

Drucker, Peter F. "The New Society of Organizations." *Harvard Business Review*, (September-October 1992): 95-105.

Houghton, N. D. "The 1954 Election in Arizona" *Western Political Quarterly* 8 (March 1955).

———. "The 1956 Election in Arizona" *Western Political Quarterly* 9 (March 1956).

Jonas, Frank. "Western Politics and the 1958 Elections." *Western Political Quarterly* 12 (March 1959): 238-46.

"The Western Scene," *Western Political Quarterly* 18 (September

1964) :3-12.

Kelso, Paul. "The 1952 Elections in Arizona." *Western Political Quarterly* 6 (March 1953): 93-102.

Lisagor, Peter. "LBJ Image Distorting His Worth." Chicago Daily News Service, McFarland State Park Archives, Florence, Arizona.

McMillan, James E. "Father of the GI Bill: Ernest W. McFarland and Veterans Legislation." *Journal of Arizona History* 35 (Winter 1994): 357-76.

_____. "First Sooner Senator: Ernest W. McFarland's Oklahoma Years, 1894-1919." *Chronicles of Oklahoma* 72 (Summer 1994): 178-199.

_____. "McFarland and the Movies: The 1941 Senate Motion Picture Hearings." *Journal of Arizona History* 29 (Autumn 1988): 277-302.

Nichols, Roger L. "A Miniature Venice: Florence, Arizona, 1866-1910." *Journal of Arizona History* 16 (Winter 1975).

Perry, James M. "A Report in Depth on Barry Goldwater: A New Look at a Presidential Candidate (The Lonely Position)." *National Observer*, 1994, in Goldwater Papers.

Rice, Ross. "The 1958 Elections in Arizona." *Western Political Quarterly* 12 (March 1959): 266-75.

_____. "The 1964 Election in the West." *Western Political Quarterly* 18 (June 1964): 431-38.

Ross, Frank E. "Arizona's U. S. Senator Is a Scholar of Wide Horizons" *Arizona Republic*, December 15, 1940.

Struass, William L "The 1960 Election in Arizona." *Western Political Quarterly* 13 (March 1960): 305-08.

Unpublished Manuscripts

Baldwin, Ava S. "The History of Florence, Arizona." Master's thesis, University of Arizona, Tucson, 1941).

Bibolet, Roland. "Interview." Lyndon Johnson Presidential Library, Austin, Texas.

_____. "Reminiscences of Roland Bibolet." McFarland State Park Archives, Florence, Arizona.

Davis, Elmer. "Broadcast." ABC Radio, July 27, 1953. "Declaration of Democratic Principles by the Majority Members of the U. S. Senate." McFarland State Park Archives, Florence, Arizona.

Flood, John. "McFarland Landmark Cases." McFarland State Park Archives, Florence, Arizona.

Foster, James and L.C. Smith. "The People's Choice: Dwight Eisenhower." Department of History, Arizona State

University, Tempe. Photocopy.

"The Gallegher Report." New York: February 28. 1967, McFarland State Park Archives, Florence, Arizona.

Huitt, Ralph K. "Senate Democratic Leadership." (Paper delivered at the 1960 Annual Meeting of the American Political Science Association, New York City)

McFarland, Ernest W. "The Operation of the Initiative and Referendum in California." Master's thesis, Stanford University, Palo Alto, California, 1924). "Memorandum on Trip to South America", 1966.

_____. "Interview." Lyndon Johnson Presidential Library, Austin, Texas.

McMillan, James E. "Ernest W. McFarland: Southwestern Progressive, the United States Senate Years, 1941-1953." (Ph.D. dissertation, Arizona State University, Tempe, 1990).

_____. "Setting the Record Straight: Ernest W. McFarland and the G. I. Bill." Presented at Arizona State University—West. GI Bill Symposium. Phoenix. November 1999, in author's possession.

_____. "Order from Chaos: U. S. Senate Majority Leader Ernest W. McFarland." Presented at Arizona Historical Society Convention. Tempe, April 2003, in author's possession.

_____."Robert S. Kerr and Ernest W. McFarland: The Parallel Careers of Two Prairie Polioticians." Presented at Oklahoma Historical Society Convention. Checotah, April 1994, in author's possession.

Moran, John. "Letter to Dr. Charles J. Meyers, Dean of Stanford University Law School." McFarland State Park Archives, Florence, Arizona.

Spingarn, Stephen J. "Interview." March 20-29, 1967, Washington, D. C. Oral History Collection, Harry S. Truman Presidential Library, Independence, Missouri.

"Statement of the Democratic Majority of the Senate." McFarland State Park Archives, Florence, Arizona.

"Vietnam: August-September 1967." McFarland State Park Archives, Florence, Arizona.

Videotapes

"Mac 14: Mildred Hagerty Interview." Phoenix: KTVK-TV, June 1984.

"Mac 15: John Moran Interview." Phoenix: KTVK-TV, June 1984.

"Mac 16: Fred Struckmeyer Interview." Phoenix: KTVK-TV, June 1984.

"Mac 17: Fred Struckmeyer Interview." Phoenix: KTVK-TV, June

1984.
"Mac 18: Brock Ellis Interview." Phoenix: KTVK-TV, June 1984.
"Mac Remembered." Phoenix: KTVK-TV, 1984.
"A Tribute to Ernest W. McFarland." Phoenix: KTVK-TV, 1971.

Interviews with Author
Aiken, Wayne. June 16, 1993, Phoenix.
Avery, Ben. June 15, 1993, Phoenix.
Bibolet, Roland: April 1990, Nogales, Arizona; June 18, 1993,
        Nogales, Arizona; August 26, 2002, phone; April 2003, phone.
Early, Billie, January 1990, Florence, Arizona.
Jenkins, Bruce, May 24, 1990, Earlsboro, Oklahoma.
Jones, Anthony O., July 29, 1986, Phoenix.
Lewis, Delbert, December, 1990, Phoenix.
        February 22, 1990, July 13, 1990, June 15, 1993, August 14,
        1996, August 16, 1996., all Phoenix.
Lyons, William, March 1987, Flagstaff.
Moran, John, August 1994, Phoenix.
Mr. and Mrs. John Permetter, May 24, 1990, Earlsboro, Oklahoma.
Phillips, William, May 24, 1990. Pinetop.
Swearingen, John, February 1990, Florence.

Letters to Author
Bibolet, Roland: December 1, 1988; December 17, 1993; December
        28, 1993; January 6, 1994; July 24, 1994; August 31, 2002.
Zobrist, Benedict K.: May 22, 1992.

McFarland's Written Arizona Supreme Court Opinions
        (cited in text)
Bacchus v. Farmers Insurance Group Exchange 1970
City of Phoenix v. Phoenix Civic Auditorium and Convention Center Association 1965
Jarvis v.State Land Dept., City of Tucson
Porter v. Empire Fire and Marine Insurance Co. 1970
Sanders v. Folsum 1969
State v. Curry 1965
State v. Goodyear 1965
State v. Goodyear 1966
State v. Jennings 1968
State v. Kananen 1965
State v. Lassen 1965
State v. Miranda 1965
State v. Overton 1977
State v. Starsky 1970

Streenz v. Streenz 1970
Transportation Insurance Co. v. Wade 1970

United States Supreme Court Decisions
Brown v. Topeka Board of Education, 1954
Escobedo v. Illinois 1964
Gideon v. Wainright 1963
Arizona v. Miranda 1966
Orozco v. Texas 1969

ACKNOWLEDGEMENTS

The biography of Ernest W. McFarland has been a long time in conception, and I hope to give appropriate recognition to all involved. A chronological approach will suffice to structure these words of thanks.

In October of 1984, shortly after McFarland's June 8 death, Arizona State University history professor Bill Phillips in conjunction with Director of Historical Publishing and Editing Beth Luey asked me, a budding Ph. D. student, to edit a selected edition of McFarland's U. S. Senate papers. Before this could happen, however, the task of bringing order to all the records Mac left behind had to be completed.

That endeavor had begun in the late 1970s when state, federal and private funds allowed the construction of the superb little archive at McFarland Historic State Park in Florence. McFarland's effects were moved to this location in the early 1980s and the organizational process was launched. Phillips supervised this lengthy project which was initiated with private donations. State Archivist David Hoober was engaged to devise a master plan to organize all the public and personal records of Mac's long and varied career, about fifty-five thousand items in all. Unlike current congressmen who personally touch less than 2% of the paper that moves through their offices, Mac handled every one of these items! A substantial grant from the National Historical Publications and Records Commission, on whose board Hoober later served, funded the processing of these records. The work was done on site at the new archive by historical consultants Carol Martel and Janet Burke, both doctoral students at ASU. My deep appreciation to all who participated in this complex endeavor. This biography would not have been possible but for them.

The book *Ernest W. McFarland: The United States Senate Papers, 1940-1952* was eventually published by Sharlot Hall Press in 1995 under the supervision of Warren Miller who has also assisted on the biography. My thanks go to Warren as a vital link.

As the senate papers project began in 1985, I decided to derive a dissertation from the research. The first part included material on the 1941 Hollywood film probe, initially a seminar paper for Robert Trennert and then an article in *The Journal of Arizona History* under the editorial supervision of Bruce Dinges; my thanks for their encouragement as the article went on to receive the C. L Sonnichsen Award as the year's best in 1988.

The dissertation was completed in 1990, directed by my mentor and friend Chris Smith who has inspired me greatly as a caring person, excellent teacher, and inspiration to my own career as a historian. The remainder of the dissertation committee including Bill Phillips, Bob Trennert, Brad Luckingham, Jim McBride, Richard Burg, and Paul Hubbard are also to be recognized.

After the dissertation, it seemed logical to expand it into a biography on McFarland's exemplary full life and career. Teaching responsibilities at Denison University, New Mexico State, and Central College in Iowa (which funded some of the research) slowed the process but by 1997 a first draft was finished beginning with a re-write and condensation of the senate years dissertation from about 500 pages to a more succinct 200.

Throughout this work, Bill Phillips, who had directed the senate papers project, once again came to the forefront as the primary editor and proofreader making precise adjustments to my initial errors and adding his own wit and scholarly suggestions to the prose. Along with Del and Jewell Lewis who have produced all of the McFarland projects, including the memorial at the state capitol, Phillips stands as the most important coordinator and critic of my work; my deepest respect and appreciation for Bill and his many contributions and friendship.

I conducted most of the research at McFarland State Park where the assistance and cooperation of park managers, Jerry Ravert and Katie Montano has been greatly appreciated as they allowed complete open access to the papers and equipment and coordinated appropriately related exhibits and presentations. They have been perfect host and hostess to my research.

Too, other national and statewide staffs where I worked must be noted: the Franklin Delano Roosevelt, Harry S. Truman, and Lyndon Johnson Presidential Libraries, the American Legion Archives, the archives at ASU, the University of Arizona, and East Central State University of Oklahoma, the Carl Albert Center at the University of Oklahoma, the Arizona and Oklahoma Historical Societies, the Pottawatomie County Historical Society in Shawnee, Oklahoma, the Pinal County Historical Society in Florence, Arizona, the library at Central Arizona Community College, the Arizona State Archives, and the Arizona Historical Foundation.

The guiding hand of the McFarland Historical State Park Advisory Committee has been instrumental in furthering the project at every stage. With Bill Phillips, Del and Jewell Lewis, my thanks go also to Tony Jones, John Swearingen, and the ageless Edna McDonald. Special appreciation and memories are extended to Mildred Hagerty,

Della Meadows, Florence resident Billie Early, all of whom passed away as the project slowly evolved.

My most special appreciation must be proffered to MHSPAC member and former McFarland administrative assistant Roland Bibolet. His interviews and correspondence provided invaluable insight into Ernest McFarland, and his engaging personality and encouragement were added benefits to the ongoing work. Thanks Roland.

The latter stages of the biography have brought in five more integral co-workers: Richard Sims, Director of the Sharlot Hall Museum, Robert Aulicino, director of book design and production, MHSPAC member Bill Miller, who has coordinated computer technology, Michael W. Rubinoff of ASU as proofreader and indexer, and Henry Padilla, who digitalized the McFarland photography collection. All have contributed immensely to fine tuning the work although any existent errors of omission or commission can only be attributed to the author.

Final thoughts and recognition are once again accorded to Del and the late Jewell Lewis, to whom this book is dedicated, who have with tremendous love and respect kept alive and furthered the McFarland legacy, and recognition goes to the subject, himself, who did so much in his post-public service years to lay the foundation for all of the research and honors given his unique career. All of you have helped stimulate research into the modern West, a primary goal of this project. Thank you.

—James Elton McMillan, Jr.

INDEX

Stone, Clifford 178
Strauss, Michael 139, 161, 175
Streenz v. Streenz (1970) 481
Struckmeyer, Frederick, Sr. 212,
    431-32
Struckmeyer, Frederick, Jr. 431,
    442, 445-46, 471-72, 480, 483,
    501, 515
Student Non-Violent Coordinating
    Committee (SNCC) 469
Students for a Democratic Society
    (SDS) 469
Subversive Activities Control Board
    192
Sullivan, Francis 105, 109, 112, 113
"Superman" (George Reeves) 303
Supreme Court, U.S. 55, 69, 157,
    159-60, 174-76, 246, 307, 310-
    12, 355, 378, 424, 435, 441, 442-
    43, 448, 464
Surplus Property Act (1944) 133
Surplus Property Board (Ariz.) 320
Swearengin, John 503
Symington, Stuart 226, 324, 404,
    408, 409, 413, 417
Taft-Hartley Act (1946) 154-55,
    239-40, 261, 276, 375, 420
Taft, Robert "Bob" 108, 118, 131-
    32, 134, 154, 166, 195, 202, 203,
    204, 205, 208, 213, 235, 239,
    245, 248, 252, 257, 260, 268,
    274, 392, 398, 490
Taylor, Gen. Maxwell 124
Taylor, Glenn 146
Taylor Grazing Act (1934) 76
Teahouse of the August Moon
    (1956) 334
Teamsters Union 363, 381
Terry, Charles, Jr. 440-41
Tet Offensive 463, 465
Thieu, Nguyen Van 453, 458
"This Is the Truth About CAP"
    booklet (1950) 186
Thomas, Elbert 106
Thompson, Raymond 350
Thorpe, Jim 11

Thunderbird Post American
    Legion Drill Team 292
Thurmond, J. Strom 202
Tobey, Charles 77, 85, 87, 89
*To Establish Justice, To Ensure
    Domestic Tranquility* (1969) 473
Travels and Trips (see Ernest W.
    McFarland)
    Europe, 1929 34-35
    Europe, 1945 123-28
    Asia, 1946 149-51
    world, 1952 270-74
    Latin America, 1966 448-49
    South Vietnam, 1967 452-59
    Africa, 1969 475-78
Truman Doctrine (1947) 166
Truman, Harry 119-21, 127, 140-
    41, 144, 170-72, 173-74, 181,
    182, 190, 198, 201-02, 203, 205,
    208, 211-12, 213, 217, 228, 231-
    32, 235, 237, 238-39, 242, 245,
    248, 252-53, 257, 261, 275, 279,
    324, 343, 394, 401, 402, 417, 419
Truman Margaret (Daniel) 506
Truman, W. C. 44
Trump, W. C. 382, 383
Tucson Central Trades Council 261
Tucson, Gas, Electric Light and
    Power Company 379
Turnbow, William "Bill" 329, 339,
    340, 341
Turner, Frederick Jackson 162
Turner, John 339
Tydings, Millard 131, 187, 193, 222
Udall, Jesse 431, 432, 447, 477,
    481, 498
Udall, Levi 329, 341
Udall, Morris 383, 395, 430, 466,
    490, 498, 514, 559n
Udall, Stewart 290, 305, 306, 324,
    326, 345, 371, 390, 395, 404, 406,
    407, 408, 409, 410, 412, 414-15,
    417, 418, 421, 422, 465, 514, 559n
Underwood, Oscar 200
United Auto Workers 184, 368
United Mine Workers of America